WORLD POLITICS
87/88

Editor

Suzanne P. Ogden

Northeastern University

Professor Ogden received her Ph.D. from Brown University and is currently an associate professor at Northeastern University in Boston. She is also an associate in research at the Fairbank Center for East Asian Research, Harvard University. Professor Ogden publishes widely in the field of Chinese politics and Chinese foreign policy. At Northeastern she teaches courses on international relations, Chinese politics, and Japanese politics. She is currently a member of the coordinating committee for the center for International Politics and Administration at Northeastern University. She has travelled extensively in Europe, Asia, and Central America, and was the Academic Adviser to the British Political Internship program in London.

Annual Editions
A Library of Information from the Public Press

Cover illustration by Mike Eagle

The Dushkin Publishing Group, Inc.
Sluice Dock, Guilford, Connecticut 06437

This map has been developed to give you a graphic picture of where the countries of the world are located, the relationship they have with their region and neighbors, and their positions relative to the superpowers and power blocs. We have focused on certain areas to more clearly illustrate these crowded regions.

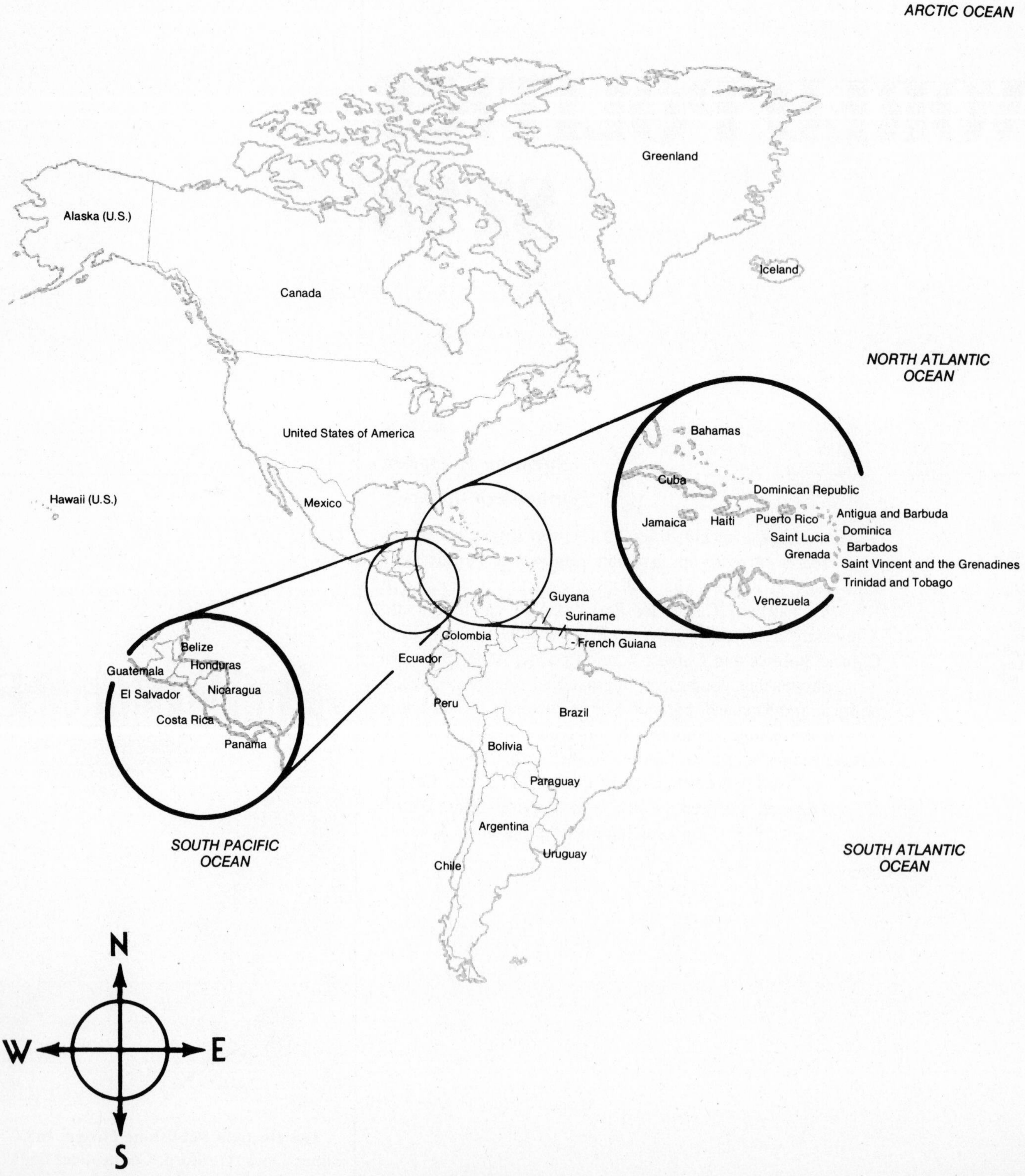

ARCTIC OCEAN

Greenland

Alaska (U.S.)

Iceland

Canada

NORTH ATLANTIC
OCEAN

United States of America

Bahamas

Cuba

Dominican Republic

Hawaii (U.S.)

Mexico

Jamaica   Haiti   Puerto Rico   Antigua and Barbuda
Saint Lucia   Dominica
Grenada   Barbados
Saint Vincent and the Grenadines
Trinidad and Tobago

Venezuela

Guyana
Suriname
Colombia   French Guiana

Belize

Guatemala   Honduras

El Salvador   Nicaragua

Ecuador

Costa Rica

Peru   Brazil

Panama

Bolivia

Paraguay

SOUTH PACIFIC
OCEAN

Argentina

Uruguay

SOUTH ATLANTIC
OCEAN

Chile

N

W   E

S

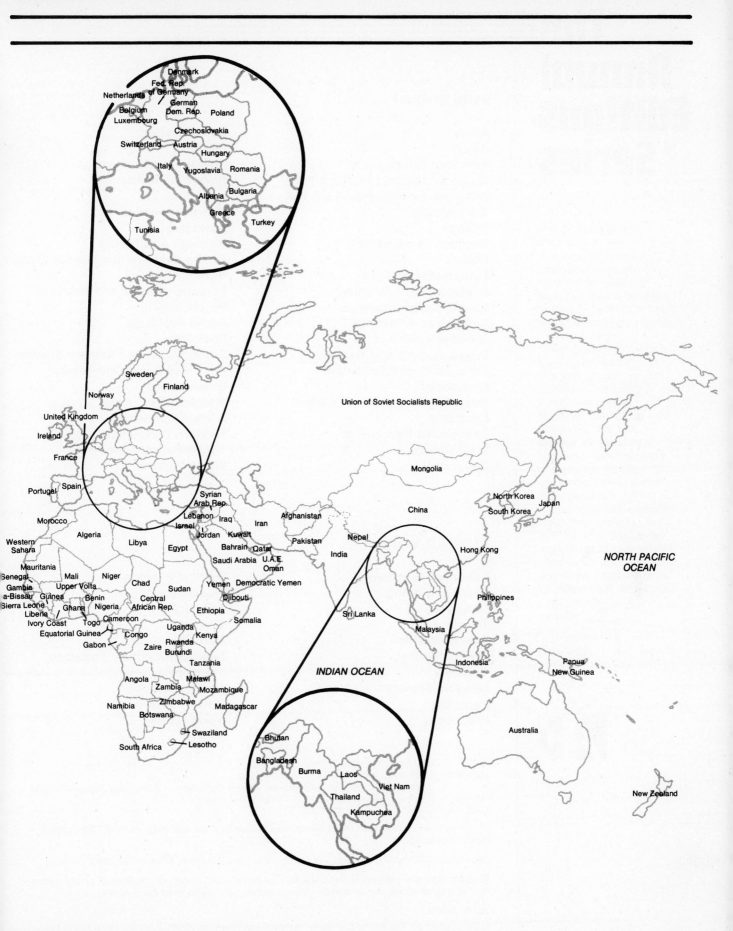

The Annual Editions Series

Annual Editions is a series of over forty volumes designed to provide the reader with convenient, low-cost access to a wide range of current, carefully selected articles from some of the most important magazines, newspapers, and journals published today. Annual Editions are updated on an annual basis through a continuous monitoring of over 200 periodical sources. All Annual Editions have a number of features designed to make them particularly useful, including topic guides, annotated tables of contents, unit overviews, and indexes. For the teacher using Annual Editions in the classroom, an Instructor's Resource Guide with test questions is available for each volume.

PUBLISHED

Africa
Aging
American Government
American History, Pre-Civil War
American History, Post-Civil War
Anthropology
Biology
Business/Management
China
Comparative Politics
Computers in Education
Computers in Business
Computers in Society
Criminal Justice
Drugs, Society and Behavior
Early Childhood Education
Economics
Educating Exceptional Children
Education
Educational Psychology
Environment
Geography

Global Issues
Health
Human Development
Human Sexuality
Latin America
Macroeconomics
Marketing
Marriage and Family
Middle East and the Islamic World
Nutrition
Personal Growth and Behavior
Psychology
Social Problems
Sociology
Soviet Union and Eastern Europe
State and Local Government
Urban Society
Western Civilization,
    Pre-Reformation
Western Civilization,
    Post-Reformation
World Politics

FUTURE VOLUMES

Abnormal Psychology
Death and Dying
Congress
Energy
Ethnic Studies
Foreign Policy
Judiciary
Law and Society
Parenting
Philosophy

Political Science
Presidency
Religion
South Asia
Third World
Twentieth-Century American
    History
Western Europe
Women's Studies
World History

Library of Congress Cataloging in Publication Data
Main entry under title: Annual Editions: World Politics.
    1. International relations—Addresses, essays, lectures.   2. United States—Foreign relations—Addresses, essays, lectures.   Title: World Politics.
ISBN 0-87967-689-2   327'.05

Eighth Edition

Manufactured by The Banta Company, Harrisonburg, Virginia 22801

Editors/ Advisory Board

EDITOR

Suzanne Ogden
Northeastern University

ADVISORY BOARD

Members of the Advisory Board are instrumental in the final selection of articles for each edition of Annual Editions. Their review of articles for content, level, currency, and appropriateness provides critical direction to the editor and staff. We think you'll find their careful consideration well reflected in this volume.

STAFF

To The Reader

In publishing ANNUAL EDITIONS we recognize the enormous role played by the magazines, newspapers, and journals of the *public press* in providing current, first-rate educational information in a broad spectrum of interest areas. Within the articles, the best scientists, practitioners, researchers, and commentators draw issues into new perspective as accepted theories and viewpoints are called into account by new events, recent discoveries change old facts, and fresh debate breaks out over important controversies.

Many of the articles resulting from this enormous editorial effort are appropriate for students, researchers, and professionals seeking accurate, current material to help bridge the gap between principles and theories and the real world. These articles, however, become more useful for study when those of lasting value are carefully *collected, organized, indexed,* and *reproduced* in a *low-cost format,* which provides easy and permanent access when the material is needed. That is the role played by *Annual Editions.* Under the direction of each volume's *Editor,* who is an expert in the subject area, and with the guidance of an *Advisory Board,* we seek each year to provide in each *ANNUAL EDITION* a current, well-balanced, carefully selected collection of the best of the public press for your study and enjoyment. We think you'll find this volume useful, and we hope you'll take a moment to let us know what you think.

Annual Editions: World Politics 87/88 is aimed at filling a void in materials for learning about world politics and foreign policy. Among the dozens of textbooks and anthologies available today, this accessible compilation of readings brings together major, current problems concerning relations among nations in an easily understandable language to which readers can relate.

The articles are chosen for those who are new to the study of world politics. The objective of this compilation is to stimulate interest in learning to understand issues that often seem foreign, remote, and irrelevant, but which actually have profound consequences for economic well-being, security, and even survival.

International relations can be viewed as a constant flow of actions and reactions that produce new situations calling for further actions. The readings in this volume convey the complexities and the interdependence of international relations confronting the world at this time. The interdependence of relationships means that events as far away as the Philippines, Japan, the Middle East, South Africa, and Latin America affect the United States, just as America's actions, and inactions, have significant repercussions for other states. International events proceed at such a rapid pace, however, that often what is said about international affairs today may be outdated tomorrow. This collection of articles about international events provides the most up-to-date commentaries available.

This eighth edition of *World Politics 87/88* is divided into eight units. The first five units are directed toward the major actors in the world: the United States, the Soviet Union, Western Europe, Japan, Eastern Europe, China, and the Third World. In the Third World unit, the focus is on those countries which have drawn considerable international attention in the past year. After presenting the major actors and analyses of their current foreign policy issues and concerns, the book turns to three broad areas of concern to international relations: the international political economy; the arms race, arms control, and disarmament; and international organization and international law. In each unit, a variety of political perspectives are offered to make readers more aware of the complexities of the problems in international relations, and to stimulate them to consider alternative perspectives on seemingly straight forward issues.

I wish to thank my colleagues and previous users of *Annual Editions: World Politics* who have taken time to comment on the collection of articles. Please continue to provide feedback to guide the annual revision of this anthology by filling out the article rating form on the last page of this book.

Suzanne P. Ogden

Editor

Contents

Unit 1

The United States as a Major Power

Four selections review the dynamics of the role of the United States as a world power. Topics include American intervention, American relationships with Third-World dictatorships, and human rights policy.

World Map — ii
To the Reader — vi
Topic Guide — 4
Overview — 6

1. **Ideology and Foreign Policy: Isolation and Intervention,** Robert W. Tucker, *Current,* May 1986. — 8

   Isolationism and *interventionism* rarely, if ever, appear in pure form in a country's foreign policy. Isolationism is a commitment to unilateralism, not indifference. Interventionism, although frequently equated with concern, is not necessarily either morally preferable to isolationism, or less perilous. *Containment* is the major expression of liberal interventionism in US foreign policy.

2. **The US and Third-World Dictatorships: A Case for Benign Detachment,** Ted Galen Carpenter, *USA Today Magazine (Society for the Advancement of Education),* May 1986. — 16

   The author criticizes the tendency of American leaders to regard any anticommunist regime, however undemocratic and repressive, as an ally, and to consider any leftist regime or insurgent movement in the *Third World* as a threat to freedom and democracy. In the long run, this approach has weakened, rather than strengthened, America's *national security.*

3. **The Human Rights Imperative,** Cyrus R. Vance, *Foreign Policy,* Summer 1986. — 22

   The former secretary of state considers some of the fallacies that subvert an appropriate US *human rights* policy. Foremost among these is the belief that the pursuit of human rights is incompatible with US *national interests.* Another is the belief that pro-US right-wing dictatorships' abuse of human rights is understandable in the context of their fight against communism, and that anticommunism is the equivalent of democracy.

4. **Ending Apartheid in South Africa,** Ronald Reagan, *Current Policy,* July 1986. — 30

   Although the United States is unalterably opposed to *apartheid,* it is also opposed to punitive sanctions against South Africa. *Disinvestment* would hurt black workers, and would result in South African whites inheriting formerly foreign-owned factories, plants, and mines. President Reagan outlines the steps that the US believes the South African government must take.

Unit 2

The Soviet Union Confronts the World

Eight articles discuss the present state of the Soviet Union's foreign policy, the impact of Chernobyl on Soviet affairs, the intricacies of Kremlin politics, and some of Gorbachev's strategies.

Overview — 34

5. **Shifting Soviet Diplomacy: The Kremlin's Overtures, the West's Distrust,** Gordon Barthos, *World Press Review,* October 1986. — 36

   Since assuming office in March 1985, *Soviet leader Gorbachev* has taken a number of initiatives to diminish hostility toward the Soviet Union. The West's deep mistrust of the Soviets should not blind them to the possibility that Gorbachev is sincerely interested in reducing international tensions.

6. **Chernobyl—The Official Story,** Walter C. Patterson, *Bulletin of the Atomic Scientists,* November 1986. — 39

   Soviet authorities, contrary to expectations in the West, presented an explicit, chilling, and factual account of the events which led up to the *Chernobyl nuclear accident* of April 1986. The Soviets thereby achieved a public relations victory for their candor, and convinced many in the West that their own nuclear industries were safe.

7. **The Soviet Union and the Third World,** Mark N. Katz, *Current History,* October 1986. — 42

   Although there has been an increase in the number of *Third World* countries that are under *Marxist* regimes and loyal to Moscow, they suffer from chronic insurgencies. Further, *non-Marxist* countries that need economic assistance which the Soviets do not supply turn to the West. Soviet leaders thus face problems not only in expanding but even in retaining their present influence in the Third World.

8. **Trade Trouble in the Soviet Union,** Maya Fishkin, *Harvard International Review,* April 1986. — 48

   As a major *exporter of commodities,* especially oil, the Soviet Union is facing falling revenues as world-wide commodity prices decline. Unable to reduce massive purchases of foreign grain, and unwilling to reduce purchases of Western high-technology goods, the only option the Soviet Union has to address a *balance of payments* problem is to borrow from abroad.

The concepts in italics are developed in the article. For further expansion please refer to the Topic Guide, the Index, and the Glossary.

9. **Misreading the Kremlin: Soviet Military Objectives,** Michael McGwire, *World Policy Journal,* Fall 1986.   **51**

The author argues that the Soviets' *conventional buildup* in Europe and *naval buildup* in the Pacific reflects a shift in Soviet military thinking in the second half of the 1960s. Ironically, this shift suggests not an increased Soviet threat but, rather, a shift in *Soviet military strategy* with favorable implications for East-West security.

10. **Will Gorbachev Reform the Soviet Union?** Vladimir Bukovsky, *Commentary,* September 1986.   **60**

Soviet leader Gorbachev is addressing a primary *contradiction between socialism and development:* if the Party continues to control economic management, military science, education, and other areas essential to development, the Soviet Union will continue to suffer from a low level of development. Yet, if the Communist party relinquishes its control, it spells the demise of socialism.

11. **Gorbachev, Citing Party's Failures, Demands Changes,** Philip Taubman, *The New York Times,* January 28, 1987.   **66**

In a broadside against *Communist party rule* and Stalin's and Brezhnev's interpretation of Leninism, Gorbachev insisted that a more open and democratic system, albeit still under Communist party rule and centralized control, was essential to revitalize the creative energies and productive power of the Soviet Union.

12. **The Soviet Union's Interests: Myths and Reality,** Yevgeny M. Primakov, *AEI Foreign Policy and Defense Review,* Vol. 6, No. 1, 1986.   **68**

A key Soviet academic discusses the discrepancy between American notions of Soviet goals in the *Middle East* and the Soviet Union's actual policies. He distinguishes between the Soviet Union's global and regional interests in the Middle East and notes how these are affected by US actions. After analyzing what Moscow considers US interests in the Middle East, he concludes optimistically that there is significant concurrence on the objective interests of the US and USSR in the Middle East.

Unit 3

American Allies: Western Europe and Japan

Nine selections review the current state of American allies, focusing on European socialism, the state of NATO, European terrorism, and economic relations with Japan.

Overview   **76**

13. **The United States and West Europe: An Age of Ambivalence,** Norman A. Graebner, *Current History,* November 1986.   **78**

Western Europeans, in part because of their less globally-oriented foreign policy, have expected less of *détente* than have the Americans. The European view is also tempered by the *geopolitics* of their position and their vulnerability to a Soviet attack. The *Strategic Defense Initiative* has heightened European concerns about the possible outcome of rising Soviet-American tensions. But their concerns about the Reagan administration's *economic policies* have also been serious.

14. **Naked NATO,** Gar Alperovitz, *The New Republic,* September 29, 1986.   **85**

It is, ironically, the conservative foreign policy establishment, rather than the liberal one, which proposes a unilateral US *withdrawal of NATO ground forces* from Europe. The conservative viewpoint is shaped by such factors as the costs to the US of NATO forces, a desire to increase US capabilities to use troops in the Third World, and exasperation with European allies. A *"no first use"* doctrine is complicated by the value of nuclear weapons as a *deterrent.*

15. **The Future of the Alliance and German-American Relations,** Helmut Kohl, *Harvard International Review,* November/December 1986.   **88**

German Chancellor Kohl indicates his strong support for the security arrangements provided by *NATO,* but believes that it must now coordinate its efforts to address the Soviet challenge beyond Central Europe. He also emphasizes the importance of a solution to *"the German question"*—the division of Germany into two parts—and indicates he will make every effort to end that division.

16. **Greece and the Atlantic Alliance,** Andreas Papandreou, *Harvard International Review,* November/December 1986.   **91**

Greek Prime Minister Papandreou criticizes *NATO* for not revising its unidimensional understanding of what has become a very complex international system since NATO was formed. *Greece* is particularly concerned about the permanent US leadership role and centralizing trends in the *Atlantic Alliance,* and has sought to maintain an independent foreign policy. Greece's primary concern is Turkey, which lies outside the East-West concerns of NATO.

The concepts in italics are developed in the article. For further expansion please refer to the Topic Guide, the Index, and the Glossary.

17. **Britain's Contribution to Maintaining Western Interests Outside the NATO Area,** Timothy Renton, *Harvard International Review,* November/December 1986.   93

Britain is increasingly concerned that although its national defense resources are devoted to the common *defense* in *NATO,* it has significant economic, political, and military concerns beyond those arising from the Atlantic Alliance. NATO members must, minimally, consult on the implications of regional security problems outside the Treaty area.

18. **Euro-Communism: 10 Years Later, Down and Almost Out,** *US News & World Report,* July 14, 1986.   96

Marxism, in the form of Euro-Communism, is disappearing from European political culture. Disenchantment with the Soviet Union, the decline of the heavy industrial base in Europe, and inflexibility within the Communist party structure are three main reasons for the erosion of support of Euro-Communism.

19. **Europe: Spreading Fear of Terrorism,** Gerd Langguth, *World Press Review,* November 1986.   98

Left-wing terrorism, which includes Marxist, ethnic, and Middle East-based groups, is a continuing problem in Western Europe. Liberal democracies, lacking the totalitarian mechanisms necessary to combat terrorism, will never be able to stop it.

20. **An Island unto Itself: The Roots of Japan's International Isolation,** Susumu Ohara, *Speaking of Japan (Tokyo),* May 1986.   101

The increasing *isolation* of Japan from the international community is an issue which worries the Japanese. Japan is largely to blame for this, and must take the initiative to change its relations with other states through *internationalization.* Although many of the problems are economic, their roots are in the Japanese ways of thinking and living.

21. **Breaching the Line: Nakasone Stays Out of Range on Military Budget,** Charles Smith, *Far Eastern Economic Review,* January 15, 1987.   104

Although Japan has now breached its defense spending ceiling of one percent of the GNP, debates over defense spending will continue to have less to do with security issues as such than with political values. The government's decision as to just how much one percent of the GNP will amount to must avoid the two extremes of a continuance of Japan's embarrassing dependence on the US for national defense, and alienating Japan's neighbors, once the victims of Japan's militarism.

Unit 4

Socialist States: Allies and Adversaries of the USSR

Five articles consider the world's socialist states and their relationships with the Soviet Union by examining Poland and the latest developments in China.

Overview   106
22. **Sino-American Relations: Policies in Tandem,** John Bryan Starr, *Current History,* September 1986.   108

Within China's *security zone,* which includes Japan, Korea, Taiwan, and most of Southeast Asia, the policies of China and the US are (except in the case of Taiwan) compatible. Although China has tried to encourage *trade and foreign investment* through new lands and policies, foreigners are still reluctant to invest further in China. Much of the reluctance derives from *foreign currency restrictions* and a concern about *political risk* factors.

23. **China's Limited Accommodation with the USSR: Coalition Politics,** David M. Lampton, *AEI Foreign Policy and Defense Review,* Vol. 6, No. 3, 1986.   114

Sino-Soviet relations have been marked since 1982 by *limited accommodation.* China's policies toward the USSR, although disguised by moral statements concerning China's "principled stand," are largely the product of *geopolitics,* a concern for the *balance of power,* and internal politics. The Soviet Union is as much a part of China's *"open policy"* as is the West. Still, compared to Sino-American relations, the scale of Sino-Soviet ties is small.

24. **Poland: Internal Situation Picking Up,** Wen Youren, *Beijing Review,* December 29, 1986.   124

The imposition of martial law in Poland in 1981 brought unrest to an end and permitted the economy to recover. Although there are still serious *economic problems* in Poland, the economy is making progress. The Polish government is listening to the views of those dissidents who disagree with its policies but still support socialist objectives.

The concepts in italics are developed in the article. For further expansion please refer to the Topic Guide, the Index, and the Glossary.

25. Boldness, Staunchness, Action, Janos Kadar, *New Times* (Moscow), October 20, 1986.   **125**

In an interview with a Soviet correspondent, Hungarian Party General Secretary Janos Kadar discusses *economic reforms* which began in 1968. These have *combined socialism with market principles*, and economic instruments have replaced administrative mechanisms for managing the economy. Since 1985, even greater decentralization of economic power has occurred, permitting local enterprises greater autonomy in decision making.

26. China Will Not Retrogress, An Zhiguo, *Beijing Review,* March 2, 1987.   **129**

Recently China has begun to reform and liberalize in many ways. The driving force behind this *overall modernization* is economic in nature, and, as the author of this article points out, the power of this economic reform will continue to change China.

Unit 5

The Third World

Twelve selections review the current state of the Third World by focusing on Africa, Asia, Latin America, and the Middle East.

Overview   **130**

A. AFRICA

27. Africa's Economy in Crisis: The Facts and Figures, *The New York Times,* May 29, 1986.   **132**

This chart outlines the current state of *Africa's economy.* All members of the *Organization of African Unity* are listed.

28. Moscow and Africa: A 1986 Balance Sheet, Michael Clough, *CSIS Africa Notes,* March 21, 1986.   **133**

Those African countries which became *allies of the Soviet Union* from the 1950s to the 1970s did so as a result of a conscious decision, not as the result of Soviet penetration. They believe that the Soviet Union was a *"natural ally"* of radical Third World states, and the only source of protection against capitalist imperialism, regional aggression, and internal subversion. In the 1980s, the perspective of many African states has changed, and Moscow's fortunes in Africa are flagging.

29. Race Politics in South Africa: Change and Revolt, Kenneth W. Grundy, *Current History,* May 1986.   **137**

A cycle of *violence* is affecting both the black and white populations of *South Africa.* Deaths result from the operations of the police and army, but also from black violence against blacks believed to be associated with the white authorities, and intercommunal fights among blacks. Changes in the laws undergirding *apartheid* are not enough to satisfy what has become a growing demand by blacks for power. Meanwhile, South Africa's policy of confrontation with its neighbors continues.

B. ASIA

30. The Process of Assimilation of Hong Kong (1997) and Implications for Taiwan, John P. Burns, *AEI Foreign Policy and Defense Review,* Vol. 6, No. 3, 1986.   **143**

China's policies toward Hong Kong will be determined by collaboration with Hong Kong's managerial class in the short run. But, the present Hong Kong government is really a lame duck, which must negotiate all significant policies with Beijing even though Hong Kong does not revert to Chinese sovereignty until 1997. China will, however, be careful not to seriously disrupt the economic and political life of the former colony.

31. Ji Reaffirms China's Policy Towards Hong Kong, *Beijing Review,* March 2, 1987.   **149**

This interview with Ji Pengfei, director of the Hong Kong and Macao Affairs Office of the State Council, reaffirms *China's policy toward Hong Kong,* which is that there will be an orderly assimilation of the long-term British crown colony into the Chinese sphere.

32. Three Decisions Vital to Anti-Vietnamese War, Yang Mu, *Beijing Review,* December 29, 1986.   **151**

According to Beijing, *Democratic Kampuchea* has been resisting the Vietnamese-installed puppet regime successfully for ten years by relying on *guerrilla warfare.* By organizing a *coalition government,* the Kampuchean people have an authoritative anti-Vietnamese government.

C. LATIN AMERICA

33. The Next Earthquake, Curtis Skinner, *Commonweal,* July 11, 1986.   **153**

The *oil price plunge* in 1986 initiated by Saudi Arabia came on top of an already desperate economic situation, and has made *Mexico's foreign debt* unpayble. The only alternative to a *debt default* is a unilateral *payment moratorium.*

34. **Contadora Primer,** *International Policy Report,* November 1986.   **156**
This report reviews the *Contadora countries* in Latin America, and outlines
the treaty that has been proposed by them. How the treaty would work, how
it would get the Soviets out of the involved countries, how it would be verified, and who has agreed to it are covered.

35. **US Role in El Salvador: The Quagmire of Dependency,** Jim   **161**
Chapin, *Commonweal,* August 15, 1986.
The *military* has, under pressure from the US, reduced the level of *terror*
in *El Salvador.* Instead, they have followed a policy of *mass depopulation*
of those rural areas in which rebels flourished. The US has provided the
Duarte government with an enormous aid package to attack communism
in many spheres: the union movement, religion, culture, and politics.

D. *THE MIDDLE EAST*

36. **Islam in the Politics of the Middle East,** John L. Esposito,   **165**
Current History, February 1986.
Political Islam has become such a powerful force in the Mideast because
of the repeated failures and crises of authority and legitimacy in most modern
Muslim states. Islam in various forms has taken the place of *nationalism* and
socialism as the key factor in ideology and politics since the 1970s. Each
regime and opposition movement adapts Islam to its own purposes, with the
result that there is an enormous diversity among them in institutions, principles, and practices.

37. **The Middle East Peace Process and the US,** Richard W. Murphy,   **172**
USA Today Magazine (Society for the Advancement of Education),
July 1986.
The climate for a peaceful settlement of the *Arab-Israeli dispute* and *the Palestinian issue* has recently improved. But obstacles remain, the toughest one
being the issue of who will represent the Palestinians in negotiations. The
author believes that the decision must be resolved through agreement among
the Palestinians, Jordanians, and Israelis. The costs of inaction are high,
not just for Israel, but for all the Middle East.

38. **The Superpowers in the Palestine Conflict,** Helmut Hubel,   **175**
AEI Foreign Policy and Defense Review, Vol. 6, No. I, 1986.
The Soviet-American confrontation provides the necessary background for
understanding the major crises in the Middle East, even though the basic
reasons for these crises are indigenous. The author addresses the question
as to whether one or both superpowers could bring an end to the Palestinian conflict. The only realistic possibility is that both superpowers, together
with their Mideastern allies, seek a reconciliation on specific, clearly defined
issues.

Unit 6

The International Political Economy: Aid, Investment, Trade, and Finance

Six articles examine the international political
economy. Topics include the IMF (International
Monetary Fund), exploitation of the developing
countries, impacts of international aid on recipient
nations, and debt management.

Overview   **184**
39. **Evaluating the MNC Contribution,** Timothy W. Stanley and   **186**
Stephen E. Thomsen, *Harvard International Review,* April 1986.
Just at the point at which the *lesser developed countries* can begin to take
a more favorable view of investments by *multinational corporations* (MNCs),
the MNCs have become reluctant to invest in them. *Restrictive investment
policies* are partly responsible. Several new international instruments have
been created to encourage new MNC investment and intergovernmental consultation on problems arising from foreign investments.

40. **Rewriting GATT's Rules for a Game That Has Changed,** *The*   **190**
Economist, September 13, 1986.
The trade talks on the *General Agreement on Tariffs and Trade* (GATT) will
decide whether international trade patterns are determined by political clout
and the "management" of trade, or by the principle of *comparative advantage. Market-sharing* goes against GATT's principle of prohibiting *selective
protectionism.* Problems which the talks must address are safeguards against
"unfair" trade, dispute settlement, rules on subsidies for agriculture, and
property rights.

41. **GATT: The Eighth Round,** V. Zolotukhin, *New Times* (Moscow),   **193**
December 15, 1986.
A new round of *multilateral trade negotiations* in Geneva is to address more
specific problems within the *General Agreement on Tariffs and Trade* (GATT)
framework established in September, 1986. The *Soviet Union,* which would
like to eventually become a full-fledged member of GATT, was not even permitted observer status in the September talks. Moscow believes the arguments used to keep it from establishing ties with GATT are politically biased.

The concepts in italics are developed in the article. For further expansion please refer to the Topic Guide, the Index, and the Glossary.

42. **The Continuing Failure of US Foreign Aid,** James Bovard,   **196**
USA Today Magazine (Society for the Advancement of Education),
September 1986.
An examination of the history of *US foreign aid* indicates that, although it
has improved the life-style of the rulers and bureaucrats in *lesser developed
countries,* it has failed to benefit the peoples of these countries, to increase
production, or to encourage them to help themselves. America's *Food for
Peace* program, *AID,* and other foreign aid instruments have actually had
negative effects on aid recipients.

43. **All Participants Must Work Together to Ensure Resolution**   **203**
of Debt Problems, J. de Larosiere, *IMF Survey,* December 1, 1986.
The managing director of the *International Monetary Fund* believes that the
indebted countries of *Latin America* have made considerable progress recently in turning around their external *account deficits.* This has been facilitated by the more realistic *exchange rates* which have come into effect, by
the dramatic decline in *international interest rates,* by the improved financial
basis of *commercial banks* which lend to indebted countries, and by the more
manageable *inflation rates* in the indebted countries.

44. **Latin America's External Debt: The Limits of Regional Cooper-**   **208**
ation, Esperanza Durán, *The World Today,* May 1986.
The *International Monetary Fund readjustment programs* which international banks demanded as a precondition for their continued credit to the *debt-
ridden Latin American countries* imposed intolerable social and political
burdens. The sacrifices demanded by austerity, moreover, did not appear
to have been worthwhile, as these countries' *external debts* continued to
grow. Growth, in fact, appears to have been sacrificed in order to repay these
debts.

Unit 7

The Arms Race, Arms Control, and Deterrence

Ten selections discuss the current state of the arms
race and deterrence by considering the future of
deterrence, nuclear alternatives, Soviet offers for
disarmament, and the difficulty of verification.

Overview   **214**
45. **Nuclear Weapons, Arms Control, and the Future of Deterrence,**   **216**
George Schultz, *Current Policy,* November 1986.
The US Secretary of State reviews the history of US thinking about *nuclear
weapons.* Although thus far nuclear weapons seem to have brought *deterrence,* the stability of the nuclear balance in the future is not guaranteed.
The Reagan administration has done much to reverse dangerous trends in
the military balance by strengthening both America's conventional and
nuclear deterrent forces.

46. **Are There Alternatives to Nuclear Threat Systems?** John   **221**
Marks, *The Humanist,* September/October 1986.
The author is convinced that politics relating to the *nuclear international security* arena can be transformed rather than the old system being rearranged,
thus guaranteeing new areas of agreement for continued *superpower coexistence.* The US and USSR must realize that *mutual shared security* is the
alternative to nuclear threat systems.

47. **Beyond Theory to Reality: Can the World Disarm?** Peter   **225**
Grier, *The Christian Science Monitor,* November 18, 1986.
Although a *nuclear-free world* sounds good, this option has its problems for
the US strategic community. The greatest ones are that it increases the risk
of a conventional war in Europe, and that it would increase tension and suspicion, since any state that cheated and acquired just one nuclear weapon
would be able to blackmail all others.

48. **Gorbachev Offer: Two Other Arms Hints,** Bill Keller, *The New*   **227**
York Times, March 2, 1987.
This article reviews some of the latest proposals by Soviet Premier Mikhail
S. Gorbachev concerning *arms reduction in Europe.*

49. **Interim Restraint: US and Soviet Force Projections,** *US Depart-*   **229**
ment of State, Special Report No. 151, August 5, 1986.
Continued US compliance with *SALT I* and *SALT II* has been contingent upon
Soviet reciprocity and maintaining *US national security* in the face of a *Soviet
arms buildup.* The Soviets' continued *noncompliance* has made it necessary
for the US to base future decisions concerning its strategic force structure
on the nature and magnitude of the Soviet threat, not on standards established in the flawed SALT structure.

50. **Do the Soviets Cheat?** Rich West, *SANE Newsletter,* May/June   **233**
1986.
The author investigates President Reagan's allegations that the Soviets have
cheated on *arms control agreements* with the US. He concludes that most
of the allegations are false, or that the US has also violated them.

The concepts in italics are developed in the article. For further expansion please refer to the Topic Guide, the Index, and the Glossary.

51. **Back from the Brink,** McGeorge Bundy et al., *The Atlantic*   235
Monthly, August 1986.
In a search for an *arms control* plan which would reduce the risks of nuclear war, these authors propose that the US base its military plans, defense budgets, weapons deployments, etc., on the assumption of *no first use of nuclear weapons.* They emphasize the importance of strengthening *conventional forces* as an alternative to first use of nuclear weapons. NATO's reliance on nuclear first use has adversely affected its capacity to fight a conventional war.

52. **US and Soviet Responsibility for Disarmament,** Si Chu, *Beijing*   242
Review, December 29, 1986.
Since the US and USSR possess over ninety-five percent of all *nuclear weapons,* they must take the lead in disarming. So far, however, their declared willingness to take the lead in reducing nuclear weapons by fifty percent has been mere propaganda. *China's resolutions on conventional and nuclear disarmament,* which have been adopted by the United Nations, is China's contribution to maintaining world peace.

53. **A Soviet Official on Verification,** Roland M. Timerbaev, *Bulletin*   244
of the Atomic Scientists, January/February 1987.
This Soviet official contends that the US is using *verification* issues to avoid agreements on *arms control and disarmament.* New Soviet initiatives have disposed of verification as a real issue. Now the real obstacle to a treaty on the *total prohibition of nuclear weapons tests* is the US. Further, if it goes ahead with its *Strategic Defense Initiative,* verification will face virtually insurmountable difficulties.

54. **Irresponsible Act,** *New Times* (Moscow), December 15, 1986.   247
According to this report, it was irresponsible of the US to exceed the quotas set by *SALT II* by building one extra B-52 bomber. The US is thereby forcing the Soviet Union into a continued *arms race.*

Unit 8

International Organization and International Law

Five articles discuss the importance of international law on world peace as affected by international organization.

Overview   248
55. **World Court Supports Nicaragua After US Rejected Judges'**   250
Role, Paul Lewis, *The New York Times,* June 28, 1986.
The World Court supported Nicaragua's claim that the United States had broken *international law* and violated Nicaraguan sovereignty by aiding the *Contras,* by attacks on Nicaraguan oil installations, ports, and shipping, by mining Nicaraguan harbors, and by an illegal trade embargo. The US claim of acting in *collective self-defense* was rejected by the Court. The US rejected the Court's ruling on the grounds that it lacks jurisdiction over this conflict.

56. **Who Will Protect Freedom of the Seas?** John D. Negroponte,   253
Current Policy, No. 855, July 1986.
The *Third Law of the Sea Conference* was called in part to address the concern on the part of the US and USSR that the *freedom of the seas* not be further eroded. Although the conference temporarily halted that erosion, further setbacks may occur unless the maritime states take action to protect that freedom. The Assistant Secretary of State does acknowledge that the US has displayed a split personality on the law of the sea.

57. **Highlights of the Convention on the Law of the Sea,** *The*   256
UNESCO Courier, February 1986.
The *Convention on the Law of the Sea* addresses issues concerning the international areas of the sea and delimits the areas over which states have jurisdiction. It covers such issues as mineral exploitation, marine scientific research, navigational rights, pollution, territorial seas, economic zones, and international seabed areas.

58. **Wanted: An International Criminal Court,** Paul Wilkinson,   258
World Press Review, November 1986.
To address *terrorism,* the states in the Western alliance need to relinquish their right to sovereign control and adopt a single forum for cooperation: a *criminal court and code* for dealing with international terrorists. They should also take concerted diplomatic actions and economic sanctions against terrorist states. Most important, however, is the settlement of the underlying source of conflict that breeds terrorism: the *Palestinian issue.*

59. **Countering the Threat of Terrorism,** Rushworth M. Kidder,   259
The Christian Science Monitor, May 21, 1986.
International cooperation is vital if *terrorism* is to be reduced. Although many obstacles obstruct such cooperation, an international consensus is growing on how to address terrorism. Diplomatic, social, legal, and security measures are being undertaken by states concerned with combatting terrorism. The public, the military, the police, and the media must all be involved in these efforts.

Abbreviations   265
Glossary   266
Index   274
Article Rating Form   277

The concepts in italics are developed in the article. For further expansion please refer to the Topic Guide, the Index, and the Glossary.

Topic Guide

The topic guide suggests how the selections in this book relate to topics of traditional concern to world politics students and professionals. It is very useful in locating articles which relate to each other for reading and research. The guide is arranged alphabetically according to topic. Articles may, of course, treat topics that do not appear in the topic guide. In turn, entries in the topic guide do not necessarily constitute a comprehensive listing of all the contents of each selection.

TOPIC AREA	TREATED AS AN ISSUE IN:	TOPIC AREA	TREATED AS AN ISSUE IN:
Africa	27. Africa's Economy in Crisis 28. Moscow and Africa	Germany	15. The Failure of the Alliance
American Interventionism	1. Ideology and Foreign Policy	Gorbachev's Policies	5. Shifting Soviet Diplomacy 10. Will Gorbachev Reform the Soviet Union? 11. Gorbachev, Citing Party's Failures
American Isolationism	1. Ideology and Foreign Policy	Great Britain	17. Britain's Contribution to Maintaining Western Interests
America's National Interest	1. Ideology and Foreign Policy 2. The US and Third-World Dictatorships 3. The Human Rights Imperative	Greece	16. Greece and the Atlantic Alliance
Apartheid	4. Ending Apartheid in South Africa 29. Race Politics in South Africa	Hong Kong	30. The Process of Assimilation of Hong Kong
Arms Control and Disarmament	49. Interim Restraint 50. Do the Soviets Cheat? 51. Back from the Brink 52. US and Soviet Responsibility for Disarmament 54. Irresponsible Act	Human Rights	3. The Human Rights Imperative
		Hungary	25. Boldness, Staunchness, Action
		International Law	56. Who Will Protect Freedom of the Seas? 57. Highlights of the Convention on the Law of the Sea 58. Wanted: An International Criminal Court
Chernobyl	6. Chernobyl		
China and the West	22. Sino-American Relations 24. Poland: Interior Situation Picking Up		
China's National Interest	22. Sino-American Relations 23. China's Limited Accommodation with the USSR 26. China Will Not Retrogress	International Trade and Finance	8. Trade Trouble in the Soviet Union 33. The Next Earthquake 40. Rewriting GATT's Rules for a Game That Has Changed 41. GATT: The Eighth Round 44. Latin America's External Debt
Communism, Containment of	1. Ideology and Foreign Policy 2. The US and Third-World Dictatorships	Islam	36. Islam in the Politics of the Middle East
Détente	13. The United States and West Europe	Japanese Isolation	20. An Island unto Itself
Deterrence	13. The United States and West Europe 14. Naked NATO 45. Nuclear Weapons	Japan's Defense	21. Breaching the Line
		Kampuchea	32. Three Decisions Vital to Anti-Vietnamese War
El Salvador	35. US Role in El Salvador	Marxist Regimes	7. The Soviet Union and the Third World
Euro-Communism	18. Euro-Communism		
Foreign Aid and Investment	4. Ending Apartheid 35. US Role in El Salvador 39. Evaluating the MNC Contribution 42. The Continuing Failure of US Foreign Aid	Mexico	33. Poverty and Politics in Mexico
		Middle East	12. The Soviet Union's Interests 36. Islam in the Politics of the Middle East 37. The Middle East Peace Process and the US 38. The Superpowers in the Palestine Conflict
Geopolitics	12. The Soviet Union's Interests 13. The United States and West Europe 23. China's Limited Accommodation with the USSR		

TOPIC AREA	TREATED AS AN ISSUE IN:	TOPIC AREA	TREATED AS AN ISSUE IN:
NATO	14. Naked NATO 15. The Future of the Alliance 16. Greece and the Atlantic Alliance 17. Britain's Contribution to Maintaining Western Interests	**Strategic Defense Initiative (SDI)**	13. The United States and West Europe
		Taiwan	30. The Process of Assimilation of Hong Kong
Nicaragua	55. World Court Supports Nicaragua After US Rejected Judges' Role	**Terrorism**	58. Wanted: An International Criminal Court 59. Countering the Threat of Terrorism
No First Use	14. Naked NATO	**Turkey**	16. Greece and the Atlantic Alliance
Nuclear Security	46. Are There Alternatives to Nuclear Threat Systems? 47. Beyond Theory to Reality 49. Interim Restraint	**Verification**	53. A Soviet Official on Verification
		Vietnam	32. Three Decisions Vital to Anti-Vietnamese War
Nuclear War	9. Soviet Military Objectives	**Western Europe**	13. The United States and West Europe 14. Naked NATO 15. The Future of the Alliance 17. Britain's Contribution to Maintaining Western Interests 18. Euro-Communism 19. Europe: Spreading Fear of Terrorism
Palestine	37. The Middle East Peace Process and the US 38. The Superpowers in the Palestine Conflict		
Poland	24. Poland: Internal Situation Picking Up		
Soviet Military	9. Soviet Military Objectives	**World Court**	55. World Court Supports Nicaragua After US Rejected Judges' Role
Soviet National Interests	12. The Soviet Union's Interests		

The United States as a Major Power

In recent years, the United States has seen its national interests advanced worldwide. It would be arrogant to assume, however, that when other states' actions advance America's national interest, or at least do not challenge it, this should be credited to US foreign policy. Although this may be true in some cases, in others it is an erroneous assumption that may lead to the misdirection of US foreign policy. In a world of complex interdependence, and a world in which the power configuration is diffuse, one state cannot direct the action of other states at will.

The Soviet Union's recent stance on arms control and its diminished support for revolution abroad, for example, may have less to do with America's foreign policy than with internal political and economic pressures on the Soviet leadership. Further, it is possible that the Soviets are not reacting to US policy initiatives, but rather generating their own initiatives to which the US is responding. Gorbachev's disarmament proposals may, on the one hand, reflect his assessment that this is the only sensible alternative for the Soviet Union to pursue in light of Reagan's insistence on continuing with the Strategic Defense Initiative (SDI) or may, on the other hand, reflect his assessment of what would contribute most to his consolidation of power at home. Although we can hardly dismiss US foreign policy as irrelevant to what the Soviets do, we cannot blindly conclude that Reagan's tough line on foreign policy produced a Soviet foreign policy more congenial to America's national interest. In addition, the unique personality, experience, and character of a policy formulator in another state merge together to shape his or her response to United States foreign policy and its formulators. Reagan, for example, may be viewed by other leaders as a tough president who "stands tall," as a rigid and ideological leader, or as a mere buffoon.

Regardless of how much credit America can take for what happens in the world, America's key allies and adversaries seem to confirm the direction of American foreign policy, especially in the European theater. Compared to the 1970s, America's relationships with its major allies are stable. The European peace movement, which was opposed to the emplacement of American nuclear missiles in Western Europe, has lost its momentum. There is less divisiveness within NATO, and fewer attempts by the Europeans to blame the US for their economic difficulties. Although Canada and the United States have problems, such as acid rain, cooperation dominates the relationship. Japan too seems to be accommodating America's concerns about Japan's defense and economic aggressiveness so as to fend off the "Japan bashing" tactics of Congress. In addition, the Japanese, together with the Europeans and Americans, are collaborating to bring about the stabilization of international currency exchange rates. Similarly, US relations with its Communist adversaries are improving. Soviet-American tensions are at their lowest level in at least a decade. Sino-American relations are steadily improving, although Washington is certainly concerned about the political upheavals in the People's Republic of China in early 1987, and their potential impact on democratizing forces and economic liberalization, as well as on China's relationship with the US.

Nevertheless, the "Iran-Contra Affair," which erupted in late 1986, did serious damage to the credibility of American leadership in the Western alliance. By doing precisely what it had insisted that its allies not do, namely, negotiating with terrorists (attempting to regain American hostages held in Lebanon by selling arms to Iran), the US now faces the strong possibility of a diminished international leadership role, especially when it tries to take the moral high ground. Further, the negotiations with terrorists and the transfer of profits from the Iranian arms sales to illegally fund the Contras to fight the Nicaraguan Sandinista regime has also damaged the Reagan administration's political clout with Congress and the American people. Congress, which in any event is now completely controlled by the Democrats, is likely to assert its foreign policy-making role more forcefully, to scrutinize carefully every foreign policy initiative of the White House, and to pose considerable obstacles to President Reagan's continuing support for the Contras. Although the full ramifications of the Iran-Contra scandal cannot yet be known, already it seems to have led to yet further hostage-taking. American efforts to have a suspected terrorist who is held by the West Germans extradited to the US has, in turn, led to further kidnappings and such instability in Lebanon that American allies, such as Saudi Arabia, Kuwait, and other major oil producers, implored the US to make a "show of force." This resulted in the stationing of the US Sixth Fleet off the Lebanese coast, but with the apparent effect of further destabilizing the situation in Lebanon.

In short, it seems that American foreign policy on terrorism, the Middle East, and Central America have backfired in the last year, and no policy victories are on the horizon. Whether or not a victory in another foreign policy area, such as arms control and disarmament, could salvage the reputation of the Reagan administration for history remains to be seen.

Using the international system as the level of analysis, however, shows the United States to be more successful. American efforts through the International Monetary Fund (IMF) and World Bank to cope with the issues of massive indebtedness and debt restructuring have started to bear fruit in spite of some casualties. In addition, the willingness on the part of the US to grapple seriously with its own balance of payments problems, as well as to bring down the value of the American dollar, has brought with it more willingness on the part of the international community to listen to the US on international economic and financial matters.

The articles in this unit indicate some of the dilemmas which the US faces in its foreign policy decisions. Article #1 indicates the dimensions of the debate surrounding the issue of when and where to intervene, and whether isolationism is evidence of indifference about international affairs, or a commitment to unilaterialism. Article 2 suggests that the US has been actively interventionist in the Middle East and Nicaragua because of its irrational obsession with Communist expansion. Interventionism has, however, weakened rather than strengthened America's national security, and has exposed America's inconsistent moral standards and insensitivity to the complexities of Third World politics. If the United States does remain actively interventionist in the affairs of other countries, such as in supporting human rights, it must reject the belief that supporting human rights policies in countries under right-wing anticommunist dictatorships is incompatible with its national interests (Article 3). The Reagan administration is clearly on the record against interventionism in the affairs of South Africa on behalf of human rights for another reason: even though it is opposed to apartheid, it is afraid of the negative impact on South African blacks of an active interventionism, which would mandate disinvestment of US corporate holdings there (Article 4).

Looking Ahead: Challenge Questions

If you were to prioritize America's foreign policy concerns, which would be primary? Which would be secondary? What are the major variables which should be used to determine whether a foreign policy issue is of primary or secondary concern to the US? Can you give any instances in which the US has sacrificed its national interest for the pursuit of moral principles? Should sub-Saharan Africa, excluding South Africa, be at the top of the list of areas where America's national interests are at stake?

Since World War II, are there instances of American intervention abroad that has served to make America's commitment to principles or to allies less credible rather than more? When America's allies did not support US military intervention abroad, what reasons did they give? What elements create an image of credibility? By what means can the US maintain credibility without projecting its military power abroad? What role does the existence of large numbers of US controlled nuclear weapons and significant conventional forces play in creating an image of US credibility?

Is US foreign policy in the mid-1980s more motivated by ''internationalism'' than in the past? Is internationalism in conflict with America's national interest?

IDEOLOGY AND FOREIGN POLICY
ISOLATION AND INTERVENTION

ROBERT W. TUCKER

Mr. Tucker is a professor at Johns Hopkins' School of Advanced International Studies.

There are two fundamental and enduring dispositions in foreign policy: isolationism and interventionism. They rarely—if indeed, ever—appear in pure form. What inclination may prompt, circumstance and interest will nearly always qualify. In our own case, a concern to secure political isolation from Europe served as a principal justification for both a policy of territorial expansion in this continent and one of extending our influence over the entire hemisphere.

Nineteenth-century American isolation from Europe was the result of an almost uniquely benign set of circumstances. A detached and distant position and a favorable balance of power in Europe not only made that status viable but virtually ensured its success. No serious adventure could be undertaken in the Western Hemisphere by a continental power without the assistance or, at the very least, the acquiescence of Great Britain. Despite an occasional lapse, Britain found it generally in her interest to discourage such adventures by others. These circumstances apart, hemispheric isolation also expressed the evident interests of the nation and reflected the limited power at our disposal. Not only had we no plausible interest to intervene in European politics, we did not have the means of doing so. It is only between the two world wars that we acquired the interest and power to do what policy and tradition rejected. In consequence, it is only between the wars that we went from a status of being isolated to a policy of being isolationist.

Given our interwar experience, the stigma that has since attached to isolationism is understandable. Even so, the stigma and judgment it reflects have become a prejudice. Many no longer even know what isolationism means; they only know it is a label to be avoided. Since the 1970s, isolationist views have been frequently paraded as a "new internationalism," presumably to differentiate them from the "old inter-nationalism" that had led to Vietnam. Whereas the old internationalism of the cold war was interventionist, the new internationalism is anti-interventionist. This terminology, a complete reversal of conventional usage, reflects a determination not to be marked by the dread epithet.

There need be no mystery about the meaning of isolationism as a policy. It means today what it meant yesterday. An isolationist policy is one of general political detachment. It avoids entering into certain relationships, notably alliances, and undertaking certain actions, notably military interventions. Historically, our policy of isolation was defined primarily by our political detachment from Europe, then the center of the state system. At present, a policy of isolation is most reasonably defined by reference to the set of relations that have been critical in determining our post-war position of primacy in the world. It is our alliance relations with Western Europe and Japan that provide the litmus test. Those who support our major alliances, and accept all that this support must imply, cannot be considered as isolationist however much they may oppose intervention elsewhere. Isolationism is not like pregnancy; a little of it is quite possible as long as it does not substantially affect the central balance of power in the world. The conviction that we must be either isolationist or interventionist, committed virtually everywhere or nowhere, reflects an absolutism that has prompted us in the past to excesses in policy and may do so again if we fail to disenthrall ourselves from it.

THE NEED TO REJECT EXTREMES

Isolationism as a disposition has often been equated with indifference. The equation may be quite misleading when applied to a small or even a middle power. Even in the case of a great power it may neglect other motivations. In our own case, a deep and pervasive fear of the domestic effects of intervening in European politics persisted until World War II. In part, this fear resulted from America's ethnic

From *Current*, May 1986, pp. 4-12. Originally from *The National Interest*, Fall 1985, pp. 16-25. Reprinted by permission of The National Interest.

composition. Europe's conflicts divided us and placed American nationality under considerable strain. In part, too, there was an almost obsessive fear that foreign involvement—and above all war—must erode constitutional processes and betray the American domestic promise. Isolationists entertained widely divergent visions of that promise. Yet it was the same conviction about the threatening domestic effects of foreign involvement that in the 1930s could unite such otherwise different figures as the socialist Norman Thomas and the conservative Robert A. Taft.

The isolationist disposition is also rooted in the commitment to unilateralism. The importance attached to retaining complete independence of action in foreign policy requires no special explanation. To be able to separate one's fate from the fate of others is always desirable, though rarely possible. The isolationist disposition responds to the deep-rooted desire to have complete control over one's destiny. That desire is apparent today and it has taken more than one expression.

These considerations qualify the equation of isolationism with indifference, particularly when applied to a great power. They do not refute that charge. For the mark of great power is that, by virtue of the resources at its disposal, it can affect the fate of others. If it refuses to do so, this must at least in part be traced to indifference.

Interventionism, by contrast, is equated with concern. This does not somehow make it politically or morally preferable to isolationism. To find in isolationism a sin of the spirit because it denotes indifference is no more persuasive than to see in interventionism a virtue because it denotes concern.

Interventionism does not have a set of uniform consequences. There have been all kind and manner of interventionists in history. What can be said of all interventionists—the successful and the unsuccessful, the just and the unjust—is that they have sought to impose their will on a recalcitrant world. Great powers have been especially inclined to change the world and they have never lacked reasons for doing so. In the case of revolutionary great powers, this disposition is often transformed into an obsession to recreate the world and not merely to change it.

Men and nations being what they are, the world is difficult to change, let alone to recreate. The means of those who desire to change the world need not always involve force, but they normally have done so. In our own history, the nation's mission of regenerating the world by bringing to it the blessings of freedom was for long to be implemented through the power of moral example. This is why, as Louis Hartz long ago pointed out, we have always been able to see ourselves as regenerating the world while remaining politically withdrawn—that is, isolated—from it. Of course, in this hemisphere we were often neither withdrawn nor particularly regenerative. Elsewhere, however, this distinctly American disposition persisted until well into this century. Long after it was given up, at the time of the war in Vietnam, the plea was made by many lapsed interventionists to restore it, the argument being that we might once again do by the power of example what we could no longer do by the power of our arms. The argument is unpersuasive. Even those who only want to see the expansion of freedom in the world may have to employ force. It is difficult to change the world without also imposing one's will on it—or at least, without *first* imposing one's will on it.

From a perspective that rises above the mere rationalization of interest, it is difficult to choose between the perils of indifference and the perils of concern. At the least, though, experience should have taught us by now that it is not only the perils of indifference that are to be guarded against. It is true that the identification of the collective self with something larger than the self has been a principal source of what justice men have been capable of showing in their collective relations. Yet in a world marked by great disparities of power, this identification, which is the tap root of concern, has also been a principal source of injustice.

INDIFFERENCE VS. CONCERN

Any foreign policy we have in the future will be some combination of isolationist and interventionist elements. It may also be internationalist. But the common view that internationalism constitutes a third distinct way in foreign policy, a way by which the hazards of both isolationism and interventionism are avoided, is mistaken. Internationalism, when it is not simply employed as pretense, can mean no more than a disposition to take seriously into account the views and interests of others (not only of allies), as well as to cooperate whenever possible and feasible in common enterprises. As such, internationalism is no small thing; but it is also no alternative way in foreign policy either, since it is always subordinate to distinctly national interests. With its corollary of multilateralism, internationalism is at best a moderator of nationalism, with its natural inclination to unilateralism. It can diminish, but not resolve the eternal dilemmas of foreign policy.

THE CREATION OF CONTAINMENT

These dilemmas have been particularly apparent since Vietnam, when the great post-war foreign policy consensus fell apart. That consensus was articulated and led by the liberals in the Democratic Party and the moderate Republicans. The liberal intellectuals in particular constituted the great voice for intervention, first against the Axis powers and subsequently against the Soviet Union once Germany and Japan were defeated. They were true believers in the rightness of American purposes in the world—above all the purpose of extending freedom—and in our power to achieve those purposes. They entertained little fear over the domestic effects of foreign policy. That involvement—and above all war—might threaten constitutional processes and betray the American domestic promise were the fears of conservative isolationists, not of liberal interventionists.

Containment was the principal policy expression of liberal interventionism. From the outset, however, there was uncertainty and controversy over the scope containment would have. In its inception, containment had no determinate form or outcome. It is true that in the sweeping language of the Truman Doctrine—with its indiscriminate commitment: "We must assist free peoples to work out their destinies in their own way"; its sense of universal crisis: "at the present moment in world history every nation must choose between alternative ways of life"; and its messianic hope of redeeming history: "To insure the peaceful development of nations, free from coercion . . . to make possible lasting freedom and independence for all"—we can see the subsequent course of a policy that led to Vietnam. Even so, the Truman Doctrine did not foreordain Vietnam. Instead, it was the American intervention in Korea, an intervention prompted far more by conventional balance of power calculations than by the universal pretensions of the Truman Doctrine, that did so. Korea stands out as the decisive event in the evolution of containment policy. At the outset of the war, it was still uncertain whether America would extend its alliance commitments beyond the Western Hemisphere, the North Atlantic region, and the defensive perimeter in the Pacific running from the Ryukyus to the Philippine Islands. Korea put an end to this uncertainty, for the war led to the sudden extension of containment throughout Asia.

The wisdom of this extension of containment to Asia, where it was to apply primarily as a barrier to Chinese expansion, did not pass unchallenged. To many, it was seen as the misapplication of a strategy that was sound only when applied to Europe. In Europe, we were protecting kindred states against a conventional military threat. Not so in Asia, where the attempt to carry out a policy of containment would not have the same degree of support from those to be protected, and could not avoid the prospects of creating highly dependent relationships. Moreover, it was argued that even where the effort to contain communist expansion through military means might prove relatively effective, it must result in the overextension of American power.

At issue in the debate over Asian policy was a broad disparity of view over the conditions, and even the meaning, of American security. In the years that followed the Korean war, this issue was not put to a clear test. In consequence, America's Asian policy was supported for over a decade by what may be termed a negative consensus. Whereas in Europe our alliance commitment had solid domestic support, in Asia the commitments made by the Truman and Eisenhower administrations evoked little enthusiasm. But so long as they did not entail a serious price they evoked little opposition as well.

Vietnam put this negative consensus over Asian containment to the test and revealed its fragility. Vietnam also led to the transformation of those who bore primary responsibility for having taken us into the war, the liberal interventionists. Beginning in the mid-1960s, this transformation was consummated in the mid-1970s. It achieved its most complete expression in the vision of a new world proclaimed at the outset of the Carter administration. The former liberal interventionists thought that they had disavowed the old politics, with its parochial interests, its one-way dependencies, its hierarchical ordering and marked inequalities, its obsession with equilibrium and power balances, and above all its reliance on forcible methods. In place of the old politics, a new politics was presumably emerging, a politics characterized by global interests, mutual dependencies, far less hierarchy and concern with equilibrium, and markedly less reliance on forcible means.

QUESTION OF SCOPE

At the same time, this vision of a new world was not one in which America would compromise, let alone abandon, the great purposes of post-war policy. We were still to be freedom's exemplar in the world. We were still to be as committed as before to the extension of freedom. Human rights were the lodestar of the Carter administration's foreign policy. Nor was continuity with the past limited to the championing of freedom. In the new world, it was assumed that American leadership would still prevail and that a roughly similar role and interest would be assured. Only the disagreeable, counterproductive, and morally offensive features of this role would be altered. In their place, new policies and means would give a new sense of purpose to an idealism too long ignored or repressed.

Thus although Vietnam discredited the principal means of containment, it did not lead to the rejection of the aspirations that had been so important in prompting the intervention. The lapsed liberal interventionists of the Carter administration, while insistent that we no longer had the power to shape the world according to our desires—and that maturity consisted in recognizing and adjusting to this—did not accept the prospect of a world in which American influence would decline. Instead, they hoped for and foresaw a developing world moving in a manner ultimately congenial to us. To be sure, we needed, in a phrase of the day, "to get on the side of change," but we needed to do so in order to guide and to manage change. The aspirations of the past were still to be pursued, though now by methods different from and less harsh than those that were employed in the past.

This vision, as we know, did not stand the test of events. It did not do so because the new world it postulated was one that bore little resemblance to the world of the late 1970s. The dilemma of still desiring certain ends though no longer willing to employ the necessary means was at the heart of the Carter administration's difficulty, and ultimately its failure, in foreign policy. The same dilemma continues today to characterize the outlook of the Democratic Party and its liberal mainstream. Above all, an opposition to the threat or use of force marks a startling change of position when compared to an earlier era. This opposition appears as a compound of a moral aversion to force and a political judgment about what force can—or rather cannot—accomplish in today's world, particularly as employed in support of an untenable status quo.

Is the outlook of yesterday's liberal interventionists and their present day heirs in the Democratic Party fairly characterized as isolationist? As early as 1971, President Nixon observed that "the great internationalists of the post-World War II period have become the neo-isolationists of the Vietnam War period . . . ." Nixon's charge was based largely on liberal opposition to the war. The isolationist charge may be put more broadly and persuasively. Recently Charles Krauthammer has done so in an essay in *The New Republic*, "Isolationism, Left and Right" (March 4, 1985). Krauthammer characterizes left isolationism, which he equates with the ideology of the Democratic Party mainstream, as an isolationism of means though not of ends. "There is no retreat from the grand Wilsonian commitment to the spread of American values." But there has been a striking change in the approved means for achieving those values. "Force is ruled out, effectively, if not explicitly." A deep reluctance to commit American power, Krauthammer believes, is due to the conviction that the international status quo is unjust. "And for those on the wrong side of history, as the left likes to say, force is not only wrong, it is futile."

This view may account for the opposition to force in some circumstances. It does not account for such opposition on virtually every occasion in which the prospect of intervention has arisen in the past decade or so. The liberal rejection of intervention must also be attributed to other causes—to doubts about our own power, to fears about the domestic effects of intervention, etc. The appeal to an unjust status quo serves as much as an excuse as it does a reason. It serves to obscure quite traditional reasons for not wishing to intervene.

If the liberal Democrats' stated reasons for rejecting interventionist means are often suspect, is not their commitment to ends that in the past have been largely inseparable from such means also suspect? Krauthammer credits, as do others, this continued commitment to "truly internationalist" ends, though he also finds in the persisting liberal attachment to multilateralism "a cover for inaction" (as in an earlier era it was a cover for unilateralism). But what does it mean to care deeply about certain ends—for example, the cause of freedom—yet not so deeply as to risk either blood or (much) treasure for them? Is this not like the man who declares his love for omelets but cannot stand having eggs broken? The suspicion must arise that despite protestations to the contrary, he has only a very limited taste for omelets. So too, the suspicion must arise that despite protestations to the contrary, liberals who profess still to care deeply about the cause of freedom in the world no longer do so. Even in their previous incarnation, they never cared quite as much for extending freedom as they were wont to insist. The liberal interventionists of yesterday hated and feared communism with as much intensity as they loved extending freedom. In some measure, their changed position is due to an abatement of this hatred and fear.

The question persists whether it is reasonable to characterize the liberal-democratic position today as isolationist. That a change in position has occurred, however we may precisely characterize this position, is apparent. But does the present position reasonably qualify as isolationist? The answer cannot be held to depend on the continued profession of "internationalist" ends. Nor can it be determined by the persisting, and often misleading, devotion to multilateralism. It might be settled by examining where and in what circumstances today liberals are now ready to countenance intervention. But unless one assumes, for example, that an unwillingness to intervene in Nicaragua today also points to an unwillingness to intervene in Western Europe tomorrow, this test cannot prove very satisfactory. It may of course be argued that in principle one cannot be a Third World isolationist, by and large, and a first world interventionist. But in the post-war period not a few have taken just

OPPOSITION TO FORCE

this position. They have done so for reasons that appear as compelling as those given for pursuing an interventionist policy virtually anywhere and everywhere.

At any rate, there are now some indications that many liberal Democrats may be moving to reclaim at least part of a position they once held. Among congressional Democrats there is a growing sensitivity to the charge of negativism on defense issues. There is also evidence of a growing willingness to support anticommunist insurgent movements. These signs of a shifting position may yet prove deceptive. But they may also register the beginning of a trend toward a more assertive foreign policy. Clearly, the stage has been set for a liberal reconversion of sorts in foreign policy. The Reagan administration's foreign policy has been quite successful with the electorate. The thought cannot have escaped many liberal Democrats that this policy would not require any wrenching change on their part.

WHO ARE TODAY'S INTERVENTIONISTS?

What has happened to the liberal interventionism of yesterday? Are the present heirs of liberal interventionism to be found in what is now the mainstream of the Republican Party?

There is clearly much to be said for the view that an historic reversal of role has taken place. The conservative interventionist believes in the rightness of American purposes in the world, just as he believes in our power to achieve those purposes. What we need, he insists, is the will to use our power. Nor does he seem to fear, again in marked contrast with his conservative isolationist forebears, the domestic effects of an activist foreign policy.

These are the recognizable traits of yesterday's liberal interventionists. At the same time, most of today's conservative interventionists may be readily distinguished from their liberal predecessors. The beliefs that are shared with an earlier generation are no longer held with the same intensity. The post-war interventionist made almost a fetish of his internationalism. His conservative successor is far less inclined to do so. Although the conservative interventionist now accepts the world, he still does not particularly like it. The states of the Third World strike him, more often than not, as thoroughly unattractive and almost congenitally anti-American. Our allies test his patience by their unwillingness to bear their share of the common defense and by their susceptibility to both the threats and the promises of the adversary. It is certainly true that from the American vantage point there is much more to dislike in today's world than there was in the post-war world. Still, the point remains that the conservative interventionist does not view the world as did his liberal predecessor. Not

only does he like it less, but liking it less he does not have the exuberance over foreign policy that his liberal predecessor did.

Thus the role reversal in foreign policy is not a simple matter. In each case the transformation is qualified, since in each case an outlook persists that is partly reminiscent of now abandoned positions. Moreover, the changes in position that have occurred have not been uniform. Among conservatives, there is a division between those who support the use of American power in behalf of broad ends or purposes reminiscent of the Truman Doctrine, and those who support only the much more limited use of our power. With few exceptions, however, neither side seriously questions the basic commitments of American policy. Instead, the issue is where and why and in what domestic circumstances we should intervene in the rest of the world.

Are those conservatives who would restrict the use of American power in the Third World to conventionally (and quite narrowly) defined security interests isolationists? Charles Krauthammer, among others, thinks that they are. In his view, a species of right isolationism has arisen, and though it has yet to capture a party, its proponents are presumably growing in strength and confidence. Right isolationism is a policy marked by nationalism and unilateralism, one that is insistent on relying exclusively on our own resources for our defense, and one that wants to disengage selectively in order to reduce the current imbalance between means and ends and to restore a greater freedom of action. Krauthammer finds in Secretary of Defense Caspar Weinberger a signal example of today's right isolationism.

This is surely a very expansive view of isolationism. There is no reason to doubt Mr. Weinberger's commitment to our major alliances with Western Europe and Japan. Nor is there reason to question his appreciation that we have a continuing vital interest in retaining access to the Persian Gulf, for without this interest he would have little reason to support so zealously the large interventionary capability we are developing. Where, then, is Mr. Weinberger isolationist? It is only elsewhere, in the Third World, that he can be so charged.

In the developing world, the secretary has laid down a set of conditions he believes must be met before we should seriously consider intervention. What has moved Mr. Weinberger to propose this set of rather exacting conditions is not his alleged isolationist sentiments, but his frequently expressed fear that today's fragile foreign policy consensus might be quickly shattered by an ill-advised use of our military power. The secretary lives in the shadow of Vietnam. He believes that the price of another Vietnam—even perhaps a mini-Vietnam—may be very high. Today, as yester-

*ROLE
REVERSAL*

day, the zealous interventionist believes that all political leadership must do in intervening is to lead. Mr. Weinberger does not think this is nearly sufficient.

Even if he is wrong, his caution does not make him an isolationist. Nor does his insistence on ensuring that intervention not be undertaken unless the nation's interest is apparent, and we have the means necessary to carry through the intervention. Clearly, Mr. Weinberger is engaged in an effort to limit the uses of American power. Clearly, in this effort he betrays a penchant for unilateralism. Still, this does not qualify him as an isolationist unless we define isolationism in a manner that bears only limited relation to its historical and conventional meaning.

This, I think, is what Charles Krauthammer has done. By his standards, to avoid being termed an isolationist, it is not sufficient to be willing to use power. One must also be committed to using it in the right way. The right way is the internationalist-multilateralist way, not the nationalist-unilateralist way. Even then, the avoidance of isolationism is incomplete unless one is also committed to employing power on behalf of very broad purposes—purposes that clearly recall those entertained by the Truman Doctrine. These are indeed exacting standards, so much so that one is left asking: who are the interventionists (or "true internationalists") today?

The answer is admittedly different today from what it was before World War II. Then one was an interventionist even though limiting the nation's interests to physical security alone, for the nation's physical security could be assured only by intervening in the European conflict. Today, this is no longer true. Instead, it is the isolationist who stands only for physical security, for a concern with physical security and little more must lead to the end of alliances. Rather than contributing to our physical security, these alliances constitute the principal threat to it. At least, this is the case if it is assumed, as it generally is, that the prospect of America's involvement in a nuclear conflict is most likely to arise as a result of events that imperil the security of our major European allies.

The true interventionist today, then, must stand for something greater than the nation's physical security. Disagreement arises over *what* America stands for and *how* this should affect the conduct of the nation's foreign policy. Those like Charles Krauthammer argue that our nationalism is unlike all other nationalisms in that we stand for an idea—the idea of freedom—that transcends the narrow confines of national interest. Accordingly, we should be prepared in foreign policy to commit ourselves to the pursuit of freedom, subject only to our now reduced means. To do less, they believe, is for the nation to betray its idea of itself. And for American conservatism to urge doing less, they argue, is to betray what it has traditionally held to be the highest of political values—liberty.

There is in this vision no acknowledgment of the self-interestedness that marks all foreign policy, including this nation's policy. There is no awareness evident here that in state relations the perils of concern have been at least as great as the perils of indifference, and that given the disparities of power among nations this will doubtless continue to be the case. There is no apparent appreciation of the tragic limitations that attend foreign policy, given even the noblest of intentions.

These are conservative insights. In the history of thought about foreign policy they have been regularly associated with conservatives. Liberals have just as regularly resisted them, if only for the reason that they express a pessimistic view about men's capacity for disinterested behavior. They suggest a skepticism about the prospects for change in foreign policy. They counsel that power should be employed as sparingly as possible and only on behalf of well defined and long sanctioned interests.

Above all, the conservative view emphasizes the limits of statecraft, not merely the material limits but the distinctly *political* limits. In the post-war years, this view was largely alien to the liberal interventionists. It was only after Vietnam that they took up the limits of power theme, and then it was to argue not so much about the limits, as the virtual impotence, of power. Not a few conservative interventionists today have adopted the earlier liberal outlook. Although they want us to be prudent, they also want us to be prudent in a cause and for a purpose that has betrayed prudence in the past and is all too likely, if taken up, to do so again.

This does not mean that American foreign policy should look only to the nation's physical and material well-being. If this must be the first charge on policy, it ought not to be the only one. The alliance we entertain with free nations is rightly considered as a value in itself. But this value, or interest, is quite different from our interest in promoting freedom in the world at large. Often the two interests are treated almost as though they were synonymous. They are by no means so.

Our alliance with the free nations is a value in itself because nations, like individuals, need friends and kindred spirits. Their need may not be nearly as great—they are, after all, more self-sustaining than individuals—but it is still very considerable. Despite our continental proportions, without the democratic nations of Western Europe our own national life would be diminished, for we would be shut out from

*TRUE
INTERVENTIONISM*

societies that begot and that continue to nourish our culture and institutions.

Still, there is a very great difference between protecting the freedom of those who already have it, and who have a demonstrated capacity to maintain it, and extending it to those who do not have it, and who offer little assurance that they have the ability to sustain it. The issue is not the value of freedom. Instead, it is what power can accomplish in spreading freedom. It is also whether universalizing freedom is a proper interest of foreign policy. Krauthammer observes that in the case of Germany and Japan we brought democracy in on the point of a bayonet. But surely this is not intended as a general prescription for American foreign policy. We brought democracy to Germany and Japan on the point of a bayonet because it was the consequence of a war we entered into primarily for conventional security considerations. First came the security interest; then came the bayonets; finally came democracy.

While freedom is the highest of political values, this does not make its universalization a proper interest of foreign policy in the sense that its pursuit justifies the sacrifice of blood and treasure. There are many things of value that are not the proper interests of foreign policy. Conservatives, despite their deep attachment to liberty, should be the first to recognize this. Their recognition of it does not qualify them as isolationists.

THE CENTRALITY OF ALLIANCES

Whether it is considered to do so or not, however, is unlikely to affect greatly the course of the nation's foreign policy. It is unlikely to do so for the same reasons that the domestic debate and shifts in position of the past fifteen years have not greatly affected the course of the nation's foreign policy. Since the late 1960s we have had an extraordinary succession of administrations, each one characterized by a distinct outlook and promise in foreign policy. During the same period, we have seen striking change in the foreign policy positions taken by political elites. Yet the proverbial man from Mars, returning to the scene after an absence of a decade and a half, would find that the nation's role and interests in the world had not altered substantially. It is not the change in policy that would attract his attention but the continuity.

Why this is so should be readily apparent. The strategic arms balance apart, the American position in the world is still defined and determined by our major alliance relationships. It is these relationships that constitute the core of our foreign policy, that account for its inner logic and coherence, and that have done so since virtually the close of World War

II. Were the great Western alliance to break apart, and the resources of our allies to be placed increasingly at the disposal of the Soviet Union, the world we have known since the 1950s would change profoundly, and with it the American role and position. Our physical security might not be jeopardized. In all likelihood it would not be, given the surfeit of deterrent power conferred by nuclear weapons. But the other features of our present relationship with the world would surely change. They would change for the worse, though how much for the worse is impossible to say.

The centrality of our major alliance relationships in the post-war scheme of things may one day end. The present realities of world power are not immutable, though neither are they subject to sudden change. The time may come when the nations of the Pacific and East Asia count for more in the scales of world power than do the nations of Western Europe. Despite the anticipation of a growing number, that time has not yet arrived. Until it does, the prospect is that we will continue to have what we have had since World War II: a Eurocentric policy.

Thus the continuity in American foreign policy must be attributed in the first place to the persisting role and importance of our major alliance relationships. Debate over these relationships has largely been over how best to manage them, not over the desirability of continuing to manage them at all. Those raising the issue of desirability have yet to receive a serious, let alone a sympathetic, hearing. They have not been given such a hearing largely because we cannot clearly grasp what a different policy might be like, and advocates of a new, though now presumably a global, unilateralism have provided very little guidance here.

In abandoning the Western alliance, we might free ourselves from the constraints of allies, but we would not free ourselves from the constraints of limited resources. Rather than needing less for defense, we might well need more, if we were to maintain, and perhaps even add to, our position elsewhere in the world. The contrary argument assumes that without our present commitment to Europe we would be in a much better position to close the gap between our commitments elsewhere and our power. But this would be true only if the threat posed by the Soviet Union to our positions elsewhere remained the same. It would remain the same, though, only if the West European states proved able and disposed to do what heretofore they have not done—to defend themselves.

What if they were not so disposed? In that event, Moscow would have much less to worry about in the theater of greatest importance to it. Freed from this concern, while progressively strengthened by the resource base Western Europe would then afford it, Moscow might

THE VALUE OF ALLIANCE

be able to turn its attention elsewhere and with greater effect. Rather than closing the gap between our commitments and our power, Soviet ascendance in Europe consequent upon a U.S. withdrawal there might well have the effect of widening this gap. Having abandoned what had heretofore been the center of our interest for the periphery, we would find the periphery increasingly difficult to secure against the improved power position of the Soviet Union.

Nor is it apparent why, in these circumstances, we should continue to make the effort to defend the periphery, or at least most of it, against the Soviet Union. For the defense of peripheral interests takes on significance, for the most part, because of their relationship to the interests that compose the core or center. If our commitment is no longer to the core, why then to the periphery? Why should we, for example, abandon the Western alliance yet continue to address our efforts to the security of the Persian Gulf? To secure access to oil needed primarily by our allies? Why defend their extra-European interests if we no longer care to defend their European interests?

These considerations suggest that the real alternative to a Eurocentric policy would not be a policy of global unilateralism but one of hemispheric isolation, since it is to this hemisphere that we would likely find ourselves increasingly tempted, if not forced, to return. To the degree the new unilateralists appreciate this, they do not really believe it is desirable to abandon our commitment to Europe. They cannot but conclude that the consequences associated with isolationism are largely the effects that might be expected to follow from the abandonment of Europe, and that Europe, not the rest of the world, would determine these effects. This explains why current visions of an alternative to a Eurocentric policy appear either vague or confused when the attempt is made to translate them into coherent policy. The impression given is that the new unilateralists have not thought seriously about what their policy might be, and that their vision remains just that.

Our major alliance relationships continue to form today, as they formed yesterday, the vital core of our foreign policy. They represent the realm of necessity in policy. By contrast, virtually the rest of the world constitutes the periphery of policy. For the most part, it is the periphery over which we have argued, often very bitterly, and continue to do so today. We have debated endlessly and acrimoniously where we have had the luxury, because the freedom, to do so. We are doing so again today over Central America, despite the repeated assertions of the administration and its supporters that the form of government Nicaragua has represents an issue of necessity for us.

In fact, an issue of necessity has arisen in the periphery on only two occasions since the Korean war. It did so in Cuba in 1962 and it did so—or it clearly threatened to do so—in the Persian Gulf in the late 1970s. In both instances, the periphery was crucial because events there, had they gone unchecked, would have had a direct and adverse impact on the core. To prevent this from happening, we threatened, and could not but threaten, to intervene.

The distinction between core and periphery, vital and non-vital interest, is not one that can always be readily drawn. It is an old and familiar story that in great conflicts even apparently peripheral interests can take on critical significance in terms of the relationship that may be drawn between them and core interests. Such conflicts are characterized by their pervasiveness and seeming intractability. The discrete issues arising between adversaries are seldom viewed in isolation. Accordingly, the inner dynamic of the conflict makes it difficult to draw a distinction between what may otherwise be seen as marginal and central.

It is this feature of great conflicts that has weighed heavily on us, and rightly so. Yet it has often been accorded the status of dogma. In the form it has frequently taken, its essential message is this: there is no periphery, only a core. For what is perceived as the periphery, the argument runs, will, if treated as such, soon become the core. Experience should have taught us by now the perils of this view. Given its most notorious application in the case of Vietnam, the argument has already served us badly. It may do so again if we insist on applying it in the future as we applied it in the past.

PERIPHERY OF POLICY

The U.S. and Third-World Dictatorships:
A Case for Benign Detachment

The U.S.'s current foreign policy "tragically identifies the U.S. and—even worse—its capitalist democratic system with the most reactionary elements around the globe."

Ted Galen Carpenter

Mr. Carpenter is a foreign policy analyst at the Cato Institute, Washington, D.C.

IT is a central dilemma of contemporary American foreign policy that the world's leading capitalist democracy must confront an environment in which a majority of nations are neither capitalist nor democratic. U.S. leaders have rarely exhibited ingenuity or grace in handling this delicate and often frustrating situation.

The current turmoil in Central America is illustrative of a larger problem. American officials assert that this vital region is under assault from doctrinaire communist revolutionaries trained, funded, and controlled by the Soviet Union. Danger to the well-being of the U.S. is immediate and serious, Administration spokesmen argue, and it is imperative that the Marxist-Leninist tide be prevented from engulfing Central America. Accomplishing this objective requires a confrontational posture toward the communist beachhead (Nicaragua) combined with massive support for all "friendly" regimes, ranging from democratic Costa Rica to autocratic Guatemala. Washington's Central American policy displays in microcosm most of the faulty assumptions underlying America's approach to the entire Third World.

The current strategy of the U.S. betrays a virtual siege mentality. It was not always thus. Throughout the 19th century, U.S.

policymakers exuded confidence that the rest of the world would emulate America's political and economic system, seeing the U.S. as a "beacon on the hill" guiding humanity to a better future. As late as the 1940's, most Americans and their political representatives still believed that democracy would triumph as a universal system. The prospective breakup of the European colonial empires throughout Asia and Africa was generally viewed as an opportunity, not a calamity. Scores of new nations would emerge from that process, and Americans were confident that most would choose the path of democracy and free enterprise, thus isolating the Soviet Union and its coterie of Marxist-Leninist dictatorships in Eastern Europe.

The actual results were acutely disappointing. No wave of new democracies occurred in this "Third World"; instead, decolonization produced a plethora of dictatorships, some of which appeared distressingly friendly to Moscow. This development was especially disturbing to Washington since it took place at a time when America's Cold War confrontation with the U.S.S.R. was at its most virulent. The nature and magnitude of that struggle caused American leaders to view the Third World primarily as another arena in the conflict. Consequently, the proliferation of left-wing revolutionary movements and governments seemed to undermine America's own security and well-being.

Washington's response to this adversity has been a particularly simplistic and un-

fortunate one. American leaders increasingly regarded any anti-communist regime, however repressive and undemocratic it might be at home, as an "ally," a "force for stability," and even a "friend." At the same time, they viewed leftist governments—even those under democratic procedures—as little more than Soviet surrogates, or at least targets of opportunity for communist machinations.

A portent of this mind-set among the U.S. policymakers surfaced during the earliest stages of the Cold War. Pres. Harry Truman's enunciation of the so-called Truman Doctrine in 1947 proclaimed the willingness of the U.S. to assist friendly governments resisting not only external aggression, but also "armed minorities" in their own midst. It was an ominous passage, for the U.S. was arrogating the right to intervene in the internal affairs of other nations to help preserve regimes deemed friendly to American interests. Although Washington had engaged in such conduct throughout Central America and the Caribbean for several decades, those incidents were a geographical aberration in what was otherwise a noninterventionist foreign policy. The Truman Doctrine raised the specter that America's meddlesome paternalism in one region might now be applied on a global basis.

Although Truman stressed that the *status quo* was not "sacred," his doctrine soon made the U.S. a patron of repressive, reactionary regimes around the world. It was a measure of how far that trend had developed by 1961 that Pres. John F. Kennedy could proclaim in his inaugural address America's determination to "support any friend, oppose any foe" in the battle against world communism. Today, leading foreign policy spokesmen such as Henry Kissinger, Alexander Haig, and Jeane Kirkpatrick express a fondness for "friendly" authoritarian regimes that would have seemed incomprehensible to most Americans only a few decades ago.

A false realism as well as moral insensitivity characterize American policy toward Third World dictatorships. There is a disturbing tendency to view such regimes in caricature, regarding right-wing governments as valuable friends whose repressive excesses must be ignored or excused, while perceiving leftist insurgent movements and governments as mortal threats to America's national interest, justifying a posture of unrelenting hostility. For example, the Reagan Administration pursues a confrontational policy toward the Marxist government of Nicaragua, terminating all aid programs, imposing a trade embargo, and supporting rebel guerrillas. At the same time, Washington lavishes economic and military aid upon equally repressive "allies" in South Korea, Taiwan, Zaire, and elsewhere.

The consequences of this simplistic and morally inconsistent strategy are highly unfortunate. America finds itself involved far too often in futile or mutually destructive confrontations with left-wing regimes. Even worse is the evolution of a cozy relationship between Washington and a host of right-wing authoritarian governments. A pervasive perception of the U.S. as the sponsor and protector of such dictatorships has undermined America's credibility as a spokesman for democracy, caused Third World peoples to equate both capitalism and democracy with U.S. hegemony, and established a milieu for rabidly anti-American revolutions. It is an approach that creates a massive reservoir of ill will and, in the long run, weakens rather than strengthens America's national security.

A flawed policy

Washington's policy toward Third World dictatorships is seriously flawed in several respects. One fundamental defect is the tendency to view largely internal struggles exclusively through the prism of America's ongoing cold war with the Soviet Union. Secretary of State John Foster Dulles was an early practitioner of this parochial viewpoint during the 1950's, when he insisted that the emerging nations of Asia and Africa "choose sides" in that conflict. Nonalignment or neutralism Dulles viewed as moral cowardice or tacit support for the U.S.S.R. Such an attitude only antagonized nonaligned leaders who were concerned primarily with charting a postcolonial political and economic course for their new nations and cared little about an acrimonious competition between two alien superpowers. The chilly relationship between India, the Third World's leading democracy, and the U.S. throughout this period was due in large part to Washington's hostility toward Prime Minister Jawaharlal Nehru's policy of nonalignment.

American policymakers have learned few lessons from Dulles' errors in the subsequent quarter-century. During the 1960's, Washington still saw internal political conflicts in nations as diverse as Vietnam and the Dominican Republic exclusively as skirmishes in the larger Cold War. A decade after the victory of one faction in the complex tribal, linguistic, and economic struggle in Angola, former Secretary of State Henry Kissinger describes that war as part of "an unprecedented Soviet geopolitical offensive" on a global scale. Kissinger's former boss, Gerald Ford, likewise interprets the episode purely as a struggle between "pro-Communist" and "pro-West" forces. Former UN Ambassador Jeane Kirkpatrick views such countries as Mozambique and Nicaragua not as nations in their own right, but as components of the Soviet empire. Similarly, Pres. Reagan's bipartisan commission on Central America describes the multifaceted conflicts of that troubled region as part of a Soviet-Cuban "geo-strategic challenge" to the U.S.

This failure to understand the complexities and ambiguities of Third World power rivalries has impelled the U.S. to adopt misguided and counterproductive strategies. One manifestation is an uncritical willingness to embrace repressive regimes if they possess sufficient anti-communist credentials.

At times, this tendency has proven more than a trifle embarrassing. During a toast to the Shah of Iran on New Year's Eve, 1977, Pres. Jimmy Carter lavished praise on that autocratic monarch: "Iran, because of the great leadership of the Shah, is an island of stability in one of the more troubled areas of the world. This is a great tribute to you, Your Majesty, and to your leadership, and to the respect and admiration and love which your people give to you." Apparently concluding that America's vocal enthusiasm for the Shah and his policies during the previous quarter-century did not link the U.S. sufficiently to his fate, the President emphasized: "We have no other nation on earth who [sic] is closer to us in planning for our mutual military security."

Barely a year later, the Shah's regime lay in ruins, soon to be replaced by a virulently anti-American government. Carter's assumption that the Shah was loved by the Iranian people was a classic case of wishful thinking. CIA operatives in the field warned their superiors that the American perception was a delusion, but those reports were ignored because they did not reflect established policy. Blind to reality, the Carter Administration identified itself and American security interests with a regime that was already careening toward oblivion.

One might think that American leaders would have gained some humility from the wreckage of Iranian policy and at least learned to curb vocal expressions of support for right-wing autocrats. Unfortunately, that has not been the case. Less than four years after Carter's gaffe, Vice Pres. George Bush fawned over Philippine dictator Ferdinand Marcos: "We stand with you sir. . . . We love your adherence to democratic principle [sic] and to the democratic processes. And we will not leave you in isolation."

It is a considerable understatement to suggest that the burgeoning Philippine opposition (which contained many legitimate democrats, such as Salvador Laurel and Butz Aquino) did not appreciate effusive praise for the man who suspended the national constitution, declared martial law, governed by decree, and imprisoned political opponents to perpetuate his own power. From the standpoint of long-term American interests (not to mention common decency and historical accuracy), Bush should have considered how a successor Philippine government might perceive his enthusiasm for Marcos. During his second presidential campaign debate with Walter Mondale, Reagan not only defended this nation's intimate relationship with the Marcos regime, but also implied that the only alternative to Marcos was a communist takeover—which proved to be a gross distortion of reality.

Ill-considered hyperbole with respect to right-wing autocratic governments places the U.S. in an awkward, even hypocritical posture. Equally unfortunate is the extensive and at times highly visible material assistance that Washington gives such regimes. For more than three decades, the U.S. helped train and equip the military force that the Somoza family used to dominate Nicaragua and systematically loot that nation. Similarly, the American government provided lavish military hardware to the Shah of Iran as well as "security" and "counterinsurgency" training to SAVAK, the Shah's infamous secret police. Throughout the same period, Washington gave similar assistance to a succession of Brazilian military governments, a parade of Guatemalan dictatorships, the junta that ruled from 1967 to 1974, and several other repressive governments. Most recently, the U.S. gave the Marcos regime economic and military aid totaling more than $227,000,000, plus millions more in payments for the military installations at Clark Field and Subic Bay. Despite ample signs of that government's increasingly shaky tenure, the Reagan Administration asked Congress to increase aid by nearly 20%. Congress exhibited little enthusiasm for that approach, approving instead a significantly smaller sum and attaching various "human rights" restrictions.

Warm public endorsements of autocratic regimes combined with substantial (at times lavish) material support produce an explosive mixture that repeatedly damages American prestige and credibility. Many of those governments retain only the most precarious hold on power, lacking significant popular support and depending heavily upon the use of terror to intimidate opponents. When repressive tactics no longer prove sufficient, the dictatorships can collapse with dramatic suddenness—as in Iran. American patronage thus causes the U.S. to become closely identified with hated governments and their policies. The domestic populations see those regimes as little more than American clients—extensions of U.S. power. Consequently, they do not view the ouster of a repressive autocrat as merely an internal political change, but as the eradication of American domination.

Moreover, there is a virtual reflex action to repudiate everything American—including capitalist economics and Western-style democracy. The U.S. unwittingly contributes to that process. By portraying corrupt, autocratic rulers as symbols of the "free world," we risk having long-suffering populations take us at our word. They do not see capitalism and democracy as those systems operate in the West, enabling people to achieve prosperity and individual freedom. Instead, Third World people identify free enterprise and democratic values with the corruption and repression they have endured. Historian Walter LaFeber, in *Inevitable Revolutions*, describes how that reasoning has worked in Central America: "U.S. citizens see [capitalist democracy] as having given them the highest standard of living and the most open society in the world. Many Central Americans have increasingly associated capitalism with a brutal oligarchy-military complex that has been supported by U.S. policies—and armies."

Hostility to the left

The flip side of Washington's promiscuous enthusiasm for right-wing autocrats is an equally pervasive hostility toward leftist Third World regimes and insurgent movements. There have been occasional exceptions to this rule throughout the Cold War era. For example, the U.S. developed a cordial relationship with communist Yugoslavia after Premier Josef Tito broke with the Soviet Union in 1948. A similar process occurred during the early 1970's, when the Nixon Administration engineered a rapprochement with China, ending more than two decades of frigid hostility. These achievements are instructive and should have demonstrated to American policymakers that it is possible for the U.S. to coexist with Marxist regimes. However, that lesson has not been learned, and such incidents of enlightenment stand as graphic exceptions to an otherwise dreary record.

More typical of America's posture is the ongoing feud with the Cuban government of Fidel Castro. The campaign to oust or, failing that, to make him a hemispheric pariah, was shortsighted, futile, and counterproductive from the outset. It served only to give him a largely undeserved status as a principled, courageous revolutionary and to drive his government into Moscow's willing embrace. Soviet defector Arkady Shevchenko recalls a 1960 conversation with Nikita Khrushchev in which the latter viewed America's hostility toward Cuba with undisguised glee. Describing U.S. efforts to "drive Castro to the wall" instead of establishing normal relations as "stupid," Khrushchev accurately predicted that "Castro will have to gravitate to us like an iron filing to a magnet."

Apparently having learned little from the Cuban experience, the Reagan Administration seems determined to make the same errors with the Sandinista government of Nicaragua. Washington's attempts to isolate the Managua regime diplomatically, the imposition of economic sanctions, the "covert" funding of the contra guerrillas, and the use of apocalyptic rhetoric to describe the internal struggle for power in that country all seem like an eerie case of *deja vu*. Reagan's depiction of the contras as "the moral equal" of America's own Founding Fathers constitutes ample evidence that U.S. policymakers have not learned to view Third World power struggles with even modest sophistication. One need not romanticize the Sandinista regime, excuse its suppression of political dissent, or rationalize its acts of brutality (*e.g.*, the treatment of the Miskito Indians), as the American political left is prone to do, to advocate a more restrained and detached policy. Administration leaders fear that Nicaragua will become a Soviet satellite in Central America; Washington's current belligerent course virtually guarantees that outcome. As in the case of Cuba nearly three decades ago, the U.S. is creating a self-fulfilling prophecy.

The American government's hostility toward left-wing regimes in the Third World has even extended to *democratic* governments with a leftist slant. An early victim of this antipathy was Iranian Prime Minister Mohammed Mossadegh. Evidence now clearly shows extensive CIA involvement (including planning and funding) in the 1953 royalist coup that enabled the Shah to establish himself as an absolute monarch. Mossadegh's "crime" was not that he was communist, but that he advocated policies inimical to powerful Anglo-American economic interests. A year later, the left-leaning reformist government of Jacobo Arbenz in Guatemala suffered the same fate. This time, American complicity in the overthrow of a democratically elected government was even more blatant. The U.S. Ambassador to Guatemala reportedly boasted that he had brought the counterrevolution to a suc-

cessful conclusion barely "forty-five minutes behind schedule." Even Reagan's bipartisan commission on Central America concedes U.S. assistance in the coup, and Washington's role has been amply documented elsewhere.

Buoyed by such successes, the U.S. helped oust Patrice Lumumba, the first elected Prime Minister of the Congo (now Zaire), in 1960. Like Mossadegh and Arbenz, Lumumba had committed the unpardonable sin of soliciting communist support. There is also some evidence of American complicity in the 1973 military coup that toppled the government of Chilean Pres. Salvador Allende. We do know that the Nixon Administration sought to thwart Allende's election in 1970, discussed a coup with disgruntled elements of the military immediately following that election, and ordered steps to isolate and destabilize the new government economically. No less a figure than Henry Kissinger, then serving as National Security Advisor, concedes that the U.S. authorized covert payments of more than $8,800,000 to opponents of the Allende government during the three years preceding the coup. Given the relatively modest size of the Chilean economy and population, an infusion of such an amount of money certainly created a considerable political impact, but Kissinger and Nixon both blame Allende's downfall entirely on internal factors. The Marxist president's pursuit of disastrous economic programs together with his systematic attempts to undercut the conservative middle class and harass political opponents undoubtedly galvanized the opposition, weakening his already precarious political position. Nevertheless, it would be naive to accept at face value the Nixon Administration's protestations of innocence regarding the coup, especially in light of Kissinger's ominous assertion that Allende was "not merely an economic nuisance or a political critic but a geopolitical challenge."

It is reprehensible for a government that preaches the virtues of noninterference in the internal affairs of other nations to have amassed such a record of interference. The level of shame mounts when American meddling undermines a sister democracy and helps install a repressive autocracy. Yet, in Iran, Guatemala, Zaire, and Chile, that was precisely what happened. Post-Mossadegh Iran endured the Shah's corrupt authoritarianism for 25 years before desperately embracing the fanaticism of the Ayatollah Khomeini. Guatemala after Arbenz has witnessed a dreary succession of military dictatorships, each one rivaling its predecessor in brutality. The ouster of Patrice Lumumba facilitated the rise to power of Mobuto Sese Seko in Zaire. His regime is regarded as one of the most corrupt and repressive on any continent.

Perhaps Chile is the saddest case of all. Although deified by Western liberals, Allende had his unsavory qualities. His enthusiasm for Marxist economic bromides pushed his nation to the brink of disaster.

He also exhibited a nasty authoritarian streak of his own, including an intolerance of political critics. Nevertheless, his actions remained (although sometimes just barely) within constitutional bounds. Moreover, he was the last in an unbroken series of democratically elected rulers stretching back more than four decades—an impressive record in Latin America. The Pinochet dictatorship that replaced Allende is conspicuous for its brutal and systematic violation of individual liberties. Yet, Kissinger can assert that the "change in government in Chile was on balance favorable—even from the point of view of human rights." Such a view reflects either willful blindness or an astounding cynicism.

Strategic, economic, and ideological justifications

Those individuals who justify America's existing policy toward the Third World cite strategic, economic, and ideological considerations. On the strategic level, they argue that the U.S. must prevent geographically important regions from falling under the sway of regimes subservient to the Soviet Union. Otherwise, a shift in the balance of global military power could jeopardize American security interests, perhaps even imperil the nation's continued existence. Economically, the U.S. must maintain access to vital supplies of raw materials and keep markets open for American products and investments. It is not possible, this argument holds, for an economy based upon free enterprise to endure if the world is dominated by state-run Marxist systems. Finally, beyond questions of strategic and economic self-interest, the U.S. must thwart communist expansionism in the Third World to ensure that America and its democratic allies do not become islands in a global sea of hostile, totalitarian dictatorships.

All these arguments possess a certain facile appeal, but they hold up only if one accepts some very dubious conceptions of America's strategic, economic, and ideological interests. Moreover, proponents have often employed these arguments as transparent rationalizations for questionable foreign policy initiatives.

The notion that the United States must assist and defend right-wing regimes while opposing leftist insurgencies or governments for its own strategic self-interest depends on several important subsidiary assumptions. Those who justify America's Third World policy on this basis generally define "strategic interests" in a most expansive manner. In its crudest form, this approach regards Third World states as little more than bases or forward staging areas for American military power. Such a rationale is convincing only if one assumes that the United States truly possesses "vital" strategic interests in regions as diverse as Southeast Asia, the Persian Gulf, Central Africa, and South America, and that

successor regimes in regional "keystone" nations would be hostile to those interests.

One can and should question whether the U.S. actually has strategic interests, vital or otherwise, in areas thousands of miles removed from its own shores. How a plethora of small, often militarily insignificant nations, governed by unpopular and unstable regimes, could augment U.S. strength in a showdown with the Soviet Union is a mystery. One could make a more plausible argument that attempts to prop up tottering allies weaken America's security. These efforts drain U.S. financial resources and stretch defense forces dangerously thin. Worst of all is the risk that a crumbling Third World ally could become an arena for ill-advised American military adventures. As we saw in Vietnam, the entrance to such quagmires is easier to find than the exit.

The inordinate fear of successor governments is equally dubious, for it assumes that such regimes would inevitably be leftwing and subservient to Moscow. Neither assumption is necessarily warranted. The ouster of a right-wing autocracy does not lead ineluctably to a radical leftist government. Vigorous democracies succeeded rightist dictatorships in Portugal and Greece. Moreover, even in cases where a staunchly leftist government does emerge, subservience to Moscow can not be assumed. Such pessimism may have had some validity in the bipolar ideological environment of the late 1940's and early 1950's, but, given the diffusion of power away from both Moscow and Washington in the past 30 years, it is now dangerously obsolete. When China and the U.S.S.R. are mortal adversaries, Yugoslavia charts a consistently independent course, and such a country as Rumania—in Moscow's own geopolitical "backyard"—dares exhibit maverick tendencies on selected foreign policy issues, the assumption that a Marxist Third World state will be merely a Soviet stooge is clearly unwarranted.

Economic factors

The economic thesis for current U.S. foreign policy is no more persuasive than the strategic rationale. Assumptions that rightist governments serve as pliant instruments of American economic objectives or that left-wing regimes become commercial adversaries can not be sustained as a general rule. It is true that countries ruled by right-wing autocrats tend to be friendlier arenas for U.S. investment, but the price in bureaucratic restrictions and "commissions" (*i.e.*, bribes) to key officials is often very high. Moreover, governments of whatever ideological stripe usually operate according to principles of economic self-interest, which may or may not correspond to American desires.

Washington received a rude awakening on that score in the 1970's, when its closest Middle East allies—Iran and Saudi Arabia—helped engineer OPEC's massive oil

price hikes. Neither U.S. client was willing to forgo financial gain out of any sense of gratitude for political and military support. Much the same situation occurred in 1980, when the Carter Administration invoked a grain embargo against the Soviet Union for the latter's invasion of Afghanistan. The U.S. encouraged, even pressured, its allies to cooperate in that boycott. Nevertheless, the Argentine military junta, a regime that the U.S. had routinely counted upon to stem the tide of leftist insurgency in Latin America, promptly seized the opportunity to boost its grain sales to the U.S.S.R.

Just as right-wing regimes exhibit a stubborn independence on economic matters, revolutionary leftist governments are not inherent commercial enemies. When the U.S. has allowed trade with leftist countries to occur, that trade has usually flourished. The lucrative oil and mineral commerce with the Marxist government of Angola is a case in point. Similarly, once the emotional feud with mainland China ceased in the 1970's, commercial and investment opportunities for the United States also began to emerge. Although a Marxist state dominating the global market in some vital commodity might conceivably attempt to blackmail the U.S., that danger is both remote and theoretical.

Economic realities exert a powerful influence that often transcends purely political considerations. Most Third World governments, whether right-wing or left-wing, benefit from extensive commercial ties with the industrialized West, particularly the U.S. America is often the principal market for their exports and is a vital source of developmental capital. Revolutionary rhetoric, even when sincerely believed, can not change that fundamental equation. It is no coincidence that Third World governments have rarely instituted economic boycotts; most embargoes originate as a deliberate U.S. policy to punish perceived political misdeeds.

Rather than adopting economic sanctions as a device for political intimidation, the U.S. should relish the prospect of promoting commercial connections to the greatest extent possible. Nothing would more readily provide evidence to left-wing leaders that a system based on private property and incentives is vastly superior to the lumbering inefficiencies of Marxist central planning. On those rare occasions when the U.S. has pursued a conciliatory, rather than a truculent and confrontational, approach, the results have been gratifying. The Marxist regime in Mozambique, for instance, first looked to the Soviet bloc for economic as well as ideological guidance, only to confront arrogant Russian imperialism and a recipe for economic disaster. The disillusioned leadership now has begun to turn away from the U.S.S.R. and open its country to Western trade and investment, a process that is likely to accelerate in the coming years.

The most misguided justification for

America's attachment to right-wing Third World states lies in the realm of politics and ideology. Proponents assume an underlying ideological affinity between authoritarian systems and Western democracies. They insist that, while rightist regimes may be repressive, such governments are natural U.S. allies in the struggle against world communism. Conversely, revolutionary leftist movements are "totalitarian" in origin and constitute accretions to the power of that global menace.

No one has advanced this thesis more passionately and at greater length than former U.S. Ambassador to the United Nations Jeane Kirkpatrick. While conceding that "traditional" autocracies sometimes engage in practices that offend American "sensibilities," Kirkpatrick clearly finds those regimes more palatable than their leftist adversaries. She asserts that "traditional authoritarian governments are less repressive than revolutionary autocracies," are "more susceptible to liberalization," and are "more compatible with U.S. interests." That being the case, American aid to keep such friendly regimes in power is not only justified, but becomes something akin to a moral imperative.

Even if one concedes that the repression practiced by leftist dictatorships is more pervasive and severe than that of right-wing dictatorships, a more fundamental issue still exists—American complicity. The U.S. has neither the power nor the requisite moral mandate to eradicate injustice and oppression in the world. At the same time, as the most powerful and visible symbol of democracy, America does have an obligation not to become a participant in acts of repression and brutality. Our sponsorship of right-wing autocracies violates that crucial responsibility. Assisting dictatorial regimes makes the U.S. government (and by extension the public that elects it) an accomplice in the suppression of other people's liberty. In a profound way, such complicity constitutes a stain on our democratic heritage.

Kirkpatrick's contention that traditional autocracies are more susceptible to liberalization likewise misses a fundamental point. She asserts that autocratic regimes sometimes "evolve" into more democratic forms, whereas no analogous case exists with respect to revolutionary socialist governments. Yet, her own examples—Spain, Greece, and Brazil—do not involve evolutionary transformations, but, rather, the *restoration* of democratic systems that right-wing elements had destroyed. History demonstrates that, while communist revolutionaries oust competing repressive systems, rightist insurgents habitually overthrow democratically elected governments. There is only one instance of a successful communist uprising against an established democracy—the takeover of Czechoslovakia in March, 1948. Conversely, right-wing coups and revolutions have erased numerous democratic regimes.

Spain (1936), Guatemala (1954), Brazil (1964), Greece (1967), the Philippines (1972), Chile (1973), and Argentina (1976) represent only the most prominent examples. It may be more difficult to eradicate leftist (especially totalitarian) systems than it is to replace rightist regimes, but right-wing autocratic movements pose the more lethal threat to functioning democracies. No fact more effectively demolishes the naive notion of an underlying affinity between democracies and rightist dictatorships. The two systems are not allies; they are inherent adversaries.

An alternative

A new foreign policy must eschew inconsistent moral posturing as well as amoral geopolitics. The most constructive alternative would stress "benign detachment" toward *all* Third World dictatorships, whatever their ideological orientation.

The concept of benign detachment is grounded in the indisputable reality that, for the foreseeable future, the U.S. will confront a Third World environment in which a majority of nations are undemocratic. It would unquestionably prove easier to function in a community of capitalist democracies, but we do not have that luxury. Democracy and capitalism may emerge as powerful doctrines throughout the Third World, but such a transformation would be long-term, reflecting indigenous historical experiences. We certainly can not hasten that process by abandoning our own ideals and embracing reactionary autocrats. In the interim, the U.S. must learn to coexist with a variety of dictatorships. Benign detachment represents the most productive and least intrusive method of achieving that objective.

This approach would reject the simplistic categorization of right-wing regimes as friends and Marxist governments as enemies. It would require redefining America's national interests in a more circumspect manner. No longer should Washington conclude that the survival of a reactionary dictatorship, no matter how repressive, corrupt, and unstable it might be, somehow enhances the security of the U.S. A policy of benign detachment would likewise repudiate the notion that there is an underlying kinship between rightist autocracies and Western democracies. Right-wing dictatorships are just as alien to our values as their left-wing counterparts.

America's primary objective should be a more restrained and even-handed policy toward repressive Third World regimes. Cordial diplomatic and economic relations should be encouraged with *all* governments that are willing to reciprocate, be they democratic, authoritarian, royalist, or Marxist. This would require normalizing diplomatic and commercial relations with such countries as Cuba, Nicaragua, and Vietnam while curtailing aid to so-called allies.

Conservatives invariably protest that this position is a manifestation of a liberal double standard. It is not. In fact, conservatives ignore the actual effects such policies have had in the past. Take the case of mainland China. Throughout the 1950's and 1960's, Washington's attempts to isolate the People's Republic of China only caused that nation to turn inward and fester, producing a particularly oppressive and regimented system. Since the U.S. abandoned its misguided strategy in the early 1970's, China has become a far more open and progressive nation. Deng Xiaoping and his followers now eagerly welcome Western trade and investment, particularly in the field of high technology. Equally important are the changes sweeping the domestic economy. Chinese officials are dismantling crucial elements of Marxist central planning, decentralizing production, creating incentives, and even legalizing certain forms of private property. All those developments should be gratifying to Americans who believe in the virtues of a market economy. Moreover, the first, albeit hesitant, signs of political liberalization in China are beginning to emerge. Prominent Chinese spokesmen even assert publicly that Karl Marx was not infallible and that many of his ideas are irrelevant in the modern era—sentiments that would have merited the death sentence only a few years ago.

While the U.S. initiative in establishing cordial political and economic relations with China can not account entirely for this movement toward liberalization, there is no question that it helps facilitate progressive trends. Conservatives who advocate isolating Cuba, Vietnam, Nicaragua, and other Marxist nations would do well to ponder that point. Liberals who endorse economic sanctions against South Africa should consider whether their suggested strategy is not counterproductive as well.

A policy of benign detachment is not isolationist—at least insofar as that term is used to describe a xenophobic, "storm shelter" approach to world affairs. Quite the contrary, it adopts a tolerant and optimistic outlook, seeing Third World states not merely as pawns in America's cold war with the Soviet Union, but as unique and diverse entities. Extensive economic relations are not merely acceptable, they are essential to enhancing the ultimate appeal of capitalism and democracy. There is even room for American mediation efforts to help resolve internecine or regional conflicts, provided that all parties to a dispute desire such assistance and our role harbors no danger of political or military entanglements. The U.S. need not practice a surly isolation. America can be an active participant in Third World affairs, but the nature of such interaction must be limited, consistent, and nonintrusive.

A policy of benign detachment would bring numerous benefits to the U.S. No longer would America be perceived as the patron of repressive, decaying dictatorships, or as the principal obstacle to indigenous change in the Third World. Our current foreign policy tragically identifies the U.S. and—even worse—its capitalist democratic system with the most reactionary elements around the globe. This foolish posture enables the Soviet Union to pose as the champion of both democracy and Third World nationalism. It is time that America recaptured that moral high ground. If the U.S. allowed the people of Third World nations to work out their own destinies instead of trying to enlist them as unwilling combatants in the Cold War, Russia's hypocritical, grasping imperialism would soon stand exposed. Mos-

cow, not Washington, might well become the principal target of nationalistic wrath throughout Asia, Africa, and Latin America. Moreover, the inherent inequities and inefficiencies of Marxist economics would soon become evident to all but the most rabid ideologues.

Equally important, a conciliatory noninterventionist posture toward the Third World would reduce the risk of U.S. military involvement in complex quarrels generally not relevant to American security. Savings in terms of both dollars and lives could be enormous. Our current policy threatens to format a plethora of "brush fire" conflicts with all the attendant ex-

pense, bitterness, and divisiveness that characterized the Vietnam War.

Finally, and not the least important, reducing our Third World commitments would put an end to the hypocrisy that has pervaded U.S. relations with countries in the Third World. It is debilitating for a society that honors democracy and fundamental human rights to embrace regimes that scorn both values. A nation that believes in human liberty has no need for, and should not want, "friends" who routinely practice the worst forms of repression. A policy of detachment would restore a badly needed sense of honor and consistency to American foreign policy.

THE HUMAN RIGHTS IMPERATIVE

Cyrus R. Vance

CYRUS R. VANCE *was secretary of state from 1977 to 1980.*

The last 5 years have not been easy for those who believe that a commitment to human rights must be a central tenet of American foreign policy. The concept and definition of human rights have been twisted almost beyond recognition. Long-standing principles of international law and practice have been chipped away. Doublespeak has too often been the order of the day. Yet the time may be coming when Americans will be able to sweep aside the illusions and myths that have been used, often deliberately, to fog the human rights debate. The time may be coming when the opportunities presented by a strong human rights policy can again be seized.

These signs do not presage merely a belated recognition that former President Jimmy Carter was correct in committing U.S. foreign policy to human dignity and freedom. One can sense a rising desire among Americans to see a return to the fundamental beliefs on which their country's human rights policy must rest and from which it draws its strength. If so, and if their leaders will respond to this desire, Americans will be able again to pursue their ideals without sacrificing their traditional pragmatism.

President Ronald Reagan is fond of calling America a "city upon a hill." But the Puritan leader John Winthrop, who first uttered those words in the 17th century, intended them as a warning about the importance of adhering to the values that eventually shaped America's founding and development—particularly those later reflected in the U.S. Constitution in the Bill of Rights—not as a boast about military or economic power. As a country, America cannot be, as Reagan suggests, the "last, best hope of man on earth" unless it is prepared to restore to its rightful place in American national life respect for and protection of human rights at home and abroad.

Let me define what I mean by human rights. The most important human rights are those that protect the security of the person. Violations of such rights include genocide; slavery; torture; cruel, inhuman, and degrading treatment or punishment; arbitrary arrest or imprisonment; denial of fair trial; and invasion of the home. In the United States, many of these protections are enshrined in the Bill of Rights.

Second is that bundle of rights affecting the fulfillment of such vital needs as food, clothing, shelter, health care, and education—in the scheme of President Franklin Roosevelt's four freedoms, the freedom from want. Americans recognize that fulfilling these rights depends largely on the stage of a country's economic development. But the United States can and should help others attain these basic rights. Americans must never forget those whose empty stomachs and grinding poverty dominate their daily lives. Nor must they forget that governmental inaction, governmental indifference, and governmental corruption can threaten these rights just as seriously as the most dramatic acts of God.

Third, there is the right to enjoy civil and political liberties. These include not only freedom of speech, freedom of the press, freedom of religion, and freedom to assemble and to petition the government to redress grievances, which are guaranteed by the First Amendment to the Constitution, but also the right that most Americans take for granted—the freedom to move freely within and to and from one's own country.

Civil and political rights also must include the liberty to take part in government, the affirmation of Thomas Jefferson's declaration that the only just powers of a government are those derived from the consent of the governed. By exercising this freedom, citizens may insist that their government protect and promote their individual rights.

Finally, there is a basic human right to freedom from discrimination because of race, religion, color, or gender.

Almost all of these rights are recognized in the United Nations Universal Declaration of Human Rights, a document that the United States helped fashion and that draws heavily on the American Bill of Rights, the British Magna Carta, and the French Declaration of the Rights of Man and of the Citizen. Each of these documents has played a vital role in the historical evolution of respect for human rights. But after World War II, the world witnessed an unprecedented human rights revolution, including measures to institutionalize the international enforcement of human rights.

A genuine reversal of the administration's human rights policy could change profoundly the way America is seen in the world.

Until then, the idea that a regime could be held accountable to international standards and to the world for the treatment of its people was regarded largely as an idiosyncrasy of the democratic West, invoked only when it served a Western power's interests. A sovereign government, tradition held, could rule its people or its territory as it saw fit.

Even countries like the United States and Great Britain, which professed to follow higher standards, did not seem to believe that those standards applied to treatment of people without white skins. There was no international outcry when the United States used harsh methods to subdue opposition forces in the Philippines at the turn of the century or brutally drove native Americans onto reservations. The British could employ the most extreme tactics in repressing native populations around the globe, and few whites thought the worse of them for that. And countries without the respect for law were even less concerned about others' rights.

Such attitudes changed radically after World War II, principally because of the horror felt around the world when the Holocaust was exposed and when the full extent of Joseph Stalin's purges became clear. Individuals and countries suddenly realized that without standards, there were also no limits. The war also revealed that the far-flung colonial systems were bankrupt. Great powers could no longer hold sway over peoples they had for so long considered, in the English writer Rudyard Kipling's words, "lesser breeds without the Law."

Against this historical background, substantial progress has been made over the last 40 years. Since 1945, the world has codified a wide range of human rights. That process is in itself an enormous achievement. The power of these codes is demonstrated when movements like Poland's outlawed independent trade union Solidarity cite international norms to justify popular demands for greater liberty. Even countries that show little respect for human rights feel a need to pay lip service to them. But codes alone are not enough. It also has been necessary to develop international institutions to implement them.

First, in 1945, the United Nations Charter was adopted, enshrining human rights both as a basic objective of the newly created body and as a universal obligation. Article 55 of the charter states that the United Nations shall promote "human rights and fundamental freedoms for all without distinction as to race, sex, language, or religion." Article 56 obliges member countries "to take joint and separate action in cooperation with the Organization" to achieve those purposes.

In 1946, the Commission on Human Rights was established in the United Nations; Eleanor Roosevelt, the former U.S. first lady, was elected its first chairman. In 1948 came the Universal Declaration of Human Rights, a basic though nonbinding declaration of principles of human rights and freedoms. The 1940s and 1950s also saw the drafting of the Convention on the Prevention and Punishment of the Crime of Genocide and the preparation of two separate human rights covenants—one on political and civil rights and the other covering economic, social, and cultural rights.

During much of the 1950s, Washington stood aloof from treaties furthering those rights and limited itself to supporting U.N. studies and advisory services. But during the 1960s, America resumed its leadership, and in 1965–1966, the two covenants were finally adopted by the United Nations and presented for ratification by member states.

Largely in response to American pressure, the world moved to implement these codes more effectively. To this end, Western Europe, the Americas, and later, Africa, established their own human rights institutions. On another front, the U.N. system for several years confined its public human rights activities to only three cases: Chile, Israel, and South Africa. But beginning in the Carter years, further U.S. prodding led the international community to broaden its concern to include the examination of human rights violations in many countries, including communist countries. Progress, though sometimes halting, has been made in a process that has no precedent.

Dangerous Illusions

Many opportunities and obstacles lie ahead. But first the illusions that cloud, and fallacies that subvert, American human rights policy must be dispelled. Only then can a coherent and determined course be charted.

The first and most dangerous illusion holds that pursuing values such as human rights in U.S. foreign policy is incompatible with pursuing U.S. national interests. This is nonsense. As Reagan stated in March 1986: "A foreign policy that ignored the fate of millions in the world who seek freedom would be a betrayal of our national heritage. Our own freedom, and that of our allies, could never be secure in a world where freedom was threatened everywhere else."

Moreover, no foreign policy can gain the American people's support unless it reflects their deeper values. Carter understood this when, as president, he championed human rights. In addition to enabling millions of people to live better lives, this commitment helped redeem U.S. foreign policy from the bitterness and divisions of the Vietnam War. It reassured the American people that the U.S. role abroad can have a purpose that they could all support.

Human rights policy also requires practical judgments. Americans must continually weigh how best to encourage progress while maintaining their ability to conduct necessary business with countries in which they have important security interests. But the United States must always bear in mind that the demand for individual freedom and human dignity cannot be quelled without sowing the seeds of discontent and violent convulsion. Thus supporting constructive change that enhances individual freedom is both morally right and in America's national interest.

Freedom is a universal right of all human beings. America's own national experience, as well as recent events in Argentina, Haiti, and the Philippines, attests to the power of the drive for freedom. In a profound sense, America's ideals and interests coincide, for the United States has a stake in the stability that comes when people can express their hopes and build their futures freely. In the long run,

no system is as solid as that built on the rock of freedom. But it is not enough simply to proclaim such general principles. The more difficult question remains: What means of support should be provided to those whose rights are denied or endangered? And to answer this question, two underlying groups of questions must be addressed.

First, what are the facts? What violations or deprivations are taking place? How extensive are they? Do they demonstrate a consistent pattern of gross violations of human rights? What is the degree of control and responsibility of the government involved? Will that government permit independent outside investigation?

Second, what can be done? Will U.S. actions help promote the overall cause of human rights? Can U.S. actions improve the specific conditions at hand, or could they make matters worse? Will other countries work with the United States? Does America's sense of values and decency demand that the country speak out or take action even where there is only a remote chance of making its influence felt?

If the United States is determined to act, many tools are available. They range from quiet diplomacy, to public pronouncements, to withholding economic or military assistance from the incumbent regime. In some cases, Washington may need to provide economic assistance to oppressed peoples and, in rare instances like Afghanistan, limited military aid. Where appropriate, the United States should take positive steps to encourage compliance with basic human rights norms. And America should strive to act in concert with other countries when possible.

A second illusion that must be exposed is one pushed by many critics of Carter's human rights focus. Wrapping themselves in a rhetorical cloak of democracy and freedom, these critics pursue a curious logic that leads them to support governments and groups that deny democracy and abuse freedom. They insist on drawing a distinction for foreign-policy purposes between "authoritarian" countries that are seen as friendly toward the United States and "totalitarian" states seen as hostile. Authoritarian governments, the argument continues, are less repressive than revolutionary autocracies, more susceptible to liberalization, and more compatible with U.S. interests. Generally speaking, it is said, anticommunist autocracies tolerate social inequities, brutality, and poverty while revolutionary autocracies create them.

Sadly, this specious distinction, rooted in America's former U.N. representative Jeane Kirkpatrick's November 1979 *Commentary* article "Dictatorships and Double Standards," became a central element of the new human rights policy set forth at the start of the Reagan administration. Kirkpatrick's thesis damaged America's image as a beacon of freedom and a wise and humane champion of human rights. If it were simply an academic exercise, this version of the authoritarian-totalitarian distinction might cause little mischief. But it has a deeper political purpose. The implication that such a distinction provides a basis for condoning terror and brutality if committed by authoritarian governments friendly to the United States is mind-boggling.

The suggestion that America should turn a blind eye to human rights violations by autocrats of any stripe is unacceptable. Such thinking is morally bankrupt and badly serves U.S. national interests. To the individual on the rack it makes no difference whether the torturer is right- or left-handed—it remains the rack. In short, a sound and balanced human rights policy requires condemnation of such conduct, no matter who the perpetrator is.

Recent events give some hope that this cruel and insensitive philosophy is being buried. In his March 14 message to Congress, Reagan stated that America opposes "tyranny in whatever form, whether of the left or the right." Debate over whether this statement reflects a policy reversal will continue until the new posture inspires a pattern of concrete actions. But it must not be perverted into a ploy to gain votes in Congress for increased military aid for the Nicaraguan *contra* rebels. A genuine reversal of the administration's human rights policy could change profoundly the way America is seen in the world and also unleash powerful forces that would encourage truly democratic alternatives. Such a policy surely would have strong bipartisan support.

A third human rights illusion, deriving from the second, is the fallacy inherent in the so-called Reagan Doctrine enunciated in the president's 1985 State of the Union address. Speaking about U.S. policy toward armed insurgencies against communist regimes, he declared: "We must not break faith with those who are risking their lives—on every continent, from Afghanistan to Nicaragua—to defy Soviet-supported aggression and secure rights which have been ours from birth.... Support for freedom fighters is self-defense."

No doubt there will be situations in which the United States should aid insurgencies—as in Afghanistan, where such aid promotes human rights and clearly serves American interests. There, the Soviet Union invaded a small neighboring country with overpowering military force, deposed the existing government, and imposed its own hand-picked government that, with the support of massive Soviet firepower, slaughtered tens of thousands of Afghans and turned millions more into refugees. It is critical to note that in supporting the Afghan rebels, Americans are not merely supporting an anticommunist rebellion. The United States is vindicating universal principles of international law and helping the Afghan people to determine their own future.

Yet the Reagan Doctrine, taking shelter under the banner of human rights, commits America to supporting anticommunist revolution wherever it arises. By implication, the doctrine offers no such assistance to opponents of other tyrannies. As the case of Nicaragua shows, the support the doctrine promises can include American arms. Consequently, despite repeated administration denials, the doctrine clearly holds out the possibility of ultimate intervention by U.S. forces.

This policy is both wrong and potentially dangerous to America's interests and its standing in the world. As with virtually all doctrines, it is automatic and inflexible by nature. That inflexibility blinds policymakers in a double sense. It blinds them to the realities and available alternatives in individual situations, and it blinds them to the principles of respect for national territorial sovereignty and nonintervention—cornerstones of international order.

The Reagan Doctrine's evident bias toward military options could easily prompt Washington to overlook better ways to achieve worthy goals. Even where economic incentives or restrictions may be sufficient, and even where U.S. policy may lack regional support and might work against broader U.S. interests, the Reagan Doctrine suggests that, at a minimum, America should fund military forces.

Beyond this strategic misconception, the Reagan Doctrine obscures the hard but essential questions of means and consequences. To avoid self-delusion, Americans must recognize that anticommunism cannot always be equated with democracy. Nor is anticommunism a shield against the consequences of unrealistic and imprudent action. At the very least, the United States must ask whom it intends to support. Do they believe in democratic values? Can they attract sufficient support in their country and region to govern if they take power? How would such a change affect the citizens of their country? Does America risk raising hopes or expectations that it cannot or will not fulfill? Can America deliver enough aid to decisively affect the outcome? Finally, will such a policy have the domestic support needed to sustain Washington's chosen course of action?

Ironically, many champions of the Reagan Doctrine call themselves realists. Yet any policy that tempts the country to ignore these basic questions cannot be called hardheaded or realistic. The doctrine's dogmatism and seductive ideological beckoning to leap before looking, are, in fact, strikingly unrealistic. So systematically ignoring the principles of sovereignty and nonintervention is not in America's national interest.

New Hope for Progress

A key strength of this country has always been its respect for law and moral values. To follow the Reagan Doctrine would undermine America's moral authority. What the United States and the Soviet Union have to offer the world must be distinguished by more than the simple declaration that, by definition, whatever Washington does is right and whatever Moscow does is wrong.

President John Kennedy once said that the United States is engaged in a "long, twilight struggle" in world affairs. But if that is so, America's principles and interests both are more likely to thrive if the country keeps faith with the ideals for which it struggles.

Principle must be the foundation of America's course for the future, but policy will be sustained only if it is also pragmatic. That must not mean that pragmatism should dominate. U.S. foreign policy must never become realpolitik unconnected with principle. Yet promoting ideals that have no chance of being put into practice risks becoming mere posturing. Nor should Americans focus simply on the great issues and ignore the fact that, at heart, human rights concern individual human beings. Indeed, it matters greatly what America can do in concrete cases, in individual countries, for any one person to live a better life.

The charge to U.S. human rights policy has rarely been put more clearly than by Felice Gaer, executive director of the International League for Human Rights. Testifying before a subcommittee of the House Committee on Foreign Affairs in February 1986, she said: "The United States needs to do more than make declarations and to provide free transport for fleeing dictators.... The U.S. Government has leverage to use—if it chooses to use it. It has the power to persuade governments."

The United States has many opportunities, and faces many problems, in trying to advance human rights abroad. In a few countries, there is reason to give thanks for recent progress. In others, recent shifts in stated U.S. policy provide hope for future progress.

Chile is a case in point. The regime of General Augusto Pinochet recently has increased pressure on Chilean defenders of human rights. Members of the Chilean Commission for Human Rights, the country's most important secular human rights organization, face almost daily threats, physical intimidation, and overt violence. Last November, the commission's office was invaded and ransacked. Its documents, compiled for a U.N. investigation, were confiscated by armed plainclothes police. The intruders beat the office caretaker with their fists and a revolver, causing a concussion. When the caretaker's daughters tried to help her, they were threatened with death. Before leaving, the invaders shouted, "Now you will know the hand of CNI [the Chilean national intelligence agency]."

On January 15, 1986, two commission officers were attacked and stoned in front of a police station by a mob of progovernment protesters while the civilian police stood idly by. The victims were the commission's president, Jaime Castillo, a founder and past president of the Christian Democratic party and former minister of justice in the democratic government of Eduardo Frei in the 1960s, and the commission's vice president, Maximo Pacheco, a former minister of education in the Frei government. The windows of the car in which they were riding were shattered by rocks, and Castillo was struck in the head with a rock and lacerated in the face and back by splintering glass. Fortunately, the two men were able to keep the car moving and escaped with their lives. Since then the pressure has continued. Pacheco has been harassed, his household servant kidnaped, and his daughter and her child subjected to threats of kidnaping and violence. The Chilean government has brushed aside all protests.

Despite such brutalities, there is still reason for hope. Chile does have a long tradition of popular rule before 1973—when Pinochet seized power in a bloody military coup—on which to build. A foundation for human rights does exist beneath the rubble created by the military dictatorship. Moreover, U.S. policy toward Chile has begun to change. From the outset, the Reagan administration opposed a U.N. resolution condemning Chile for human rights abuses. In March 1986, however, the administration changed its position and sponsored its own resolution condemning Chile. Much credit must go to America's courageous ambassador, Harry Barnes, Jr., to Secretary of

State George Shultz, and to those members of Congress who have long pressed the Chilean government to restore respect for human rights and to hold early, free, and fair elections.

In future dealings with Chile, the United States must make its views on human rights clear. Washington must stress that U.S.-Chilean relations will be affected by Santiago's conduct. America must state bluntly that unless Chile's human rights policies and conduct change, the United States will, among other actions, vote against all future international bank loans to Chile.

In Argentina, meanwhile, promise has become reality. Under the leadership of President Raúl Alfonsín, respect for freedom and for individual dignity has been restored to that country. As the publisher Jacobo Timerman—who was tortured under Argentina's old military regime—and others have pointed out, the Argentine people can be thankful to Americans who kept faith in the dark days of the late 1970s, when thousands of Argentines "disappeared" and many were murdered at the hands of the military.

Above all, Argentina's return to democracy is truly a triumph of popular courage and determination, a victory of the faith and will of the oppressed over their oppressors. Americans must continue to support the Alfonsín government both politically and economically as it confronts massive economic difficulties. Washington should be forthcoming and steady in providing help, bilaterally and through the international financial institutions.

Encouraging news recently has come from the Philippines and Haiti as well. In Haiti, the heir to one of the world's worst traditions of government finally was driven from power. This island country remains desperately poor and faces a difficult future. But at least its destiny is being determined largely by men and women who seek a better life for all Haitians. America can and must help, beginning with immediate emergency food aid, while it urgently assesses Haiti's longer-term needs. In the Philippines, the problems are even more complex, but the victory achieved is even more inspiring. All Americans have marveled at the magnificent commitment of the Filipino people to freedom, at the physical and moral courage of President Corazon Aquino, at the support of the Roman Catholic church under the leadership of Jaime Cardinal Sin, and at the unforgettable sight of peaceful, unarmed men and women facing down tanks and guns with their "prayers and presence." The United States should offer whatever support it can as that country seeks to rebuild both politically and economically.

One of the most striking developments of the 1980s has been the answer to Stalin's question concerning how many divisions the pope has. From Poland to the Philippines, the world has heard the answer: Quite a few. Much remains to be done in the Philippines, and the doing will not be easy. But what has been shown in Buenos Aires, in Port-au-Prince, and in Manila is that peaceful, democratic change is possible in today's world, that such change carries with it great promise, and that there is much that American human rights policies can do to promote it.

In many other countries the pace of change has been maddeningly slow, and in some, nonexistent. Both opportunities and pitfalls abound. This is particularly true in Central America, and nowhere more so than in Nicaragua. Furnishing military aid to the *contras* is a disastrous mistake. The United States should listen to the virtually unanimous advice of its Latin American neighbors who urge it not to give such aid and to give its full support instead to the Contadora process. Despite temporary setbacks, this regional peace effort provides a framework for ending Central America's agony while safeguarding the hemisphere's security interests. But whatever their viewpoint, Americans all should be able to agree that human rights are denied and abused in Nicaragua, and have been for decades—by the late dictator Anastasio Somoza Debayle and his supporters and by the Sandinistas. Americans must continue to demand an end to all such abuses.

To avoid self-delusion, Americans must recognize that anticommunism cannot always be equated with democracy.

In the Pacific, human rights are of special importance in South Korea. The United States has major national interests in South Korea and its future. Americans fought side by side with the South Korean people in defending the country. Seoul is an important ally, America's seventh largest trading partner, and a critical force for stability in Northeast Asia. And South Korea's future will be vitally affected by the way its government responds to popular demands for greater pluralism and respect for the rights and dignity of all of its citizens. America must exert its influence to that end. The next 3 years will be especially important as international attention to South Korea increases when Seoul hosts the Asian

Games in fall 1986 and the summer Olympic Games in 1988.

South Korea differs from the Philippines in its political traditions and cultural heritage. The Filipino people have democratic roots several decades long, while South Korea's slow movement toward more open government is a relatively recent development. These differences should caution Americans in drawing conclusions and predicting how each government will act to open up its society. Failure to be realistic can lead to false hopes and expectations.

This does not mean playing down human rights issues in U.S. relations with South Korea. Quite the contrary, as a friend and ally, the United States must speak more candidly and forcefully than it has about the need for South Korea's leaders to open up the political process more rapidly and to recognize and respect the right of all its citizens to be free from repression and secure from arbitrary arrest, imprisonment, and the invasion of their homes. A pragmatic as well as principled policy also would make clear that the United States will continue to help South Korea defend itself against the threat of attack from North Korea, while maintaining America's strong interest in South Korea's economic development and prosperity.

The Soviet Union clearly presents the most difficult problems in balancing human rights principles and pragmatism. Two critically important truths must always be kept in mind. First, human rights must always be on America's agenda with the Soviet Union. On that there can be no compromise. Second, human rights almost never can be on the agenda alone. The facts of the nuclear age require dealing with Moscow on matters that can determine the fate of the planet—avoiding nuclear war and preventing regional conflicts that could lead to nuclear war. No American government can honor its commitment to the human family if it fails to pursue human rights with Soviet leaders; it cannot honor its commitment, however, if it does not also pursue the cause of peace.

The United States must continue to prod the Soviet Union to honor its commitment to the human rights provisions of the Helsinki Final Act. America must also prod the Soviets to relax their grip on those people, from the dissident scientist Andrei Sakharov to thousands of unknown individuals, who are most oppressed by Soviet rule. America must do so because those individuals have few other advocates in world councils. America must do so because, in speaking out, it reminds the world of the difference between the vision of Jefferson and the perverse outlook of Stalin. And America must do so because it can have an effect. Sometimes America may act through quiet diplomacy; at other times, through forceful public statements. Still other situations may call for the use of incentives or rewards on the one hand and threats and punishments on the other.

Americans must also remember the special plight of Soviet Jewry. Specifically, Moscow must be pressed to increase the level of Jewish emigration at least to that achieved in the mid- and late 1970s. It was possible then; it should be possible now.

Since martial law crushed the Solidarity movement in December 1981, human rights conditions have been a major problem in Poland. American economic sanctions that initially were imposed have been dismantled step by step as the Polish government met certain conditions: Martial law was lifted and many political prisoners were released. The calibrated American response has been, on the whole, an intelligent application of U.S. human rights policy.

Yet despite what some take as normalization of the situation, the last year has seen severe incursions on academic freedom and purges, together with the harassment and even imprisonment of some of Solidarity's leading figures. Further U.S. assistance to help Poland overcome its economic catastrophe should be keyed to Warsaw's willingness to reverse the setbacks of the last year and to move toward genuine national reconciliation involving the Polish government, the Roman Catholic church, and Solidarity.

Finally, there is South Africa. The United States has maintained diplomatic relations with South Africa for many years. During World War II, although many of the strongest advocates of apartheid were pro-Nazi, the South African government itself fought with the Allies to free the peoples of Europe from fascist tyranny. South Africa is a source of important raw materials, occupying a strategic position along the sea routes running from the Indian Ocean and the Middle East into the Atlantic Ocean. Yet productive relations with South Africa are impossible because of sharp differences over apartheid, over the right of South Africa's blacks to live decent lives, and over their right to participate as full citizens in governing their country.

South Africa has institutionalized discrimination of the most vicious sort and resists fundamental change of this abhorrent system. What the United States seeks in the near term is clear: the dismantling of apartheid, root and branch, and the sharing of political power among whites, blacks, mixed-blood "Coloreds," and Asians alike.

The United States should make unmistakably clear to President P. W. Botha and all South Africans that Americans are committed to the total abolition of apartheid and to genuine power sharing. The U.S. government must underscore that South Africa cannot adopt one policy for worldwide public consumption and a second, less stringent policy for private discussion in Pretoria. America must make unmistakably clear that time is running out and that major steps must be taken now. The South African government also must be told that, without prompt action, the United States will impose more stringent economic restrictions than those approved by Reagan in September 1985. And America should work with like-minded countries to pressure South Africa to make those decisions that are necessary now to stop further repression and a bloody civil war later.

The world has a long agenda in the pursuit of human rights. There will be, I fear, no final victory over tyranny, no end to the challenge of helping people to live decent lives, free from oppression and indignity. But this generation has set the highest standards for human rights in human history. It has achieved much; it has proved repeatedly that no idea is so compelling as the idea of human freedom. America was "conceived in Liberty, and dedicated to the proposition that all men are created equal." It is America's task, a century and a quarter after Abraham Lincoln spoke, to do its utmost to help redeem that promise for men and women everywhere.

Ending Apartheid in South Africa

President Reagan

Following is an addresss by President Reagan before members of the World Affairs Council and Foreign Policy Association in the East Room of the White House, Washington, D.C., July 22, 1986.

For more than a year now, the world's attention has been focused upon South Africa—the deepening political crisis there, the widening cycle of violence. And, today, I'd like to outline American policy toward that troubled republic and toward the region of which it is a part—a region of vital importance to the West.

The root cause of South Africa's disorder is apartheid—that rigid system of racial segregation, wherein black people have been treated as third-class citizens in a nation they helped to build.

America's view of apartheid has been, and remains, clear. Apartheid is morally wrong and politically unacceptable. The United States cannot maintain cordial relations with a government whose power rests upon the denial of rights to a majority of its people based on race. If South Africa wishes to belong to the family of Western nations, an end to apartheid is a precondition. Americans, I believe, are united in this conviction. Second, apartheid must be dismantled. Time is running out for the moderates of all races in South Africa.

But if we Americans are agreed upon the goal, a free and multiracial South Africa associated with free nations and the West, there is deep disagreement about how to reach it.

First, a little history—for a quarter century now, the American Government

has been separating itself from the South African Government. In 1962, President Kennedy imposed an embargo on military sales. Last September, I issued an Executive order further restricting U.S. dealings with the Pretoria government. For the past 18 months, the marketplace has been sending unmistakable signals of its own. U.S. bank lending to South Africa has been virtually halted. No significant new investment has come in. Some Western businessmen have packed up and gone home.

The Call for Sanctions

And now, we've reached a critical juncture. Many in Congress and some in Europe are clamoring for sweeping sanctions against South Africa. The Prime Minister of Great Britain has denounced punitive sanctions as "immoral" and "utterly repugnant." Well, let me tell you why we believe Mrs. Thatcher is right.

The primary victims of an economic boycott of South Africa would be the very people we seek to help. Most of the workers who would lose jobs because of sanctions would be black workers. We do not believe the way to help the people of South Africa is to cripple the economy upon which they and their families depend for survival.

Alan Paton, South Africa's great writer, for years the conscience of his country, has declared himself emphatically: "I am totally opposed to disinvestment," he says. "It is primarily for a moral reason. Those who will pay most

grievously for disinvestment will be the black workers of South Africa. I take very seriously the teachings of the gospels. In particular, the parables about giving drink to the thirsty and food to the hungry. I will not help to cause any such suffering to any black person." Nor will we.

Looking at a map, southern Africa is a single economic unit tied together by rails and roads. Zaire and its southern mining region depends upon South Africa for three-fourths of its food and petroleum. More than half the electric power that drives the capital of Mozambique comes from South Africa. Over one-third of the exports from Zambia and 65% of the exports of Zimbabwe leave the continent through South African ports.

The mines of South Africa employ 13,000 workers from Swaziland, 19,000 from Botswana, 50,000 from Mozambique, and 110,000 from the tiny, landlocked country of Lesotho. Shut down these productive mines with sanctions, and you have forced black mine workers out of their jobs and forced their families back in their home countries into destitution. I don't believe the American people want to do something like that. As one African leader remarked recently, "Southern Africa is like a zebra. If the white parts are injured, the black parts will die too."

Well, Western nations have poured billions in foreign aid and investment loans into southern Africa. Does it make sense to aid these countries with one hand and with the other to smash the industrial engine upon which their future depends?

Wherever blacks seek equal opportunity, higher wages, and better working conditions, their strongest allies are the American, British, French, German, and Dutch businessmen who bring to South Africa ideas of social justice formed in their own countries.

If disinvestment is mandated, these progressive Western forces will depart and South African proprietors will inherit, at fire sale prices, their farms and factories and plants and mines. And how would this end apartheid?

Our own experience teaches us that racial progress comes swiftest and easiest not during economic depression but in times of prosperity and growth. Our own history teaches us that capitalism is the natural enemy of such feudal institutions as apartheid.

Violence and Change

Nevertheless, we share the outrage Americans have come to feel. Night after night, week after week, television has brought us reports of violence by South African security forces, bringing injury and death to peaceful demonstrators and innocent bystanders. More recently, we read of violent attacks by blacks against blacks. Then, there is the calculated terror by elements of the African National Congress: the mining of roads, the bombings of public places, designed to bring about further repression—the imposition of martial law and eventually creating the conditions for racial war.

The most common method of terror is the so-called necklace. In this barbaric way of reprisal, a tire is filled with kerosene or gasoline, placed around the neck of an alleged "collaborator," and ignited. The victim may be a black policeman, a teacher, a soldier, a civil servant. It makes no difference. The atrocity is designed to terrorize blacks into ending all racial cooperation and to polarize South Africa as prelude to a final, climactic struggle for power.

In defending their society and people, the South African Government has a right and responsibility to maintain order in the face of terrorists. But by its tactics, the government is only accelerating the descent into bloodletting. Moderates are being trapped between the intimidation of radical youths and countergangs of vigilantes.

And the government's state of emergency next went beyond the law of necessity. It, too, went outside the law by sweeping up thousands of students, civic leaders, church leaders, and labor leaders, thereby contributing to further radicalization. Such repressive measures will bring South Africa neither peace nor security.

It's a tragedy that most Americans only see or read about the dead and injured in South Africa—from terrorism, violence, and repression. For behind the terrible television pictures lies another truth: South Africa is a complex and diverse society in a state of transition. More and more South Africans have come to recognize that change is essential for survival. The realization has come hard and late; but the realization has finally come to Pretoria that apartheid belongs to the past.

In recent years, there's been a dramatic change. Black workers have been permitted to unionize, bargain collectively, and build the strongest free trade union movement in all of Africa. The infamous pass laws have been ended, as have many of the laws denying blacks the right to live, work, and own property in South Africa's cities. Citizenship, wrongly stripped away, has been restored to nearly 6 million blacks. Segregation in universities and public facilities is being set aside. Social apartheid laws prohibiting interracial sex and marriage have been struck down. It is because State President Botha has presided over these reforms that extremists have denounced him as a traitor.

We must remember, as the British historian Paul Johnson reminds us, that South Africa is an African country as well as a Western country. And reviewing the history of that continent in the quarter century since independence, historian Johnson does not see South Africa as a failure: ". . .only in South Africa," he writes, "have the real incomes of blacks risen very substantially. . . . In mining, black wages have tripled in real terms in the last decade. . . . South Africa is the. . . only African country to produce a large black middle class. Almost certainly," he adds, "there are now more black women professionals in South Africa than in the whole of the rest of Africa put together."

Despite apartheid, tens of thousands of black Africans migrate into South Africa from neighboring countries to escape poverty and take advantage of the opportunities in an economy that produces nearly a third of the income in all of sub-Saharan Africa.

It's tragic that in the current crisis social and economic progress has been arrested. And, yet, in contemporary South Africa—before the state of emergency—there was a broad measure of freedom of speech, of the press, and of religion there. Indeed, it's hard to think of a single country in the Soviet bloc—or many in the United Nations—where political critics have the same freedom to be heard as did outspoken critics of the South African Government.

But, by Western standards, South Africa still falls short, terribly short, on the scales of economic and social justice. South Africa's actions to dismantle apartheid must not end now. The state of emergency must be lifted. There must be an opening of the political process. That the black people of South Africa should have a voice in their own governance is an idea whose time has come. There can be no turning back. In the multiracial society that is South Africa, no single race can monopolize the reins of political power.

Black churches, black unions, and, indeed, genuine black nationalists have a legitimate role to play in the future of their country. But the South African Government is under no obligation to negotiate the future of the country with any organization that proclaims a goal of creating a communist state and uses terrorist tactics and violence to achieve it.

U.S. Ideals and Strategic Interests

Many Americans, understandably, ask: given the racial violence, the hatred, why not wash our hands and walk away from that tragic continent and bleeding country? Well, the answer is: we cannot.

In southern Africa, our national ideals and strategic interests come together. South Africa matters because we believe that all men are created equal and are endowed by their creator with unalienable rights. South Africa matters because of who we are. One of eight Americans can trace his ancestry to Africa.

Strategically, this is one of the most vital regions of the world. Around the Cape of Good Hope passes the oil of the Persian Gulf, which is indispensable to the industrial economies of Western Europe. Southern Africa and South Africa are repository of many of the vital minerals—vanadium, manganese, chromium, platinum—for which the West has no other secure source of supply.

The Soviet Union is not unaware of the stakes. A decade ago, using an army of Cuban mercenaries provided by Fidel Castro, Moscow installed a client regime in Angola. Today, the Soviet Union is providing that regime with the weapons to attack UNITA [National Union for the Total Independence of Angola]—a black liberation movement which seeks for Angolans the same right to be represented in their government that black South Africans seek for themselves.

Apartheid threatens our vital interests in southern Africa, because it's drawing neighboring states into the vortex of violence. Repeatedly, within the last 18 months, South African forces have struck into neighboring states. I repeat our condemnation of such behavior. Also, the Soviet-armed guerrillas of the African National Congress—operating both within South Africa and from some neighboring countries—have embarked upon new acts of terrorism inside South Africa. I also condemn that behavior.

But South Africa cannot shift the blame for these problems onto neighboring states, especially when those neighbors take steps to stop guerrilla actions from being mounted from their own territory.

If this rising hostility in southern Africa—between Pretoria and the front-line states—explodes, the Soviet Union will be the main beneficiary. And the critical ocean corridor of South Africa and the strategic minerals of the region would be at risk. Thus, it would be a historic act of folly for the United States and the West—out of anguish and frustration and anger—to write off South Africa.

Key to the Future

Ultimately, however, the fate of South Africa will be decided there, not here. We Americans stand ready to help. But whether South Africa emerges democratic and free or takes a course leading to a downward spiral of poverty and repression will finally be their choice, not ours.

The key to the future lies with the South African Government. As I urge Western nations to maintain communication and involvement in South Africa, I urge Mr. Botha not to retreat into the *laager*, not to cut off contact with the West. Americans and South Africans have never been enemies, and we understand the apprehension and fear and concern of all of your people. But an end to apartheid does not necessarily mean an end to the social, economic, and physical security of the white people in this country they love and have sacrificed so much to build.

To the black, "colored," and Asian peoples of South Africa, too long treated as second- and third-class subjects, I can only say: in your hopes for freedom, social justice, and self-determination, you have a friend and ally in the United States. Maintain your hopes for peace and reconciliation, and we will do our part to keep that road open.

We understand that behind the rage and resentment in the townships is the memory of real injustices inflicted upon generations of South Africans. Those to whom evil is done, the poet wrote, often do evil in return.

But if the people of South Africa are to have a future in a free country where the rights of all are respected, the desire for retribution will have to be set aside. Otherwise, the future will be lost in a bloody quarrel over the past.

Components for Progress Toward Peace

It would be an act of arrogance to insist that uniquely American ideas and institutions, rooted in our own history and traditions, be transplanted to South African soil. Solutions to South Africa's political crisis must come from South Africans themselves. Black and white, "colored" and Asian, they have their own traditions. But let me outline what we believe are necessary components of progress toward political peace.

First, a timetable for elimination of apartheid laws should be set.

Second, all political prisoners should be released.

Third, Nelson Mandela should be released—to participate in the country's political process.

Fourth, black political movements should be unbanned.

Fifth, both the government and its opponents should begin a dialogue about constructing a political system that rests upon the consent of the governed—where the rights of majorities and minorities, and individuals are protected by law. And the dialogue should be initiated by those with power and authority—the South African Government itself.

Sixth, if postapartheid South Africa is to remain the economic locomotive of southern Africa, its strong and developed economy must not be crippled. And, therefore, I urge the Congress—and the countries of Western Europe—to resist this emotional clamor for punitive sanctions.

If Congress imposes sanctions, it would destory America's flexibility, discard our diplomatic leverage, and deepen the crisis. To make a difference, Americans—who are a force for decency and progress in the world—must remain involved. We must stay and work, not cut and run.

It should be our policy to build in South Africa, not to bring down. Too often in the past, we Americans—acting out of anger and frustration and impatience—have turned our backs on flawed regimes, only to see disaster follow.

Those who tell us the moral thing to do is to embargo the South African economy and write off South Africa should tell us exactly what they believe will rise in its place. What foreign power would fill the vacuum if South Africa's ties with the West are broken?

The Need for Coordination

To be effective, however, our policy must be coordinated with our key Western allies and with the front-line states in southern Africa. These countries have the greatest concern and potential leverage on the situation in South Africa. I intend to pursue the following steps.

• Secretary Shultz has already begun intensive consultations with our Western allies—whose roots and presence in South Africa are greater than our own—on ways to encourage internal negotiations. We want the process to begin now, and we want open channels to all the principal parties. The key nations of the West must act in concert. And, together, we can make the difference.

We fully support the current efforts of the British Government to revive hopes for negotiations. Foreign Secretary Howe's visits with South Africa's leader this week will be of particular significance.

• And second, I urge the leaders of the region to join us in seeking a future South Africa where countries live in peace and cooperation. South Africa is the nation where the industrial revolution first came to Africa; its economy is a mighty engine that could pull southern Africa into a prosperous future. The other nations of southern Africa—from Kinshasa to the Cape—are rich in natural resources and human resources.

• Third, I have directed Secretary Shultz and AID [Agency for International Development] Administrator McPherson to undertake a study of America's assistance role in southern Africa to determine what needs to be done and what can be done to expand the trade, private investment, and transport prospects of southern Africa's land-locked nations. In the past 5 years, we have provided almost $1 billion in assistance to South Africa's neighbors. And this year we hope to provide an additional $45 million to black South Africans.

We're determined to remain involved, diplomatically and economically, with all the states of southern Africa that wish constructive relations with the United States.

This Administration is not only against broad economic sanctions and against apartheid; we are for a new South Africa, a new nation where all that has been built up over generations is not destroyed, a new society where participation in the social, cultural, and political life is open to all people—a new South Africa that comes home to the family of free nations where it belongs.

To achieve that, we need not a Western withdrawal but deeper involvement by the Western business community, as agents of change and progress and growth. The international business community needs not only to be supported in South Africa but energized. We'll be at work on that task. If we wish to foster the process of transformation, one of the best vehicles for change is through the involvement of black South Africans in business, job-related activities, and labor unions.

But the vision of a better life cannot be realized so long as apartheid endures and instability reigns in South Africa. If the peoples of southern Africa are to prosper, leaders and peoples of the region—of all races—will have to elevate their common interests above their ethnic divisions.

We and our allies cannot dictate to the government of a sovereign nation. Nor should we try. But we can offer to help find a solution that is fair to all the people of South Africa. We can volunteer to stand by and help bring about dialogue between leaders of the various factions and groups that make up the population of South Africa. We can counsel and advise and make it plain to all that we are there as friends of all the people of South Africa.

In that tormented land, the window remains open for peaceful change. For how long, we know not. But we in the West, privileged and prosperous and free, must not be the ones to slam it shut. Now is a time for healing. The people of South Africa, of all races, deserve a chance to build a better future. And we must not deny or destory that chance.

The Soviet Union Confronts the World

The leadership issue in the Soviet Union seems to have been resolved well enough for the time being to enable the Soviet leaders to direct their attention to the solution of pressing domestic and foreign policy problems. The Communist party's General Secretary, Mikhail Gorbachev, appears to have become the Soviets' leader at the right historical moment; not only was the Soviet Union in need of a man determined to clear away major bureaucratic obstacles in order to inaugurate substantial political and economic reforms, but also the Soviet Union's foreign policy had come to a dead end. Soviet foreign policy desperately needs the image Gorbachev projects: a cautious, concerned, well-educated, and perceptive leader, who understands the needs of his adversaries, who would consider it virtually unthinkable to use nuclear weapons, and who has better things to do with finite Soviet resources than to waste them on support for revolution in places of marginal relevance to the Soviet Union's national interest. Although this may only be an image and not reality, image is all-important in foreign policy.

Afghanistan has required significant sacrifices from the Soviet citizenry. Any foreign policy initiative which would require even further sacrifices by the populace would encounter serious resistance. This may partially explain why the Soviets now appear committed to a withdrawal from Afghanistan, and why the arms race must, in Gorbachev's view, be brought to a halt. In terms of technology and finance, the Soviet's huge standing army on both the European and Asian fronts imposes serious economic burdens. There appears to be a strong sentiment among the Soviet military leaders, moreover, that they would have more money for defense if the economy was not stagnating. The performance of Soviet agriculture in the last several years has been abysmal, industrial production lethargic, and the technological gap is growing ever wider between the Soviet Union and the West. Under such conditions, it would be short-sighted for the Soviet military to further sap the strength of the economy through siphoning off further resources for its own sector.

From the Soviet perspective, there is much to be gained from decreased tensions with the US: increased trade, technological transfer, continued grain sales, and a diminished sense of threat to the Soviet Union's security.

The Soviet Union must ponder as much as the United States does about just what fruits certain Middle-Eastern entanglements will bear. Although countries such as Syria are willing to take Soviet arms, they are limited in their willingness to listen to Soviet advice. Many regimes in the Middle East are not very attractive to Moscow, offering little more than their hatred of the United States.

When Gorbachev considers Central America, even greater doubts must surface. Apart from a launching area for further revolutions, which the United States is in a far better position to counter than the Soviet Union is to support, Nicaragua offers little to the Soviet Union. With a miniscule population of some three million and no strategic resources, why should the Soviet Union continue to pour money into Nicaragua when there are twenty-five times this number of people in Mexico and it is located next door to the US? The Soviets' Cuban experience must have caused serious debate within the Soviet leadership over the wisdom of further ventures close to the US; for although Cuba can be rationalized as a strategic foothold and listening post close to the US, the continued support of Castro has cost the Soviet Union hundreds of millions of dollars each year.

Before Gorbachev's time, the Soviet Union did become involved in many states of secondary importance to its national interest in an effort to spread socialism worldwide: Ethiopia, Angola, Nicaragua, Cuba, Afghanistan, Kampuchea, and Mozambique. Today, one could easily argue that even from Moscow's perspective, they are not "involved" but "stuck" in these countries. The Soviet Union continues to put in far more than it gets out of its engagement in these underdeveloped countries.

The Soviets' ability to have an effective foreign policy is further impeded by its restless Eastern European allies, though these problems seem to have abated since Gorbachev's accession to power in March 1985. Indeed, without so much as a whimper, the Warsaw pact countries signed on to another twenty years of military subordination to the Soviet Union. Still, economic problems, pressure for greater economic and financial ties with the Western capitalist states, and nationalism continue to undermine Soviet control of Eastern European governments. Added to these problems in effectively marketing communism abroad are the setbacks to the prestige of Communist and Socialist parties in Western European countries over the past few years.

Viewing the Soviet Union's foreign policy in its totality, however, there are two extremely important bright spots. The first is progress in Sino-Soviet relations. Although still in the process of rebuilding the trust, if not the intimacy, of their former relationship, there has been progress in trade, diplomacy, and cultural exchange. Any reduction of hostilities is greatly welcomed by the Soviet Union, especially since it shares 4000 miles of border with the People's Republic of China. This does not mean that the two countries are willing to embrace each other as "socialist brothers" as they did in the 1950s, but only that the relationship is moving in a positive direction.

The second significant advance in Soviet foreign policy is toward more positive relations with the United States. Gorbachev's openly conciliatory stance toward the US has encouraged extended summitry and negotiations for extensive disarmament. Gorbachev has tried to find common ground on which both the United States and the Soviet Union can agree, rather than focusing on areas of conflict within the relationship. His efforts to bring about a better relationship between the two superpowers have earned him a vast amount of good will worldwide. While it would be premature to write tomorrow's history books with the Soviet Union as the leading advocate and practitioner of principles of peaceful coexistence, Gorbachev has certainly taken some important steps toward relaxing world tensions. Perhaps most significant toward the improvement of relations with the United States is that in 1987, Gorbachev released dozens of imprisoned dissidents and called for a broad-ranging reform of the antidemocratic and bureaucratic practices of the Soviet Union's Communist party.

Thus, if we examine Soviet foreign policy in the last few years, we cannot help but notice the dramatic difference that Gorbachev has made. He has taken bold initiatives to diminish the hostility of other countries toward the Soviet Union. Although caution is always in order, ideology must not blind the US to the possibility that Gorbachev is sincerely interested in reducing international tensions (Article 5). The new willingness of the Soviet Union to expose its mistakes and weaknesses to the outside world in order to create greater trust is illustrated by the stunning candor of the Soviets in admitting the errors which led to the Chernobyl nuclear accident in 1986 (Article 6). Even the Soviets' conventional buildup in Europe and naval buildup in the Pacific may be interpreted in a positive light. A shift in Soviet military strategy indicates a worst-case assumption: a nuclear war could happen, but it would be accidental, not purposeful (Article 9).

The fact that Gorbachev has done more than just make public relations gestures for foreign consumption suggests that he is sincerely attempting to bring about disarmament and to address serious problems within the Soviet socialist system, problems which have generated many of the conflictual issues with the West. Gorbachev has not minced words in his attack on the practices of the Communist party of the Soviet Union, and is committed to addressing its abuses of power at the expense of Soviet citizens (Article 11). Gorbachev, like China's preeminent leader Deng Xiaoping, faces a basic dilemma: although he is aware of the tension between socialism and rapid development, and although he realizes the socialist system must undergo a thorough reform if the country is to move ahead, he is also concerned about the implications for Communist party rule if the critiques of socialist practices in the Soviet Union go too far (Article 10).

The Soviets' developmental difficulties at home are, of course, compounded by their problems abroad. Rather than being able to develop a profitable economic and political relationship with Marxist regimes in Third World countries, the Soviets instead find themselves drained of resources trying to buttress these pro-Moscow regimes against repeated insurgencies. Since the Soviets' ability to supply economic aid to poor countries is limited, it finds itself losing the battle with the Western capitalist states to attract non-Marxist regimes to its side (Article 7). In fact, the Soviets' economic problems at home have become increasingly severe in the face of falling revenues for oil and other commodities which the Soviet Union relied upon for trade with the West. Thus the Soviet Union is now forced to borrow from abroad in order to pay for the grain and technology which its own economic system is incapable of producing (Article 8).

Looking Ahead: Challenge Questions

Thinking as a Soviet citizen heavily socialized in Marxist values, what kinds of initiatives would you suggest that the Kremlin take in the foreign policy field? Would they be similar to the ones Gorbachev has chosen? What would be the reasons for constructing a Soviet foreign policy along the lines that you have chosen? How would you expect the United States to respond to your proposals? Would you be surprised if the United States did not respond favorably? From the perspective of Moscow, does it appear that the United States is negotiating from a position of strength? If so, what are the constituent elements of that strength? Does history indicate that countries are more willing to negotiate from a position of strength, or from a position of weakness? In this regard, what has been the history of successful and unsuccessful Soviet-American negotiations?

What would be the most probable analysis that Soviet decision-makers are making concerning their setbacks in the Third World? Do you think the Soviets are still interested in promoting revolution in preindustrial Third World countries? If so, what area of the world do you think the Soviets will choose next to advance the socialist revolution and why?

What foreign policy tools do the Soviets use most in promoting their objectives abroad? In what way are these tools similar to or different from those used by the United States? Are they more effective than those used in American foreign policy? What do the Soviets want from the global community? Are these things incompatible with American national interests or the national interests of other countries? Why or why not?

Shifting Soviet Diplomacy

The Kremlin's overtures, the West's distrust

GORDON BARTHOS

When Soviet leader Mikhail Gorbachev launched his famous "charm offensive" soon after gaining power in March, 1985, it was seen as largely cosmetic by most Kremlin watchers. Gorbachev's wit and his wife's stylish clothes turned heads in the West but won few hearts.

For a year now, the Soviet leader has been working overtime to build substance into his smile and to steer the Soviet Union toward better relations with its adversaries, but from Moscow's point of view the results have been frustrating. Try as he might, Gorbachev cannot seem to spark much interest in Washington or elsewhere, or to reap much credit for trying to improve the atmosphere between Moscow and the hostile capitals that encircle it.

The field of arms control is the most obvious example. In January, Gorbachev put on an audacious hat and proposed to rid the world of nuclear weapons by the year 2000. The skeptics in Washington and elsewhere dismissed the idea as propaganda. And when Gorbachev reached for a modest gesture — his year-long moratorium on nuclear test blasts — the critics yawned and again wrote it off as posturing.

Some Soviet watchers believe that this Western mistrust of the Kremlin's every move may blind us to important changes in the way the Soviets are approaching world affairs. Since the beginning of this year Gorbachev has made repeated overtures, not only to the U.S. but also to Europe, China and Japan — Moscow's historic rivals to the West, South and East.

These moves bring to mind the early days of Nikita Krushchev's government, when the Soviets offered "peaceful coexistence" with the West. But Krushchev moved too impetuously and without full support from his Politburo. When he erred, he was pushed from power. With Krushchev's history in mind, Gorbachev is moving more cautiously, and that instinctive caution is likely to be reinforced by the West's lukewarm reaction to his overtures.

In methodical fashion, Gorbachev has started to address some of the problems that arose under his predecessors. His key overtures in recent months include a highly publicized offer in June to accept some U.S. "Star Wars" research into ballistic missile defenses, provided Washington agreed not to build and deploy such weapons. This was a major concession. The Soviets formerly had wanted a halt to everything connected with Star Wars, President Reagan's plan for an anti-missile defense system.

At the same time, Gorbachev offered an olive branch to Western Europe. He announced that the Soviets were prepared to live with the existing French and British nuclear arsenals, provided they were not modernized. The Kremlin had formerly insisted that these arsenals be scrapped as the price of a Soviet-U.S. arms accord.

On the touchy issue of the Reagan-Gorbachev summit, the Soviets seem to be edging away from their demand that substantive arms control agreements should be negotiated beforehand and simply signed at the summit. Now they seem to be leaning toward the idea that a summit would be a good thing even if no major arms-cutting deal could be reached.

Gorbachev announced in July that the Soviets plan to withdraw 7,000 troops from Afghanistan, a move calculated to ease tensions with three countries that have objected to the 1979 Soviet invasion — China, Pakistan and the U.S. At the same time he hinted at a withdrawal of Soviet troops from the Mongolian border with China, something Peking has long made a precondition for better relations with Moscow.

The Soviets recently announced they were opening formal talks with Israel to reestablish consular links severed after the 1967 Mideast war. If talks were to lead to renewed Soviet diplomatic recognition of Israel, the risk of war in the Middle East would be eased because Moscow could no longer be counted on to come to the aid of countries planning attacks on Israel.

He also called for a Pacific conference to talk about reining in the superpowers' nuclear rivalry in the region — including their naval rivalry. This has been a growing concern among the Pacific Ocean countries.

None of these proposals will bring a new era of cooperation and trust between the Soviet Union and its major

 From *Toronto Star*, August 11, l986 as it appeared in *World Press Review*, October 1986, pp. 20-22. Reprinted by permission.

Time for 'New Political Thinking'

There have been as many changes in the Soviet Ministry of Foreign Affairs in the past eight months as in the preceding 10 years — most of them in the ministries and in the diplomatic corps. If we include the few changes introduced by Yuri Andropov, Mikhail Gorbachev's predecessor, then we are talking about a complete overhaul.

The changes mark the return of the foreign ministry to Communist Party control. Over the years, and especially in the last years of Leonid Brezhnev's era, Andrei Gromyko, as Minister of Foreign Affairs, assumed great authority, consulting his peers only for formality's sake. All of that is over. It is the role of Anatoly Dobrynin to guard against such tendencies. Dobrynin, former ambassador to the U.S., is now one of 11 central committee secretaries who, along with the 12-man Politburo, run the Soviet Union.

According to a Western official recently returned from Moscow, the new Minister of Foreign Affairs, Eduard Shevardnadze, is not the powerful figure that he appears to be. Although he is a member of the Politburo, his role is limited to executing the decisions of his master, Gorbachev.

As for Dobrynin, he is Gorbachev's chief adviser. A sort of visionary in the style of former U.S. Secretary of State Henry Kissinger, whom he often encountered during his years in Washington, Dobrynin commissions the studies and proposes policy options for Gorbachev and the Politburo — of which he is not a member. It is a situation that could generate conflicts, especially if Dobrynin seems to have the last word on nominations of diplomatic personnel.

In an article in the June issue of the party monthly, *Kommunist*, Dobrynin says that "the time has come for new political thinking." This "new thinking" calls for a global approach to diplomacy that encompasses "all the elements of world politics — military, political, economic and humanitarian." Dobrynin hits the nail even harder by specifying that humanitarian concerns require the refinement of the "civilized norms of international cooperation." [Indeed, the Soviet Union has said that it would like to become a member of the General Agreement on Tariffs and Trade (GATT).]

If the human rights issue gives rise to "calumnious anti-Soviet campaigns," Dobrynin adds, one must respond not only with polemics but with "constructive" treatment of the problem. This requires "taking into account the traditions and conditions of each country," thus demonstrating a "high degree of professionalism" and a "broad vision of the world." The formulas are certainly not the herald of a liberalization, but perhaps they signal a less dogmatic approach to human rights matters.

Another area of Dobrynin's "new thinking" concerns the role of the military in international relations. Gorbachev had already offered some innovative ideas on this subject last March in his closing address to the Party Congress, when he declared that security "is increasingly a political function that can be accomplished only by political means." In other words, he added, it is time to "establish relations between countries on a more solid basis than that of arms."

Dobrynin also emphasized this when he said, "The nature of arms today is to allow no nation the hope of defending itself by military means — by building even the most powerful defense system." The dual notions of national and international security, he added, have become inseparable.

While Soviet leaders still stress military parity, that idea now seems secondary to the idea of the survival of mankind in the face of today's arsenals. Such survival, according to Dobrynin, requires "an approach to international relations not from the perspective of narrow interests that pit nation against nation, but from the perspective of our common interests and aspirations." This language is, no doubt, designed to discipline the military and to legitimate the flexibility that Soviet leaders have voiced in recent arms negotiations.

These developments have created less uproar than the restoration of the Ministry of Foreign Affairs to party control, but the real surprise is that there has been no apparent reaction from the individuals concerned. Thus the creation in the foreign ministry of a new department responsible for arms negotiations will probably undercut the authority of the Minister of Defense, until now the sole judge in the matter.

It is significant that in his *Kommunist* article Dobrynin asks the civilian research institutes — and not the armed forces — to produce a series of studies on the "interdependence of offensive and defensive nuclear and conventional weapons," on verification procedures, on "global and regional strategies leading to the elimination of various types of arms" and on the consequences of "conversion from a war economy to a civilian economy." All of this is an attempt to learn "what is reasonably sufficient in terms of reducing current arsenals, and to dispel the legends and myths" that have grown around these problems. In Dobrynin's view these "myths" are propagated not only by the U.S.; one also must examine the "Soviet Pentagon" to find their origin.

The future will tell whether these new stirrings will lead to significant change. For the moment they shed light on the new tactics of Soviet diplomacy. But it is only at the negotiating table that the "new political thinking" will be put to the test.

— *Michel Tatu, "Le Monde," Paris (liberal), Aug. 7.*

adversaries. Profound problems remain — the superpowers' combined arsenal of 50,000 nuclear weapons, more than 100,000 Soviet troops in Afghanistan and 400,000 Soviet Jews who want to leave the country but cannot. Yet Gorbachev's overtures must be viewed as part of a strategy to decrease the Soviet Union's isolation on the world stage.

"It is high time to begin an effective withdrawal from the brink of war, from the equilibrium of fear, to normal, civilized relations between nations," Gorbachev told the 27th Party Congress. The cornerstone of his approach, Gorbachev added, would be "a readiness for mutually acceptable compromises" in political matters, and actions that "give nobody grounds for fears, even imagined, about their security" on the military scene.

2. THE SOVIET UNION CONFRONTS THE WORLD

If the Kremlin cannot have warm relations with Washington, at least it can avoid open hostility by seeming to be in a mood to negotiate and compromise, experts say. "If the Soviet Union comes to be perceived in the outside world as an increasingly circumspect superpower, one more willing than the U.S. to curb military expenditure, this could indeed be an inducement to the U.S. to modify its policies," says Oxford University Kremlin watcher Archie Brown.

There is a danger for Gorbachev from within the Soviet power structure if he moves too far too quickly. His energetic program is strikingly reminiscent of Krushchev's plan of attack — although Gorbachev, with his KGB security police background, is less prepared to tolerate dissent. Krushchev,

---

"There is danger within for Gorbachev if he moves too far too quickly."

---

too, came to power committed to massive internal reform and to "peaceful coexistence" with the outside world.

Between 1953 and 1958 he lifted the iron hand of Stalinist repression at home, launched his massive "virgin land" program to open up 70 million acres of new land in Siberia and sent up

the world's first space satellite. Abroad, he challenged Soviet orthodoxy by announcing that war with capitalist countries "is not fatalistically inevitable," met with U.S. President Dwight Eisenhower, allowed Yugoslavia (but not Poland or Hungary) to go its own idiosyncratic way and forged friendly relations with India and Egypt.

But Krushchev moved too impulsively in some areas, and that was his undoing. He misjudged American resolve during the Cuban missile crisis, and then had to give in. He let ideological disputes with former ally Communist China degenerate into open hostility. And he banked on a spectacular Siberian project that faltered. By 1964 Krushchev was on the outside looking in. (Aug. 11)

Chernobyl—the official story

At an August 1986 conference in Vienna the Soviet Union presented its report on the April reactor accident, resulting in a public relations victory for the Soviets and conviction among Westerners of the safety of their own nuclear industries.

Walter C. Patterson

Walter C. Patterson, an independent analyst and commentator on nuclear affairs based in Britain, attended the post-Chernobyl review conference in Vienna. He is the author most recently of Going Critical: An Unofficial History of British Nuclear Power *(1986).*

THE CHERNOBYL accident in April apparently has convinced the world nuclear industry that nuclear power is safe—or at any rate safe enough. This somewhat disconcerting conclusion emerged from an August 25–29 conference in Vienna, sponsored by the International Atomic Energy Agency (IAEA). There the Soviet Union presented its official report on the world's worst nuclear accident. The conference's conclusion was not embodied in a formal communique, nor did it adopt any resolutions. Nevertheless, industry and government delegates from East and West clearly concurred that nothing they had learned should hamper the further expansion of nuclear power. Since the delegations were drawn from the nuclear community in each participating country, the conclusion is perhaps not unexpected. The process by which it emerged, however, is worthy of comment, not least as a guide to how the nuclear community will cope with Chernobyl henceforth.

With some 600 nuclear experts from 62 countries and 21 organizations, national and international, present, the gathering was nominally a "technical working conference," but intensive diplomacy by the IAEA won agreement for both the opening and closing days of the conference to be open to the media, represented by more than 200 journalists. No one who attended the first day's session will soon forget it.

Western suspicions that the Soviet authorities would resort to obfuscation and cover-up were swept aside by a deluge of information—explicit, vivid, and chilling. The official Soviet report ran to 388 pages. In a five-hour tour de force the head of the Soviet delegation, Academician Valery Legasov, deputy chairman of the Kurchatov Institute of Atomic Energy, introduced the report. Even in translation his speech was gripping; his description of the final hours, minutes and seconds before the Chernobyl explosion left both delegates and journalists visibly disturbed.

Legasov also brought with him a 25-minute videotape entitled simply "26 April," which was shown to the conference on the opening morning and then twice again by overwhelming demand. The film offered a grim contrast to the Soviet television documentary being shown in the delegates' lounge. The doggedly cheerful documentary devoted most of its time to the efforts of the workers at the site and at Hospital 6 in Moscow. Legasov's videotape, however, recounted all too starkly the events of April 25–26 that had made all the subsequent heroics and cleanup efforts necessary. It described the Chernobyl plant and the RBMK-1000 reactor design; it then followed the course of the last experiment on Chernobyl Unit 4, to its catastrophic denouement.

The unit had been scheduled for shutdown for annual maintenance. In 1984, in similar circumstances, the staff had carried out an experiment to see how long after the steam supply was shut off the free-wheeling number 8 turbogenerator could supply electricity to run essential equipment; the experiment, though executed without difficulty, had been unsuccessful, since the electrical supply had dwindled too rapidly. Improved electrical equipment had since been added, and the experiment was to be tried again. But this time—perhaps because the previous attempt had been without incident—the experimental program was "not properly prepared and had not received the requisite approval."[*]

At 1:00 a.m. on April 25, the staff began reducing reactor power from the maximum 3,200 megawatts to 1,600 megawatts. At 1:05 p.m. turbogenerator number 7 was shut down. At 2:00 p.m., to keep it from interfering with the experiment, the emergency core cooling system was disconnected. At this point, the electricity grid control center in Kiev notified Chernobyl to keep supplying power until late in the evening. The experiment was suspended and the plant continued in operation, with the emergency core cooling system disconnected.

Finally, at 11:10 p.m., power reduction recommenced. The

---

[*]U.S.S.R. State Committee on the Utilization of Atomic Energy, *The Accident at the Chernobyl Nuclear Power Plant and Its Consequences* (Aug. 1986), p. 15.

experiment was to be carried out at a power level of 700–1,000 megawatts. However, with the automatic control system switched off, the operator could not stabilize the reactor quickly enough and power dropped to only 30 megawatts thermal. The ensuing buildup of neutron-absorbing xenon in the core then made it impossible to raise power above 200 megawatts. In an effort to offset the xenon poisoning, the operator withdrew more and more control rods. Operating instructions directed that the reactor should never be operated with fewer than the equivalent of 30 of its 211 control rods in the core. By 1:22 a.m. of April 26, only some six to eight rods' worth of absorber were still in place, and, in the dismaying words of one Soviet delegate, the reactor "was free to do as it pleased." At 1:23, with the reactor in this precariously unstable condition, the experiment began. It lasted only 40 seconds.

Legasov's videotape had tracked the changing power level of the reactor as a green line extending gradually along a simple graph. In the upper right-hand corner of the diagram was an equally simple schematic of the core of the reactor, with control rods sliding imperceptibly in and out. As Legasov's narrative reached its dreadful climax, the green line on the graph turned almost vertically upward; a blazing red glow swelled to fill the reactor core. It was not Hollywood animation, but it made its point.

In due course, the conference participants agreed that the reactor had suffered a "prompt critical excursion." The science editor of Britain's *Financial Times* put it more bluntly: it was a "slow nuclear explosion," taking perhaps a second rather than a nanosecond, but a runaway nuclear chain reaction nevertheless. The precise sequence of events in the crucial second or so remained unclear. Experts postulated that the fierce power surge—perhaps as much as 100 times the nominal design power—had shattered the fuel into incandescent fragments; the fragments had transferred their heat almost instantaneously to the water coolant, flashing it to steam with a pressure shock violent enough to blast a gaping crater through the concrete above the reactor. This "steam explosion" exposed the red-hot core; air rushed in, mixing with the hydrogen formed when zirconium fuel cladding reacted with steam. Within two or three seconds a hydrogen explosion showered the refueling hall and the surroundings with blazing core material, starting about 30 fires.

No Western advance commentary on the Soviet report had come close to conveying the true horror of the accident. Legasov's videotape included footage filmed from a helicopter jolting above the hole torn in the top of the reactor building, apparently only a day or two after the accident. Deep in the grey twisted ruins could be glimpsed the glow of the burning core. After the first afternoon session, journalists watched in fascination as the nuclear community faced up to the reality of their industry's first catastrophic accident—the accident they had believed could never happen.

FEW OF THOSE journalists, however, could have anticipated the transformation that was to take place by the following Friday. On August 25 the conference mood was bleak and tense; by August 29 it had become cheerful, convivial, verging on the euphoric. The possible reasons for this metamorphosis can only be inferred. On Tuesday, Wednesday, and Thursday conference participants withdrew behind closed doors, away from the media's gaze. Four working groups met in parallel sessions, to consider the short- and long-term technical aspects of the accident, the emergency measures taken, and the radiological consequences. After each morning and afternoon session, Morris Rosen, director of nuclear safety for the IAEA, chaired a press conference lasting an hour or more.

Inevitably, however, time constraints proved frustrating. Some journalists wanted the working-group chairmen to summarize the findings of the sessions, but four summaries took up at least half an hour, further limiting the time for questions. Answers from the panel all too often turned into extended lectures aimed at the lowest common denominator of understanding among the media. Though understandable, this was unfortunate: the media representation was of the highest caliber, including many of the most experienced reporters covering the nuclear scene internationally. At the end of the conference one British delegate was heard to remark that the questions from reporters were better than those asked by delegates in the closed working groups.

In both the working groups and the press conferences two themes dominated: the long-term health effects of the accident and its implications for nuclear safety worldwide. The treatment of these two themes during the conference, in the press conferences, and in informal briefings through

A May 9 photograph released by the Soviet news agency TASS shows the damage done to Chernobyl reactor 4. (*AP/Wide World Photo*)

the week, suggests how the grimness of the opening day could have evolved into the sweetness and light of the closing plenary session.

The immediate health effects were clearly horrific; the

Evidence of impressive competence in other areas—especially the emergency measures implemented in the hours after the accident—took the edge off earlier suggestions that the Soviets could not be trusted to operate nuclear plants.

Soviet presentation left no doubt of that. They were nevertheless limited: 31 fatalities to date. The press conference panelists—comparing this with fatalities in car accidents, plane crashes, and other modern technological mishaps—insisted on the need to keep the health effects of the Chernobyl accident in perspective. As to the longer term, many people would suffer cancers as a result of exposure to radiation from Chernobyl, some of which would certainly be fatal. The precise numbers, however, could not be predicted with any confidence, nor would it be possible to say that Chernobyl caused any particular cancer. Dan Beninson, chairman of the International Commission on Radiological Protection, declared himself convinced that Soviet estimates were unnecessarily high; the number might be only 2,000, in a population of many millions over a 70-year lifetime.

In successive press conferences such comparisons were pressed ever more emphatically. By setting the long-term Chernobyl fatalities against a background of all the other deaths occurring during the same period in the same population, the health effects of the accident could be made to appear unimportant. Even the central Soviet estimates, implying 24,000 fatal cancers and hundreds of thousands of nonfatal cancers, could be thus discounted. (A British delegate was heard to remark that there is no such thing as an "extra" death; the quota is one death per person.) By implication, if Chernobyl didn't get you something else will, so why worry about a nuclear accident? Bemused observers from outside the nuclear community watched the emergence of this new approach to radiopathology. Indications are that this may henceforth become a central tenet of nuclear industry philosophy. Morris Rosen commented that it was not for him to say what society would consider acceptable. Compared to the health effects from other types of energy production, society might even consider such a casualty list an acceptable price to pay for "cheap, clean nuclear electricity."

Furthermore, Western conference participants found that the Soviet data reinforced their already firm conviction that the Chernobyl accident had little, if any, relevance to nuclear safety elsewhere. The Soviet report itemized the advantages and disadvantages of the RBMK design and described how Soviet engineers had endeavored to incorporate features offsetting the disadvantages. Lord Marshall, chairman of Britain's Central Electricity Generating Board, briefing journalists, claimed, however, that Legasov had admitted that the RBMK design had not merely disadvantages but defects. No official translation appeared to bear out this allegation, but it became the focus of Western reaction to the technical discussions. At the outset, Western delegates declared that the RBMK design could not be licensed in Britain or the United States. They laid great stress on its "positive void coefficient" —that is, the positive feedback between reactivity and steam —claiming that no Western design would be so vulnerable to catastrophic malfunction.

EVEN SO, BY THE CLOSE of the conference the Western delegations had drastically muted their criticisms of Soviet nuclear technology. The evidence of impressive Soviet competence in other areas—especially the emergency measures implemented in the hours after the accident—had taken the edge off earlier Western suggestions that the Soviets could not be trusted to build and operate nuclear plants. In response to press questions, Legasov demanded that Western delegates put their technical doubts directly to his delegation, rather than obliquely in briefings to journalists. Instead the Western delegations began to hedge, declaring that they did not know enough to be able to offer definitive opinions as to Western licensability of Soviet plants modified after the accident. Onlookers reflected that the Western delegations might have been reluctant to challenge Soviet nuclear safety directly, lest the Soviets reciprocate with a similar challenge about the safety of Western nuclear plants. Human error is not unique to the Soviet Union.

As a result, the final plenary saw a comradely closing of the nuclear ranks, amid an outpouring of mutual congratulations on the week's efforts. For the Soviets the conference was a public relations triumph. Their forthrightness and candor all but blotted out the memory of the initial Soviet failure to warn their neighbors about Chernobyl. The IAEA, too, won plaudits for its role as an honest broker and a conduit for improved East-West dialogue.

Questions nevertheless remain. The nuclear power industry has suffered its first unambiguous catastrophe and come to terms with it. The nuclear community clearly expects the rest of the world to do likewise—to put Chernobyl behind it and press on. The rest of the world, however, may not be quite so sanguine.

The Soviet Union and the Third World

"With Marxist states in the third world facing insurgencies or chronic instability and non-Marxist states requiring economic assistance that the Soviet Union does not supply, Soviet leaders appear to face difficulties not only in expanding but in maintaining their influence in the third world. . . . There is no indication, however, that the Soviet Union will pull back from its commitment to its Marxist allies in the third world."

MARK N. KATZ

Mark N. Katz is a research associate at the Kennan Institute for Advanced Russian Studies of the Smithsonian Institution's Woodrow Wilson International Center for Scholars. He is the author of *The Third World in Soviet Military Thought* (Baltimore: Johns Hopkins University Press, 1982), and *Russia and Arabia: Soviet Foreign Policy toward the Arabian Peninsula* (Baltimore: Johns Hopkins University Press, 1986).

SINCE the 1960's, the third world has become one of the major arenas of Soviet–American rivalry. The Soviet Union has had important successes in the third world—especially during the 1970's—but it has also had significant failures and even now experiences serious problems.

There has been a dramatic increase in the number of third world countries that have experienced Marxist–Leninist revolutions, coups or takeovers. These include North Vietnam and Cuba in the 1950's, South Yemen and the Congo in the 1960's, and South Vietnam, Kampuchea (Cambodia), Laos, Benin, Ethiopia, Mozambique, Angola, Afghanistan, Nicaragua and Grenada in the 1970's. Further, all these Marxist–Leninist regimes are pro-Soviet. The only pro-Chinese Marxist–Leninist government was the Pol Pot regime in Kampuchea that lasted from 1975 to 1978; then Vietnam invaded and replaced Pol Pot with a pro-Soviet Vietnamese puppet regime. Because of its ability to provide more economic and military assistance, Moscow has prevented new Marxist regimes from allying themselves with China, its main Communist rival.

In addition, over the years the Soviet Union has established close relations with non-Marxist states in the third world, signing treaties of friendship and cooperation with India, Iraq, Syria and North Yemen. And the Soviet Union has close military ties with Libya.

But Soviet leaders have also experienced setbacks with non-Marxist (or in some cases, quasi-Marxist) regimes. Pro-Soviet radical leaders have been overthrown and replaced by more conservative leaders in countries like Ghana, Mali and Chile. During the 1970's, Egypt and Somalia abrogated their treaties of friendship and cooperation with Moscow and expelled all Soviet advisers. Other countries that once had close ties to the Soviet Union did not break with them dramatically, but gradually their friendly relations cooled. Among these countries are Guinea, Guinea-Bissau, Algeria, Burma, Uganda and Peru.

Soviet leaders soon noticed that they could not rely on non-Marxist–Leninist regimes either to "continue on the path toward socialism" or to remain allies of the Soviet Union.[1] Without strong influence over these regimes, the Soviet Union could not prevent them from following their independent national interests, which often differed from Soviet interests. And attempts by the Kremlin to exert influence over these non-Marxist regimes in order to keep them allied to the Soviet Union backfired and led them to improve their ties to the West instead.

By the mid- to late 1970's, many Soviet writers concluded that the only reliable third world regimes were "states of socialist orientation."[2] Each of these states had a Marxist–Leninist vanguard party in power and often had a treaty of friendship and cooperation with the Soviet Union as well.[3] Most had institutions similar to those of the Soviet Union and other Communist regimes: a Marxist–Leninist party with a Politburo, Secretariat and Central Committee; an intelligence service, usually organized by the East Germans; a corps of political officers in the ranks of the armed services; a "popular militia" that could serve to counter a coup attempt by the army; and a central planning organization and economic ministries to insure state control over most (if not all) of the economy. A country with these institutions and a large number of Soviet, Cuban and East German economic and military advisers was much less likely to change its foreign policy orientation.

Soviet leaders can indeed boast that no third world country ruled by a pro-Soviet Marxist–Leninist vanguard party has ever been overthrown by internal forces. The one such regime that did fall from power recently—Grenada's—was overthrown not by internal forces but by a foreign invasion.

Nevertheless, these states of socialist orientation present serious problems for the Soviet Union. In six Marxist regimes (Afghanistan, Angola, Kampuchea, Ethiopia, Mozambique and Nicaragua) there are insurgencies that the regimes have been unable to defeat. Troops from established socialist states have sometimes intervened (witness the Cubans in Angola, the Vietnamese in Kampuchea and the Soviet Union in Afghanistan), but these troops have been unable to defeat the insurgents.[4]

RIVAL FACTIONS

Another such state—South Yemen—does not face an insurgency, but has experienced chronic infighting among rival factions of the Marxist leadership. This rivalry erupted in fierce fighting in January, 1986; up to 10,000 were reported to have died; and fighting could break out again in the future.[5] Finally, all third world countries ruled by Marxist–Leninist parties, including long-established regimes like the regimes of Vietnam and Cuba, are experiencing severe economic difficulties. Their attempts to construct a socialist economy has led to economic stagnation.

While the "socialist commonwealth" greatly expanded in the 1970's, the weakness and unpopularity of the newer Marxist–Leninist regimes meant that the Soviet Union and its allies have had to support them; in some cases this support has been necessary just to keep them from being overthrown. At a time when the Soviet Union itself is facing severe economic difficulties, this is a costly and seemingly unending burden. Soviet academic writers have commented on the poor economic performance of the states of socialist orientation compared to the states of capitalist orientation in the third world. There seems to be general acknowledgement that the socialist states pose significant problems for the Soviet Union. In addition, some observers argue that the Soviet Union should put greater emphasis on making friends with the more stable nonsocialist third world governments on the basis of common interests, if not common ideology.[6]

There is no indication, however, that the Soviet Union will pull back from its commitment to its Marxist allies in the third world. Although Soviet military writers seldom discuss openly the insurgencies taking place against third world Marxist–Leninist regimes, their writing about insurgencies in general indicates that they believe counterinsurgency operations can succeed.[7] Even some of the "regional peace proposals" the Soviet Union has made for countries like Afghanistan are designed to end external support for the opposition movements while leaving the Marxist regime firmly in power.

Will the Soviet Union succeed in helping its weak Marxist allies in the third world to defeat the opposition movements they are fighting and to establish their power? Will the Soviet Union be able to assist Marxist revolutionaries to come to power in other countries (an event that has not yet happened in the 1980's)? And will Soviet leaders expand their relations, especially in the military sphere, with non-Marxist third world states?

THE MIDDLE EAST

In the Middle East, Moscow's closest allies are Syria, Libya, Iraq and South Yemen. Of these, only South Yemen has a Marxist–Leninist government. Iraq and Syria are ruled by rival branches of the Baath party; Libyan leader Muammar Qaddafi espouses his own brand of Islamic socialism.

Soviet support of the Arabs and United States support of the Israelis in the Arab–Israeli conflict have won many friends for the Soviet Union in the Arab world. But the Soviet Union has also experienced many disappointments, particularly President Anwar Sadat's expulsion of all Soviet personnel from Egypt. Moscow's relations with Egyptian President Hosni Mubarak are cordial, but hardly friendly. Some conservative Arab states like Jordan and Kuwait have purchased Soviet arms; yet these countries have strictly limited their ties to Moscow. The Arab monarchies, in particular, have no illusion about whether the Soviet Union would help their internal opponents overthrow them if possible.[8]

The Iran–Iraq War has complicated Soviet policy in the Middle East; although Moscow has supplied Baghdad with substantial military assistance (especially after Iranian forces crossed into Iraq in 1982), Moscow's close allies, Libya and Syria, have backed Iran. Other Arabs have criticized the Soviet Union for providing arms to Libya and Syria without the condition that they cannot retransfer the arms to Iran.[9] Further, because of Moscow's initial neutrality in the Iran–Iraq War and its continued support of Iraq's archrival, Syria, Iraq has turned toward the West in recent years. Baghdad has obtained arms from France; and it restored ties with the United States in late 1984. But since Iraq relies mainly on Soviet arms, it cannot afford to become estranged from the Soviet Union, at least while the war continues.[10]

2. THE SOVIET UNION CONFRONTS THE WORLD

The prospects for Marxist revolution in the Middle East appear dim, because the main opposition to Middle Eastern governments has been dominated by Islamic fundamentalists, not leftists. No fundamentalist Islamic movement appears to be in a position to seize power at present. But if an Islamic regime were able to topple a pro-American regime, the Soviet Union would be pleased, because United States influence would be reduced. An Islamic regime, however, would not necessarily be pro-Soviet, as revolutionary Iran has shown. In addition, Islamic fundamentalist movements like the Muslim Brotherhood in Syria can threaten pro-Soviet regimes as well as pro-American ones.

The Soviet Union has made slight progress in increasing its cooperation with non-Marxist regimes in the Middle East since General Secretary Mikhail Gorbachev came to power. Oman and the United Arab Emirates both recognized the Soviet Union for the first time in 1985. But in the Arab world there is no longer much hope that the Soviet Union will provide the Arabs with the wherewithal to defeat Israel; nor does the Soviet Union seem ready to help them develop economically. However, while the Soviet Union may not give the Arabs as much as they want when there is actual fighting between them and Israel, the Soviet Union has little interest in seeing peace established between the Arabs and the Israelis. Other analysts have argued that if such a peace were established, the Arab states would have less need for the Soviet Union because they would have less need for Soviet weapons and more need for the kind of economic assistance that is available mainly from the West.

Whether this argument is valid will not be known unless or until there is a general peace in the Middle East. However, the Soviet Union has been willing to give more help to those Arab states and groups—like Syria, Libya and radical Palestinian factions—that have been least willing to compromise with Israel. As long as the Arab–Israeli conflict remains unresolved and the United States continues to support Israel, the Soviet Union is likely to retain some allies in the Arab world and perhaps gain others.

SOUTH ASIA

Another article in this issue is devoted to Soviet aims in Afghanistan. It is sufficient to note here that since the Soviet invasion of Afghanistan in 1979 to protect the tottering Marxist regime, the Soviet Union has been unable to defeat the mujahideen, and the mujahideen have been unable to drive Soviet troops out of their country.

The prospects for Marxist revolution in South Asia are not good. Soviet leaders may hope that Pakistan's General Mohammad Zia ul-Haq will be overthrown or replaced by opposition leader Benazir Bhutto or someone else who might be less willing to help the mujahideen in Afghanistan. The mujahideen's resistance would be hampered without the sanctuaries provided in Pakistan's North-West Frontier Province and the aid that is channeled through Pakistan.

The Soviet Union has friendly relations with India; it continues to sell weapons to India and to license India to produce Soviet weapons, like MiG's. New Delhi sees Moscow as a useful ally against Pakistan and China, its main rivals. And even though the Indian government under Indira Gandhi indicated that it was not alarmed about the Soviet invasion of Afghanistan, India has been unhappy that it has failed to persuade the Soviet Union to withdraw its troops. Prime Minister Rajiv Gandhi's government has moved to improve relations with the United States. Although India is not likely to give up its close relationship with Moscow, there are significant differences between the two that will block Soviet efforts to become more closely allied with New Delhi.[11]

SOUTHEAST ASIA

Although pro-Soviet Marxist regimes came to power in Vietnam, Kampuchea and Laos, the "domino theory" that other countries in Southeast Asia would also become Communist has so far proved false. Some of the nations of ASEAN (Association of Southeast Asian Nations: Thailand, Malaysia, Singapore, Indonesia, the Philippines and Brunei) have authoritarian regimes of questionable popularity, but most have experienced strong economic growth over the last decade and enjoy standards of living higher than those in Indochina.

There are Marxist guerrilla groups operating in Thailand, Malaysia and Burma, but these have—or once had—links with China rather than the Soviet Union. The Marxists in Burma control some territory, but the central government seems to be in no danger of falling. The Communist guerrillas in Thailand and Malaysia have been contained.

A growing Marxist insurgency in the Philippines is led by the New People's Army (NPA). Like the other Marxist groups in Southeast Asia, the NPA is Maoist, though its actual ties with China are tenuous. The NPA has reportedly turned down recent offers of Soviet support.[12] Toward the end of the Ferdinand Marcos regime, the NPA was very strong, but Corazon Aquino's peaceful succession to power has limited the appeal of the NPA and has led to defections from its ranks. It is too early to tell whether the insurgency will come to an end, but it is apparently on the defensive.

As for the Soviet Union allying itself with the non-Marxist regimes of the area, this appears to be extremely unlikely as long as Vietnam occupies Kampuchea. At this writing, these nations see very little to gain from closer ties with the Soviet Union.[13]

AFRICA

In sub-Saharan Africa, three of Moscow's closest allies—Angola, Ethiopia and Mozambique—are fighting insurgent movements. In Ethiopia, guerrillas in Eritrea and other provinces are struggling to make their regions independent of Addis Ababa. In Angola and Mozambique, South African-backed guerrillas are attempting to overthrow the Marxist regimes. In all three cases, the Marxist regimes have thus far been unable to defeat the rebels.

The likelihood of Marxist revolution does not seem great in Africa, except in Namibia (where an insurgency led by the leftist South-West Africa People's Organization—SWAPO—continues), in South Africa (if the opposition to the government should become dominated by Marxists) and, perhaps, in the Western Sahara (although the Moroccan government is doing well against the Algerian-supported Polisario [Popular Front for the Liberation of Saguia el Hamra y Rio de Oro] guerrillas). Elsewhere in Africa, a Marxist regime might come to power through a coup d'état by a self-proclaimed Marxist-Leninist. But as the Soviet Union knows, such leaders are often overthrown themselves—unless the Soviet Union and its allies are able to gain enough influence to prevent this.

The Soviet Union has also befriended non-Marxist states in Africa, usually providing them with military assistance. But non-Marxist African states desperately need the economic assistance that the Soviet Union has been unable or unwilling to provide. Only the West can provide this aid. Thus while non-Marxist African states may want to receive Soviet weapons on concessional terms, they have little incentive to become so close to the Soviet Union that they alienate Western donors.[14]

LATIN AMERICA

In Latin America, the Soviet Union's oldest and best ally is Cuba, where Fidel Castro came to power in 1959. Cuba has long been a stable Marxist state and does not face a sustained insurgent movement. Since 1979, Nicaragua has had a Marxist regime against which "contra" revolutionary forces are still fighting.

There were several Marxist insurgencies in Latin America in the 1960's; but these all failed; witness Bolivia, Venezuela, Colombia, Guatemala and the Dominican Republic. The most likely candidates for Marxist revolution in Latin America in 1986 are those Central American nations near Nicaragua: El Salvador, Guatemala and Honduras. However, guerrilla activity in these countries peaked around 1981; since then, Marxist forces have usually been on the defensive. Whether or not Marxism eventually comes to Central America remains to be seen, but the guerrillas will have to increase their activity there a great deal in order to succeed.[15]

Elsewhere in Latin America, the Sendero Luminoso (Shining Path) has unleashed a campaign of terror in Peru. This group, however, claims to be Maoist, and the Soviet Union has a long-established arms relationship with the Peruvian government.[16] Marxists are also believed to be gaining strength within the Chilean opposition, although this group is not yet in a position to overthrow the military government of General Augusto Pinochet. Marxist revolution is apparently not a significant threat to the larger, more developed Latin American nations. To the smaller, weaker nations threatened by Marxism, the United States can be more of a hindrance and the Soviet Union less of a help simply because of geography.

With regard to the non-Marxist states of the region, Latin America provides the Soviet Union with many potential friends because, above all others, this area traditionally tried to avoid "United States imperialism." But like other regions of the third world, Latin American governments are interested in obtaining economic assistance, and this is not available from the Soviet Union to the same degree that it is from the West (although the Soviet Union has established strong commercial links with some Latin American nations, most notably Argentina). Non-Marxist Latin American governments are suspicious of Soviet intentions, since they perceive the Soviet Union as working actively to promote revolution against other Latin American governments. Only if there were a severe deterioration in United States–Latin American relations would the Soviet Union significantly improve its ties with the non-Marxist governments of Latin America.

CONCLUSION

The most obvious challenges to Soviet interests in the third world are the insurgencies being fought against pro-Soviet Marxist–Leninist regimes. Should such a regime be toppled by an indigenous opposition movement (and not by external intervention as in Grenada), the Soviet Union would lose an ally; and an important—and unwelcome—precedent would be set: for the first time, a guerrilla movement would have toppled a Marxist–Leninist regime in the third world. Other guerrilla movements might fight all the harder after seeing another guerrilla movement succeed. Further, these guerrilla movements might receive increased Western aid, thus making it more difficult for the Soviet Union and its allies to defend Marxist regimes.

Western aid to these insurgent groups is a growing problem for the Soviet Union. The United States has given assistance to the Afghan guerrillas since the administration of President Jimmy Carter and has given aid to the Nicaraguan contras since the early years of Ronald Reagan's administration, but recently a "Reagan Doctrine" has emerged to give assistance to the opponents of other pro-Soviet Marxist–Leninist regimes in the third world.[17]

2. THE SOVIET UNION CONFRONTS THE WORLD

It is perhaps no accident that after Gorbachev came to power in the spring of 1985, even stronger counteroffensives were launched against the guerrillas in Nicaragua, Angola, Mozambique, Ethiopia and Afghanistan (the strongest Vietnamese offensive against the resistance in Kampuchea preceded Gorbachev's accession to power). In all these campaigns, the Marxist–Leninist regime (often with external assistance) made significant progress and the guerrillas were put on the defensive. In none of them, however, were the guerrillas defeated; thus they continue to pose a threat to Soviet interests.[18]

However, in another respect these insurgencies serve Soviet interests: as long as the opposition is never strong enough to seize power, its existence encourages the Marxist regime to rely on the Soviet Union and its allies. No other country is likely to supply the Nicaraguan, Angolan and Ethiopian governments with military assistance equivalent to that provided by Moscow and Havana even if these regimes were willing to expel the Soviet and Cuban troops. In Mozambique, Soviet and Cuban assistance has been limited— possibly because the Soviet Union and Cuba recognize that South Africa has too many advantages—and the Mozambicans have turned to Zimbabwe, Portugal and other Western countries for military aid. As a result, Soviet influence in Mozambique appears to have declined.[19]

This consideration might apply to Kampuchea as well: as long as Vietnam is bogged down fighting there, it will need Soviet military assistance. But Vietnam would probably continue to seek Soviet military assistance because of the hostility between Beijing and Hanoi. Similarly, the continuation of the conflict in Afghanistan does not help the Soviet Union; the Marxist regime there (like the one in Phnom Penh) is in no position to break from the intervening power that props it up.

With Marxist states in the third world facing insurgencies or chronic instability and non-Marxist states requiring economic assistance that the Soviet Union does not supply, Soviet leaders appear to face difficulties not only in expanding but in maintaining their influence in the third world. This is very different from the situation a decade ago, when Soviet influence in the third world seemed to be expanding rapidly.

Yet there are still important avenues for Soviet expansion in the third world. There is no shortage of conflict between and within third world nations. Even when there is no clear East–West aspect to a particular conflict, it is often easier for third world nations to obtain weapons from the Soviet Union than from the West.

In addition, the possibility of Marxist revolutionaries coming to power must not be discounted. This could happen in countries that are very poor, have a right-wing regime, and have crushed the moderate opposition, leaving only armed extremists. These will not necessarily be Marxist to begin with, but if the Soviet Union and other Marxist states become their main source of political and military support, these movements could become dominated by Marxists.

Apparently, the Soviet Union did not anticipate that the new Marxist regimes that came to power in Asia, Africa and Latin America during the last decade would require so much assistance for so long just to remain in power. But if the Soviet Union can retain its present position in the third world and even expand it with moderate effort, it will try to do so. If the difficulties the Soviet Union is experiencing in the third world increase and if ever greater efforts are needed just to maintain Moscow's position, then the Soviet Union may be forced to make difficult decisions about which of its third world allies it will try to maintain and which are not so important. These are choices that the Kremlin would prefer not to face.

[1]For an examination of Soviet writing on this issue, see Mark N. Katz, *The Third World in Soviet Military Thought* (Baltimore: Johns Hopkins University Press, 1982), pp. 133–136.

[2]For a discussion of the concept of "states of socialist orientation," see Francis Fukuyama, *Moscow's Post-Brezhnev Reassessment of the Third World*, R-3337-USDP (Santa Monica: Rand Corporation, February, 1986), pp. 83–85.

[3]Colonel G. Malinovsky, "National'no-osvoboditel'noe dvizhenie na sovremennom etape," *Voenno-istoricheskii zhurnal*, no. 24 (December, 1979), pp. 25–36.

[4]On these insurgencies, see Mark N. Katz, "The Anti-Soviet Insurgencies," *Orbis* (Summer, 1986).

[5]John Kifner, "Battle for Southern Yemen: How the Fury Began," *The New York Times*, January 30, 1986, p. A4.

[6]For an examination of Soviet academic writing on this subject, see Jerry F. Hough, *The Struggle for the Third World: Soviet Debates and American Options* (Washington, D.C.: Brookings Institution, 1986), chapt. 4.

[7]See for example Major General M. Fesenko, "Ognevoe parazhenie nazemnykh sredstv PVO," *Voenno-istoricheskii zhurnal*, no. 5 (May, 1984), pp. 66–73; and Admiral P. Navoitsev, "Deistviia VMS protiv berega," *Voenno-istoricheskii zhurnal*, no. 8 (August, 1984), pp. 47–52.

[8]On the Soviets and the Middle East, see Robert O. Freedman, *Soviet Policy toward the Middle East since 1970*, 3d ed. (New York: Praeger, 1982); and Mark N. Katz, *Russia and Arabia: Soviet Foreign Policy toward the Arabian Peninsula* (Baltimore: Johns Hopkins University Press, 1986).

[9]See for example Kuwait's *Al Watan*, January 4, 1986, pp. 14–16, in Foreign Broadcast Information Service, *Soviet Union*, January 7, 1986, p. H15.

[10]Ties with the United States were broken in 1967. See Frederick W. Axelgard, ed., *Iraq in Transition: A Political, Economic, and Strategic Perspective* (Boulder, Colo.: Westview Press, 1986).

[11]On the Soviet Union and South Asia, see Stephen P. Cohen, "South Asia after Afghanistan," *Problems of Communism*, vol. 34, no. 1 (January–February, 1985), pp. 18–31.

[12]Paul Quinn-Judge, "Philippine Insurgents Are Turning Down Soviet Support," *The Christian Science Monitor*, November 26, 1985, pp. 1, 12.

[13]On Soviet policy in Southeast Asia, see United States Congress, House Committee on Foreign Affairs, *The Soviet Union in the Third World, 1980–85: An Imperial Burden or Political Asset?* 99th Congress, 1st session (Washington, D.C.: U.S. Government Printing Office, 1985), pp. 104–121.

[14]On the Soviets and Africa, see Peter Clement, "Moscow and Southern Africa," *Problems of Communism*, vol. 34, no. 2 (March–April, 1985), pp. 29–50; and Paul Henze, *Rebels and Separatists in Ethiopia: Regional Resistance to a Marxist Regime*, R-3347-USDP (Santa Monica: Rand Corporation, December, 1985).

[15]On the Soviet Union and Latin America, see Cole Blasier, *The Giant's Rival: The USSR and Latin America* (Pittsburgh: University of Pittsburgh Press, 1983).

[16]On the Sendero Luminoso, see Cynthia McClintock, "Sendero Luminoso: Peru's Maoist Guerrillas," *Problems of Communism*, vol. 32, no. 5 (September–October, 1983), pp. 19–34.

[17]On the "Reagan Doctrine," see Stephen S. Rosenfeld, "The Guns of July," *Foreign Affairs*, vol. 64, no. 4 (Spring, 1986), pp. 698–714.

[18]David B. Ottaway, "U.S. and Rebel Sources See Soviets Bolstering Support for Third World," *The Washington Post*, June 11, 1986, p. A36.

[19]Fukuyama, op. cit., pp. 69–75.

Trade Trouble in the Soviet Union

Maya Fishkin

The recent collapse in petroleum prices has focused world attention on debt-ridden oil producers such as Mexico and Nigeria, as well as countries such as Saudi Arabia and the United Kingdom, two of the wealthier petroleum exporters. Surprisingly, however, the problems confronting the world's largest oil producer—the Soviet Union— have been largely ignored, despite the fact that the USSR is the third largest exporter of crude to the West. Energy exports are Moscow's major source of hard Western currency, which is needed to finance capital imports crucial to the Soviets' ambitious development plans. These plans have been jeopardized by the dramatic deterioration in the USSR's balance of payments. Faced with growing import needs and falling export revenues, Moscow will more than likely be forced to turn to the international credit markets for relief.

The balance of payments problem is intensified by the structure of the Soviet Union's controlled economy. The difficulty stems from the official inconvertibility of the ruble, a policy designed to maintain government control of internal prices. The resulting partial insulation of the economy from import-led inflation and world recession comes at the cost of an artifically-determined balance of payments devoid of any automatic adjustment mechanism. Soviet planners compare their "shopping list" of Western imports with projected hard currency revenue from exports. Since there is no floating exchange rate that adjusts in response to disequilibria, trade imbalances are not automatically corrected. As a result, balance of payments deficits can only be eliminated by a conscious decision to reduce imports, increase exports, or borrow from abroad. Faced with a continuing fall in oil earnings, the Soviets must respond by pursuing at least one of these policy prescriptions—each of which poses distinct problems for Moscow.

Of these three choices, it seems least likely that the USSR will opt to limit imports. Indeed, Soviet import demand has never been greater, especially in light of the government's interrelated goals of revitalizing the stagnant domestic economy and raising Soviet living standards. In his opening address to the twenty-seventh Communist Party Congress, Mikhail Gorbachev announced plans to double Soviet output and to achieve dramatic improvements in labor and capital productivity by the year 2000. Yet so far, the Soviet leadership has been unable to introduce the extensive system of individual incentives needed to achieve these ambitious targets. Moscow also seems unable to use its traditional growth formula of building new industries with large quantities of capital and labor. The growth of labor inputs has slowed appreciably; female participation in the labor force is already quite high, and population growth in the industrialized areas of the USSR has fallen dramatically since the 1960's.

Any hopes for faster development hinge on the ability of Soviet industry to undergo intensive technological innovation, though it is difficult to imagine how such innovation might materialize within the Soviet Union. Although the USSR possesses a well-developed research sector staffed with highly trained cadres of personnel, the transition from theoretical and experimental advances to industrial applications has proven to be a stumbling block. Wide-scale integration of sophis-ticated techniques into Soviet production processes has yet to occur, and any plan to accelerate Soviet growth will have to rely heavily on imports of Western technology.

The continuing arms race is also pressuring the Soviets to increase their imports of high technology goods. The Reagan Administration's refusal to compromise on the Strategic Defense Initiative may heighten this trend by forcing Moscow to divert greater amounts of its export earnings to finance the acquisition of Western technology with military applications.

Finally, the Soviets will continue to make massive purchases of foreign grain. Due to the poor performance of the nation's agricultural sector, grain purchases have averaged nearly $7 billion per year since 1981. The acquisition of sufficient grain supplies may be particularly important in lending credibility to Mikhail Gorbachev's apparent commitment to raise Soviet standards of living; much of the grain imported by the USSR is used to feed livestock, and increased per capita meat consumption has long been a primary goal of the Soviet leadership.

The USSR's growing import requirements come at a time when Moscow is anticipating its lowest hard currency revenues in years. In the past the Soviet Union's most successful exports to the West were highly fungible goods. Hence, over 80 percent of Moscow's hard currency earnings come from the sale of raw materials such as oil, natural gas, timber, gold, and other minerals; more than three-fifths of the earnings come from oil exports alone. This unbalanced export composition proved to be highly successful during the tumultuous 1970's, when supply shocks

Reprinted with permission from the *Harvard International Review*, April 1986, pp. 32-34. Copyright 1986 by the Harvard International Relations Council.

sent commodity prices soaring. However, this emphasis on raw materials has been costly in the 1980's, as world-wide commodity prices have fallen and the Soviets are experiencing a steady drop in hard currency receipts.

The decline in petroleum prices has been particularly distressing, with the USSR's oil export revenues falling from a peak of $26.3 billion in 1983 to $22.8 billion in 1985. The precipitous drop in the spot price of oil during January and February of 1986 accelerated that trend. Experts predict that the Soviet Union will receive only $13 to $16 per barrel of crude in 1986, compared to $26 to $28 per barrel in 1985. Dr. Daniel Yergin, President of Cambridge Energy Research Associates, estimates that current oil prices will reduce Soviet export earnings by as much as $6 to $7 billion this year.

The substantial loss of oil revenues will be compounded by sluggish demand for Soviet natural gas in Western Europe. The Yamal pipeline, so long opposed and even embargoed by the Reagan Administration, is now expected to bring in less than $2.5 billion per year—only one-fourth of the Soviets' original estimate.

The value of Soviet hard currency earnings from its exports to the West has further suffered from the 30 percent depreciation of the dollar against Western European currencies during the past year. Although the world petroleum markets operate on a US dollar basis (and Soviet oil revenues are subsequently dollar-denominated), most Soviet purchases abroad are made in Western Europe and Japan. The conversion from dollars to deutschemark and yen only aggravates Moscow's loss of real buying power.

In the past, the Soviet Union has been able to respond to declines in oil prices and revenues by expanding its production and exports. However, this avenue may be closed now, since many experts believe that Soviet oil production has plateaued. Indeed, last year the USSR pumped three percent less crude than in 1984. Abram Bergson, George F. Baker Professor of Economics Emeritus at Harvard University, suggests that the problem stems from the short term orientation of Soviet petroleum goals, and hence of Soviet planners. While drilling and production on fields with proven reserves have been extensive in the past few years, not enough resources have been devoted to the search for new reserves.

Consequently, many oil fields in Western USSR have now been largely depleted. More disturbingly, the Western Siberian fields—relatively new fields that provide over three-fifths of all Soviet output—have experienced as much as a seven percent decline in overall crude production. In addition, any plans to expand Siberian oil drilling capacity must take into account some rather intractable problems of infrastructure and transportation. Given the present level of crude prices, an intensification in expensive Siberian exploration efforts may prove unprofitable.

To combat its falling revenues, Moscow may try to increase oil shipments to the West by shifting exports away from its Eastern bloc allies. This shift has already been attempted to a limited degree, though Moscow will probably not channel more of its oil exports to the West. The reluctance is at least partially due to the wide differential between the price now paid to the Soviets by their Eastern bloc allies and the lower petroleum prices that Moscow receives on the open markets in the West. The price paid by East European nations for Soviet crude is based on the so-called Bucharest formula of 1974—a five-year moving average of world prices. During the oil shocks of the 1970's, the Bucharest formula effectively provided Eastern Europe with a subsidy on Soviet petroleum. However, oil prices have been falling since 1981, and the Soviet Union now finds itself the beneficiary of the Bucharest arrangement. Although worse off, the Eastern Europeans will likely continue to look to Moscow for most of their energy needs. Constrained by their own balance of payments problems, they value the ability to pay for Soviet oil by exporting "soft" (uncompetitive on Western markets) goods to the USSR. Soviet oil sales are therefore beneficial to both sides, despite the skewed pricing arrangement, and it seems highly likely that the USSR will continue to send over half of its total energy exports to Eastern Europe.

Faced with significant constraints on its energy exports, the Soviet Union might try to raise hard currency revenues by expanding other export categories. Even here, however, the Soviets face formidable obstacles.

In the past, the USSR has been an important exporter of gold, and there is some evidence that Moscow has been rather active in the gold markets recently. Nonetheless, the Soviet Union is justifiably reluctant to flood those markets and risk a collapse in bullion prices. These same fears condition Soviet sales of industrial and high-quality diamonds; indeed, the prospects of raising extra revenue by exploiting the USSR's vast reserves of precious minerals are limited. Other relatively small sources of hard currency, such as tourism and luxury products like caviar and furs, are even more difficult to exploit on any large scale.

The only remaining avenue for increasing Soviet revenues is an expansion in sales of processed and semi-processed goods to the West. The Soviets have tried to achieve this for some time, but they have trouble competing with the superior quality of Western products, despite dumping prices. Even when the initial quality of such goods is satisfactory, Western buyers are skittish about future availability of replacement parts and reliable service. The problem of image is further compounded by the lack of sophistication of Soviet marketing techniques.

General and often unwarranted suspicion and hostility encountered by Soviet sellers in Western markets presents yet another, albeit rarely acknowledged, obstacle to expanded exports. Periodic warnings, especially from the United States, remind prospective buyers about the perils of being economically dependent on an ideological adversary.

Finally, the USSR is one of the few US trading partners without most favored nation (MFN) status. Many of its exports are still subject to the high tariffs established in the 1930's.

Faced with a dramatic fall in current export revenues, bleak prospects for enhancing hard currency earnings in the future, and growing import needs, the Soviet Union will be increasingly prone to borrow heavily from the West. Yet, Soviet planners have acted quite conservatively in the international credit markets in the past. While the East European nations' ratios of debt service to export earnings have at times exceeded 22 percent, such a ratio for the Soviet Union has never risen above four percent. However, this situation may now be changing: both European and American scholars believe that Soviet reluctance to assume higher levels of debt is rapidly dissipating. The significant deterioration in the Soviet Union's trade balance combined with the lack of means to remedy the problem has provided Moscow with strong incentives to seek relief by borrowing on a scale not previously seen.

European and even American banks will not hesitate to provide the Soviet

Union with the short and long term credits it seeks; indeed, with the exception of the 1917 Bolshevik repudiation of Tsarist Russia's foreign debt, the USSR has been an irreproachable customer. There is a great deal of confidence, especially in the European banking community, that commercial lending to the Soviet Union represents a safe investment. After all, even the substantial sums needed by Moscow this year will seem insignificant when compared to the overall size of the Soviet economy. Furthermore, experts believe that conservative Soviet planners will never allow their debt service ratio to rise anywhere near the critical levels reached by many third world and East European nations in the 1980's. The inevitable stigma attached to any inter-national default would be too heavy to bear for a nation that takes pride in its status as a superpower. Even consider-ations of image aside, Moscow's good credit rating in Western credit markets has paid handsomely in the past; the Soviets are rarely asked to pay more than a small fraction of a percentage point over the benchmark London inter-bank offer rate (LIBOR) in interest.

There is very little the Reagan Administration can do to stop the flow of private credits to the Soviet Union. Nonetheless, this shift in the USSRs international economic be-havior presents the United States with another valuable policy tool. Moscow will now be particularly responsive to offers of favorable conditions on official US loans—loans that could be arranged in exchange for political concessions. Even-tually, an entire range of economic issues, from granting MFN status to offering favorable terms on Western loans, could be included within the broader context of strategic and political negotiations between the two superpowers. The recent per-ceptible warming in superpower relations and the deteriorating economic environ-ment of the Soviet Union present the United States with a rare chance not only to attain many of its long-standing geopolitical goals, but to reach a greater level of economic interdependence with its traditional adversary.

Misreading The Kremlin:
SOVIET MILITARY OBJECTIVES

Michael MccGwire

Michael MccGwire is a senior fellow in the Foreign Policy Studies Program at the Brookings Institution.

Churchill's image of Russia as a riddle, wrapped in a mystery, inside an enigma, is immensely compelling to the West. But as a description of the modern Soviet state, it is no longer accurate. Despite the fact that it is partly a closed society, the Soviet Union generates a great deal of evidence about itself: the outcomes of major decisions are largely visible; ideology, doctrine, and plans are publicly articulated. And because the Soviet Union is a centrally planned system, such outward signs can often be traced back to policies and decisions forged at high levels of power, even if we cannot determine exactly *how* those decisions and policies were arrived at. Thus the external evidence the West receives can, if properly interpreted, reveal a great deal about underlying Soviet policy.

It is that necessary proper interpretation that Westerners often fail to achieve—or even attempt. The Soviet view of the world, informed by an amalgam of Marxist-Leninist theory and traditional Russian instincts, is substantially different from the Western view. In the area of military thought, however, the reasoning and logic of both Russia and the West stem from the same roots: all countries structure their military planning around the central objectives they consider most important. In theory, then, Western analysts should be able to trace the ideas and concerns that influence Soviet military decisions.

In practice, this is done all too rarely, and the consequences of this failure should not be underestimated. Misunderstanding the Soviet Union's military objectives could be fatal in war, but it also exacts costs in peacetime, since it leads to incorrect assessments of Moscow's larger foreign-policy goals. For example, Western observers have often claimed that because of the economic and social failures of the communist system, the Soviets must rely on military power as the primary instrument of their foreign policy. Crude measures of Soviet military strength or details of Soviet weapons capabilities have been used to claim that Moscow is bent on geopolitical expansion or military dominance.

Such an analysis overlooks the fact that even in peacetime Soviet behavior is shaped and distorted by the imperative Moscow feels to prepare for the contingency of world war. This is not, as certain observers suggest, a contingency the Soviets seek; in fact, one of their primary goals is to avoid it. Yet because they believe that, if world war does break out, it is crucial that the Soviet Union *not lose*, they have structured their military objectives in ways that look threatening to the uninformed Western eye.

Thus the additions the Soviets have made to their military forces over the past two decades—in particular, the conventional buildup in Europe and the naval buildup in the Pacific—have been widely misunderstood. These additions were the result of a basic shift, largely ignored or unappreciated by the West, that took place in Soviet military thinking during the second half of the 1960s. The irony is that this shift, if properly under-stood, suggests not an increased Soviet threat but rather a change in Moscow's military strategy that has generally favorable implications for East-West security.

Postwar Soviet Military Planning

In order to understand the logic behind the Soviet Union's military strategies, one must try to view the world from Moscow. Particularly, one must avoid the assumption that U.S. intentions are self-evidently benevolent. The Soviets cannot be expected to take at face value Washington's assertions that its weapons programs—whether Kennedy's missile buildup or Reagan's Strategic Defense Initiative—are intended to stabilize deterrence and are hence in the Soviet Union's interests. One must also avoid the assumption that Western understanding of nuclear strategy is superior to Moscow's.

Western presumptions generally do not take account of the Soviet Union's historical experiences and the impact they have had on Soviet military planning. Current Soviet plans for the contingency of world war have their roots in the 1948–53 period. With Germany's wartime invasion still fresh in the Soviets' memories and the specter of U.S. anticommunism looming ever larger, Moscow took the threat of a premeditated Western attack very seriously. It responded by planning for an offensive into Europe, with the objective of deterring Western incursions or, if that proved unsuccessful, of repelling such incursions and then going on to defeat NATO, thereby denying the United States a bridgehead in Western Europe.

Although by the end of the 1950s the Soviets had largely discounted the threat of deliberate attack from the West, the possibility of world war was still inherent in the international system. Hence Moscow felt itself required to be able to mount a successful invasion into Western Europe if such a war seemed unavoidable. This element of Soviet strategy has remained in place over time; what has changed is the underlying assumptions about how to achieve this goal, which have been successively refashioned to accommodate new weapons and technology and shifts in NATO doctrine.

The strategic concept of operations held in the 1950s might best be characterized as "improved World War II": nuclear weapons were considered as just another increase in firepower. The early 1960s, however, saw a radically different strategic concept. The revolutionary nature of nuclear missile warfare was recognized, and Soviet military planners made the judgment that a world war would inevitably be nuclear and would escalate to massive strikes on Soviet soil. This judgment provoked a new strategy based on intercontinental nuclear preemption. Despite the fact that the Soviet intercontinental capability was limited during the first half of the 1960s, Moscow judged that if a nuclear exchange were inevitable the damage to Russia would be less devastating if it could get in the first blow—even a modest strike. Thus if the Soviets decided that world war could not be avoided, they would not only launch a ground offensive in Europe and preemptive nuclear strikes on targets located on the periphery of the Soviet Union, but would also—at least in theory—make a massive preemptive nuclear attack on North America.

From *World Policy Journal*, Vol. III, 4, Fall 1986, pp. 667-695. This essay is adapted from Michael MccGwire's book, *Military Objective in Soviet Foreign Policy*, published by Brookings Institute.

2. THE SOVIET UNION CONFRONTS THE WORLD

During the second half of 1966, however, the Soviets made a major adjustment in their assumptions about the course a world war would take. No longer did they consider it inevitable that world war would result in a nuclear strike on Russia. Several factors combined to bring about this shift. NATO's switch from a strategy of "massive retaliation" to one of "flexible response" indicated that, if NATO had its choice, the early stages of a war in Europe would be conventional; it could also be read as U.S. reluctance to make good on its nuclear guarantee of Europe, now that the growing Soviet intercontinental capability made America itself vulnerable to nuclear attack. This impression was reinforced by the concept of "assured destruction," which suggested a wider U.S. reluctance to resort to strategic nuclear weapons except in response to a direct attack on American soil.

Thus Moscow concluded that in the event of world war it might be possible to deter the United States from initiating an intercontinental nuclear exchange. In the 1950s and early 1960s, the Soviets had accepted such an exchange as inevitable, and assumed that decisions taken by NATO and the United States would determine the nature of a world war. But after the December 1966 shift in military doctrine, Moscow hoped to be able eventually to influence the course of war themselves. For the first time since the development of nuclear missiles, the Soviets were able to contemplate making plans and devising strategies based on the assumption that during a world war they might be able to avoid the nuclear devastation of Russia.

Once the avoidance of the homeland's nuclear destruction became a feasible strategic objective, Soviet strategic priorities changed accordingly. The overarching goal of the Soviet government has been, and remains, to promote the long-term well-being of the Soviet state. Working to support this national objective are three first-order objectives: to ensure that the Communist party retains power; to preserve the Soviet Union's capacity for independent action; and to avoid world war. As we have seen, if this last goal proved impossible to maintain, it was to give way to the goal of not losing the war.

The exact means of achieving this would depend, of course, on the nature of world war. And, as described above, Moscow's assessment of the course world war would take changed radically in December 1966. Thus the priorities that guided planning before that date—what we might call the 1960s objectives—are distinct from those the Soviets began to implement after that date—the 1970s objectives.

Under the earlier, pre-1966 hierarchy of objectives, when Soviet planners assumed that a world war would automatically go nuclear, such a war was seen as the decisive clash between capitalism and socialism—a fight to the finish, with defeat being equivalent to extinction. Thus in order not to lose, the Soviets had to ensure both that the socialist system was preserved and that the capitalist system was destroyed.

After 1966, however, the goal of avoiding the nuclear devastation of Russia gained priority. This meant that the Soviets would have to refrain from launching nuclear attacks on the United States, since that would invite retaliatory attacks on Russia. Thus the goal of extirpating the capitalist system had to be replaced by the goal of gravely weakening the capitalist system—and this goal had to remain subordinated to the overriding objective of avoiding Russia's destruction by nuclear weapons. Such shifts in strategy implied a fundamental change in the political nature of a world war. No longer would it be a fight to the finish between two social systems; instead, it would be one crucial campaign in the ongoing struggle.

Strategic Implications of the New Hierarchy of Objectives

The new objectives developed after 1966 required, of course, a complete restructuring of Soviet military planning and strategy. To achieve the governing objective—avoiding the nuclear devastation of Russia—Moscow had to ensure that North America be spared nuclear attack. And if the U.S. military-industrial base was going to remain intact during the course of a world war, it was essential that the United States be denied any advanced position in the eastern hemisphere that would allow it to build up the military capacity for a ground offensive against the Soviet Union. Thus the defeat of NATO in Europe and the eviction of U.S. forces from the continent became a strategic imperative. It was also essential that U.S. forces be prevented from establishing a new bridgehead at some subsequent stage of the war.

As a result, Moscow has come to think of world war as occurring in two phases. In the first, the Soviets would initially conduct intense operations leading to the defeat of NATO forces in Europe. If, after this step, it were not possible to make an acceptable peace, the Soviets would move to occupy key areas throughout the rest of Europe and to establish an extended defense perimeter. This first phase could last three to four months, although the Soviets would hope that the initial stage of intensive operations, primarily in the western theater of military action, would last no longer than three weeks.

The second phase of a world war is considered likely to be long and drawn-out, its course impossible to predict. A primary Soviet objective would be to prevent the United States from establishing an eastern-hemisphere bridgehead from which to launch a land attack on the Soviet Union. Thus an extended Soviet defense perimeter would be necessary. Since the Soviets would need to economize force by exploiting natural defensive barriers, the Sahara Desert would likely be the southern boundary of the defense perimeter, which would then angle down to meet the Indian Ocean at the Horn of Africa. From there, it would run north past the inhospitable shores of the Arabian Peninsula, up through Baluchistan to Afghanistan, and then along the Chinese border to the Pacific. To the west, there would be some sort of "Atlantic Wall," including Iceland and the British Isles.

The problem remained of how to defeat NATO in Europe without precipitating nuclear strikes on the Soviet Union. In particular, there was the risk that NATO would resort to nuclear weapons, causing the conflict to escalate to an intercontinental exchange. The Soviets responded to this danger in two ways. In the 1967–68 period, they set out to develop the military capability to launch preventive strikes against the means of nuclear delivery and related NATO command-and-control facilities, and to mount a blitzkrieg into Western Europe—in both cases, using only conventional means. Such operations would make it much more difficult for NATO to resort to nuclear weapons. And even if NATO's nuclear capability were not completely destroyed, it would be greatly reduced and the escalatory momentum would be lessened. This military adaptation to the danger of escalation was reinforced in the second half of the 1970s by a political campaign that had two objectives: to persuade NATO to declare a policy of no first use of nuclear weapons; and to convince the United States that resorting to nuclear weapons in Europe would inevitably lead to an intercontinental exchange, causing the nuclear devastation of North America.

Another danger the Soviets had to take into account was the possibility that the United States, when confronted with the impending defeat of NATO in Europe, would strike at the Soviet Union. Such a strike could not be defended against; the only way to prevent it was deterrence—the threat of massive nuclear retaliation on the United States. This required the Soviets to ensure that their deterrent force be able to survive a surprise attack. The impending availability of the necessary intercontinental ballistic missile (ICBM) capability had been one factor underlying the December 1966 decision. But because deterrence during wartime would require a much higher level of credibility than deterring a premeditated or preemptive strike in peacetime, the Soviets had to insure against the possibility that the United States would devise some way of rendering the Soviet fixed-silo deterrent force impotent. Since the Soviets were having trouble developing mobile land-based missiles, they turned to ballistic-missile submarines (SSBNs) for their insurance force.

In addition to these changes in strategic concepts, the 1970s hierarchy of objectives made it necessary for the Soviets to revise their thinking about nuclear preemption. The strategy of the 1960s had emphasized preemptive nuclear strikes, both against the United States and within the European theater, if war should start with a conventional phase. But under the 1970s objectives, strategy focused on avoiding escalation. Thus while in the 1960s the Soviets were leaning forward, poised to preempt, in the 1970s they had to lean backwards, avoiding any suggestion of being prepared to initiate nuclear conflict, since this might trigger a strike from NATO or the United States.

This adjustment in doctrine did not mean, however, that the Soviets had concluded that a world war could not or was unlikely to escalate to a nuclear exchange. Rather, avoiding a nuclear exchange was considered so desirable a goal that the Soviets were willing to undertake the heavy costs of restructuring their forces around a strategy that would make such avoidance more likely, even if the chances for success remained slim. And because they recognize the slimness of those chances, the Soviets have stayed prepared for a world war that does involve significant strikes on Russia and America, with nuclear weapons being used in some or all theaters. In other words, the 1970s hierarchy of military objectives that emerged from the December 1966 decision did not replace the previous strategy for waging global nuclear war. The original strategy remains in reserve, to be resorted to if escalation becomes unavoidable.

Nor does the shift in doctrine mean that, in theory, the Soviets have formally renounced the possibility of preemption under any circumstances. In practice, however, the Soviets perceive that a U.S. second-strike force would survive a preemptive attack. As a consequence, Soviet strategy is no longer based on nuclear preemption; it appears that Soviet forces are prepared for NATO and the United States to strike first.

The Restructuring of Soviet Forces

Such a sweeping readjustment of Soviet strategy resulted, of course, in a substantial restructuring of Soviet forces. The 1970s hierarchy of objectives altered Soviet calculations about the necessary size of the ICBM force, about the type and size of medium-range missiles needed, and about the need for missile defenses. Furthermore, the reassessment changed the cost-benefit calculus of arms control from negative to positive.

The restructuring process began in the 1967–68 period and continued through the 1970s; by 1976, most of the 1970s objectives and associated operational concepts had been adopted. The most immediate impact of this process was on Soviet thinking about ballistic-missile defenses. By the 1968–69 period, the Soviets had reversed their long-standing position on the need for such systems. Since Soviet strategic weapons now needed to be able to deter U.S. strikes during wartime, rather than to deliver preemptive Soviet strikes, the Soviets had to be certain that under all circumstances their ICBMs could not only be launched but would also strike their targets in the United States. As a result, limiting the deployment of U.S. antiballistic missile (ABM) systems became more important than deploying Soviet ABM systems. This priority was enshrined in the 1972 ABM treaty.

The 1970s hierarchy also changed the basis by which Moscow calculated its need for ICBMs. If wartime deterrence were to fail, and the United States were to strike at the Soviet Union, then the scale of devastation would be directly related to the size of the U.S. arsenal—the smaller that arsenal, the better. At the same time, a relatively small Soviet arsenal should be enough to deter the United States: if the U.S. president were not deterred from striking Russia by a threat to destroy the 20 largest American cities, he would not likely be deterred by the threatened destruction of 200 or even 500 cities. Deterrence would be effective either at a fairly low level of threat or not at all.

Thus the Soviets concluded that their interests would best be served by fewer rather than more missiles, as long as they could persuade the United States to make comparable reductions in its arsenal. This new willingness to accept arms limitations and hence to negotiate seriously on arms control was a major factor behind the East-West detente of the 1970s. In theory, it would even have been worth the Soviets' while to accept ceilings for their own forces that were lower than those for the United States, as long as U.S. inventories were thereby reduced below existing levels. In practice, though, Moscow had to consider the need to retain negotiating leverage, as well as the military necessity for enough weapons to match the United States in the postexchange phase of a global nuclear war.

Their immediate decision, therefore, was to curtail the deployment of ICBMs so as to match the U.S. capability. This left the Soviets with about a thousand third-generation systems targeted on North America. Since

these missiles were significantly inferior to their U.S. counterparts, Moscow planned to go ahead and replace them with fourth-generation systems. This replacement program was cut somewhat short of fulfillment, however, by the signing of the Strategic Arms Limitations Treaty (SALT II) in 1979—a worthwhile sacrifice, in Soviets' eyes, since they placed great importance both on arms control as a process and on its potential contribution to detente.

Another area the 1970s hierarchy affected was the requirement for medium-range missiles. Under the new strategy, these missiles were to be used in the event of nuclear escalation that did not involve intercontinental strikes but remained limited to the theaters. Theater nuclear war would have particular problems, different from those inherent in global nuclear war. Speed of response would be a critical factor and the exact locations of the military targets involved in theater war might not be known in advance. This required the Soviets to develop a new type of medium-range missile that would have a flexible targeting capacity and be relatively invulnerable to preventive conventional attack.

Yet Soviet military interests would be best served by the elimination of all nuclear weapons in the European region—as indicated by Mikhail Gorbachev's latest proposals. This would improve the chances of success for a conventional blitzkrieg, while removing the danger that NATO would try to defend itself by resorting to nuclear weapons, which could precipitate intercontinental escalation.

The Regional Impact of the New Strategic Concept

Although the new objectives that stemmed from the December 1966 doctrinal decision changed the cost-benefit calculus of strategic arms control, and hence facilitated detente, other outgrowths of the decision had the opposite effect of increasing U.S.-Soviet tension. For example, the 1970s hierarchy of objectives required a restructuring of Soviet forces at the theater level that looked, to the Soviet Union's potential opponents, very much like a major and unprovoked military buildup with aggressive implications. Public awareness of this restructuring did not emerge in the West until the second half of the 1970s; then, just as the curtailment of Soviet strategic forces in the early 1970s had reinforced the Western trend toward detente, so did the buildup of Soviet theater forces in the late 1970s contribute to the move away from detente.

Although the 1970s hierarchy of objectives was not formulated until the 1967–68 period, Moscow had already accepted the fact that a nuclear war might begin with a conventional phase. Furthermore, certain procurement decisions made during the previous 10 years, under earlier sets of strategic objectives, ended up facilitating the restructuring of Soviet ground and air forces. For example, new aircraft for frontal aviation were already under development, and a radically new type of infantry fighting vehicle was ready to enter service. Tanks had never stopped being developed and produced, and the lessons Vietnam had to teach about the military potential of helicopters were already being digested. To the arms and equipment already in the procurement pipeline were added the weapons decided upon during the 1967–68 period, which began to enter service in the mid-1970s. All these different flows combined to produce an impressive buildup in the fighting power of Soviet ground and air forces.

The restructuring of naval forces did not have these advantages. The 1970s hierarchy of objectives necessitated radical changes in warship design, and there was relatively little being developed that was relevant to the new concept of operations. Two adjustments were particularly important, one concerning the need for sustained operations, the other the use of nuclear weapons.

Under the 1960s hierarchy, the navy's primary mission was to counter the strategic strike capability of Western aircraft carriers and SSBNs. To this end, Soviet naval units were to be deployed, even in peacetime, within weapons-range of these sea-based nuclear delivery systems. The Soviet units had to be able to survive a Western preemptive attack long enough to launch their weapons, after which they were expendable. Nuclear warheads were essential to this mission; since Soviet strategy then dictated a preemptive strike against North America, escalation was not a concern.

Under the 1970s hierarchy, however, the danger of escalation became a central consideration, and authority to use nuclear weapons might be withheld as long as the war did not escalate to major strikes on the Soviet Union. Thus naval forces had to carry a full load of conventional weapons as well as nuclear ones, which required much larger magazines. Meanwhile, naval constructors could no longer design ships for short, sharp actions in the initial stages of a war; instead, they had to think in terms of protracted naval warfare, which might involve such sustained missions as gaining and maintaining command of large areas like the Norwegian Sea. All these requirements added up to a need for much larger surface ships and submarines. These new classes of larger units began to enter service between 1980 and 1982. As they proliferated, the Soviets' capacity for waging conventional war at sea would markedly increase — as would also their capability for projecting force in peacetime. Like the Soviet buildup in ground and air forces, this deployment of an expanded naval capacity struck the West as a signal of offensive intentions.

The 1970s hierarchy of objectives of course generated different strategic requirements for different regions. Those for Europe and the Atlantic were particularly demanding. In the event that world war became unavoidable, NATO had to be defeated and U.S. forces evicted from the continent — preferably without either side resorting to nuclear weapons. If, at this stage, it were not possible to negotiate peace on satisfactory terms, Warsaw Pact forces would need to complete the subjugation of Western Europe and establish an extended defense perimeter within a few months. The way Soviet forces were restructured to meet these new requirements caused understandable concern in NATO about Moscow's intentions — a concern heightened by the Soviet deployment of the SS-20 medium-range ballistic missile.

The SS-20 was not, however, dictated by the 1970s objectives and comes more properly under the 1960s hierarchy. Its deployment in 1977 seems to have stemmed not so much from the new strategy as from the availability of components of the SS-16 ICBM, from the military inadequacies of the first- and second-generation SS-4 and SS-5, and from the failure of plans to replace them with third-generation medium-range systems at the end of the 1960s. When the Soviet leaders woke up to the political and military costs being incurred by the SS-20 deployment, they moved to curtail it. But this response was too little and too late.

The Soviets divide the European theater of war into three theaters of military action (what they refer to as TVDs). Overriding priority goes to the western TVD, which extends from the Baltic to the Alps and roughly matches NATO's central front. In the Soviets' contingency plan for world war, to avoid losing they would have to succeed in this TVD and evict U.S. forces from the continent. Thus a Soviet offensive into Western Europe would not result from some urge to aggression, and its failure would not reflect a miscalculation of the costs of opportunistic expansion. Rather, an attack on Western Europe would constitute a strategic imperative — an outgrowth of a Soviet conviction that world war had become inevitable. To meet their military objectives in this TVD, the Soviets need a certain margin of superiority, since a heavy local preponderance of forces would be required to breach NATO's defenses.

Second in importance to the western TVD is the southwestern TVD — the Balkans, Turkey, and the Mediterranean. Soviet dominance of this TVD would allow Warsaw Pact forces to provide direct support to operations in the western TVD, to pin down NATO's southern forces, and to deploy naval units to intercept supplies being shipped from North America to ports on France's Mediterranean coast. Furthermore, control over the Turkish straits could be critical. NATO might try to shift the strategic axis of the war away from the central front by making a northerly thrust out of the Black Sea toward the Baltic. Thus if NATO held the Turkish straits, it would be in a position to launch a marine invasion of the northwestern Black Sea coast and then mount a major land offensive up through Romania, Moldavia, and the Ukraine, toward Poland. Thus the Soviets must plan to seize the Turkish straits during the initial stages of the war.

The northwestern TVD ranks a poor third in priority (southern Scandinavia and the Danish Straits come within the western TVD). Because of the western TVD's overriding importance, Moscow is unlikely to commit substantial ground forces in the north until it is assured of success on the central front. It would, however, be necessary to take over the northern-

most part of Norway in order to facilitate operations in the Norwegian Sea, enhance the defense of the Northern Fleet area, and provide a 250-mile buffer between NATO and the base complex on the Kola Peninsula. Once NATO had been defeated in the western and southwestern TVDs, the rest of Norway could be expected to surrender without undergoing military occupation.

If Soviet operations in the European-Atlantic region during the first phase of a world war were successful, the central problem in the next phase would be establishing control over Britain and France without precipitating nuclear strikes on the Soviet Union. In the phase following that, the dominant concern would be to establish an effective defense perimeter in order to prevent the return of Western forces. The obvious pitfall here is over-extension; on the other hand, Germany's experience in World War II highlighted the fatal danger of allowing the enemy to control Northern Africa. Thus it would be in the the Soviet Union's interest to institute the extended defense perimeter described above, which would take in Southwest Asia and the Horn of Africa. The problems of occupation would be minimized, since much of the perimeter would run through desolate areas, remote from population centers; and in any case, many of the states involved are favorably disposed toward Moscow. In military terms, the Soviets would have an easier time defending this extended perimeter than NATO's southern boundary. And there are several other advantages: the area would include a large proportion of the petroleum resources in the eastern hemisphere; it would cover the southern sea route to the Soviet Far East; and it would provide military access to the Indian Ocean.

Soviet strategy toward the Asia-Pacific region was also affected by the December 1966 decision. Under the 1960s hierarchy of strategic objectives, a Soviet decision to launch nuclear strikes on the United States would have required a concomitant decision to attack China with nuclear weapons, in order to prevent it from emerging from a Soviet-American conflict as the undamaged victor. Under the 1970s hierarchy, though, such a simple solution was barred by the need to avoid any action that might encourage a U.S. strike on Russia. Instead, the Soviets had to rely on conventional weapons to keep China from taking advantage of Soviet involvement in a European war to seek military gains in Asia. This shift in strategy coincided with the deterioration of Sino-Soviet relations and resulted in a buildup of the Soviet forces facing China from 20 to 45 divisions by 1975 — again, an action that troubled Russia's opponents.

A further addition of 10 more Soviet divisions was made in the first half of the 1980s. This deployment is likely to have been a response to various developments of the previous decade: the normalization of Sino-Japanese relations; the growing Sino-American rapprochement, which was extending into the defense field; and the Soviets' 1976–77 decision to develop the Sea of Okhotsk as a secure area for deploying SSBNs. That decision required a further buildup of the Soviet Pacific Fleet and a reinforcement of the Kuril Islands against amphibious assault, which removed the possibility of negotiating the return of the four southern islands to Japan.

In the second phase of a world war, the Pacific defense perimeter would probably be extended to encompass an intimidated but unoccupied Japan, the Korean and Liao-Tung Peninsulas, and Manchuria. Nevertheless, the Soviets would have to cover the possibility that three or four years into the war (when there might be no satellite surveillance), the United States would somehow manage to mount a successful invasion of the Soviet Union through northwest China, thereby outflanking the bulk of the Soviet forces in the far eastern TVD. In such a case, the Soviets would have to consider giving up eastern and central Siberia and concentrating on the defense of the west Siberian plain, establishing an inner defense perimeter to the east of the Yenisey River. This contingency requires the Soviets to locate as many as possible of their main military facilities within this defended core — particularly those installations that contribute to the credibility of the wartime deterrent, such as ballistic-missile early-warning radars. (The radar at Abalakova, near Krasnoyarsk, which has prompted U.S. accusations that the Soviets are violating the ABM treaty, is inside this defense perimeter.)

The adoption of the 1970s hierarchy of objectives had significant effects on Soviet views of the southern TVD, which constitutes part of the Indo-

Arabian region. Under the 1960s hierarchy, the region was of military interest only as a potential launch area for SSBNs carrying Polaris and Poseidon missiles. But the new objectives reinforced the importance of the southern sea route linking western Russia to the Soviet Far East—which had assumed a new salience anyway after the Sino-Soviet border clashes in 1969. Further, the 1970s hierarchy made the Horn of Africa a strategic fulcrum of the extended defense perimeter, thus increasing the geostrategic significance of the TVD.

This requirement for an extended defense perimeter has generally changed Moscow's war-related interests in the Third World. Under the 1960s hierarchy, which assumed that any world war would escalate to intercontinental nuclear exchange, Soviet strategy focused on the threat posed by U.S. sea-based strategic delivery systems that in peacetime were within striking range of the Soviet heartland. Soviet forces had to be maintained within weapon-range of these strike units, in order to be able to attack them at the onset of a war. The primary areas of Soviet concern were the eastern Mediterranean and the northwest quadrant of the Indian Ocean; strategy dictated that the Soviets have access to airfields and naval support facilities in at least one country bordering those waters. By the end of the 1960s, this access was being provided by Egypt and Somalia.

Under the 1970s objectives, however, nuclear weapons could no longer be used against U.S. strategic strike units at the beginning of war, since that might trigger escalation. A peacetime naval presence in the Mediterranean continued to be necessary, since U.S. carriers there could threaten the success of Soviet operations in the southwestern TVD during the early stages of a world war. But now, war-related requirements throughout the Third World were mainly concerned with establishing the extended defense perimeter and with the second phase of a world war. This focus introduced a new factor into Soviet deliberations about what Third World nations it was important to have influence with. Arms sales to the Third World became a primary means to achieve this: not only would they raise the costs of Western military intervention and sometimes earn hard currency, but they were also a way to preposition heavy equipment in what would become forward defense areas. The buildup of the Libyan tank force may, in part, reflect such Soviet considerations.

As this discussion makes clear, the changes in strategy dictated by the December 1966 doctrinal decision were sweeping and thorough. Implementing them was a lengthy, complicated process. In the 1976–77 period, the Soviets evaluated the results of their restructuring efforts to date and reviewed developments in NATO's capability and doctrine. This period probably saw slight revisions on strategy—decisions on reviving the requirement for a long-range bomber, on the need for a new type of medium-range missile, and on reintroducing the operational maneuver group to ground force operations. Other far-reaching decisions affected the navy, as the importance of the Arctic as a deployment area for SSBNs was downgraded and a new importance ascribed to the more easily defended Sea of Okhotsk off the Pacific, and as more emphasis was laid on mobile land-based missiles as part of a survivable deterrent force.

But such modifications do not imply that there was any fundamental adjustment to the December 1966 doctrine on the likely nature of a world war, or any significant changes in the structure of the 1970s hierarchy of objectives, which continue to be valid. What is somewhat new is the Soviets' recent insistence that there can be no victors in a nuclear war. This suggests that they are unwilling to allocate resources to implementing the fallback set of 1960s objectives, beyond those necessary to keep the United States from dictating its own terms in the wake of an intercontinental nuclear exchange. Moscow may also be increasingly reluctant to accept the military logic of reverting to the 1960s strategy if escalation seems inescapable. Instead, it may prefer to follow Washington's lead of pursuing limited nuclear options rather than the military logic of full-scale escalation.

Misinterpreting the Evidence

Commonly, Western observers have charged that the Soviets have engaged in a "relentless buildup" of military capacity. This claim does not take account of the strategic objectives underlying Moscow's military procurement program. Certainly, a buildup in capability occurred in the 1970s,

as the Soviets restructured their ground and supporting air forces to bring them into line with the 1970s hierarchy of objectives. But having achieved that restructuring, the Soviets resumed their policy of reequipping their forces on a routine, continuous basis. Given the size of the forces, large quantities of ordnance are involved; but the actual buildup had largely ceased by the end of the 1970s.

The term "relentless buildup" is even less appropriate to describe events in the other branches of service. In strategic rocket forces, for example, the deployment of fourth-generation ICBMs was curtailed to conform to SALT II; and compared with earlier generations, the development and deployment of fifth-generation ICBMs has lagged. In the case of medium-range missiles, the long-delayed replacement of the obsolescent first- and second-generation systems by the fourth-generation SS-20 was finally achieved in the first half of the 1980s, about 20 years after the original deployment of SS-4s and SS-5s.

Similar patterns hold true for the Soviet air forces. Since the mid-1970s, production of the medium-range Backfire bomber has been running at about 30 aircraft a year, divided equally between the long-range air force and the naval air force. To reequip these forces with Backfires will take some 20 years, at the end of which time both forces will be significantly smaller than they were in the 1970s. The adaptation of the long-range turboprop Bear, first deployed in the late 1950s, as a platform for the Soviet version of the air-launched cruise missile (ALCM) can be seen as a matching response to the arming of U.S. B-52 bombers with ALCMs.

In the Soviet navy, the new classes of surface ships entering service in the 1980s were much larger than their predecessors, with greater endurance and combat sustainability. But in the late 1970s, the replenishment and landing ship programs were curtailed, and a sharp reduction occurred in the delivery rate of SSBNs, which had been running at a lower rate in the second half of the 1970s than in the first. Nor was there a compensating increase in the delivery rate of nuclear-powered attack submarines, whose production appears to be running well below capacity.

When one analyzes the evidence, it becomes clear that the development of Soviet forces over the past 25 years has been a complex process—not some simple-minded "relentless buildup." The development of the Soviet intercontinental delivery capability is, instead, more accurately described as the costly and laborious process of catching up with and then remaining abreast of the United States—first in numbers, then in quality, and finally in the diversity of delivery systems. This development involved a considerable amount of waste, as successive generations of missiles were deployed and replaced until they finally approached the capabilities of U.S. systems. The buildup of Soviet ground forces in the 1970s and naval surface forces in the 1980s is best described as the costly restructuring of forces required by a new concept of operations. The Soviets were moving away from the inherently unstable strategy of intercontinental nuclear preemption to one that would abstain from nuclear strikes on North America, except in retaliation, and would seek to avoid the use of nuclear weapons in Europe.

The assertion that the Soviets relentlessly built up their offensive forces is generally intended to support the claim that Moscow seeks military domination of the world. But that connection is hard to maintain. By far the largest buildup took place in the Far Eastern theater, where the number of divisions nearly tripled and the number of tactical aircraft increased by sixfold. No one suggests, however, that the Soviets are planning to invade China. If a military buildup on that scale does not imply expansionist intentions in Asia, then why should smaller buildups imply them elsewhere?

Indeed, if the Soviets have been seeking military domination of the world, how does one account for the structure and deployment of their forces since World War II? In a drive for world dominance, the Soviets would deploy no more forces facing NATO than would be necessary to secure the European borders of the Soviet empire. These deployments would be designed to tie down Western military resources while freeing the maximum number of Soviet forces for use elsewhere. Furthermore, one would expect the Soviets to exploit the advantage of their adjacency to the Persian Gulf area, which is the weakest part of the U.S. girdle of containment, instead of giving the southern theater the lowest priority in terms of men, arms, and equipment. And why did the Soviets not develop a worldwide capability to project force, comparable to that of the U.S. Navy and Marines? Why, having developed a limited naval capability to operate (if not survive) in distant waters by the end of the 1960s, did they cut back these deployments in the second half of the 1970s?

If the Soviets believe in territorial expansion, why didn't they take over Sinkiang in the mid-1960s, when China was embroiled in its cultural revolution? In the late 1960s, with more than half a million Americans tied down in Vietnam, the British committed to withdrawing from east of Suez, and the U.S. tilt to China and arming of Iran yet to come, why didn't the Soviets use their military preponderance to achieve gains in Iran? It is implausible to argue that they were waiting to take advantage of some Vietnam syndrome that was to develop some five or more years in the future. And during the time that this syndrome did still have a restraining influence on U.S. policy, why didn't the Soviets take the opportunity presented by the Somalian invasion of Ethiopia to establish military dominance of the Horn of Africa?

Merely to ask all these questions is to realize that the image of a nation pursuing a "relentless buildup" to support a quest for world military domination is fundamentally inaccurate: the evidence does not support such a hypothesis. One of the underlying mistakes that Western observers make, however, is to analyze the evidence of Soviet behavior in light of Western vulnerabilities rather than Soviet strategic requirements. It is Soviet policy to cover against the worst case of world war. This is contingency planning on the grand scale; it represents prudent precautions, not paranoia. The Soviets do not have the advantage of 3,000 miles of ocean on one side and 5,000 on the other, nor do they enjoy the luxury of overwhelming predominance in their own hemisphere. The Soviet Union sprawls across half the Eurasian land mass, the traditional enemies on its borders are now all ranged against it, and it has no significant or reliable allies. Facing west, with their backs to the Urals, the Soviets see the NATO alliance curving around their flanks, with a fully restored Germany in its center. Turning east, they see 4,500 miles of border, on the other side of which are a billion Chinese; beyond lies the Soviets' age-old enemy, Japan. Facing either direction, they see considerable U.S. forces deployed in forward positions. To the south, they face the worry of Moslem irredentism.

The Soviet military must plan for the contingency of world war, the objective being not to lose. In the Euro-Atlantic region, this means defeating NATO on land, evicting U.S. forces from the continent, and establishing a defense perimeter that could run from the Norwegian Sea to the Cape Verde Islands and east across North Africa. In the Asian-Pacific region, China must be deterred from taking advantage of Soviet involvement in Europe, Japan must be neutralized, the United States must be held at bay, and Soviet forces must be ready to seize Manchuria once victory is assured in Europe. In the Indo-Arabian region, the Soviets must establish themselves in the Horn of Africa, and be ready to seize Chah Bahar at the head of the Arabian Sea and perhaps to drive south from Azerbaijan to Tabriz in Iran.

Just to recapitulate these requirements gives a sense of their scale, and the history of World War II suggests that they are not overstated. It is these requirements that have determined the composition, deployment, and supporting infrastructure of Soviet armed forces. These forces' strength depends on the relative priority of the tasks they are assigned to and on how likely Moscow considers war to be. Because Europe is of such central importance, the Soviet forces there have always been numerous and well equipped. But even in this vital region, the strength of Soviet forces is not sufficient to give them high confidence that they would be successful in war.

This relative restraint supports the conclusion that the Soviets saw the restructuring of their forces facing NATO during the 1970s as a military necessity and were aware that the political consequences would be negative. The threat implicit in that buildup adversely affected Soviet relations with Western Europe and ensured that the Soviet deployment of the SS-20 would be perceived as political intimidation. Similarly, the Soviets' buildup of forces in Asia and the Pacific has contributed to the deterioration of their relations with Japan.

This was not the Soviets' intent; they do not, generally, see military force as a primary instrument of policy.[1] They are aware that it has political utility only in a limited range of circumstances — retaining political control throughout the Soviet security zone, for instance. In other circumstances, they realize, threatening to use it can in fact be counterproductive; on those occasions when they have resorted to military threats, they have usually been acting out of short-term frustration rather than from long-term policy considerations. The one area in which the Soviets do see a role for military power is in the U.S.-Soviet relationship: they are convinced that their matching America's military strength persuaded Washington to view the Soviet Union as a superpower with worldwide interests and to negotiate with it on limiting strategic weapons systems.

The actual use of military force is quite different from the role of military power. The reluctance with which the Soviets have resorted to military force in their national security zone demonstrates their sensitivity to the political costs of coercive intervention. Outside this zone, the Soviets have used military force only in supportive interventions; and the force has been used in protective rather than punitive ways.

Moscow's use of force in the Third World has also been constrained by the danger that superpower confrontation could escalate to world war. The Soviets' dread of war is genuine and deep-seated. Though they believe war to be less likely than they did during the early postwar years, when a premeditated Western attack seemed a live possibility, they still do fear war — not one resulting from a deliberate decision to attack, but one caused by an uncontrollable chain of events, a slippery slope into the abyss of world conflict.

The United States, on the other hand, assumes that war could only come about through some Soviet initiative that the West had failed to deter. Following this line of reasoning, U.S. officials dismissed Soviet claims that the confrontational style of U.S. policy during the first Reagan administration was making war more likely.[2] They argued that these claims were propagandistic and that the Soviets could not help but recognize that war was in fact less likely, since the Reagan style of policy had enhanced deterrence.

This fundamental disjunction in the two sides' perception of the danger of war is at the root of much misunderstanding. If one thinks war is unlikely, then seeing foreign policy as a game like football is not unreasonable: a series of plays is won or lost; a loss for one side is a gain for the other. This zero-sum thinking pervades the U.S. approach to the superpower relationship and means that deep-seated Russian concerns about war are dismissed as rhetoric. But Yuri Andropov was not indulging in rhetoric when he accused the Reagan administration of having a flippant attitude to the issues of peace and war. The Soviets have grown increasingly frustrated at their inability to get across these concerns; as one senior Soviet advisor put it, "the danger of war [in U.S. policy] lies in the fact that politics are carried on as if there were no danger of war."[3]

Living with the Soviets

The harsh facts of the adversarial U.S.-Soviet relationship — massive nuclear inventories, opposing forces deployed around the world, troops confronting each other directly across the European divide, totally different concepts of the dangers of war — are daunting, to say the least. But they become somewhat less so if one focuses on the *why* of Soviet behavior rather than the *what*.

For example, the Soviet military posture facing NATO denotes an offensive concept of operations. In war, the Soviet objective would be to defeat NATO, oust U.S. forces, and establish control over Western Europe. To execute that offensive concept, Soviet forces at key points on the central front must outnumber NATO forces by as much as six or eight to one. This almost certainly requires overall superiority in the theater, by a ratio of as much as three to two.

There is, therefore, an inherent asymmetry between the two sides' requirements. If the Soviets are to keep from losing a world war, they have to carry out a successful offensive in Europe, whereas for NATO not to lose it has only to check that offensive. Thus it might seem that NATO must either reconcile itself to living with a significant margin of inferiority or else be prepared to engage in a permanent arms race, since the Soviet Union would continually strive to preserve the edge it needs for a successful offensive. The situation is, however, mitigated by two important factors.

First, the occupation of Europe is not something the Soviet Union desires for its own sake. An invasion would be contingent on a Soviet decision that world war was unavoidable; and avoiding such a war is one of the Soviet Union's first-order national objectives.

Second, the Soviets distinguish between the way they *structure* their forces for the contingency of world war, and the extent to which they *flesh out* that structure to make those forces fully capable of carrying out their assigned missions. Forces in Europe clearly have highest priority. Nevertheless, the less likely the Soviets consider war, the less importance they will attach to having the necessary margin of advantage permanently in place in the European theater.

Such seems to have been the case in the late 1970s. The adoption of the 1970s hierarchy of objectives had caused Soviet ground and air forces facing Europe to be fundamentally restructured. Although this greatly increased their capacity for conventional deep strikes and a blitzkrieg offensive, the actual force levels deployed were not sufficient to guarantee success. That this level of deployment was the result of conscious policy rather than miscalculation is suggested by Moscow's readiness in 1979 to begin negotiating seriously on mutual and balanced force reductions. For as long as the Soviets see arms control negotiations promoting the objective of avoiding world war, they will tend to place less stress on the lower-order objective of not losing a war should one break out.

The Soviets show a similar flexibility in the area of strategic nuclear inventories. The change from the 1960s strategy of intercontinental nuclear warfighting to the 1970s concept of wartime deterrence did away with the theoretical requirement for numerical superiority in nuclear arsenals. In addition, resources devoted to nuclear weapons are resources denied to the Soviet economy. And smaller arsenals would promote the Soviets' strategic objective, if wartime deterrence should fail, of limiting the nuclear devastation of Russia. Since the late 1960s, therefore, Moscow has consistently demonstrated its interest in negotiating limits on strategic weapons.

The sticking point here has to do with U.S. domestic politics and psychological needs as much as with U.S.-Soviet relations and military requirements. The Soviets have lived with U.S. nuclear superiority for 40 years and are willing to settle for approximate equivalence if that effectively caps the arms race. In fact, some evidence even suggests that, if SALT II had been ratified and negotiations on reductions had continued, Moscow would have been willing to accept a halt on new deployments and to live with its mixed inventory of third- and fourth-generation missile systems. But so far, Americans have been reluctant to accept the idea of equivalence with the Soviet Union—even an "equivalence" tilted in favor of the United States and its allies, as SALT I and SALT II provided for.

The Soviet desire for significant arms limitations has met a further obstacle in the U.S. Strategic Defense Initiative (SDI). Since SDI will initiate an arms race in space, it makes war more likely; by undermining the Soviets' deterrent, it might cause them to lose a war. Furthermore, space-based systems have potential as offensive weapons. Because of these dangers, and because a race to deploy space weapons would be extremely costly, Moscow would like to see SDI curtailed. The only negotiating lever the Soviets have in this regard, however, is U.S. worry about the first-strike capability of Soviet heavy land-based ICBMs. Thus SDI has altered the arms-control equation: at the present time, Moscow cannot afford to make concessions on offensive systems except in exchange for U.S. constraints on SDI. If the Reagan administration accepted such constraints, serious strategic arms reductions might well be possible.

The Third World is another area where Soviet policy and strategy do not pose the problem that they could. Since Western influence predominates in the Third World, it might seem that a Soviet attempt to advance the cause of socialism there must inevitably lead to East-West military conflict. But such a supposition is based on assumptions that date from the time of European imperial competition, when European nations used military and commercial means to establish their domain over large areas that often lacked formal structures of government, and did not hesitate to use force against their competitors. The present situation is different. The Third World is now composed of independent states; the Soviet Union believes that historical processes will move those states toward socialism when circumstances are appropriate; and since the Soviets believe in the inherent superiority of their socioeconomic system, the primary instruments of their policy are not military but political, social, and economic.

This worldview has encouraged the Soviet Union to adopt a fairly relaxed approach to the competition for influence in the Third World. They take advantage of opportunities as they arise, but they are still prepared to win some and lose some. Military support to Third World countries has been provided in the shape of arms, equipment, and training, aimed at enhancing their capacity for self-defense as well as increasing Soviet political influence. Moscow also supported national liberation movements, but these movements have become relatively scarce. And the Soviets have strictly limited their use of military force to support client states—largely out of fear that a superpower confrontation in the Third World could escalate to a world war.

The Costs of Worst-Case Thinking

And yet, despite these underlying positive conditions for U.S.-Soviet relations, Western policymakers have tended to rely on worst-case assumptions about Soviet intentions. Worst-case assumptions do have a place in all contingency plans, where the focus is on one's own vulnerabilities. For at this level of threat analysis—what one might call the military and tactical or "colonel's" level—the hostile intentions of one's opponent have to be taken for granted and one has to prepare to meet that opponent's capabilities. But this kind of worst-case analysis, while suitable for contingency planning, is wholly inappropriate at the political and strategic, or "ministerial," level of analysis that should underlie foreign policy.

At this ministerial level, the primary concern should be with the most likely course of events. One cannot ignore the opponent's military capabilities, but these must be measured against his security requirements to discover whether there is the type of surplus capability that would indicate an aggressive plan of action. Thus it is crucial to try to gauge the opponent's interests and intentions—major elements of a nation's motivations. Of course, determining any country's interests, even one's own, is a difficult task; it is relatively easy, however, to identify what is *against* an enemy's interests. Doing so can help one avoid making the simplistic assumption that what is bad for oneself must be good for one's opponent.

These general principles hold for U.S.-Soviet relations. Soviet intentions must be examined directly. To claim that they should be ignored is to fall into the "colonel's fallacy." At the national level, intentions are remarkably consistent; radical change only comes during political shifts like the Bolshevik Revolution. Thus after more than 65 years of Soviet behavior and pronouncements, there has emerged a fairly clear picture of Soviet intentions, particularly regarding peace and war.

This picture does not always jibe with the West's image of the Soviet Union. Moscow does see the United States as an adversary—but this perception results as much from the global status of the two superpowers as from the ideological struggle for socialism in a world dominated by capitalism. The Soviets' communist theory does predict that in the long run socialism will prevail—but this has not led to the type of territorial expansion through military aggression that the West generally expected of the Soviets during the decade after World War II. This was not really surprising, given the Soviets' experience of war during the previous 30 years and the communist belief that in the last analysis the course of history is determined by economic developments rather than violence—by broad masses of people, not armies.

Those who believe that the Soviet Union has an urge for military aggression are not persuaded by this explanation of Soviet behavior. Instead, they consider Soviet restraint to be the direct result of the Western policy of conventional containment and nuclear deterrence. And even those who acknowledge that the evidence accumulated since 1945 does not support the hypothesis of a Soviet Union bent on world domination are prone to argue that "it is better to be safe than sorry." This assumes that worst-case assumptions are cost-free.

But that is not true. The costs of worst-case assumptions are pervasive. For these assumptions affect everything, from NATO military strategy to U.S. foreign policy, from the domestic allocation of resources to attitudes toward arms control. The economic costs are obvious; less so are the distortions that unjustified worst-case assumptions introduce into Western policies—military, domestic, and foreign.

For example, the assumption that the Soviets had an interest in seizing Western Europe led NATO to adopt the doctrine of flexible response in 1967. This switch was intended to increase the credibility of the Western deterrent. No longer would NATO strategy call for automatically resorting to nuclear weapons—a strategy that many considered increasingly incredible. Instead, NATO would initially use conventional means to check a Soviet assault on Europe. This conventional phase would serve the double purpose of allowing NATO to be certain that it faced a major attack and giving the Soviets the opportunity to see the error of their ways and withdraw.

Because the central assumption of Soviet expansionism was ill-founded, adopting this doctrine had the paradoxical effect of increasing the capabilities threat facing NATO on the central front while at the same time making war more likely. If the Soviets were to make a drive into Western Europe, they would not be responding to some aggressive urge that could be deterred by a threat of punishment. Rather, a Soviet offensive would be a by-product of the momentous decision that world war was unavoidable. That decision became slightly less unthinkable once the NATO doctrine of flexible response opened a window of conventional opportunity, for if the Soviets skillfully exploited that window, they might be able to prevent NATO from resorting to nuclear weapons in the theater—or at least decrease the likelihood of a U.S. strike on Russia.

Flexible response was a particular application of the strategy of deterrence. Deterrence has been a mainstay of U.S. policy since the early 1950s; it has also been one of the most powerful means of perpetuating worst-case assumptions. For if deterrence is to have any meaning, one must assume that the adversary is indeed tempted to take the action one is attempting to deter. The assumption of a Soviet urge to aggression has therefore become a cornerstone of Western policy, encouraging Western policymakers to ignore questions about Soviet intentions.

The requirement that nuclear deterrence be credible has also fostered a particular style of U.S. policy. Even in the days of the U.S. atomic monopoly, the American people would support deterrence only if they perceived the Soviet Union as an enemy that deserved brutal punishment. Then, as the United States was brought within range of Soviet strategic systems, the U.S. public had to be persuaded that defending Europe was worth risking the nuclear devastation of America. These domestic political constraints have forced U.S. policymakers to paint the issues in stark moral terms. The result has been a foreign policy that tends toward intransigence, as a demonstration of resolve, and shies away from negotiation and compromise.

Worst-case assumptions also work to restrict the flexibility and focus of foreign policy. The assumption that the Soviets aim at world military domination has required that physical containment be the primary U.S. foreign-policy objective. The Soviets have had to be excluded from involvements around the world; the possibility that Western interests would be better served by enlisting Soviet collaboration has been ignored.

A higher-level U.S. objective, such as "securing cooperative Soviet behavior," would open up more constructive policy options. Containment could continue to be an important supporting objective, but it would be only one among many: fostering consultation on matters of mutual interest, increasing trade interdependence, encouraging rising expectations in Russia by improving the Soviet standard of living, and collaborating in such areas as space exploration or the stifling of dangerous international developments before they become unmanageable. Currently, such options are incompatible with containment, which remains the primary objective.

During the detente of the early 1970s, Washington did relax its worst-case assumptions and adopt an objective at a higher level than containment. This allowed a broader range of initiatives, which had benefits both for the U.S.-Soviet relationship and for East-West relations in Europe. But the assumptions of Western deterrence conflicted with those of detente, and the pressure to return to the more restrictive policies could not be resisted.

The systematic misunderstanding of Soviet motivations is harmful in itself. Worst-case thinking closed Western policymakers' minds to the possibility of changes in Soviet policy that could be in Western interests. Serious Soviet proposals were discarded as propaganda, and valuable opportunities were missed. This was certainly true in arms control. The West focused on an exaggerated Soviet threat and on its own vulnerabilities, thus blinding itself to the evidence that the Soviets have such a serious interest in reducing nuclear arsenals that they are willing to make major concessions to reach an agreement. It did not enter Western minds that Moscow might have been willing to cap the arms race at the levels existing when SALT II was signed, forgoing their fifth-generation ICBMs (except perhaps for the small single-warhead replacement for their remaining third-generation systems). Yet the evidence suggests that these possibilities were at least worth exploring.

Instead, worst-case thinking has dominated policy-making to a dangerous extent. Assumptions that the Soviets would eagerly seize any chance to destroy the United States make it almost impossible to reach an arms control treaty that does not enshrine U.S. superiority. Assumptions about the likelihood of Soviet preemption have shifted U.S. attention from preventing crises to controlling them once they begin—even though by the time a crisis is in progress and thoughts turn to preemption it is probably too late to try to manage events. And, perhaps most insidiously, worst-case assumptions about Soviet intentions have tended to breed a false complacency about the danger of inadvertent war.

Furthermore, Western deterrence dogma has certain destabilizing effects that are too often ignored. If one believes that war can only come about through some Soviet initiative that the West has failed to deter, then anything that enhances deterrence should make war less likely. The trouble is that measures intended to strengthen deterrence, such as the deployment of Pershing II missiles in Europe, are likely to raise international tensions and in the process make war not less but *more* likely. As tensions rise, so do the chances that intentions will be misread, setting off a dangerous chain reaction in which each side feels compelled to demonstrate its resolve to the other.

The "better safe than sorry" approach has strong appeal, and it was to be expected that policymakers would tend toward the colonel's fallacy in the immediate postwar years, when the memory of Hitler's expansion was still vivid. But the fallacy has persisted—partly because the threat perceptions of the 1948–53 period were institutionalized by the policy of deterrence and by the NATO staff structure, and partly because without an exaggerated threat it is difficult to secure political support for sustained defense spending in a democracy.

In any case, the present situation is somewhat ironic: the West has always prided itself on the sophistication of its strategic theorizing, while disparaging the Soviets as paranoid. Yet Moscow seems to have avoided the fallacies the West has fallen into. The Soviets structure their forces for the contingency of world war and make worst-case assumptions about the nature of such a war. But that is appropriate at the level of military and technical analysis. The West's mistake lies in using this approach at the political and strategic level—the ministerial level at which broad issues of foreign and defense policy are decided.

The Soviets, on the other hand, have been reasonably successful at keeping the two levels of analysis distinct. Once clear of the 1948–53 period, they steadily moved away from preoccupation with the idea of a premeditated Western attack. By the 1960s, although the potential opponent was still the West, whose objective in a war would be to overthrow the Soviet system, the Soviets saw the true danger as war itself—inadvertent war. If it came, it would be the result of some Western action; but Moscow did not assume that the West had an *urge* to go to war. Thus the Soviet Union has avoided the trap of worst-case thinking that has proved so costly to the West.

The Challenge to the West

With the benefit of hindsight, one can see that in the 1976–77 period Soviet policies were moving in a direction generally favorable to improved East-West relations. The Soviets had largely completed the restructuring of their theater forces, and investment in defense had leveled off. They were ready to accept SALT II and keen to move on to a third round of negotiations on limiting strategic weapons, and may even have been considering forgoing their fifth generation of ICBMs. Important elements of their naval buildup were soon to be curtailed. Those in the Kremlin who had argued for direct Soviet military intervention had lost. War was considered to be relatively unlikely; U.S.-Soviet detente lay at the heart of Soviet foreign policy.

By the 1984–85 period, the prospects had changed. The Soviets now believed that the likelihood of war had risen significantly. Some resources had been switched from the civilian to the defense sector; the number of active divisions and the production of certain armaments had increased. The construction of two fifth-generation ICBMs had been authorized, and the development of a third, the replacement for the heavy SS-18, was proceeding. Although the relationship with the United States continued to be at the heart of Soviet foreign policy, the future nature of that relationship was uncertain. Both the value and the very possibility of detente were in question. And besides these immediate manifestations of changes in Soviet policy, there could be other unfavorable changes that would only become apparent in future years.

The prognosis is not rosy. But in its dealings with the Soviets, the West has several strikes in its favor. For one thing, the Soviets' belief in historical inevitability makes their world-vision much less dangerous than that of the great empire-builders—Arab-Moslem, European-Christian, or Aryan-Nazi. The Soviets lack the sense of urgency that would launch them on a crusade or jihad to achieve their ends.

The West is also fortunate in Marxism's emphasis on the primacy of socioeconomic factors, both domestically and in the struggle between social systems. The mass of Russians may place the security of their homeland above their personal comfort; but this does not mean that guns always have precedence over butter within the Soviet economy. Priorities depend on how likely war is considered to be. The overriding importance attached to defense industries in the 1930s, and again in the late 1940s and early 1950s, when the danger of war was seen to be high, should not obscure the concerted attempts since 1953 to increase the relative share of the civilian sector of the economy.

Another factor in the West's favor is the Soviets' view of world war. They are serious about the danger that war will break out, and about doing their best to avoid such a war if at all possible. Clearly this seriousness serves everyone's best interests; the corollary, though, is that Moscow is serious about not losing such a war if it proves unavoidable.

Soviet forces have been structured to meet this contingency, in a way that looks threatening to their potential opponents. But the actual level of the threat this force posture poses is to some extent within Western control, since the resources the Soviets devote to fleshing it out depend on their perception of the danger of war. Thus, although NATO seems at this point to have no alternative to living with Soviet forces that are structured for an offensive against Western Europe, the assertiveness of that threat will diminish as Moscow thinks war less likely. Meanwhile, the Soviets have good military reasons for negotiating reductions in their arsenal of strategic nuclear weapons and resisting the deployment of weapons in space.

Yet the West's worst-case assumptions about the Soviet Union's intentions have tended to foreclose opportunities for improving East-West relations; U.S. policies often yield results that are exactly the opposite of what the United States desires. The colonel's fallacy is costly because it calls for military responses to problems that are primarily political. So far, it has not led the West into war. But the damage it has caused is considerable. It has encouraged the steady buildup of armaments—a major source of friction in the superpower relationship and a cause of serious discord in NATO. It has led the West to view the competition for world influence in military and zero-sum terms, neglecting the comparative advantage the West has in socioeconomic instruments of policy. Perhaps most seriously, the colonel's fallacy type of worst-case thinking ignores the extent to which militarizing the competition exacts a high cost in human suffering and jeopardizes future world order.

The West faces a challenge that may best be summarized in the form of three questions. Is the West politically mature enough to distinguish between the way Soviet forces are structured for the contingency of world war (including plans to take over Western Europe), and Soviet intentions regarding the use of military force as an instrument of policy? Is the West politically astute enough to perceive that the threat posed by Soviet capabilities is directly related to the Soviet estimate of the likelihood of war, and that U.S. attitudes and behavior are the most important factors in that estimate? And is the West wise enough to appreciate that attempts to solve its security dilemma by military means alone can only make the problem worse?

Notes

[1] Malcolm Mackintosh, an assistant secretary in the British Cabinet and a special advisor to the government on Soviet military affairs for more than 20 years, concludes that "the Russian people are not and never have been a militaristic nation devoted to the solution of their problems or the achievement of their goals by war." Mackintoch, "The Russian Attitude to Defence and Disarmament," *International Affairs*, Vol. 61 (Summer 1985), p. 33.
[2] That Soviet protestations were sincere is suggested by the diversion of KGB assets in 1981–83 to seeking evidence of preparations for war and monitoring operational warning indicators. Murray Marder, "Defector Told of Soviet Alert," *Washington Post*, August 8, 1986.
[3] The comment was made by Georgi Arbatov, director of the Institute for the Study of the U.S.A. and Canada. Cited in Charles Kiselyak, "Round the Prickly Pear: SALT and Survival," *Orbis*, Vol. 22 (Winter 1979), p. 833.

Will Gorbachev Reform
the Soviet Union?

Vladimir Bukovsky

VLADIMIR BUKOVSKY, who left the Soviet Union in 1976 after
twelve years in Soviet prisons, work camps, and psychiatric
"hospitals," is the author of *To Build a Castle: My Life as
a Dissenter*. His previous articles in COMMENTARY are "The
Soul of Man Under Socialism" (July 1979) and "The Peace
Movement & the Soviet Union" (May 1982). A much-ex-
panded version of the present article (written during Mr.
Bukovsky's tenure as a Visiting Scholar at the Hoover Institution) will form the opening chapter of a collection of
essays by various authors to be published by the Institute
for Contemporary Studies under the title *The Future of
the Soviet Empire*.

THE current "crisis" of the Soviet system about which everybody has been
talking must seem very strange to an outside
observer: there are no starving crowds or dead
bodies along the roads, no riots or clashes with
the police, virtually nothing to show or hide on
the evening news. Of course, Soviet economic performance is appalling: GNP growth has declined
almost to zero; and a 30-percent decrease in oil
production has been aggravated even further by the
recent drop in the price of oil. To this, add obsolete industrial equipment, chronically ill agriculture, and nearly catastrophic environmental
problems, and the resulting picture will seem
frightening enough. Yet within the Soviet system,
only a fundamental challenge to the principles
upon which the regime is built can be seen as a
true crisis, and then that challenge can only be
taken with full seriousness if it is described in the
terminology of Marxism-Leninism.

Such a description is precisely what has been
given by Professor Tatyana Zaslavskaya in her
famous "Novosibirsk Document." This influential scholar (the new Soviet leader Mikhail Gorbachev himself uses many of her definitions in his
speeches) sees the cause of Soviet economic problems in

the lagging of the system of production relations, and hence of the mechanism of state
management of the economy which is its reflection, behind the level of development of
the productive forces.

Lest anyone wonder about the actual meaning

of her definition, Professor Zaslavskaya quotes a
classic Marxist formula describing what actually
happens in a time of contradiction between "productive forces" and "the system of production
relations":

There ensues either a period of acute socioeconomic and political cataclysms within the
given formation, which modify and readjust
production relations to the new mode of production, or there comes an epoch of a general
crisis of the given social formation and of its
downfall caused by a social revolution.

Nor, she adds, is a socialist society miraculously
exempt from this general rule:

Attempts at improving production relations,
bringing them into greater correspondence with
the new demand of productive forces, . . . cannot run their course without conflict.

The Soviet people, then, should brace for a new
spell of class struggle in their classless society
(or a struggle of "interest groups," as Professor
Zaslavskaya tactfully calls them), because a

radical reorganization of economic management essentially affects the interests of many
social groups, to some of which it promises improvements, but to others a deterioration in
their position.

And no class (or "interest group") in history has
been known to give up its position without a
struggle.

Not surprisingly, Professor Zaslavskaya becomes
vague and inconsistent, even evasive, when she

defines the "social group" whose interests are antagonistic to the goal of social progress, and whose position, therefore, must "deteriorate" in the forthcoming class struggle. She talks about an "intermediate link of the management" which has acquired more rights and responsibilities than those on the top and at the bottom. She alludes to some bureaucrats at the top who do not want to have more responsibilities requiring better professional qualifications than they possess. She also mentions some officials who "occupy comfortable positions with high incomes and vaguely defined responsibilities." And she describes a general tendency within the Soviet system to reward those who are more docile instead of those who are more gifted and efficient.

However, these generalized descriptions of personality types and tendencies cannot serve as a substitute for a clear definition of a social group (with common economic interests and a certain place in the system of production relations, as required for Marxist analysis). She comes very close to naming this mysterious group when she says that the "central element in the system of production relations is the dominant form of ownership of the means of production"—a classic Marxist formula. But if she went a bit further and actually named the culprit, she would no longer be an influential Soviet scholar but a dissident, because every schoolboy in the Soviet Union knows that under socialism the means of production belong to the Communist party apparatus, acting on behalf of the "proletariat."

This is exactly the group (or "New Class," as Milovan Djilas called it long ago) which occupies the cushiest positions with high incomes and vaguely defined responsibilities, which rewards the docile instead of the gifted, and whose interests are opposed to a radical reorganization of economic management. When Professor Zaslavskaya speaks about the need to shift from "administrative methods to economic means of management," when Gorbachev, echoing her, emphasizes the need to give more "independence and rights" to enterprises, and when he, finally, says that "It is impossible to achieve any tangible results in any sphere of activity as long as a party official substitutes for a manager," one has little doubt as to whose interests will be affected by this "reorganization."

The emerging dilemma is truly paradoxical: if the party retains its control over the economy, socialism will be endangered and will finally collapse; if, however, the party loses its control over the economy (and, therefore, its control over Soviet society), what Gorbachev calls "the position of socialism in the modern world" will collapse just as surely.

In short, the implacable logic of Marxist-Leninist analysis predicts the inevitable demise of socialism. Here indeed is a fundamental crisis of the entire system.

THAT system grew out of the compromise between revolutionary ideology and reality that the Communists were forced to make from the very beginning.

According to Lenin's own theory, the state was supposed to "die out" under socialism. Yet so long as the Communist state was encircled by powerful capitalist enemies, its power had to grow in order to survive and to promote revolution throughout the world. The Soviet state emerged out of this contradiction, according to the laws of dialectics.

The new system of government was proclaimed to be a "dictatorship of the proletarians," which in practical terms meant a dictatorship of the "advance-guard of the proletarians"—the Communist party—ruling on behalf of the proletarians. At that time, the proletarians—industrial workers and poor peasants—constituted barely 10 percent of the population, while the party members constituted about 10 percent of the proletarians. Leaving aside the scope of terror needed for such a tiny minority to rule dictatorially, "partocracy" was the only possible way to resolve the new regime's fundamental contradiction.

Thus, behind the backs of everyone and every governmental institution, there developed a party "shadow government"—the Central Committee of the CPSU and its respective Departments—overseeing and directing every aspect of work in accordance with ideological requirements. Today, after nearly seventy years, this network of party cells penetrates every institution, from top to bottom, in order to guarantee that each party directive will be carried out to the letter.

The Foreign Ministry of the USSR, like a foreign ministry in any normal state, is preoccupied with its professional duties of maintaining relations, promoting trade, negotiating agreements, and in general advancing the national interests of the Soviet state. But at the same time, the International Department of the Central Committee is promoting world revolution and making sure that the interests of Communist ideology are given priority over any considerations of diplomacy.

The Ministry of Education is concerned with preparing qualified specialists in every sphere of activity, but its counterparts in the Central Committee are concerned with making a good builder of Communism out of every student. And the Central Committee's task is given priority when it comes to promotions and appointments, as well as to the content of educational programs.

The Ministry of Defense is responsible for the security of the country, and for training good soldiers and officers. But a corresponding Department of the Central Committee, acting through a Chief Political Directorate of the Army, makes sure that these soldiers are good *Soviet* soldiers, the liberators of humanity from the chains of capitalism.

The Ministry of Culture is charged with promoting art, literature, and entertainment. But being subordinate to the Department of Propaganda of the Central Committee, its main concern is effective propaganda on behalf of the official ideology. Accordingly, it becomes a ministry of political censorship, weeding out the "wrong" tendencies and promoting the "right" ones.

The intelligence service has the job of collecting military and strategic information about potential enemies, but disinformation, organization of mass movements, "liberation movements," international terrorism, drug smuggling, etc.—in short, organization of any activity which might destabilize, confuse, or scare other countries into submission—is even more important.

The double structure—established in every sphere of life and on all levels: national, district, regional, local, with vertical and horizontal subordination—is a perfect instrument of control and an ideal system for maintaining socialism at home and spreading it abroad. For the Soviet state is not a state in the traditional meaning of the word; it is the material and operational base of the world socialist revolution. Internally, it maintains a regime of occupation; externally, a state of permanent ideological war. Each needs and feeds the other.

Of course, the double structure of the Soviet state did not appear overnight, but evolved during the civil war and the subsequent struggle within the party. Initially, party control over the governmental apparatus was introduced because most of the specialists were former "class enemies" and could not be trusted. Even in the Red Army during the civil war, former czarist officers had to be conscripted by the Communists to lead the troops. Since they had to fight against their former colleagues and friends in the White Army, instances of "treason" were quite likely. Therefore, political commissars were appointed to each unit to watch over the officers.

The same was true in other areas, such as education or industry, where old czarist teachers and engineers were equally mistrusted as "class enemies." The party was small (some estimates show 115,000 members on January 1, 1918; 250,000 in March 1919), and consisted of mostly uneducated people (even by 1927 only 1 percent had graduated from universities, 8 percent had graduated from elementary school, while over 25 percent were registered as "self-educated," and 2 percent were completely illiterate). For a party of proletarians, this was as it should be.

To say that is not to make a joke, but to point to a very serious contradiction which was never resolved by the leadership. On the one hand, a party of proletarians ruling on behalf of the working class must have in its ranks a clear majority of workers. And indeed, demand for real proletarians was so great that only complete imbeciles were left in the factories or on the farms where they started. On the other hand, this practice, continuing almost until the present day, created an ill-educated and incompetent party bureaucracy.

As far as the "specialists" were concerned, in due course most were replaced by the new "Soviet specialists," often members of the party. Thus, in the army only 4,500 former czarist officers out of 50,000 were still serving by 1930. The number of party "specialists" in the governmental apparatus increased from 5 percent in 1923 to 20 percent in 1927. But the practice of party control through political commissars persisted, creating conflicts between the more competent specialist and his party controllers, who were usually less competent but more influential.

The considerable resentment thus accumulated acquired a new dimension after Lenin's death in 1924 and became an essential part of the internal struggle in the party under the new General Secretary, Stalin.

Stalin had to build his personal authority in a tough competition with "old revolutionaries," who even in 1927 constituted three-quarters of the leadership, while being only 1.4 percent of the total membership. By combining promotion of new members with purges of old, and by increasing the power of the party apparatus, Stalin consolidated his position. This meant an even more complete double structure. In 1925, the apparatus constituted only 2.5 percent of the membership; by 1939, it was 10 percent. After the mass terror of the 1930's, the party could not be challenged by anybody. Its power became enormous, its privileges huge. Total membership was 1,589,000 and at least half of them were no longer proletarians. Thus, the formation of a double structure was completed by the end of the 1930's, with its innermost core—the party apparatus—reaching its maximal power.

This new class of bosses, of professional leaders, and of organizers was and has remained the very embodiment of revolutionary ideology, its priests and caretakers. For without the ideology, they are nothing but a bunch of careerists and cynical parasites. As long as ideology reigns, however, they are omnipotent. There is no law, human or natural, which they cannot cancel: "Our task," declared one of them, "is not to study the economy, but to change it. We are not bound by any law. There are no such fortresses which Bolsheviks could not storm."

After Stalin's death, the appalling state of the Soviet economy and its centralized inflexibility forced Khrushchev to attempt a reorganization. Basically, he tried to subordinate the party to the economy, so to speak, by giving priority to economic factors over ideological ones. To no avail. The people he shifted and shuffled were the same old party bureaucrats, and bureaucracy only multiplied as a result of all his desperate efforts to loosen central control of the economy.

Khrushchev was pensioned off as a "voluntarist" who rocked the boat too much, but the problem refused to depart with him. His successors, Kosygin and Brezhnev, divided the functions of state and party leadership between them. Kosygin represented the interests of the government (and, therefore, the need for reforms), while Brezhnev embodied the interests of the party apparatus. However, it soon became clear which of these two sets of interests was the more important. Kosygin's reforms turned out to be modest: all he achieved was to insist that state-run enterprises should be self-sufficient and should bring profits instead of losses. Even this simple economic wisdom was never fully accepted. Kosygin's reforms were largely watered down by his colleagues from the party apparatus and then quietly sabotaged by the middle management of the bureaucracy.

Still, Kosygin's efforts were not entirely in vain: his campaign for reforms generated debates within the Soviet hierarchy, and a barely noticeable split into two trends: "managers" and "ideologists" (the actual terms they used). Certainly, there was no questioning by the managers of Communist ideology or its ultimate goals. Rather, the argument was over how to achieve these goals better and more efficiently. According to Marx, said the managers, economic relations are the essence of history, a material force which moves society, and we are Marxists, are we not? Indeed, we are, replied the ideologists, but Lenin wrote that the "idea which comes to possess the masses becomes a material force," and we are Leninists, are we not?

As this debate proceeded, a number of interesting new industrial experiments were carried out, and these were written up ecstatically in the Soviet newspapers of the 1960's. But this early euphoria evaporated as it became evident that the experiments illustrated all too clearly the superiority of capitalist over socialist methods. Although these capitalist methods would undoubtedly foster more rapid economic growth, the state would no longer maintain its control over economic life. More importantly, party control of the economy would be rendered both superfluous and impossible. As between economic growth and party control, the choice fell on the latter. And with good reason.

There are currently 18 million party members, roughly 6.5 percent of the population, or about 10 percent of its adult part. The ruling elite, the *nomenklatura*, is estimated at between 3 and 5 million, families included. It is impossible to determine how many of them are "ideologists," but whatever they believe in, they stand to lose a great deal, perhaps even everything, from a real diminution of party control. Because it is to the party, not to their skills or talents, that they owe their positions, they would have no chance of remaining on the same level in any other socio-political system (if, indeed, there is such a level of power and privilege under any other system). Besides, many might be held responsible for crimes and corruptions committed in the service of the regime, if this regime were ever to change dramatically (as has happened in China).

For these reasons, the partocrats prefer a longer course of economic decline, a slower way of death, should the worst become inevitable. Dangerous as such a continuous decline of the Soviet economy is, it would mean only a *gradual* defeat of the socialist forces, with the ultimate catastrophe postponed for perhaps fifteen to twenty years. By contrast, radical economic reforms mean for the partocrats an immediate ouster and a loss of status, and without even any guarantee that the cause of socialism can thereby be saved.

On the other hand, the "managers" apparently think that they do not stand to lose anything, except their ideological chains. Being competent specialists, better educated, and more confident, they believe they will remain on the same level (or even higher) in a more competitive society. The top echelon of "managers" in the *nomenklatura* probably hope to become the sole masters of the country once the partocrats are removed.

Somebody has already said of this new class of managers or "meritocrats" that they are "the grave-diggers of Communism." In the long run, perhaps, they may turn out to be just that. But let us have no illusions: these "reformers" are no more eager than the old partocrats to bury Communism. Being specialists, they are willing to run the risk of reforms in order to save the socialist cause. Being younger, they do not want to preside over the downfall of their regime. It is less clear, however, how much they understand of the system's limitations on the one hand or the possible consequences of needed reforms on the other.

A ND Gorbachev? Is he one of them, as many seem to believe? We do not really know, but assuming that he is, he will find himself basically in the same situation Khrushchev did twenty years ago. His reforms will have to be implemented through the same party apparatus whose power they inevitably serve to diminish. And since the General Secretary has no other instrument of control over the country, by reducing the power of the party apparatus he will be reducing his own as well.

During Andropov's brief reign, according to some accounts, "hundreds of persons who held real power either in Moscow or in the provinces were removed. Thousands of middle-echelon officials were replaced or shifted to other duties." The purge continues, but even if Gorbachev places like-minded people in every position of influence in the country, he is bound to discover what Napoleon discovered when he appointed his brother to be the "king" of a conquered country: the brother became a real king in due course, and acted accordingly. Khrushchev made a similar discovery: it was the very people he himself had chosen and promoted who removed him when they felt he had gone too far.

This structural constraint alone makes far-reaching reforms quite impossible. Yet if they do not reach far enough, they will not work. The time when the government could govern, leaving the party to conduct propaganda, is long past. Once revolutionary enthusiasm died, the party had to rely on its exclusive right to promote and to dismiss, to enrich and to impoverish any individual in the country. Now, if people are going to be promoted according to their talents and rewarded according to their performance, who will bother to join the party? And if people are not treated according to their merits, where is the reform?

So far Gorbachev has not unveiled his plan of reorganization. We can only guess its main features from the hints he has dropped in his early speeches. Amid invigorating appeals for better discipline, he emphasizes once again Kosygin's principle of "self-sufficiency," which must be introduced this time "in reality," and he threatens, like Khrushchev, to eliminate many bureaucratic governmental institutions. His constant theme is the need to give more rights and independence to enterprises, to simplify central planning, and to institute a "revolutionary shift" to the latest technology. Thus far the program looks like a fairly minimal adjustment within the system.

But Gorbachev's other ideas are bound to be more controversial. For example, his remedy for agriculture is believed to be the "family-based productive link system" (zveno) which was tested in experiments of the 1960's with spectacular results but was rejected as an attempt to restore capitalism. The question remains whether Gorbachev will actually try to pursue such ideas.

Two variables will largely determine the answer: first, the behavior of the West; second, the behavior of the Soviet population.

If the West, repeating the mistake it made in the 1970's version of détente, provides assistance on a great scale, then the Soviet regime can get away with minimal reforms for another decade before coming to its next major crisis. In other words, the scale of reform will be inversely proportional to the scale of Western economic assistance.

Moreover, if the West goes on protecting and perpetuating the external Soviet empire by recognizing Soviet client-states and providing them with economic help (Central Europe, Mozambique, Angola, and, perhaps soon, Vietnam), then the economic burden of empire will continue to be reduced and the risk of its collapse will be diminished, thus slowing down the drive for more radical changes in the Soviet economy. If, however, the West dissociates itself from these regimes, and instead supports resistance movements, then the pressure to improve the performance of the Soviet economy will increase dramatically. Equally, any slowdown in military competition, or any sweeping arms-control or arms-reduction agreements, will only serve to reduce the need for reforms.

A⁣s FOR the second variable, the possible response of the Soviet people, the question is how far reform must go in order to evoke their enthusiasm. How big must the new incentives be in order to increase productivity to the required level?

One must remember that at least three generations have grown up under the present system, watching the slow destruction of their country, culture, and fellow countrymen. There is hardly a family which has not experienced repression at some point or other. For three generations these people have been obliged to listen to and to repeat the obvious lies of official propaganda and to be cheerful at the same time because it is antisocial not to be cheerful in a socialist paradise. This contradiction between reality and propaganda alone is sufficient to produce profound psychological damage, to say nothing of the ever-present fear, suspicion, and misery.

The current condition of the Soviet people is not simply one of disillusionment, apathy, or resignation. It is a biological exhaustion, a fatigue of human material. The signs of this are high infant mortality, low birthrate (below replacement level among the Russians and some other nationalities), life expectancy of about sixty, and an exceptionally high percentage of children born physically and mentally handicapped (about 6-7 percent by the end of the 1970's, and projected to be 15 percent by the end of the 1990's). The latter is partly due to massive environmental pollution, but it is mainly a product of alcoholism.

Contrary to popular belief, the current epidemic of alcoholism has little to do with traditional Russian drinking habits. Thus a pre-revolutionary Russian encyclopedia indicates that in 1905 about 50 percent of men and 95 percent of women were total abstainers. (For comparison, per-capita consumption was much smaller than in the United States today.) A document smuggled out of the Soviet Union in 1985 shows an enormous increase in alcohol consumption. It asserts that, in 1979, only 0.6 percent of men and 2.4 percent of women were abstainers, and only 5 percent of young people under age eighteen. In 1983, according to this document, there were 40 million "medically certified alcoholics" in the Soviet Union, and the number was estimated as growing to 80 million by the year 2000, which would be 65 percent of the working population.

In addition to these signs of degeneration, there is widespread dissent. This should not be understood in narrowly political terms; it is broader and deeper than that. Professor Zaslavskaya explains it in the "Novosibirsk Document" as follows:

Even with the most rigid regimentation of behavior in the economic sphere, the population is always left with a certain choice of reactions to the governmental restrictions, which it does not necessarily . . . accept. Hence a possibility of overt and covert conflicts between the interests of the groups and of the society. When the established norms and rules affect the vital interests of certain groups of the population, . . . the latter often find a way to shirk the restrictions and to satisfy their demands. When the state takes more strict measures to curb undesirable types of activities, the population responds by finding more subtle patterns of behavior, which will secure satisfaction of its demands in the new conditions, etc. Thus, reciprocally oriented behavior and interactions, of the state on the one hand, . . . and of socioeconomic groups, on the other, represent an important part of the social mechanism of economic development.

Needless to say, the same kind of implicit "dialogue" occurs between the regime and society in all spheres of life, not just in economic relations. In the latter sphere this "dialogue" has led to the development of a black market of many semi-legal activities, and of corruption and theft of public property. In other spheres, it has led to cultural, nationalist, and political dissent.

The black market is everywhere. A general shortage of consumer goods and food, of services and materials, has made it necessary for the people to develop their own system of distribution. The government has tried to fight it tooth and nail (since the early 1960's, a wide variety of these activities is punishable by death), but the system has continued to grow into a huge and intricate network of underground business and industry. Quite often even the party bosses, top governmental executives, and the police have become involved or have been bribed to cover up this activity. Few have been caught.

One can only guess what effect corruption on this scale is having on the top echelon of power. As far as the general population is concerned, however, the effect has clearly been profound. If nothing else, people have become less dependent on official favors and state distribution, while becoming more and more cash-oriented.

To sum up, nearly seventy years of ruthless and unscrupulous Communist rule have destroyed the trust which may have existed originally between the Soviet rulers and the people. The people can hardly expect significant improvements as a result of any within-the-system reforms because the very idea of this system has outlived itself. But even if the system is dismantled, it could take a couple of generations before the people recover completely. Collectivized farmers have to learn how to be peasants, "proletarians" have to learn how to be workers, surviving craftsmen have to teach their skills to new generations.

Surely, Gorbachev cannot count on the millions of "medically certified alcoholics" to sober up suddenly and to become Stakhanovites, even if he pays them five times the present level of wages. If they were capable of sobering up, they would already have joined one or another of the semi-legal businesses existing in the country. Whatever Gorbachev's reforms are going to be, then, they must appeal to those who are interested in working and earning, which means that they must compete in incentives and rewards with the black market.

It is of some interest to note what Gorbachev wants to do with the economy; it is far more interesting to see what the economy will do with Gorbachev as he learns what Lenin discovered sixty-five years before him: that the "marketplace is stronger" than socialism. The best guess is that Gorbachev will choose socialism—which is to say the rule of the party—over the marketplace. Thus he has only three options: He could introduce no changes, and then philosophically watch over the slow disintegration of the empire, the loss of superpower status, and the final collapse of the system, perhaps within fifteen or twenty years. Second, he could adopt a Chinese-type version of Lenin's New Economic Policy (NEP), only to see himself swept away by rising inflation, unemployment, industrial unrest, and disintegration of the party system—and with no real hope of avoiding the final collapse. Third, he could follow the example of Brezhnev in getting the West to bail him out with enough aid and trade to postpone the day of reckoning for several more decades.

In the final analysis, then, it is the West that must choose between the death of Communism in the 20th century and its survival into the 21st.

GORBACHEV, CITING PARTY'S FAILURES, DEMANDS CHANGES

ASKS SECRET VOTES

Philip Taubman

Special to The New York Times

MOSCOW, Jan. 27—Mikhail S. Gorbachev, charging his Communist Party with stagnation and systematic failures, called today for secret balloting and a choice of candidates in the party's elections of its officials.

Mr. Gorbachev, in a six-hour speech in a plenary meeting of the party's Central Committee, also said the leadership was considering giving Soviet voters at large a choice of candidates in general elections to local government bodies.

Hinting at resistance to those and other proposed changes in the Soviet system, Mr. Gorbachev said, "We are often asked whether we are not making too sharp a turn." He sought to assure his audience that he was not leading the country away from the basic principles of Communism.

NEW LAWS PROPOSED

In his speech, Mr. Gorbachev proposed the adoption of new laws to institutionalize some of the changes he has set in motion, including legislation to guarantee open debate and to protect citizens against abuses of power.

Focusing his drive for renewal on the ruling party for the first time, he said that the party was largely responsible for economic and social stagnancy in the 1970's and the early 1980's.

"Conservative sentiments, inertia, a tendency to brush aside everything that did not fit into conventional patterns and an unwillingness to come to grips with outstanding socio-economic questions prevailed in policy-making and practical work," he said.

ALLUSION TO STALIN PERIOD

Alluding to the Stalin period, Mr. Gorbachev said that many problems were rooted in a time when "vigorous debate and creative ideas disappeared from theory and the social sciences while authoritarian evaluations and opinions became unquestioned truths that could only be commented on."

Western diplomats said the speech seemed to mark the beginning of a new phase in Mr. Gorbachev's efforts to consolidate power and revitalize a society that atrophied under the rule of Leonid I. Brezhnev from 1964 to 1982.

If Mr. Gorbachev's efforts are successful, the result is unlikely to resemble what Western societies recognize as democracy.

The Soviet Union would remain under single-party rule. The multi-candidate election slates within the party would still be handpicked by the party. Decisions of lower party bodies could still be overruled by leaders at the next highest level.

But Mr. Gorbachev appears to hope that a dose of what he calls "control from below" may be enough to refresh the party, and make it an engine of change instead of a dead weight.

The Communist Party is an elite minority—about one of every 10 adults is a member—that Lenin envisioned as the guiding force in Soviet society.

Virtually all key posts in government, industry, education, academia and journalism are held by members of the Communist Party.

The party system ranges from the national bodies—the Politburo, which makes policy, and Secretariat, which carries out policy—to party cells in every Soviet institution, factory and farm. The function of all these party entities is to keep an eye on the government bureaucracy.

Mr. Gorbachev today portrayed some party officials at the provincial and local levels as petty tyrants who stifle local initiative, suppress dissent and often succumb to bribery and favoritism.

The essence of his message was that the party, if it intends to lead a changing society, must break free from the stultifying legacy of Stalin and Brezhnev and return to the more dynamic role that Mr. Gorbachev said had been envisioned for it by Lenin.

Although the changes outlined by Mr. Gorbachev would not diminish the unchallenged authority of the Communist Party, diplomats said they might introduce a small element of democracy in a system that has long stifled dissent and free choice.

Under current procedures, party leaders at the local, provincial and national level are handpicked by the national party leaders and are endorsed by party members in a show of hands.

Mr. Gorbachev said multiple candidates and secret balloting should be used in the election of party officials at the local and provincial level and at the level of the various republics that make up the Soviet Union.

VAGUE ABOUT TOP BODIES

Mr. Gorbachev hinted at some unspecified changes in the selection of the membership of the top party bodies—the Politburo and the Secretariat—which have been chosen by the party leadership itself.

"The Politburo's opinion is that further

democratization should also apply to the formation of the central leading bodies of the party," Mr. Gorbachev said without elaborating.

He suggested holding an unusual party conference in 1988, the first such session since 1941, to discuss organizational changes within the party. Normally party programs and top personnel changes are approved during party congresses convened every five years. The party statutes provide for so-called conferences for major decisions between congresses.

Mr. Gorbachev also dealt with policy issues raised by anti-Russian rioting in December in Alma-Ata, the capital of the republic of Kazakhstan. The rioting, with Kazakh nationalist overtones, followed the appointment of an ethnic Russian party leader to lead the nominally Moslem republic.

Saying that there had been other unspecified incidents similar to the Alma-Ata riots, he said:

"One should admit that the errors that were allowed to occur in the sphere of ethnic relations and their manifestations remained in the shadow. Ethnic feelings deserve respect. They should not be ig-nored, but they should not be encouraged either. Let those who like to play on nationalist or chauvinistic prejudices entertain no illusions and expect no loosening up."

Mr. Gorbachev opened his speech with indirect criticism of the Stalin and Brezhnev years. Although he did not name the two leaders, there was no doubt about the targets of his criticism.

"Lenin's ideas of socialism were interpreted simplistically and their theoretical depth and significance were often left emaciated," he said of the Stalin period. "Spurious notions of Communism and various prophecies and abstract views gained currency."

In recent weeks, Soviet television showed a documentary about Lenin that depicted him as an opponent of an all-powerful party apparatus and an advocate of democratic socialism.

INFUSION OF NEW LEADERSHIP

Mr. Gorbachev, in an allusion to the Brezhnev years, said the rapid turnover in the party officials since he took office in early 1985 was required because the "renewal of the composition of the Cen-tral Committee and the Government and their replenishment with new cadres had not been insured for a long time."

Mr. Gorbachev called for a constant infusion of new leadership into the party, but he did not specifically recommend a new retirement policy, as some Soviet officials and Western diplomats had predicted he would.

Complaining about "faceless" literary and artistic works, he said he supported the recent cultural thaw "because we cannot hope to succeed without decisively changing the public mentality and remolding popular psychology, thinking and feelings."

On his policy of greater openness in the discussion of public issues, Mr. Gorbachev said:

"This is a powerful lever for improving work at all levels of our development and an effective form of control by the whole people. Evidently, the time has come to begin elaborating legislation guaranteeing openness."

He also said that legislation was being drafted to give people the right to file complaints in court against "illegal actions of officials, infringing the rights of citizens."

The Soviet Union's Interests: Myths and Reality

Yevgeny M. Primakov

YEVGENY M. PRIMAKOV is director of the Moscow Institute of World Economy and International Relations and a member of the U.S.S.R. Academy of Science. Formerly director of the Moscow Institute of Oriental Studies, a Middle East correspondent for *Pravda*, and a Moscow Radio commentator, he is a graduate of the Moscow Institute of Oriental Studies.

Introduction

I have had long talks with Harold Saunders, an American authority on the Middle East, whom I hold in high esteem, about the Soviet and U.S. interests in the Middle East. I highly value the opinions of my colleague, who for a long time has been involved either directly or indirectly in the formulation and implementation of U.S. policy in the region. Unlike others, he has a realistic view of the Middle East situation. But I cannot fully agree even with him, first of all, about my country's motivation in the Middle East and the goals determining its policy.

The points of view concerning Soviet interests and policy that have currency among U.S. scholars and politicians and that, unfortunately, have become rather deep-rooted and persistent have nothing to do with the real state of affairs. In view of this, an objective analysis of the aims and goals of Soviet Middle East policy seems to be of great importance: without such analysis it would be difficult to avoid miscalculations and mistakes. In addition, it is also all the more important today because the U.S.S.R. and the United States are warily resuming contacts on the Middle East and in this context the correct reading of the interests of the other side is essential.

A Word on Methodology

Before discussing Soviet interests in the region, one should, perhaps, dwell on the methodological aspect. Soviet scholars believe in real, objective interests—interests of a people, a nation—that apply to all countries without exception. But alongside the objective interests there are also other, subjective interests dependent on the nature of the forces in power in a state and its individual policy makers.

It is my conviction that in the Soviet Union the interests of the state coincide with the objective national interests. I am not speaking of the extent to which the policy of the state ensures compliance with these interests in every instance; at any given moment that coincidence depends on many factors affecting the implementation of a policy and, consequently, making it either fruitful or unfruitful. But what matters most is that no clash of objective and subjective interests exists in the U.S.S.R., because there are no pressure groups who can impose their group or personal interests in opposition to the objective interests of the people.

For example, the U.S.S.R.'s policy in the Middle East is not colored by or subjected to the electioneering objectives, the influence of groups or parties possessing large financial and organizational means. In this respect, Soviet society has nothing in common with its American counterpart.

American Notions of Soviet Interests

After this introductory methodological remark, I would like to begin with the Western, especially American, notions regarding Soviet interests in the Middle East. Although it is true that some of these notions are already things of the past, most of them still have currency not only among the learned community but, what is much more important and sometimes dangerous, among those who are directly involved in political decision making in the United States.

Being quite varied, these notions of Soviet interests owe their existence to their authors' adherence to the "mirror approach," that is, the belief that the two countries, each in its own way, defend similar interests in the Middle East. At the same time, many people in

Yevgeny M. Primakov, ''The Soviet Union's Interests: Myths and Reality,'' *AEI Foreign Policy and Defense Review*, Vol. 6, No. 1 (1986), pp. 26-34. Copyright 1986, American Enterprise Institute. Reprinted with permission.

the United States proceed from the concept of the "zero-sum" game: what is profitable to the United States is unprofitable to the U.S.S.R., and vice versa. Certainly, there are both concurrence and divergence of U.S. and Soviet interests. But to define them from the opposite corner, neither the mirror approach nor the zero-sum game is applicable. It is very clearly seen in the complete discrepancy between a number of American notions of the goals of the Soviet Middle East policy and the actual tasks the U.S.S.R. has pursued.

First Notion: The U.S.S.R. allegedly advocates the status quo, the maintenance of the "no war, no peace" situation in the Middle East. In other words, it opposes the settlement of the Middle East conflict. Such conclusions in no way reflect the actual Soviet stand. I shall try to show below why the Soviet Union is interested in quite the contrary—in achieving stability in the Middle East. Such stability is naturally possible only if there is a lasting settlement of the Middle East conflict and in turn only if the interests of all parties to the conflict are taken into account.

Second Notion: It is alleged that the Soviet military presence in Afghanistan is an evidence of the preparation for a Soviet "jump" into the Persian Gulf area. I think that such theoretical constructions have already been refuted by events themselves. In the first place no jump followed the introduction of a limited Soviet armed forces contingent into Afghanistan, although the American press wrote so much about it at the time. What matters is not that from the military point of view the "Afghan springboard" is unnecessary for such a jump. Much more important is that in all the talk about such plans there is not a grain of truth about the real thinking in Moscow. Perhaps it is unnecessary to dwell on this subject in much detail; it may be unnecessary to disprove once again the inventions about the expansionist nature of Soviet policy, aimed allegedly at an "unrestrained advance" toward the warm seas. I will only put a question: how do these pseudointentions comply with the Soviet proposals on the demilitarization and neutralization of the Persian Gulf and the appeal of the Warsaw Treaty countries for a simultaneous application of nonproliferation zones of NATO and Warsaw Treaty activity to other regions, including the Gulf?

Regarding the specific Soviet action vis-à-vis Afghanistan, I would like to emphasize several points: first, it was undertaken in response to a request from a country subjected to outside armed aggression. Second, it was undertaken in a certain international context, when the United States intensified its tough confrontation with the U.S.S.R. Let us remember the 1977 U.S. decision to set up rapid deployment forces; the 1979 NATO decision to increase its members' military budgets substantially and constantly in the future, irrespective of the possible improvements of the international situation; the 1979 NATO decision to deploy medium-range missiles in Western Europe; the permanent basing of the U.S. Navy in the Indian Ocean; and the attempt to play the "Chinese card" against the Soviet Union. Today it is admitted in the United States that the question of the U.S. ratification of SALT II was actually "buried" before the Afghan developments. It was killed when the campaign against the nonexistent "Soviet brigade" in Cuba was launched. All this took place, as I stress, long before the difficult Soviet decision to bring a limited contingent of Soviet troops into Afghanistan—a country with a common border of 2.5 thousand kilometers with the U.S.S.R.

Third, the Soviet action, as was announced at once, was of a temporary nature. A possible solution to the problem lies in the guarantee of the cessation of the intervention of the anti-Afghan forces based in Pakistan and Iran and armed by the United States and some other countries. Such a "package" solution seems to be fully realistic if it is not blocked by the United States (however paradoxical it may seem on the face of it). There are many people in the present U.S. administration who believe that the "containment" of the U.S.S.R. in Afghanistan is an effective way of "wearing it out," and they do everything possible to prevent, for instance, Pakistan from agreeing to a settlement with Afghanistan.

Third Notion: The Soviet Union is allegedly searching for oil, as its own oil resources have been exhausted, and it has to plan for external sources to satisfy the future oil requirements of its economy. Accordingly, the U.S. Central Intelligence Agency prepared reports on the subject, which later were linked with the Afghan events. I remember the sensation caused by the publication of these reports, giving rise to many articles and even monographs in the United States, elaborating the CIA ideas. What has remained of all these conclusions today? Serious American researchers, even those who had supported the CIA ideas at the time, soon made a realistic assessment of the situation and were courageous enough to admit the incompatibility of the arguments contained in the CIA reports with the real state of affairs. (By the way, the CIA researchers themselves soon revised their conclusions on the subject.) Despite their forecasts, the Soviet Union continues to increase its oil production and its prospective oil resources. Further increase is somewhat restrained because more and more oil is extracted in regions of difficult access. This certainly does not mean that the U.S.S.R. is not interested in the purchase of a certain, relatively small, amount of oil. It gets this oil from some Arab countries as payment for its credits, and it would be shortsighted to say that this mutually beneficial form of economic cooperation will not continue to develop.

Fourth Notion: Soviet policy allegedly aims at "warming up the situation" in the Arab countries with monarchic or, in general, conservative (nonradical) regimes. Such a reading of the Soviet political line stems from poor knowledge of its theoretical principles and ignores the practical objectives of the Soviet Union. The U.S.S.R. has always proceeded from the premise that revolutionary situations cannot be exported to other countries and that revolution ripens on the local soil as a result of the development of internal contradictions. As historical experience has shown, attempts to force revolution frequently yield directly opposite results.

Sympathy and support rendered by the Soviet Union to revolutionary forces are another thing. But this happens after these forces are victorious as a result of the objective development of the revolutionary process, not superimposed from outside. Enough has now been said about the theoretical aspects of the matter.

Regarding the "practice" mentioned earlier, the Soviet Union is interested in stability, naturally. It does not seek the pseudostability of the situation, which, as some people in the West believe, can be achieved by preventing socioeconomic and political changes by conservation of the social status quo. Such "stability" is never feasible. It will not be allowed by history itself. Stability cannot be achieved by artificially inflaming a situation in a country. That, as a rule, does not lead to the triumph of truly progressive forces but is fraught with the threat of socially backward, at times dictatorial, regimes and, in addition, creates a pretext for outside intervention.

There are no instances of Soviet intervention in the home affairs of such countries. On the contrary, one may cite instances of an opposite nature. The Soviet Union, for example, was the first state to recognize Saudi Arabia's sovereignty. The positive experience of the mutually advantageous Soviet-Kuwaiti relations is already of twenty years' standing. The same may be said of our relations with Jordan or Morocco.

Fifth Notion: The U.S.S.R. allegedly supports extremist and terrorists forces in the Middle East, another notion without basis in reality. As is known, the Soviet Union on principle has been and is against terrorist acts and terror in general.

The U.S.S.R. fights resolutely against state terror-ism, that is, the policy pursued at the state level against individual countries that strive for independence and refuse to subordinate their interests to those of other states. State terrorism is exemplified by the policy pursued by Israel vis-à-vis Lebanon or the American administration's policy vis-à-vis Nicaragua.

Sixth Notion: The U.S.S.R.'s policy is allegedly to exploit so-called "Islamic fundamentalism." In the 1970s and 1980s, the impact of Islam on the political processes in the Near and Middle East has certainly increased. Soviet scholars proceed from the premise that this impact is relatively stable. But this conclusion is not tantamount to a desire to "play up" this phenomenon, or to a positive attitude toward it. The report of the Central Committee of the Communist Party of the Soviet Union (CPSU) to the twenty-sixth Congress of the party stressed that both the liberation forces and the reaction-raising counter-revolutionary movements may make use of Islamic slogans. Consequently, what matters is the actual content of a given movement. Does this formulation contained in one of the most important Soviet documents resemble argumentation in favor of the exploitation of Islamic fundamentalism? Could the conclusion of Soviet scholars that, depending on the state of class forces, Moslem movements may acquire both positive and extremely reactionary coloring be interpreted as such exploitation?

Soviet Interests

Now I would like to dwell on the Soviet interests in the Middle East. We should, obviously, distinguish between the interests regarded, on the one hand, from the point of view of the global situation and, on the other hand, from the point of view of the regional situation, although the two are connected.

We determine Soviet interests in the Middle East in the global context by our desire for stability and peace in the region. The fact that the United States makes use of a "universal" approach to the issues of its confrontation with the Soviet Union is taken into consideration. The United States prepares, according to U.S. Defense Secretary Caspar Weinberger, for a confrontation simultaneously at the strategic and at the regional levels. It is in this context that one may regard the attempts to prepare a first strike at the U.S.S.R. with the use of both intercontinental ballistic missiles and medium-range missiles. Pershing II and cruise missiles deployed in Western Europe and aimed at centers of control in the European part of the U.S.S.R. gravely threaten the Soviet Union's security. Another place of arms is being established in Japan and South Korea. Ships of the U.S. Seventh Fleet are armed with the Tomahawk cruise missile of 2,500 kilometers range.

We cannot but regard American activity in the Middle East in this light. When a battalion of U.S. marines was brought to Lebanon to impose on it a separate agreement with Israel, the Soviet Union could not avoid noticing that the battalion was equipped with thirty naval units, including two aircraft carriers, a battleship, and 300 battle planes. Such a formation cannot, naturally, be considered only as a "local force" having nothing to do with the strategic level.

Moreover, before that another American battalion had been permanently deployed in the Sinai area under the separate Camp David agreements. It had been noted that the battalion was part of the Eighty-second Air-Borne Division, a task force of rapid deployment troops. According to scenarios published in the United States, the escalation of actions to land these forces at the appointed place looked something like this: first, a battalion of the eighty-second division would land to prepare a beachhead for the landing of the entire division, which would then support the transfer of all other rapid deployment units there. As it happened, the United States "found" no unit to be permanently deployed in the Sinai, in direct proximity to the boundaries of four states—Israel, Saudi Arabia, Jordan, and Egypt—other than a battalion of the notorious eighty-second division!

A similar situation arose in the spring of 1984 regarding the possible U.S. escort of tankers threatened by the Iran-Iraq hostilities in the Gulf. The United States demanded, as a condition, to set up a system of land bases for the permanent deployment of American armed forces, a demand absolutely inappropriate to the suggested action.

The United States carried out these actions in a certain context, allowing the Soviet justification for concluding that the preservation of the existing situation of "no war, no peace" would facilitate U.S. attempts to make its military presence in the region felt and to escalate it. If we add that separate solutions, as experience has shown, do not bring about stabilization of the situation, but on the contrary impair it and make the general settlement more remote, then it becomes clear why the U.S.S.R. is against separate solutions as well as continuation of "no war, no peace" in the Middle East.

Thus a lasting stabilization of the situation in the Middle East is in the Soviet Union's interests. It would not be amiss to point out once more in this connection that the Middle East is a region adjoining the U.S.S.R.'s borders, its so-called "soft underbelly."

But stabilization in the Middle East is impossible without first a just and overall settlement of the Arab-Israeli conflict. It is quite obvious that the elimination of that conflict, as well as the solution to stabilization problems other than an Arab-Israeli settlement, requires time. It is in the interests of the Soviet Union not to allow the Middle East conflict to acquire the character of a direct Soviet-American confrontation in the period necessary to achieve such stabilization or at least to turn in its favor. But this attitude should not be interpreted as a readiness of the Soviet Union to retreat. There is a line the Soviet Union would not allow to be crossed. A retrospective look at the events of 1967 and 1973 in this connection (but not in connection with the falsehoods about the Soviet Union's "readiness" to send its troops to the Middle East) shows that the U.S.S.R. cannot agree to giving Israel an opportunity to threaten the existence of a number of Arab regimes. A similar Soviet response was probable in 1983, when certain Western circles wanted to make Israel deliver a blow at the air defense installations in Syrian territory.

The conclusion is clearly justified that without an overall settlement of the Middle East conflict there will be a constant danger of Soviet-American confrontation there. Therefore, we have much need for mutual restraint. But "rules of conduct," however thoroughly thought over, agreed upon in detail, and linked to specific situations, cannot serve as an alternative to an overall settlement. This should also be emphasized because there is a strong trend in American political sciences to concentrate on the formulation of rules of conduct, which are regarded as a panacea even against a situation threatening war. "Self-restraint" of the great powers being quite essential especially in a crisis situation, the formulation of such rules is fraught with some danger, because they may be taken for the "limits of the permissible." Thus interpreted, which is inevitable, they may even stimulate activity, which in itself would lead to a dangerous aggravation of the situation.

While the interest of the Soviet Union (though initially of a regional nature) in firm relations with the countries of the region is first and foremost political and economic, it is also linked to the global situation. And there again, the Soviet Union is not guided by a "selective approach" determined by the ideological and political proximity of a regime. This proximity is certainly taken into consideration, but it is not absolute and does not prevent the U.S.S.R. from pursuing a policy of expanding relations with all countries of the region.

Such a broad approach is also regarded as an obstacle to U.S. attempts to involve the countries of the region in anti-Soviet plans and actions. The U.S.S.R. cannot ignore the U.S. conclusion of a strategic alliance with Israel, stating outright that it is directed against the Soviet Union. It would be naïve to think that Moscow did not also notice that under the present administration the United States tried unsuccessfully to push some Arab countries into a "strategic consensus" aimed against the U.S.S.R. Largely because of the constructive Soviet stand, U.S. attempts to get access to the Egyptian base at Ras Banas for permanent deployment of its troops in Egyptian territory on the Red Sea shore also failed. This U.S. failure occurred even though Egypt has manifestly become less remote from the United States since the Camp David agreements. In this connection, one may also mention the futile U.S. maneuvering to force Egypt to agree to the return of its ambassador to Tel Aviv as a condition of the return of its ambassador to Moscow. As we know, President Mubarak did not agree to it. One may, finally, recollect that the United States failed to make any country of the Arab Peninsula approach it with the request to escort tankers in the Gulf; the United States insisted on such an official request. All this shows that countries of the Middle East, irrespective of their social and political set-up, are interested in maintaining relations with the Soviet Union and do not want a one-sided orientation to the United States. The Soviet Union, naturally, takes this into account.

All this does not represent any attempt on the part of the Soviet Union to force the United States from the Middle East. The U.S.S.R. never and under no circumstances opposed U.S. participation in the Middle East settlement, which unfortunately cannot be said about the United States. There is no need to quote numerous statements of American leaders to this effect or describe their deeds—they are well known.

Here again we see the flimsiness of the "mirror juxtaposition" of the Soviet and American approaches. The natural absence of any wish on the part of the U.S.S.R. to force the United States from the Middle East is by no means tantamount to its consent to the imperial motives of U.S. policy.

The response of the Soviet Union to the resumption of diplomatic relations between Iraq and the United States is characteristic of the Soviet stand. It was calm, fully refuting forecasts current in the United States that the Iraqi-American normalization might worsen the U.S.S.R.'s relations with Iraq.

A number of Soviet interests in the Middle East may be regarded mainly through the "regional prism." I will mention one of them—the development of objective socioeconomic and political processes in the countries of the region unhindered by obstacles from the outside. The development of these processes has nothing in common with the "pushing up" of a revolutionary situation. I would like to add that permanent instability in the Middle East as a result of the unsettled regional conflict in no way promotes the process of radicalization of political power in the Arab countries.

Ideological sympathies of the Soviet Union for the revolutionary forces and the policy of supporting them are manifested mainly in counteracting external forces that would block the objective liberation process; in other words, the Soviet Union seeks to prevent outside intervention intended to change by force the nature of a regime establishing itself.

Further, one should say that Soviet interests in the region are directly linked to its economic cooperation with the countries of the Middle East. The Soviet Union wants to expand that cooperation to develop its own economy. The Middle Eastern countries provide a market for the expanding engineering industries of the U.S.S.R. The Soviet Union also has an interest in compensatory agreements under which Soviet credits are repaid by the products of enterprises built with Soviet aid.

At the same time, the Soviet Union does not seek any special position that would ensure its oil purchases. As already mentioned, the U.S.S.R. has sufficient energy resources of its own. Oil imports from the Middle East are, however, important because of both the growing oil requirements and the proximity of the Middle Eastern oil sources to consumers in the European part of the U.S.S.R.

The question of arms sales should not, of course, be passed over in silence. The Soviet Union does sell arms to a number of countries of that region in view of their struggle against the expansionism of Israel, which receives the most sophisticated American weapons. But it must be said that several times the Soviet Union has proposed to the United States an agreement to control arms deliveries to the Middle East in the context of the process of an overall political settlement of the Arab-Israeli conflict.

U.S. Objective Interests: A Soviet Perspective

Now we should address American interests in the region viewed from the "Soviet corner." They should be divided into objective national interests, which, I must stress once more, should be recognized, and subjective interests formulated among other things on the basis of internal political struggle and considerations of the moment.

It seems that the U.S. objective interests include:

• stability of the situation in the Middle East, which precludes a real possibility of an armed confrontation with the U.S.S.R.

• neutralization of the region from the point of view of the confrontation with the Soviet Union

• unhindered import of oil to the United States and its allies

• broad relations with the countries of the region, but not as a means of harming similar relations with the U.S.S.R.

• objective development of the socioeconomic and political situation in the countries of the region

The last U.S. interest deserves to be discussed in more detail. There was a time when it was believed in the United States that conservation of traditional relations and corresponding political superstructures in the Arab countries provided a way of strengthening or at least preserving American positions there. This view was convincingly refuted by a number of American specialists. But it seems that their opinion has not yet properly influenced U.S. practice in the Arab world.

Of special significance for the guarantee of American objective interests is the recognition by the United States of the necessity to settle the Palestinian question on a just basis and to give up its essentially unconditional support of Israel, especially when Israel manifested its expansionist course by refusing to accept the exchange offered to it: the return of Arab lands occupied since 1967 for peace with Arab countries.

Of course, the U.S. administration cannot ignore in its home situation the importance of the "Israeli factor," the public opinion of the United States. At the same time, admitting the importance of that factor amounts to admitting the necessity of guaranteeing the existence of the State of Israel. If the United States had not gone beyond this objective, nobody would have spoken against it. From the very beginning the Soviet Union recognized the right of Israel to exist. But the consideration of the Israeli factor in the home situation of the United States cannot justify its assistance and support for the expansionist anti-Arab course of Israel.

It is sometimes asserted in the United States that it cannot influence Israel, that all attempts to do so have yielded opposite results. I cannot agree with that assertion. As we know, practice is a criterion of truth. Only once did the United States use a club—when Israel invaded south Lebanon in 1978, occupying Lebanon's territory up to the Litani River. At that time Israel's action was absolutely against the U.S. interests in view of its policy of implementation of the Camp David agreements. Acting under White House instructions, Brzezinski, then the president's national security adviser, informed Israel that if its forces were not immediately withdrawn from the Lebanese territory, the United States would stop arms deliveries (Brzezinski writes about this in his memoirs). The pressure proved fully effective; after a few hours Israel started to pull its forces out.

Regarding the just settlement of the Palestinian question, without which no settlement in the Middle East is, naturally, feasible, it must ensure the legitimate right of the Palestinian people to self-determination. Today—and I hope that all students of the Middle East, both in the U.S.S.R. and in the United States realize this—it is impossible to reduce the Palestinian problem to the problem of refugees alone. Palestinians have become a historical entity, a people. Consequently, recognizing that fact, one cannot endow that people with the right to only limited self-determination, denying it a possibility to create its own national state.

It is known that the Soviet Union responded unenthusiastically to the Jordanian-Palestinian agreement signed in February 1985 by King Hussein and Yasser Arafat, not considering it to be a step in the right direction. But this response was motivated not by a negative attitude to Jordanian-Palestinian rapprochement, but by the fact that the agreement was silent on two cardinal issues: the creation of a Palestinian national state and the representation of the recognized leader of the Palestinian people, the PLO, in the settlement process. The U.S.S.R., as seen from its proposals regarding the Middle East settlement published on July 29, 1984, does not preclude the formation of a confederation with another state, once the national Palestinian state has been established.

Subjective Definition of U.S. Interests

Objective interests were discussed earlier. But the United States also formulates "interests" that, though far from being objective, serve as the basis for its practical activities in the Middle East.

The subjective interpretation of U.S. interests seems to have played no small role in the "glorification" of separate deals on the Middle East. The United States disavowed almost instantly the joint Soviet-American Declaration on the Middle East of October 1, 1977, which had opened the way for the resumption of the Geneva peace conference. Why? Did the United States act in such an unprecedented manner because it had reassessed the impact of the Joint Declaration on the Middle East situation? No. The reason for the repudiation of the agreement with the U.S.S.R., when the ink in the signatures under the joint document was still wet, lay, on the one hand, in U.S. efforts to exclude the Soviet Union from the solution of the Middle East problem and, on the other hand, in the interests of an influential group in the United States, the so-called Israeli lobby. It is absolutely clear to me that having repudiated the joint Soviet-American document, the U.S. president completely ignored the requirements of the Middle East situation.

The U.S. administration's wish not to harm its relations with Israel even to the smallest extent is visible in the subjectively formulated and interpreted U.S. interests in the Middle East. Its practical line has not infrequently been subjugated to this wish, being far not only from complying with the actual requirements of the political settlement in the Middle East, but also with elementary logic. American attempts to exclude the U.S.S.R. from participation in the process of peaceful settlement in the Middle East may serve as an example. I would certainly not like to explain such attempts wholly by the U.S. desire to please Israel; there are evidently other reasons. Still, the Israeli factor is quite manifest in these motives. Meanwhile, it is absolutely clear that no advance to a just and lasting peace in the Middle East is feasible without Soviet participation. At times, American officials have become aware of and have even spoken about it, though more often such admissions are made before occupying a governmental post or after leaving an office. I remember talks with Brzezinski in 1976, when he was active on Mr. Carter's team, fighting the presidential elections. Brzezinski said at the time that one of Kissinger's mistakes had been his unwillingness to act jointly with the Soviet Union in the Middle East. But as soon as Brzezinski had become the president's national security assistant, he apparently changed his opinion.

In their attempts to isolate and sometimes even to mislead the Soviet Union, some U.S. officials have acted in a cynical way. For example, Kissinger, as seen in his memoirs on negotiating the Geneva conference with the Soviet Union in 1973, wanted only to bring the Arab countries and Israel together and then to pull them apart for separate deals. There seems no need to add that such actions are motivated by the interests of a personal political career and considerations of prestige and have little, if anything, to do with the task of bringing stability to the Middle East.

The Israeli factor also makes itself felt in the approach to U.S. contacts with the Palestine Liberation Organization, although it is clear to all unbiased observers that such contacts and, in the final account, the recognition of the PLO would be in full accord with objective U.S. interests.

Such a U.S. approach is cardinally different from that of the Soviet Union. The U.S.S.R. recognizes Israel and its right to exist, although we oppose the state terrorism of Tel Aviv and, what is more, know that there are persons among Israeli leadership who were and still are involved in terrorist activity. Working for an all-round Middle East settlement, the Soviet Union does not preclude the possibility of contacts with the representatives of Israel's government, even in the absence of diplomatic relations with Israel, which were severed when it committed aggression against Arab states in 1967. During the UN General Assembly sessions former Soviet Foreign Minister Gromyko met Foreign Ministers Eban, Allon, and Shamir.

But let us go back to the U.S. course of separate agreements in the Middle East. President Carter considered the Camp David agreements almost the acme of his foreign policy, and his aides thought that the Egyptian-Israeli treaty would be an offering on the altar of his reelection. But he won no such victory. At the same time, the separate Egyptian-Israeli agreements neither brought about a general settlement, nor were even instrumental in its achievement. The situation in the region has proved to be no more stable, as Lebanon's bleeding wounds have convincingly shown. It may also be added that separate deals ultimately and inevitably create a situation when, in the absence of an overall settlement, another aspect of the Middle East conflict becomes more and more apparent (Harold Saunders and some other American scientists write about it): and if the region goes nuclear, then all dangers threatening the world because of that conflict will immediately multiply.

At times, the concrete formulation of American interests raises the problems under discussion to the rank of "vitally important." In other words, their significance is artificially exaggerated, which, naturally, induces corresponding measures that are absolutely inappropriate. Of the interests so exaggerated, mention may be made, for instance, of defining U.S. oil interests in the Middle East as vital. At present the United States satisfies from 3 to 5 percent of its oil requirements by imports from the Gulf area. As stated earlier, the United States has an interest in the unhindered transportation of that oil, though it is not decisive for the "to be or not to be" of the American economy. By declaring its oil interests in the Gulf area vital, the United States goes far beyond the problem of oil transportation. In fact, the United States desires to preclude any shifts in the entire chain (beginning with the production of oil and determining its price and ending with its sale), which might harm American capital. Let us recollect the nervous response in the United States to the nationalization of oil production in some Arab countries. This nationalization did not result in a stop or even reduction of oil deliveries to the United States or its allies. This U.S. "vital interest," then, was linked not to the desire to ensure normal functioning of the American economy, but to the uneasiness regarding profits of American oil concerns.

As far back as 1974 Kissinger frankly spoke of the feasibility of American armed intervention in the Arab Peninsula in case the oil situation in the region changed against U.S. interests. He had in mind a "hypothetical situation" when oil deliveries would have been stopped.

Conclusion

An unbiased analysis makes it quite clear that there is a large field of concurrence on the objective interests of the Soviet Union and of the United States in the Middle East.

At the same time, the subjective formulation of U.S. interests in the region and the practical line pursued to secure these interests hinder the rapprochement of points of view. In the final account, they make the stabilization of the situation in that region of the world more remote, although this goal is extremely important both for the Soviet Union and for the United States.

American Allies: Western Europe and Japan

The United States faces a constant challenge in its effort to maintain a strong alliance with its allies while protecting its own national interests. On the one hand, the US is viewed by its Western European and Japanese allies as both a staunch supporter and as a major source of concern when they formulate their own policies. On the other hand, the allies have problems arising out of situations in which American interests are not central. In such cases, American interests are likely to be subordinated to their own and may even be in conflict with American interests.

The advance of Europeanism, in short, challenges "Atlanticism" (US dominance in a US-European partnership). Europe's challenge to the US is increasingly regional, rather than national. For example, the European members of NATO are frequently at odds with the US over security issues such as the percentage of national budgets committed to NATO funding, the number of American troops in Europe, and the level of conventional forces in NATO. Similarly, the strength of the European Economic Community (EEC) makes financial and trade concerns more European than national. But, the solidarity of the EEC is now threatened because of the excesses in agricultural production, particularly in France. These excesses, due in part to extensive EEC subsidies to farmers, have resulted in wine lakes, butter and cheese mountains, and so much surplus beef and grain that storage facilities are inadequate. It has been unfortunate for US-European relations that, at just this moment of crisis, the US has responded to domestic interest groups lobbying for protection of their own produce by imposing tariffs on a variety of European agricultural goods, including wine and cheese. The anger and resentment over what the Europeans consider American insensitivity to their problems have combined with the mistrust of the US created by its duplicitous dealings in the Middle East in the Iran-Contra scandal to create new problems in the Atlantic Alliance in 1987.

A regional challenge is not yet evident in US-Asian relations. Here, the United States is facing the economic challenges of a number of governments, each acting independently of the others: Japan, South Korea, Taiwan, Hong Kong, and Singapore. But for the time being, Japan still captures most of the headlines concerned with the economic power of East Asia. Some view Japan's aggressive economic performance as a nationalistic threat. Because the issues are so diffuse, trade issues spill over into security issues. Therefore, the US suffers a balance of payments deficit in its trade with Japan, in the view of many Americans, because the Japanese do not pay their share of their own defense bill, because of Japanese protectionism, and because of nefarious Japanese business practices.

Since the US-Japan relationship is bilateral, it lends itself to emotional manipulation, with conclusions emanating from nationalistic sentiments rather than facts. Little attention is paid to such facts as US domination of the Japanese food import sector, US protectionist policies for its own weak industries, the superiority of Japanese goods and of Japanese marketing strategies, or the extra effort that the Japanese make—and which the Americans are unwilling to make—to develop international markets. Often overlooked is the role that Japanese culture plays. Much of Japan's success can and should be attributed to Japanese cultural traits such as honesty, diligence, loyalty, the importance of the group, and, most of all, the emphasis on quality and efficiency. In short, just because the Japanese are outperforming the Americans does not mean they are doing something illegal or immoral.

Still, Japan clearly must do something about its international image if it wishes to find itself welcome in international circles. It is, after all, not just the United States or the industrial economies of Europe which are angry about Japanese economic aggressiveness. Countries in the developing world, notably the former Japanese-occupied countries of Southeast Asia, are also alienated by Japanese business practices. In 1985, student demonstrations erupted in several Chinese cities in protest against the massive influx of Japanese consumer goods at the expense of the development of China's consumer goods and high-tech industries (and jobs). The Chinese government, which oversees a still largely state-controlled economy, knowingly gambled that Japan would gain a strong economic position, in the belief that Japanese investment and technology transfer would be worth the risk. Japan can hardly be blamed for making the most of every business opportunity available in China, but, in merely doing what they do best, Japan may turn China into an adversary rather than a friend.

The Sino-Japanese relationship is illustrative of issues in which US interests are peripheral to Japan's central concerns. Like the Europeans, the Japanese relationship with the US on foreign policy formulation is consultative, not dependent. A combination of their own enhanced power, ceaseless American prodding to develop greater defense capabilities, and a recent history of US foreign policy decisions seemingly taken without concern for their impact on Japan, has spurred Japan's independent stance. This is exemplified in the Japanese defense budget.

Although Japanese politicians must respond to American pressures to increase defense expenditures, they must also respond to internal pacifist sentiments. Thus, while the US strategic partnership is central to Japan's defense, all the extraordinary pressures put on Japan by the US since 1947 only succeeded a full forty years later in moving the Japanese to spend a tiny fraction more than one percent of their GNP for defense.

Nevertheless, the Japanese cannot take an isolationist

stance and formulate policies without consulting allies. Japan is far too integrated into the international economic and financial system to allow for such unilateralism. Thus, under pressure from its trading partners since the latter half of 1985, the Japanese have slowly pushed the yen up to higher levels vis-à-vis other hard currencies to decrease the competitive edge of Japanese goods in the marketplace. They have opened up corporate markets to foreign investments; shown an increasing willingness to expose their telecommunications and high-tech sector to competition from the outside; agreed to further "voluntary restraints" on exports to the US in the areas of machine tools and automobiles; and pushed interest rates down to stimulate economic growth. In short, Japan clearly wants to be a well-integrated, well-liked member of the international community, and to rid itself of the image of an "economic animal."

The articles which follow address many of the aforementioned issues in US relations with its allies in Western Europe and Japan. In the case of Western Europe, it is evident that geopolitics play an important role in how Europeans approach potentially conflictual issues with the Soviet Union. The Europeans are worried about the Strategic Defense Initiative, for example, because it might heighten the tensions between the Soviet Union and members of the NATO Alliance (Article 13).

What role NATO members should play beyond the European theater is another source of concern for the Europeans, who feel pressured by the US to support its military actions outside the NATO framework. Although the Federal Republic of Germany's Chancellor believes NATO must coordinate its efforts to address the Soviet challenge beyond Europe (Article 15), Germany legally cannot, and would not really want to, use its forces outside of German territory. Greece, on the other hand, criticizes NATO for being concerned only with the Soviet threat, and with ignoring such threats as those presented by Turkey (Article 16). Britain is likewise concerned about problems other than the East-West concerns of NATO, and urges NATO members, at a minimum, to consult about problems outside the Treaty area (Article 17). America's exasperation with the limited willingness of NATO members to help it address more than European regional issues has led to mounting pressure for a unilateral US withdrawal of its NATO ground forces from Europe so that the US could increase its funding of American capabilities in the Third World (Article 14). On the other hand, the US cannot help but be pleased that Euro-Communism is on the wane, thereby diminishing any prospect that the Soviet Union could gain more influence and control in Western Europe through parliamentary means (Article 18).

As for Japan, there is evidence of increasing sensitivity on the part of the Japanese to the US concerns about their willingness to take greater responsibility for their own defense. Prime Minister Nakasone has minimally exceeded the earlier defense spending ceiling of one percent of the GNP, thus addressing both US demands for greater Japanese contributions to their own defense and Japanese concerns that their country not continue its extreme dependence on the US. On the other hand, the Japanese must, like the Germans, be careful not to build up too powerful a military out of fear of upsetting their Asian neighbors, the former victims of Japanese military aggression (Article 21). Finally, Japan has also become more sensitive to the concerns of the broader international community, which perceives Japan as economically aggressive. Concern about Japan's increasing isolation from the international community has led some Japanese to call upon their government to internationalize its relations with other states. (Article 20).

Looking Ahead: Challenge Questions

What are the kinds of issues which still inhibit European unity? Are these insoluble problems for the immediate future? What role might a powerful charismatic European leader of the European Parliament play in integrating Europe on noneconomic issues? Is the resolution of economic issues the basic building block for resolving political issues, or must political issues be addressed first? What effect might greater European unity have on the NATO alliance?

Is Japan's relationship with the United States and Western Europe moving in a positive direction? Are the Japanese becoming more integrated with the Western world? Does it appear that Japan is more interested in being considered the leader of the Asian world, or a partner of the Western world? What measures could Japan take to improve its standing with its trading partners that would not at the same time damage the Japanese economy? If Japan's trading partners create protectionist barriers against Japanese imports, causing a contraction of the Japanese economy, what would be the effect on the international trading system and the international economy? Rather than looking to Japan to find the solutions to the balance of payments deficits in Japan's trade with Western European countries and the US, what might those countries themselves do to improve their trade positions? To what extent does the United States really want to press Japan to rearm? How valid is the view that Japan's trade advantage is the result of its small defense budget?

The United States and West Europe: An Age of Ambivalence

This reviews United States-West European relations since the early 1980's. Disagreements during this period "led some Western observers to wonder whether the North Atlantic alliance had become obsolete. . . . [But] mutual interests in peace, security and economic progress were sufficiently clear to support the proposition that institutionalized cooperation was still preferable to unbridled national action."

NORMAN A. GRAEBNER

Norman A. Graebner has written and edited some 20 books, including two recently published volumes of essays. His latest book is *The National Security: Its Theory and Practice, 1945–1960* (New York: Oxford University Press, 1986).

THE destruction of the European equilibrium in World War II created a new and promising relationship between the United States and the countries of West Europe. The Soviet Union's emergence as the continent's superpower—the first such superpower since Napoleon—demolished any remaining imperial ambitions held by Britain, France, Germany and Italy and forced them to rely on the United States. In the resulting military-economic arrangements, formalized by the Truman Doctrine, the Marshall Plan, and the formation of the North Atlantic Treaty Organization (NATO), the United States became the senior partner.

Geography and history preserved a variety of individual national purposes among the European states, but the realities of economic dislocation, political instability and international insecurity—all creatures of the recent war—were so overwhelming that the newly established trans-Atlantic ties became essential. Whatever the ultimate success of European recovery, the continued presence of the Soviet antagonist in the East would sustain the trans-Atlantic connection and the American commitment to Europe's defense. After NATO's creation in 1949, Soviet policy, with good reason, tried to weaken Europe's ties to America, while United States policy tried to maintain European confidence in American power, reliability and peaceful intentions.

By midcentury, the unity of purpose between America and Europe that underwrote their alliance was marked by divergent views toward every aspect of a changing world. Europeans rejected overwhelmingly the exaggerated fears of the Soviet Union that dominated the official American outlook as early as Harry Truman's presidency. They also rejected the American propensity to see the Kremlin's hand in every third world upheaval and challenged Washington's conviction that the security interests of the United States were global.

As long as Europe's major concerns remained economic reconstruction and discouragement of any Soviet attack on West Europe, its leaders and analysts accepted America's burgeoning involvements in Asia and elsewhere as the price of United States economic cooperation and strategic support. But with the return of West Europe's prosperity in the 1950's and the corresponding increase in European confidence, the mounting arms race and persistent tensions in United States–Soviet relations began to open strains in America's relations with its European allies. After the early 1970's, European officials and writers questioned a wide spectrum of American policies toward Europe and the world as unnecessarily fear-ridden, overdemanding and tension-producing. Many West Europeans, enjoying perennial peace with no apparent danger, viewed the trans-Atlantic relationship as only an expression of American interest, and held the United States responsible for whatever strains existed in that relationship under the assumption that they owed far less to the alliance than the alliance owed to them.

Despite 35 years of successful containment, Europeans and Americans in positions of command have

From *Current History*, November 1986, pp. 353-356, 387-389. Copyright 1986, Current History, Inc. Reprinted by permission.

never resolved the military dilemmas inherent in alliance strategy. For many the reliance on the American nuclear arsenal remains potentially disastrous. Throughout history, governments have justified war as an instrument of national policy only when the price of capitulation or defeat seemed less acceptable than the costs of resistance. Under what circumstances would nuclear extermination cost less than the avoidance of nuclear war? What military or political consequences could be less attractive than nuclear annihilation? Those who favor a reduction of nuclear forces (if not their total elimination) have failed to offer an alternative strategy, despite the horrors of nuclear war. In the absence of any financially acceptable alternative, Europeans no less than Americans entrust the future of Europe to the assumption that nuclear weapons create their own effective deterrents.

In any crisis, Europeans acknowledge reluctantly, NATO's nuclear strategy would place West Europe completely under the decision-making power of the United States. Beyond the discouragement of Soviet aggression against Europe—a danger that Europeans regard as remote—the whole European defense effort is of little use. West European governments have tended to avoid commitments outside Europe that would require the employment of force.

What troubled some European leaders during the 1970's was the vast increase in Soviet power that appeared to give the Kremlin new military options. In 1977, West German Chancellor Helmut Schmidt noted West Europe's added vulnerability because of new Soviet missiles, the mobile SS-20's with three warheads each, capable of reaching all West European targets, including those in Britain. Schmidt warned the NATO partners that the Soviet Union had "upset the military balance in Europe and created for itself an instrument of political pressure on the countries within the range of the SS-20, for which the West so far has no counterbalance." In December, 1979, NATO voted to deploy in Europe 108 United States Pershing 2 and 464 cruise missiles to offset the Soviet SS-20's and thereby to create an effective theater nuclear force in Europe. The decision to place more weapons in Europe did not necessarily make the threat of European suicide more convincing. If Europe required a deterrent to offset the SS-20's, that deterrent, some Europeans argued, need not be located in Europe.

Europeans agreed overwhelmingly that the long-range American nuclear arsenal was adequate for the protection of Europe. For that reason, they thought that President Ronald Reagan's massive pursuit of military superiority after January, 1981, was unnecessary, destabilizing and dangerous. To Europeans it made considerable difference whether the Reagan rearmament program was the beginning of a new crusade against the Soviet Union or an end in itself. What

troubled them especially was the flow of official statements that indicated Washington's intention to face the Soviets down with superior power everywhere from Central America to the Middle East. European analysts questioned the assumption that additional military might would make the administration's anti-Soviet posture more effective. Chancellor Schmidt warned the Reagan administration that its effort to regain nuclear superiority would merely inaugurate a new arms race. Europeans found President Reagan's decision of August, 1981, to assemble and stockpile neutron weapons disquieting; such weapons could only be destined for a European theater of war.

Throughout the autumn of 1981, massive demonstrations in Europe condemned the deployment of United States nuclear arms to offset the Soviet SS-20's. Neither European nor American observers could agree on the meaning of these demonstrations. Some regarded them as evidence of a growing European neutralism and pacifism; some viewed them as a passing phenomenon, encouraged by Communist propaganda. Despite huge demonstrations in Hamburg, Bonn, London and Paris, and the hesitancy of Belgium and the Netherlands, in March, 1982, the NATO defense ministers reaffirmed the plan to deploy the United States cruise and Pershing 2 missiles in Europe, beginning in 1983, with the proviso that Washington commence arms talks with Moscow. Schmidt favored the emplacement of theater weapons if the arms talks stalled but, he argued, there "might have been fewer demonstrations in Europe if there had been less loose talk out of the United States, telling the Europeans we were not living in a postwar period but in a prewar period. That had a psychologically devastating effect."

President Reagan's first major arms control initiative—his proposal of November, 1981, for eliminating United States and Soviet medium-range missiles from Europe—demonstrated his recognition of the rising anti-Americanism and neutralism in West Europe. If the allies occasionally shared the administration's sense of outrage at Soviet behavior, they understood that tough language, large increases in defense spending and symbolic sanctions would irritate Kremlin leaders without intimidating them or compelling them to conform to Washington's designs. By the spring of 1982, the Reagan administration, urged on by Secretary of State Alexander Haig Jr., began to display some moderation toward the Soviet Union. In May, Haig delivered a conciliatory speech before the United States Chamber of Commerce, stressing the need for political dialogue with Moscow. And the President announced that Soviet behavior was no longer an obstacle to negotiations. Thereafter the Reagan administration opened negotiations with Soviet leaders on both long-range and medium-range missiles.

Europeans were troubled less by President Reagan's huge military program than by his administration's outspoken animosity toward the Soviet Union. Unable to govern United States–Soviet relations, Europeans lauded every change in policy or attitude that reduced East–West tensions across Europe. By 1978, much to Europe's dismay, Washington had dismissed the détente established by Presidents Richard Nixon and Jimmy Carter because détente had failed to control Soviet behavior in Africa and the Middle East.

Whatever cordiality had once existed in American–Soviet relations evaporated completely with the Soviet invasion of Afghanistan in late December, 1979. President Reagan and his team caught the new anti-Soviet crusade at high tide. At his confirmation hearings in early January, 1981, Alexander Haig reminded members of the Senate Foreign Relations Committee that "the years immediately ahead will be unusually dangerous. Evidence of that danger is everywhere." President Reagan himself declared at the White House in February that Soviet leaders were ready "to commit any crime, to lie [and] to cheat" in their headlong quest for world domination. The new administration's tough anti-Soviet stance assumed the death of détente or, at the least, Soviet disinterest in it.

For West Europe, détente remained essential to its prosperity and peace of mind. Chancellor Schmidt made that clear in an interview with *The Economist* (London) in October, 1979: "One of the necessities for the alliance as well as for Germans is to get along with the eastern power. We don't want to get back into the cold war." West Europeans did not share the American concern for Afghanistan that prompted President Carter to announce his Carter Doctrine for the American defense of southwest Asia. *Die Zeit* (Hamburg) expressed Europe's detachment from the crisis: "Europe must not become a zone of tension if tension prevails in other regions. . . . The West cannot win in Berlin the battle that it lost in Afghanistan." Europeans argued that détente was divisible, that any settlement was better than none and should be pursued regardless of Soviet behavior elsewhere.

Europeans simply expected less of détente. They saw little danger to their security in Soviet policies that troubled the more globally oriented United States. They denied that the Soviet Union had gained more than the West from détente. For them, the years of relaxation had demonstrated the bankruptcy of the Soviet system and the unreliability of the Soviet Union's East European allies. Europeans did not regard the Soviet Union as a benign presence; but they overwhelmingly rejected the American fears that "the Russians are coming." They saw no need of any confrontation with the Soviet world. Moreover, they thought that the Soviet Union was so beset with internal and external problems—Poland, Afghanistan, food shortages and other domestic troubles—that it desperately wanted better relations with Europe.

Early in the cold war, Europeans accepted their vulnerability to Soviet attack as the price of existing at the center of the East–West confrontation. Western strategy assumed that the next war would be fought in Europe, and the Europeans accepted that assumption, knowing that the major cold war issues were European and that West Europe itself would be the primary objective of any war. By the 1970's, however, many Europeans no longer regarded Europe as the center of the cold war. For them it was not self-evident that West Europe need suffer disaster because of the perennial failure of Washington and Moscow to settle their differences or terminate their global confrontations in regions and over issues that concerned most Europeans remotely, if at all.

To protect Europe from a Soviet–American war begun elsewhere, French President Charles de Gaulle repeatedly demanded that Britain and France have some voice in determining United States policies outside Europe. "If there is no agreement among the principal members of the Atlantic Alliance on matters other than Europe," he asked, "how can the Alliance be indefinitely maintained in Europe?"

United States officials had long attributed all Communist-led assaults on the status quo to the existence of a Kremlin-based monolith. Detecting no limits to Soviet aggressiveness, they tended to view any Soviet–Communist aggression, as in Korea or Afghanistan, as a prelude to a generalized use of force. Europeans rejected such notions of global danger. They challenged the Reagan administration's initial assumption that Soviet expansionism was the universal source of turmoil. The Reagan view of Central America was especially disturbing to West Europeans because it directly challenged their own perceptions of third world revolutions and change. Many Europeans questioned President Reagan's decision to convert El Salvador into a major arena of Soviet–American confrontation and his attempt to influence the Salvadoran civil war with aid, advisers and military equipment.

In criticizing the American role, *Il Messaggero* (Rome) warned in February, 1982: "It is probably the best way . . . to repeat the strategic error made twenty years ago with Castro and to revive the domino theory already experienced in Vietnam." In April, editor André Fontaine of Paris's *Le Monde* observed that "President Reagan still sees in any third world crisis the hand of the Soviet Union. From here that appears ridiculous. You don't need Russians to create situations like Nicaragua and El Salvador." Europeans (and many Americans) regarded the issues of Central America as regional rather than global, indigenous rather than external.

President Reagan's extended crusade against the Sandinista government of Nicaragua received no support in Europe. Europeans rejected his admonition, directed largely at Congress and the American people, that Nicaragua had become a beachhead of Soviet penetration of the Western Hemisphere. Europeans looked askance at the President's long, divisive effort to wrest $100 million in military aid from Congress for the anti-Sandinista rebels. At the Bonn economic summit of May, 1985, the Europeans rejected President Reagan's plea for support of his trade embargo against Nicaragua. British Foreign Minister Sir Geoffrey Howe warned that an embargo would push the Sandinista government more completely into the Soviet–Cuban camp. German Foreign Minister Hans-Dietrich Genscher reminded the President that Europeans did not believe in trade sanctions to achieve political ends. So bitter was the Spanish reaction to American policy in Nicaragua that the President faced massive anti-American demonstrations when he visited Madrid after the Bonn summit.

Several days later, the European Economic Community (EEC), under the prodding of Claude Cheysson, former French foreign minister, doubled its aid to Central America, including Nicaragua, in deliberate defiance of the American embargo. Europe's rejection of American policy in Nicaragua became even more complete when the World Court, in June, 1986, denounced the United States for backing Nicaragua's anti-Sandinista rebels and violating the United Nations charter.

IN PURSUIT OF ARMS CONTROL

West Europe adopted a dual-track program that would deploy the American-made Pershing 2 and cruise missiles to offset the Russian SS-20's if every effort to eliminate such weapons from Europe failed. When the intermediate-range nuclear force (INF) talks in Geneva produced no agreement, the major European governments, having calmed their domestic debates and diffused their antinuclear crusades, began to accept the new medium-range missiles in late 1983. Thereupon the Soviet delegates walked out of the Geneva talks. In the absence of any agreement, the number of missiles in Europe began to mount.

United States Secretary of Defense Caspar Weinberger informed NATO defense ministers in December, 1984, that the Soviet Union had built 387 SS-20's with 1,161 warheads. Clearly the planned deployment of 108 Pershing 2's and 464 cruise missiles did not approach the Soviet defense levels. Soviet leaders pointed to the remarkable accuracy and speed of the Pershings as well as the British and French nuclear arsenals. Only some agreement could stop the acceleration of the nuclear arms race across Europe.

During the autumn of 1984, European observers detected a changed mood in Washington as President Reagan, responding to the pressures of his reelection campaign, reassured the voters that he was indeed a man of peace. In a speech before the United Nations on October 24, the President promised that he would

seek an arms limitation offer from the Soviet Union. That month, Soviet Foreign Minister Andrei Gromyko visited the White House to renew an attempt to improve East–West relations. Europeans hoped that the President would concentrate on foreign affairs in his second term. After four years of American military expansion they believed it was time to negotiate some agreements on arms control.

What troubled European analysts as they contemplated renewed United States–Soviet negotiations was President Reagan's unshakable devotion to his Strategic Defense Initiative (SDI), popularly known as Star Wars, an expensive program to perfect a space-based antinuclear missile shield. With wide support in the American defense community, the President announced early that he would withhold SDI from any arms negotiations. The Soviet Union, demonstrating its profound respect for American science and technology, made it clear that it would accept no agreement on arms control that did not include SDI. During December, Secretary of State George Shultz, accompanied by his arms control adviser, Paul Nitze, left for London, Brussels and Bonn to ease Europe's concern regarding SDI. The United States, he said, would not permit the search for an effective defense against nuclear attack to become a substitute for arms control negotiations.

Secretary Shultz's lengthy talks with Gromyko in Geneva on January 7–8, 1985, did not guarantee any future agreements, but they committed both powers to strive for greater cooperation. The Shultz–Gromyko formula included a comprehensive three-talk process, one for long-range missiles and bombers, one for mid-range missiles, and one for space and defensive weapons. Europeans, like Americans, hoped that the forthcoming arms talks would lead to significant accords on other East–West issues as well.

After a lapse of 15 months, the Geneva arms talks opened in March. The barriers to agreement were considerable: the deep disagreement over Star Wars, the growing complexities emanating from new technologies, the fragile restraints of existing arms treaties, and the lingering distrust of the Soviet Union shared by many of President Reagan's chief advisers. Observers predicted that the administration would never see merit in any Soviet proposal unless the President imposed his own views—assumed to favor agreement—on the civilians who opposed any concessions. Defense Department officials complained that Moscow's interpretation of the second strategic arms limitation treaty (SALT 2), President Jimmy Carter's unratified arms agreement, had become so loose that it amounted to outright violations.

Reagan officials were surprisingly ineffective in addressing the mounting concerns of the European allies on SDI. Britain's Prime Minister Margaret Thatcher endorsed the Star Wars research program during her visit to Washington in February, 1985. But leading European experts and many American scientists predicted that SDI would never produce results commensurate with its promise and its cost. To gain support in Europe, American officials suggested early that European firms would be permitted to compete in the bidding for specific defense projects. In March, 1985, Weinberger gave the European governments 60 days to decide whether they wanted to enter a technological partnership with the United States.

The immediate reaction was cool. In London, Foreign Secretary Howe expressed his government's skepticism, saying that SDI reflected a Maginot Line mentality. West Germany's Genscher argued that SDI would damage the strategic unity of the alliance and would undermine the arrangements that had served Europe so well. Eventually the Thatcher government in London signed an agreement on SDI research. In March, 1985, Chancellor Helmut Kohl of West Germany announced that his government had reached an agreement permitting West German participation in Star Wars research. Opposition leaders in both London and Bonn accused Thatcher and Kohl of subservience to the United States.

During the late summer and autumn of 1985 Europe's attention shifted from the stalemate on arms control to the forthcoming summit scheduled for Geneva in November. What fascinated Europeans and Americans alike, in addition to the effort being made by Washington and Moscow to narrow the gap on arms control, were the personalities of the two leaders and the promise of a remarkable spectacle. Mikhail S. Gorbachev, the new Soviet General Secretary, marched toward the summit amid televised press conferences, ubiquitous meetings with world leaders, a successful visit to Paris, and claims that he had initiated the Soviet–American exchanges on arms proposals. Even as American officials declared the Soviet proposals old and unacceptable, they acknowledged Gorbachev's success in establishing the Soviet position as moderate and reasonable. Refusing to budge on SDI, President Reagan tried to put Gorbachev on the defensive by adding regional conflicts to the summit agenda.

Despite the maneuvering, the propaganda and the struggle for advantage, the European press predicted smiles but meager results. London's *Daily Telegraph* anticipated a change in style, but not in substance. Warning against overexpectation, *Die Zeit* declared that Reagan and Gorbachev could not build an enduring bridge in two or three days. The summit itself, the first in six years, was fundamentally a media event, with both sides striving for a propaganda advantage while the issues became lost in imagery. Experience had taught that summits were not good for conducting business. The two leaders agreed to nothing except to meet again in 1986 and 1987. "And

because President Reagan," asserted Ian Davidson in London's *Financial Times,* "seems determined not to give the Soviets the one thing they want most, the explicit ban on Star Wars deployment, . . . the joint declaration that their negotiations will do better in the future seems based on a dose of illusion."

Back in Washington, President Reagan received a Defense Department report documenting Soviet cheating on the 1972 Anti-Ballistic Missile (ABM) and SALT 2 treaties. On December 31, 1986, the unratified SALT treaty would expire. Whatever the state of Soviet compliance, Europeans opposed any formal dismissal of the treaty as a guide for American defense policy. Despite Europe's known preferences, in late May, 1986, the President announced that the United States would no longer be bound by the SALT 2 formula and would violate its central provisions before the end of the year unless the Kremlin changed its behavior. In giving the Soviet Union time to reconsider, the President announced in June that he would dismantle two Poseidon nuclear submarines to keep within the confines of SALT 2.

Europe's reaction to the Reagan threat was bitter. "It's a disaster," fumed Helmut Kohl. Some Europeans thought the atmosphere was more dangerous than at any time since World War II. *The Economist* reported that half the Britons polled distrusted the President's judgment and believed the United States no less a threat to peace than the Soviet Union.

In Washington, even while they argued that the President was justified in his response to Soviet cheating, officials admitted that the administration had failed to anticipate the European reaction. Gorbachev, recognizing Europe's nuclear anxiety, filled the air with new arms proposals while Defense Department officials, reading the fine print, rejected them. European leaders—Thatcher, French President François Mitterrand and Kohl—could see no danger in responding positively to Russian overtures. They favored negotiations, finding hope in the assumption that President Reagan, unlike some of his advisers, favored an arms agreement as the one means available to overcome the legacies of huge federal debts and trade deficits that he could no longer reverse.

Ultimately, Europe's dissatisfaction with the Reagan administration centered on its economic policies. Throughout the 1980's, Europe lagged behind the United States and East Asia in job creation and technological progress. Unemployment reached 18 million by 1984 and threatened to rise even higher. Helmut Schmidt attributed the structural economic problems facing both Europe and the United States to America's fiscal disarray, caused by inadequate taxes, a grossly inflated military budget, and huge federal deficits that required massive borrowing, much of it from West Europe and Japan.

High interest rates, the product of overborrowing,

sustained an overvalued dollar that curtailed critical American exports, producing unprecedented trade deficits and a dangerous protectionist crusade. High interest rates magnified the financial burdens of third world countries, threatened the American banking structure with disaster, and deprived Europe of the investment capital it required to transform its industrial base. Europeans were troubled especially by the Reagan defense program, which consumed dollars by the hundreds of billions and exceeded what they regarded as essential for European and American security.

A RECOVERY PROGRAM

Shortly before the Bonn economic summit of May, 1985, Secretary Shultz prescribed his own recovery program for Europe. Protectionist trade barriers, he warned, would damage business in general without conferring any lasting benefits even on those sectors of the economy endangered by imports. He observed, second, that the dollar could not be cheapened or stabilized by government interventions in the world currency markets. With this argument, Shultz confronted leaders of the European Economic Community, who argued that trade barriers could be eliminated only if the trading nations engaged in negotiations aimed specifically at monetary reform. Third, Shultz urged joint action by Europe, Japan and the United States to sustain economic growth as the surest guarantee against protectionism and depression. Rather than relying on exports to the United States to sustain their economies, Europe and Japan should encourage spending inside their countries.

At Bonn, President Reagan promised to encourage economic growth by reducing the American budget deficit. At the same time, he pressed West Germany and Britain especially to accept larger deficits of their own to fuel economic growth as the United States had done in previous years. Europe's spokesmen at Bonn agreed on the need to create prosperity and jobs by encouraging new business, but they rejected outright the plea that they copy America's recovery by running up colossal deficits and covering them with foreign investments—an escape from immediate disaster available only to the United States. West Germany was afraid that any move to stimulate its domestic economy would ignite inflation, although American officials believed that West Germany had not fully exploited its growth potential.

Shultz's preachments against protectionism faced opposition in both Europe and the United States. Troubled by the growing American trade deficits, in late 1984 the Reagan administration closed the American market to European steel pipes. Earlier, it had restricted imports of European specialty and bulk steel. Next, the administration threatened Europe with retaliation against its agricultural subsidies. The American share of Europe's agricultural imports had fallen from 26 percent in 1974 to 20 percent in 1983, while the Europeans successfully maintained their agricultural competitiveness in other markets. By 1984, the United States had run up huge trade deficits in the Common Market countries. Without some price adjustment in Europe, any phasing out of American agricultural subsidies would deprive American producers of their remaining European markets. At Bonn, Mitterrand blamed the trade imbalances on fluctuating currency exchange rates and demanded negotiations to establish fixed exchange rates. At the same time the French leader moved to protect French agriculture from foreign competition through new trade arrangements. Kohl, Thatcher and Reagan warned Mitterrand that protectionism for French farmers would unleash protectionist demands around the world.

By the spring of 1986, Europe and the United States were approaching a trade war. The crisis began when Spain and Portugal, both new members of the European Economic Community, decided to tax farm imports, especially American grains and oil seeds, to raise prices to European levels. When the EEC failed to provide compensation for America's predicted losses of $1 billion, President Reagan announced United States import quotas and tariff increases on European goods. The EEC responded by threatening import restrictions in retaliation against the United States. Washington rejected EEC advice to seek compensation under the international General Agreement on Tariffs and Trade (GATT).

Again Europeans complained that the United States used GATT when it sought general agreements on trade and tariffs but ignored GATT when it believed it could obtain better arrangements through bilateral negotiations. Long before the Tokyo economic summit of June, 1986, France had pressed members of the EEC to retaliate against the Reagan trade policies. The trend toward protectionism on both sides of the Atlantic resurrected memories of the 1930's. And the trans-Atlantic disagreements over fiscal and trade policies threatened to become more pervasive with the passage of time.

Disagreements of such magnitude, whether over questions of security or trade, led some Western observers to wonder whether the North Atlantic alliance had become obsolete. Economic disagreements, unfortunately, were more intransigent because they touched the quality of life for countless individuals. Whatever the strains within NATO, however, mutual interests in peace, security and economic progress were sufficiently clear to support the proposition that institutionalized cooperation was still preferable to unbridled national action. What divided Western leaders on security issues was not their conflicting national interests but their differing perceptions of danger, both in Europe and in the third world, and their differing notions of what constituted a reasonable decision when measured by its possible effect on regional security.

Some Western leaders thought that Soviet ambition eliminated the possibility of successful coexistence and required the elimination of the Soviet system. Others believed that the West could accept the existing international order as the basis of policy. Those who shared a pessimistic view of the world were a small minority whose influence, in the United States and elsewhere, vastly exceeded their numbers. What characterized the outlook of the Western world on most security issues was not disagreement but a broad international consensus, one sufficient to control the important decisions.

America's Europe problem.

NAKED NATO

GAR ALPEROVITZ

Gar Alperovitz is the author of a new, expanded edition of
Atomic Diplomacy: Hiroshima and Potsdam (Penguin) and, with
Jeff Faux, of *Rebuilding America* (Pantheon).

QUICKLY, for $150 billion (roughly the amount the United States spends each year on NATO), identify the people urging the following positions:

Speaker A: "The fear of Soviet invasion has diminished." And, "A gradual withdrawal of a substantial portion, perhaps up to half, of our present ground forces would be a logical result."

Speaker B: America should "initiate a longer-term process to alter the nature of its military presence in Europe.... The United States will have to take the first steps, even perhaps unilaterally, through a ten-year program of annual cuts in the level of ground forces in Europe."

Speaker C: "American troops are not going to remain in Europe for very long.... There is no active public opinion in favor of keeping those troops in Europe.... Sooner or later such passive acceptance of an inherited military strategy will drain away into nothingness."

If you guessed Edward Kennedy or George McGovern or any other mainstream liberal political leader, you lose. The people primarily responsible for the growing attack on NATO are certified members of the moderate, conservative, and neoconservative foreign policy establishment. Speaker A is Henry Kissinger, Speaker B is former national security adviser Zbigniew Brzezinski, and Speaker C is neoconservative godfather Irving Kristol. While these conservatives propose unilateral military withdrawal, many liberals favor maintaining America's military commitment to NATO—or even expanding it as part of a "no-first-use" nuclear policy.

New York Times columnist William Safire scathingly criticizes liberals and moderates who do not as yet understand that the days of NATO in its current form are—or should be—numbered: "Three hundred thirty thousand Ameri-

cans man a Maginot Line intended only as a trigger for a U.S. nuclear attack on the Soviet Union if the Russians invade Europe.... [This] theory is hopelessly outdated. Our policy is frozen because too many hard-liners here think a pullout would dispirit the West Europeans, and too many soft-liners are afraid to be called 'isolationist' for saying the emperor of NATO is wearing no clothes."

America's fiscal crisis adds force to the logic of the case against NATO. With a $160-$200 billion deficit and limited possibilities for further domestic budget cuts or tax increases, defense spending is almost certainly going to be trimmed. And NATO is the financial heart of the Pentagon. It consumes three times the amount spent on strategic nuclear forces. A few years ago the Government Accounting Office estimated that NATO took up 56 percent of all military resources. Other estimates range from $120 to $170 billion of the roughly $300 billion total.

Revisionists on the right want to reduce U.S. spending in Europe in order to expand it elsewhere—especially to increase America's capacity to use troops in the Third World. A recent proposal by *U.S. News and World Report* publisher-editor Mortimer Zuckerman is representative: "Some 150,000 troops should be phased out of Europe over a five-to-ten year period and redeployed as an additional strategic reserve in the United States, able to move to the world's trouble spots." The goal is to "build U.S. airlift and sealift capabilities and enhance the Rapid Deployment Force so that, if needed, America [can] project adequate military power into the Persian Gulf area, the Middle East and southwest Asia where the risks and stakes to the Western geostrategic position are the highest."

Exasperation with the European allies—many of whom have repeatedly reneged on pledges to increase their own level of military spending—fuels the criticism. European nations spend roughly 3.8 percent of their GNP on average on defense; the United States spends roughly 6.7 percent. Some NATO critics hope a U.S. decision to withdraw troops will prod Europe into increasing its commitment.

The Europeans, who live each day under the nose of the Russian bear, don't seem to believe there is a serious likelihood of attack—or if they do, they are apparently not worried enough to tax themselves for a larger defense effort. How much longer will members of Congress and taxpayers continue to support such "allies," or to believe traditional arguments stressing the Russian threat?

There is also unhappiness with European criticism of American initiative elsewhere in the world. To aggressive neoconservatives who believe America should be less worried about what the allies think, NATO increasingly feels like a ball and chain restraining U.S. foreign policy. Conflicting approaches to Nicaragua and Libya have sparked intense controversy. Kristol observes that "a major clash between the United States and Europe over Central America could soon lead to overwhelming pressures in the United States for a redefinition of its role in NATO—even to the point of the withdrawal of U.S. forces from the continent."

THERE ARE three basic issues in the new NATO debate: (1) Is there a military need for the current high levels of U.S. NATO spending? (2) If not, what non-military uses of these funds make the most sense? (3) Should the United States expand its military power in other areas? Many conservatives would like to answer "No" to the first question and "Yes" to the third, without pausing to discuss the second.

But if Congress believes that the current level of funding is more or less right for military functions other than NATO, then a cutback in NATO should logically lead to a reduction in the overall defense budget. This point has been urged by former Treasury Secretary William C. Simon and others worried about the deficit. Many neoconservatives would prefer to slide a good deal of the money now in NATO to other uses before the fiscal conservatives make their case effectively to the public.

And before the liberals wake up. Senator Gary Hart recently put a toe gingerly into the water, commenting that "we are not the Romans. We do not intend to stay in Germany for 300 years, or until we are driven out." Otherwise, Democrats aren't saying much about NATO. On the main issue the conservatives have had the field largely to themselves.

THERE ARE several obvious possibilities liberal Democrats could pursue. Both Kissinger and Brzezinski have urged a schedule of unilateral withdrawals, and it would not be difficult to develop legislation giving Europe ample notice that over, say, five years, the United States would cut $15-20 billion from its contribution to NATO each year until a floor of perhaps $50-75 billion was reached. The allies, taken together, are as rich as we are—and richer than the Russians. Such an approach would give

them time to improve their defenses if they so chose, and a substantial U.S. troop commitment would continue to prove our willingness to be mutually at risk. Legislation of this kind could have a strong populist appeal if it were sponsored by liberal Democrats and if it specified that funds saved by the United States would be allocated to domestic use, tax reduction, and/or deficit reduction.

A Democratic foreign policy that proposed seriously revising America's role in NATO might also be well-positioned to take advantage of the desire for change in Europe. At some point in the next few years, new Labor, "Alliance," or Social Democratic governments in Britain and West Germany could well come into office with their own proposals to ease the military confrontation on the Continent. Within both nations there is a far-ranging debate over "de-nuclearized zones," "non-offensive" defense systems, and general schemes to disengage the military blocs.

Soviet leader Mikhail Gorbachev recently proposed major troop reductions "from the Atlantic to the Urals." On paper these could amount to up to 500,000 men on each side (and Soviet rhetoric includes dismantling of NATO and the Warsaw Pact). Many Russian experts believe the Soviet Union is suffering from such extraordinary economic difficulties that it would welcome some relief from the huge military burden it bears in Europe, and a new American initiative could challenge the Russians to begin serious negotiations.

Yet very few of the kinds of ideas liberals might normally be expected to develop have surfaced in the NATO debate. The political fears that Safire talked about, and worries about allied morale, explain part of the caution. Although hardly anyone imagines the Western allies will change sides in the cold war, as Gary Hart observes, "Even the smallest detail in the traditional structure . . . is considered sacrosanct."

Another major complication derives from "no first use." In the spring of 1982 four former presidential foreign policy advisers—McGeorge Bundy, George F. Kennan, Robert McNamara, and Gerard C. Smith—urged that the United States commit itself to not "going nuclear" first in any confrontation with the Soviets, and to increasing conventional forces in Europe as an alternative counterweight. Their underlying judgment accorded with the view that our current conventional military presence in Europe is only large enough to serve as a "trip-wire" for nuclear war. As Safire puts it: "Legions of realists know that no conventional deterrent exists in Europe." But the conservatives hold that conventional troops can be cut—and a good deal of money saved—without significantly altering this basic reality. McNamara, Bundy and Company argue that this basic reality needs to be changed. They insist that the nuclear threshold must be raised, and that building up the deterrent of NATO's conventional forces is the only way to do it.

Last month six other policy experts joined Bundy, McNamara, Kennan, and Smith in an *Atlantic* article delineating another "no-first-use" nuclear proposal. However, this time the group toned down an explicit commitment to a serious expansion of conventional forces. Although no reason for the change was given (and although they implicitly endorsed such a policy), the coyness is almost certainly attributable to the fact that new conventional forces are very expensive—and whatever the merits of the conventional build-up argument, large additional military expenditures are politically impossible both here and in Europe.

LIBERALS ARE in a stalemate—caught between the hope of reducing nuclear weapons and the reality of financial limits on conventional forces. The stalemate in turn has temporarily bolstered the position of old foreign policy hands who object to tampering with the status quo.

The consensus that there is little prospect of a Russian attack logically should open the way to a fundamentally new détente-based European security policy. Even Brzezinski, who is no liberal, is willing to contemplate a neutralized Germany as part of a buffer between East and West. Most people on both sides, however, continue to avoid the politically difficult issue of détente: the conservatives because the last thing they want to see is a neutral area in Europe, the liberals because they can't imagine it, or fear to raise it politically.

There is an outside chance that a Reagan-Gorbachev summit meeting would reduce some intermediate-range nuclear weapons in Europe. However, given the rigidities, bureaucratic interests, and worries of the allies on both sides, prospects for more than token change appear to be limited. The current focus of discussion is primarily the ABM treaty and the Star Wars defense systems. There is also no sign that the Reagan administration has given any official thought to major shifts in conventional forces.

At a more fundamental level, however, as the attack on NATO continues to gather force, the groundwork for a post-Reagan policy shift is being laid. In the absence of more far-ranging ideas from liberals and the left, the conservative critics are likely to dominate this discussion in both political parties. The no-first-use group, for all its concern about nuclear weaponry, concedes that such weapons are still the ultimate deterrent in Europe. So long as the liberals fail to integrate their no-first-use ideas with a serious disengagement approach, conservatives—with the only proposals that might save real money—will hold most of the politically appealing cards, especially in a period when the European allies are all but certain to cut their own defense spending and to criticize U.S. policies they don't like.

As the stand-pat centrists and new no-first-use liberals slowly lose ground in the NATO debate, America's European defense policy will be shaped more and more by those who aim to increase America's willingness and capacity to use force in diverse parts of the world. And by people whose views imply ever greater reliance on nuclear weapons in the main arena of cold war conflict.

The Future of the Alliance and German-American Relations

Helmut Kohl

Helmut Kohl is the Federal Chancellor of the Federal Republic of Germany.

The Second World War left Europe destroyed and exhausted. Europe saw itself exposed to the grasp of the Soviet empire. Moscow viewed Eastern Europe, Central Europe as well as the Balkans as the spoils of war and proceeded to impose the Soviet communist system on the major part of these areas. The Soviet aim was to dominate all of Germany. Lenin said once that to dominate Germany is to dominate all of Europe. There is, in fact, a lot to be said for this. The Soviet Union failed in this endeavor. The Western powers saw through its policies and the fact that they were directed towards spreading communism over all of Germany. They countered this Soviet ploy by providing post-war reconstruction assistance and integrating the Germans as partners in the Western system.

The North Atlantic Pact was directed against the Soviet threat. However, it is much more than just a military alliance for defense purposes. We need to remind ourselves constantly that NATO is a trans-Atlantic community based on shared values.

After the first World War the United States made the fateful mistake of not involving itself in the shaping of the new order for peace in Europe. I feel that a strong commitment on the part of the United States at that time could have helped to prevent the disaster that was to come. With the formation of the North Atlantic Pact some thirty years later, the United States and Canada permanently tied their destiny to that of Europe. This was a new element in American history. The North Atlantic Pact has become the firm foundation for a historical link between the old world and the new, based on shared political and economic values. The preamble to the North Atlantic Treaty says, *inter alia*, that the parties to the treaty "are determined to safeguard the freedom, common heritage and civilization of their peoples, founded on the principles of democracy, individual liberty and the rule of law."

From the German point of view, the Alliance has stood the test of time and achieved its objectives in a variety of ways. It has been possible to preserve peace in Europe. It has been possible to adjust the military strategies of Alliance members to cope with new circumstances, despite the fact that this, in some cases, has involved heated debates. On the whole the Alliance partners have been able to keep their defense capabilities in an appropriate ratio with the growing Soviet challenge. The common interests of the Alliance members have been strong enough to make it possible to

deal with any problems that have occurred.

The political philosophy the Alliance has developed is flexible enough to be helpful in dealing with the decisions that have to be made in individual cases. Although the Harmel Report is nearly twenty years old, its content continues to have the same significance for us.

The Harmel Report states that the Atlantic Alliance has two main functions. "Its first function is to maintain adequate military strength and political solidarity to deter aggression and other forms of pressure and to defend the territory of member countries if aggression should occur." In recent years the Federal Republic of Germany has taken a number of measures that serve this objective. I am thinking in this context of its agreement to deploy US intermediate-range nuclear forces, the strengthening of its conventional defense capabilities and its extension of the basic period of compulsory military service. The latter measure was necessary to guarantee the availability of sufficient manpower to be able to fulfill Alliance obligations in the course of the next decade.

The Harmel Report states that the second function of the Alliance is to "pursue the search for progress towards a more stable relationship" with the Warsaw Pact countries. This policy is intended to contribute towards solving "the underlying political issues." The Harmel Report also states that "military security and a policy of détente are not contradictory but complementary." It continues to be the policy of the Alliance as a whole to seek dialogue with the Warsaw Pact countries on the basis of an assured defense capability as well as mutually beneficial cooperation. More than anything else we want more freedom of movement and a greater exchange of ideas across the borders separating East and West. For us the credibility of statements regarding commitment to peace depends, among other things, on whether or not there is progress in the human rights sector and whether or not the East-West borders become more permeable.

It is of special importance to us Germans that the Harmel Report includes the statement that "no final and stable settlement in Europe is possible without a solution of the German question, which lies at the heart of present tensions in Europe. Any such settlement must end the unnatural barriers between Eastern and Western Europe, which are most clearly and cruelly manifested in the division of Germany." My administration is steadily working towards a reduction of these barriers. The effects of confrontation in Europe are felt most strongly by the people in divided Germany.

II

Today, the vital interests of the Federal Republic of Germany extend beyond the NATO region. The Soviet superpower is taking advantage of the weakness of third world countries to establish Marxist-Leninist regimes there. These countries provide the Soviet fleet with new naval bases, something it is on the lookout for throughout the world. The war in Afghanistan represents a crossing of the Rubicon in the sense that Soviet troops are engaged in open warfare for the first time in an area outside the territory that the Soviet Union laid claim to after the Second World War.

It would be extremely dangerous if the Western democracies were not to react to this Soviet policy and failed to provide a coordinated response. While it is true that the Western European countries no longer have global commitments to speak of, with the exception, to some extent, of the United Kingdom and France, they nevertheless have global interests to protect due to their dependency on raw materials and exports. They share these interests with the United States, which also favors an open world system permitting the free movement of people and goods. They are aware that the Soviet Union, by means of a flanking maneuver, can threaten their independence and security. The situation in the Gulf Region has immediate implications for the security of the Federal Republic of Germany.

What to do? First of all I would consider it wrong to want to change the clear-cut provisions in the NATO Treaty regarding the geographic definition of the NATO area. This would give rise to considerable problems, since the Basic Law (constitution) of the Federal Republic of Germany only permits the employment of German armed forces for the defense of the Federal Republic. Political coordination with regard to the situations that exist outside the NATO area is taking place inside the Atlantic Alliance. The Alliance partners are thus taking into account the fact that the Alliance represents a part of the constitution of the Western world as a whole and that the Soviet challenge is being manifested today in a large number of different ways and no longer exclusively in Central Europe. This type of coordination within the Alliance cannot be close enough. Differing assessments of regional conflicts and trouble spots would create the danger of divisiveness. The Alliance partners also need to seek agreement with regard to the appropriateness of a response in specific cases and to show solidarity. This is obviously in keeping with German interests.

On the other hand, as important as it may be to have a consensus in the Alliance, it must not become a danger to Alliance cohesiveness when issues arise on which it is difficult to arrive at a consensus. There are differences in the ability of the partners to act. I have already referred to the specific case represented by the Federal Republic of Germany. Thus, the principle of political coordination should be applied with the kind of flexibility that reflects these differences. Arriving at a common assessment of the challenges facing the Western democracies continues to be a factor of central importance. We must never lose sight of the fact that the Western democracies are all sitting in the same boat. If and when a need for action arises, this need can be dealt with by one or several partners as the case requires.

The Alliance, which is restricted to its defined area, does not need to be involved. The Federal Republic of Germany has underscored its willingness to help compensate for the restrictions imposed on its armed forces by means of such things as the Wartime Host Nation Support Agreement.

III

It would be silly to deny that there have been problems between Western Europe and the United States in the recent past with regard to the perception of certain issues. These problems have not had a negative influence on the Alliance. Still, they deserve our full attention. This also applies to German-American relations.

In recent decades our awareness of one another has, on the whole, diminished rather than increased. This is true on both sides of the Atlantic. We are faced with a phenomenon that might be termed "creeping estrangement." This fact could lead to a situation in which people on one side of the Atlantic are no longer able to share the perception of life, the visions and dreams of those who live on the other side. The United States has overcome the period of weakness caused by the Vietnam War. The United States once again believes in itself and its purpose in the world. The average American is again able to derive confidence from the strength of his country. It goes without saying that his view of the world will be different from that of a young German. The majority of Americans are confident that they will be able to cope successfully with the future. In Germany, by contrast, we are faced with a movement that takes a pessimistic view of the future. This view is not supported by the majority of German young people, but it is vociferously propagated by certain groups. This problem indicates how difficult the communication problems between us can be. We need to take vigorous action to counteract this danger. We need to create opportunities for more young people on both sides of the Atlantic to attend schools or universities on the other side. We need to provide the American servicemen stationed in the Federal Republic with more information on Germany and the Germans. We need to intensify our promotion of German studies programs in the United States and US studies programs in the Federal Republic.

Another point is the question as to how we are to respond to the challenge posed by the Soviet system. There is an enormous concentration of military manpower and weapons in Central Europe, *i.e.*, on German soil, at the interface between East and West. This concentration of military strength prompts East and West to exercise extreme caution in dealings with one another. At the same time, it is a source of anxiety that is consciously capitalized on by interested parties. No administration in Bonn finds it easy to do what is necessary to maintain an adequate level of defense readiness. Every administration has to justify its defense policy measures in detail to a critical public. This is often difficult since the people of our country are unaware of the Warsaw Pact's military potential. In the West military weapons are an open issue. They cost the taxpayer lots of money and are often felt to be a burden. I am thinking in this context of the many army maneuvers and overflights by air force planes in our densely populated country. In addition, in recent years the Soviet Union has managed to create the image of a world power showing a sense of responsibility and restraint, despite the fact that in Afghanistan it is currently waging a brutal war of suppression against an entire people.

We Germans, who are forced to live in the painful situation of a divided people, need strong nerves, patience, and a rational approach. We need to make our American friends aware of Germany's very special situation. It goes without saying that German policy is strongly focused on strengthening an awareness of national unity, something that, in the final analysis, must also express itself in a multitude of personal ties. This does not change the fact that the Federal Republic of Germany is a reliable, predictable and loyal Alliance partner. In my annual addresses on the state of the nation in divided Germany I have time and again warned against the illusion that the Germans could steer a neutral course. Adherence to the community of Western nations and, in particular, to the Atlantic Alliance is an integral part of the political rationale in the Federal Republic of Germany, since without the help of our Western friends we are unable to maintain our freedom in the face of the excessive Soviet arms buildup.

This fact is in the forefront of our minds in the current disarmament and arms control negotiations. Any such agreement must be balanced, reliably verifiable and must not prejudice our security. It is our common aim to place relations with the Soviet Union on a firmer basis than in the past. In this connection I advocate a renewed meeting between President Reagan and General Secretary Gorbachev. We need to be watchful, however, so the Soviet leadership does not make use of agreements of this kind to cover up an arms buildup or to take advantage of détente for further political and military expansion as was the case in the 1970s. The Soviet Union will have to change its ways if it wants to gain the confidence of the West. Nothing could serve this purpose better than a withdrawal from the bloody and senseless Afghanistan adventure with which it has damaged its image and severely strained foreign relations.

Finally, I would like to refer to the danger of disturbances arising from economic relations between Europe and the United States. The large US current account deficits which the decline in the dollar exchange rate has not yet been able to correct, has strengthened protectionist tendencies in the United States. We owe a debt of thanks to President Reagan for having effectively resisted protectionist initiatives thus far. The prosperity of the Western nations is based on the freedom of world markets.

A reconciliation of economic interests will not be easy. The United States will have to put its own house in order first. It should not try to get other countries to solve its economic problems for it. The American budget deficit has to be reduced so that interest levels can be lowered. At the same time, Europe must remain open to the rest of the world and make a determined effort to bring relief to world agricultural markets on which the United States and other countries have a relative advantage. This cannot be done in a hurry. However, there is a need to create the feeling on both sides of the Atlantic that things are moving in the right direction. Extremely close cooperation is required here. We should not underestimate the destructive potential inherent in the further growth of economic problems between the countries of the West.

IV

In conclusion let me say that the Alliance continues to be a central pillar of German foreign policy. The opinion polls taken in Germany show a high and rising level of approval of the Alliance and the Federal Republic's integration in the West. The Alliance is capable of coping with the challenges that face it. It offers a good framework for the coordination of our policy towards the East as well as towards the trouble spots outside the NATO area.

The Federal Republic's decision to become a member of the NATO Alliance was based on fundamental values. This fact is reflected in the close and friendly relations that exist between the American and German peoples. The fact that there have been atmospheric disturbances in recent years is something that should neither be played down nor exaggerated. What we need to do is to promote an understanding of the common nature of our interests and recognition of the fact that we will either keep our freedom together or lose it together.

Greece and the Atlantic Alliance

Andreas Papandreou

Andreas Papandreou is Prime Minister of Greece.

Every system of defense is created to serve specific politico-defensive aims which are dictated by the international realities of the particular time. The commonality of the aims is recognized and accepted by the *ad hoc* collective consent of the member-states. The strength and credibility of every such institution depends on its ability to adapt itself to changing international and internal realities.

The Atlantic Alliance is a product of the cold war climate and the logic of bi-polarity. This one-dimensional approach was a decisive factor in the original shaping of the Alliance. That was one of the reasons why the possibility of the emergence of new centers of power on the international scene was underestimated. The differentiation of the international points of reference was further encouraged by the creation of new collective agencies of international economic, political, and military activity. At the same time, the traditional means at the disposal of the international system could not cope with the regional crises which in the post-war years have accounted for a

Papandreou talks with Indian Prime Minister Gandhi

substantial proportion of international political, diplomatic, and military activity.

The requirement that the Atlantic Alliance should adapt itself to the new order of things has created a number of serious frictions which have been fed by a series of developments within NATO itself. The original commonality of aims of the member-states of the Alliance has been redefined by the emergence of two coexisting trends—on the one hand, centralizing trends which make for the permanent leadership role of the United States and for a collective and unified approach to international problems; on the other hand, internal developments within the Alliance concerning the balance of forces in Europe and resulting in decentralizing trends. These trends crystallized in differences regarding the priorities in national political issues, in increased demands by the member states in the area of their national and international actions, and in the questioning of the exclusivity of American leadership. At the same time, the continuous escalation in both the quantity and the quality of nuclear weapons and the dominance of NATO's stragegic doctrines, which turned Europe into a nuclear war theater gave rise to a crisis of confidence within the Alliance itself. European public opinion and political leaderships have shown extreme sensitivity concerning the prospect of a catastrophic nuclear conflict—whether by design or accident—on European soil.

But there was a change also in the very ideological-political foundation of the Alliance. The East-West problems continue to form the framework within which NATO operates. However, development in the perception of the "traditional Soviet threat" has strengthened the views which favor a balance and co-existence between the two blocs.

The Atlantic Alliance must recognize and accept the changes which have taken place both in the international order as well as within its own ranks. The multi-dimensional and complex character of the international system is not suited to one-dimensional and uniform approaches. Insistence on seeking collective responses to international problems and the adoption of a joint, harmonized foreign policy in a Western Bloc framework have proved in the past to be counter-productive. The idea of a geographic and qualitative expansion of the jurisdiction of the Atlantic Alliance tends to downgrade the special characteristics and the composite inter-dependencies which determine the functioning of the international system. Consequently, it does not meet the need for a flexible and multi-faceted approach to international problems. It tends also to ignore the claim of the member-states for autonomous intervention in international affairs—a claim which is based on real differences in national aims and priorities within the context of the Alliance.

Greece has also special reasons to be wary of the dominance of centralizing trends within NATO. It is not only the multifaceted nature of the international system that compels Greece to demand the right for autonomous intervention on international issues. It must be remembered that for many decades Greece's foreign policy had not freed itself from the direct influence of the United States—a fact which justifiably made the

French President Mitterand welcomes Greek Prime Minister Papandreou to France

Greek people sensitive to the issue of national independence. In response to this demand for independence, the present Greek government has formulated a political position and pursued a diplomacy which seeks on the one hand to protect and promote our legitimate and lawful national interests and, on the other hand, to contribute to the effort to create a more just and peaceful world. Without failing to take account of its place in the international system and the limited ability of a small country to intervene on the international scene, Greece:

● has oriented its relations with other poles in the international system;
● has concentrated emphasis on its own surrounding major region, formulating a Balkan and Arab policy which accords with its national interest, while not coming into conflict with the declared aims of NATO; and
● has been active both within and outside the Alliance in undertaking and promoting initiatives in the area of nuclear arms control.

Whereas the national security of almost all European countries is linked to East-West issues, Greece faces a specific and crucial threat which lies outside of that framework. The manifestations of Turkish expansionism in Cyprus and the Aegean feed tensions in Greek-Turkish relations which are often regarded in the West as arising from a traditional enmity between two neighboring nations. This assessment by the United States and by NATO in practice negates the difference between the attacker and the one defending himself

from attack, and is tantamount to the resignation by the Alliance from its role of shielding its member states when their national security and integrity are threatened. If Turkey were a member of the opposing bloc, the Turkish threat would undoubtedly be blunted and, in any event, it would be something which would be collectively dealt with by NATO as a whole. Up to now the Alliance has failed to act in the face of these expansionist actions on the part of Turkey. Greece is obliged to face alone this threat to its national security and integrity. That makes it necessary for Greece to adapt its foreign and defense policies in order to deal with this Turkish expansionism.

No allied strategy for the southeast wing of NATO can be effective if it ignores the fact that Turkey's provocative stand in the area of the Aegean and in Cyprus constitutes a destabilizing factor working against the cohesion of the Alliance. Since the balance of forces in the area of the Greek-Turkish conflict is a vital national security issue for Greece, bilateral Greek-American relations are inevitably affected by the corresponding relations between the US and Turkey. Given that the Alliance does not shield Greece from the threat on its Eastern border, the balancing of the triangular relations "Greece-US-Turkey," and also "Greece-NATO-Turkey," is a basic prerequisite for ensuring that relations between Greece and the United States and that membership in NATO, shall at the very least, not operate against its vital national interest.

Britain's Contribution to Maintaining Western Interests Outside the NATO Area

Timothy Renton

Timothy Renton MP, is Minister of State for Foreign and Commonwealth Affairs for the United Kingdom.

No man is an island, and even an island nation like Britain is critically dependent on others for its security. Today we depend above all on the collective defense provided by the North Atlantic Alliance. The Soviet Union and other members of the Warsaw Pact are the greatest threat we face in every sense: in ideology and human values; in political and social organization, shutting off the Eastern part of our continent under Communist systems imposed and kept in place by the ultimate sanction of force; and in a very real way in the military field. The Warsaw Pact's conventional forces in Central Europe have the numerical edge over NATO in manpower, nearly three times the artillery, twice the number of tactical aircraft, and more than twice as many main battle tanks. Soviet nuclear weapons, having reached approximate strategic parity with three times the US's throw-weight, are presenting new and disturbing challenges at the intermediate and shorter-range level. And the Soviet chemical weapons stockpile includes 300,000 tons of nerve agents alone.

In face of this, all British Governments of the post-war period have chosen to focus their military efforts on common defense in NATO to such an extent that some 95 percent of our national defense resources are now devoted to this task. Overall, our defense expenditure is greater than that of any other ally except the United States. But is this a complete answer to the problem of security? Are there not risks for Britain, and for NATO, in focusing too exclusively on the Atlantic area? Might not the apparent stability of our own continent blind us to the very real threats that exist in the wider world, both from Communist activities and the whole range of other conflicts and strains (not forgetting terrorism)?

Britain has always taken these questions seriously. The present Government has always set its face against the policy of "Little England," and indeed of "Little Europe." History gives us no choice. We still have responsibilities to a number of dependent territories, and must—as the Falklands conflict showed—be ready to stand by them at need, which means maintaining an independent capability for out-of-area military action. Today, twenty years after the retreat from "East of Suez," we still have garrisons in Hong Kong, Cyprus, and the Falkland Islands; a military presence in strategic locations such as Diego Garcia and Ascension Island; naval forces committed to such areas as the Arabian Sea and the Caribbean; forces in the Commonwealth countries of Belize and Brunei; and various rapidly deployable units—centered on five Airborne Brigade and three Commando Brigade Royal Marines—which have their primary commitments in the NATO area but can also be used outside it in times of crisis. We fill out this framework with a world-wide program of short-term military deployments and exercises—this year, for instance, a sizeable Naval Task Group including the carrier HMS Illustrious has visited the Far East and Pacific, and in November it will join up with army and air force units for a major exercise in Oman alongside the Sultan's forces.

All these activities bolster the general level of Western military presence outside the NATO area, as well as Britains' national interests, and they deserve to be better known. But it would be quite wrong to reduce the issue to these terms. Britain has far more at stake in the non-NATO world than a handful of dependent territories. Our trade, currency, and transport links are truly global; our invisible trade surplus and overseas investments are the second highest in the world after the US. Tourist and immigration flows bring the security, ethnic and social problems of far-flung regions to our own doorsteps and vice-versa. We have long-standing partnerships with and in some cases commitments to independent third world nations in regions like the Persian Gulf, the Caribbean, Africa, and Southeast Asia. (The Commonwealth grouping is one obvious example; also, in the security field are the Five Power Defense Arrangements between Britain, Australia, New Zealand, Singaporo, and Malaysia.) I would add to all this our general stake in global peace, security, resistance to Communist encroachment, and containment of the drug and terrorist menaces—responsibilities we feel particularly keenly as a permanent member of the UN Security Council.

Most of these interests are shared by other NATO allies and members of the Western community, including friendly regional powers such as Australia and Japan. All agree that they are worth protecting. The difficult questions are about how this should be done. Short-term military action or long-term resilience, patience, building of deeper bonds with Western values—where does the balance of advantage lie? How do the intangibles, like the reaction of "world opinion" to our choice of methods, affect the balance of practical gain and loss? If military action must be taken, who should take it, individually or collectively? Is the present pattern of burden-sharing fair? Last, or perhaps first of all, what general threat and what tactics can we expect across this whole canvas in future from our opponents in the Soviet Union?

It is too early to predict whether Gorbachev's leadership has ushered in a period of greater Soviet introspection or, rather, a more subtle and skillful brand of opportunism world-wide. The "correlation of forces" in, say, Africa or the Middle East has certainly not been running Moscow's way since the great rebuilding of US out-of-area capability and concern was launched in the early 1980's. That is not to say the Russians will easily give up any of their existing bridgeheads (the story of the Aden coup is instructive) or miss chances to acquire new ones. But one general point does need stressing. Where the West scores against the Communist Bloc, all along the line, is in the far greater richness and diversity of what it has to offer the developing world—in aid, economic partnership, technological advice, and not least in workable social-political concepts. For all the anti-capitalist and anti-colonial rhetoric still heard in third world quarters, Western help in regional mediation and negotiation is still worth far more when it comes to the crunch than that of any Communist power—and often is most acceptable when offered with hands clean of any direct military involvement.

In short, our ability to defend our interests world-wide relies on more than just military strength. And in this wider balance, Britain and the other Europeans contribute a very fair share. The European Community, as befits the world's single largest trading bloc, administers large programs of economic assistance to countries skirting the Mediterranean and to a total of 66 African, Caribbean, and Pacific States linked to the community under the Lomé Convention. Its political presence is felt through regular dialogue with Arab, ASEAN and Central American groupings and through ad hoc regional-political initiatives of the Twelve. Individual members, like the UK, make further contributions suited to their particular history and geography: one thinks of Britain and the Commonwealth; French support for African countries; German defense subsidies to Southern Europe and wider technical aid programs; Spanish influence in Latin America; and so on. Through the Economic Summit grouping, the leaders of Europe consult regularly with Japan as well as North America on the broad political and strategic purposes which their economic strength can be made to serve.

European consciousness of this whole policy complex, and of the need for a more coherent and coordinated European contribution, is currently on the rise. The Single Act adopted by EC leaders at Luxembourg last year gave for the first time ever a binding treaty character to European Political Cooperation, establishing a framework in which the political initiatives of the Twelve can be seen as part of a single picture with the Community's aid and trade policies and the relevant aspects of security. One of the main tasks of the UK's EC Presidency in the second half of 1986 will be to start exploring the scope of this new and stronger mandate, and to find the areas where Europe's contribution to regional stability can most distinctively

and effectively be made.

None of this alters the fact that many of our friends and partners outside Europe—in war-torn regions like the Gulf or Southeast Asia—find themselves in situations where political and economic strength alone is no guarantee of safety, and where straightforward military defense is needed against external or internal attack. Even in these cases it is often better in every sense (risks, resources, and respect for sovereignty) for the West to help its local friends defend themselves

British Prime Minister Margaret Thatcher

rather than to intervene directly. British experience shows just how much can be done by military assistance in the form of training, personnel on loan, and visits by advisory teams to help friendly states to develop self-sufficient, disciplined forces able to maintain national security and allow for the wider development of their countries. Last year nearly 700 British servicemen were in loan service appointments in countries outside NATO, and nearly 4000 non-NATO overseas students were trained in military establishments in the United Kingdom.

This leaves a final class of situations where there is no alternative to direct military intervention by one or more Western nations. There can be no question at present, and I suspect will be none in future, of formal joint action out-of-area by NATO countries; the North Atlantic Treaty clearly limits the geographical area within which an armed attack on the territories, forces, or vessels of any of the Parties to the Treaty shall be considered an attack against them all. The decision to deploy or not to deploy out-of-area will remain one for national governments, using their own national forces. But this does not rule out *consultation* in NATO on the implications of regional security problems outside the Treaty area. On the contrary, it is both possible and desirable for the Allies to exchange notes during a crisis and work between times as well to develop longer-term security concepts compatible with their shared interests in the Atlantic region.

Although there has been a lot of soul-searching over it in recent years, this arrangement does have the one great merit of flexibility. Every out-of-area contingency is different, but there are always considerable risks, costs, and uncertainties involved. Careful thought and full room for maneuver are needed to choose the precise moment and means of intervention and the right operating partners. Britain's national experience bears this out, showing the many different uses to which even a limited range of out-of-area instruments can be put. Our forces' role in monitoring elections for Zimbabwean independence, the joint Anglo-French operation to protect the transition to independence in Vanuatu, and the Falklands conflict are examples of deployment for national purposes. We acted with others in defense of wider Western interests when we joined Mine Counter Measures contingents from the US, Dutch, French, Italian, and Egyptian Navies to search for mines in the Red Sea; when we supplied a contingent to join US, French, and Italian forces in the Lebanon MNF; and when we sent Royal Navy vessels (which are still there) to patrol in and around the Gulf of Hormuz in defense of the free passage of shipping. No doubt we can expect more, and more varied, opportunities in the future.

There are other out-of-area security contributions that do not fit any of these neat categories. One that needs no particular justification is the use of national forces for multilateral peace-keeping and monitoring exercises and for individual acts of disaster relief. Another and more complex issue is the use of military methods against terrorism. Britain and the other members of the European Twelve have, like all civilized countries, unambiguously condemned all terrorist acts and made clear that no country which supports terrorism can expect to enjoy normal relations with us. We have assisted in specific anti-terrorist actions, agreeing, for example, to the use of F-111 aircraft based in Britain for the US strike against specific targets in Libya earlier this year. On that occasion we saw it as the best way of curbing Libyan support for terrorist activity, with the lowest risk of unnecessary casualties on both sides. But this did not, of course, exhaust the range of useful instruments brought to bear on Libya by the European Allies, many of which would be equally appropriate for use in the future against any other offending state. Measures of prevention and self-protection, international exchange of information, and political and economic pressure all have a practical role to play. Most effective of all would be the building of a watertight, practical, and effective consensus among all responsible states, West and East, North and South, to reject terrorism in all its forms and make the world unsafe for all brands of this callous and destructive activity.

To sum up: Britain's long history of global involvement has left us with more direct out-of-area responsibilities than most. It gives us assets and experience that can be put to a wide range of uses in defense of both national and Western interests. But it has also taught us the costs and uncertainties of any use of force, and the value of using other, especially non-military, methods whenever possible. To resort to such means is not an admission of weakness, but often, simply, the most economical use of our strength. As Sir Geoffrey Howe said in a recent speech, "We have to take account of the effects not only on close allies but also on other nations and groups whose cooperation may be important to us . . . . The more support we can muster for protective and deterrent measures, the better our chances of reducing violence all round."

H.M.S Invincible, British aircraft carrier

The threat to Western interests is not going to lessen in coming decades. Even if its Soviet component were to remain relatively limited and cautious, there will be many other ill-wishers to fill the gap. The case is clear for those countries who have an out-of-area capability, including the capability to train others in self-help, to maintain this and be flexible and imaginative in the way they use it alone or with others. But we can and should also do more to build up and refine our non-military efforts for stability. Not just because this is the field where most European allies can most readily contribute—and increasingly do so as a single, coherent grouping—but also because this is the field of the West's most transparent, and most enduring, superiority over all democracy's foes.

EURO-COMMUNISM: 10 YEARS LATER, DOWN AND ALMOST OUT

Western Europe's Communists thought they had the answer with their very own movement. As it turned out, they lacked even the right question as potential recruits became yuppies instead

Only a decade ago, Euro-Communism promised to unlock the door to power for Western European Communists. Today, barely surviving, it gropes for rejuvenation against fearsome odds.

Euro-Communism grew out of discontent with the old order—Communist and capitalist—and fury over the role in Vietnam of Western Europe's great protector, the United States. Pioneered by Italian, Spanish and French Communists, it offered a high degree of independence from the orthodoxies of Moscow. Communism would win playing by the normally repugnant rules of democracy.

Through most of the 1970s, U.S. policymakers were deeply worried. Communists in Portugal and Italy, both members of the North Atlantic Treaty Organization, were poised to take power peacefully. The hordes of youth opposing the war in Vietnam and U.S. toughness toward Moscow, especially on arms control, were seen as a generation of new blood for the far left.

But the political and economic fervor for the movement lapsed. Leaders of national Communist parties found that they needed to coordinate policies but were unable to do so. Now, the demonstrators still appear, though their numbers are dwindling. More are interested in pursuing the pound, the franc and the mark. At the ballot box and as an intellectual force, Marxism is fading from the mainstream of European political culture.

WHY IT DECLINED

In Spain, Santiago Carrillo, leader of Communism there since the Spanish Civil War and an architect of Euro-Communism, lost his seat in parliament last month—though a united leftist front gained. In May, Dutch Communists, who have been in Holland's parliament since 1922, lost their three seats. The Belgian Communists suffered a similar drubbing last October. France's communists, who once commanded up to 25 percent of the vote, fell below 10 percent in March.

While local realities contributed to the erosion of Communist support in each case, three broad reasons explain the trend:

• An increasingly negative image of the Soviet Union. However much they vowed independence, most Euro-Communists looked to Moscow as the fount of ideology. But the Soviet socioeconomic model is increasingly unattractive to European workers. Moscow's bullying behavior—from the occupation of Afghanistan to the suppression of Solidarity, the Polish dissident movement—has added to the disenchantment.

• The decline of the Continent's heavy-industry base. Concedes Giorgio Napolitano, a top Communist member of the Italian parliament: Some Communist parties were "late in understanding inevitable change in social structure as a consequence of technological innovation." A shift toward high-tech and service industries, combined with the success of the European welfare state and a flood of nonvoting immigrant labor, has sapped the Communist working-class base.

• The rigidity of old-style party structures, despite the promised Communism with a human face. Inflexibility has stifled internal party reform and left Communism without dynamic leaders. They have been bypassed in popular appeal by pragmatic yuppie Socialist leaders such as Spain's Felipe González, who reflect the new, consumerist Europe.

The decline of the French Communist Party (PCF) symbolizes Continentwide problems. In the grip of hard-line Secretary-General Georges Marchais, the party only toyed with Euro-Communist ideas, shedding neither close ties to Moscow nor Leninist organization. In last March's elections, its candidates got only 9.8 percent of the vote, its worst performance in 50 years. Says reform leader Pierre Juquin, "The party has been unable to analyze and understand the upheavals in French society" such as the youth revolt, the ecologists and the women's movement.

Former PCF leader Annie Kriegel, now a columnist for the conservative *Le Figaro,* says the party "is menaced by the erosion of its social layer of support—the shift in the economy from blue collar to white collar." Since 1975, she notes, France has lost 1.2 million industrial jobs and gained 1.5 million service jobs.

The French party's plight has triggered defections and a protest movement from within. The dissidents, gaining in numbers, hope Marchais means it with hints that he will step down in 1988, enabling the party to adapt to new French realities.

So deep is Communist disunity that in Spain, which helped give birth to Euro-Communism, three separate parties now vie for Marxist support. Veteran leader Santiago Carrillo already has been ousted from the mainstream party that, together with a pro-Soviet group known as "the Afghans," joined ecologists and other independents for the nation's recent electoral campaign.

In Portugal, with Western Europe's most backward economy, Communists led by the charismatic Alvaro Cunhal have held on to some 15 percent of the vote. Smaller parties in Greece, Belgium and Finland have long been marginal, as has the tiny British party, with its 12,000 aging members. In Greece, the

Euro-Communists have even changed their name in an effort to broaden appeal.

The only European party still holding its own is that of Italy. The PCI is by far the largest in the capitalist world, drawing 30 percent of the Italian vote. Unlike the others, it has a tradition of genuine independence from Moscow and of being more Italian than Communist. Says *La Stampa* commentator Arrigo Levi, "The PCI is a queer thing. It shows no sign of losing strength, though it is no longer a threat."

But even the PCI suffers a modest decline from its high of 34.5 percent of the electorate and has difficulty attracting youth. To counter stagnation, the Italians have added a new wrinkle to Euro-Communism—the Euroleft. This, says scholar Lucio Colletti, is another effort to break out of isolation by iden-

tifying with the European left, such as Britain's Labor Party and West Germany's Social Democratic Party. He says that it offers the party legitimacy as a democratic force.

Kevin Devlin, an analyst for Radio Free Europe, sees the Euroleft idea as an attempt to distance the PCI from other Communist groups. "The general tendency," Devlin explains, "is to pay a lot of attention to Socialists to woo them away from the U.S."

But the Euroleft concept has not reversed the broad pattern of decline. Analysts say the European public appears to see little difference between Communists who keep the old pro-Soviet image and those who adopt a more liberal one. American officials may not be happy with Socialists and others who oppose U.S. policies, but find them infinitely preferable to a Communist al-

ternative, whatever it is called.

Now, although they once sold the idea of independence from Moscow, European Communists of all factions pin their long-term hopes on Soviet leader Mikhail Gorbachev. Their reasoning: If Gorbachev manages to modernize the Soviet economy, get an arms deal with the U.S. and make even small gestures to civil liberties, some of the gloss might transfer to the European parties.

But the record so far leaves little evidence that either the Euroleft subterfuge or Gorbachev can stop the rot. French actor Yves Montand, closely aligned with the French party for two decades before denouncing it, says skeptically: "Euro-Communism is still Communism, and Communism eventually spells Gulag."

by Robert A. Manning with
the magazine's European bureaus

Europe: Spreading Fear of Terrorism

Charting extremist organizations and their aims

GERD LANGGUTH

Gerd Langguth is Berlin's envoy to the federal government in Bonn. This is excerpted from the political quarterly "Aussen Politik" of Hamburg.

Western Europe is the area of the world most endangered by international terrorism, yet even the trans-border contacts and mutual assistance of terrorist groups do not permit the conclusion that they have a common supreme command. There is selective cooperation among them, but there is no uniform European terrorist organization. Left-wing terrorism remains a political factor and a constant danger because only a police state — an instrument that democracies do not have at their disposal — is in a position to contain such activities.

In 1984, more than 40 different terrorist groups left their bloody trail worldwide in the form of bombings, kidnappings and assassinations, according to an analysis by Tel Aviv University's Center for Strategic Studies. The highest quota of terrorist attacks that year took place in Europe. The study says that 40.5 percent of all terrorist acts took place on that continent, 20.6 percent in the Middle East, 15.5 percent in Africa, 14.6 percent in South America, 2.9 percent in Central America and 1.5 percent in North America. Eastern Europe accounted for 0.2 percent of the terrorist acts listed by the study.

Terrorism is a type of extremist combat aimed at achieving political objectives through violence. Its methods differ from the military combat of regular troops. The most important combat method employed by terrorists consists of attacks on the lives and property of others, especially through murder, kidnapping, arson, bombing and other acts of violence preparatory to such crimes.

One characteristic of terrorism is that it spreads fear among the leaders of the political system it combats. This does not preclude making the intimidation of the public a part of such actions with the ultimate aim of demonstrating the political impotence of the target nation's leadership. However, terrorism does not include spontaneous attacks such as demonstrations that turn violent. Instead, it involves the systematic destruction and destabilization of a political order.

With a few exceptions, there currently is little extreme-right movement in Europe worth mentioning. Terrorist groups are almost exclusively extreme leftists. This is best demonstrated in West Germany. The Federal Office for the Protection of the Constitution in Cologne, the intelligence service concerned with the nation's internal security, registered 148 leftist attacks in 1984. Only 11 rightist terrorist attacks were recorded during the same period, and they were perpetrated mainly by individuals and short-lived groupings.

There are several reasons why the organizational capabilities of rightist terrorism are less pronounced than those of the leftists, according to the security authorities. For one thing, the social structure of right-wing extremism appears to be less suitable for organizing an illegal machinery. For another, the right-wing extremists are geographically fragmented and lack the focal points that the left-wingers have formed. Moreover, right-wing extremism feeds on emotions such as xenophobia, and emotionalism is no suitable base for sustained terrorism.

This does not mean that the danger from extreme-right terrorism should be minimized — especially because this type of terrorism is inspired by the successes of its leftist counterpart, and even the smallest terrorist group can endanger a liberal democracy. Moreover, there are indications of an internationalization of rightist terrorism. But right-wing terrorism in Europe poses no major danger, as opposed to its leftist counterpart.

The leftist terrorist movements operating in Europe can be divided into three groups. First, there are Marxist groups that embrace Communism and are known as the New Left.

The second group consists of ethnic terrorists motivated by nationalism to fight against a supremacy regarded as alien. They include the Corsicans, the Basques, the Armenians and the Irish Republican Army, the last with strong Marxist leanings.

The third group consists mainly of organizations committing acts of terrorism in Europe and coming mostly from the Arab Middle East. Their objective is to put pressure on national governments, in some instances to persecute renegade fellow countrymen or to take action against representatives of Israel. They include Palestinians, Lebanese, Shiite Moslems and, above all, organizations operating in Libya. This raises the issue of state terrorism — terrorist actions carried out with the financial and logistical support of individual governments.

These three groups occasionally overlap, and there are collaborations of varying intensity. The convergence of these three terrorist streams explains why Europe is particularly endangered by terrorism. The European-bred, Marxist-oriented terrorist movements

From *Aussen Politik*, of Hamburg, No. 2, 1986, as it appeared in *World Press Review*, November 1986, pp. 19-21, 23. Reprinted by permission.

in the first group could hardly have been effective had they not had massive support from the Arab-Palestinian "liberation movements" — at least in the 1970s.

Some terrorists in this group were trained in Arab camps, as were rightists whose anti-Semitism made them useful tools for extremist Palestinian organizations. This and the fact that ever more "freedom movements" against Israel were formed by Arabs in the second half of the 1960s gave European terrorism its clout.

It is not easy to describe the various Arab-Palestinian terrorist organizations. In any event, the following organizations now operate in Europe as well as in Israel:

Force Seventeen is the original bodyguard of PLO leader Yassir Arafat. This group is headed by Abu Tayeb, who is fiercely loyal to Arafat. Its attacks are aimed primarily at Israeli targets, including embassies. The group is said to be responsible for the assassination of three Israelis aboard a yacht in Cyprus in 1985. That assault triggered an attack by Israeli bombers on the PLO headquarters in Tunis.

The Palestine Liberation Front apparently has three factions. A faction led by Abul Abbas is said to be responsible for the hijacking of the Italian cruise ship *Achille Lauro*. Abul Abbas is a member of the Palestinian National Congress and is regarded as an Arafat confidant. The second wing, pro-Syrian, is headed by Fatteh Ghanem, who operates from Damascus. The third group, headed by Talaat Yacub, is trying to tread a line between Syria and Arafat — but it is controlled from Damascus, which indicates a degree of Syrian influence.

Alluding to the murder of Israeli athletes at the Olympic Games in Munich in 1972, another terrorist organization calls itself the Black September Group or, occasionally, Black June Group. This is a Palestinian grouping controlled by Abu Nidal, who broke away from Arafat in 1976. Nidal is characterized by changing loyalties, vacillating among Iraq, Syria and Libya. Another group, Front for the Liberation of Palestine/Special Command, is headed by Abu Mohammed and has headquarters in Lebanon. It operates outside Israel, and its actions are targeted primarily against Israel and the U.S.

Shiite groups include primarily Hiz-ballah (Party of God), headed by Hussein Fadlallah, and the Islamic Amal under Hussein Musawi — both probably backed by Teheran. In Arab-Palestinian terrorist organizations, there is an element of state terrorism emanating primarily from Libya but also from Syria and Iran.

The most important left-wing terrorist organizations originating in Europe and forming part of the New Left include West Germany's Red Army Faction (RAF) and Revolutionary Cells. Experts estimate that the RAF has about 2,000 sympathizers and 20 to 25 hard-core activists operating underground. The number of sympathizers has declined in the past few

---

"Extreme-right terrorism is inspired by the successes of its leftist counterpart."

---

years, and the assumption is that the group no longer has the extensive network it had at the height of terrorist activities in 1977 when it managed to kidnap the industrialist Hanns-Martin Schleyer and hold him hostage for many weeks before killing him.

The Revolutionary Cells and other "autonomous" terrorist groups in Germany are "leisure-time perpetrators," primarily young terrorists who pursue an occupation or university studies during the day and plant bombs after hours. They are small and loosely organized and are usually not bent on killing but aim attacks at military installations, at industrial firms said to cooperate with the military and at political institutions. Today's generation of the RAF and the Revolutionary Cells usually contents itself with letters claiming responsibility for terrorist acts.

In France, the Action Directe is one of the most dangerous terrorist groups. In the spring of 1985 it reportedly had 15 to 20 hard-core members and between 120 and 130 sympathizers. The Action Directe has sought close cooperation with terrorists in Italy, Turkey and West Germany. In 1981 the group's most important members were behind bars, but an amnesty for

political extremists through which French President François Mitterrand tried to restore public order benefited most of the Action Directe prisoners.

In Belgium, the Cellules Communistes Combattantes, or Communist Fighting Cells, are said to have committed 27 bomb attacks, most of them against NATO installations, between October, 1984, and December, 1985. The exact strength of this group is unknown, but there are indications of ties to the French Action Directe and the German RAF. The group attributes its terrorist activities to the austerity program of the Belgian government, the necessity for an anti-war campaign, starvation in Ethiopia, nuclear energy, environmental pollution and U.S. intervention in Latin America — but its stated objective is "class struggle, in the course of which one or the other class will have to die."

Activities of the Italian Red Brigades are now rather limited because most of the group's core was put out of action through renegades. A 31-page paper on a split in the Red Brigades, unearthed in Paris at the beginning of 1985, was seen as evidence that the Red Brigades have contacts with French terrorists. In the 1970s the Red Brigades and the German terrorists were the most effective and significant indigenous European Marxist-terrorist movements.

In March, 1985, the Greek terrorist organization Revolutionary Group for International Solidarity Christos Kasimis attempted an attack on the German Embassy in Athens. It was the group's first appearance. Kasimis, after whom the organization is named, was killed by Greek police during an arson attempt in 1977. The group evidently has close ties with the RAF, as indicated by one of its pamphlets that says, "Violence against the German state is a justified and humane act."

In November, 1985, Greek terrorists attacked a vehicle of the Athens police. Responsibility was claimed by the 17th of November Organization, which reportedly has been responsible for terrorist acts in Greece since 1975. The organization is named after the day in 1973 on which students rebelled against the ruling military junta. This group is said to be responsible for several murders — notably that of a CIA collaborator in Greece in 1975. In November, 1983, it claimed responsibility for the assassination of a U.S. naval officer.

The past few years have seen European terrorist organizations increasingly striving for collaboration. International cooperation is apparent in several terrorist incidents. For example, Italian authorities are convinced that the kidnapping and subsequent holding for 42 days of the U.S. NATO Gen. James Dozier in Italy in 1981 was planned in Paris.

International cooperation is also substantiated by the fact that the German RAF and the French Action Directe have used explosives originating from the same source. In a joint communiqué released in January, 1985, headed "For the Unity of Revolutionaries in Western Europe," both groups avow that they are part of a West European guerrilla force and stress their intention to carry out joint terrorist actions. There is no reason to assume that the terrorist movements in Europe are under a common supreme command, but they exchange information and probably use Europe's easily crossed borders to elude the authorities.

It is unlikely that there is close cooperation between West German terrorists and the Irish Republican Army (IRA). On the other hand, the RAF named the assassination commando who carried out an attack in January, 1985, on the chairman of an arms manufacturing firm, after Patrick O'Hara, an Irish terrorist, died in a Belfast prison following a two-month hunger strike in 1981. The naming could also be propaganda meant to suggest cooperation with Irish terrorists.

Europe is frequently hit by imported terrorism — for example, the July, 1985, bomb attacks in Copenhagen. One of the bombs went off outside the office of an American airline while others were detonated in a synagogue. The attacks were claimed by a Beirut-based group calling itself Holy Islamic War.

European terrorist organizations sometimes cooperate with Arab groups. There are ties between Action Directe and the Armed Revolutionary Lebanese Factions, a Middle East terror organization originating in the Syrian-occupied part of Lebanon. This extremist group claimed responsibility for the slaying of the Israeli diplomat Jacob Barsimantev and the U.S. military attaché Charles Ray, and for the assassination of U.S. Ambassador Christian Chapman in Paris. There are indications that relations between RAF and Arab terrorists are improving.

Liberal democracies will never be able to stop terrorists attacks. This is because democracies cannot institute policies to the extent that totalitarian states can, nor are they generally in a position to develop perfect security systems against terrorist actions.

In Europe, terrorism probably will remain a political factor for a considerable time to come. The reason is not only the geostrategic location of Europe

---

> "The past few years have seen European [terrorists] striving for collaboration."

---

but also the lack of effective police coordination in fighting terrorism. Cooperation between national police forces is minimal and selective. For instance, it took much effort to induce the Dutch and French authorities to extradite German terrorists captured by them because the terrorists claimed to be seeking political asylum.

The main targets of terrorist attacks in Europe are installations of NATO, the German army and the U.S. The attacks on military installations and citizens of the U.S. worldwide are intended to induce the U.S. to review its foreign policy. Such attacks could buttress those in the U.S. who favor a withdrawal of U.S. troops from Europe.

The more successful the authorities are in combating terrorist groups and the more weakened these groups become as a result, the greater the danger that individual attacks will become more brutal. This is exemplified by the slaying near Wiesbaden in August, 1985, of a U.S. soldier, Edward Pimental. Although the RAF was interested only in obtaining the corporal's identity card to gain access to the air base, the man was killed.

In West Germany, new problems arise every time convicted terrorists are released from prison after serving their term. For instance, a convicted German terrorist disappeared into the terrorist underground immediately after his release. It can be assumed that most convicted terrorists remain faithful to terrorist ideas even in their prison cells.

There can be no doubt that the Soviet Union directly supports "liberation movements" in their struggle against "imperialism." But there is no conclusive evidence that the Soviet Union backs, let alone directs, the terrorist activities of the Red Army Faction, Action Directe in France or Belgium's Communist Fighting Cells. And there is no reliable evidence that an organization like the Soviet intelligence agency KGB has a steering function.

Although the East bloc has an interest in destabilizing the West, there is no proof that West European terrorists have been supported by any Eastern intelligence agencies. However, passive support can be assumed, as some terrorists can move freely in the East bloc (among them Abul Abbas, who following the seizure of the cruise ship *Achille Lauro* flew from Rome to Belgrade).

Terrorism is a weapon of the weak. The Marxist terrorists of the New Left have no real backing among the people of Europe. But by operating in concert with terrorists controlled by Libya and extremist Arab organizations, a military dimension is increasingly becoming evident. The "anti-imperialism" of European terrorists is directed primarily against military forces stationed in Europe in a bid to gain international recognition as military fighters. This is why captured terrorists demand that they be treated as prisoners of war.

Finally, there is the background element of student unrest. Terrorism in Europe would be unthinkable without the student revolts that broke out in Western democracies in the 1960s and that rank among the most important movements in European postwar history. The unrest in the U.S., where it began, was different from that in the Old World, where it became heavily ideological along the lines of political philosophies — especially Marxism.

(No. 2, 1986)

An Island unto Itself

The Roots of Japan's International Isolation

Susumu Ohara

Editor and General Manager
Japan Economic Journal

Delivered at the 31st JCA Professional Committee Meeting, Hakone, Japan, January 24, 1986.

Susumu Ohara

Born in 1932. After graduating from the Department of Anglo-American Studies of the Tokyo University of Foreign Studies, Susumu ("Shin") Ohara joined the staff of the Nihon Keizai Shimbun, *Japan's leading business daily, in 1954. He was posted to the United States in 1963 to open and head the paper's Washington news bureau, returning to the Tokyo head office as deputy foreign news editor in 1968. Mr. Ohara was named editor of the* Japan Economic Journal, *the paper's weekly international edition, in 1974 and also became general manager in 1982. In March 1986, he was appointed president of Nihon Keizai Shimbun America Inc., in New York. Mr. Ohara has written several books in Japanese and translated many books from English into Japanese, including* Japan Inc. *(1972),* The Seven Sisters *(1976), and* The Islamic Bomb *(1981).*

MANY of you here today, and I include those of you from the United States, are familiar with Japanese newspapers and their peculiarities. At the start of every new year, for example, one can find a seemingly endless tirade of special New Year's features on the state of things in Japan and what problems and tasks the nation faces in the near and distant future. Some years the major papers pick up the same theme, and some years the themes vary. I might add that neither are the electronic media immune from this holiday practice. Indeed, few are the Japanese who are able to escape the media onslaught.

Now, don't get me wrong. While some may feel it all a waste of time or simply another opportunity to attract advertisers, the practice does have its uses. The New Year's articles, though often only rehash, do sometimes serve to throw into the limelight issues the public should be aware of or made to think about.

New Year 1986 saw four of Japan's six so-called national newspapers—all big opinion leaders in a society not known for its plurality of mind—discuss essentially the same theme. It probably won't surprise you to hear that this year's subject of so much attention was, or better yet *is*, Japan's in-creasing isolation in the international community. You may or may not have taken a gander at the papers earlier this month, but you are doubtless aware that the issue is a real one. How the situation is to be resolved is another question, and let me assure you, there are no easy answers. I would like to make a few comments on the matter, if I may be permitted.

Why is the issue of an isolated Japan the subject of so much attention this New Year? Because, I think, the problem is only getting larger, not smaller, and the need for an answer only greater.

Here is the question: Will Japan be able to live harmoniously with the rest of the world in the future? If things are to continue their present course, then I would be tempted to be pessimistic and say no. But I want to be optimistic. The mass media like to use the term *internationalization* when discussing this issue; it is a pleasantly vague term and the press is not at all hesitant to use it. We are reminded constantly that internationalization is under way and assured that it will mean a bright future for Japan.

Now, I'm all for internationalization, but to be honest, I'm more than a little bit concerned about how much it will achieve. How deep will it go? I'm not asking out of concern that too comprehensive a change might prove deleterious to the foundations of Japanese society. Rather, I think the only lasting, beneficial changes will have to be on a profoundly deep level. That is the hope I pin on internationalization—that it be thorough.

It is the state of relations between the United States and Japan that cries most loudly for any benefits that can be derived from so-called internationalization. The most obvious problems lie almost exclusively in the economic arena. We all know what they are: an unprecedentedly large trade deficit, unfair trade practices, calls for pro-

Reprinted from *Speaking of Japan*, (Tokyo), May 1986, pp. 18-21.

tectionism, closed markets, hostility. And the list goes on; I don't think I need elaborate.

Until some time ago, Japanese press comments on the trade issue tended to call upon both sides to make more efforts to improve and rectify the huge imbalance. They urged Japan to open its markets wider and faster, and the United States to step up its efforts to penetrate them.

I myself was part of the chorus. I wrote along those lines to the Japanese audience in Japanese and to the American audience in English. At the 47th World Trade Conference, which was held in Chicago in 1984, I was one of the guest speakers and gave a speech entitled "Emotionalism on Both Sides of the Pacific." My conclusion then was that to overcome protectionist sentiment and any resulting retaliatory measures on both sides of the Pacific, every effort should be made to avoid emotional politicization of particular bilateral trade issues.

I was critical of what I considered to be emotional overreaction in both countries. I cited phrases like *Japan bashing* or *Japanese conspiracy,* which frequently appeared in the American press, as examples of hostility in the United States.

I also criticized emotionalism in Japan, emotionalism stemming from resentment toward things like U.S. pressure to open up markets. The emotionalism on the Japanese side, of course, differs from the American variety; Japan has yet to shake off feelings of inferiority, feelings of being America's "little brother."

"...we Japanese need to ask some fundamental questions...about our country, our society and culture, and ourselves."

That was how I felt two years ago, and that is what I tried to communicate in my speech at the World Trade Conference in Chicago. But let me tell you: I don't feel that way anymore. I no longer take the position that both sides are to blame. I have come to the conclusion that it is the outcome that matters and not the factors that lead to it. In a word, it is the Japanese side that is more to blame and that should take the initiative. Japan can no longer depend on its role as junior partner to the United States and therefore expect automatic acceptance even in the face of friction. Although Japan itself may not have yet realized it, the "little brother" role was lost years ago, when the country came to gain its present position of economic prominence. Japan has come into its own; now if only it would act as though it had.

Do not think that the Japanese are not aware

that change and a more developed sense of global responsibility are being demanded of them by the rest of the world. They cannot help but be aware of it, the way it is being drilled into them by the mass media. The press and electronic media warn of the strong feelings abroad and the possibly dire consequences should Japan ignore them. They preach, with a fervor that suggests an impending crisis, that an isolated Japan will mean the demise of its prosperity before long. The Japanese learn through their newspapers, televisions, and radios that they must find a way to live in harmony as a member of the world community.

Although the rhetoric may be thick, the Japanese like to listen to it. Whether they really believe that internationalization in the real sense can be achieved, however, is another question.

The newspapers are full of articles attacking Japanese trade policy, specifically the barriers that hold off foreign products from Japanese markets. We are playing with fire by resisting these imports, they say. But coupled with this admirable self-criticism, there is a reluctance—some might claim an inability—to do anything about it. This reluctance goes beyond the institutional, I think. It is found in the individual.

I think that few would argue with me if I said that the economic strife between Japan and the United States is indicative of other problems, problems that go deeper than just economics. Without question, the most pressing issue is the economic one, and it is the one in need of the most immediate attention. But it has also pointed out the need for other changes, changes that Japan must make in the very way it sees itself and the rest of the world, changes in things as fundamental as ways of thinking and living. While the huge trade deficit and a closed market may be viewed as problems, I rather liken them to symptoms. These symptoms did not arise out of themselves but must have roots in Japanese society itself. We can say that solving the economic issue is the priority, but how can we say anything is solved if the origins of the issue are left unexamined?

While it is all very well for journalists, television commentators, scholars, and the like to call for internationalization to go beyond the marketplace and into Japanese society at all its levels—certainly not undesirable demands—it is very likely that the majority of these individuals would feel uncomfortable working side by side with non-Japanese. The same goes for students coming from abroad to study in Japan. Their numbers are abysmally small compared to the number in the United States, or even in England or West Germany. Whatever excuses Japan likes to make about the difficulty of the language or living conditions for foreigners, it is best to remember that these are only excuses. While Prime Minister Nakasone should be applauded for his proposal to boost the number of foreign students in Japan from the current 14,000 to 100,000 by the turn of the century, I wonder how the Japanese people will react to this. Students from Third World nations, in particular, will have a hard time finding accommodations among Japanese, who have a deep-rooted aversion to them. You may often hear Japanese speak of their affinity for their "fellow Asians," but in all but a few Japanese no such affinity exists. Loathing is closer to the truth, if you will permit me to be blunt.

Indeed, we Japanese need to ask some fundamental questions, questions about our country, our society and culture, and ourselves.

Japan's image in the United States has not fared well of late, and an anti-Japanese mood is finding accommodation in some quarters of the American public. A good example of this can be found in an article entitled "The Danger of Japan," by Theodore H. White, which appeared in the *New York Times Magazine* on July 28, 1985. White accuses Japan of dismantling American industry in a new offensive to win the war. He says that the United States

---

"...Japan's trade practices are its worst enemy in the long run..."

---

must never again repeat the postwar mistake of being merciful and generous toward Japan. Such policies, he says, have allowed Japan to barricade itself against imports as it put its energy into catching up with the West and launching export assaults on markets overseas. A Japanese correspondent who interviewed White for one of the New Year's feature articles concluded that Japan has much to learn from his logic.

Of course, most Americans take a far less extreme attitude when it comes to discussing bilateral relations, and I only use the White article here to emphasize my point. But I don't know even one American who will say he or she is satisfied with the current state of affairs.

Japan must change the way it is perceived by other countries, but not through ways designed just to hide what others don't wish to see.

Bill Hosokawa, an honorary consul general of Japan in Denver, Colorado, says, "Americans respond to individualists, and my advice to the Japanese government is to develop a new cultural and public-relations initiative by dispatching people of this type to the United States." Mr. Hosokawa thinks that sending sumo wrestlers and Kabuki troupes is well and good, but their performances do little to really communicate to Americans how modern-day Japanese think, act, and view the world. He says, "I cannot overemphasize this point: American society is most receptive to individualists. And to Americans today, the Japanese are a race of faceless machines."

Let me quote another Japanese on this issue. He is Akira Irie, a professor at the University of Chicago. He believes that "Japan must seek a frank and open relationship with the United States, even at the risk of a certain amount of inefficiency." He goes on to say that, "given the degree of interdependence between the two countries today, it is meaningless to talk of features that make Japan unique or different."

It is up to the Japanese to see that internationalization will mean more than only liberalization of financial markets and boosted consumption of foreign goods. It is important that the Japanese realize that solving the trade imbalance is not enough, not nearly enough, and that it must not stop there if Japan is to ensure for itself a position of equality and respect in the world community.

Historically, the openness and frankness that Japanese so admire in Americans has never been at home in Japanese society. But things can change, and they can change fast if there is a will. Our economic successes after the war were, unfortunately, not complemented by developments of a more psychological nature. That is not to say that we cannot change. But neither is it to say that we will. The desire must be there first.

To close, I would like to say that I think Japan's trade practices are its worst enemy in the long run, and I hope changes are made before real destruction to our economy from the likes of protectionism by foreign trading partners appears. Japan shouldn't wait for warnings and threats to be realized before it acts. It should do so now, while there is still the possibility that it can earn praise from abroad for its actions.

(The title of this speech was provided by the editor.)

Breaching the line

Nakasone stays out of range on military budget

Charles Smith in Tokyo

Compared to the furore which greeted Prime Minister Yasuhiro Nakasone's failed attempt in the autumn of 1985 to scrap Japan's longstanding policy of limiting defence spending to under 1% of gross national product, there was an appearance of something approaching careless ease about the way in which Japan's cabinet decided, just before the New Year holiday, to allow a de facto breeching of the limit in 1987. However, defence lobbyists in the US and elsewhere who concluded that Japan has finally begun to base its decisions on armaments expenditure on common sense rather than an allegedly irrelevant and out-of-date political rule of thumb, could be disappointed.

Although the scrapping of the 1% limit may be seen as symbolising a break with the anti-military traditions of the past, the government seems unlikely to be able to avoid setting a new framework for future spending — possibly doing no more than substituting the word "around" for "under" in the wording of the original 1976 cabinet resolution setting the 1% limit. Whether or not a change of wording releases more funds for defence spending, it seems clear that debates on defence policy will continue to be dominated by "theology," not by a discussion of security issues as such.

Given the sensitivities of Japan's neighbours about its military past and its position as the region's only great economic power, this is probably natural enough. A sharp rise in defence spending, based on a decision by Japan to match the Soviet military build-up in Northeast Asia is no more conceivable under the "security-minded" Nakasone than under some of his more pacifist predecessors.

Defence emerged as one of the major stumbling blocks in Nakasone's programme for "settling Japan's postwar political accounts" in September 1985 when he tried to push through a cabinet decision abolishing the 10-year-old limit on defence spending, only to be forced to retract at the last moment.

In deciding to confront the defence spending issue before it was strictly necessary, Nakasone misjudged his own standing within the ruling Liberal Democratic Party (LDP) even more seriously than the state of public opinion — his chief opponents over the issue included two former prime ministers who vetoed his proposals primarily to pay off personal grievances.

A year later the cards seem to have been stacked very differently. Nakasone was careful to remain on the sidelines during the critical debate on the night of 29-30 December when two members of his cabinet and three senior LDP executives hammered out a decision under which the 1987 defence budget will be allowed to rise by 5.2% from the 1986 level, reaching 1.004% of this year's forecast GNP.

Even if he had taken an active part in the discussions the prime minister would have had less at stake than during the 1985 bargaining on defence issues. The LDP's landslide election victory in July 1986 has made it easier for the party, and particularly for Nakasone himself, to attack sensitive issues without worrying overmuch about the short-term impact on the cabinet's support rating.

The boldness with which Nakasone and his aides pushed through a controversial tax-reform proposal in early December exemplified the party's new-found readiness to challenge public opinion on sensitive issues.

Quite apart from the favourable electoral equation, changes within the LDP have made it easier for Nakasone to call the shots on defence than was the case in late 1985. His two main opponents during the 1985 debacle, former prime ministers Takeo Fukuda and Zenko Suzuki, retired after the July election as leaders of the LDP's second and third largest intra-party factions.

Their successors, Finance Minister Kiichi Miyazawa and Executive Council chairman Shintaro Abe, were directly involved in the discussions on the 1987 defence budget and are thus unlikely to launch a counterattack against the prime minister over the 1% issue. Both men in fact may have been glad to see the critical decisions on defence taken before Nakasone steps down as party leader and prime minister later this year, especially as they are themselves both potential candidates for party leadership.

The third LDP "new leader," Noboru Takeshita, may have had an equally strong interest in seeing the 1% issue tackled by the present government rather than its successor. As secretary-general of the party, Takeshita chaired the 29 December meeting at which the proposal to breach the 1% limit was discussed, but responsibility for the actual decision remains conveniently split between him and his senior party colleagues. Chief Cabinet Secretary Masaharu Gotoda, a close Nakasone aide who has consistently favoured higher defence spending, also played a key part in the discussions.

The scrapping of the 1% ceiling, combined with the downward pressure of exchange rates on the cost of imported (largely US) military equipment, means that the Defence Agency will be able to buy at least three-quarters of the military hardware specified in its original budget proposal to the Finance Ministry. The agency will be allowed 13 out of 14 new warships listed in its original draft, 12 out of a total of 16 requested new fighter aircraft and 52 of the 56 tanks included in the Ground Self-Defence Forces.

Beyond making it possible to acquire most of the hardware needed in the original 1987 defence build-up programme, however, the government's "watershed" decision on defence leaves many questions unanswered. It is still uncertain whether and how Japan will find the funds needed to implement a five-year defence build-up programme adopted in 1985 which calls for total spending of ¥18.6 trillion (US$123.7 billion) by the end of fiscal 1991. Considerably more sensitive than the question of new arms procurement is that of how the Defence Agency will meet deferred payment obligations on equipment that has already been ordered.

Although the government releases few details about the terms on which the agency buys military hardware, press reports suggest that about ¥2 trillion worth of instalments are due on existing weaponry — equivalent to roughly 1.6 times the value of this year's expenditure on new equipment. A further problem the government faces is how to raise, or even maintain, its military recruitment levels without paying substantially more to defence personnel whose wages and salaries already account for an unusually large 43% of total defence spending.

As a simple way to create a new framework for defence spending without unduly alarming neighbouring countries (or pacifist-minded voters at home) the cabinet originally planned to announce that, though the 1% ceiling was being abolished, the government would under no circumstances spend more money on defence over the coming five years than would be needed to implement the current defence build-up plan. The fact that, at the last moment, a statement of this kind was not included in the announcement suggests that someone — possibly Nakasone himself — might have had cold feet.

The government now says it plans to wait until after Nakasone's return from an impending tour of Eastern Europe to announce a new defence framework. This will be adopted as a cabinet resolution (like the original 1% guideline) and is thus not subject to approval by parliament, where three out of the four major opposition parties are strongly opposed to further increases in defence spending. Even so, defence, along with tax reform, will probably top the list of contentious issues liable to hold up normal business during the regular parliamentary session which starts at the end of January.

The new defence guideline that now seems likely to be adopted, one committing the government to maintain spending at "around" 1% of GNP, probably will be interpreted as a licence to raise spending to at least 1.2% of GNP, though the LDP's own defence lobbyists may argue that "around" means anything up to 1.5%. How much spending actually rises, however, may continue to reflect the government's reading of public opinion on the sensitive defence issue. Steering a course that avoids the two extremes of alienating Japan's neighbours and leaving the country embarrassingly dependent on US military protection (and thus open to US accusations of a "free ride") will remain a tricky task — and may be trickier than ever with the removal of a precise numerical limit on the defence budget.

Socialist States: Allies and Adversaries of the USSR

The international Communist movement of the 1980s is less international and less communistic than in earlier times. A combination of pragmatism, disenchantment with the Soviet model, and nationalism in Eastern Europe and China has forced so many changes within this movement that what remains today is structure without content.

In the early 1960s, the Chinese Communists asserted that a "socialist camp" no longer existed. This reflected their disenchantment with international socialism under Moscow's leadership, a feeling reinforced by the 1968 Soviet invasion of Czechoslovakia and Moscow's invocation of the "Brezhnev doctrine." If China had admitted to being a member of a socialist camp, it might thereby have made itself more vulnerable to a Soviet invasion justified by that doctrine, which stated that the interests of any one socialist country are not as great as the interests of the socialist community as a whole. At the time, China viewed itself as more Marxist and revolutionary than the "revisionist" and "capitalist" Soviet Union.

Now both in form and in policy content and in spite of the campaign against "bourgeois literalism," China is acting as if Marxism is irrelevant and outdated. Only shards of Communist doctrine remain in place, while the ever-pragmatic reformers enact a host of modernizing reforms which use capitalist methods and structures. No doubt with an eye toward the failure of rigid, centralized dogmatism in China and the Soviet Union, the Chinese Communists have chosen to be less communistic in order to bring about the promised goal of modernization.

This change in policy and value orientation has not, however, been accompanied by growing animosity toward the Soviets. In fact, China's confrontations with the Soviet Union were far more serious when it imagined itself the ideological equal to, or the superior of, the Soviet Union. China's reformers have now jettisoned their ideological pretensions. The Sino-Soviet relationship has also been influenced by the relationship of each country to the United States. Neither the Chinese nor the Soviets are very happy that the United States might gain the upper hand in the triangular balance of power by manipulating the one against the other. China, in particular, has tried to establish as much of an equilibrium in its relationship to the two superpowers as possible; but thus far China's economic and political interests heavily favor growing rapport with the United States.

Likewise on their western flank, the Soviets contemplate the disintegration of many of the props of the international Communist movement. Foremost among these is Soviet control of the economies of the Eastern European states.

The last decade has witnessed the steady disintegration of these ties, largely because the Soviets are no longer able to underwrite the international debt of their socialist allies due to the additional weight of their own economic failures. Thus they have been willing to tolerate economic liberalization at the expense of the socialist model of centralized state planning, and have even encouraged Eastern European states to expand their economic and monetary ties with the capitalist West. As a result, the economies of Hungary and Romania are less under the control of the Soviets than of the International Monetary Fund (IMF). The IMF tells their leaders how to run their economies if they want continued financial support. With Poland once again in the IMF, its economy will likewise be orchestrated by IMF financiers. What concerns the Soviets is that these growing East-West economic and financial ties may have far-reaching implications for economic and political influences, even control, by the capitalist West over the Soviets' Eastern European allies. The control over butter may in the long run confer more power than the control over guns.

On the other hand, strong Soviet leadership, an important component of Soviet control over the international Communist movement, has rebounded after several years of floundering. Gorbachev has reasserted Soviet leadership of, if not over, Eastern Europe. He has interfered less than his predecessors with efforts by some of those countries to improve human rights conditions, perhaps because the improvement of such conditions has become increasingly linked, under the Helsinki accords, to Western investments and hence to economic and technological development. Further, Gorbachev appears willing to accept the reality of the growing currents of independence within Eastern European countries. He recognizes that the Soviet Union can no longer force these countries into exchanging goods in barter arrangements unfavorable to themselves, particularly when they now have Western countries as alternative sources of supplies and markets. Gorbachev may even assess the efforts of these Eastern European governments to take charge of their own development as a positive trend, as long as the general tone of their foreign policy and the substance of their security measures are aligned with Moscow's. Gorbachev's willingness to propose complete disarmament by the year 2000, including removal of medium-range ballistic missiles from the territory of Eastern Europe may, in part, be a response to local pressure; but to Gorbachev's credit, it must be said that his predecessors usually responded rigidly to just such chafing from Eastern European states.

Unit 4

Perhaps Gorbachev learned from America's experience with its Western European allies that, once countries attain a certain level of economic strength and are more involved with the international community, there are countervailing pressures and options that diminish the significance of a once-dominant power. The Soviets can hardly prohibit the Eastern European states from trading with the West when they themselves do. Besides, as Eastern European growth becomes less tied to support from the Soviet Union, the Soviets can, in turn, ask them to pay a higher price for Soviet resources, notably oil.

Thus, while the Kremlin cannot be entirely happy with East Germany's growing relations with West Germany, nor with the formers' increasing economic dependence on the latter, it can do little to prevent their relations from developing. A case could be made, in fact, that of all the Eastern European countries, the Soviets need the active support and friendship of East Germany and Poland the most. Their size, wealth, and geographical position make them keys to both the Soviets' security and its technical and economic power. The Soviets, after all, look to East Germany when they cannot get technology from the West. And although Polish dissidents still challenge Communist party rule under Moscow's control, the Polish government has recently been able to relax its policies on political dissidents, and the economy is making progress (Article 24). Further, the astounding economic success of Hungary's economy, which has combined socialist and market principles, and the Soviet Union's own recent efforts to replace administrative with economic instruments for managing the economy, make it in Moscow's best interest to look the other way when orthodox Marxist principles are violated (Article 25). Except for military defense, then, the Soviet Union can no longer deal with the Eastern European countries as subordinate junior partners.

The same is true for China. China may not be as developed as the Soviet Union, but it is now developing far more rapidly than the Soviet Union, and without Soviet help. According to Beijing, they will have an equal relationship, or none at all. Since 1982, Sino-Soviet relations have been characterized by limited accommodation, and

a concern for maintaining the balance of power. But although China professes it will maintain equidistance between the two superpowers, the fact is that the scale of Sino-American relations dwarf the scale of Sino-Soviet relations (Article 23). One explanation for this is that within China's security zone, the policies of China and the US are compatible, whereas geopolitics have contributed to considerable tensions between the Chinese and Soviets. Nevertheless, China's strategic ties with the US will remain limited for the time being out of a concern for not upsetting the Soviet Union (Article 22). The Chinese insist, on the other hand, that in economic relationships with the West, the door remains "open." This is in spite of attacks on "bourgeois liberalization," which the Chinese consider a negative consequence of their relations with the capitalist world (Article 26).

Looking Ahead: Challenge Questions

Are recent developments in Eastern Europe's relationship with the Soviet Union in some sense analogous to how Western Europe's relationship with the United States has evolved? To what extent do they arise from similar or from different conditions? Why has greater autonomy for Eastern Europe come so much later than for Western Europe? Does a greater independence of eastern European countries from the Soviet Union necessarily jeopardize the security relations embodied in the Warsaw Pact? Is Moscow's control of international socialism under siege, or is it simply undergoing a metamorphosis in the form it takes?

Do China's internal reforms, which adopt some elements of capitalist economic systems, suggest that China is abandoning socialism as a political and economic doctrine? Why are China's major economic ties with capitalist countries? Does China have more to gain from a closer relationship with the Soviet Union and the socialist camp, or with the United States and the capitalist camp? What appears to be the major determinant of China's decisions concerning its relationship with other countries, ideology or pragmatism?

Sino–American Relations: Policies in Tandem

This article notes that "relations between the United States and China in 1986 are healthy but fragile. The relationship has become multifaceted, encompassing foreign policy, trade and investment, security ties and cultural relations."

JOHN BRYAN STARR

Executive Director, Yale–China Association, Yale University

John Bryan Starr is a lecturer in the department of political science at Yale University. His most recent book is *The Future of US–China Relations* (New York: New York University Press, 1982).

R ELATIONS between the United States and China, which reached something of a post-normalization nadir in 1981, have improved significantly over the last five years. The cooling of bilateral ties in the early years of the administration of Ronald Reagan was occasioned by China's reassessment of its ties with Moscow, with Washington, and with other nations in the third world.[1]

While China had nominally pledged itself to a policy of identification with the third world and to the avoidance of an alliance with either of the superpowers, Chinese and American initiatives and policy statements in 1979 and 1980 lent credence to the perception that Beijing and Washington were creating a strategic relationship designed to counter Soviet interests in East Asia. This perception served to alienate both the Soviet Union and third world states, a detriment that was not counterbalanced, in Beijing's view, by the gains deriving from its closer ties with the United States.

Moreover, the Chinese apparently believed that the future of Sino–American relations was seriously threatened by Ronald Reagan's election in 1980. Reagan was known to have close personal ties to members of the government on Taiwan and had campaigned with a promise to "upgrade" relations with Taiwan. Thus the Chinese believed that President Reagan was likely to undo the progress made in building Sino–American relations under Presidents Richard Nixon, Gerald Ford and Jimmy Carter. These two factors brought about a shift in Chinese policy: distancing Beijing from Washington and reaffirming China's independence in world affairs.

In office, however, President Reagan pursued policies toward China very different from those promised by Reagan the campaigner. By 1982, the "darkening clouds" that the Chinese had seen hovering over the state of relations the preceding year had begun to dissipate. Two years later, the relationship's improved state was symbolized by the exchange of visits between President Reagan and Chinese President Li Xiannian.

Today, the relationship is strong and multifaceted. The United States and China are pursuing remarkably parallel policies with their Pacific Basin neighbors. United States trade with and investment in China have expanded rapidly and substantially. Cultural relations, especially academic exchanges, have grown exponentially. Finally, perhaps the most significant area of development in recent years has been that of military cooperation and arms sales. For all its strengths, however, the relationship is not without its problems. In each of its facets there are obstacles to further progress.

Samuel Kim has drawn a distinction between China's attitude toward nations and events within its "security zone" and its attitude toward nations and events outside this zone. Kim notes that within this security zone, China's interests are at stake, whereas outside this zone China's norms are involved.[2] While China has become increasingly critical of certain aspects of United States foreign policy since 1981, that criticism is directed primarily at United States policies toward and actions in areas that lie outside China's security zone, where norms and not interests are at stake. Within the security zone, a strong confluence of interests between the United States and China has developed. This confluence is manifested in Chinese and American policies toward Japan, Korea, the states of the Association of Southeast Asian Nations (ASEAN) and Indochina. The exception, of course, is Taiwan.

Both China and the United States regard their relations with Japan as the keystone in developing Pacific Basin policies. The two have a comparable trade relationship with Japan; in each case, trade is large in volume and unbalanced in Japan's favor.[3] Both have an interest in seeing Japan bear an increased share of regional security costs, though this interest is mitigated in China's case by China's lingering concern over the potential revival of Japanese militarism and expansionism—a concern not shared by the United States.

Like the United States, China has an interest in maintaining stability on the Korean peninsula. China is strongly committed to maintaining close ties with North Korea in order to maintain distance between Pyongyang and Moscow. As a result, Beijing has presented itself to Washington as a potential intermediary in United States contacts with North Korea and as a potential participant in reunifying the peninsula. At the same time, there are growing unofficial ties between China and South Korea.

China's relations with the ASEAN states have improved steadily over the last five years. Most of these states continue to regard China as a potential threat to their security, and many of them have a troubled relationship with the Chinese minorities living within their borders. Nonetheless they react favorably to the fact that, in the interest of developing trade ties, China has stopped supporting insurgencies in the region. As a result, American and Chinese policies toward the ASEAN states are now closely parallel.

Although the United States and China found themselves on opposite sides during the conflict in Vietnam, that disagreement ended in the late 1970's as China's relations with Hanoi deteriorated. Like the United States, China opposes Soviet assistance to Vietnam and Vietnam's control over Laos and Kampuchea. Both Beijing and Washington support the coalition of anti-Vietnamese Kampuchean forces nominally headed by Prince Norodom Sihanouk. And Beijing and Washington have been equally cool toward recent Vietnamese overtures advocating improved relations.

The exception to this confluence of American and Chinese interests in the Pacific Basin is Taiwan. Indeed, the Chinese continue to refer to Taiwan as the most important obstacle to further improvement in Sino–American relations. While Beijing appears to be satisfied with United States adherence to the August, 1982, Sino–American joint communiqué (in which it was agreed that United States arms sales to Taiwan would be gradually reduced and ultimately terminated), the Chinese are not satisfied with current American policy on the reunification of Taiwan with the mainland.

Beijing has made what it regards as its last and most generous offer of terms for reunification.[4] In addition, it has concluded an agreement for the transfer of sovereignty over Hong Kong that it considers a model and a potential incentive for Taiwan. Despite what Beijing regards as its generosity and its probity, Taiwan has refused to enter into negotiations over the question of reunification. Faced with this intransigence, Beijing believes that only United States pressure can persuade Taiwan to negotiate. Using an earlier Chinese argument—namely, that the Taiwan question is an internal matter that can be decided only by the Chinese parties themselves—the United States has so far refused to exert pressure on Taiwan. Aside from the question of whether or not it would be appropriate for the United States to involve itself as an advocate for Beijing's position, the Chinese assumption that such involvement would be effective is highly questionable.

TRADE AND INVESTMENT

The "Open Door" policy inaugurated in 1978 by First Deputy Prime Minister (now de facto leader) Deng Xiaoping and his colleagues calls for China's increasing involvement in the world economy. As a result, foreign trade as a percentage of gross national product has increased from less than 12 percent in 1980 to more than 26 percent in 1985, with most of the growth occurring during the last two years. The prospect of substantial trade and investment was an important factor in the decision by the United States and China to normalize relations in 1979. Although businesspeople in the United States and officials in China both complain that the growth of trade and investment over the last seven years has not met their expectations, this growth is impressive nonetheless.

Total two-way trade between the United States and China in 1985 amounted to some $8.08 billion, up more than 26 percent over the previous year.[5] This trade constitutes 11.6 percent of China's total two-way trade, placing the United States third (behind

Japan and Hong Kong) among China's trading partners. United States exports to China in 1985 totaled $3.86 billion; most important were exports of civilian aircraft, logs, fertilizer, wheat, and oil and gas drilling equipment. Most important among China's exports to the United States, which totaled $4.22 billion, were crude petroleum, gasoline, tin, stuffed toys and cotton cloth.[6]

In addition to expanding trade relations, the Chinese have actively encouraged foreign investment in their economy. Laws governing the operation of equity joint ventures were promulgated in 1984. Special economic zones (SEZ's), in which preferential regulations favoring foreign investors apply, were set up in Guangdong and Fujian provinces. Subsequently, 14 cities located along the China coast were given the autonomy to sign agreements with foreign firms.

Hong Kong firms have been quick to take advantage of the preferential treatment available to them as investors in the SEZ's and coastal cities. Of the 925 joint venture agreements signed by the end of 1984, some 734, or 80 percent, involved Hong Kong companies. By contrast, American firms have been relatively slow to respond to investment opportunities in China. At this writing, fewer than 100 joint venture agreements have been signed between American firms and Chinese co-investors. This constitutes less than 10 percent of the total. Total United States investment in China is currently estimated at about $1 billion, which is far below the expectations the Chinese had when they launched the Open Door policy eight years ago.

Several obstacles lie in the path of the further, more rapid development of Sino–American trade and investment. At the moment, the most important of these obstacles is the Chinese reaction to a sharp drop in Chinese foreign currency reserves over the last 18 months, caused primarily by the very substantial balance of payment deficits China experienced in 1984 and 1985, particularly in trade with Japan. Whereas at the end of 1984 China's reserves stood at $21.3 billion (including $4.6 billion in gold), by the end of 1985 they had dropped to less than $16 billion (including $4 billion in gold).

To stem the drain on foreign exchange, in joint venture agreements Chinese negotiators have been encouraged by their government to insist on terms that involve little or no expenditure of foreign exchange by the Chinese. Most welcome are projects, like hotels, that generate foreign exchange. Most difficult to negotiate are projects that produce profits in nonconvertible Chinese currency but call for the eventual repatriation of foreign capital in convertible currency.

A second obstacle to the further development of United States–Chinese economic ties is fear of United States firms about the political risk involved in investing in China. Potential investors, quite reasonably,

look back over the period since the founding of the People's Republic of China in 1949 and note that the last decade of stability and rapid economic development was preceded by nearly three decades of frequent policy shifts and fluctuating rates of economic development. The Chinese respond by asserting that the policy shift in 1978 is irreversible. They note that the current policy has resulted in a significant increase in the standard of living of the average Chinese citizen. As a result, the policy enjoys broad popular support. By contrast, the policies that preceded it are seen as having brought about the Cultural Revolution and, as a result, have been thoroughly and permanently discredited.

Few American businesspeople are completely convinced by these arguments. They see current policies as closely associated with Deng Xiaoping, now 82 years old, and they worry that Deng's policies are likely to be called into question when he no longer influences economic and political decision making. While they are impressed with Deng's success in selecting not only a second but also a third echelon of successors, they note that examples of a smooth transition of power in socialist political systems are very few indeed.

For their part, the Chinese have expressed dissatisfaction with American hesitation to license the sale of advanced technology to China. This reluctance has resulted from American laws preventing the sale of technology with a potential military application to nations who may use this technology against the United States. An important obstacle was overcome in December, 1985, when Congress approved the United States–Chinese nuclear accord originally signed during Chinese President Li's visit to the United States in July, 1985. There was some congressional opposition to the agreement because of allegations that China was exporting nuclear technology to Brazil, Argentina, South Africa, Pakistan and Iran. Approval came too late, however, to permit American firms to participate in the bidding for a major nuclear power plant project in Guangdong province; as a result, the project will be developed in cooperation with French, British and Hong Kong firms.

The government-to-government cultural ties forged during the first two years after normalization were severed by the Chinese in 1981 to protest the United States decision to grant political asylum to the defecting tennis player Hu Na. Reestablished in 1982, these ties, together with unofficial, institution-to-institution cultural and academic exchanges that continued unabated during the interruption of official ties, are flourishing.[7] Over the longer term, they may prove to have the greatest impact on Sino–American relations.

More than 15,000 Chinese students and scholars are currently living and working in the United States; they make up more than half of all Chinese now studying abroad. The current number of scholars is greater by a factor of six or seven than that of the pre-World War II peak. Roughly half the Chinese studying in the United States are financed by their government. The rest are what the Chinese call "self-funded," receiving support from relatives, friends or American institutions. A small fraction of the number are in the United States as participants in government-to-government or university-to-university exchange programs. A growing number apply as individuals directly to graduate schools for admission into advanced degree programs. The majority continue to arrange their visits through individual faculty sponsors in American colleges and universities. As visiting fellows, these Chinese scholars ordinarily work at an American institution free of tuition.

Only a few Chinese are enrolled as undergraduates in the United States because of the Chinese view that undergraduate education is an inappropriate level at which to invest scarce financial resources. Throughout this period, Chinese studying in the United States have been concentrated in the hard sciences, the natural sciences, mathematics, engineering and computer science. Fewer than 500 Americans are living and working in China. Most are employed by Chinese colleges and universities as teachers of English or other subjects. Others are enrolled as students in Chinese language instructional programs. A few are participants in government-to-government or university-to-university exchange programs and are carrying on their own research.

While thriving, the cultural relationship between the United States and China is not free of problems. One of these is the question of reciprocity. There is an inevitable imbalance in academic exchanges, given the level of development of American science and the financial resources available to fund exchanges. Once the novelty of having Chinese scholars in American institutions wears off, this imbalance may be more prominent and arguments in favor of greater reciprocity may prevail.

On the Chinese side, the potential for a "brain drain" is of particular concern. Visiting the United States in 1979, Deng Xiaoping spoke jokingly of the need to send twice the number of needed Chinese scholars to the United States, because half of them would decide to stay in the United States. Although there are no reliable statistics on the number of Chinese scholars who have decided not to return to China, the State Education Commission in Beijing regards the problem as potentially serious.

A final problem in cultural exchanges is a lingering attitude on the part of some Chinese that interactions between Americans and Chinese will have a pernicious effect on China's politics, society and culture. While arguments against "spiritual pollution" have become somewhat more muted in recent months, those opposed to Deng's Open Door believe that China's potential gain from increased trade, investment and access to Western technology does not outweigh the corrupting effects of Western values. Those supporting the opening to the West, including Deng himself, defend the policy on what has in the past proved to be a shaky argument, namely, that China will borrow Western techniques but it will not borrow Western values.

ARMS SALES AND STRATEGIC COOPERATION

Strategic considerations have affected Sino–American relations since the beginning of the process of normalization in 1971. The two sides were drawn toward one another at a time when Sino–Soviet relations had deteriorated to the point of armed conflict and when the United States was bogged down in a conflict in Vietnam with opponents heavily supported by Moscow. As early as 1973, the United States Department of Defense began to commission studies of the implications of a limited United States effort to strengthen China's defense capabilities. Five years later, and six months prior to the announcement of the normalization of relations between the two countries, National Security Adviser Zbigniew Brzezinski visited Beijing and called for "cooperation in the face of a common threat," the Soviet Union. Following his visit, the first sale to China of "dual-use" technology (that is, civilian technology with potential military application) was approved in Washington, and shortly thereafter the United States ceased to protest sales of military equipment to China by members of the North Atlantic Treaty Organization (NATO).

Although Brzezinski was responding, in part, to the Chinese suggestion of a tripartite relationship among the United States, Japan and China aimed against the Soviet Union, in retrospect it appears that perceptions of the nature of this relationship in Washington differed from those in Beijing. Whereas Washington was thinking in terms of an alliance, Beijing was thinking in more traditional terms of a looser relationship, a "united front." This difference of perception became apparent with the Chinese invasion of Vietnam, which followed close on the heels of Deng Xiaoping's visit to the United States in early 1979. The decision to invade Vietnam was taken without consultation with the United States, though the timing lent credence to the idea that the United States had given tacit approval to China's plans during Deng's visit to Washington.

A year after the normalization of relations, Secretary of Defense Harold Brown visited China. Because his visit followed only by a month the Soviet invasion of Afghanistan, the Chinese were particularly receptive to his raising of the topic of strategic cooperation with the United States. Following this visit the United States removed China from the category assigned to Warsaw Pact nations under the Munitions Control

Act, thereby legalizing United States arms sales to Beijing. Initial negotiations for such sales involved exclusively "nonlethal," "defensive" armaments.

With the appointment of Secretary of State Alexander Haig, President Reagan began to reassure Beijing. Haig visited China six months after President Reagan's inauguration in 1981 and reaffirmed American willingness to approve, on a case-by-case basis, the sale of nonlethal military equipment to China.

Two years later, when Secretary of Defense Caspar Weinberger visited China, talks on strategic cooperation resumed. They continued during the return visit to the United States of Zhang Aiping, China's minister of national defense. Among the agreements reached during the Zhang visit was one calling for a port visit to Shanghai by United States warships. Prompted by New Zealand's actions, the Chinese insisted that any ship visiting China should not carry nuclear arms. Because the United States will not divulge information on whether a ship is carrying nuclear weapons or not, the port visit was canceled.

The gradual easing of restrictions on the export to China of military-related technology resulted in a doubling (from 2,020 to 4,097) of sales approved by the United States government between 1982 and 1984. On the other hand, China's requests quadrupled over the same period. As a result, the percentage of requests granted under newly eased restrictions actually declined from 86 percent in 1982 to 46 percent in 1984.[8]

In January, 1985, General John W. Vessey, chairman of the Joint Chiefs of Staff, visited China. During the year following this visit, several agreements were reached regarding initial sales of military material to China. The first contracts called for the sale of military helicopters and naval boat engines. In September a contract was negotiated for the sale of equipment to manufacture artillery ammunition. Subsequently, in January, 1986, an agreement was negotiated calling for the modernization of navigation and fire control radar equipment for Chinese F-8 high-altitude interceptor aircraft.

Several factors militate against further arms sales and the rapid development of security ties between the United States and China. Washington and Beijing believe that Moscow will view closer Sino–American security ties with alarm. Neither side sees an advantage in alienating the Soviet Union. Indeed, current Chinese foreign policy calls for the encouragement of a rapprochement between Beijing and Moscow. While insisting on the resolution of the "Three Obstacles" standing in the way of such a rapprochement, the Chinese nonetheless believe that improved relations with the Soviet Union will prove to be an advantage to China.[9] Similarly, close security ties between the United States and China would work to the disadvantage of the United States, because such ties would have a destabilizing effect on relations between the Soviet Union and the United States.

China is more interested in importing American technology than it is in importing the products of American technology; this is a factor in limiting future arms sales. The shortage of foreign exchange also exerts a restraining influence. More important is China's reluctance to become dependent on a foreign supplier for key military hardware.

In setting forth the program known as the four modernizations—the modernization of agriculture, industry, science and technology and defense—Chinese planners made it clear from the outset that the modernization of the military must be preceded by the modernization of industry and the development of China's capacity to supply its own military needs. China's priorities were confirmed with the decision last summer to reduce the troop strength of the People's Liberation Army by 25 percent (from approximately four million to three million men). This decision suggests that for the moment the Chinese are postponing the upgrading of military hardware in favor of the development of civilian industry.[10]

CONCLUSION

Relations between the United States and China in 1986 are healthy but fragile. The relationship has become multifaceted, encompassing foreign policy, trade and investment, security ties and cultural relations. However, from the perspective of both Beijing and Washington, each of these facets involves potential stumbling blocks, and the existence of these stumbling blocks requires careful management.

[1]For a discussion of this period, see Steven I. Levine, "China and the United States: Limits of Interaction," in Samuel S. Kim, ed., *China and the World: Chinese Foreign Policy in the Post-Mao Era* (Boulder, Colo.: Westview Press, 1984), pp. 113–134. See also Harry Harding, "China's Changing Role in the Contemporary World," in Harry Harding, ed., *China's Foreign Relations in the 1980's* (New Haven: Yale University Press, 1984), pp. 177–224.

[2]Samuel S. Kim, "China and the Third World: In Search of a Neorealist World Policy," in Kim, op. cit., pp. 178–211.

[3]Japan is China's largest trading partner, accounting for more than 27 percent of China's total foreign trade. Two-way trade last year was $19 billion, more than double that between the United States and China. There was a $6-billion trade surplus in Japan's favor.

[4]In 1981, Marshal Ye Jianying put forward the "Nine Points" on the terms of reunification. Most important among these was the promise that following reunification, the economic system would remain intact and that Taiwan would be governed as a "special administrative region." In 1983, the Chinese constitution was rewritten to include a provision for such regions, a provision that applies to Hong Kong after 1997.

[5]Trade figures for 1985 are drawn from *China Business Review*, vol. 13, no. 3 (May–June, 1986), pp. 76–77.

[6]The $360-million trade surplus in China's favor shown in these figures is disputed by Chinese authorities, who exclude Chinese goods shipped through Hong Kong from their calculations, thus showing a deficit in excess of $2 billion in United States–Chinese trade last year. This figure was cited by State Councillor Gu Mu in conversation with foreign visitors in December, 1985.

[7]For a detailed evaluation of educational exchanges, see Committee on Scholarly Communication with the People's Republic of China, National Academy of Sciences, *Sino–American Educational Exchanges: Survey of Trends, 1978–84* (Washington, D.C.: National Academy Press, forthcoming).

[8]Figures drawn from Deng-ker Lee, "An Analysis of Washington–Peking Security Ties: Gains versus Risks," *Issues and Studies*, vol. 22, no. 3 (March, 1986), pp. 11–33.

[9]The Three Obstacles are the Soviet occupation of Afghanistan, Soviet assistance to Vietnam in its conflict in Kampuchea and the presence of Soviet troops and missiles on China's northern border.

[10]This view is expounded by Roger W. Sullivan, "US Military Sales to China: How Long Will the Window-shopping Last?" *China Business Review*, vol. 13, no. 2 (March–April, 1986), pp. 6–9.

China's Limited Accommodation with the U.S.S.R.: Coalition Politics

David M. Lampton

Until recently, many Americans had the comfortable illusion that China's current "open policy" meant simply opening up to the West generally and to the United States specifically. Beijing, however, has been careful to describe its fundamental policy as "opening up to the outside world." Since 1982 it has become progressively clear that this policy also embraces the Soviet Union. What forces have been driving China in Moscow's direction, how far are events likely to proceed, and what are the interests of the United States as the process of Sino-Soviet accommodation unfolds? Some possible improvements in relations between Moscow and Beijing should be welcomed by Washington—others should not.

Factors Propelling Chinese Foreign Policy

Though Zhou Enlai has been dead for just over a decade now, his foreign policy and the principles upon which it rested are very much alive. Zhou's disciples are spread liberally throughout the foreign affairs apparatus in Beijing today.[1] What were the central features of that foreign policy outlook that shapes China's contemporary behavior?

Zhou Enlai, like Mao Zedong and philosophers and statesmen throughout Chinese history, saw the world system as an ever-shifting balance of forces. It was a system in which powers once dominant were in decline and powers once weak were on the ascendancy. For Chinese statesmen, geopolitics is primary. There are no permanent friends—and no permanent enemies. The task of statecraft was (and is) to realign continually China's relationship with external powers in such a way as to maximize China's flexibility, to prevent the formation of a coalition capable of threatening

China's fundamental interests, and thereby to ensure an international environment consistent with the needs of domestic policy. Zhou Enlai saw the world in much the same way as Metternich saw it in the nineteenth century and Nixon and Kissinger see it in the twentieth. China finds both comfort and advantage in being the reluctant object of major power courtship.

Fundamental to this view is the calculation that some countries or regions are more important than others. The United States, the Soviet Union, Japan, and Europe are the key actors. Rhetorical alliance with the third world is useful principally to keep the major powers pliable and off balance. As in the 1960s, China may pursue a "revolutionary strategy" in the third world, but Chinese foreign policy derives from its assessment of the relationship among the principal powers.

Although China's foreign policy leaders have a balance-of-power outlook, disembodied strategic and tactical orientations are no more the sole determinant of foreign policy in China than they are anywhere else. The interests and perceptions of domestic constituencies are critical, as are the opportunities and threats that the international system presents. Any particular foreign policy will be consistent with the values, interests, and needs of some regions, sectors of the population, and leaders, while it runs contrary to the interests, needs, and values of others. As the dominance of particular regions, sectors, or leadership groups in China change, so too will Beijing's external policies, within the context of the constraints and opportunities provided by the international system.[2] Foreign policies are manifestations of domestic coalitions, as are domestic policies.

The balance-of-power orientation and the primacy of domestic politics account for the fluid and opportunistic nature of Chinese foreign policy. Nonetheless, in China, as elsewhere, there is a need to rationalize self-interested behavior in a larger moral framework.

I would like to acknowledge the research assistance provided by Ms. Chu Hsiao-fen. She undertook a great deal of documentary research for this project. I must also thank Kenneth Lieberthal and Jonathan Pollack for their comments on an earlier draft of this paper.

Therefore, one finds Chinese external policies that can be understood only as a response to balance-of-power and domestic considerations explained as principled stands. One finds assertions that policy will not change even as policy is in the very process of transformation. Sino-Soviet relations are a case in point. Beijing has continually claimed that normalization of relations will not occur until Moscow alters its behavior vis-à-vis the Sino-Soviet border, Kampuchea, and Afghanistan. Even so, China's policy toward the Soviet Union has been in the process of dramatic, albeit gradual, change. Normalization is a process, not an end state, and it has been under way since 1982.

A decade ago, Winston Lord anticipated the changes in Sino-Soviet relations with which he now must deal as Washington's new ambassador to China. He commented: "It is possible that the Russians and Chinese may come to see incentives for moderating their bilateral relations—their desire for greater diplomatic flexibility in their dealings with us and others, the lessening of at least border tensions, the openings caused by leadership successions in both countries."[3]

The day that Lord foresaw has arrived. How has China's policy toward the Soviet Union changed since 1982, and what accounts for these alterations? What are American interests?

Background: The Gradual Thaw, 1982 to 1986

Without ignoring some limited (and ultimately still-born) efforts to improve Sino-Soviet relations during the 1970s, the process of limited accommodation now under way between Moscow and Beijing had its origins in 1982, the last year of Leonid Brezhnev's life. At this time, the new Reagan administration was uncertain about the weight to assign Beijing (compared with Japan) in its strategic calculus. The issue of arms sales to Taiwan was front and center in the Sino-American relationship, and Beijing had ample reason to be anxious about the level at which the new American president would conduct relations with Taipei. Indeed, in February 1982, a central work conference in Beijing produced decisions to resist arms sales to Taiwan vigorously, to emphasize the primacy of central planning and the secondary role played by market forces, to increase the emphasis accorded heavy industry (downplayed since mid-1979), and to recognize that reform was creating fertile conditions for corruption and ideological deviation.

Moscow was quick to see the opening these events provided, and General Secretary Brezhnev, while in Tashkent in March 1982, made a major policy state-ment concerning Sino-Soviet relations. Four points in his declaration were particularly important: (1) "we did not deny and do not now the existence of a socialist system in China"; (2) "we have never supported and do not support now in any form the so-called concept of two Chinas"; (3) "we are also ready to discuss the question of possible measures to strengthen mutual trust in the area of the Soviet-Chinese frontier"; and (4) "we are prepared to come to terms, without any preliminary conditions, on measures acceptable to both sides to improve Soviet-Chinese relations on the basis of mutual respect for each other's interests, non-interference in each other's affairs and mutual benefit—certainly, not to the detriment of third countries."[4]

In its initial response, Beijing chose to tie improvement of bilateral relations to altered Russian behavior along the Sino-Soviet border, in Afghanistan, and in Kampuchea ("the three major obstacles").[5] Nonetheless, by September 1, 1982, the Chinese leadership stated publicly at the Twelfth Party Congress that it considered *both* superpowers to be equally hegemonist —that American global behavior was not to be preferred to the Soviet Union's.[6] From Moscow's perspective, this presumably was a comparatively favorable assessment. At a minimum, this declaration marked an end to Beijing's "American tilt." Shortly after the close of the Party Congress in Beijing, Brezhnev, speaking in Baku, called for "the normalization and gradual improvement of relations between the U.S.S.R. and the People's Republic of China on the basis that I would describe as one of commonsense, mutual respect and mutual advantage."[7]

Since the Twelfth Party Congress, there has been gradual improvement in Sino-Soviet relations with respect to trade, cultural exchange, and state-to-state relations. There even have been hints at the possibility of improved party-to-party links. From the fall of 1982 to the present, this process has unfolded through a series of trips back and forth, bilateral talks convened twice annually, back-channel interactions, and a series of agreements concerning trade; cultural, scientific, and educational exchange; and technological cooperation. This complex chronology is detailed elsewhere;[8] only the highlights need concern us here.

Shortly after the close of China's Twelfth Party Congress, it was announced that Soviet Deputy Foreign Minister Leonid Ilichev would journey to Beijing to open (on October 4, 1982) talks at the vice-foreign-minister level. Since those discussions, seven additional rounds have taken place, with even-numbered sessions held in the U.S.S.R. and odd-numbered sessions convened in China. The seventh round was held in Beijing in October 1985, and the eighth held in

Moscow in April 1986. These talks have not generally been the occasions on which dramatic announcements have been made. Rather, the most visible signs of progress have been meetings, statements, and agreements that have punctuated the periods between rounds.

As the first round of talks got under way in October 1982, Chinese General Secretary Hu Yaobang said that China was willing to establish relations with "any party . . . if they wish to be friends with us."[9] At the conclusion of the first round of talks, Premier Zhao Ziyang was reported to have said that the talks would continue and that China's ongoing opposition to Soviet hegemonism and the Beijing-Moscow dialogue were not contradictory.[10] A little more than three months after Foreign Minister Huang Hua traveled to Moscow for Brezhnev's funeral in November 1982 (where he received a warm reception), Hu Yaobang said that "for politicians, hatred is something which they can forget after a night's sleep. I do not agree with the view that it is difficult to move the piled-up resentment between China and the Soviet Union."[11]

With the succession of Andropov to power in the Kremlin, Moscow reiterated Brezhnev's offer to nurture economic, scientific, and cultural relations to build a foundation for the improvement of relations in other spheres.[12] In March 1983, the two sides signed a trade agreement that called for more than a doubling of trade in that year from $200 million to $470 million. By April it was announced that the two sides had resumed border trade. This trade had been suspended about twenty years earlier. In June, border trade was further expanded to include Soviet Central Asia (the Soviet Republic of Kirghiz). In September, newly promoted Deputy Foreign Minister Kapitsa visited China. The two sides agreed to broaden their bilateral relationship to include culture and education; ten students were to travel each way to study language. In April 1984, the two sides further expanded the relationship along this dimension by signing a protocol on the exchange of students and experts. They agreed to send seventy students to each other's country and to exchange two educational groups during the 1984–1985 academic year.[13]

On February 9, 1984, General Secretary Andropov died, and Beijing dispatched Vice-Premier Wan Li to his funeral. Moscow lost no time in reiterating its desire to continue the improvement of bilateral relations,[14] though Chernenko's own poor health and the prospect of yet another succession in Moscow meant that dramatic departures in Sino-Soviet relations were unlikely. Nonetheless, shortly before President Reagan was to arrive in China in April 1984, Beijing

acknowledged that the vice-chairman of the Soviet Union's Council of Ministers, the person who had headed the U.S.S.R.'s economic assistance program to China in the 1950s, Ivan V. Arkhipov, would visit China. And, in an effort to protect its nascent ties with Moscow, Beijing carefully deleted the anti-Soviet components of President Reagan's remarks while he was in China. Despite Beijing's efforts to avoid offending Moscow during Reagan's stay, the Arkhipov visit was abruptly postponed by the Soviets.

Although the second half of 1984 witnessed a deceptive lull in the development of Sino-Soviet relations, in November both sides agreed that Arkhipov would visit China from December 21 to 29, 1984. Moreover, although political relations made little observable progress during the first three quarters of 1984, Moscow boosted imports from China, thereby producing a bilateral trade surplus that was greatly welcomed in Beijing's Ministry of Foreign Trade. Moscow was holding out the economic carrot for Beijing to gnaw on.

Arkhipov's journey to China was a milestone by every measure. He was received by Premier Zhao Ziyang, Peng Zhen, and Chen Yun, though he did *not* meet with Deng Xiaoping. Three agreements were signed with Vice-Premier Yao Yilin (one on economic and technical cooperation, one that established a Joint Commission for Economic, Trade, Scientific, and Technical Cooperation, and a third that dealt with scientific and technical cooperation).[15] Perhaps most important, the Agreement on Economic and Technical Cooperation called for "planning, construction, and reconstruction of industrial enterprises and other projects." The two sides agreed to sign a five-year trade agreement in 1985 (to cover the period 1986–1990) once the details had been worked out. And for 1985, the two sides agreed to boost trade to about $1.8 billion.[16]

Though Chernenko died in March 1985, new Secretary General Gorbachev quickly signaled that he wanted to sustain the forward momentum. Gorbachev met with Vice-Premier Li Peng who attended Chernenko's funeral (Li was raised by Zhou Enlai). At their meeting, Gorbachev called for a "serious improvement" in relations, and Li conveyed Chinese Secretary General Hu Yaobang's greetings, "the first such message in nearly 20 years."[17] In his first speech on foreign policy (delivered March 11), Gorbachev repeated his desire for improved relations. In April, a protocol on cooperation between the U.S.S.R. Ministry of Higher and Secondary Specialized Education and the Chinese Ministry of Education was signed for the academic year 1985–1986. The agreement provided for the exchange of 200 students and trainees.[18]

By July 1985, Vice-Premier Yao Yilin was in Moscow where he signed the long-term trade agreement (1986–1990) that had been promised the preceding December. Sino-Soviet trade was to double by 1990. The announced value of the agreement was about $14 billion. In September, the Soviet and Chinese foreign ministers met in New York, agreed to exchange visits at a time left unspecified,[19] and reportedly discussed innerparty conditions in both countries.[20] This meeting produced speculation in press and diplomatic circles that a restoration of party-to-party ties was possible; Beijing quickly sought to dispel this line of reasoning by saying, "It is still premature to consider the resumption of CPC-CPSU relations" until the "three major obstacles had been removed."[21]

Given Beijing's record of obscuring each move forward in relations with Moscow by statements that progress was not possible until the "three major obstacles" had been removed, China's disavowal merely further fueled speculation that consideration was (and is) being given to a broadening of relations to the party-to-party sphere.

In October, as the seventh round of talks at the vice-foreign-minister level took place, a delegation from the Supreme Soviet of the Soviet Union visited China. Politburo member Peng Zhen met with the group and said that "the fact that the highest organs of state power of China and the Soviet Union have resumed relations after a suspension of more than 20 years reflects the expansion of relations between the two countries over the past few years."[22]

By year's end, Kapitsa was once again in Beijing to discuss the exchange of foreign minister visits in 1986 and to brief the Chinese on the recently concluded Soviet-American summit in Geneva.[23] One Eastern bloc diplomat was reported by *Far Eastern Economic Review* to have commented that this showed that "Gorbachev intends to treat China like a world power," in contrast to his predecessors who were never quite able to bring themselves to do so.[24] This broadening of the relationship to include strategic and global issues is significant. Highlighting the progress of Sino-Soviet relations well beyond economic and cultural ties is the two-week visit of Georgiy A. Arbatov, Moscow's premier expert on the United States, who delivered briefings on the global situation and on Soviet-American arms control negotiations in October 1985.

Nineteen-eighty-five concluded with Vice-Premier Li Peng, who received some training in the Soviet Union, stopping over in Moscow on his way back to China after a trip to France, Czechoslovakia, and Bulgaria. While in Moscow he met with General Secretary Gorbachev, and "the meeting proceeded in a friendly and calm atmosphere." The purpose of the trip, according to Beijing, was to further "Sino-Soviet relations in the fields of economy, trade, culture and education."[25] Significantly, Li apparently made his stop in Moscow without having received regular prior authorization for the stop from his superiors in Beijing. Upon his return to China, he was reportedly criticized by Deng Xiaoping.

The spring of 1986 saw more advances in the substance, scale, and intimacy of the relationship, although Beijing continually reiterated that an improvement in party-to-party relations would have to await a change in Soviet behavior around China's periphery. From March 15 to 21, Arkhipov was back in China where the two sides held the first meeting of the Sino-Soviet Commission for Economic, Trade, Scientific, and Technical Cooperation. At the end of the sessions, the two sides signed a protocol concerning the conditions for engineering and technical personnel exchanges.[26] Moreover, both sides agreed to try to exceed the level of trade called for in the long-term trade agreement that had just been signed the previous July. Finally, the two sides agreed that China would send a study group of nuclear power generation experts to the Soviet Union.

Shortly after the commission meetings, the eighth round of Sino-Soviet consultations was held in Moscow in April, and nothing specific was agreed to although the Soviets did propose raising the level of dialogue above the vice-foreign-minister level. This suggestion was promptly rejected by Beijing as "unrealistic," although the Chinese characterized the talks themselves as "useful."[27]

As we look analytically at the condensed chronology, several things stand out. First, there has been a slow, but dramatic, improvement in Sino-Soviet relations, evidenced in the gradual increase in the number and type of delegations going back and forth between the two countries, by the range of institutions involved, and the breadth of issues embraced. By the end of 1985, the Soviet Union was China's sixth largest trading partner. Second, the Chinese have portrayed "normalization" as an end state, while in fact it is a process that has been under way since 1982. This semantic gymnastics has permitted China to garner the (economic) benefits of improved relations with Moscow while maintaining the "principled" public stance that normalization could not occur until the "three major obstacles" were removed. This tactic also reflects Beijing's concern that improved relations with Moscow could damage its ties with Washington.

China is pursuing "economic diplomacy," and economic advantage is the principal value being maximized.[28] Third, despite the improvement in relations, the scale of Sino-Soviet ties is comparatively small. In 1985, Sino-American trade was 3.37 times as large as Sino-Soviet trade. In 1985, more than 15,000 Chinese students and scholars were in the United States, while no more than 200 Chinese students and trainees were in the Soviet Union. In 1984, well over 100 delegations per month traveled between the United States and China while the numbers going between China and the Soviet Union were infinitesimal by comparison. Fourth, it is extremely unlikely that an improvement in relations could produce an alliance such as that of the 1950s, if for no other reason than China derives too much benefit from the West and its role as the reluctant object of superpower affections.

In the future, continued moderate and gradual progress in Sino-Soviet relations is likely; more dramatic change is entirely conceivable in the midterm. The questions to which we now turn are: What forces are propelling Beijing in the direction of limited accommodation with the Soviet Union? Can we outline the contours of a coalition of interests supportive of better relations with Moscow? What are America's interests as this process unfolds?

A Policy Coalition:
The Roots of Accommodation in China

Momentous shifts in a nation's foreign policy do not generally occur unless several constituencies have interests and perceptions that converge on the new direction. The search for single causes is misplaced. Though China is an authoritarian regime, bargaining within the elite—and a desire to build consensus wherever possible—means that coalitions must be built in order to adopt and implement policy. Although the closed nature of the Chinese foreign policy process makes it difficult to specify coalition members with precision, plainly many interests are being served by the move toward Moscow.

Inasmuch as many people in the emerging third Chinese echelon of national leadership were trained in the Soviet Union, many have speculated that the warming trend in Sino-Soviet relations reflects the increased influence of these new individuals. Though this factor is probably of some importance, the limited accommodation under way between the two Communist powers has its origins in other, more fundamental considerations. It is worth keeping in mind that Taiwan's President Chiang Ching-kuo spent twelve years in the Soviet Union and the experience had an impact—close relations with Moscow were not among them.

China's "open policy" includes the Soviet Union because of changes in Beijing's perceptions of the international strategic environment and pressures emanating from the domestic political system. China's foreign policy leadership has come to view the Soviet Union as less an immediate threat than was the case in the 1970s. As in the early 1970s, when Mao Zedong perceived that the limits to American intervention abroad had been reached in Vietnam, so China's leaders now believe that Soviet imperialism has reached its high-water mark. "For example," as one Chinese analyst writes, "40 years ago, the Soviet Union was able to defeat the utterly evil fascist Germany, but now it cannot conquer a small country like Afghanistan, though it has sent 100,000 troops there."[29]

Not only is the Soviet Union mired down in Afghanistan and saddled with draining economic and military commitments in Eastern Europe, Cuba, Vietnam, Africa, and the Middle East, but also the Soviet economy is in doldrums that China does not expect Moscow to overcome any time soon, even *if* Gorbachev is serious about economic reform:

> The Soviet economy is now at a turning point. Over the past year or so, its growth rate has been slowing down, reaching the lowest point since the war. In the period of the current 5-year plan (1981–1985), the average annual growth rates for the total production of society and the national income will only reach 3.5 and 3.2 percent respectively. If the situation continues to develop like this, the national strength of the Soviet Union will inevitably be affected.[30]

Another factor has also affected Beijing's calculus. Since the Reagan administration came to power, American capacity and perceived "will" to offset Soviet armed might have increased. The United States is no longer the reluctant Goliath to which Beijing delivers sermons on the "lessons of Munich," as was the case in the middle and late 1970s. With the strength of the Soviet Union and the United States perceived by Beijing to be in approximate balance, China's foreign policy leadership appears to believe that there is little likelihood of a global war in the next two decades. In the words of Foreign Minister Wu Xueqian, "The development of forces for peace has outstripped the growth of those for war."[31] This window of stability provides China the opportunity to maneuver between the superpowers—to use the anxiety of each superpower to extract benefits from the other. What danger to global stability exists results from the nuclear arms race. Beijing, therefore, desires to preserve a stable international order that will allow China to proceed with its domestic modernization and reunification plans and to use negotiation to achieve as much assistance from each power as possible.

One other part of the geopolitical picture has changed as well. Japan, under Prime Minister Nakasone, is moving gingerly, but perceptibly, to increase military spending. Although Deng Xiaoping urged Tokyo to strengthen Japan's self-defense capability during his October 1978 trip to Tokyo, quite a different tune is being sung in Beijing today. China, like much of Asia, fears a remilitarized Japan and is coming to perceive that its security and economic development interests might best be served by a Soviet Union that presents less threat to Japan, as opposed to a Japan that is more adequately armed to protect itself. This fear of Japanese military power is exacerbated by the resurgence of anti-Japanese nationalism in China, a feeling fueled by a surge in imports from Japan and a large trade imbalance in Tokyo's favor.

Beijing is highly motivated to improve Sino-Soviet ties because current domestic priorities give overwhelming preeminence to economic growth and reform. To maximize economic expansion, Beijing has kept a tight rein on military expenditures, much to the disquiet of some in the Chinese armed forces. From 1979 through 1983, Chinese military expenditures as a percentage of gross national product dropped by about one-third.[32] In 1985, China announced that it would reduce the size of its armed forces by 20 to 25 percent. As Zhou Enlai and Mao Zedong moved toward the United States in the early 1970s in order to reduce foreign policy threats so that resources could be concentrated on domestic political and economic priorities, so in the 1980s Deng Xiaoping is doing likewise vis-à-vis the Soviet Union.

The Chinese leadership also perceives an opportunity in the new Gorbachev leadership, believing that he is more serious about internal economic reform in the Soviet Union than his Kremlin predecessors. In the words of Beijing's periodical *World Economy*, "Although some of Gorbachev's propositions on reform were also made by Brezhnev and Andropov in the past, most people believe that he is more energetic about reform."[33] If Gorbachev is serious about internal reform, so the logic goes, he has no choice but to reduce friction and economic drains abroad, drains which in the case of Vietnam may total as much as $4 billion per year.[34]

Economic considerations are important, too. China is eager to continue importing goods from abroad and needs to expand export markets—anywhere. In late 1984 and early 1985, China's foreign exchange re-

serves declined about 30 percent, leaving barely enough foreign exchange in reserve for four or so months of imports. In the January–July 1985 period alone, Beijing reported a cumulative trade deficit of $7.89 billion. By boosting exports to the U.S.S.R. and the Eastern bloc and by arranging barter agreements to conserve foreign exchange, China can augment its capacity to import and soften the effect of protectionist policies in the United States and elsewhere in the West. The Chinese best speak for themselves:

> Stones from other hills may serve to polish the jade of this one . . . . The Soviet Union and the East European countries have a relatively stable overseas market, namely the CEMA market . . . . At the same time, they have developed trade with the developed capitalist countries at an accelerated speed . . . . However, due to various causes known to all, they, particularly the Soviet Union, have lost the Chinese market and China has also lost the Soviet market. At a time when the West practices trade protectionism and imposes various restrictions on our export commodities, we should promptly adjust our market strategy and strengthen our economic and trade relations with the Soviet Union and the East European countries so that we can have a relatively stable overseas market. However, this does not in the least mean a reduction in our trade with Western countries.[35]

The Soviets have not been slow to appeal to the trading instincts of the Chinese, saying in late 1984:

> The United States has imposed restrictions on 33 of China's commodities, especially clothing and piece goods; our country, however, has not erected such tariff barriers. Generally, China suffers large trade deficits with the United States; however, China enjoys a trade surplus with the Soviet Union. The Americans always trade in dollars, whereas the Soviet Union agrees to set up a direct commodity barter with its trading partners, which is much more convenient. The geographical proximity of the two countries lessens transportation costs, and the similarity in the structure of foreign trade management between the two countries is also conducive to the signing of contracts.[36]

In the last sentence of the above quotation, the Soviets are gently observing that to do business with the West, China's bureaucracy must change. This is not necessary in order to deal with the Soviet Union. This may be an important observation to China's millions of cadres who find their bureaucracies under pressure to change in order to interact effectively with the West.

Moreover, given the difficulty the Chinese have in meeting Western product quality, style, and reliability standards, the Eastern bloc countries and the Soviet Union are frequently easier markets in which to sell than the West. Finally, in light of the world petroleum glut, which coexists with a Chinese export capacity, declining Soviet production, and an energy shortage in Eastern Europe, the Chinese see broad vistas for their petroleum exports to the Eastern bloc:

We can switch to the Soviet and East European markets the commodities which are subject to various restrictions or are unsalable on the Western market but which are much sought after on the Soviet and East European markets . . . . Taking into account the fact that the Soviet Union will find it difficult to increase its petroleum exports to East European countries while the latter are in great need of petroleum, we can increase our petroleum supplies to the East European countries. Meanwhile, we can increase the import of suitable technology and equipment from the Soviet Union and East European countries and expand border trade with the Soviet Union.[37]

As noted in the earlier chronology, an important component of the 1984 agreement with the Soviet Union was that the U.S.S.R. would assist China in renovating some of the industrial plants constructed during the 1950s. With respect to China's economy as a whole, a substantial amount of technology will come from the Soviet Union and Eastern bloc countries, given China's strategy of renovating older facilities rather than importing whole plants.

Two domestic considerations provide impetus for limited accommodation with Moscow as well. Because a disproportionate share of current Chinese foreign investment is going into China's coastal areas, the western and northwestern reaches of the country have become a clear second priority in the development plan. Last year I met with one leader of a major western province-level unit who scarcely concealed the displeasure he felt at western China's low development priority. With poor transportation links to China's eastern seaboard, leaders in these areas hope to forge closer economic ties to Central Asia, the

Soviet Union, and the Middle East. According to Huang Baozhang, vice-chairman of the Xinjiang Regional People's Government, "As the CPC Central Committee had implemented a policy of opening up to the outside world, Xinjiang had also decided to implement a policy of opening up to the Soviet Union and to the West [of China]."[38]

In short, Beijing is placating the western regions of China by allowing them to develop, and benefit from, their own economic ties to the Soviet Union and other regions to China's west. In Beijing's own words, "The Chinese Government has especially provided Xinjiang with a specific share of the total volume of goods turnover envisaged in the trade agreement between the Chinese and Soviet governments."[39]

Warming relations with Moscow also signal to China's populace, the West, and elite members disgruntled with the consequences of reform that China has no intention of entirely shedding the planned character of its economy or uncritically accepting Western values and influence. From the perspective of central planners like Chen Yun, reform has weakened the levers of central economic control. For ideologists like Deng Liqun and others like Peng Zhen, Li Xiannian, and Hu Qiaomu, who are worried about the "spiritual" effects of the open policy, the Soviet model of central planning and tight social control has many appealing aspects.

Tactical considerations are important in China's calculus, too. Though Washington, Beijing, and Moscow all profess to eschew the crude concept of triangular diplomacy, all three have been ardent practitioners of the art. Beijing wants to remind Washington of China's diplomatic options when Congress and the executive branch are deciding issues such as technology transfer, financial support for the United Nations Fund for Population Activities, development financing, weapons and military technology sales to Taiwan, and trade policy. Moreover, since at least October 1985, with the visit of Vice President Bush to Beijing, China has been pushing Washington to take affirmative steps to nudge Taipei in the direction of accommodation with the mainland. In his January 1986 speech to the Standing Committee of the National People's Congress, Foreign Minister Wu Xueqian expressed the hope that the "United States will support with actual deeds, not hamper, China's efforts to realize peaceful reunification."[40] Beijing's moves toward the Soviet Union have many origins, but one is certainly the desire to encourage Washington to be more receptive to China's policy preferences, including those with respect to Taiwan.

By moving closer to Moscow, China's foreign policy leaders also hope to produce more flexibility in Hanoi. As Richard Nixon went to Moscow in 1972 to put pressure on Hanoi to end the conflict with the United States, so Beijing is taking the same route in the mid-1980s. Though there are as of yet no clear signs that Moscow will exert such pressure, there have been several tantalizing hints in this regard. In June 1985, Vietnamese Party Secretary General Le Duan traveled to the U.S.S.R., received a comparatively cool reception, and came away having endorsed the accommodation under way between Beijing and Moscow.[41] In March 1985, during the events surrounding Chernenko's funeral, Gorbachev received China's high-level delegation led by Li Peng while not extending the same courtesy to Heng Samrin, leader of the Hanoi-backed government in Phnom Penh.[42]

Because of the diversity of considerations motivating Beijing, the improvement of Sino-Soviet relations is likely to continue. This multiplicity of motives means that improved relations with the Soviet Union is a policy with many constituencies in China. We can make an informed guess about the general nature of these constituencies. The coalition members likely include many in the central foreign trade apparatus who find their trade monopoly slipping away as decentralization has proceeded, those in the planning system who find it easier to deal with a planned economy than the free-wheeling West, the western areas of China that see economic benefits to trade with the U.S.S.R., enterprises and ministries that produce goods without a market in the West or that face stiff competition from the West in domestic markets, the propaganda apparatus and organs of state control that find present open policies eroding their functions, leaders at all levels who received training in the U.S.S.R. (*liu su pai*) and see their futures imperiled if the single route to the top becomes training in the West (*liu mei pai*). This coalition is given added power because ties to the U.S.S.R. need *not* come at the expense of China's ties to the West. This is a policy that implies no immediate losers —no hard choices. This is what Hu Yaobang and Zhao Ziyang apparently call "economic diplomacy."[43]

In our observation of the diversity of interests that appear to be served by improved Sino-Soviet ties, it is incumbent to note that one Chinese leader has thus far declined to associate himself publicly with the limited accommodation under way—Deng Xiaoping. This raises the fundamental question, Is the Chinese elite divided over policy toward the Soviet Union?

Though Deng has not publicly met any of the visiting Soviet dignitaries or made any major conciliatory gestures, little evidence suggests that he actually opposes the process that has been under way since at least

1982. Indeed, if such a consistent and durable policy trend could occur in the face of his direct and intense opposition, this would call for a reevaluation of our assessment of his role in the system and for reconsideration of American expectations that both domestic and foreign policies in Beijing will survive his passing. Rather than being opposed, more likely Deng sees economic and tactical advantages to the thaw. He may choose to identify with the process when key political accommodations are made in the future but sees no immediate purpose to be served by publicly identifying with the process now. Finally, he may well believe that, given his previous intimate identification with improved Sino-American ties, a sudden association with Moscow would send a highly counterproductive message to Washington. In the end, the Beijing elite (Deng included) desires to extract as much economic and technological benefit from *both* sides as possible; it does not want the relations with one to jeopardize its interests with the other.

Because there is a strong coalition behind improved relations with the Soviet Union, much improvement has occurred with little Soviet "give" on the "three major obstacles." Looking to the future, we can expect a further reduction in tensions along the Sino-Soviet border and continuing expansion of economic, scientific, educational, and cultural intercourse, as long as Soviet behavior does not deteriorate from the Chinese perspective. If Moscow makes the painful decisions to reduce its debilitating commitments in Afghanistan and Vietnam, improvement in bilateral relations could be dramatic, though relations would achieve a degree of intimacy far less than that which the two nations enjoyed in the 1950s.

American Interests as the Process of Sino-Soviet Accommodation Unfolds

What are American interests as this process of accommodation proceeds? U.S. interests lie in three areas.

First, the strategic rationale in Washington for a move toward China was that Soviet military planners must be faced with the need to divide their military power between the western and eastern reaches of their vast country. Whatever accommodation occurs between Moscow and Beijing should not enable Moscow to move sizable military resources to further threaten NATO. Such an occurrence would call into question part of the strategic premise of our relationship with China.

Second, it would be a serious mistake on Beijing's

part to try to leverage ties with Moscow into a more assertive posture vis-à-vis Taiwan. American policy has been unwavering in its commitment to a peaceful resolution of that problem.

Third, the closer Beijing's ties with Moscow become, the more thorny will become technology transfer issues between China and the United States, with technology leakage to the U.S.S.R. a key concern.

Finally, Beijing must recognize that the political basis in the United States for good Sino-American relations has been a broad-based coalition of political conservatives and liberals. What made this coalition possible was the recognition in America that Chinese and Soviet interests in the world were quite separable. Nothing China does in the future should cause Americans to reexamine that assumption. Moreover, the Sino-American relationship was further strengthened by both sides' perception before 1982 that Soviet behavior was inherently destabilizing and that cooperation was needed between Washington and Beijing to ensure stability. With the adoption of the "independent foreign policy" line, China's leaders have come very close to asserting that American and Soviet behavior in the world are equally objectionable. Premier Zhao Ziyang's March 25, 1986, statement to the National People's Congress does not increase the strength of Sino-American relations: "Both of them [the United States and the Soviet Union] should give up their pursuit of military supremacy and cease their aggression and intervention against other countries."[44]

Fortunately, the rationale for Sino-American ties has broadened substantially beyond the strategic considerations that dominated thinking throughout the 1970s and early 1980s. The task of leadership in both Washington and Beijing is to define once again a durable basis for the relationship in the second half of the 1980s and for the 1990s.

Notes

1. Disciples of Zhou Enlai certainly include Li Shenzhi, Huan Xiang, Ji Pengfei, Yao Guang, Han Xu, Qian Jiadong, Li Zewang, and Chen Chu.

2. Kenneth Lieberthal, "Domestic Politics and Foreign Policy," in Harry Harding, ed., *China's Foreign Relations in the 1980s* (New Haven, Conn.: Yale University Press, 1984), pp. 43–70; see also, Susan Shirk, "The Domestic Political Dimensions of China's Foreign Economic Relations," in Samuel S. Kim, ed., *China and the World* (Boulder, Colo.: Westview Press, 1984), pp. 57–81.

3. Winston Lord, "The United States, the Soviet Union, and the People's Republic of China," Department of State, *News Release*, March 23, 1976.

4. *FBIS*, USSR: *Daily Report*, March 24, 1982, p. R3; from Moscow, TASS in English, March 24, 1982.

5. *AFP* (Hong Kong) in English, October 13, 1982; in *FBIS*, USSR: *Daily Report*, October 14, 1982, p. B1.

6. See Hu Yaobang's Speech to the Twelfth Party Congress, September 1, 1982, in *Beijing Review*, no. 37 (1982), pp. 15 and 31.

7. *FBIS*, USSR: *Daily Report*, September 30, 1982, p. B1; Moscow in Mandarin to China, September 28, 1982.

8. Gerald Segal, *Sino-Soviet Relations after Mao*, Adelphi Paper no. 202 (London: International Institute for Strategic Studies, 1985).

9. Cited in Segal, from Beijing Radio in Russian, October 17, 1982, in Summary of World Broadcasts, Far East 7163, A2, 1.

10. Tokyo, KYODO in English, October 24, 1982; in *FBIS*, USSR: *Daily Report*, October 25, 1982, p. B1.

11. Cited in Segal, from FE 7263, A3, 9, and CHI-83-039-Annex.

12. Moscow in Mandarin to China, November 28, 1982; in *FBIS*, USSR: *Daily Report*, December 8, 1982.

13. Moscow in Mandarin to China, April 17, 1984; in *FBIS*, USSR: *Daily Report*, April 18, 1984, p. B3.

14. Moscow in Mandarin to China, February 17, 1984; in *FBIS*, USSR: *Daily Report*, February 21, 1984, p. B1.

15. For texts of the agreements, see *FBIS*, USSR: *Daily Report*, April 25, 1985, pp. B1–B5.

16. "Soviets to Modernize Chinese Industries," *New York Times*, December 29, 1984.

17. Segal, p. 17.

18. Moscow, TASS International Service in Russian, April 5, 1985; in *FBIS*, USSR: *Daily Report*, April 5, 1985, p. B1.

19. Richard Nations, "Point, Counterpoint," *Far Eastern Economic Review*, December 19, 1985, p. 16.

20. *Wen Wei Po* (Hong Kong), September 30, 1985, p. 2.

21. *Zhongguo Xinwen She* (Beijing) (China News Agency) in Chinese, October 5, 1985; in *FBIS*, China: *Daily Report*, October 7, 1985, p. C1.

22. *Xinhua* (Beijing) in English, October 11, 1985; in *FBIS*, China: *Daily Report*, October 15, 1985, p. C1.

23. *The Daily Yomiuri*, December 9, 1985, p. 1; also, *Far Eastern Economic Review*, December 19, 1985, p. 16; see also, *South China Morning Post*, December 14, 1985, p. 10.

24. Richard Nations, "Point, Counterpoint," p. 16.

25. *Xinhua* (Beijing) in English, December 23, 1985; in *FBIS*, China: *Daily Report*, December 24, 1985, p. C1.

26. *Liaowang* (Outlook), carried in Beijing in Russian to U.S.S.R., April 5, 1986; in *FBIS*, China: *Daily Report*, April 8, 1986, pp. C1–C2.

27. *Xinhua* (Beijing) in English, April 16, 1986; in *FBIS*, China: *Daily Report*, April 16, 1986, p. A1.

28. *Wen Wei Po* (Hong Kong) in Chinese, December 20, 1985, p. 2; in *FBIS*, China: *Daily Report*, December 20, 1985, p. W1.

29. *Renmin Ribao*, October 15, 1985, p. 6; in *FBIS*, China: *Daily Report*, October 16, 1985, p. K21.

30. *Shijie Jingji* (World Economics), no. 8 (August 10, 1985), pp. 50–52; in *FBIS*, China: *Daily Report*, September 25, 1985, p. C1.

31. "Wu Xueqian Speaks at NPC Standing Committee Session," *Xinhua* (Beijing) domestic service in Chinese, January 16, 1986; in *FBIS*, China: *Daily Report*, January 17, 1986, p. K3.

32. See *World Military Expenditures and Arms Transfers 1985* (Washington, D.C.: United States Arms Control and Disarmament Agency, 1985), p. 58.

33. *Shijie Jingji* (World Economy), no. 8 (August 10, 1985), pp. 50–52; in *FBIS*, China: *Daily Report*, September 25, 1985, p. C3

34. Parris Chang, *Asian Wall Street Journal*, December 30, 1985, p. 12.

35. *Shijie Jingji Daobao* (World Economic News), August 19, 1985, p. 9; in *FBIS*, China: *Daily Report*, September 10, 1985, p. A2.

36. Moscow Radio Peace and Progress in Mandarin to China, December 25, 1984; in *FBIS*, USSR: *Daily Report*, December 28, 1984, p. B2.

37. *Shijie Jingji Daobao* (World Economic News), August 19, 1985, p. 9; in *FBIS*, China: *Daily Report*, September 10, 1985, p. A2.

38. Hong Kong, *Wen Wei Po*, October 4, 1985, p. 1; in *FBIS*, China: *Daily Report*, October 8, 1985, p. W5.

39. Beijing in Russian to the USSR, September 15, 1985; in *FBIS*, China: *Daily Report*, September 19, 1985, p. C3.

40. *FBIS*, China: *Daily Report*, January 22, 1986, p. K20; also, *FBIS*, China: *Daily Report*, January 17, 1986, p. K4.

41. Richard Nations, "A Mild Chill in Moscow," *Far Eastern Economic Review*, July 11, 1985, pp. 10–11.

42. "Moscow Fare: Chopstick Diplomacy?" *New York Times*, April 3, 1985.

43. Hong Kong *Wen Wei Po* in Chinese, December 20, 1985, p. 2; in *FBIS*, China: *Daily Report*, December 20, 1985.

44. Beijing Television Service in Mandarin, March 25, 1986; in *FBIS*, China: *Daily Report*, March 28, 1986, p. K23.

POLAND

Internal Situation Picking Up

The 5th anniversary of the imposition of martial law in Poland has seen the nation's problems balanced by economic and social improvements.

Wen Youren

On December 13, 1981 the Polish government announced a state of emergency across Poland and imposed martial law, which lasted for one and a half years. Since then Poland has achieved considerable success in rehabilitating the national economy and securing social stability.

Before martial law, Poland was enduring its most critical postwar domestic crisis. Its economy was on the verge of collapse. Political upheavals caused by the Solidarity Trade Union threatened the stability of the government. The imposition of martial law, however, immediately brought the unrest to an end and laid a foundation for economic recovery. Over the past five years Poland has taken many measures to restore the economy and to carry out economic reform.

The process of recovery is a long and slow one. National income fell 25 percent between 1978 and 1982. During the same period, industrial output dropped 10 percent and farm production 20 percent. Economy began to revive slowly in 1983. Industrial output this year is 8 percent higher than in 1978, but national income is still 8 percent lower. Production of grain and oil-bearing crops registered record highs this year. Animal husbandry has picked up since 1984, but meat production this year is still expected to be 10 percent lower than in 1978.

Since 1982 Polish enterprises have undertaken various kinds of reforms, centring around responsibility for their own profits and losses and self-management of the workers, and they have made certain achievements. But because the Polish reforms are taking place in the context of a sluggish economy, plus a lack of experience and other obstacles both domestic and international, the reform line has not been fully adhered to. The Polish authorities have admitted that they were over-optimistic about an early improvement in the economic situation and that improvements will take a much longer time than expected. Wage increases have exceeded those in labour productivity, and inflation has not been brought within reasonable limits. The index of price increases, amounting to 15 percent in 1985 and 17 to 18 percent this year, has far exceeded earlier predictions. Foreign debts (interest included) grew from US$23 billion in 1980 to US$31.3 billion in June 1986.

In the area of politics, the Polish government has done much to promote socialist democracy and legal system, and to win over the majority of the people. It has learnt from experience that there are differences of views and opinions among the people and that the duty of the government is to conduct dialogues and consultations with the dissidents to reach agreement when important issues arise. During the past 5 years the role of the Parliament and local assemblies has clearly improved. Trade unions, which were reestablished after the abolition of the Solidarity Trade Union, have become politically active. Some policies on important issues have been discussed publicly before being passed. With its position strengthened, the Polish government has, over the past 5 years, announced four general amnesties, including the release this year of all political prisoners. It insists that dialogue must be carried on with those who, though having different views, are concerned about the prosperity of their country, while those who do not abandon their anti-socialist activities are to be excluded from national reconciliation. The Polish government believes that the process of normalization has advanced remarkably since the imposition of martial law and many people are paying more attention to the government. One American newspaper has cited the progress made by the Polish government in reaching reconciliation with its critics.

Polish leader Wojciech Jaruzelski claimed in a speech on December 1, "We have to a great extent realized social stability." But at the same time he admitted, "We still have serious economic problems which affect the living conditions of the people and thus affect the social mood." The 10th Congress of the Polish United Workers' Party in July this year decided to go ahead with the economic reform's second phase in an effort to accelerate the country's economic development. At the same congress the Party also decided to further enrich the "socialist democratic model" of Poland. In a December 10 article commemorating the 5th anniversary of martial law, the Polish armed forces' organ *Zolnierz Wolnosci (Freedom Fighter)* pointed out that today's top priority for Poland is economic development. Therefore, the results of the second phase of economic reform will undoubtedly exert an important impact on Poland's future.

Reprinted by courtesy of *Beijing Review*, Vol. 29, No. 52, December 29, 1986, pp. 12-13.

BOLDNESS, STAUNCHNESS, ACTION

JANOS KADAR

General Secretary of the Hungarian Socialist Worker's Party,
interviewed by the Editor-in-Chief of New Times Vitaly Ignatenko

Comrade Janos Kadar gave me an appointment for 11:30.
His office, overlooking the embankment and the serene river, is filled with books. There is a large original portrait of Lenin considering a chess move. Photographs on the walls show historical episodes in the life of the party and its international links. A smaller portrait of Lenin hangs above the General Secretary's desk.

Janos Kadar comes into the office. He smiles and shakes hands. His handshake is strong.

"Well, let's get down to business," he motions me to the table. "I'm ready for your questions."

Comrade Kadar, you ended your concluding speech at the 13th Congress of the HSWP by quoting the words Janos Arany, the classic Hungarian poet, used to describe one of his main characters: "The greater the danger the braver he is." If you look at the history of the struggle for socialism in Hungary, to what extent does it reveal this trait in the Hungarian people?

Our great poet formulated the historical experience and aspirations of the people on the eve of the Hungarian bourgeois-democratic revolution and the liberation struggle.

In my concluding address to the congress I quoted his words to remind people of a historical fact: when the situation required it our people and our working class worked and struggled with redoubled energy and boldly took up the cause of national independence and social progress. I wanted to stress that to cope with our domestic and foreign problems what is needed above all is boldness, staunchness and action.

The promulgation of the Hungarian Soviet Republic in 1919 was a widely known historical instance of bold action for socialist ideals. This happened at a time when the forces of young Soviet Russia, then being torn by Whiteguards and the troops of the invaders, were far from our country. From the moment the Hungarian Soviet Republic was formed it had to wage a difficult struggle for survival, the preservation of Hungarian sovereignty and the future of the nation. For several months our people successfully withstood political and diplomatic threats, economic pressure and armed intervention, and it was only military force enlisted by the former ruling classes, mobilized and equipped by the Entente powers, that succeeded in defeating the Hungarian Soviet Republic.

Even under the counterrevolutionary regime the finest sons and daughters of our people continued the struggle because they knew that the first Soviet Republic in Hungary, which fell, "will be followed by a second, which will be victorious." This

was how Lenin characterized the period. Being aware of this, Hungarian patriots and internationalists at home and in many European countries fought against fascism and war, for an independent, democratic and free Hungary. The country, plunged into the second world war and exposed to mortal danger through the fault of the ruling classes, was liberated as a result of the heroic and selfless struggle of the Soviet Army.

After the nazi occupiers had been driven out of Hungary, our people were able to take their destiny into their own hands. At that period, too, Communists and other patriotic and progressive forces had to tackle formidable problems, for they had inherited a devastated country. Their efforts bore fruit: they managed to establish and strengthen the popular government and mobilize the people to restore the country and build a new social system. As a result of dedicated work we made great advances in the struggle for democratic and socialist goals over a short period.

After several years of progressive development, serious mistakes on the part of the leading group headed by Rakosi and the growing distortions of policy brought the country to crisis in 1953. In 1956 betrayal by the revisionist group headed by Imre Nagy and the actions of internal and external counterrevolutionaries gravely threatened the people's government. Hungarian Communists, Hungarian advocates of socialism, backed by the Soviet Union, the socialist countries, the international communist movement and progressive people everywhere, upheld our constitutional system, restored legality, and created conditions for the further building of socialism.

Thirty years ago Western propaganda claimed that socialism in Hungary was dead. Now more and more often it asks why the republic survived and why it continues to march forward. Of course, they find it hard to admit that Hungary's example is proof of the viability of socialism. They attempt to offer their own explanation: Hungary is doing well because, they say, it is using capitalist methods.

Yes, I am aware of that. But let us go back to those years. When the danger was behind us and the popular government was no longer threatened, the tasks of building socialism again came to the fore. Perseverance and hard work were still needed to solve them. After the consolidation of political power and the social system, the next major challenge in the early 1960s was to finish building the foundations of socialist society and to reorganize agriculture along socialist lines. There were snags along the way as well. We were aware that unless we came to grips with the problem, the fundamental political basis

Reprinted from *New Times*, (Moscow), October 20, 1986, pp. 3-6.

125

of our state—the alliance between workers and peasants—could not be strong and Hungarian agriculture would not be able to meet the country's food needs. If we had mishandled this problem we would have caused grave damage to the unity of the working classes and the country's economic position would have deteriorated.

With active help from all strata of society, the party and the working class—in the period of the establishment of agricultural cooperatives—managed to strengthen the foundation of our popular state, i.e., the alliance between workers and peasants, and boost agricultural output. The socialist reorganization of agriculture is a historic achievement of our system. It marks not only a major political step forward but helps considerably raise the living standards of the working class, the peasantry, all the working people, and makes it possible to meet the people's needs. We also have large quantities of goods for export.

In the mid-1960s new major tasks arose before us in the process of socialist development. The sources of extensive growth of the economy having been exhausted, it was necessary to make our system of economic management more flexible and carry out a comprehensive reform. The essence of the management system, in operation for 18 years now, is as follows: a socialist planned economy taking into account the laws of the market, the use of economic as opposed to administrative methods of management, and a certain degree of autonomy and incentive for cooperatives and state-owned enterprises. The experience of recent years has shown that the economic reform introduced in 1968 took into account the general laws of the building of socialism and the specific features of our country and its economic structure, and helped to develop the national economy and consolidate socialist elements in our society.

Among other complex problems we have tackled over the past forty years are: ensuring the unity of the nation for achieving our main objective of building a socialist society, extending socialist democracy, bringing about a dramatic improvement in the living conditions of the people, and big advances in the level of education and quality of life.

Determination, restraint and firm adherence to principle were needed to stand our ground in the international arena. Hungary, as a socialist country, an ally of the U.S.S.R. and a member of the Warsaw Treaty and CMEA, is a link in the socialist community, and as such it occupies a recognized place among nations.

This brief outline of my country's history since liberation cannot of course give a complete picture of how often the firmness of the Communists and the dedication and staunchness of the Hungarian people have been put to the test. Looking back over the past forty years, we find more and more proof that if there is a clear goal, and correspondingly firm leadership, if all creative forces are united, then a nation which has become master of its own destiny is able to overcome all its difficulties and attain its historical objectives. It was with reference to the path we have covered and thinking about the goals now facing us that I quoted one of the main characters of Janos Arany.

Your party congress has set new targets for the country's economic development and identified its new forms. What have been the most notable features of the experience of the past year and a half?

In March 1985 the 13th party congress formulated a clear-cut programme for the further building of an advanced socialist society, for revealing and tapping the potential of the socialist system. The congress set the following objective: constantly aware of the need for economic balance, especially the balance of payments and the state budget, commodity stocks and wages, increase effectiveness of the national economy and thus create a basis for raising the people's living standards. Important conditions for a fuller use of the potential of the so-

cialist system are the acceleration of scientific and technological devlopment, efforts to reveal people's creative forces, and the strengthening of the unity and cohesion of the nation by improving democratic institutions.

Since the congress ended we have started to implement its decisions. Unfortunately, it has to be said that as regards the main goal—accelerated economic development—we are not pleased with the start that has been made or with the present state of affairs. In addition to objective factors—international economic conditions, a very cold winter in 1985, and the present drought—we should look for the causes of this in shortcomings in our own work.

While we have not managed to achieve the desired goals in the economy, we have started to carry out the congress decisions in some other important fields. After the congress we held elections to the National Assembly and the local councils under a new electoral law which makes it binding to put up at least two candidates in every constituency. The elections took place in a favourable political atmosphere and have brought positive results. Change for the better has been achieved in the work of the trade unions and other bodies representing the interests of the working people.

As part of the effort to improve the system of economic management, councils of enterprises have been set up which give them still greater autonomy and responsibility for economic activity. A special law establishes the norms of honest economic activity and obstructs dishonest economic practices. Following the congress decisions, the local councils have become more independent. While the state retains its monopoly over the issue of money and control of currency resources, we have set about creating a banking system that keeps separate the functions of banks of issue, state financing and trade. We hope this will lead to the kind of credit and financial practices which will better serve the purpose of enhancing production activity.

Although the overall economic processes are still not favourable, economic performance has improved in some branches. Many large enterprises have managed to raise output, increase exports and achieve good results in the use of manpower. We have expanded our multiform cooperation with the socialist countries. Our economic ties with the Soviet Union are developing dynamically. Between 1986 and 1990 we hope to increase trade between the two countries by 30 per cent.

The Central Committee of the HSWP and the government of Hungary have taken a number of measures to meet our economic objectives and targets for this year. These measures serve to develop the production structure, stimulate technical progress and export, provide greater incentives for enterprises and workers to improve economic performance, make better use of working time, and strengthen labour discipline. In every field we attach great significance to the human factor and better tapping of the intellectual and creative potential inherent in society. A fine example is offered by the participation of our specialists in the VEGA space programme, and this also speaks volumes about the potential of science in Hungary.

Western propaganda has been rather ingenious in attaching various labels to socialist countries. For example, Hungary has been described as a country of "limited socialism" or "limited pluralism" and sometimes, somewhat indulgently, as a "communist state." It seems to me that you, Comrade General Secretary, have already commented on that by saying: "I wish it were so. Unfortunately, this is not yet the case. But we would like it to be the case and we are working towards this end." Is there any need for a further reply?

I think there is. First, about our immediate objectives and longer-term prospects. At present we are building an advanced socialist society, with communism as our ultimate goal.

Our party is firmly convinced that the congress decisions are correct and—given improved work and concentration of effort —they can be fulfilled to good effect. In our work we can rely on the political maturity and industry of our people. Internationally, our bilateral and multilateral cooperation with the socialist countries provides a solid buffer.

Perhaps you are in a better position than anyone else, Comrade Kadar, to trace the progress of the community of free socialist nations. How would you formulate new tasks! And what methods do you think will be useful in solving them!

Since the second world war decisive changes in the world balance of forces have been brought about by the fact that the socialist system, first established in the U.S.S.R., has become a world system.

Another momentous change in recent decades, also linked with the above change, is the collapse of the "classical" colonial system. The peoples that have freed themselves from the colonial yoke are ever more resolutely opposing the insidious machinations of the imperialists and working to consolidate the independence of their countries and build independent national economies, with more and more of these countries choosing the non-capitalist path of social and economic development.

The social and economic progress of the Soviet Union and the other socialist countries, and the international authority of our community add to the appeal of socialism and provide a reliable bulwark for every progressive and peace-loving movement. I believe therefore that the most important thing for the socialist community at present is that our countries, separately and together, should further reveal the advantages of the socialist system.

Historical experience shows that we should never forget that the socialist community is made up of independent national states. They are linked by the identity of basic goals and interests. This gives strength to proletarian, socialist internationalism. But the system in any given socialist country can only be secure and effective—and this is one of the main conclusions the Hungarian Communists have drawn—when the Marxist-Leninist party—the leading force in society—makes decisions that simultaneously and equally take into account the general and fundamental laws of socialism and the local conditions and national traditions in the given country. All this is necessary if the masses are to support our goals, if the advantages of the socialist system are to be used fully, and if we are to be reliable partners of our socialist allies and of all the champions of peace.

There is no doubt that each party and each socialist country should formulate the strategy and tactics to solve these tasks in accordance with their own possibilities, but it is also true that it cannot do without the experience of the community of socialist states. The present situation makes it more urgent than ever before for the socialist countries to strengthen their cohesion.

In their foreign and home policies the Hungarian Socialist Workers' Party and the Hungarian government seek, in keeping with our common principles and the identity of our main interests and goals, to foster links with the Soviet Union and the other socialist countries covering all the important areas of political, economic and social life.

The social and economic progress of the socialist countries and the international authority and influence of our community are inconceivable without the existence of the Soviet Union, the historic achievements of the Soviet Communists and all Soviet people.

We in our country followed with interest and sympathy the 27th congress of the Communist Party of the Soviet Union which, in considering new social and economic phenomena and inter-national relations and creatively applying Marxist-Leninist theory, approached the key issues of our era in a new way, stimulating further reflection and action. We are convinced that the acceleration of the Soviet Union's social and economic development and the implementation of the large-scale programme adopted by the congress will not only bring considerable change in the life of the Soviet people, but will give an impetus to the development of other socialist countries.

Not only this country, but the whole world, and all peace-loving people approve and support the foreign policy strategy of the CPSU, which aims at ending the arms race, preventing nuclear war, preserving peace, and solving the global problems on which the survival of mankind depends.

The Hungarian Socialist Workers' Party, the government of Hungary and our people are convinced supporters of the Soviet foreign policy initiatives, and attach great significance to concerted actions by socialist countries on major issues of world politics. We for our part are doing everything in our power to ensure that our common initiatives in the world arena yield results.

We consider it an honour that Budapest should have been the venue of the meeting of the Warsaw Treaty Political Consultative Committee last summer and that it was in our capital that it adopted the appeal containing a programme for reducing armed forces and conventional armaments in Europe, which would go a long way towards strengthening peace and security in our continent.

One of the key areas of joint work between the socialist countries is economic cooperation. We share a determination to raise our work in this area to a new level meeting higher standards, as recent sessions of CMEA have also shown. One way of achieving this is through broader scientific and technological cooperation and specialization, and the setting up of joint enterprises. The same end will be served by the establishment of direct links between enterprises. A higher level of economic cooperation would offer greater possibilities for the development of the whole community and the individual states it comprises, and strengthen the international economic positions of our countries.

The states that make up the socialist world system embarked on revolutionary transformations at different times and in different historical conditions, starting out from different levels of productive forces. They differ in size of territory and population. Multiform cooperation among the countries of the socialist community has never come automatically. We are convinced, therefore, that contributing towards stronger unity and cooperation by its policies is an important task of the Marxist-Leninist party which guides the building of socialism. It is only if the party constantly and consciously seeks to contribute by its policies to unity and cooperation among socialist countries that it can best serve the twin goals of raising the living standards of its own people and the cause of social progress in the world.

By way of conclusion I can say: we believe that the Hungarian Communists and people, the Hungarian People's Republic can contribute to our common cause primarily by successfully tackling the tasks of construction on the agenda in their own country.

Our country and our people are not alone in struggling and working for a peaceful socialist future. We are trying to live up to our role in solving our common tasks because in this way we serve the vital interests of our own people. Making use of time-tested methods and looking for new opportunities, we will promote cooperation with our Soviet friends and other fraternal socialist countries and pool our efforts in work and the struggle to strengthen peace and international security and solve the global problems facing mankind.

4. SOCIALIST STATES: ALLIES AND ADVERSARIES OF THE USSR

On this morning of October 1 all the Hungarian papers carried the news of the agreement on an early meeting between Mikhail Gorbachev and Ronald Reagan in Reykjavik. This is good news.

It is in many ways an unusual autumn. September saw the successful conclusion of the Stockholm conference and the Vienna session of the IAEA. Preparations have got under way for the Vienna meeting which will mark the next stage in the Helsinki process. And there seem to be favourable signs at the Geneva negotiations. At the beginning of our talk, Comrade Kadar, we referred to the Hungarian poet Arany. Now I am reminded of Pushkin's "Boldino autumn." (This phrase is used to denote a particularly fruitful period, like the autumn in Boldino where the poet Pushkin wrote so many masterpieces.) Do you believe there are grounds for talking about a "Boldino autumn" in international politics?

As far as I remember, the "Boldino autumn" was the autumn when Pushkin's creative potential was most fully revealed. Certain hopes and perspectives have been generated in international politics today. Responsible political leaders in the Soviet Union and the other socialist countries and—more broadly—throughout the world—sincerely wish international issues to be solved by negotiation, taking into account the interests of all the parties concerned. Accordingly, the leading bodies of the Hungarian People's Republic welcomed the Geneva summit during which the sides made a statement of fundamental importance. They jointly stressed that neither side would seek military superiority, that there can be no winners in a nuclear war and that nuclear war should be prevented. Regrettably, the Geneva summit has not brought notable progress, although the Soviet Union has come out with many sensible proposals, with regard to the interests of both sides. Important proposals and initiatives have also been put forward by the latest meeting of the Warsaw Treaty Political Consultative Committee. The socialist countries have also taken vigorous steps at various international negotiations, for example, at the current session of the U.N. General Assembly and at meetings within the framework of the European cooperation and security-building process. World public opinion gives its due to the successful conclusion of the Stockholm conference. For our part, we expect a similar conclusion to the Vienna and Geneva negotiations.

Relations between the Soviet Union and the United States are of particular significance for international politics and it is very important to see progress in their bilateral relations. I am glad that Mikhail Gorbachev and Ronald Reagan are shortly to meet in Iceland to prepare the schedule for a visit by the CPSU General Secretary to the U.S. I am convinced that all who want durable and secure peace will welcome the summit meeting as a step towards new possibilities in improving the international situation.

Budapest

China Will Not Retrogress

An Zhiguo

China's struggle against bourgeois liberalization has evoked widespread concern and comments abroad.

While some commentators have rightly said that it would not retard the progress of China's modernization, others worry that it will bring the reform and open policy to a premature end. This latter fear, it seems to me, originates from a lack of understanding of the basic forces operating in China and perhaps failure to analyze them scientifically.

The fight against bourgeois liberalization and the policy of reform, opening up and economic invigoration do not conflict with each other. The former means combating a tendency to negate the socialist system and Party leadership and advocate capitalism.

Economic structural reform aims to remove fossilized economic methods, overcome defects in the economic structure and establish a planned commodity economy which is based on public ownership and full of vitality. Political reform is intended to overcome overcentralization of power and confusion in the different roles of the Party and the government; to expand socialist democracy, strengthen and improve the Party leadership and consolidate the people's democratic dictatorship. To put it in a nutshell, reform is the self-improvement of the socialist system, not its negation.

Opening the outside world is aimed at breaking down autarky: absorbing advanced foreign science, technology, managerial expertise and outstanding culture; and using foreign capital to expedite China's socialist construction. It is not directed at importing the capitalist system. Opening to the outside world is fundamentally different from "complete Westernization" as preached by the trumpeters of bourgeois liberalization.

Zhao Ziyang recently said that the Party's political line—effective since the Third Plenum of the 11th CPC Central Committee in 1978—is, proceeding from China's reality, to build socialism

The campaign against bourgeois liberalization will not affect China's present economic policies. Rather, it can only steer economic reforms to the right track.

with Chinese characteristics. This has two major aspects: One is upholding the four cardinal principles (i.e., upholding the socialist road, the Party's leadership, the people's democratic dictatorship, and Marxism-Leninism and Mao Zedong Thought—*Ed.*); the other is upholding the policy of reform, opening up and economic invigoration. The two are interrelated and neither can be dispensed with.

Of the four cardinal principles, the Party leadership and the socialist road are the most important. In China today, failure to criticize those who oppose socialism and the Party's leadership; and allowing the erroneous ideological trend that worships capitalism blindly and advocates "complete Westernization," will inevitably bring about political instability, splits and turmoil. Should that occur, implementation of any guidelines and policies, however correct, would be impossible. Combating bourgeois liberalization is therefore aimed precisely at a smooth implementation of the policies of reform, opening up and economic in-

vigoration in condition of continued political stability and unity.

Since the open policy began in 1979, China's import and export trade has developed rapidly, the scale of its foreign economic and technical co-operation has expanded, the area of co-operation has been widened and the methods of co-operation have been diversified.

Currently, there are 7,730 Sino-foreign joint ventures, Sino-foreign co-operative enterprises and wholly foreign-owned businesses. Cultural exchanges have expanded too. Experience has shown that the open policy helps quicken the progress of China's socialist modernization.

Meanwhile, the reforms under way nationwide have accelerated production and benefited people in general. In 1978, China's national income averaged 315 yuan per capita, the figure reached 735 yuan in 1986. People in over 90 percent of the rural areas have eliminated poverty and backwardness, and urban people's welfare has improved. As long as the current line and policies continue, it is estimated that total industrial and agricultural output value in 1990 will be double that of 1980, and that the goal of quadrupling 1980 production by the year 2000 can be achieved. Since the masses support the current line and policies are full of confidence in the future, how could China abandon these policies whose efficacy has been tested and return to its former, fossilized economic methods and closed-doorism?

Although it is only eight years since China started the policies reform, opening up and invigorating the economy, their benefits have been quite obvious. While combating bourgeois liberalization, China will continue these policies—long term.

Reprinted by courtesy of *Beijing Review*, March 2, 1987, p. 4.

129

The Third World

- Africa (Articles 27-29)
- Asia (Articles 30-32)
- Latin America (Articles 33-35)
- The Middle East (Articles 36-38)

The "Third World," a group of close to one hundred "lesser developed countries" (LDCs) which have little more in common with each other than their inability to achieve sustained growth, is today riven with external conflict, internal unrest, and massive indebtedness. Many of their problems have economic roots. Other problems do not, but they exacerbate the economic difficulties. Sectarian, religious, ethnic, and national conflicts contribute to the drain on scarce economic and financial resources. Further, the use of dictatorial powers and the abuse of human rights in certain countries has silenced or alienated those who might otherwise have contributed more to their country's developmental process. Fragmented policies have often wasted precious resources in civil violence as in Lebanon; in conflict with the government, as in Haiti, Uganda, Angola, Nicaragua, and the Philippines; or in conflict with their neighbors, as in the Iran-Iraq war and elsewhere in the Middle East.

Development in the LDCs is further hindered by environmental problems, the end results of extreme poverty: deforestation, desertification, erosion, and salinization of the soil. The abuse of the environment, and even what are called "natural disasters" are both the cause and the effect of poverty. They also reflect the inability or unwillingness of governments to protect the environment, for as is now increasingly realized, the bulk of "natural disasters" occur in underdeveloped countries, just as they used to occur in what are now the developed countries.

The international community shares a feeling of despair about the LDCs. Developmental aid has not brought development, and loans have seemingly brought even more indebtedness. All too many LDC governments choose to use their scarce resources either to oppress their own populations or to wage war against their neighbors. Further development is at the whim of an undisciplined and erratic international economy governed only by the marketplace. Prices for commodities, the products upon which most LDCs rely in order to finance development, are at their lowest level since the early 1930s. Those countries that are seriously attempting to develop, discover that when they at last manage to industrialize certain sectors, those manufactured goods already glut the marketplace. High

interest rates on loans and, until recently, the increasing costs of energy have further discouraged the leaders of, and the potential investors in, these countries.

When the world was forced to confront the eviction of Duvalier, the right-wing dictator from Haiti, and the reliance upon brutality, terrorism, and fraud to gain electoral victory for Marcos, the former right-wing dictator of the Philippines, it again raised serious questions about the kinds of values undergirding the distribution of foreign aid. What was wrong with these aid programs that what aid did not flow into the pockets of the ruling elite, was used to brutally oppress the country's people? In part it shows that the aid recipients were able to successfully barter their anticommunist proclivities for aid with few strings attached. This has been particularly true of US bilateral aid, but multilateral aid programs have suffered from similar problems. Although the IMF's attachment of "conditions" to loans has led to other sorts of difficulties for indebted Third World countries, one cannot help but wonder that if strings, such as a demand for austerity budgets and basic economic reforms, had been attached to bilateral foreign aid decades ago, many more LDCs might have escaped the trap of underdevelopment.

However, when individual countries attach conditions to bilateral aid, whether demanding the expenditure of foreign aid in a certain sector, political or economic reforms, or an improvement in human rights conditions, it is usually viewed (and often rightly so) as an attempt to control aid recipients, a form of "neoimperialism." Recipient countries often bitterly resent such controls, and view them as attempts by the donor to economically exploit them, even to "underdevelop" them, and to use them as pawns in the East-West power struggle. Although international financial institutions that have demanded reform and austerity of aid recipients have also been blamed for the ensuing political instability, it is more difficult for aid recipients to see decisions made multilaterally as having the same manipulative and sinister intentions as those made by one country.

In their focus on the major trouble spots in the Third World, the following articles address some of the issues just mentioned. Given the level of American aid in El Salvador, it is most unlikely that any government there could come to power or carry out a major policy if it were unacceptable to the US (Article 35). Mexico's foreign indebtedness is so vast that, barring a moratorium on repayment of the debt, or debt default, Mexico has few alternatives to acceding to the demands of its debtors and opening up the economy to foreign investors. From Mexico's viewpoint, this would risk making the economy vulnerable to foreign control (Article 33).

In Africa a number of governments are, in an effort to please Western aid donors, promising to reduce the role of the central government in economic growth, substituting for it an enhanced role for the private sector (Article 27). This is part of the latest strategy not just of Western aid donors, incidentally, but also of the IMF. Further, now that the Soviet Union is no longer viewed by the African states as their "natural ally," largely because the Soviets are unable to provide generous economic aid, the African states must turn to the Western states for support. They are, therefore, far more amenable to accepting their donors' suggestions than they used to be (Article 28).

Perhaps as much a consequence as a cause of economic underdevelopment in the LDCs is the warfare that saps the energies of so many of them. Vietnamese-occupied Kampuchea, for example, can hardly be expected to develop when the country has been bogged down in a struggle against the occupying forces and their puppet regime for ten years (Article 32). Awareness of how disruptive even rumors of an occupation have been on the economy of Hong Kong has contributed to China's cautious approach toward integrating both Hong Kong and Taiwan in a peaceful manner (Article 30). But nowhere is the devastating impact of internal dissent and warfare on development so evident as in the Middle East. There, political Islam, the Palestinian issue, nationalism, socialism, and ethnic and religious differences have contributed to endless warfare and political instability. In such a context, devleopment hardly has a chance. The region's governments are plagued with crises of authority and legitimacy. In the midst of these crises, a new type of Arab citizen and a new concept of legitimacy are forming, both of which reflect the rise of democratic forces (Articles 36 and 37).

South Africa, on the other hand, is riven by racial violence. The violence is not just between blacks and whites, but also among blacks themselves (Article 29).

A final issue affecting development is the Soviet-American confrontation in the LDCs. Although both the US and USSR have contributed to development through aid programs, they have often done so for the political purpose of furthering their own ambitions in the Third World. Further, their military aid (and military sales) to the LDCs have contributed to the level of devastation which these countries can wreck both on others and on themselves. Lebanon, Iran, and Iraq have all suffered far more than they would have from violence had there been fewer arms merchants from both East and West to respond to their desires for more lethal weaponry. Nevertheless, the Soviet-American confrontation is not the major reason for most of the crises in the LDCs. Usually, indigenous issues are far more important than superpower rivalries in explaining the origins of the political crises which have led to war. Thus, if a peace settlement is to occur, the local parties to the dispute must be the key participants (Article 38).

Looking Ahead: Challenge Questions

What are the major sources of conflict within and between countries of the Third World? To what extent are their problems the result of incompetent governments, internal social and economic conditions which shackle effective policy, or alternatively, foreign involvement? How do the various government and rebel groups within these countries use the East-West conflict to their advantage? Do you believe the industrialized states who gave aid to Third World countries did so largely to maintain them as economic dependencies, or to cultivate them as pawns in the East-West struggle? In the case of those countries which pulled themselves out of the Third World to become "newly industrialized countries," was the type of aid they received the same kind as that given to those countries which have not succeeded in developing? If the aid was virtually the same in form, what factors account for the differences in growth?

Africa's Economy in Crisis: The Facts and Figures

Figures are from 1984. South Africa and Morocco are not included; they are not members of the Organization of African Unity.

Country	Per capita production level (dollars)	Debt (millions of dollars)	Net aid (millions of dollars)
Indian Ocean countries			
Comoros	235	203.0	24.4
Madagascar	245	2,119.8	159.6
Mauritius	1,004	560.0	19.6
Seychelles	2,296	57.5	2.2
East Africa			
Ethiopia	114	1,550.2	397.2
Burundi	214	346.0	160.5
Tanzania	219	2,600.0	81.4
Uganda	237	1,031.0	146.0
Kenya	261	3,811.0	414.6
Somalia	275	1,429.0	303.0
Rwanda	293	281.0	149.4
Djibouti	313	179.0	40.1
Sudan	393	7,892.0	542.0
Southern Africa			
Mozambique	147	1,044.0	250.0
Malawi	177	885.0	163.0
Lesotho	214	140.0	103.0
Zambia	410	4,775.0	255.0
Angola	568	859.0	92.0
Swaziland	669	278.9	29.0
Zimbabwe	740	2,124.0	282.0
Botswana	1,210	356.1	101.0
Central Africa			
Equatorial Guinea	65	126.0	11.2
Zaire	93	5,001.0	238.0
Central African Republic	241	277.2	120.0
São Tomé and Principe	343	75.2	7.9
Cameroon	792	2,792.0	142.0
Congo	1,100	1,603.0	44.0
Gabon	2,618	975.0	73.0
Sub-Saharan Africa			
Chad	116	157.9	115.0
Burkina Faso	119	529.9	188.0
Mali	137	1,176.0	278.0
Guinea-Bissau	174	214.2	66.0
Niger	243	668.1	251.0
Cape Verde	256	118.0	39.9*
Gambia	272	311.7	42.7
Senegal	364	2,026.0	32.7
Mauritania	425	1,700.0	156.0

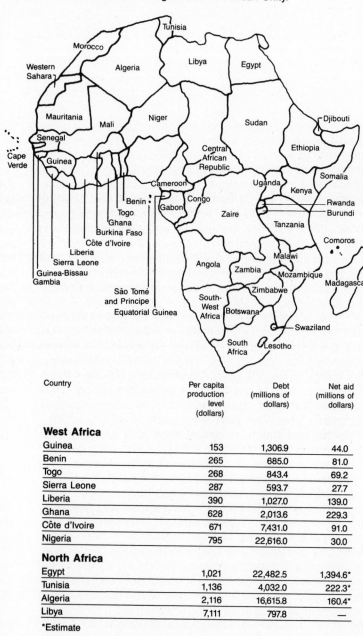

Country	Per capita production level (dollars)	Debt (millions of dollars)	Net aid (millions of dollars)
West Africa			
Guinea	153	1,306.9	44.0
Benin	265	685.0	81.0
Togo	268	843.4	69.2
Sierra Leone	287	593.7	27.7
Liberia	390	1,027.0	139.0
Ghana	628	2,013.6	229.3
Côte d'Ivoire	671	7,431.0	91.0
Nigeria	795	22,616.0	30.0
North Africa			
Egypt	1,021	22,482.5	1,394.6*
Tunisia	1,136	4,032.0	222.3*
Algeria	2,116	16,615.8	160.4*
Libya	7,111	797.8	—

*Estimate

Source: Organization of African Unity

Moscow and Africa:

A 1986 Balance Sheet

Michael Clough

When President Reagan took office in 1981, it was generally assumed that his administration would adopt a conservative globalist approach to African issues. For a complex mix of reasons, it did not. Instead, Assistant Secretary of State for African Affairs Chester Crocker won the support of the White House and Secretary of State Alexander Haig for a strategy toward southern Africa and the rest of the continent that, although conservative in disposition, was still more regionalist than globalist.

It was not until 1985 that a somewhat disparate assemblage of politicians, officials, and opinion leaders coalesced in support of a more aggressive, ideological, and interventionist posture toward radical socialist regimes in the Third World. The most controversial of the African manifestations of this new drive from the right has been the buildup of pressure for direct U.S. assistance to Jonas Savimbi and his UNITA guerrillas in Angola (see "United States Options in Angola" by John A. Marcum in *CSIS Africa Notes* no. 52, December 20, 1985). Ironically, this new wave of globalism is cresting just as it is becoming clear that many of the special relationships that Moscow seemed to have cemented in Africa between the 1950s and the mid-1970s have proven to be illusory and ephemeral.

False Analogies

On the basis of false analogies with the rise of communism in the Soviet Union and Eastern Europe, globalists are inclined to explain decisions by Third World states to align with the Soviet Union in terms of Soviet "penetration" and "subversion." Such theories cannot be reconciled with actual events in any African country. From Egypt and Guinea in the 1950s to Angola, Mozambique, and Ethiopia in the 1970s, every African country that has become an ally of the Soviet Union has done so as a result of a conscious and unforced decision. Before the decision by national

leaders to seek Moscow's support, the Soviet presence in most of these countries was minimal at most. To explain why independent African leaders, many of whom lacked a prior ideological affinity with the Soviet Union, chose to associate with the communist camp requires an understanding of the so-called "natural ally" thesis.

Repeatedly invoked by Soviet officials, the natural ally thesis holds that the Soviet Union and radical socialist states in the Third World share a common project (building socialism) and a common enemy (capitalist imperialism). For example, Karen Brutents, an influential official in the international department of the CPSU Central Committee, wrote in 1979:

> It is certain that in future, support from the Soviet Union, the socialist countries, and the international working-class movement will continue as always to be vital to the national liberation struggle. Without this support it is impossible to ultimately defeat neocolonialism and advance along the road of social progress. Without this support it would be impossible to ensure that the developing countries' growing international authority is a stable process.

The positive strand of this thesis — the claim that the Soviet Union and radical socialist states share a commitment to building socialism — has only a limited and fading appeal for most Third World leaders. Far more important is the negative strand which holds that the Soviet Union is the only reliable source of protection against capitalist imperialism, regional aggression, and internal subversion.

In their own explications of the natural ally thesis, Third World leaders invariably stress its defensive strand. In 1979, for example, Mozambique's President Samora Machel referred to the socialist countries as "a reliable rearguard for the victory of our liberation struggle," calling them the "natural ally for the defense of our political and economic independence." According

Originally published as *CSIS Africa Notes* briefing paper series, Issue No. 55, March 1986, pp. 1-4. (Washington, DC). Reprinted with permission.

to a 1978 party document, FRELIMO's "political alliance with the socialist countries constitutes an important strategic factor for dissuasion of the aggressive plans of imperialism."

A necessary corollary of the natural ally thesis is the argument that a "natural antagonism" exists between the United States and radical socialist governments in the Third World. The assumption that the United States is fundamentally opposed to regimes that embrace socialism has been a prime consideration in the decision of many such regimes to tilt toward the Eastern bloc. In a world dominated by two superpowers, the perception that one of the superpowers is fundamentally hostile will, in accordance with the familiar principle that "the enemy of my enemy is my friend," inevitably cause states to seek the support of the other superpower.

In the mid-1970s, many if not most radical socialist Third World leaders perceived the United States as a potential adversary. From their vantage point, U.S. interventions in Iran, Guatemala, Lebanon, Cuba, the Dominican Republic, Zaire, Southeast Asia, and Chile provided ample grounds for such an assessment. In Africa, the governments that took power in newly independent Angola and Mozambique had more immediate reasons for concern. In the wake of the Ford administration's abortive intervention in the Angolan civil war in 1975, they were understandably fearful that the United States would work in concert with South Africa to subvert their governments. This fear has since ebbed in much of Africa, replaced by pragmatic interest in economic and security connections with the West, and Soviet fortunes in the continent have stagnated. (See, for example, "Benin Joins the Pragmatists" by L. Gray Cowan in *CSIS Africa Notes* no. 54, February 28, 1986.)

The Treaty Scorecard

During the 1970s the Soviet Union entered into treaty relationships with five African countries: Egypt (May 1971), Somalia (July 1974), Angola (October 1976), Mozambique (March 1977), and Ethiopia (November 1978). Egypt and Somalia abrogated their treaties with Moscow in 1976 and 1977 respectively, and are now counted among Moscow's strongest foes on the continent. Since 1978 only one additional African country — Congo — has signed a treaty of friendship and cooperation with Moscow, and that treaty did not contain a military clause. Moreover, the decisions of Mozambique's President Machel to seek military assistance from the West and sign a nonaggression pact (the Nkomati Accord) with South Africa in March 1984 have rendered its treaty with Moscow relatively meaningless.

Military Assistance

Military assistance trends provide a second indicator that the Soviet gains of the mid-1970s have not caused a significant shift in the strategic orientation of most African states. Between 1976 and 1980, roughly one-third of Africa's 51 independent states received the bulk of their military supplies from the Soviet Union and its allies. In percentage terms, this constituted a small increase over preceding periods. Most of that increase, however, can be accounted for by the emergence of radical socialist governments in the five Portuguese-speaking territories that gained their independence in 1974-75.

Since 1980 the number of African states dependent primarily on the Soviet Union for military support has declined; and the number of arms transfer agreements between the Soviet Union and African states as a percentage of total agreements signed by African states has also declined slightly. The countries that have signed major arms purchase agreements with Moscow in the 1980s are Angola, Congo, Ethiopia, Mozambique, Tanzania, Algeria, and Libya. Tanzania's arms purchases from the Soviet Union have never translated into close military links between the two countries. Moreover, Tanzania's appetite for arms decreased sharply in the early 1980s following the end of its intervention in Uganda to assist in the overthrow of the Idi Amin regime. Since 1982 three countries previously dependent on Moscow (Congo, Mozambique, and Algeria) have turned to the West for military assistance. As of 1985 only Angola and Ethiopia (and, in a very different sense, Libya) could be counted as significant military dependencies of the Soviet Union. (For a summary of recent developments in the Soviet-Libyan relationship, see "Africa: Year of Ironies" by Helen Kitchen in the February 1986 "America and the World 1985" issue of *Foreign Affairs*, pp. 566-567.)

In 1986 more African countries — a total of 41 — will receive military training assistance from the United States than ever before. (For background, see "Some Observations on U.S. Security Interests in Africa" by Noel C. Koch in *CSIS Africa Notes* no. 49, November 19, 1985.) Included on the list of countries that the Reagan administration proposed to aid were Algeria, Benin, Congo, Madagascar, and all of the former Portuguese territories except Angola. (A proposed package of military training and nonlethal supplies for Mozambique was blocked by Congress in July 1985.) A decade earlier, most globalists would have considered all of the radical socialist regimes in these countries to be firmly in the Soviet camp.

The UN Vote Criterion

Another frequently used (and usually misused) indicator of alignment is voting behavior in the United Nations. An examination of how African countries have voted on three issues that the Soviet Union regards as "key" — Afghanistan, Kampuchea, and illegal use of chemical and biological weapons — provides another demonstration of the limits of Soviet influence. No more than nine African countries have ever voted with the Soviet Union on *any* of these issues, while at least 23 countries have voted against the Soviets on *all* three issues in each of the past five years. The number of countries voting with the Soviets on any of these issues has declined from nine in 1980 to six in 1984. In 1984 only Libya voted with the Soviet Union on all three of these key issues. (See "The UN: A Not So Dangerous Place?" by Michael Clough in *CSIS Africa Notes* no. 45, July 24, 1985.)

The Zimbabwe Watershed

A major symbolic watershed in Soviet relations with Africa occurred in April 1980 when Robert Mugabe's Zimbabwe African National Union-Patriotic Front (ZANU-PF) won an overwhelming victory in Zimbabwe's first independence election. A radical socialist government coming to power through an election following a negotiated settlement brokered by a conservative British government represented a sharp contrast to the transitions to independence that had occurred in Angola and Mozambique.

Mugabe pointedly declined to invite East Germany, Poland, Hungary, or Czechoslovakia to participate in Zimbabwe's April 1980 independence celebrations, and reportedly cold-shouldered an attempt by Moscow to trade Foreign Minister Andrei Gromyko's presence for an agreement to issue a joint communique cementing Soviet-Zimbabwean ties. The USSR was represented instead by a low-level Politburo member, and Zimbabwe delayed until February 1981 before allowing Moscow to open an embassy in Harare. In contrast, Prime Minister Mugabe made a triumphant visit to Washington in 1980.

Of more consequence substantively was the fact that Mugabe turned over the task of integrating and training the Zimbabwean military (including the recent retraining of an army brigade initially placed under North Korean tutelage) to the British; chose to rely on Western support for protection against pressure from South Africa; and charted a moderate economic course. (See "Whither Zimbabwe?" by Michael Clough in *CSIS Africa Notes* no. 20, November 15, 1983.)

Why did Mugabe decide to snub the Soviet Union and tilt westward? Most analysts point to the fact that Moscow had consistently favored Joshua Nkomo and the Zimbabwe African People's Union (ZAPU), ZANU-PF's historic rival within the nationalist movement, during the liberation struggle. In this view, Mugabe's post-independence posture was motivated by bitterness over Soviet failure to aid ZANU in the past and suspicion that the Kremlin might still harbor hopes of seeing Nkomo emerge on top in an independent Zimbabwe. These considerations were undoubtedly a factor in Mugabe's thinking. They were not, however, the only or even the most important determinants of his decision to rely so heavily on London and Washington.

Given the nature of the economic and regional security problems facing his government at independence and his favorable experiences with the Thatcher government and the Carter administration during the transition period, Mugabe had good reason to conclude that maintaining his country's historic ties with the West would pay higher dividends in areas of primary importance. Moscow lacked the economic wherewithal of the United States and Britain. Just as important, a close relationship with London and Washington seemed a better bet to deter South African intervention than did Soviet arms. These factors would not have been sufficient had the Mugabe government not also believed it could trust the West. Here the Carter administration's steadfast refusal to support the short-lived internal settlement and the Thatcher government's impartial performance during and after the April 1980 elections had to weigh strongly and positively in Mugabe's calculations. If the West had lacked either the resources or willingness to support his government, Mugabe would have eventually had little choice but to cut a deal with the Kremlin.

The argument that the historic differences between ZANU-PF and the Soviet Union prevented the Mugabe government from aligning with the East also overlooks the critical role played in Zimbabwean developments by President Machel of Mozambique. If Mugabe had desired a rapprochement with Moscow, Machel undoubtedly could have served as a go-between. Instead, however, Machel, influenced by his own government's experiences, appears to have encouraged Mugabe to chart a moderate course and develop close ties with the United States and Britain. (See "What Does the Case of Mozambique Tell Us About Soviet Ambivalence Toward Africa?" by Winrich Kühne in *CSIS Africa Notes* no. 46, August 30, 1985.)

If the above analysis is correct, the setback the Soviets suffered in Zimbabwe was far more fundamental and far-reaching than is implied by arguments that focus on unique historical antagonisms between ZANU and Moscow. That setback evidenced a structural weakness in the Soviet position in Africa, one that can be eased marginally by better intelligence and tactical decision making by Soviet leaders, but not eliminated.

Why Stagnation?

What accounts for Moscow's flagging fortunes in Africa? Three factors have been most important: (1) The Soviet Union proved to be a poor patron. As most Soviet analysts now acknowledge, the Soviets lack the skills, capital, and markets necessary to compete effectively with international agencies, multinational corporations, and Western governments in the economic realm. In addition, while Soviet military assistance has ensured the short-term survival of the regimes in Angola, Ethiopia, and, to a lesser extent, Mozambique, it has failed to provide security and stability. (2) By 1978 the easy opportunities for Soviet gains afforded by the collapse of Portuguese colonialism and the fall of Ethiopia's Haile Selassie had been exhausted. (3) Since 1976, the United States has pursued a more active and regionally sensitive policy. U.S. policymakers have endeavored, with surprising and largely unremarked success, to convince African leaders that diplomatically and economically it is the West, and not the Soviet bloc, which is relevant to solving Africa's basic problems. In short, in the latter 1970s and early 1980s the regional and international environment became, as many skeptical regionalists predicted it would, much less conducive to growing Soviet influence in Africa.

Soviet Priorities and Imperatives

The mere fact that Moscow has experienced some setbacks in Africa does not mean that its leadership would fail to act to ensure that the extension of the Reagan doctrine to the continent would be neither cheap nor quickly successful. Africa is not near the top of

Moscow's list of global priorities, nor do Soviet leaders seem inclined to commit significant resources to achieve new successes on the continent. They cannot afford, however, to allow either the MPLA in Angola or the Dergue in Ethiopia to be defeated by Western-backed insurgents. This is the message that Soviet officials, publicists, and academics have consistently sought to communicate to the United States since at least 1983.

In late 1983, for example, Soviet officials at the United Nations met with South African officials to warn them that Moscow would not allow the MPLA to be defeated militarily by UNITA. "In view of the friendly nature of Soviet-Angolan relations," one Soviet official commented in June 1984, the Soviet Union "cannot be indifferent to the problem of Angola's security." More recently, an influential Soviet commentator declared in reference to the Reagan doctrine, "the United States has no right to arm and train murderers and bandits or to interfere in the affairs of sovereign states. Attempts to arrogate that right to itself, to don the uniform of international gendarme, can only meet with resolute opposition from the Soviet Union." The marked increase in the level and sophistication of Soviet support for the MPLA since Moscow warned Pretoria provides good reason to take these statements seriously.

Conservative globalists ought to understand better than most Americans why Soviet leaders are unlikely to back down in Angola and Ethiopia. Moscow's fears concerning the possible global repercussions of defeats in these two symbolically important countries derive from the same concerns about credibility that underlay the "domino theory" used by U.S. officials in the 1960s to rationalize an escalating U.S. commitment to defend South Vietnam.

Michael Clough currently teaches in the Department of Political Science at the University of Wisconsin, and is a 1985-86 CSIS adjunct fellow. From 1980 to 1985 he was assistant professor of National Security Affairs at the U.S. Naval Postgraduate School in Monterey, California. He coauthored with Helen Kitchen *The United States and South Africa: Realities and Red Herrings* (CSIS Significant Issues Series, 1984), and was editor of and contributor to *Changing Realities in Southern Africa: Implications for American Policy* (Berkeley: Institute of International Studies, University of California, 1982). Articles by Dr. Clough have appeared in *Foreign Policy, Problems of Communism, Africa Report, CSIS Africa Notes, Current History,* and other periodicals. This issue of *CSIS Africa Notes* is adapted from his final chapter in *Reassessing the Soviet Challenge in Africa,* a collection he has edited for publication in 1986 by Berkeley's Institute of International Studies. Other contributors to this forthcoming volume include Paul Henze, Martin Lowenkopf, John Marcum, and Donald Jordan.

Race Politics in South Africa: Change and Revolt

"One doubts that the government is prepared to legitimize its own demise. It is clear, however, that President Botha has been led to appreciate the need for dramatic political steps to end the [black] unrest. . . . Still, intimidation is the language of apartheid, and this regime is fluent in its use, at home and abroad."

KENNETH W. GRUNDY

Professor of Political Science, Case Western Reserve University

Kenneth W. Grundy is the author of *The Militarization of South African Politics* (Bloomington: Indiana University Press, 1986) and *Soldiers without Politics* (Berkeley: University of California Press, 1983), a study of blacks in the South African armed forces. He has taught at universities in Uganda, Zambia and Ireland.

THERE was bitter irony in South African police activities during Christmas, 1985. The bastion of "Western Christian civilization" banned caroling in Cape Town's black and "coloured" townships, required special permits for traditional candlelight services, and used violence to break up a multiracial candlelight sing and procession.

To the regime, candles, hymns and vigils have evidently become revolutionary symbols. The police action was no more harsh, no more repressive, than official behavior in hundreds of other circumstances throughout the year. But aimed as it was at Christmas celebrations involving black people, it accented the South African government's insecurity.[1]

In the months since August, 1984, more than 1,000 blacks and just over 20 whites have been killed in political protests. Of late, the pace of violence aimed directly at the white community has quickened (land mines on roads near the borders with Botswana and Zimbabwe, and the bombing of a shopping center south of Durban). At its June, 1985, national conference held in Zambia, the African National Congress (ANC) decided to escalate armed struggle and to hit "soft" civilian targets as well as "hard" government facilities, especially security force targets.[2] This recent tactical shift that strikes randomly at white civilians has led whites to pressure the government to deal more fiercely with insurgents and with neighboring governments that allegedly provide sanctuary. One distraught farmer whose wife and two children died in a land-mine explosion, said "You can tell Oliver Tambo [president of the ANC] to beware of awakening the tiger in the Afrikaner."[3]

Unlike past unrest, civil disobedience, protest and violence touch virtually every part of the black population today. Racial group interests, articulated by the most dynamic and powerful spokespersons, are irreconcilable. At this stage they cannot be negotiated away. Each successive episode of spasmodic protest (Sharpeville, Soweto, and the current violence beginning in the eastern Cape in 1984) lasted longer, was deeper, was geographically more extensive, involved more people, was harder for the authorities to cap, and had shorter "quiet" periods in between.

Despite the government's declaration of a state of emergency and its efforts to hide the realities through controls on the media, the unrest has taken on a momentum difficult to end. Deaths lead to funerals, which become political demonstrations that precipitate more violence. The very presence of police and soldiers triggers the outrage that ends in bloodshed.

Some two-thirds of the deaths and a higher proportion of the injuries are the direct result of police or army operations. The other third result from black murders and mob violence aimed at blacks regarded as associates of the authorities. Black policemen, police informants, town councilors, agents of the government and their families and those who fail to cooperate with the militants' calls for boycotts are the targets. To a lesser extent, conflict between various protest organizations and their supporters has added to the unrest—Inkatha (largely Zulu) against United Democratic Front (UDF), and

From *Current History*, May 1986, pp. 197-200, 227-228. Copyright 1986, Current History, Inc. Reprinted by permission

UDF against various black consciousness groups.[4] Sometimes these battles take place in the guise of ideological disputes, but they occasionally reflect tribal divisions.

There is another form of black-on-black violence that is potentially more disturbing—the horribly brutal intercommunal fights, some of which are fomented by police agents. Some involve migrant laborers against settled township residents. More serious are ethnic disputes, often involving Zulus as one of the parties. They may be known as "faction fights" when only a single ethnic group is involved. In Natal, such fights account for a high proportion of the deaths. One such incident outside Durban in January, 1986, which involved Zulus and Pondos (a branch of the Xhosas), left at least 36 dead and over 40,000 homeless.[5]

At present black opinion seems to be badly divided. Moderate blacks favor negotiation, but are divided on tactics and policy choices. More militant blacks, especially members of the UDF and some covert supporters of the ANC, argue that it is too late for negotiation. South Africa must be made ungovernable, they say, and "sellouts" must be silenced. It is possible that as the government seems less and less secure, an embryonic civil war may begin within the black majority as black leaders insist that blacks cannot successfully confront white power unless all blacks support one particular strategy.

There is little sign of abatement. The protests touch all regions, all ages, all life-styles and all issues. They embody a number of strategies and tactics—from legal protest and petition, work stoppages and consumer boycotts, to sabotage and assassination. There is also a measure of anomic mob violence—the expression of frustrations difficult to vent legitimately. Although the revolutionary groups in exile, the ANC and the Pan-Africanist Congress (PAC), have increased their direct involvement, much of the unrest is spontaneous and locally generated.

The parlous state of the South African economy compounds the problem. The economy has slowed; black unemployment is high; capital and skills flee the country; new investment, especially from abroad, is scarce; and a good part of the country's $24-billion debt comes due shortly. The rand fell to an all-time low in August and September, 1985. The government's repressive policies fuel the economic malaise. Political instability and economic nonperformance feed on one another.

GOVERNMENT RESPONSES

Government policy has been indecisive and insensitive. A combination of vague promises, marginal reforms and rigid enforcement of existing security laws has failed to stem the protest. President P. W. Botha told a National party (NP) congress that the NP is "committed to the principle of a united South Africa, one citizenship and a universal franchise, *but within structures chosen by South Africans.*"[6] In the idiom of the NP, that qualifying phrase means that racial separation will remain the root of whatever constitutional structures are devised under NP rule.

President Botha may say publicly that apartheid is "outdated" and inappropriate for South Africa, but government policy continues to be based on racial group identity. "Group" separation continues. New homelands are moved along to "independence." Each "group" is reputed to have control over its "own affairs" and to share in decisions on common affairs. Although Botha insists that no one group will dominate the others, in effect and by intention the white "group" remains paramount.

Possible changes in policy satisfy no one but the President and his wing of the NP. The reactionary Conservative party (which broke away from the NP in 1982) and its electoral ally farther to the right, the Herstigte Nasionale party, continue to pose a threat to the NP by registering by-election and local and provincial election victories, and by demanding more stringent enforcement of racial apartheid and an end to concessions to blacks. Within the NP, its right wing resists compromise. NP moderates and, to their left, the official opposition in Parliament, the Progressive Federal party (PFP), sense that the government is not prepared to take significant steps to share power with popular, moderate blacks. To white liberals, the government's offer is too little too late, cosmetic change to defuse the tension. Blacks are virtually unanimous in their conviction that the government is not prepared to bring them into the central government in any meaningful fashion.

Although symbolically remarkable, the repeal of both the Prohibition of Mixed Marriages Act (1949) and those provisions of the Immorality Act (1958) that apply to sexual relations across the color line says nothing to the issue of power. Likewise, the repeal of the law barring racially mixed political parties applies only to parties contesting elections within the system. It does not change the segregated and racist basis of Parliament, which totally excludes the black 73 percent of the population (68 percent if one excludes blacks in the "independent" homelands). The large-scale constitutional revision of 1983 does not speak to black political grievances and legal powerlessness.

In addition, the government has spoken vaguely of more important social and political changes (see most recently the speech by P. W. Botha at the opening of Parliament in January, 1986), but even if all of Botha's intimations were legislated they would still be unlikely to satisfy black militants or even black moderates, the latter fast becoming irrelevant to the struggle. For example, the government proposes improved property rights for urban blacks leading to freehold ownership (as against leasehold rights), but these rights would still apply only to segregated residential areas. The President promises black participation in government, but invariably he is referring to local or provincial positions or, if he refers to central government, roles outside Parliament.

When the government claims it will negotiate with black leaders, it refers to "elected" black leaders, homeland leaders, or those who renounce violence. Even Nobel

Peace Prize winner Bishop Desmond Tutu and the Reverend Allan Boesak, a UDF patron and president of the World Alliance of Reformed Churches, both of whom eschew violence, are too radical for Pretoria. The dilemma is that blacks reject any individuals the government will meet with and the government refuses to talk with credible black leaders.

A recent survey among urban blacks asked an open question: "Which leader or organization would you most like to represent you in solving problems or grievances?" Over 60 percent identified with leaders or movements that call for black rule and universal suffrage in a unitary state.[7] The ANC or its jailed leader, Nelson Mandela, garnered 31 percent support in the survey; 16 percent favored Bishop Tutu; and 14 percent, the UDF. Only 8 percent opted for KwaZulu Chief Minister Mangosuthu Buthelezi or his Inkatha party, and 8 percent mentioned government or pro-government organizations.

Fully 80 percent of the respondents agreed with the proposition that

> compromise is no longer possible. . . . The next step must be a unitary arrangement in which all blacks and whites together vote for their leaders, to participate without regard to race or group in one central government.

Only 20 percent favored a transitional federal structure, an option still too "revolutionary" for the government to entertain. Any apparent middle ground for compromise is narrow or nonexistent.

Government leaders have also promised that influx control (the pass-law system) would be phased out, that a common identity document for South Africans of all races would be issued to replace the hated "passes" that blacks are currently required to carry at all times, that further constitutional amendments would accommodate urban blacks, that blacks residing in homelands not yet independent would retain their South African citizenship, and that a form of dual citizenship would be arranged for homeland citizens in so-called "independent national states" (Transkei, Bophuthatswana, Ciskei and Venda). But these are promises grudgingly conceded. They do not mean a significant redistribution of power or wealth or opportunity. In the view of popular black leaders, there has been little real political change.

Blacks have grown accustomed to hearing government commissions, staffed by reformers in the NP, calling for elaborate change. Yet the government is fearful of its own less-reformist white constituency. The bogey of white backlash is trotted out before every election and party congress. So the NP elite waters down or ignores the recommendations of reformers, bending minimally to retain power. In September, 1985, in the latest such exercise, the President's council called for the abolition of influx control and the pass laws, an orderly urbanization policy not based on racial discrimination and developed in concert with blacks and uniform identity documents for all South Africans. Presumably the only restriction on urbanization would be housing availability.

The business magazine *Financial Mail* called this a "blueprint for a funeral." The "jugular" of apartheid has been "nicked," it went on, "in what could easily become the most important social change in SA's recent history."[8] One doubts that the government is prepared to legitimize its own demise. It is clear, however, that President Botha has been led to appreciate the need for dramatic political steps to end the unrest. Even if all his recommendations were implemented, the lack of political rights, the Group Areas Act (residential segregation), race classification, unequal education and employment opportunities and racist attitudes remain. To the ANC, nothing short of a complete transfer of power to "the people" in a "united, democratic and nonracial country" will suffice.

Some outspoken black critics call for a national forum to rewrite the ground rules for South African society. The black clergy, the UDF, liberal whites, and some homeland leaders (Buthelezi and KaNgwane's Chief Minister, Enos Mabuza) join the chorus. They do not agree on who should participate and the nature of their charge. More moderate are the PFP, Inkatha and perhaps the Solidarity party in the Indian House of Delegates. These are parties that function, albeit in protest, within the present legal structures of homelands and the Parliament. Missing, of course, are the real combatants, the government and the UDF. The ANC, the Azanian People's Organization (AZAPO), and the National Forum, the black consciousness-socialist body, reject the convention idea out of hand.

The government says that it is prepared to negotiate (the operative word should be consult) only with blacks who renounce violence and revolution. But the government's own policies virtually guarantee that no popular black voice would so qualify and that no popular black would risk sitting down with the government. The UDF, the South African Council of Churches, black clergy like Bishop Tutu and Anglican Bishop Suffragen of Johannesburg, Reverend Simeon Nkoane, moderate black trade unionists, even the Black Sash and the South African Institute of Race Relations, have renounced violence but have not abandoned their call for a revolution in power relationships. So the government is left with pliable homeland leaders, suspect "elected" town councillors, and a few others who have been, ipso facto, rejected by the people. The government refuses to admit that the vast majority of blacks see Botha's reforms as a re-formation of apartheid, not its abolition.

The government is also troubled by the ANC's Nelson Mandela, who poses an enormous threat, although he has been in prison for 23 years. If he should die in prison, the political consequences might be grave. He underwent prostate surgery late in 1985. The government sought to negotiate his release at that time, but it has insisted that he renounce violence and go into exile. Mandela has proudly refused those terms. Botha has even offered a prisoner trade with the Soviet Union and Angola. Meanwhile, Mandela's stature grows; he holds firm and the government's standing declines.

Dreading lost votes and a greater division in the white electorate because of concessions, the government has characteristically responded to unrest with force. One Cabinet minister offered this representative opinion:

> In the short term, the priority must be to get the security situation under control. Kid-glove handling will do SA more international harm than the shock effect of the tough, hard but efficient approach.[9]

The use of force has been so insensitive and heavy-handed that commentators have begun to wonder if the police and the South African Defense Forces (SADF), or individuals within the forces, may be pushing the government along by a ferocity that the government feels it must vindicate and rationalize.[10] Top UDF leaders, clergy and trade unionists have been detained. There have been deaths in detention and charges of widespread torture. Some detainees have been charged with treason, because the government tries to prove that there are links between UDF and the ANC. More recently, there has been a pattern of intimidation of political opponents by death squads allegedly answerable either to the authorities or to the political right wing. These death squads appear to be immune from apprehension and prosecution. Reverend Nkoane has twice been attacked. Victoria Mxenge, a lawyer who was defending UDF members being tried for treason, was assassinated in August; her husband had been assassinated earlier. Eastern Cape leaders Matthew Goniwe and Fort Calata were found murdered. Winnie Mandela's house in Brandfort was torched. The list goes on.

In July, the government declared a state of emergency. Mass funerals were banned in specific magisterial districts, but that order has been impossible to enforce. All UDF meetings are banned. In some areas, schoolchildren who boycott classes are arrested, yet in other areas schools are regarded as hotbeds of trouble and have been closed by the authorities. Police violence is widespread, as trigger-happy, mean-spirited or just frightened police attack peaceful (but provocative) protesters. Much of this violence is now hidden from scrutiny by censorship aimed mostly at foreign television crews.[11] Still, intimidation is the language of apartheid, and this regime is fluent in its use, at home and abroad.

REGIONAL POLICY

With the signing of the Nkomati Pact of Nonaggression with Mozambique early in 1984, it appeared that South Africa's relations with neighboring governments were about to enter a normal, more quiescent phase.[12] Having bullied neighboring governments, South Africa apparently intended to stabilize the region through force of arms and planned to institute a new, economically expansive order to complement its diplomatic and its earlier military offensives. But Nkomati unraveled.[13]

As the domestic situation deteriorated, Pretoria and particularly the hawks in the SADF and the State Security Council, the country's powerful inner cabinet, tried to eliminate any threat on South Africa's borders and to sever links between revolutionaries within South Africa and their support groups in neighboring states. Even if Pretoria failed to achieve these goals in the region, preemptive or retaliatory incursions would notify nearby capitals that they were vulnerable to South African military force. Hence, they had better abandon their assistance to revolutionaries, send the ANC packing or, even better, cooperate with Pretoria in its defense of the status quo.[14]

A list of just a few of the more important crossborder incursions illustrates the point. Repeated raids into Angola continue, ostensibly to attack South-West Africa People's Organization (SWAPO) concentrations and bases. These military operations also include air and land support for Jonas Savimbi's UNITA (União Nacional para a Independência Total de Angola), the regionally based opposition to the Angolan government. In September, the SADF admitted for the first time since 1975 that it was providing "material, humanitarian and moral" to UNITA.[15] When the Luanda government launched a massive attack in August against UNITA's stronghold in the southeast, direct SADF intervention was crucial to turning back the offensive.[16]

Earlier, on May 22, SADF special units were apprehended in Angola near Cabinda in the act of preparing to sabotage oil storage tanks at the Gulf Oil facility, fully 880 miles from the Namibian border. The operation was clearly not aimed at SWAPO or at collecting intelligence on the ANC, despite the official cover story.

Across the continent, South African aid to the Resistência Nacional Moçambicana (MNR), in open defiance of the Nkomati agreement, has become undeniable. In August, Mozambicans in cooperation with Zimbabwean military forces captured the MNR headquarters at Gorongoza in central Mozambique. Among the documents collected were a desk diary and several notebooks with minutes of meetings between top MNR officials and South African envoys, particularly military men. These documents revealed a deep division between SADF intelligence operatives and officials in South Africa's department of foreign affairs.[17] After the disclosures, Chief of the Armed Forces General Constand Viljoen asserted on television that the military had willfully and without authority from the government violated the nonaggression agreement. On more than one occasion, the foreign minister had not been informed about SADF moves in Mozambique.[18] General Viljoen was also critical of the department of foreign affairs.

Violent raids into Botswana (June, 1985) and Lesotho (December, 1985), December reports of incursions into Swaziland, further threats of action against Zimbabwe, and the economic blockade and pressures that contributed to the military coup in Lesotho in January, 1986, reveal a South Africa groping for a new regional order in which Pretoria can virtually dictate policy to neighboring states.[19] This is the reemergence of a policy of destabilization and preemptive and retaliatory violence.[20] Economic pressures are a regular part of these tactics. Although this aggressive policy has no long-range hope of success, in the short run weak and insecure governments in the region may be forced to conform to Pretoria's dictates, at least insofar as their links with the ANC are concerned.

One might ask why South Africa seems to waver (as it has over the last half dozen years) in its approach to various black states? Is South Africa unsure of its goals? Are there rifts among the policymaking elites that in fact lead to two or more foreign policies? If so, what is the nature of those divisions? Where do the hawks and the normalizers (there are no doves) find support? Or is South Africa consciously playing a "good guy/bad guy" routine in order to keep its neighbors off balance?

FIRST STEPS TOWARD RESOLUTION

Within South Africa, most leaders have few illusions about the extent and the probable impact of external relations on their own domestic future. They understand that interference from abroad can lighten or add to their burdens, but in the final analysis any changes will result from Pretoria's policies and from the initiatives and responses of the black populace and its leaders.

Some signs of movement are apparent. Most important for the white regime, some townships have become ungovernable. Throughout the country, "elected" town councillors have fled, have been assassinated or have resigned. In some areas, a general disorder prevails. In others, informal forms of local self-government have appeared. Thus a dyarchy of sorts is being established; there are some parts of South Africa where government officials dare not go unless they are accompanied by overwhelming force. This does not amount to effective government for Pretoria or for its opponents. Just how the existence of separate though unequal claimants to rule will be resolved is still unclear.

In addition, various white leadership groups have tried to open a dialogue with the ANC. On September 13, 1985, a group of seven business leaders traveled to Zambia for talks with Oliver Tambo and a team of ANC leaders.[21] The PFP and liberal clergymen have also visited. In October, the government withdrew the passports of Afrikaner students from the University of Stellenbosch after they had sought to meet their "banned" ANC counterparts. Admittedly, these are just the first steps in what must, of necessity, be a long process of exchange. Talks are not negotiations. But they do open communications with what is officially regarded as the enemy, possibly to divide the belligerents and thereby to facilitate eventual compromise.[22] The prospects of that happening look slim.

Within the NP, there is serious talk (as there has been for some time among the opposition) that President Botha is ill-suited to lead South Africa out of the current crisis. He is, the rumors suggest, too inflexible, too cautious, too unimaginative, and too clearly identified with interests not inclined to accept significant power shifts. The names of possible replacements are hardly more assuring—Gerrit Viljoen, minister of cooperation, development and education; Chris Heunis, minister of constitutional development and planning; R. F. "Pik" Botha, minister of foreign affairs; and F. W. de Klerk, Transvaal leader of the NP and minister of home affairs and of national education. Of course, the armed forces pose another alternative, although there is little evidence that the military desires to assume outright responsibility for the state.

These names emerge as if change at the helm, in itself, will open new avenues for resolution. This is not likely, although without new leadership little will be altered. Other critics have suggested the creation of a government truly open to the participation of a variety of parties and interests, much like Great Britain's coalition War Cabinet. The current civil upheaval requires a national, total, cooperative effort. Unfortunately, those with real power do not seem inclined to support a collaborative effort that would, after all, require all parties to compromise a great deal.

Botha surely realizes that unmitigated repression is not working; but he also senses that thoroughgoing reform would lead the right to bring down his government. That is Pretoria's dilemma.

---

[1]A political cartoon in the *Cape Times* pictured sword-wielding Roman soldiers standing under a Christmas star and announcing to the three kings searching for Jesus: "This is an illegal gathering under the riotous assembly provision of the Internal Security Act. I'm giving you three minutes to disperse." Quoted in the *Cleveland Plain Dealer*, December 25, 1985, p.1.

[2]Howard Barrell, " 'All for the Front': The ANC Conference," *Work in Progress* (Johannesburg), no. 38 (August, 1985), pp. 9–13; and "Let Us Act Together," *Sechaba* (London), August, 1985, pp. 11–15.

[3]Quoted in the *Cleveland Plain Dealer*, January 14, 1986, p. 4.

[4]Richard de Villiers, "UDF under Attack: Inkatha and the State," *Work in Progress*, no. 39 (October, 1985), pp. 33–34.

[5]*The Star* (Johannesburg), Weekly Air Edition (WAE), January 27, 1986, p. 1.

[6]*Financial Mail* (Johannesburg), vol. 98, no. 1 (October 4, 1985), p. 60.

[7]Ibid., vol. 97, no. 12 (September 20, 1985), p. 64.

[8]Ibid., pp. 42–43.

[9]Ibid., vol. 97, no. 9 (August 30, 1985), p. 66.

[10]See Glenn Frankel, "Army's Repressive Role Alarms Black, White South Africans," *Washington Post*, October 23, 1985; and "Police Must Be Disciplined" and "Bring the Army Back in Line," *The Star*, October 1 and 2, 1985.

[11]*The Star*, WAE, November 18, 1985, p. 11; and *The New York Times*, December 29, 1985.

[12]See Kenneth W. Grundy, "Pax Pretoriana: South Africa's Regional Policy," *Current History*, vol. 84, no. 501 (April, 1985), pp. 150–154.

[13]Richard Weisfelder, " 'Peace' from the Barrel of a Gun: Nonaggression Pacts and State Terror in Southern Africa," in

5. THE THIRD WORLD: Africa

Michael Stohl and George Lopez, eds., *Foreign Policy and State Terror* (Westport, Conn.: Greenwood Press, 1986).

[14]For a critique of the policy see "Hawks Ascendant," *Financial Mail,* vol. 97, no. 13 (September 27, 1985), pp. 36–41. It is defended by right-wing Member of Parliament Louis Stofberg in *The Star,* WAE, January 27, 1986, p. 14.

[15]"Angola: What South Africa Faces," *South Africa Digest,* October 4, 1985, p. 906; and "Minister Discloses Links with UNITA," *Paratus* (Pretoria), vol. 36, no. 10 (October, 1985), pp. 22–23.

[16]*Africa Research Bulletin* (political series), vol. 22, no. 10 (November, 1985), pp. 7825C–7827B.

[17]The notebooks are quoted at length in "Counting on Colonel Charlie," *Africa News,* vol, 25, no. 9 (November 4, 1985), pp. 8–12. For background and analysis see John S. Saul, "Mozambican Socialism and South African Aggression: A Case Study in Destabilization" (Paper read at the annual meeting of the African Studies Association, New Orleans, November 25, 1985).

[18]*Africa Research Bulletin,* vol. 22, no. 10 (November, 1985), pp. 7815B–7816A.

[19]On the Lesotho coup see *The Star,* WAE, January 27, 1986, pp. 1, 3 and 7.

[20]See Kenneth W. Grundy, *The Militarization of South African Politics* (Bloomington: Indiana University Press, 1986), chap. 6.

[21]See "A Moment in History," *Leadership* (Johannesburg), vol. 4, no. 3 (1985), pp. 25–30.

[22]Howard Barrell, "The Tactics of Talks: ANC and Business," *Work in Progress,* no. 39 (October, 1985), pp. 4–8.

The Process of Assimilation of Hong Kong (1997) and Implications for Taiwan

John P. Burns

JOHN P. BURNS is senior lecturer, Department of Political Science, University of Hong Kong. Mr. Burns has written articles on rural politics in China and on administrative reform in both China and Hong Kong. The author gratefully acknowledges the advice of Leo Goodstadt, David M. Lampton, Terry Lui, Miron Mushkat, and Ian Scott, who made useful suggestions for the revision of this paper.

HONG KONG'S transition to Chinese rule began in September 1984 when the United Kingdom and the People's Republic initialed a draft Joint Declaration on the future of the colony. According to the agreement, on July 1, 1997, when the British-held lease on 92 percent of the territory's land area expires, Hong Kong will become a "special administrative region" (SAR) of China, enjoying a "high degree of autonomy."[1]

Under the formula "one country, two systems," China has pledged that "the socialist system and socialist policies shall not be practiced in Hong Kong" and that the territory's "previous capitalist system and life style will remain unchanged" for fifty years beyond 1997. The future SAR government will be composed of local inhabitants, to implement the popular slogan "Hong Kong people ruling Hong Kong." Its chief executive, China declares, will be "selected by election or through consultations held locally" and will be appointed by Beijing. The executive will be "accountable" to the legislature, which will "be constituted by elections."

In addition, Beijing has stipulated that the Hong Kong people will continue to enjoy all the rights and freedoms that they now have; that an independent judiciary will operate under the present legal system, relying on the common law; that Hong Kong will continue as a free port and a separate customs area; that the Hong Kong dollar will be freely convertible; that the Hong Kong government will be able to issue its own travel documents and to control immigration; that Hong Kong will be responsible for law and order, civil aviation, shipping, trade with foreign countries, and education policy; and that Chinese troops stationed in Hong Kong will not interfere in local affairs. The central government will be responsible for foreign affairs and defense. Finally, the agreement stipulates that Chinese authorities will include these principles in a "basic law" or mini-constitution for Hong Kong, which defines the territory's future political system and which codifies the SAR's relationship to Beijing.

Chinese policy toward Hong Kong is carried out by a variety of actors, with different interests and, we can speculate, different preconceptions about the territory. To accomplish its goal, official Chinese policy, defined by Deng Xiaoping and his allies, seeks to capture Hong Kong's strong, largely unreformed executive and to place in power co-opted local capitalists who, under Chinese Communist party direction, will maintain the territory's stability and contribution to China's economic development program. More conservative or leftist elements in Beijing's leadership may, however, be able to establish competing agendas for Hong Kong's post-1997 government.

Strategically important groups in Hong Kong have reacted to this process in a variety of ways. Some businessmen have allied themselves with Chinese authorities to take power in the transition. Others have protested, either by reducing their commitments locally (the businessmen) or by voicing their concerns over future developments (the professionals). Still others have withdrawn altogether: they have sent large amounts of capital abroad or have themselves emigrated.

Hong Kong's transition to Chinese rule has certain implications for Taiwan. First, Taiwan must accept Chinese rule in Hong Kong and cooperate with the new SAR government if it wishes to preserve important regional economic links and if the Kuomintang

(KMT) wishes to continue its activities in Hong Kong. Second, insofar as the "one country, two systems" concept is perceived to be successful in Hong Kong and insofar as the Taiwanese economy becomes increasingly dependent on trade with China, some elements in Taiwan may be tempted to advocate negotiating a similar agreement with China. Third, the relationships of Hong Kong and Taiwan to China, however, differ geographically, economically, and politically. Fourth, so long as the People's Republic seeks to reunify Taiwan with China by peaceful means, Chinese authorities must treat Hong Kong carefully.

The Chinese Actors

On the Chinese side, various actors are implementing Hong Kong policy. They have different interests in Hong Kong, which range from short-term attempts to extract as much capital from the territory as possible, to long-term political and strategic concerns.

The most authoritative local source of China's Hong Kong policy is the Hong Kong branch of the New China News Agency (NCNA), headed by Xu Jiatun, a recently retired party Central Committee member. The NCNA acts as the local operational arm of both the party and the state in Hong Kong. Xu heads the Hong Kong and Macau Work Committee, which oversees the activities of the estimated 2,000 party members working in Hong Kong and which reports to the party's Hong Kong and Macau Office of the Central Committee in Beijing.[2] Xu also presides over the local arm of the Chinese state in Hong Kong (organized into foreign affairs, social services, culture and education, economics, research, and so forth), which reports to the Hong Kong and Macau Offices of both the Foreign Ministry and the State Council.[3] Local political actors also include the Hong Kong arms of both the Guangdong Provincial Public Security Bureau and the national Ministries of Public and State Security, charged with intelligence gathering activities in the territory.

Local economic actors include the traders, such as China Resources, and more recently Wang Guangying's Everbright, and a host of other Hong Kong–registered but mainland-controlled companies doing business here. The Hong Kong branch of the Bank of China sets policy for its network of thirteen PRC-controlled banks in the territory. According to one estimate, these organizations employ over 20,000 "mainlanders in white collar jobs" (cadres) in the territory.[4]

At the central level, an array of institutions either make Hong Kong policy or have interests in Hong Kong. Central political institutions include the three Hong Kong and Macau offices mentioned above (party, State Council, and Foreign Ministry), the party Secretariat, the party Politburo, and the Ministries of Public and State Security. Insofar as Hong Kong media influence the mainland, the party Central Committee's Propaganda and United Front Work Departments also have an interest in Hong Kong. Finally, the Central Committee's Organization Department controls the recruitment and deployment of party members in Hong Kong.

The central economic institutions concerned with Hong Kong policy include units of the State Council, such as the State Planning and Economic Commissions, the Ministry of Finance, the Bank of China, the Ministry of Foreign Economic Relations and Trade (MOFERT), the Customs Administration, foreign trade corporations, and other organizations such as the Chinese International Trust and Investment Corporation (CITIC). Finally, intermediate-level units within China, such as provincial trade corporations and provincial governments, have established their own operations to do business in Hong Kong.

The different roles played by these units, and their different interests in Hong Kong, have spawned a wide range of perceptions of the territory and its relationship to China.

China's Perceptions of Hong Kong

China's perceptions of Hong Kong exist on a continuum ranging from the most general, remote, and political of understandings (held in Beijing and at senior levels in Hong Kong) to the most particular, intimate, and usually economic of understandings (held by those directly charged with making money in Hong Kong).

The most general view assumes the superiority of socialism and Socialist institutions (and thus the inferiority of capitalism and bourgeois institutions) and believes in the necessity and ultimate "correctness" of Communist party rule.[5] To implement the party's policies in Hong Kong, like everywhere else, China should rely on uniting with its friends (the united front) and on implementing the "mass line." In addition, the general, more remote view sees that Britain and its allies in Hong Kong control the economic and political arenas in nearly conspiratorial fashion (Britain can, for example, "play the public opinion card" at will); that most Hong Kong people are patriotic and eager to embrace the rule of the motherland; that the Hong Kong economy is fragile and depends on help from the mainland; and that Hong Kong is built on undesirable speculative and corrupt practices. These views in their more extreme form may be held by Beijing officials with less direct responsibility for Hong Kong policy and by those identified in Hong Kong sources as "the conservatives" or "leftists."[6]

To a greater or lesser extent, the stereotype is tempered by the knowledge that China has real economic interests in Hong Kong: from 35 to 40 percent of China's annual foreign exchange earnings come from the colony, China uses Hong Kong's port facilities as a transshipment center, and Hong Kong provides an important focus for the transfer of technology (including management technology) to China. Nonetheless, a mixture of these views can be found not only among officials in Beijing, but also among their colleagues who head China's establishment in Hong Kong.[7]

At the other end of the continuum are those individuals in China's institutions in Hong Kong who are personally responsible for economic decisions in the territory and who are able to use economic criteria to make those decisions, those who were born and educated in Hong Kong, and those who speak Cantonese.[8] Although this group also holds a critical view of Hong Kong, it is based more closely on the economic realities of life in the territory and less on party dogma. They recognize that interests in Hong Kong are complex, that British authority is declining, that the local population has mixed feelings about the future, and that Hong Kong's economic well-being rests on many factors, including entrepreneurship, relaxed government controls, and the play of market forces.

China's Strategy

By appealing to Chinese nationalism and by defining Hong Kong as a foreign policy issue, authorities in Beijing have insulated Hong Kong from the conflict that has dogged post-Mao domestic politics. As Hong Kong becomes further integrated with China, however, conflicts within China's leadership may have consequences for policy in the territory.

China's policy for assimilating Hong Kong involves action in the following areas. First, during the transition period, China seeks to expand its political influence gradually in Hong Kong. United front elements within Hong Kong have stepped up their recruitment activities and have begun to play a more active role in local politics.[9] In October 1985, for example, the left-wing Federation of Trade Unions launched a drive to expand its membership substantially.[10] It has recently reorganized its structure and opened new branches.[11] In addition, during the past several years, NCNA has launched a campaign to woo the local media.[12] After the signing of the Joint Declaration, several of Hong Kong's more than twenty daily newspapers (including *Ming Bao, Dongfang Ribao, Xingdao Ribao,* and *South China Morning Post*), perhaps

wishing not to offend Hong Kong's new masters, became noticeably less critical of China.[13] For several years, official China has wooed Hong Kong's intellectuals and academics through, for example, exchange programs for teachers.[14] Mainland authorities plan to recruit increasing numbers of Hong Kong youth to study in China.[15] Finally, and probably least significantly for the moment, the party plans once again to recruit members from among Hong Kong's population.[16]

Second, China seeks to preserve and to increase Hong Kong's economic contribution to the mainland. To accomplish this, Chinese authorities have encouraged Hong Kong businessmen to invest substantial sums in newly established special economic zones, such as Shenzhen, which lies on Hong Kong's northern border. Authorities in China have also expanded their investments in Hong Kong,[17] while local PRC-controlled banks, led by the Hong Kong branch of the Bank of China, have become increasingly active. In 1985, for example, the Bank of China increased the number of loans it made to Hong Kong businesses at a rate far higher than did local banks.[18]

Third, China has allied itself to a group of large businessmen in Hong Kong, who it believes will most likely preserve the political and economic status quo.[19] These business leaders include among many others Sir Y. K. Pao (chairman of World-Wide Shipping), T. K. Ann (chairman of Winsor Industrial Corporation), and David K. P. Li (chief manager of the Bank of East Asia). The alliance is institutionalized in its leadership of the Basic Law Drafting Committee in Hong Kong.[20] In the political arena, both parties seek to maintain the power of a strong executive (whom Beijing will appoint after 1997). Currently, the British colonial governor's authority is in theory nearly absolute,[21] a position that China and these business leaders wish to maintain in the new chief executive.[22]

In addition, the alliance seeks to place the business community in positions of formal power, as Hong Kong's post-1997 chief executive, and in local advisory councils of state.[23] As Hong Kong's Lord Kadoorie pointed out: "The people who govern Hong Kong should be chosen from those members of the community who created the prosperity [the capitalists]. . . . All Hong Kong is one big business, and it must have a good management and a well-chosen board of directors," in short, a "benevolent oligarchy."[24] By implication, a popularly elected, powerful legislature (perhaps with political parties), which pressure groups in Hong Kong could use to establish a welfare state or to redistribute the wealth, are inappropriate for Hong Kong.[25] The Communist party will exercise real power in this situation.[26]

In the years leading up to 1997, Chinese authorities are eager to establish Hong Kong's political framework in the "basic law" as soon as possible (and in any case before the British or people in Hong Kong can tamper with the existing institutions). For these reasons Beijing has publicly warned authorities in Hong Kong not to make "big changes" to the territory's political institutions.[27] China has announced that it will release a draft of the basic law in 1988,[28] several years earlier than expected, but just after the British government plans a major review of government machinery in Hong Kong.[29] In any case, British authorities are publicly committed to seek the "convergence" of any changes in Hong Kong's political institutions with those proposed by China in the basic law.[30]

The basis of the alliance between the businessmen and the Communist party is short-term shared interest. With party backing, the businessmen can fend off claims from groups in Hong Kong for increased social welfare, and they can be sure of a disciplined and docile labor force. The alliance is short term, however, because in the process the business community will forgo an opportunity to create institutions for resisting party encroachment if and when the relationship goes bad. Even under the "noninterventionist" British regime, conflicts of interest between the business community and political authority sometimes emerged. For example, businesses sometimes protested against rising public utilities tariffs, tax increases, and increases in the cost and size of the civil service and public expenditure generally. On these issues, and on such future potential issues as immigration control, education policy, and control of the exchange of information, *if* the Communist party establishes policies that conflict with the interests of the business community, business leaders will have no recourse but to accept them.

In the long term, Hong Kong can look forward to the growing influence of the Chinese Communist party leading ultimately to direct party rule. The authority of the British-controlled Hong Kong government will continue to decline throughout the transition period. Although both colonial officials and the NCNA insist that the current government is not a "lame duck," leftists in Hong Kong have defined the government's legitimate role as that of a "caretaker," which amounts to much the same thing. All significant policies will increasingly have to be negotiated with Beijing before they can be determined or implemented.

As Hong Kong becomes more integrated with the mainland, it will become more of a domestic issue in China's politics.[31] "Leftists" or "conservatives" in

China, who are critical of "spiritual pollution," "bourgeois liberalism," and other unorthodox ideas, see Hong Kong as a source of these imports. Critics of China's open policy may also decide that reform is needed in Hong Kong. Indeed, many thoughtful mainlanders may wonder why Hong Kong should be allowed to enjoy special, even coddled, treatment (including capitalism, a free press, and the right to travel), while they must go without. Although it is difficult to determine the extent to which these tendencies in China will influence Hong Kong affairs in the future, they should be acknowledged.

Some observers predict that when China takes over Hong Kong, the party, while permitting relative freedom in the economic arena, will restrict political activities and civil liberties in the territory.[32] Although the Joint Declaration promises civil liberties in Hong Kong beyond 1997, critics point out that in China these rights are given by the state (and are not inherently possessed by the people), that Chinese citizens are not now free to criticize the government, that the party exercises rigid control over the press on the mainland, and that other rights can be exercised in practice only under party leadership.[33] If Chinese authorities decide to restrict freedoms in these areas in Hong Kong, the business allies of the party, completely dependent on party support, could do little but accept the result.

The Reactions of Strategic Elites

In general, influential people in Hong Kong have reacted to China's strategy either by accommodating to the changes, by protesting against the changes, or by withdrawing.

Some businessmen have protested against these arrangements by reducing their level of investment in Hong Kong and by holding foreign currency deposits in unprecedented amounts. Some businesses are for the first time selling stock in privately owned undertakings, such as Swire's wholly owned Cathay Pacific Airlines and Stanley Ho's Macau gambling monopoly. Other local businesses are investing overseas at higher rates. These are not strategies that indicate high levels of confidence in the future.[34]

Some Hong Kong professionals, many of whom could lose their privileged position in Hong Kong (maintained by restrictive practices) in the transition to 1997, have voiced public protest. Their protests have centered on the process of drafting the basic law and its likely contents and Britain's plans to reform Hong Kong's political institutions. They have argued that political reform in Hong Kong should proceed independently of China's plans,[35] that by criticizing political reform in Hong Kong China has been meddling in Hong Kong politics,[36] that British authorities should implement direct elections of Hong Kong's legislature,[37] and that Hong Kong's post-1997 executive should be "accountable" (that is, subordinate) to the legislature,[38] as stipulated in the Joint Declaration. Further, some protested against the way in which Chinese authorities and their business allies set up the Basic Law Consultative Committee in Hong Kong, a body designed to advise on the contents of the basic law. Although the constitution of the committee required that its leaders be "elected," in its meeting to select a standing committee, authorities interpreted this to permit "democratic consultation," or party selection.[39] After several days of protests following the initial meeting, the committee relented and "elected" its leaders. These disagreements point to difficulties ahead: China, Britain, and Hong Kong may not share the same meaning for many of the terms used in the Joint Declaration.

Because these protest strategies have been relatively ineffective, a significant number of strategic leaders who have doubts about the future have undoubtedly sent capital abroad, have emigrated, or have made plans to emigrate. Although no data on the movement of capital or people are available, it is widely believed in Hong Kong that most big-business men and many professionals have made contingency plans to leave Hong Kong in the event of economic or political disorder.[40] Some countries, such as Canada, have recognized this and have established "economic immigration programs." According to the Canadian government, in 1984 the largest group of business immigrants came from Hong Kong, in numbers that have increased substantially during the past few years, due in Canada's view to the "1997 jitters."[41] Hong Kong citizens have invested substantial sums in Australia and the United States as well.

If strategically important elites leave Hong Kong in large numbers, they will deprive the future SAR of the talent and entrepreneurial skills necessary to maintain the territory's economic position vis-à-vis China. This in turn will undermine virtually the only justification for China to maintain the status quo intact.

Implications for Taiwan

Chinese authorities have attempted to persuade the KMT on Taiwan to negotiate reunification of the country under the formula "one country, two systems." As recently as February 18, 1986, Beijing called on Taiwan to discuss a "1997-style" reunification.[42] In addition to the terms granted to Hong Kong in the Sino-British Joint Declaration, Beijing has promised

Taiwan control over its own armed forces and intelligence services and maintenance of international contacts. The KMT has adamantly refused these terms.[43] Rather, Taiwan has made plans to attract investment funds from Hong Kong[44] and has announced its intention to ease immigration restrictions on Hong Kong residents.[45] The nervousness of Taiwan authorities is obvious in their dealing with the issue of whether to permit trade with the mainland. While they have banned direct trade with China, they have permitted indirect trade through Hong Kong,[46] which in 1984 reached U.S. $550 million.[47] Insofar as Taiwan becomes increasingly dependent on China trade, forces within the territory may be more accommodating to a political settlement with China.

In addition to serving as a middleman in China-Taiwan trade, Hong Kong also provides other services, such as a regional center for Taiwan's China Air Lines and a base for pro-KMT activities, which are currently protected under British law in Hong Kong. To preserve its position in Hong Kong, Taiwan authorities have recently decided not to withdraw during the transition to 1997 but to engage the Communist party actively in the colony with a view to protecting the interests of Hong Kong residents and to carry out propaganda for the KMT.[48]

In several fundamental respects, however, the positions of Hong Kong and Taiwan differ. Hong Kong, geographically contiguous to the mainland, is much more economically dependent on China than is Taiwan, at least for the moment. This could change, however, in the face of world economic problems and protectionism in export markets. Hong Kong is ruled by an alien government that lacks legitimacy, while Taiwan is ruled by a Chinese government that has legitimacy. And finally Hong Kong's state is autonomous from society, while Taiwan's state is linked to society by a strong, well-organized political party. All of these factors permit Taiwan to resist China's calls for reunification.

So long as Taiwan resists China's policy of reunification, Beijing must treat Hong Kong carefully. If the policy of "one country, two systems" is perceived to fail, China may have to wait considerably longer to gain sovereignty over Taiwan, or resort to force. China's desire to regain sovereignty over Taiwan must weigh at least as heavily on the minds of Beijing's leaders as its consideration of Hong Kong's economic value to the mainland in inhibiting rash action in the colony. If Taiwan's leaders reach an accommodation with Beijing, which now seems very unlikely in the short or medium term, then Hong Kong's position will be protected only by Beijing's perception of the territory's economic value to the mainland's development goals.

Conclusion

Hong Kong's transition to Chinese rule means growing Communist party rule in Hong Kong. At least initially, this will probably be indirect, exercised through the offices of co-opted business leaders. In the long term, however, one can expect formal party influence to grow and the party's presence to be felt in the political, economic, and social arenas. Hong Kong will then be dependent on party policies determined in Beijing. The extent to which Hong Kong will be able to influence those policies through its own party members remains to be seen.

To say that the Chinese Communist party will rule Hong Kong in the future is to state the obvious. The real questions are, What will be the nature of the party in the year 2000, and what will be its policies? Insofar as the party remains divided over development strategy—and this seems likely given the complexity of the process—in spite of some policy successes, capitalist Hong Kong will continue to be a target of conservative criticism. Authorities in Beijing may be willing to compromise political freedom and noninterventionist policies in Hong Kong to win support for further reforms in China. Still, so long as the Hong Kong economy can service China's development needs, authorities in Beijing are likely to permit the continued existence of some form of capitalism in the territory for some time to come. This, in turn, depends on many factors, some of which are beyond Hong Kong's control, such as world economic conditions and the fate of protectionism in Hong Kong's major markets.

1. See "A Draft Agreement Between the Government of the United Kingdom of Great Britain and Northern Ireland and the Government of the People's Republic of China on the Future of Hong Kong," (Hong Kong: Government Printer, 1984).

2. See *South China Morning Post* (hereafter SCMP), October 21, 1985, and November 4, 1984.

3. See *Dagong Bao*, April 6, 1985, for a discussion of the State Council's Hong Kong and Macau Affairs Office, in Foreign Broadcast Information Service, *China–Daily Report* (Washington, D.C.: Department of Commerce) (hereafter *FBIS*), April 8, 1985.

4. *SCMP*, November 4, 1984. If they live in Hong Kong for seven years or more, even these "cadres" become eligible to be "Hong Kong people," according to the Sino-British Joint Declaration. (See Annex I, Article 14.) Critics point out that given this vague definition, the way is open for Beijing to rely on these relatively recent arrivals to rule Hong Kong.

5. These, together with a belief in Marxism, Leninism, Mao Zedong Thought, and a belief in the "dictatorship of the proletariat" constitute the "four cardinal principles," which legitimize the current leadership's rule and which are enshrined in the state constitution.

6. See *Zhengming* [Hong Kong], October 1, 1985; in *FBIS*, October 3, 1985. *Zhengming*, June 1, 1985; in *FBIS*, June 6, 1985. *Zhengming*, August 1, 1985; in *FBIS*, August 7, 1985. My discussion focuses on Chinese "elite" perceptions of Hong Kong. At the "mass" level, resentment of Hong Kong in China was indicated in 1985 by the soccer riot in Beijing, which followed Hong Kong's defeat of China's national soccer team in World Cup competition.

7. PRC officials in Hong Kong lead very sheltered lives. Their families and children remain in China, so they do not learn from family or school contacts about society in Hong Kong; they live in their own dormitories or housing complexes; and most are unable to speak Cantonese.

8. See *SCMP*, October 21, 1985, for a list of "local" NCNA employees, for example.

9. See *Zhengming*, May 1, 1985; *FBIS*, May 8, 1985.

10. *SCMP*, October 9, 1985. The activity of leftist unions must, however, be seen in the context of a long-term decline in trade union membership generally in Hong Kong, a trend that has affected the leftist unions as well.

11. *SCMP*, January 13, 1986.

12. In addition, Shenzhen Broadcasting Station now relays

Ji Reaffirms China's Policy Towards Hong Kong

Ji Pengfei, director of the Hong Kong and Macao Affairs Office of the State Council, reaffirmed China's policy towards Hong Kong in an interview with *Beijing Review* on February 21. He was commenting on the January 16, 1987 Communique of the Enlarged Meeting of the Political Bureau of the Central Committee of the CPC (see *Beijing Review* No. 4, p. 5).

Question: The people of Hong Kong have been very much concerned on learning about the change of personnel in the Party Central Committee and the struggle against bourgeois liberalization. Some fear that China will not continue to implement its policies of reform, opening to the outside world and invigorating the economy. Would you comment on the reaction?

Answer: Such fears are not called for. The 1978 Third Plenary Session of the Party's 11th Central Committee summed up historical experiences and, starting from the realities in China, put forth a line, principles and policies for building a socialist society with Chinese characteristics. The basic points are to uphold the four cardinal principles (the socialist road, the people's democratic dictatorship, leadership of the Communist Party, and Marxism-Leninism and Mao Zedong Thought) and to persist in reform, opening to the outside world and enlivening the economy; these two basic aspects are linked and neither one can be dispensed with. Thanks to the implementation of the line, China has in the past eight years made great achievements in its socialist modernization drive, achievements that have won worldwide

recognition. Since this line and these policies have proven beneficial to the nation and people, we will continue to follow them for a long time to come. The personnel change in the Party's Central Committee and the struggle against bourgeois liberalization are aimed at fully and correctly carrying out the line of the Third Plenum of the Party's 11th Central Committee and not at altering it.

Q: Some people are worried as to whether the personnel change in the Party Central Committee and the anti-bourgeois liberalization struggle will affect implementation of the policy of "one country, two systems" and the policy to keep the capitalist system in Hong Kong intact for 50 years after China resumes exercise of sovereignty over Hong Kong in 1997. What's your comment on this question?

A: The scientific concept of "one country, two systems" has been advanced by Comrade Deng Xiaoping by pooling the collective wisdom of the Party's Central Committee; it was advanced in accordance with the principle of seeking truth from facts and showing respect for history and realities. As a basic policy of the state formulated to realize the cause of reunifying the motherland, the idea of "one country, two systems" will not change because of any personnel changes. Comrade Deng Xiaoping has explicitly stated: "'One country, two systems' is a policy that has been adopted by the National People's Congress; it is a law. How will it change? If a policy is correct,

no one will be able to change it."

I've just said that the personnel change in our Party's Central Committee and the struggle against bourgeois liberalization are aimed at better implementing the line of the Third Plenary Session of the Party's 11th Central Committee and building a socialist society with Chinese characteristics on the mainland. They do not have anything to do with the policy towards Hong Kong. The policy of maintaining the capitalist system in Hong Kong for 50 years and upholding Hong Kong's prosperity and stability has already been laid down in the Sino-British Joint Declaration and ratified by the National People's Congress, so it will not change.

Q: Will the struggle against bourgeois liberalization involve Hong Kong, which is under the capitalist system?

A: No. The struggle against bourgeois liberalization does not affect Hong Kong at all. According to the principle of "one country, two systems," the mainland is carrying out socialism, and Hong Kong, capitalism. The mainland must persist in the four cardinal principles, while Hong Kong continues to operate according to the system of capitalism. In fact, even on the mainland, the scope within which we combat bourgeois liberalization is also strictly limited. It will be confined within the Chinese Communist Party. It will be carried out only in the political and ideological fields, and we will never allow "leftist" practices to be repeated. It is not a political campaign and will never flare up into one. So, I see no reason to fear

Reprinted by courtesy of *Beijing Review*, March 2, 1987, pp. 14-15.

149

that the struggle against bourgeois liberalization will involve Hong Kong.

Q: Will the personnel change in the Party Central Committee and the struggle against bourgeois liberalization affect the drafting of the Basic Law of the Hong Kong Special Administrative Region?

A: No, not at all. The drafting of the Basic Law is going on in an orderly manner as scheduled. Now all the special-subject groups are hard at work preparing for the 4th plenary session of the Basic Law drafting committee to be held in April. I am pleased to see that all the committee members, both from the mainland and Hong Kong, are active in the discussions and eager to put forward proposals reflecting the policies of the Chinese government for Hong Kong in a serious and responsible manner and in the spirit of democratic consultations, mutual respect and trust, and have reached common understanding on many issues. As for questions on which agreement has not been reached for the time being, members of both sides can continue to seek their settlement through democratic consultations. I am sure that the drafting of the Basic Law will be completed on schedule by 1990 through their joint efforts.

Q: Will the co-operative efforts of China and Britain to implement the Sino-British Joint Declaration on the question of Hong Kong be affected by the personnel change in the Central Committee and the anti-bourgeois liberalization struggle?

A: No, they will not. The Chinese government and the British government have worked well together to implement the Joint Declaration signed two years ago. The Sino-British Joint Liaison Group is very successful in its work; it has solved a series of important problems, including Hong Kong's status in the General Agreement on Tariffs and Trade, its status in the Asian Development Bank, its residents' travel documents, transitional arrangements of civil aviation accords between Hong Kong and other countries and regions, the setting up of Hong Kong's independent shipping register, and its public servants' pension system. The Sino-British Land Commission has also made marked progress, having settled questions of land leases that extend beyond 1997 and other problems in that connection. The friendly Sino-British co-operation, along with its encouraging results, has been widely acclaimed by people of all fields in Hong Kong. Their confidence in Hong Kong's future has been enhanced. I am sure that the friendly co-operation between China and Britain in carrying out the Joint Declaration will continue.

Three Decisions Vital to

Anti-Vietnamese War

Yang Mu

On December 25, 1978, with the support of the Soviet Union, Viet Nam, self-proclaimed the third military power in the world, invaded Democratic Kampuchea. On January 7, 1979, Vietnamese troops occupied Phnom Penh, the capital of Kampuchea, and on the 10th installed the puppet regime of Heng Samrin. At that point, Hanoi declared that within four months the Domocratic Kampuchean troops would be wiped out and the whole territory of Kampuchea would be under the control of the Heng Samrin regime.

The Democratic Kampuchean troops were not wiped out within four months, instead, they have been keeping up resistance against Viet Nam for eight years. During that time they have gained in strength. This is because:

(1) Viet Nam has perpetrated an outrageous violation on a small, weak nation, provoking its people to resist and others to protest all over the world.

(2) Viet Nam is going against a growing tide of peace, independence and development throughout the world, nourishing the. Kampuchean people's spirit. This is an irresistible force which Viet Nam will eventually succumb to.

(3) The Democratic Kampuchean resistance forces have followed a wise course. Its milestones are a transition followed by three strategic decisions.

The transition was to take on guerrilla warfare in the tropical jungle, ending the forces' passive posture and giving them a secure base in the west border areas to hit back.

Viet Nam had been carrying out sporadic border attacks before the invasion. In the first half of 1978, Viet Nam launched ten large-scale attacks across the border. The scale of these attacks grew after Viet Nam signed the treaty of friendship and co-operation with the Soviet Union on November 3, 1978.

Kampuchea, however, underestimated Viet Nam's ambition and unpreparedness sealed its fate. Realizing too late what was at hand, Kampuchea's forces resisted as best they could with conventional warfare. Their units were separated, surrounded, and had their supply lines cut. Democratic Kampuchea lost many of its soldiers and civilians in the process.

Far from being wiped out in four months, Democratic Kampuchea has been keeping up resistance for eight years while all the time gaining strength, because its national salvation war has won world-wide support.

In May 1979, the leaders of Democratic Kampuchea met in the jungle and decided that faced with such heavy odds the people's forces should wage a guerrilla war. In June of that year, the approaches of the guerrilla war were formulated in a series of meetings. This was the turning point. Thereafter the resistance forces established base areas primarily along the Kampuchean-Thai border from which to attack Viet Nam's occupation.

The three strategic decisions were to set up the coalition government of Democratic Kampuchea; to penetrate and take the fight into the interior of the country and to issue their eight-point proposal for a political solution to the Kampuchean problem.

First Strategic Decision: Coalition Government

The leaders of the three resistance forces in Democratic Kampuchea, Norodom Sihanouk, now president of the Coalition government of Democratic Kampuchea (CGDK), Son Sann, now prime minister of CGDK and Khieu Samphan, now vice-President in charge of foreign affairs, held their first meeting in Singapore in September 1981. The Singapore declaration signed on that occasion announced that supporting relevant resolutions of the United Nations and the declarations of international conferences on the Kampuchea problem, the three parties agreed to form a coalition government. In June 1982, the CGDK was established in Kuala Lumpur, the capital of Malaysia.

At the time, Viet Nam's newspapers described the coalition as built on sand, and some Western news agencies suggested it would last no more than six months. But the 4-year old coalition has proved that it is strategically sound. By joining the three parties, the Kampuchean people have an authoritative anti-Vietnamese government, which represents their national interests, organizes the patriotic forces and gives united leadership. The coalition forestalls Viet Nam splitting Kampuchea's resistance forces, thus further isolating Hanoi. The coalition has also enhanced its prestige and gained broader international support by its unified policies. The number of countries voting in the United Nations for the withdrawal of the Vietnamese from Kampuchea increases year by year. Last year, it was 114, this year 116.

Second Strategic Decision: Fighting in Hinterland

The resistance forces, having successfully defeated the first six dry-season offensives, had to abandon most of their bases along the Kampuchean-Thai border and moved their main force into the interior in the 7th dry season (November 1984-March 1985).

Son Sann and some high-ranking officers have said that they had only two choices under the heavy bombardment of the Vietnamese: to die along with their positions, or retreat temporarily to avoid unnecessary deaths. They chose the latter. After the 7th dry season offensive, the Vietnamese press and radios boasted about their "great victory," claiming that the forces of the CGDK "no longer existed." International observers, however, predicted that the fighting by the resistance forces inside Kampuchea would be significant, making the military situation for the Vietnamese more difficult.

This has been borne out by the fact that the CGDK forces have upset Hanoi's plans. After its military occupation of Kampuchea in 1979, Viet Nam put nearly 10 divisions on the western front, and the rest elsewhere. The aim was to pin the resistance forces along the western border and then eliminate them. After the

resistance forces gave up their bases along the border and became active around Tonle San Lake and Phnom Penh, Viet Nam had to withdraw troops from the border area to defend its major cities in the interior—its forces were thus dispersed. Besides it is hard to close the border and find the main strength of the resistances. The Vietnamese, having landed themselves in a passive position, were unable to start new large scale offensives after the 7th dry-season offensive. The dispersal has also hampered their coordination.

The Three Strategic Decisions—forming a coalition government, fighting in the hinterland and raising the eight-point proposal for a political solution—have proven vital to the anti-Vietnamese war. So long as they are abided by to the end, the Vietnamese will be driven out and a new Kampuchea born.

After moving into the interior, the armed forces of the coalition have been able to overcome ammunition shortages and have gained a foothold in a large area in the interior. Because in the process they strengthened their ties with the people. They have built on those ties and have gained the confidence of the people. They can secure food from the local people and weapons and drugs from outside easily.

Their unity—represented by the CGDK—enables the factions to fight their common enemy.

Third Strategic Decision: Political Solution

On March 17, 1986 the CGDK issued an Eight-Point Proposal for the Political Solution to the Kampuchean Problem. The main points of this proposal are: that Viet Nam should negotiate its troop withdrawal from Kampuchea with the tripartite CGDK; that it should completely withdraw from Kampuchea in two phases on a set schedule; that after the first phase of the Vietnamese troop withdrawal, Heng Samrin and his faction should enter into negotiations with the CGDK to form a four-part coalition government of Kampuchea.

The eight-point proposal expressed the desire of the CGDK for peace and its restraint towards Viet Nam. It also embodies the CGDK's desire for national unity. It makes use of the proposals for a solution which have been put forward by other countries. The proposal also looks to the future and maps out the rebuilding of Kampuchea and principles of Kampuchea's future policies.

The document itself represents the unity of the CGDK; it is the three factions' common programme. On the whole, the United Nations resolutions adopted over the years and the International Conference on Kampuchea Declaration of 1981 are commonly recognized as the basis for a solution to the Kampuchean problem. At present the eight-point proposal also shares that status.

The eight-point proposal has been rejected outright by the Vietnamese authorities, showing once again that Hanoi stubbornly refuses to withdraw its troops. Over 60 countries have formally expressed support for the eight-point proposal of Democratic Kampuchea. Its significance will become more obvious as time goes on.

Poverty and Politics in Mexico:
THE NEXT EARTHQUAKE

CURTIS SKINNER

Curtis Skinner is a writer who specializes in Latin American affairs. He has lived for ten years in Mexico.

The collapse in international oil prices has put the fear of the people into Mexico's De la Madrid government, and for good reason. A projected shortfall of $6 billion this year has pushed Mexico back to the brink of default on its outstanding foreign debt of $97 billion and made three years of grinding economic austerity imposed on the poor and working classes into a mere "exercise in hunger." Having colluded with the International Monetary Fund (IMF) to cut popular living standards by almost half since 1982 in order to pay the country's commercial bank creditors, President Miguel De la Madrid is extremely reluctant to take further belt-tightening measures for fear of driving a sorely-pressed population into open revolt.

To avoid a forced default by Mexico that would set a dangerous precedent for the rest of debt-strapped Latin America, the Reagan administration is arm-twisting U.S. banks to come up with at least half of the $4 billion in fresh credits Mexican finance officials say they will need in 1986.

Enter the Baker Plan, the Reagan administration's touted "growth solution" to the third-world debt problem. The plan, formulated by Treasury Secretary James Baker at last October's IMF-World Bank joint meeting in Seoul, calls for increased lending on more flexible terms by multilateral agencies and commercial banks to debtor countries who undertake "structural reforms" to promote foreign and domestic private investment and liberalize trade. The gist of the Baker scheme—which proposes an inadequate $29 billion in fresh credits to fifteen countries over the next three years, but offers no relief for existing debt burdens—is using third-world debt dependency as a wedge to dismantle nationalist barriers to United States capital and exports. Having pursued a market-oriented economic strategy for the past year, De la Madrid expressed support for the Baker initiative at last January's Mexicali meeting with President Reagan and appears willing to take further liberalizing measures consistent with the plan. This policy may win Mexico its new loans and increase export earnings, but it will do so by further sacrificing popular living standards, perpetuating the debt trap, and retreating from the country's decades-long effort to develop an independent, industrial economy.

The seeds of Mexico's debt bondage lie, ironically enough, in the country's emergence as an oil power. In the late 1970s, the Jose Lopez Portillo administration borrowed heavily in international credit markets to finance an ambitious industrial development program based on enormously expanded petroleum production. A huge chunk of this money, however—perhaps as much as half of the total—was never invested in Mexico at all, but ended up deposited in Swiss bank accounts by corrupt government functionaries or used by businessmen for secure investments and real estate purchases in the United States and Europe. The cost of servicing Mexico's variable-interest loans, meanwhile, increased substantially starting in 1979, as the United States pursued a tight monetary policy to fight inflation. In August 1982, with only $200 million remaining in its central bank, Mexico was forced to suspend commercial debt principal payments and go cup-in-hand to Washington for a $10 billion bailout. This encouraged other Latin American countries to publicly acknowledge their unserviceable debts and so touched off the world debt crisis. As part of the rescue package, the incoming De la Madrid government agreed to follow a three-year austerity program monitored by the IMF.

De la Madrid tried hard to be a good boy for the bankers. Mexico played a key role blocking the formation of a Latin American debtors' cartel in 1983-84, and the country's harsh economic retrenchment strategy served as Washington's model for the region. As is often the case with IMF "structural adjustment" programs, the austerity burden fell mainly on the poor and working classes. The government slashed vital consumer subsidy programs, allowing the prices of such food staples as rice, beans, and tortillas to increase severalfold. De la Madrid also sold off dozens of parastatal enterprises, contributing to a 40 percent unemployment rate that has thrown legions of grown men on the streets of Mexico City to sell Chiclets and eat fire for handouts. In collaboration with Mexico's quasi-official trade union organization, the Confederation of Mexican Workers (CTM), the government held wages well below annual inflation rates averaging 60 percent over the last three years, cutting the standard of living for most Mexicans almost by half. By late 1985, workers earning the minimum wage (about three dollars a day) were spending over 70 percent of their income on the basic food basket.

5. THE THIRD WORLD: Latin America

De la Madrid's assault on popular living standards was rewarded with a major debt rescheduling, but financial "recovery" on the IMF's terms continued to elude Mexico. A critical problem was the steady decline in international oil prices beginning in 1983. Oil exports account for 70 percent of Mexico's foreign exchange earnings and the price shortfall severely undercut government savings.

Another important factor, less often acknowledged by the political-business elite who exhorted Mexican workers to tighten their belts for the good of the country, was the headlong flight of capital from Mexico. Economists estimate that up to $60 billion left the country from 1977 to 1984, and up to $5 billion may have been siphoned out the first six months of 1985 solely through the practice of under-invoicing exports and over-invoicing imports. This capital flight—by far the largest of any debtor nation—has done enormous harm to the country by depleting foreign exchange reserves, reducing the government's tax base, drying up investment resources, and stifling economic growth. As a result, the government found itself compelled to increase its borrowing and deficit spending, consequently driving up interest rates, worsening inflation, and devaluing the peso. By September 1985, Mexico had fallen out of compliance with its IMF austerity goals and was barred from further borrowing; in October, only two months after signing a new commercial debt rescheduling agreement, Finance Minister Jesús Silva Herzog (who was ousted last month as finance minister following sharp differences within the De la Madrid cabinet) had to request from the bankers a six-month-extension on principal payments.

Consequently, the Saudi Arabian-instigated oil price plunge this year caught Mexico at its most vulnerable moment since 1982. The country's outstanding foreign debt is bigger than ever, with servicing charges estimated at $11 billion, and the total public debt service burden (foreign and domestic) accounting for almost half of Mexico's 1986 federal budget. In this desperate strait, De la Madrid has two apparent choices: to declare a unilateral debt payment moratorium or opt for the temporary relief afforded by the Baker Plan. Having ruled out the first as "irresponsible," the Mexican president is pressing ahead to open his protected economy to foreign trade and investment, as called for under the Reagan scheme. Among recent liberalizing measures, De la Madrid has revised foreign investment laws to permit majority equity by non-Mexicans in new companies; opened Mexico's internal market to the foreign-owned *maquiladora* assembly-and-export plants; lowered general import requirements; and announced Mexico's decision to join the General Agreement on Tariffs and Trade (GATT). The Baker/De la Madrid strategy for attracting business and promoting exports requires keeping wages "competitive" (low), maintaining a brutal rate of peso devaluation, and taking further steps to privatize the mixed economy and eliminate state subsidies. Consistent with this approach, De la Madrid announced another round of budget cuts and state enterprise sales in a major February 1986 speech on economic policy and the debt.

The net effect of these measures would be to strengthen foreign over domestic capital and restructure the economy to the dictates of the world market. The competitive pressures unleashed by joining GATT and dismantling protective barriers may force stronger companies to become more efficient. However, they will certainly drive many small Mexican manufacturers out of business, resulting in the loss of thousands of jobs, as will the *maquiladoras'* foray into the domestic market. Lifting equity restrictions on foreign investment also works against national industrial development. Studies in *Excelsior* and in *Statistical Abstract of Latin America* have shown that transnational corporations usually enter the market by taking over an existing Mexican firm—displacing domestic capital—and use their size and technological "know-how" to dominate the most dynamic industrial sectors, particularly capital goods. In current bilateral trade and investment negotiations, the United States is pressing Mexico to water down its provisions for technology transfer and to strengthen patent protections, which would help the transnationals maintain their technological monopoly.

Meanwhile, Mexico's policy of wage restraints, consumer subsidy cuts, and divestment of state enterprise constrains development of the domestic market. Though some of the money-losing public corporations up for sale are pure bureaucratic boondoggles, others provide subsidized goods and services to business and consumers that cannot profitably be replaced. If this strategy produces immediate fiscal savings and economic growth as a short-term distortion, in the long run it undermines the country's financial integrity by: reducing the state's internal revenue base, increasing the carrying cost of the unemployed and marginal sectors, and compelling excessive reliance on fickle foreign markets for economic security. It is a recipe for continued dependence on external borrowing and petroleum exports.

De la Madrid faces a mounting political challenge to this unpopular program. After fifty-six uninterrupted years in power, the ruling Institutional Revolutionary Party (PRI) is caught in the throes of a legitimacy crisis provoked by prolonged economic decline, the party's spectacular mismanagement of the national oil patrimony (a deeply felt issue), and recent examples of gross bureaucratic corruption and electoral fraud. The PRI's ability to co-opt and buy off disaffected social groups in time-honored fashion has been sapped by years of austerity. Now the party faces an unprecedented challenge to its authority from the political right and left as well as from a burgeoning grassroots movement. Though no rival organization is capable of competing on equal terms with the PRI's huge political machine, this popular mobilization could wrest some important social concessions from De la Madrid while laying the groundwork for political change.

On the electoral front, the rightist National Action Party (PAN) has been a thorn in the PRI's side, particularly in the important northern states of Chihuahua, Sonora, and Nuevo León. While PAN advocates a vague laissez-faire business philosophy, its appeal to many Mexicans is not ideological. Some supporters see National Action as more responsive to local interests than the highly-centralized PRI, but most votes for PAN, Mexico's largest opposition party, are votes against the government.

The PRI has responded to PAN's growing power at the polls with ham-handed fraud and repression, provoking PAN street protests that have turned violent. Ballot-box stuffing and falsified voting lists robbed PAN gubernatorial candidate Adalberto Rosas Lopez of a likely victory in the important Sonora race last July. In December and January of that election year, a rash of PAN-led mass protests broke out around the country against PRI vote-rigging in municipal elections. In the southern state of Chiapas, PAN militants occupied municipal offices in numerous towns and had to be forcibly removed by the police at the cost of seven lives. Demonstrators in the important central provincial city of San Luis Potosi torched the municipal palace on New Year's Eve and were also dispersed with bloodshed by the security forces.

Given this confrontational background, the local elections scheduled for Chihuahua this July stand as a watershed in Mexico's political history. President De la Madrid is under considerable pressure from the United States, backed by the creditor bankers, to avoid a repeat of last year's farce that would further discredit the PRI and undermine the system's long-term stability. On the other hand, PRI hardliners like CTM chief Fidel Velasquez oppose any weakening of the party's control at this time of acute economic strain. At stake is the state governorship, which PAN candidate and Ciudad Juárez mayor Francisco Barrio Berrazas stands to win in clean elections, according to the polls. The bets are that the PRI, never before having relinquished a governorship, will turn to massive fraud once again. Should this occur, there is a high potential for statewide violence since PAN controls over 60 percent of Chihuahua's municipalities, including the major cities.

Another symptom of a deep lack of confidence in the PRI and growing mass politicization is the emergence of independent self-help groups in the wake of last September's devastating earthquakes in Mexico City. The quakes—which caused $6 billion in damage, killed up to 20,000 people, and left another 130,000 homeless—have had a profound impact on the Mexican psyche, greatly adding to the prevailing climate of crisis and insecurity, but also inspiring impressive examples of popular initiative to cope with the tragedy. Rejecting government assistance, numerous volunteer groups sprang up around the city in the days following the disaster to channel private relief to the victims, known as *damnificados*. The De la Madrid administration, meanwhile, has come under strong criticism for corruption and inefficiency in aid administration, and for its failure to provide long-term relief for the *damnificados*, tens of thousands of whom are still camped out on city streets. The United Front of Earthquake Victims, a grassroots organization claiming 100,000 members, has held regular street demonstrations demanding new housing and urging that money spent repaying the foreign debt be used for earthquake reconstruction.

The key roadblock to both progressive political change and a socially responsible resolution of Mexico's debt crisis is the PRI's stranglehold on the country's major labor organizations and the weakness of the left, two aspects of the same problem. Since the "union insurgency" movement for political independence and internal democracy was crushed in the 1970s, the left, divided into eight small parties, has had a minimal presence in the mass organizations that carry decisive social weight in Mexico. However, the oil price plunge and redoubled austerity have given union bureaucrats like CTM chief Velasquez new cause for worry about restiveness in the ranks. The left wields a tremendously potent political weapon by linking De la Madrid's wage policy to Mexico's national subjugation under the foreign debt, forced oil sales, and the Baker Plan. The Communist-led United Socialist Party of Mexico (PSUM), Trotskyist Revolutionary Workers Party (PRT), and social democratic Mexican Workers Party (PMT) have moved aggressively to exploit the issue in recent months. A left-organized Mexico City demonstration on February 6 drew 50,000 marchers from 122 workers', peasants', and political organizations to demand wage increases, a debt moratorium, and repudiation of the Baker Plan. Passing in front of the U.S. embassy, marchers shouted, "Thieving government, you're sold to the gringos."

With oil prices in a long-term decline, Mexico's foreign debt is unpayable, as even De la Madrid cabinet members privately acknowledge. The only question is whether default is managed to benefit the bankers or the Mexican people. The De la Madrid policy of continuing full interest payments with fresh credits and rolling over the accumulated principal lets the banks keep the loans formally in good standing and their profits intact. The cost to Mexico is ever-deepening debt dependency, and the banks also lose in the long run by increasing their overall exposure as they postpone the day of reckoning.

The alternative to this *de facto* default is a unilateral payment moratorium or flat-out debt annulment on Mexico's part. Mexican business sleaders and government officials have warned direly that such a step would provoke crippling economic retaliation from the United States, including a trade embargo and suspension of new credits. These fears are exaggerated. Mexico is neither Cuba nor Nicaragua. It is in fact the United States' third-largest trading partner after Canada and Japan. A $35 billion trade cut-off would have sharply negative effects for the U.S. economy, particularly in a Southwest already battered by plunging oil prices, and is not a credible policy option for the Reagan administration. As for a credit suspension, Mexico only stands to gain by halting the downward debt spiral, and in any case, could make up the loss from its payments savings.

A three-to-five-year total debt payment moratorium, with future interest payments limited to 20 percent of the total value of exports, would give Mexico vital breathing space to put its financial house in order, pursue economic development, and begin to redress workers' living standards. A more equitable, but riskier, option is simply to cancel the debt, preferably in conjunction with other Latin American debtors. As Fidel Castro noted at last summer's debt conference in Havana, repudiating the regional public debt would help compensate for the "illegitimate transfers" Latin America has made to the developed world in recent years in the form of excessively high interest rates, an overvalued dollar, deteriorating terms of trade, and capital flight. But the real point is that the working classes of poor nations like Mexico should not be held responsible for debts they neither contracted nor benefited from—especially when the creditors are the wealthiest financial institutions and governments in the world. (Citibank, Mexico's largest creditor, made *$1 billion* in 1985 profits.) For Mexico and much of the rest of the third world, progress depends on a clean break from the debt tar baby.

CONTADORA PRIMER

O N JUNE 6, 1986 THE CONTADORA countries—the mediators—placed the latest version of the Contadora treaty on the table for the consideration of the Central American countries.

Symbol	Description
Central America—Parties to the Treaty
Contadora Group—Mediators
Contadora Support Group

THE CONTADORA countries are Mexico, Panama, Colombia and Venezuela— so-named for Contadora island, off the western coast of Panama, where they held their first meeting in 1983.

The Contadora Support Group is composed of Argentina, Brazil, Peru, and Uruguay—four Latin American democracies who lent strong diplomatic support to the Contadora process beginning in 1985.

The actual parties to the treaty are the Central American countries: Guatemala, El Salvador, Honduras, Nicaragua and Costa Rica. They would sign the treaty and make peace among themselves.

Note that the United States is *not* a party to the agreement. This was intentional: to allow the Central Americans to make peace with or without Washington's okay.

On the following pages of this report, the key provisions of the proposed Contadora treaty are outlined, with special emphasis on how these provisions would be enforced in Nicaragua, through the efforts of a Commission on Verification and Control and an International Corps of Inspectors.

How It Would Work

Chapter 3, para. 33
Stop Aid To Contras

Timing: On signing

Chapter 3, para. 25
Restrict Foreign Military Exercises

Timing: Six months after ratification

Chapter 3, para. 28
Withdraw Military Advisers

Timing: Six months after signing

Chapter 3, para. 19
Bar All Arms Imports

Timing: Eight days after ratification

Chapter 3, para. 30
Stop Aid To Salvadoran Guerrillas

Timing: On signing

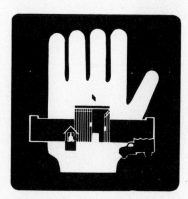

Chapter 3, para. 25
Close All Foreign Military Bases

Timing: Six months after signing

How It Would Get the Soviets Out

Although this page deals with Nicaragua, the Contadora treaty imposes the same obligations on all five signatories. El Salvador and the other Central American countries also would have to stop importing arms and expel foreign military advisers under the treaty. The verification commission would operate equally in El Salvador and the other countries. We stress the impact on Nicaragua because here the treaty satisfies the chief stated objectives of the Reagan administration, and yet both it and the American media have overlooked this virtue of the treaty.

HELICOPTERS AND TANKS

Chapter 3, para. 19:

Nicaragua undertakes "not to acquire, after the date of the entry into force of the Act, any more military *materiel*, with the exception of replenishment supplies, ammunition and spare parts needed to keep existing *materiel* in operation, and not to increase their military forces, pending the establishment of the maximum limits for military development within the time-limit stipulated for the second stage."

ADVISERS

Chapter 3, para. 27:

Nicaragua undertakes to "withdraw, within a period of not more than 180 days from the signing of this Act and in accordance with the studies and recommendations of the Verification and Control Commission, any foreign military advisers and other foreign elements likely to participate in military, paramilitary and security functions."

How It Would Be Verified

INTERNATIONAL CORPS OF INSPECTORS

(Technical inspection body: investigates)

VERIFICATION AND CONTROL COMMISSION

(Adjudicatory body: analyzes and recommends.)

Part II, para. 3(B): "The International Corps of Inspectors shall have at its disposal all the resources in personnel and finances, as decided by the Commission, necessary to ensure the strict observance of the commitments on security matters."

"The Commission shall carry out its investigations by making on-site inspections, gathering testimony and using any other procedure which it deems necessary for the performance of its functions."

"The Commission shall be accorded every facility and prompt and full cooperation by the Parties."

"We fully agree this must be done with corresponding verification and control mechanisms. An agreement like this cannot work without verification and control mechanisms."
President Daniel Ortega,
May 26, 1986

Ports and Harbors Military Bases

Border Stations Airfields

The International Corps of Inspectors (ICI), under the supervision of the Commission on Verification and Control, will use a variety of resources and methods to ensure the provisions of the Contadora treaty. Illustrated on the above map, the ICI uses jeeps, helicopters and observation posts to verify compliance at ports, border crossings, military bases and airfields.

 # WHO HAS AGREED?

	Costa Rica	El Salvador	Guatemala	Honduras	Nicaragua	United States (degree of support)
Sept. 1984	👎	👎	*	👎	👍	*"One-sided."* —State Department
April 1986	👍	👍	👍	👍	👎	*"We interpret these provisions as requiring a cessation of support to irregular forces."* —Special envoy Philip Habib
June 1986	👎	👎	👍	👎	👍	*"Inadequate."* —Asst. Sec. Elliott Abrams *"A paper agreement."* President Reagan

There have been three Contadora drafts; chart shows reaction of country to each draft. All countries have approved at least one draft—but never at the same time.

All three drafts have been fair and balanced. The September, 1984 version most favored Nicaragua. In September, 1985 the Contadora Group produced a modified draft and in April 1986 asked the Central Americans for their final reactions. Nicaragua objected to some of the changes.

The Contadora Group then produced a third draft in June 1986, and as Nicaragua swung in favor, three of the others swung against.

Objectively, the differences among the three drafts are minor. Nearly all of the provisions pictured in this report have been in all three versions. Two factors account for the wide swings in position by the signatories. First, they overreacted to minor textual changes. Second, they sometimes announced in favor when they knew the other side would not accept.

The United States is *not* a party; yet because of the influence it wields over Costa Rica, El Salvador, and Honduras, U.S. acquiescence is necessary. The United States objected to the first Contadora treaty. In April 1986 U.S. special envoy Philip Habib pledged to abide by the second treaty. U.S. officials objected strongly to the third, current draft of the treaty.

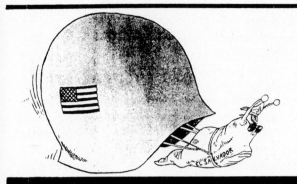

The quagmire of dependency

JIM CHAPIN

JIM CHAPIN, *writer, political consultant, and a former national director of the Democratic Socialists of America, is the Chair of World Hunger Year.*

"In El Salvador, it's good for your health to have an American connection."

Bernard Packer
Former head of AIFLD in El Salvador

EL SALVADOR has fallen out of the American media in the last two years. And it has fallen out of the American political process. These two facts are not unconnected. In the absence of serious American political discussion of events in El Salvador, the involvement of the United States in that country has steadily increased. While American politicians and journalists have exercised themselves over $100 million in aid to Nicaraguan *contras*, they have ignored the ever-growing commitment of the U.S. to the Duarte government in El Salvador, and where that commitment might lead. Other than occasional statements about Duarte and his struggle against the military (a struggle which goes nowhere), the media, lacking any clear "story line," has largely abandoned its coverage of the issues. With all but a few left-wing and New Right Congressmen supporting the Duarte government, American policy toward that country has not been subjected to any sustained criticism from main-stream politicians or journalists.

While our watchdogs in Congress and the media have been sleeping, the United States has taken on a role as the primary sponsor of the Duarte government exceeding that of even a few years ago. In 1985, U.S. aid to El Salvador topped half-a-billion dollars, more than $120 per Salvadoran, a level of support exceeded only by what we give to Israel. However, if one takes into account the higher GNP of Israel, U.S. aid to El Salvador is almost exactly equivalent: one-fifth of each country's GNP. It is a sum higher than the entire national budget of El Salvador a few years ago. Given this level of support, we shouldn't be surprised that El Salvador and Israel rank at the very top of the short list of countries that regularly support

U.S. positions in the United Nations. The list would be much longer if we paid other countries at the same rate!

The conflict in El Salvador is going nowhere and going somewhere at the same time. Like most historical events, it leads in ambivalent directions, rather than providing the simple good guys/bad guys dichotomies beloved of American journalists, politicians, and public opinion. Just as the accession of Cory Aquino (with the support of the same military leaders who bolstered the Marcos regime for two decades) will not solve the problems of the Philippines, so Duarte's uneasy alliance with the military and the United States opened only the *possibility* of an end to the persistent conflict in El Salvador. Nothing that has happened in the last year would lead one to think that an end to the conflict is any nearer.

In fact, one can make a case that almost *every* force in El Salvador seems weaker now than a year ago, with two very important exceptions: the American government and the Salvadoran military which it sponsors. The continuance of the war over time has resulted in the destruction of the old Salvadoran oligarchy. The forces of the death squads have been politically scattered: the right-wing quasi-Fascist bloc built up by Roberto D'Aubuisson under the name of ARENA (Republican National Alliance) has shattered, with various individuals trying to pick up its pieces; and the traditional military-backed party, the PCN (Party of National Conciliation), collapsed in the 1985 election. The right wing has recourse to one remaining major political bastion: the legal system — the Supreme Court and the Attorney General's office — which has been threatening to overturn the 1979 nationalization of coffee, but has been thwarted by Duarte's intention to execute Phase II of the land reform.

The military has generally continued to protect former death-squad members, and no major figure has been successfully tried for anything up to and including killing Salvadoran archbishops and American nuns, shooting AFL-CIO representatives, or plotting to kill American ambassadors. Even so, the experience of the military in the years without an American presence has been so grim that the army has concluded that *nothing* can be allowed to interfere with the American pipeline, especially since the demands of the American masters are so limited in scope.

Even attempts to prosecute a gang who kidnapped rich businessmen for ransom have so far led nowhere. One major figure, Lt. Col. Roberto Mauricio Staben (a CIA favorite and commander of the American-trained Arce battalion) has already been released, and Rodolfo Isidro Lopez Sibrian (who was never punished for his role in killing AIFLD — American Institute for Free Labor Development — workers) apparently will escape punishment.

The most dramatic event of the last year was the September 10, 1985 kidnapping of Duarte's daughter Ines, who had been his campaign manager in 1984. The FMLN (Farabundo Martí Liberation Front) held her for forty-four days, and was able to get a number of its people released in return for her. Many commentators have claimed that this episode demonstrated Duarte's power: the army was unhappy, to say the least, but had to succumb to the family interests of the president. Colonel Sigifredo Ochoa, who has always been an anti-Duarte lightning rod in the military, was violently critical. Ochoa was re-assigned to Washington, where he has so far failed to report.

The military remains unwilling to punish even the most flagrant violators of the law. But it has, under American pressure, reduced the level of terror in the country. In fact, on the two occasions when the military put its eggs in the basket of the (potentially anti-American) right, from 1972 to 1979, and again in 1982-84, the result was a vast increase in rebel strength that, according to some military analysts, came within a year or so of toppling the regime altogether. If anything, under Duarte and with American support, the military has become more powerful as an independent force in the last few years. Its "professionalization" may be laying the groundwork for it to function independently of the old oligarchy, just as the equally "professional" Chilean military has been functioning for the last dozen years.

At the height of death-squad activity, thousands of people died every year. Nothing like that is happening now. What is happening is rather interesting: a bifurcated and more sophisticated strategy which is a "clean-up" version of what the Guatemalan military successfully accomplished without much American aid. This strategy couples an easing of political restriction in the cities with an increase of violence in the rural areas.

In the Salvadoran version, increased violence does not involve mass slaughters of local Indian populations (most of them were killed in 1932), but only rare and probably not centrally planned incidents. More common is the policy of mass depopulation of the rural zones backing the rebels. That policy has known several phases. Until 1982 units of the armed forces would enter villages in search of the insurgents, often disrupting and displacing the populace. After 1982, this policy had to be abandoned in certain areas because rebel control had grown too strong. Since 1984, however, with the increased assistance of U.S.-supplied aircraft and bombers, the policy of depopulation has resumed in earnest. This so-called "clean warfare" relies on heavy bombing from above and the use of troops on the ground. The government has waged strong campaigns that have driven the rebels out of areas they had possessed for years, such as the Guazapa Volcano or parts of Chalatenango province. As a result, today half-a-million people, more than 10 percent of the country's population, are displaced persons.

American intervention in recent years has been more than military. It has taken place on a wide front. The theory of "low intensity conflict" — which was developed by French counter-insurgents in Algeria and Vietnam, then used by us in Vietnam, and now is being implemented by the Reagan administration all around the world — requires that we see the world as the Communists do, as total. *Everything* is grist for the conflict: religion, culture, the union movement, politics, etc. Here, as elsewhere, "anti-Communists" unwittingly make imitation the sincerest form of flattery.

The AFL-CIO, acting through the AIFLD, has worked to destroy the Popular Democratic Unity (UPD), the moderate labor union federation which it helped to put together in 1980. Why? Because that federation was not sufficiently pro-Duarte. Bernard Packer, the AIFLD representative in Salvador, began a group called the Democratic Workers' Federation in 1984. Although Packer himself became so controversial he had to be replaced, his policy remains. His group carried out a pro-Duarte rally three months ago.

The anti-Duarte elements of UPD joined with unions of teachers and public administrators to form the National Unity of Salvadoran Workers (UNTS) in February of this year. These groups carried out a number of larger and more enthusiastic anti-Duarte labor rallies on February 21, March 25, and on May Day. The old UPD unions (who were a major base of support for Duarte in 1984) have been unhappy not only with Duarte's economic policies and his failure to negotiate, but also with his use of security troops to smash strikes and with the torture by acid and electricity of some members and relatives. Chris Norton, writing in *NACLA Report on the Americas,* says the AFL-CIO has followed "the logic of recent U.S. policy in El Salvador. In many respects, the UPD has indeed functioned as the independent, centrist union which AIFLD worked twenty-three years to build. The problem is that in the context of a policy that has defined Duarte as the acceptable left end of the political spectrum, and then pulled him to the right, such a union base is seen as a dangerously destabilizing force."

Meanwhile, the newest aspect of American cultural imperialism, evangelical Protestantism, has moved into the country in a big way. USAID has signed a cooperation agreement allowing a Protestant group to distribute food to refugees, and the military has given them access to the camps, barracks, and jails, and has helped them on housing projects. According to Campus Crusade for Christ, the number of Protestant baptisms has risen from 70,000 in 1975 to 250,000 last year. They now claim that some 20 percent of the country's population are active members. Walter Dean Burnham has suggested that fundamentalist religion has filled the social space in the United States that in other countries would be filled by socialism, and now the Protestants in Central America seem to be consciously positioning themselves as anti-Marxists in support of American policy.

The Catholic church in El Salvador has been institutionally weak judging by the number of vocations to the priesthood, for example, even by normal Latin American standards. The relatively few priests and nuns cover the whole ideological spectrum from left to right, but it has been possible for the archbishops to emerge as the voice of "moderate" public opinion. Archbishop Arturo Rivera y Damas, perhaps responding to the murder of his predecessor, Archbishop Oscar Romero, has been more cautious. He supported the Christian Democrats fairly strongly until this year, but has distanced himself increasingly, condemning the indiscriminate bombing of civilians by the government air force, but also condemning the attacks on the economy by the guerrillas.

American aid has not overcome the decline in the economy. Inflation has run at 30 percent a year. Unemployment and underemployment are estimated at 50 percent. Real income has dropped 30 percent so far in this decade. And the largest American firm in the country, Texas Instruments, has just closed its factory. Duarte, under pressure from his American paymasters, has had to devalue the currency and raise taxes. The only economic good news has been the Brazilian drought which has doubled the price that El Salvador can get for its coffee exports.

As Duarte has been pulled right by the pressure of U.S./IMF economic policies and urged to compromise with the army and the political right, some of the space to his immediate left has opened. There have been public protest marches and strikes, something one did not see much of at the height of the death squads. Political groups just to the left of Duarte, the social democratic and Christian democratic wings of the FDR (Democratic Revolutionary Front), have made tentative appearances in the capital for the first time in five years. Their representatives met with representatives of Duarte in Lima this April, and Duarte, on the second anniversary of his election as president (June 1), called once more for negotiations. Guillermo Ungo of the FDR responded with guarded hope.

Meanwhile, the FMLN, faced with the collapse of its military strategy, has retreated from the Nicaraguan/Cuban example to the Vietnamese example. In a way it is an ironic choice, for the Vietnamese never fully realized how vast American firepower was, and they, too, kept getting trapped into direct confrontations with it.

El Salvador is a tiny country, the size of Massachusetts, with about one-fourteenth the population of Vietnam (which is the thirteenth most populous nation in the world). Despite American attempts to make Nicaragua into the "North Vietnam" of the conflict, the analogy fails. Nicaragua does not border El Salvador, and the two nations which do (Honduras and Guatemala) are both American allies. As long as we are willing to continue to increase aid at the present rate — and if necessary to back it up with American troops — the blunt fact is that given the present circumstances *no government can come to power in El Salvador without at least American toleration.*

The FMLN, not fully wanting to recognize this state of affairs, has decided to "come out of the closet" and to form a single Marxist-Leninist party. This should be an interesting enterprise, since many of the leaders and parties involved have been as willing to kill each other as to kill government forces. At a meeting of the five FMLN organizations in Perquin last summer, it was agreed that the purely military struggle had failed, and that it was time for a prolonged popular struggle. The new slogan is "one party, one army, until the taking of power." As always, the Salvadoran rebels, reflecting the grimmer history of their nation, have been less attractive and more bloodthirsty than the Sandinistas.

The political wing of the revolutionary movement, the FDR, has been unhappy with the evolution of the Marxist-Leninist military wing, but it has even less power (lacking a United States base) to influence them than Duarte does the army. When Duarte came to power, he had a strong base of support in El Salvador. The direction of the last year's politics has narrowed that base. More and more, the key to Duarte's position is in Washington. Instead of building a strong political system in El Salvador, what we have done is to create a government and military that is totally dependent upon us.

ONE MIGHT be forgiven for thinking that this war will go on forever with no result (even the archbishop has spoken despairingly of the war as "apocalyptic and interminable"), but in fact we should remember that the revolutionary forces have at least twice come somewhat close to victory, once in 1979-80, and once at the end of 1983. On each occasion the United States increased the level of its involvement and stopped them. But when the government drifts to the right (or, as now, is pulled there by its American sponsors) the rebel forces gain strength and the U.S. must escalate its efforts to maintain the government in power.

This, not anything that has happened or may happen in Nicaragua, is the "Vietnam model." For that reason alone, we should pay more attention to what is happening in El Salvador. Even a "pocket Vietnam" is a pocket we should avoid.

The choices before the United States are not easy. Duarte appears to be an arrogant and often inefficient man who insists on trying to run his government single-handedly. His party, unable to carry out the policy of its natural constituency, is tending to become a collection of corrupt hangers-on. So far,

EVEN AS THE latest attempts at negotiations between the Duarte government and the revolutionary front appear to have come to nought, pressures on religious groups in El Salvador grow ominous. Accusations that church human-rights groups are linked to the rebels have come from three women rights workers who were jailed by the government, then freed in exchange for public confessions of guerrilla connections. Church officials have denied the accusations (although it is common sense to assume that in a civil-war climate their agencies might well be infiltrated by *both* rebel and government agents) and have expressed concern that "to call someone a Communist here is practically a death sentence." The government and the U.S. embassy are publicizing the accusations widely — but without instituting any judicial process to prove them. A number of church workers have received death threats.

THE EDITORS

the United States is supporting Duarte "the way a rope supports a hanged man": by pushing him to carry out unpopular right-wing economic policies, limiting his ability to control the army (most of our military aid goes directly to the armed forces rather than through civilian government), and opposing any serious negotiations with the rebels.

As for the revolutionaries, Edward Sheehan, whose low opinion of the Sandinistas is known to readers of this magazine, has suggested that "in power, the FMLN might make the Sandinistas seem like Swedish Socialists." I would agree, with the single qualification of removing the "might." The violence that the Marxist-Leninist wing of the FMLN has shown toward the general population and towards each other has no parallel in Sandinista behavior.

This is not to say that negotiations serve no purpose. Neither the army nor the FMLN can win the military struggle (unless the U.S. withdraws its aid to the army). The ironic effect of present American policies is to complete a "forced-draft" urbanization and "modernization" of El Salvador, by destroying the rest of the traditional peasant base of the Salvadoran society. The effect of "liberalization" in the cities is to allow an expression of attitudes to the left of those the U.S. government wants, but these attitudes can only be suppressed by letting the death squads go back to their old ways.

THE present situation in El Salvador limits American options. We cannot abruptly withdraw our support. Aside from the level of American credibility already invested in the regime, a victory for forces (which at their best are roughly equivalent to those presently ruling Vietnam) would be bad for El Salvador, bad for the U.S., and bad for Central America. We can't continue the present policy of indefinitely increasing support for the government, because that decreases both the government's real domestic strength and its room to maneuver with flexibility. If the Salvadoran government thinks our support is unlimited, it has no incentive and no ability to make necessarily difficult changes.

We need to put our aid through the civilian, not the military, sector, and at the same time insure that the money not be used to create a "kleptocracy" (a government made rich by stealing from its people) dependent upon us for its very survival. We need to support a domestic force for peace in El Salvador, and we have to understand that if there is no such force there, then our effort is wasted. Our policy of demanding a victory *and* an end to the death squads at the same time simply can't work: death squads are the price of "victory." Liberalization permits rising left-wing opposition, which, denied political space, will find military space. The natural direction of a military-dominated regime is a slide to the right, which reduces government support.

The U.S. can't demand a "frozen social revolution" as the price of our continued support. We must allow a real opportunity for all political forces (including Marxist, Leninist, and Communist) to push their case, else the war will go on indefinitely. We have to deal with the reality that a liberalized political system will probably not produce a capitalist political economy. The "capitalist" (in many ways pre-capitalist) economy in El Salvador that exists today is the result of generations of savage repression. Lifting that repression will probably not produce a result satisfactory either to political conservatives at home or even to moderate Democrats.

The United States under Reagan, here and elsewhere, is seeking victory when it should be seeking peace. "Perpetual war for perpetual peace" increases rather than reduces Soviet influence, because it confronts the Soviets in the arenas where they function best: social wars and weaponry. Where our society functions best is in the arts of peace: business, communications, and culture. In effect, peace would be our best "weapon." But the Reagan administration, wedded to a strange admiration of their alleged Communist foes, wants nothing so much as to imitate them. We must hope that the next U.S. administration will not attempt to "build democracy" as we are now doing in El Salvador: by substituting our dollars and military support for the social base that an indigenous democracy requires. It is an appealing shortcut, but a fatal one.

Islam in the Politics of the Middle East

"Islamic governments and movements manifest a broad range of positions in their ideology, actors and policies. Islam has been used to legitimate monarchies, military regimes, and a theocracy. These self-styled Islamic regimes span the ideological spectrum, from Libya's radical socialist 'state of the masses' to the conservative monarchy of Saudi Arabia. Islamic actors display a similar diversity: clerical and lay, traditionalist and modernist, highly educated and illiterate, moderate and terrorist."

JOHN L. ESPOSITO

Professor of Religious Studies, College of the Holy Cross

John L. Esposito writes on Islam's role in effecting sociopolitical change. Among his publications are *Islam and Politics* (Syracuse: Syracuse University Press, 1984), *Voices of Resurgent Islam* (New York: Oxford University Press, 1983), and *Women in Muslim Family Law* (Syracuse: Syracuse University Press, 1982).

ISLAM has emerged dramatically in the politics and headlines of the Middle East. Islamic resurgence and Islamic fundamentalism are only a few of the banners used to describe events as diverse as Libyan Muammar Qaddafi's espousal of Islamic law and ideology (1971), General Zia ul-Haq's coup d'etat in Pakistan (1977), Iran's "Islamic revolution" and the seizure of the Grand Mosque by militants in Saudi Arabia (1979), the assassination of Egypt's Anwar Sadat (1981), the revolt of the Muslim Brotherhood in Syria (1982), and terrorist attacks against American personnel and interests in Lebanon and Kuwait (1983–1985).[1]

Why has religion become such a visible force in Middle East politics? There is no single answer. Rather, a confluence of events has contributed to the widespread reemergence of Islam in politics. This phenomenon is not simply a reaffirmation of the presence and continued vitality of religion as a social force in Muslim societies but, most important, a response to the failures and crises of authority and legitimacy that have plagued most modern Muslim states. The experience of failure—military, political, socioeconomic and cultural—has paved the way for Islam as an alternative ideology for state and society.

The resurgence of Islam in Muslim politics is rooted in a broader religious revivalism that has encompassed personal as well as political life. The personal dimension is reflected in increased emphasis on the performance of religious observances: mosque attendance, fasting during the month of Ramadan, and abstention from alcohol and gambling. This has been accompanied by more religious programming in the media, a proliferation of religious literature, the growth of new Islamic associations—in particular vibrant missionary *(dawa)* movements. These movements are devoted not only to their traditional task of converting non-Muslims but also to the Islamization of Muslim populations, i.e., the deepening of religious commitment and observance.

For many, religious revivalism has simply meant greater piety; for others, it has included a reassertion of Islam as a total or comprehensive way of public and private life. As a result, both incumbent governments and opposition movements have appealed to Islam to legitimate their actions and policies. State Islam has taken many forms under Libya's Muammar Qaddafi, Pakistan's Zia ul-Haq, Sudan's Gafaar Nimeiry, and Iran's Ayatollah Ruhollah Khomeini. Muslim countries have introduced Islamic laws and regulations, implemented Islamic taxes and established Islamic banks, finance corporations and insurance companies on an interest-free basis. At the same time, opposition movements, ranging from political parties and groups to radical revolutionaries, have also appealed to Islam for legitimacy. Islam has become the battle cry for the *mujahideen* freedom fighters of Afghanistan and for the Islamic Jihad terrorists of Lebanon.

Four themes capture the general mood of Islamic revivalism: disenchantment with and rejection of the West; disillusion with the political and socioeconomic realities of Muslim life; a quest for identity and authenticity—an attempt to root the development of Muslim society in indigenous cultural values; and the reassertion of Islam as an alternative ideology for state and society.

Many Muslims (in common with others in the third world) have become progressively ambivalent toward the West. Western models of political, social and economic development are viewed as inappropriate transplants from an alien historical/cultural experience that have been uncritically applied to Muslim societies. Western liberal nationalism, capitalism and socialism are perceived as having failed to meet the political and socioeconomic needs of Muslim societies.[2]

In much of the Muslim world, political systems have not been able to provide a base for national unity and political legitimacy. Despite constitutional and parliamentary forms of government, Muslim rulers are often regarded as autocratic heads of corrupt, authoritarian regimes that are propped up by Western governments and multinational corporations. Neither Western capitalism nor Marxist socialism has been able to redress widespread poverty and the maldistribution of wealth. Capitalism is condemned as consumerism and unbridled materialism blind to issues of social justice. Marxist socialism is rejected as a godless alternative that reduces human life to the material and thus strikes at the heart of religion. Modernization is accused of fostering the Westernization and secularization of Muslim societies: a blind, uncritical pursuit of progress at any cost, "valueless" social change. Infatuation with and imitation of the West, sometimes characterized as "Westoxification" or "Westomania," is blamed for a general moral and cultural decline and a loss of identity and values that have led to the breakdown of Muslim society, the disruption of family life, increased crime and promiscuity and spiritual malaise.

Attributing the failure of Muslim societies to straying from Islam, revivalists believe Islam's revitalization depends on a return to Islam in both individual and community life: a restoration of Islamic identity, pride and values. Islam is reaffirmed as a total way of life. This belief is rooted in the revivalists' understanding of Islamic history. They believe that both revelation (the Koran) and the example of Mohammed and the early community support the belief that the Islamic community is (or should be) a religiopolitical community or state governed by Islamic law (the Shariah). Revivalists view the spectacular early spread of Islam and the creation of an Islamic empire or commonwealth as validating the truth of Islam's message and mission and as a sign of God's

guidance. Success, power and wealth are seen as the signs of a faithful community. Subjugation and decline are the fruits of departure from the path of Islam. Thus Islamic political activists believe that Muslims must reestablish or reorient their government and society through the implementation of Islamic law in order to regain their rightful place in the world.

THE IDEOLOGY OF ISLAMIC REVIVALISM

The ideological framework for Islamic activists may be summarized by the following beliefs:

1) Islam is a comprehensive way of life. Religion is integral to politics, state, law and society.

2) Muslim societies fail because they depart from this understanding of Islam by following Western secular and materialistic ideologies and values.

3) Renewal calls for an Islamic political and social revolution that draws its inspiration from the Koran and from Mohammed, who led the first Islamic movement.

4) To reestablish God's rule, Western-inspired civil law must be replaced by Islamic law, which is the blueprint for Muslim society.

5) While the Westernization of society is condemned, modernization as such is not. Science and technology are accepted, but they are to be subordinated to Islam in order to guard against the infiltration of Western values.

Radical movements go beyond these principles and operate on the following assumptions:

1) A Western Judeo–Christian conspiracy pits the West against the Islamic world. It results from the combination of neocolonialist ambitions and the power of Zionism.

2) Establishing an Islamic system of government is not simply an alternative but an Islamic imperative, based on God's command. All Muslims must obey. Those who fail to comply, governments or individuals, are no longer Muslim; they are unbelievers, or atheists—the enemies of God. True Muslims are obliged to wage holy war *(jihad)* against these infidels. This belief provided the rationale for the assassination of President Sadat of Egypt by members of Egypt's al-Jihad, for whom Sadat's failure to implement Islamic law made him the hypocritical head of an atheist state.

3) Christians and Jews, who are not judged "true believers," are no longer regarded as the "people of the book" but as unbelievers.

ISLAMIC ACTIVISTS: WHO ARE THEY?

Islamic activists and organizations range from moderate to radical. Contrary to popular stereotypes, most Islamic revivalists are not uneducated, antimodern reactionaries seeking refuge in the seventh century. Many combine a traditional religious upbringing with degrees in education, science, engineering and medicine. They are graduates of Cairo, Khartoum, Teheran and the American University of Beirut as well as Harvard, Indiana, Oxford and the Sorbonne. While the ulema (clergy) play a more important role among the Shiites, the leadership of Sunni organizations is predominantly lay rather than clerical. Activists include members of the lower middle and middle class, both city dwellers and villagers; they are educated, pious and highly motivated; many are upwardly mobile students and young professionals recruited from mosques and schools.

Most Islamic organizations, like the Egyptian, Sudanese and Jordanian Muslim Brotherhoods, Kuwait's Islamic Reform Society and Pakistan's Jamaat-i-Islami, work within existing political systems. They participate in elections, organize students and run youth centers, clinics and legal aid societies. However, government suppression or what are perceived as hostile actions, directly or indirectly supported by Western powers, can radicalize moderates, transforming reformers into revolutionaries.

A minority of Islamic organizations, like Egypt's al-Jihad and Lebanon's Hezbullah, pursue a policy of violent confrontation, believing that the political realities of Muslim life require armed struggle or *jihad*. Radicals view their governments as anti-Islamic regimes who either control religion or repress the attempts of authentic Islamic movements to implement Islam. Violent acts and armed revolution are viewed as necessary and appropriate responses to the enemies of God—despotic rulers and their Western allies.

THE POLITICS OF RESURGENT ISLAM

A series of crises served as catalysts for Islamic revivalism. Among the more significant events were the 1967 Arab–Israeli war, the 1971 Pakistan–Bangladesh civil war, the Arab–Israeli war and Arab oil embargo of 1973, and the growth of political dissent and civil war in Iran and Lebanon.

In many ways, 1967 marked a turning point in Arab politics. Israel's quick and decisive defeat of a combined Arab force (Egypt, Syria and Jordan), with staggering Arab military, economic and territorial losses (Gaza, the Sinai, the Golan Heights, the West Bank and especially the holy city of Jerusalem), seemed the clearest sign of Arab Muslim impotence. Israeli rule over a unified Jerusalem and the transfer of Israel's capital from Tel Aviv to Jerusalem made the occupation of Jerusalem an Islamic as well as an Arab issue. While some attributed the loss to the continued influence of a backward religious tradition, for others "the disaster" (as it was called) raised many questions about the direction of Muslim governments and about the West as a model for development. The mood of disenchantment and soul-searching unified clergy and laity, literate and illiterate, traditionalist and modernist in a quest for identity and authenticity. They shared a desire to renew and restore, to bring about a revitalization of Muslim societies that would root their present more firmly in past history, culture and values. As a result, the framework and the terminology of political discourse and action shifted.

Since the 1970's, Islam has displaced nationalism and socialism as the dominant factor in the ideology and politics of Middle East regimes and opposition movements. Middle East governments exploit and experiment while Islamic organizations proliferate and engage in political and social action.

THE DIVERSITY OF MUSLIM POLITICS

Thus, political Islam is not a monolith; it has taken many different forms. The specific causes of Islamic revivalism in the Middle East and its diversity of expressions are seen in the individual countries and movements from Libya to Pakistan.[3]

Libya was the site of one of the earliest and most controversial state implementations of Islam. When Muammar Qaddafi seized power in 1969, he self-consciously emulated his hero—Egypt's President Gamal Abdel Nasser. However, it was not long before the slogans and ideology of Arab nationalism and socialism gave way to Qaddafi's espousal of Islam as the Third Way, the alternative for Libya and the Muslim world. Qaddafi announced the introduction of Islamic law in the early 1970's. Islamic regulations prohibiting alcohol and gambling and Islamic punishments for theft and adultery were introduced. However, the full implementation of Islamic law was soon ignored as Qaddafi delineated his Third Way in a series of three slim volumes, *The Green Book*.

Setting aside traditional interpretations of Islamic law, Qaddafi's *Green Book* was to provide the blueprint for a new Libyan society and an example for the Arab world. He radically redefined Islam and Arab nationalism, stamping them with his own interpretation. Indeed, the *Green Book* replaced the Shariah as the program for Libya's political and social order and the basis for its cultural revolution. Qaddafi's personal ideological statement, the Third International Theory, proclaims a revolutionary alternative to capitalism and communism. Mixing populist rhetoric with political, social and economic experimentation, he has attempted to implement an ideological revolution in Libya and to export it internationally.

The Libyan Arab Republic has become the Socialist People's Libyan Arab Jamahiriya (rule of the masses) with Qaddafi as its philosopher-ideologue, guiding a decentralized populist government of revolutionary people's committees that control government offices, schools, the media and many corporations. Qaddafi's radical socialist redefinition of Islam and its cultural revolution have alienated landed and business sectors as well as traditional religious authorities (the ulema), who have condemned his radical reinterpretation of Islam and its socialist policies.

Egyptian politics of the 1970's offers a vivid picture of government and opposition uses of Islam. From the beginning of his presidency, Anwar Sadat appealed to Islam for legitimacy and popular support. Whereas Nasser had been the father of Arab nationalism, Sadat took the title "The Believer President." He lifted the constraints placed by Nasser on the Muslim Brotherhood, whose leaders were released from prison. Sadat's government supported Islamic student organizations in university elections both to neutralize the influence of Nasserist and leftist forces and to enhance his rule. The use of Islam was extended to the Egyptian–Israeli October War of 1973. It was the Ramadan War; its battle cry (Allahu Akbar, God is Most Great) was the traditional Islamic battle cry; its code name was Badr, the first major victory of Mohammed. The relative success of Egyptian forces (combined with the effectiveness of the Arab oil embargo) was a source of immense pride in the Muslim world.

By the mid-1970's, Sadat's use of Islam was beginning to backfire. State support for Islamic revivalism resulted in mounting criticism of the regime by the Muslim Brotherhood and Islamic student organizations. Sadat's initiatives, like the Camp David accords, support for the Shah of Iran, and changes in Muslim family laws, brought criticism not only from moderate Islamic groups but from a new crop of radical organizations. The radicals rejected the "Islamic legitimacy" of a government that appealed to Islam but did not reinstitute an Islamic state based on Islamic law. Many radical groups were led by former Muslim Brothers whose prison experience or life underground had convinced them that a more radical revolutionary course was necessary. They viewed most Middle East regimes as anti-Islamic governments who either repressed Islamic movements or coopted religion through control of the religious establishment.

Radical Islamic organizations like the Islamic Liberation Organization (Mohammed's Youth) and Takfir wal Hijra (Excommunication and Emigration) attempted a coup d'etat in 1974 and kidnapped and executed a former government minister in 1977. Despite government crackdowns and executions, groups like the Army of God (Jund Allah) and the Holy War Society (Jamaat al-Jihad) mushroomed underground. Members of the latter group finally assassinated Sadat in October, 1981.

In Egypt, the government's use of Islam thus served as a two-edged sword. As Islam became legitimate, it became the yardstick whereby the government was judged un-Islamic by its opposition.

PROTEST AND REVOLUTION IN IRAN AND LEBANON

A turning point in Iranian history and a singular event in contemporary Islamic politics took place in 1978–1979. A seemingly enlightened, entrenched monarch, an American ally, was overthrown by a popular revolution. The source of its leadership and ideology, Shia Islam, was particularly astonishing. The Shah and the Ayatollah Khomeini represented incongruous national alternatives. Postrevolutionary Iran influenced the emergence of Shia political activism in quiescent Shia minority communities in Sunni-dominated states like Saudi Arabia, the Gulf states and Pakistan. In Lebanon, Shia Islam has become a major political force; radical Shia groups have been blamed for attacks against American, French and Israeli personnel across the Middle East.

Shia Islam provides an ideological framework for protest and revolution. Although they share a common faith, Shia and Sunni Muslims follow different political ideologies. In contrast to the Sunni majority, the Shiites, who constitute about 15 percent of the world's Muslims, believe that Islamic history reveals that they are a disenfranchised minority. Unlike the Sunnis, who perceive a past characterized by success and power, the Shiites see themselves as oppressed and disinherited, prevented by Sunni governments from assuming their rightful place in Islam.

The pivotal issue that has divided Sunni and Shia is the leadership of the Islamic community. Sunni Muslims believe that Mohammed died without designating an heir and that his successor (caliph) can be selected or elected as head of state. The Shiites (the "party of Ali") believe that Mohammed designated Ali, his cousin and son-in-law, as the divinely inspired religiopolitical leader (Imam) and that leadership of the Islamic community belongs to his descendents, i.e., remains within the family of the prophet Mohammed. Despite this belief, the Shiites have lived under Sunni rule throughout most of Islamic history.

One event in particular, the martyrdom of Ali's son Hussein, embodies the Shia world view and has provided the ideological basis of contemporary Shia politics. In 680 A.D., the Imam Hussein challenged the leadership of the Sunni Caliph Yazid, who was regarded as a usurper. Hussein and his followers were vanquished by Yazid's army at Karbala in Iraq. The memory of this "martyrdom," including a willingness to sacrifice and die for God, constitutes the religious paradigm for Shia Muslims, and it is reenacted ritually in a moving drama each year. This "passion play" recounts the struggle of the small righteous party or army of God against Satan, the overwhelming force of evil. The battle of Karbala is the model for Shia Islam's sacred task, the age-long battle against tyranny and oppression that is to continue until the coming of the *mahdi*, a messianic leader, whose rule will usher in an age of righteousness and social justice.

Coupled with the 1973 Arab oil embargo, Iran's Islamic revolution of 1978–1979 seemed to many Muslims the clearest sign of a resurgent Islam. Many Muslims saw these two events as signs of the return of Islamic political and economic independence after a long period of subjugation to and dependence on Western interests. Yet many others were puzzled both by the fall of the Shah and by the manner in which it occurred. The White Revolution (the Shah's ambitious modernization program) had been swept aside by the Islamic revolution.

The promise of rapid modernization was apparently eclipsed by those who promised a retreat to the past. Discontent with the fast pace of modernization (Westernization) and the increasing autocracy of the Shah led to the development of an alliance of traditional religious leaders, merchants and lay intellectuals, both secular and Islamic. Members of this alliance shared common concerns about political participation and freedom, military and economic dependence on the United States, and the progressive Westernization of Iranian education and society. The preservation of Irano–Islamic culture and the fear of losing national identity and autonomy became common rallying points.

Shia Islam emerged as the most viable vehicle for mass mobilization against a regime whose authoritarian suppression turned reformers into revolutionaries. It provided a common set of symbols, a historic identity and a value system that was non-Western, indigenous, and broadly appealing. Moreover, Shia Islam possessed an ideological framework of protest and opposition to social injustice within which a variety of political and religious factions could function. The religious establishment was relatively independent and, unlike the ulema in Sunni countries, it possessed a hierarchical organization with charismatic ayatollahs, a number of whom (the Ayatollahs Khomeini, Mohammed Taleqani and Kazem Shariatmadari) had suffered because of their opposition to the Shah's government. Moreover, lay reformers like Ali Shariati and Mehdi Bazargan enjoyed respect, especially the respect of an increasingly alienated and militant younger generation. Finally, the mullah (the local religious leaders)–mosque system proved to be a natural, informal, nationwide communications network.

A coalition of heterogeneous groups spanning Iran's political spectrum, from liberal democrats to Marxists, from secularists to conservatives and Islamic modernists, joined under the banner of Islam. While they shared a unity of purpose—opposition to the Shah and a desire for a more indigenously rooted modernity—their religious and political positions and agenda were diverse. The sharp differences among the revolutionary factions came to a head after the fall of the Shah. Few Iranians anticipated a clerically dominated state guided by the Ayatollah Khomeini.

Today, the clergy control the Islamic Republic party and many key government positions. Under Khomeini's doctrine of governance of the jurist (velayat-e-faqih), the Islamic Republic of Iran is guided by Islamic law as interpreted by its supreme leader or jurist. Islamic government has been implemented as much by punitive restrictions as by inspiration. All opposition—monarchists, Marxists, liberal constitutionalists—has been silenced in the name of the state's Islamic ideology. The clergy, like Ayatollah Shariatmadari, and early supporters of Khomeini, like Iran's first postrevolutionary President, its Prime Minister and its foreign minister, have fled the country, have resigned or have been executed. Press and media censorship are enforced, restrictions on women's dress and employment have been introduced—all in the name of Islam.

LEBANON

Lebanon offers the second major example of militant Shia politics. Since the late 1970's, organizations like Amal and Hezbullah have mobilized Shia Muslims in protest and revolutionary movements. As a result, a religiopolitical community, long a distant third in political and economic power in a confessional state dominated by Maronite Christians and Sunni Muslims, has become a formidable force.

In the mid-1970's, Shia Islam, whose followers were predominantly rural, poor and disorganized, spawned its first protest movement. The "Movement for the Dispossessed" evolved into "The Battalions of the Resistance," whose acronym is Amal, "Hope." Amal was originally organized by Imam Musa Sadr, an Iranian-born and Iranian-educated leader of Lebanon's Shia community, to defend the rights of a people who had over the years become Lebanon's largest confessional group. It attracted upwardly mobile professionals, businessmen and clergy. Iran's revolution and the Israeli invasions of 1978 and 1982 with Israel's subsequent occupation and "Iron Fist" policy, contributed to the radicalization of Shia youth, in particular, and the consequent growth of Amal as well as more extremist groups like Hezbullah (Party of God) and the shadowy Islamic Jihad (Holy War).

Under Nabih Berri (Musa Sadr having disappeared mysteriously in Libya in 1978), Amal has asserted its leadership as a relatively moderate organization. Its goal is a pluralistic Lebanese state in which the Shiites enjoy their rightful proportional share of power. Amal's militias have battled with Israeli, Lebanese and PLO (Palestine Liberation Organization) forces. At the same time, Berri has been a force for moderation, mediating the release of American hostages and serving as a member of Lebanon's Cabinet.

In contrast to Amal, Hezbullah has close ties with Iran, is strongly influenced by Lebanese clerics like Sheik Mohammed Hussein Fadlallah, advocates the creation of an Islamic state, and is believed to be responsible for extremist actions like the bombing of the American Marine barracks in 1983. Finally, there is the Islamic Jihad, an organization that often takes credit for assassinations and suicide attacks, but about which little is known.

ISSUES AND PROBLEMS

Islamic governments and movements manifest a broad range of positions in their ideology, actors and policies. Islam has been used to legitimate monarchies (Saudi Arabia and Morocco), military regimes (Pakistan, Libya and Sudan), and a theocracy (Iran). These self-styled Islamic regimes span the ideological spectrum, from Libya's radical socialist "state of the masses" to the conservative monarchy of Saudi Arabia. Islamic actors display a similar diversity: clerical and lay, traditionalist and modernist, highly educated and illiterate, moderate and terrorist. Islamic organizations vary from the relatively moderate Muslim Brotherhoods of Egypt and the Sudan to the radical Egyptian al-Jihad and the Lebanese Hezbullah.

5. THE THIRD WORLD: The Middle East

The euphoria engendered by events in 1973 and reinforced by Iran's revolution has been challenged by recent realities. Oil revenue has decreased dramatically; Iran and Iraq are locked in a seemingly endless war; Lebanon has been shattered; and the Arab–Israeli conflict seems no closer to resolution. Islamic revivalism has often meant government manipulation of Islam to delay or control elections, ban or restrict political parties, impose press censorship, or suppress political and religious dissent. The vast majority of moderate Islamic activists have been overshadowed by a radical minority who assassinate, kidnap and bomb in the name of Islamic political and social justice.

The realities of current Muslim politics raise two questions: whose Islam? and what Islam?

Is the implementation of Islam the primary function of kings, military rulers and the clergy? Is it to be entrusted to elected Parliaments? Many Muslims today insist that greater political participation is required in a modern Islamic state that takes seriously the traditional notions of community consultation *(shura)* and consensus *(ijma)*. This expectation is common to most Muslims, whether they are Islamic or secular in orientation. It united factions in their revolt against the Shah and, more recently, was a basis for the MRD (Movement to Restore Democracy), which pressured Zia ul-Haq for elections in Pakistan. Government sensitivity to these concerns has led to parliamentary elections in Jordan and Kuwait and to a Saudi commission to consider the creation of a Parliament.

Will Islamic renewal be directed toward restoration or reconstruction? Islamic revivalists run the gamut from conservative traditionalists, who seek to restore past norms and values through the reimplementation of traditional Islamic laws, to modern reformers, who seek to reinterpret tradition, to reformulate Islam to meet the changing conditions of modern life.

Whatever its orientation, Islamic revivalism does not mean a rejection of technology. Technology has become part and parcel of Muslim life. Technology and science (mass communications, travel, education) are harnessed to spread Islam. The danger is not technology but the loss of identity and values. The issue is not television and education but the content of media programs and educational curricula. The target of revivalists is the uncritical imitation of the West that has led to the secularization of Muslim societies and the displacement of Islamic attitudes and values by foreign, Western values that affect political, social and family life. Fear of cultural assimilation or domination and the threat of political and military dependence on the superpowers make an explosive mix.

The anti-Americanism that has sometimes accompanied Islamic politics is not the product of an instinctive hatred of America, but a response to the threat to Muslim identity of American political and cultural domination. Iran and Lebanon provide two examples. For many Iranians, United States–Iran relations—from the CIA*-

*United States Central Intelligence Agency

coordinated return of the Shah from exile in 1953 and the CIA training of the Shah's secret police to the substantial American military and economic presence and support for the regime until its fall in 1979—provided proof that the United States was pro-Shah and anti-Islamic, i.e., opposed to Iranian self-determination. Similarly, in Lebanon the United States is viewed as part of the problem, rather than the solution. United States support for an unpopular Christian President and its close relations with Israel, even after Israel's invasion of Lebanon and its occupation of the south, have drawn the anger and firepower of Lebanese radicals. United States government installations have been bombed and American citizens, who had long been a welcome presence, are now victims of kidnapping and murder.

Attempts to Islamize Muslim states and societies have raised many important issues, including the nature of Islamic government, the scope of Islamic law, the feasibility of introducing traditional social welfare taxes and Islamic interest-free banking, the status of minorities and women, and the expression of political and religious dissent. If Muslims are to modernize without simply Westernizing, then they will have to formulate appropriate models for political, social and legal change. Since there are no ready-made answers, the process of formulation and implementation will include experimentation and exploitation by established governments and opposition groups alike, as each seeks to control and lead. Thus wherever Islam is part of public life, tension and conflicts can be expected in the struggle for ideological supremacy and power.

Yet several important points must be remembered. The process of modernization in the West extended over several centuries. The establishment of modern states, the creation of a sense of national identity and political legitimacy and the development of appropriate economic and social institutions took time and experimentation. The process was accompanied by heated debates, riots, revolutions (American, French and Russian). The accommodation of religion and science and the resolution of issues of modernization (the family, women's role in society, the rights of minorities) have remained a challenge to modern Judeo–Christian communities. Issues of political and cultural identity and religious values, as well as the pace and impact of modernization, remain important concerns in the West today, inspiring a variety of reform and revivalist movements: Christian and Jewish revivalism in the United States, liberation theology and Christian-based communities in Central America.

The political and economic realities of the post-World War II independence period (the Arab–Israeli conflict, poverty, illiteracy) have hampered the process of self-determination in the Muslim nation of the Middle East. Until political and educational reforms permit a more consensual approach to indigenously rooted national political systems, Middle East governments, like current Middle East politics, will remain fragile, precarious and potentially volatile.

170

[1]For detailed studies on Islam's role in Middle East politics, see John L. Esposito, *Islam and Politics* (Syracuse: Syracuse University Press, 1984); Edward Mortimer, *Faith and Power: The Politics of Islam* (New York: Random House, 1982); Ali E. Hilal Dessouki, ed., *Islamic Resurgence in the Arab World* (New York: Praeger, 1982).

[2]See, for example, Khurshid Ahmad, "The Nature of the Islamic Resurgence," in John L. Esposito, ed., *Voices of Resurgent Islam* (New York: Oxford University Press, 1983); Mustafa Mahmud, "Islam vs. Marxism and Capitalism," in John J.

Donohue and John L. Esposito, eds., *Islam in Transition: Muslim Perspectives* (New York: Oxford University Press, 1982).

[3]See James P. Piscatori, ed., *Islam in the Political Process* (Cambridge: Cambridge University Press, 1983), pp. 155–159; John O. Voll, *Islam: Continuity and Change in the Modern World* (Boulder: Westview, 1982); John L. Esposito, ed., *Islam and Development: Religion and Sociopolitical Change* (Syracuse: Syracuse University Press, 1980) and Robin Wright, *Sacred Rage* (New York: Simon and Schuster, 1985).

The Middle East Peace Process and the U.S.

"If [the U.S.] should opt out of the peace process, those who believe in the role of force and in absolute solutions will take our place."

Richard W. Murphy

Mr. Murphy is Assistant Secretary of State for Near-Eastern and South Asian Affairs.

WHY is the U.S. so actively involved in seeking a solution to the Arab-Israeli dispute and the Palestinian issue since there is neither a crisis in the region nor any agreement on even the outlines of a possible settlement?

The Middle East peace process has ebbed and flowed. It gained momentum in the late 1970's and produced the first great step toward Arab-Israeli accommodation— the Egypt-Israel peace treaty and the Camp David Accords. However, the bright promise of a broader peace and a solution of the Palestinian issue which we hoped would flow from Camp David was denied. It gave way to retrenchment, stagnation, and the tragic war in Lebanon. Now, there is new momentum toward peace. Israel and Jordan have again begun to search for ways to break the stalemate.

In Israel, the unity government has withdrawn Israeli troops from Lebanon and launched a program of economic reform, its first two priorities. Israel's leaders are wrestling again with the controversial questions of peace with the Arabs and the future of the 1,400,000 Palestinians who live under Israeli occupation. Prime Minister Shimon Peres has made clear his desire to lead Israel into direct negotiations with Jordan based on UN Security Council Resolutions 242 and 338 in search of lasting peace and a just solution to the Palestinian problem.

Jordan's King Hussein, recognizing the futility of confrontation and concerned about the stability of the region and the unfulfilled aspirations of the Palestinians, has boldly called for peace with Israel and a solution to the Palestinian issue. In statements which break new ground in the Arab world, Hussein has called for negotiations with Israel "promptly and directly" . . . "in an environment free of belligerent and hostile acts." The King's initiative is all the more remarkable, since he is ready to engage in a negotiating process with no guaranteed outcome whereas, for years, Arab states have refused to consider negotiations with Israel without assurances of the final result.

Prime Minister Peres has responded to the King's initiative by acknowledging Hussein's sincerity and his genuine desire for peace, and the King has replied by calling Peres a man of vision. Such expressions of mutual respect by an Israeli prime minister and an Arab leader both constitute a remarkable public dialogue and symbolize a new atmosphere of hope and compromise. Jordan has taken a further step in signalling its commitment to peace with Israel by restoring diplomatic relations with Egypt. By breaking with the rejectionists who sought to isolate Egypt for making peace with Israel, Jordan is associating itself with Egypt's courageous decision to lead the way toward a broader peace in the region

Pres. Hosni Mubarak of Egypt shares Hussein and Peres' concerns for future stability in the region. He, too, has supported renewed momentum in the peace process and has played a constructive role in support of practical steps toward direct negotiations. Although there have been strains in the Egypt-Israel relationship, both states are committed to their peace treaty. In the Egyptian approach, there is a healthy element of self-interest, since Egypt seeks a broadening of the peace process to vindicate its historic choice for peace with Israel.

The willingness of Jordan, Israel, and Egypt to renew the search for a broader peace has been mirrored by a similar

Bill Fitz-Patrick/The White House

Pres. Reagan with King Hussein of Jordan at the White House, Feb. 13, 1984.

movement within some moderate elements of the Palestinian community in support of peace and accommodation with Israel. These are important changes in the political landscape of the Middle East. The desire of King Hussein to engage in negotiations with Israel; his focus on the process, rather than the outcome; the positive response from Israel; and the support of Egypt and moderate Palestinian elements offer new hope that a solution can be found.

Obstacles

Although the climate for peace has improved markedly, some major obstacles still stand in the way of direct negotiations. The toughest of all is the question of who shall represent the Palestinians in negotiations. Both Israel and Jordan agree that Palestinians must participate in the process that will address their legitimate rights as a people as well as the security of Israel and Jordan. Both states also acknowledge that the Palestinians who take part must be respected, credible representatives of their community, since they will be called on to make compromises that must be part of any realistic settlement.

Thus far, there is no agreement on who

those Palestinians should be. The PLO demands the exclusive right to represent the Palestinians, and King Hussein has associated Jordan with the PLO in his Feb. 11, 1985, peace initiative. Many Palestinians who support the PLO are prepared to accept the terms which Israel, Jordan, and the U.S. believe should be the basis for negotiations—acceptance of the existence of Israel and UN Security Council Resolutions 242 and 338. However, the PLO, as an organization, has yet to transcend its internal divisions and to meet these conditions clearly and unequivocally, nor has it been willing to forswear all violence as a means of achieving its ends. Constituent elements of the PLO have been involved in new acts of terror and assassination, including the murder of three Israelis in Cyprus, the hijacking of the *Achille Lauro* and the killing of Leon Klinghoffer, and the attacks on the airports and the murder of travellers in Rome and Vienna.

Recently, PLO chairman Yasir Arafat made a qualified statement (the "Cairo Declaration") concerning an end to violence. The meaning and effect of this limited undertaking will have to be judged by the situation on the ground. Still, it must be understood that all violence everywhere in connection with the Middle East con-

flict obstructs the goal of direct negotiations for peace and must be eradicated.

King Hussein has joined Prime Minister Peres in deploring these and other acts of terror and violence as harmful to the peace process. He has also worked hard and successfully to prevent the use of Jordanian soil for terrorist attacks against Israel and the West Bank. Israel believes that the PLO is disqualified for a role in the peace process because of its failure to renounce all violence and to recognize Israel. Hussein, however, continues to believe that the PLO must be involved, as the only organization with broad-based support throughout the Palestinian community. He believes that the PLO has the capacity to transform itself, if given the opportunity.

The view of the U.S. toward the Palestinian representation issue is that Palestinians of goodwill who seek peace and accommodation with Israel and who command respect in their community should come forward to play this role. We also believe that those who continue to practice violence and terror count themselves out of the process. However, the ultimate decision on which Palestinians are acceptable must be agreed on by the Palestinians, Jordanians, and Israelis, among themselves.

The Reagan Administration's policy toward U.S. recognition of the PLO is another issue. We have said clearly and consistently that the PLO must first accept Resolutions 242 and 338 and recognize Israel's right to exist before we will engage it in a dialogue. Meanwhile, the relationship between the U.S. and the PLO is not a central issue in the peace process. The Palestinians must negotiate with Israel, together with Jordan, not with the U.S. They must produce representatives who have demonstrated their willingness to seek peace with Israel. The PLO, as an organization, has not yet met this challenge, which was put to it more than a year ago by King Hussein.

Another question that must be resolved in the search for peace is how to structure some kind of international support for direct negotiations. King Hussein, whose peace initiative faces harsh opposition from Syria and other rejectionists, has called for an international conference to provide an umbrella he needs for entering into negotiations with Israel. We understand the King's need, and have agreed to explore with Israel and Jordan the question of modalities for an internatonal conference which would lead to direct negotiations. Prime Minister Peres has also responded positively to the King's desire by offering to consider some international mechanism acceptable to all the parties to support direct talks. The sticking point has been the role of the Soviet Union. Our view and Israel's is that the U.S.S.R., by its failure to restore diplomatic relations with Israel and its negative policies, has failed to demonstrate that it would play a constructive role in the peace process. Another question is the role of Syria, which has shown no interest, to date, in joining the peace process.

Where are we now in our efforts to surmount these hurdles and move on to direct negotiations, which the U.S., Israel, and Jordan all desire? What has been the impact of recent acts of terrorism on our efforts? It is true that the *Achille Lauro* hijacking and subsequent terrorist incidents diverted our attention, temporarily, from the peace process. Indeed, it is the aim of the terrorists whose goal is to intimidate all those who seek compromise. Thus, both Israel and Jordan have been victimized by increasing terrorist acts in recent months. We are determined, however, not to allow terrorism to halt our efforts for peace, and Israel and Jordan share our determination.

In their separate visits to Washington in 1985, King Hussein and Prime Minister Peres urged that we do everything possible to sustain the positive momentum of recent months, and both leaders expressed their urgent desire for this in their eloquent statements at the UN. We are maintaining our close dialogue with Israel and Jordan and continuing to search for ways to resolve the issues of Palestinian representation and international auspices.

Some critics of U.S. policy have argued that we have underestimated the difficulty of these obstacles. They claim that, in our search for a process of negotiations, we have underestimated profound substantive differences which still divide the parties and the absence of any consensus within Israel, as well as among the Palestinians and among the Arabs, on an acceptable solution. According to this view, the parties have shown they can at least cope with the *status quo*, although it is unsatisfactory, and that it is a mistake to try to change it for some uncertain alternative. In short, they argue, in the absence of a serious crisis, leave well enough alone.

The costs of inaction

However, the *status quo* is not stable. The Middle East is a dynamic region in which the forces of pragmatism and compromise contend with extremism, confrontation, and religious fundamentalism. The Arab-Israeli conflict provides a volatile focus for these conflicting forces within Israel, among the Palestinians, and in the Arab world. These tensions are serious. The history of other conflicts proves that they will not evaporate under benign neglect. Unless the elements who support moderation and compromise are actively supported and encouraged, the future is likely to bring greater strife and danger for all.

The costs of inaction are high for Israel, whose future security and well-being can be assured in the long run only if peace is achieved and the Palestinian dilemma is resolved. The human and material cost which years of conflict have imposed on Israel has been immense. It is a great tragedy of the modern era that a nation which was born as a symbol of the highest values of peace and redemption—not only for the Jewish people, but for mankind—has been deprived of the right to realize this dream. The threat of yet another war, the uncertainty and tension of the current uneasy situation, and the strain imposed by control of a large, resentful Palestinian populace in the West Bank and Gaza are a great burden to Israel's social and democratic fabric. That is why Prime Minister Peres and many other Israelis have expressed the urgent need for a just solution to the Palestinian dilemma and peace with all its Arab neighbors to insure Israel's security.

The need for peace and accommodation is no less urgent for the Palestinians. Their desire for justice and a greater role in fulfilling their own aspirations also demands a response. This community, particularly its younger generation, is also challenged by the forces of extremism and fundamentalism, which feed on frustration and despair.

For Jordan, like Israel, peace and a resolution of the Palestinian issue are essential for future well-being. That is why King Hussein, whose nation already includes a majority of Palestinians, wants urgently to define a new relationship with the Palestinians now living under Israeli control.

The stakes are high for Israel, the Palestinians, and Jordan to come to terms with each other and to reconcile their respective interests and aspirations. If Israel is denied its right to permanent peace, security, and recognition, if the Palestinians are denied their legitimate rights, and if Jordan's quest for peace is thwarted, all will be victims.

We reject the theory that the interests of Israelis, Palestinians, and Jordanians in this conflict are irreconcilable and that this is a zero-sum game. We are certain that, with flexibility and a willingness to compromise, the urge for peace—which is strong in Israel, among the Palestinians, and in Jordan—can be translated into negotiations and ultimately agreement which provide justice and security for all.

Why do we say the U.S. also has an important stake in such a solution? Our deep interest in the security of Israel, an ally whose strength and welfare are vital to us; our friendship with Jordan and Egypt, whose continued moderation and stability and well-being are of key importance; and our traditional commitment to human values, which are threatened by adverse forces in the region, require us to commit ourselves as a nation.

Diplomacy abhors a vacuum. If we should opt out of the peace process, those who believe in the role of force and in absolute solutions will take our place. We have a duty to ourselves and our friends to continue our diplomatic efforts, notwithstanding the obstacles, in support of our friends who yearn for peace and believe in compromise and moderation. We must continue to encourage flexibility and accommodation by all the parties to a conflict in which there are no black-and-white answers and in which all the protagonists have compelling equities.

Whenever I visit Israel, I am encouraged by the vigor of debate over the peace process, Israel's future, and the Palestinian issue. The Jewish people, in Israel and throughout the world, because of their own experience, have a unique perspective on the suffering of others. I have always believed that their faith and tradition, to which the world owes so much, will help build peace between Israel and its Arab neighbors. Peace is also a holy creed of Islam and the Arab people, whose culture offers the spiritual and moral strength needed for peace and reconciliation. These two peoples, both descendents of the sons of Abraham, are destined, in the words of Prime Minister Peres, "to live side by side, from time immemorial, till the end of time." They deserve our continuing, active support in their search for peace.

The Superpowers in the Palestine Conflict

Helmut Hubel

HELMUT HUBEL is a research fellow at the German Council on Foreign Relations, Bonn. His dissertation is on northern European security and Soviet foreign policy. He is now working on Middle East and European security.

Introduction

THE conflict between the two mightiest states on earth is not only a result of rivalry for power. Both nuclear superpowers are also the leaders of two opposing systems of society, founded on totally different concepts of *Weltanschauung*, ideology, and economy. During the past twenty years the two blocs have lost their homogeneity (if they have ever been as unified as people sometimes assume); new, rather independent powers, for example, the People's Republic of China, have evolved. Nevertheless, the two superpowers still influence world politics decisively, and outside the context of American-Soviet competition the developments in various regions of crisis—Central America, Southern Africa, the Middle East, or elsewhere—cannot be sufficiently comprehended.

It would be analytically wrong and politically dangerous, however, to understand the major crises in the third world only as a consequence of a policy of one of the superpowers or their rivalry. The basic reasons for these crises are indigenous, although the way they are staged is often influenced by the East-West conflict. When analyzing these crises, one should not forget that in most cases no clear demarcations of spheres of influence exist. Also many of the countries concerned do not wish to be part of the Eastern or of the Western world. Weak internal structures and regional conflicts were often used as an opportunity and a pretext for the great powers in history to gain presence and exert their influence. This situation has remained unchanged. Regional crises often intensified the superpowers' rivalry and sometimes decisively influenced their general relationship.

As far as the Palestine conflict[1] is concerned, only since the Six Day War of 1967 have both superpowers become fully engaged, the United States on the side of Israel, the Soviet Union on the side of the Arab states. Providing modern military equipment, economic help, and diplomatic support did not ensure, however, that either superpower could significantly influence its respective partner's behavior. On the contrary, in most cases the regional parties skillfully used their patron's backing to pursue their own goals. The United States gained substantial and partially decisive influence on the developments only during the war of 1973. Afterwards, in peace diplomacy, Washington became dependent again on the regional leaders and was not able to impose solutions.

This may explain, as far as external influence is concerned, why the conflict over Palestine has remained unsolved in its very essence. Despite Egypt's peace with Israel, the question remains, Who shall rule in former Palestine? Israel, the winner of three major wars, has now been in control of all the land west of the Jordan for eighteen years. The Kingdom of Jordan would like to be rid of the Palestinian problem, as too would Israel. Without cooperation of the Palestinians in the occupied territories and the consent of Arafat's PLO, however, King Hussein will not be able to make peace with Israel. Moreover, he is still dependent on the support, or at least the toleration, of the Arab world.

Since 1984 some new developments in the Palestine conflict have taken place that seem to have opened up new opportunities for a political solution. Despite all these diplomatic activities, which will be discussed later in detail, the essential question remains whether there is still anything at all to negotiate. Time has not stood still, and new realities have come into existence —not only in the occupied territories but also in the minds of many people in Israel and elsewhere. Interestingly enough, discussions in Israel and the United States on this problem have concentrated on whether there is still time left for a political compromise.[2]

Helmut Hubel, "The Superpowers in the Palestine Conflict," *AEI Foreign Policy and Defense Review*, Vol. 6, No. 1, 1986, pp. 34-43. Copyright 1986 American Enterprise Institute. Reprinted with permission.

5. THE THIRD WORLD: The Middle East

In my view there are very few indications that a comprehensive solution to this conflict is feasible under present circumstances:

- The majority of Israel's population, because of security considerations or convenience, is not prepared to give up considerable parts of the occupied territories. Moreover, any compromise over the Jerusalem question seems to be impossible.
- Although the Palestinian population in the occupied territories longs for a solution, the PLO is not prepared—and is perhaps unable—to show flexibility in principal matters.
- Never was the Arab world so weak and divided as today. Opportunities for a negotiated peace, which may seem to exist at present, could quickly fade away should the Iran-Iraq war come to an end. Without Khomeini's threat many Arab states might harden their resistance to Israel. A victorious Iran, in contrast, in combination with Syria could successfully initimidate those Arabs who prefer peace with Israel.

To summarize, as far as the regional parties are concerned, many arguments point to a continuation of the Palestine conflict without any clear solution. The question remains whether one or both superpowers could bring an end to this conflict. To answer this question, the pages that follow will first analyze the American and Soviet role and influence. Second, the recent developments in peace diplomacy will be discussed in detail: is there a chance that Washington unilaterally or together with Moscow could sponsor peace? Third, I will present the European and German outlook on these problems: what are the experiences and results of former European involvement in peace diplomacy?

The Role of the Superpowers in the Middle East

The Quest for Influence. Since the decline of the Ottoman Empire, the Middle East has been an area of opportunity for outside powers to gain presence and influence.[3] The region's military-strategic importance, the oil, various rivalries between Arab leaders, and finally the Jewish settlements in Palestine intensified competition between the great powers. After World War II and especially since the Suez crisis of 1956, when Great Britain and France had to retreat from their former positions, the United States has set about establishing itself as the predominant power.

With the intensifying conflict between East and West in Europe, the Middle East gradually became an additional arena of American-Soviet rivalry, as the crises in Turkey and Iran had already indicated in 1946–1947. Whereas Europe became divided with its Eastern part under Soviet control, no clear demarcation of stable spheres of influence was reached in the Middle East. Turkey, in NATO since 1952, and Israel after 1967 were the only lasting exceptions.

Although the Jewish state had been recognized immediately by the American government, it survived its first war with the Arabs only because Stalin decided to support Israel militarily in 1948. Since the early 1960s and especially after the Six Day War of 1967, Israel and the United States became tied together in a unique relationship. Because of the strong moral commitment of many Americans to the survival and security of Israel and the active Jewish community in the United States with its influence in policy making, this relationship has to be characterized today as a mutual dependency, despite Israel's urgent and growing need of American economic and military aid.

With minor exceptions the rest of the region remained what it had been for decades. It offered quickly changing circumstances with easy opportunities to gain new friends through arms deliveries, economic aid, and diplomatic support, but it also often posed insurmountable difficulties to keeping these partners as reliable friends. This is the lesson the United States had to learn with Libya and Iran, the Soviet Union with Egypt and to a considerable degree with Iraq as well.

Both superpowers considered the Middle East and the adjacent marine areas to be of such strategic importance that they sought footholds and a permanent presence that would deny the adversary special advantages. For several decades and surely until today the Soviet navy was no match for the leading sea power. Since the 1960s, however, the Red Fleet has managed to establish a certain presence in the Mediterranean, in the Red Sea, and in the Indian Ocean with some facilities on shore. Moreover, the United States regarded the Soviet Union's increased force projection capabilities from its homeland as dangerous enough to seek some counter-balance or at least a "tripwire" as a deterrent in the region.

Moscow, however, has always seen the American alliances with Turkey, Iran (under the shah's rule), and Pakistan as part of the "capitalistic encirclement" and sought to circumvent it by developing a close relationship with nationalistic Arab states. Anwar al-Sadat's reversal of alliances, though, deprived Moscow of its central base of influence. Since the mid-1970s the Soviet Union could therefore count on only minor partners (South Yemen) or rather unreliable ones (Iraq and Syria).

The other states in the region continued to pursue a policy that combined aspirations toward nonalignment with a certain security cooperation with Western partners. Whereas they preferred to buy sophisticated military equipment from the West and to enjoy a certain security umbrella provided by Western powers, most of them tried to prevent a close military relationship with foreign troops permanently based on their soil.

Several motives fueled the dynamics of American-Soviet rivalry for influence. For the Soviet Union it was primarily a military-strategic consideration toward a region that it has always tended to consider its own backyard. Reducing Western positions in this area would, of course, contribute to Soviet advantages in the global East-West competition. Given its rather weak share in world economy, economic or energy interests do not seem to have played a major role—despite the fact that for political reasons Moscow has always tried to develop economic links with its immediate neighbors. Despite its gradually declining oil production (which has been, up to now, largely compensated by increased energy production from gas and nuclear power), access to Middle Eastern oil fields does not seem to be a short-term factor in Soviet policy toward the Middle East. Moscow has been more interested in receiving Western petrodollars in exchange for its military equipment from partners in the Arab world (as in the case of Libya).

For the United States, especially after Great Britain had withdrawn from "east of Suez," influence in the Middle East was essential to secure both military and economic interests. Aware that most of its West European partners and Japan regarded the Middle East as vital for their economic stability, Washington was determined to preserve its position in southwest Asia, not only to contribute to the stabilization of the world economy (especially after two major oil crises), but also to preserve the Western alliance and to secure its leadership in the Western world.

The West Europeans and Japan, of course, welcome the containment of Soviet power. In the economic sphere, however, they remained rivals among each other and of the United States. All of them wanted to "recycle" the petrodollars by increased exports. In this economic competition some partners, France, for example, evidently pursued their own course farther and concluded bilateral agreements with partners in the region on both economic and military matters.

After the Soviet intervention in Afghanistan and its expulsion from Iran, the United States regarded cooperation with the conservative rulers of the Gulf as a strategic necessity. One should not neglect the economic side, however, as the AWACS deal and follow-up projects have shown. As a consequence, the old problem for Western powers in the Middle East became virulent again: to pursue its global strategic interests, the United States needed a close cooperation with important Arab states. This cooperation was hampered, however, by the strong American commitment to Israel's security, as long as only one Arab government recognized the Jewish state.

One has to speak, therefore, of a real dilemma of American policy in the Middle East: how to reconcile the strong commitment to Israel's security, which is a direct consequence of the internal policy process, with U.S. responsibilities as a global power and as the leader of the Western world. U.S. policy toward the Palestine conflict has always been to give Israel's security interests priority, even at the expense of other interests. Some French and other West European politicians have regarded this preference as a major deficiency, for which they have tried to compensate by developing their own policy toward the Palestine conflict (see the section on the European perspective).

American and Soviet Positions Today. At the beginning of this decade the problems of the Middle East seemed to coincide with the East-West conflict. Many observers in the West and East regarded these regional crises as powder kegs with a high risk of explosion. The United States considered the Soviet invasion in Afghanistan a threat to vital Western interests in the Persian Gulf, taking into consideration the Iranian revolution and the vulnerabilities of the Arab kingdoms and sheikdoms. The outbreak of the Iran-Iraq war, however, also demonstrated the limited possibilities for outsiders—including both superpowers—to influence developments decisively in this region of turmoil. The Soviet Union continued its entanglement in its undeclared war against Afghanistan and has not been able to profit from the American expulsion from Iran. On the contrary, the conservative Arab Gulf states, who mainly feared an Iranian export of revolution, strongly increased their cooperation in security matters among themselves and with the Western powers. Moreover, Washington undertook a set of military and diplomatic preparations to be able to respond with its own military power, if the conflicts should escalate. The members of NATO agreed that the United States should be supported in these efforts, as in the 1982 American-German agreement on wartime host support demonstrated, for example. (Bonn agreed to provide additional troops and facilities to support American reinforcements.)

In the early 1980s Washington managed to consolidate one important element of the Camp David agreements, the Egyptian-Israeli peace, by establishing a multinational force and observers (MFO) in the Sinai. The presence of Western peace-keeping forces was a clear symbol of the American and West European determination to engage in a peaceful settlement of the Palestine conflict. To those Arab states who rejected the Egyptian-Israeli peace and to the Soviet Union, the MFO meant a significant improvement of the American diplomatic and military position in that crucial area.

The Egyptian-Israeli peace treaty, however, solved only their bilateral problems and left the core of the Palestine conflict open. In this perspective, Israel's war in Lebanon (which had been essentially designed by the Israeli minister of defense at the time, Ariel Sharon) aimed to solve the Palestinian problem by destroying the PLO as a military and political power. With the Reagan initiative of September 1, 1982, the American administration seemed to have understood these implications of Israel's intervention. The Western powers' unfortunate entanglement in Beirut, however, shifted, almost totally, world attention to the Lebanese quagmire for the following year and a half. At that time Israel's government set out to sabotage any diplomatic solution of the Palestinian problem—and succeeded. After the retreat of the Western peace-keeping forces from Beirut, no impetus was left for any new American initiative.

The Soviet Union behaved very cautiously during the Israeli invasion and tried hard to prevent any confrontation with the United States in Lebanon. Moscow, however, deterred Israel from a direct attack against Syria (which the United States also sought to prevent), quickly reequipped the Syrian army, and significantly increased its air defense by manning the new SAM 5 sites with Soviet military personnel. This cautious but determined reaction was sufficient to consolidate Syrian intransigence and to prevent any American-European success in Lebanon. After the American government had deliberately ignored Syrian interests in the Golan Heights and had pressed the Lebanese government to sign a treaty with Israel, Syria's president Assad could easily take revenge.

In cautiously backing Syria and some Lebanese factions, the Soviet Union managed to "prove" to the Arabs that the Americans were not able to bring an end to the Lebanese crisis, as they had promised. Moscow, however, did not gain any substantial advantage from the American predicament beyond a modest improvement of relations with some Arab states, such as Egypt. Its political influence continued to be not more than a "denial capacity." Syria's President Assad

sought jealously to increase his own influence in Lebanon. The PLO, scattered over several Arab countries, became torn between Arafat's majority group and the Syrian-backed dissidents who wanted to destroy any movement toward a political solution. Arafat knew that he could survive politically only if he cooperated with Jordan and Egypt.

This placed the Soviet Union in a difficult position. First, it did not want to lose its stakes in Syria and in Lebanon. Second, it tried to preserve a unified Palestinian movement susceptible to Soviet tutelage. Third, the rivalries and hostilities among the Arabs made it difficult to reach the center of Arab politics and to break the American "monopoly" in the search for a solution to the Palestinian problem. Moreover, it remains a significant weakness of the Soviet position that Moscow entertains diplomatic relations neither with Saudi Arabia, the most important of the conservative Arab Gulf states, nor with Israel.

Therefore, many politicians and observers continued to believe that if anyone could induce both the Israelis and the Arabs to a compromise, it could only be the United States.

A New Chance for Progress toward Peace?

Recent Developments in Peace Diplomacy. For several years the Lebanese crisis has been linked in various ways to the Palestinian problem. Nevertheless, the developments since Israel's intervention absorbed international attention for several months. With Israel's unilateral retreat, Lebanon's continuing internal crisis moved into the background, and the major conflict was again on the scene of international diplomacy. After Menachem Begin left politics, a new Israeli government much less unified—at least on the question of the occupied territories—came into power. The most interesting developments, however, took place among two of Israel's Arab neighbors, which brought hope of renewed peace diplomacy.

King Hussein of Jordan was put into the front line of the Palestine conflict after President Reagan declared his preference for the "Jordanian option" in his initiative of September 1, 1982. On the one hand, Reagan alleviated Hussein's fears that the solution to the Palestine conflict could be sought in Jordan, as Israel's Minister Ariel Sharon, for example, had postulated. On the other hand, the king could not wait in retreat any longer until others took the initiative. Arafat, however, having physically survived both an Israeli and a Syrian-inspired siege in Lebanon, saw no other chance for his political survival as leader of the PLO than to cooperate more closely with Egypt and Jordan.

This paved the way for Hussein and Arafat's agreement of February 11, 1985, which contained, of course, only a minimum of common understanding, postponing the basic differences over an eventual solution. Whereas Jordan's king seemed to be preoccupied mainly with the possibility that the Palestinian problem might dangerously undermine the Hashemite rule, Arafat obviously struggled for political survival, hoping for better options in the future. Aware of Arafat's fragile position vis-à-vis Syria and the rebels within his own organization, Egypt and Jordan tried to involve the United States in the peace process again and to open up a direct American–PLO dialogue. They were cautious enough not to offend the Soviet Union, stressing the necessity of an international peace conference.

The American government, however, saw no reason not to abide by its commitment to Israel, refusing to negotiate with the PLO unless it recognized Israel's right to exist. Again Arafat explicitly rejected this condition. Some compromise formulas concerning an involvement of Palestinian representatives close to the PLO in a joint Palestinian-Jordanian delegation were discussed during the mission of Assistant Secretary of State Richard Murphy in April 1985. The subsequent visit of Secretary of State George Shultz, however, did not produce any visible results. The American government, of course, was very well aware that Israel was not prepared to respond to a major initiative. Lacking a clear majority in parliament, Israel's Prime Minister Peres was still preoccupied with his army's retreat from Lebanon and with his country's grave economic crisis. He preferred not to expose himself to an additional battle that promised to become the toughest in the history of Israel.

Both superpowers, besides continuing the dialogue with their respective partners in the region, again took up talks over the Palestine conflict and other problems of the Middle East. A similar exchange of views, although less formal, had been already undertaken earlier during critical phases of the Iran-Iraq war. In his UN speech of September 24, 1984, President Reagan, among other things, proposed talks between the superpowers on regional conflicts. After his reelection such talks on Middle Eastern problems took place in Vienna on February 19 and 20, 1985. We do not know whether this meeting between Richard Murphy and Vladimir Polyakov contained more than a formal exchange of views. In any case, more than a resumption of the dialogue that had broken down in 1977 could not be expected. There is also little evidence that the Geneva summit meeting of November 1985 contained more than a brief exchange of views on the Palestine conflict.

The Superpowers between Competition and Partial Cooperation. As long as the East-West conflict continues to dominate world politics—and there are no indications to assume otherwise in the foreseeable future—no general conciliation between the two leading powers seems feasible. The only realistic prospect is that both superpowers together with their allies seek a *modus vivendi* on clearly defined issues, knowing that this will not change their principal differences. Such an understanding was reached in Europe in the early 1970s.

Détente in Europe was possible only because both superpowers were aiming at a more stable bilateral relationship at that time. The American-Soviet summit meetings of those years dealt mainly with the core of their bilateral relationship: the strategic arms issue. In combination with the SALT I and the ABM treaties, Washington and Moscow addressed a wider range of problems and also reached some understanding on "rules of behavior" in third world areas, at least as the Americans then believed.

Soon, however, the war of October 1973 highlighted the continuing rivalry between both powers. Later the events in Angola, Ethiopia, and finally in Afghanistan destroyed any hopes of a lasting "code of conduct" between the two leading powers vis-à-vis third world issues, which at least some people in the West had entertained. Despite all rivalries, however, one common interest was still valid: neither Washington nor Moscow wanted to be dragged by another party into a confrontation that might lead to a dangerous escalation of hostilities. As far as the Middle East was concerned, this interest prevailed during the last crises, such as in Lebanon in 1982 or the Iran-Iraq war. This was not, however, more than a mostly tacit understanding.

For several reasons a lasting agreement on third world problems did not materialize:

• The American-Soviet relationship was never stable enough to allow a longer-term concerted policy.
• Washington and Moscow largely regarded unforeseeable developments in the third world as provoked by or advantageous to each other.
• The Soviet Union, although not intending to create revolutions, never recognized any "status quo" and sought to minimize Western influence by increasing its own political and, in some cases, military presence.

Regarding the Palestine conflict, two major efforts were undertaken in the 1970s to coordinate American and Soviet policy. The first, in December 1973, was the Geneva conference to reach a comprehensive settlement of the conflict. As Henry Kissinger has described in detail, the decision makers in Washington did not believe in the feasibility of this approach and instead worked successfully at excluding the Soviet Union from the peace process.[4] For Moscow the Geneva conference was, of course, the opportunity to effect what has always been the principal goal of Soviet policy: to be recognized as an equal power in all aspects of world affairs.

The second approach for a concerted policy was the Vance-Gromyko declaration of October 1, 1977, which alluded to the Geneva project. It had no chance to materialize because of the total inefficiency of the Carter administration's preparations. Sadat, however, felt compelled to take the initiative and to go to Jerusalem and pave the way for an agreement with Israel. The early Carter administration's inconsistent strategy hampered its relationship both with Moscow and with its partners in the Middle East. The Egyptian leader as well as the Israelis became suspicious of a "superpower *diktat*." The Soviet leadership found its chronic mistrust only confirmed: Washington was not "sincere" and was obviously unreliable, revealing itself unable to pursue a steady foreign policy.

Certain lessons can be drawn from the experience of the past decade:

• Any American-Soviet common understanding of Middle Eastern problems (as well as of other third world issues) is feasible only if both powers are cooperating generally and negotiating on central political issues, especially strategic arms. Success can be expected only if such an understanding is part of a longer-range strategy that includes all relevant aspects of American-Soviet relations.

• Because the superpowers' relationship obviously oscillates between cooperation and tension, there is little prospect for a basic and lasting agreement on problems in a volatile region with such a quickly changing environment as the Middle East.

• The question remains open whether, despite all problems, a rather limited American-Soviet cooperation is possible.

On this last point, there are at least a few indications of common or parallel interest. First, both superpowers agreed to the UN partition plan for Palestine in 1947, recognized the state of Israel, and have defended its right to exist. Second, both consider the Palestine conflict extremely dangerous, with the potential for leading to a worldwide conflict. Measures to reduce the danger of escalation could help defuse the situation. Third, in the experience of both superpowers, their respective partners have quite often managed to use their protection for their own interests, interests that were not shared by their patrons. In the same way that the Soviet leadership might regard it useful to minimize certain dependencies on Syria by expanding ties with Israel and the United States, Washington could broaden its maneuvering room by pursuing a dialogue with the Soviet Union and Syria. Fourth, the Jews living in the United States and in the Soviet Union create links to the state of Israel. In the 1970s when the prospect of an American-Soviet understanding existed (including one on the Middle East), an exceptionally high number of Jews were allowed to emigrate from the Soviet Union. It may well be that the Israeli as well as the American government wishes to replicate that pattern. The price would undoubtedly be to allow Moscow to participate in the peace process.

To be realistic, we find no indications in the foreseeable future of a major breakthrough in American-Soviet relations in general that might in turn reinforce tendencies for a partial cooperation in the Middle East. Today we still have to wait and observe how the superpower relationship actually develops and whether the further evolution of the Palestine conflict really offers new opportunities.

The European Perspective

The Venice Declaration and Its Results. The Venice Declaration of 1980 was the peak of an independent European outlook toward the Palestine conflict. In this declaration the Europeans called for a comprehensive settlement of the conflict that would safeguard the security of all states in the region, including Israel, but that dealt with the Palestinian problem, incorporating the PLO in future negotiations. The Europeans also declared their readiness to engage in a settlement providing concrete guarantees. The declaration was presented as a supplement to the Camp David agreements, which had hitherto failed to reach a comprehensive solution of the conflict.[5]

Although the members of the EC had already developed this attitude during the 1970s, the timing of their declaration was remarkable. The new tensions between the two superpowers, which had accumulated after the Soviet invasion of Afghanistan, threatened to endanger a significant European interest in the continuation of détente, which Europeans still regarded as a major achievement. Now a new confrontation between East and West loomed in the Middle East, in an area where European security was also at stake.

The Europeans had already learned from the Arab-Israeli conflicts of 1967 and 1973 that their military security was immediately affected when the superpowers confronted each other in that area. During the October war of 1973 they tried to resort to neutrality, although they were aware that the supply lines between the United States and Israel crossed Western Europe. Arab efforts to forge an "oil weapon" to press the Europeans to adopt a pro-Arab policy toward the Arab-Israeli conflict reaffirmed the Europeans' search for—as they saw it—a "more balanced" position.

After the Iranian and Afghan crises the West European leaders were told during their visits to the Gulf that the kingdoms and sheikdoms today constituting the Gulf Cooperation Council also preferred to stay out of the superpowers' rivalry and hoped for a mediating role of the West Europeans. Feeling threatened by the repercussions of the Palestine conflict, they urged the major West European countries to work toward a settlement with the participation of the PLO. Having prevented, with the help of Saudi Arabia, major economic difficulties during the second oil crisis, the Europeans saw their own political ambitions regarding the Palestine conflict reinforced.

It was this combination of factors that convinced the European leaders—French President Giscard d'Estaing, British Foreign Minister Lord Carrington and his prime minister, and West German Chancellor Helmut Schmidt—of the necessity of taking the initiative within the European Political Cooperation. They came to realize, however, that their ambitions were regarded with mistrust, particularly from the Israeli and American governments. The Arabs also, although welcoming this initiative, did not show any further readiness for a compromise with Israel. The Europeans very soon recognized that they could not produce a breakthrough toward a comprehensive solution.

Moreover, a new American president who set about creating a renewed American leadership in world affairs brought the Europeans back in line with his own peace diplomacy. The test case was the Sinai peacekeeping force that had been envisaged in the Camp David agreements. With the participation of four West European countries the European Community actually engaged in consolidating a peace treaty that some of its members had criticized before for not being comprehensive and that was rejected by Egypt's partners in the Arab world.

In Western Europe the major proponents of a more independent outlook had left office. The new French president, Mitterrand, in particular tilted his country's Middle Eastern policy toward Israel, at least initially bringing him closer to the United States. Mitterrand cooperated with Washington not only in the case of the Sinai MFO but also during the Lebanese crisis. Israel's intervention demonstrated the weakness of the Arab world, which had rarely shown itself so split and indecisive. (Only Syria as the immediate neighbor reacted strongly, but this created, except in the case of France, no major problems for the Europeans.) Absorbed to a considerable degree with the continuing Iran-Iraq war and confronted with a glut on the oil market, the Arabs did not even seriously contemplate resorting to the "oil weapon" again. (Some West Europeans had, of course, already started to diminish their oil dependence on the Arab world considerably, and the Western world had agreed within the International Energy Agency on safeguards against energy bottlenecks.)

During the Lebanese crisis only the French (and Greeks) tried again to keep a distinct role in the Palestine conflict by cooperating with the PLO, the rest of the EC preferring a low profile. Moreover, President Reagan's initiative of September 1, 1982, was supported in Europe because it seemed to show the only realistic way toward a comprehensive settlement of the Palestine conflict. Because of the continuing Gulf war, the West Europeans chose to cooperate closely with Washington. As a consequence, no spectacular new initiative in the Palestine question seemed to be appropriate. Finally Europe became preoccupied again with its own security problems during the debate over intermediate nuclear forces.

For historical reasons the Federal Republic of Germany is one of the most outspoken advocates for Israel's right of existence and security. Chancellor Adenauer already understood the close American-Israeli relationship and its importance for Bonn. Later governments, especially the Social Democratic-liberal ones, therefore, only very cautiously moved toward a more balanced approach vis-à-vis the Palestine conflict. In fact, in 1973 the West German ambassador to the UN was one of the first Europeans to speak about the right of self-determination for all peoples, including the Palestinians. This statement, however, reflected more the particular situation of divided Germany than any specific ideas for a political solution of the Palestine conflict.[6]

Together with elements of the traditional French ambition to play a distinctive role in the Middle East, the point of Palestinian self-determination became part of the EC's Venice Declaration. Nevertheless, the government of the Federal Republic continued to respect Israel's sensitivity and did not press its views on the Palestinian question, contrary to the French or even Austrian leaders. Some differences between Chancellor Schmidt and Prime Minister Begin were more personal, although these differences also reflected an Israeli uneasiness about German efforts to circumvent their "special responsibility," as they saw it, toward the Jewish state. The Federal Republic had actually increased its cooperation with partners in the Arab world considerably, which also fit in with German economic interests in the Middle East.

Furthermore, the visits of Chancellor Kohl to Amman, Cairo, and Jerusalem demonstrated the German willingness to pursue a balanced approach toward Israel and its Arab neighbors who wished to live in peace with the Jewish state. Toward the PLO Bonn continued its restraint.

The Arabs as well as the Israelis regarded the question of the sale of the Leopard II tank as the major test of West Germany's future policy in the Middle East. With Chancellor Kohl's statement that this highly sophisticated weapon would not be for sale to Saudi Arabia, Bonn has avoided a major change in its traditional reserved policy.[7] If other official weapons sales take place, which are still under discussion, this would indicate an increased role of the Federal Republic of Germany in the Middle East, with possible new commitments in the Palestine conflict.

A Future Role for Europe in a Peace Process? As sketched above, the early 1980s have demonstrated the rather limited possibilities for the West Europeans to go significantly beyond American peace diplomacy and to act as a real supplement. The limits of West European maneuverability are evident because, as long as they themselves are so dependent on the American security umbrella, most of these countries cannot afford to pursue a course clearly distinct from American Middle Eastern policy.

Only France has considered it opportune to distance itself explicitly from Washington's policy, at least occasionally. Except for some advantages in bilateral relations with Arab partners, this independence did not provide Paris with enough options to create a breakthrough in peace diplomacy. President Mitterrand also had to recognize that the Egyptian president saw the key to progress not in Paris, but in Washington.

As a matter of fact, what the West Europeans can do is to try to influence American policy through close cooperation. This has been the lesson for East-West relations in general; from a West German perspective this is also valid for problems of the Middle East. Beyond that they can, in cooperating with partners in

the region, support tendencies toward peaceful solutions. Nevertheless, the key to progress remains with the parties directly involved.

As for the Soviet Union's role in the Middle East, the West Europeans have not been able or did not want to make up their minds how to deal effectively with this problem. In principle, they agree with the American view that Soviet power and influence should be contained. The question always has remained how to achieve this goal. One should not forget, for example, that de Gaulle's tilt toward the Arab world in 1967 was strongly motivated by his concern that the Soviet Union might otherwise increase its influence there considerably. Since then the French tendency has often been to deprive the Soviet Union of opportunities by indirect means.

Europeans still wonder whether it might one day be possible to include the Soviet Union constructively in a permanent solution to the Palestine conflict. From the European perspective it might be better to try to include the Soviets than to create new perils unintentionally by explicitly excluding them.

Options for the Future

When thinking about the superpowers' relationship in the Middle East, one cannot ignore the fact that a remarkable asymmetry exists between the American and Soviet involvement. Although the Soviet Union is geographically much closer to the region and regards it as its backyard, its presence is quite restricted. Lacking strong economic and cultural relations, it is "only" a military superpower. Moreover, the Soviet Union does not even have comprehensive diplomatic access to the region. After expulsion from Egypt, it retained mainly partners from the radical left in the Arab world. Lacking diplomatic relations with the conservative Gulf states (with the exception of Kuwait), Moscow still has difficulties in reaching and influencing that center in Arab politics that has evolved around Egypt, Jordan, and Saudi Arabia.

As far as the Palestine conflict is concerned, the Soviet Union's options are still essentially restricted by its lack of official relations with Israel. As Israel's attitude toward a political solution of the Palestine conflict remains decisive, Moscow, in refusing to resume diplomatic relations, has virtually excluded itself from any participation in peace diplomacy. Its difficulty is only too apparent: a resumption of diplomatic relations with Israel not only would entail a break with the policy pursued since 1967, but also would run the risk of losing the last partners on the "left" (especially Syria) without assurance of gaining new ones.

There have been certain signals, however, that Moscow would like to broaden its access to the Arab world. For example, the Soviet Union has resumed diplomatic relations with Egypt and has courted Saudi Arabia to establish such relations. The hour of decision will come for the Soviet leaders if Jordan, together with Palestinian representatives, enters negotiations with Israel. Only after "losing" Jordan and Palestinian representatives to an American-led peace process might Moscow reconsider its position and try to adjust to the new situation. Otherwise, it might be excluded from the peace process forever. Before this should happen, however, it might be "safer" for the Soviet leaders to continue their inflexible course. Their latest so-called peace plan[8] was aimed primarily at placating as many Arabs as possible without offering any concrete steps toward a political process. The primary purpose of this plan is quite obviously to establish the Soviet Union as an equal cosponsor of peace negotiations with the United States.

Despite many frustrations in the past, most of the Arabs and many observers in the world today still consider the United States as the only power that can effect real results leading toward a permanent settlement of the conflict. Superficial observers always tend to point to Israel's heavy dependency on American economic and military aid. A strong and resolved president, they argue, could press an Israeli government to a compromise that could fulfill at least some of the Palestinian aspirations. These observers, however, tend to forget or to ignore the American political culture and the way American foreign policy toward the Middle East is formulated.

First, American public opinion continues to support a strong solidarity with the Jewish state, which is supplemented by a widespread conviction that Israel is the only trustworthy friend of America in an area of turmoil. Second, Israel's base of influence in the American decision-making process has always been the Congress where the Israeli lobby continues to exert a great influence on the president. Finally, despite all frustrations with Prime Minister Begin, Ronald Reagan has continued to be a president with distinct sympathies toward the Jewish state. Under present circumstances it seems to be unthinkable that he or any other American president would hold back essential economic or military aid in order to force an Israeli government to make major concessions without an evident benefit to the country's security.

It is my guess that the present American administration will not undertake any major effort in peace diplomacy unless the PLO virtually excludes itself from a direct participation in peace talks, thereby giving a mandate to "independent" Palestinians and the king of Jordan. But then the real problems would only begin: could Palestinian representatives and King Hussein actually agree to a territorial compromise that would leave basic Palestinian aspirations, for example, for East Jerusalem, unfulfilled? Would anybody protect the Jordanians and "independent" Palestinians against the opposition from the Arab world that would then have to be expected? Unfortunately, it seems most probable that the answers would be negative.

Two modest options seem to remain. First, the United States and the West Europeans, together with Arab governments preferring peace with Israel, can encourage those who are ready to reach a political compromise and isolate those who press for a new military confrontation. Second, the United States, the West Europeans, and the Soviet Union should seek an understanding of how the Palestine conflict can be permanently contained, if it cannot be solved. A machinery for crisis management should be worked out to limit the dangers of escalation.

Notes

1. I prefer this term because it comprises the problem of Israel's legitimacy as well as the contradicting quests for land between Israel, the Palestinians, and Arab states in former Palestine.

2. See Meron Benvenisti, *West Bank Data Project: A Survey of Israel's Policies* (Washington, D.C.: American Enterprise Institute, 1984) and the controversial reactions to his pessimistic conclusions.

3. The following section is based mainly on my publications *Die sowjetische Nah- und Mittelost-Politik* (Bonn: Europa Union Verlag, 1982) and *Die USA im Nahost-Konflikt* (Bonn: Europa Union Verlag, 1983).

4. Henry Kissinger, *Years of Upheaval* (London: Weidenfeld & Nicolson, 1982), esp. pp. 747–853.

5. For an extensive analysis see various contributions in David Allen and Alfred Pijpers, eds., *European Foreign Policy-Making and the Arab-Israeli Conflict* (The Hague: Nijhoff, 1984).

6. The evolution of the Federal Republic's policy toward the Middle East is described in Karl Kaiser and Udo Steinbach, eds., *Deutscharabische Beziehungen* (Munich: Oldenbourg, 1981).

7. See the communiqué of Jidda, October 11, 1983, in *Bulletin des Presse- und Informationsamtes,* Bonn, no. 105, p. 966–67, and Kohl's press conference at the same place, *Frankfurter Allgemeine Zeitung*, October 12, 1983.

8. *Pravda*, July 30, 1984.

The International Political Economy: Aid, Investment, Trade, and Finance

In the international political economy of the 1980s, aid, trade, investment, and finance all hover around a central issue: indebtedness. The inability of many key developing countries to repay their international debts has spawned efforts to reschedule debts and to rethink aid, investment, trade, and financial strategies. The International Monetary Fund (IMF) and World Bank have attached conditions to loans requiring growth-oriented structural and macroeconomic reforms. Implementation of such reforms has, however, often resulted in austerity, a contraction of the domestic economies, and political instability. "Conditionality" requires the recipients of loans to tighten their belts at home by ending overspending on foreign imports. Without such actions the recipients of loans have been incapable of escaping indebtedness and achieving sustained growth and development.

The IMF and World Bank are now trying new strategies that go beyond loans, rescheduling of payments of interest on the loans, and attaching conditions to loans to address the structural impediments to development. They are asking industrialized states and their commercial banks to cooperate still further by providing adequate flows of capital to the indebted states. The problem in getting the industrialized countries to cooperate at this point is the lackluster performance of their own economies. Further, they are disenchanted with the recipient countries' inability either to develop or to repay their debts and, therefore, are reluctant to invest more funds.

Another aspect of the new IMF-World Bank strategy is to encourage the development of private business and investment within the indebted countries. The emphasis on international financial aid to the public sector would shift to investment in the private sector. The problem is gaining confidence at home and abroad so that such investments will really bear fruit.

Finally, if the indebted states are to have the slightest opportunity for development, the industrialized countries must keep the international economic environment healthy. The IMF and World Bank strategy includes noninflationary expansion of the international economy and the maintenance of a strong international trading system by avoiding protectionism. Protectionism usually generates countermeasures which fuel economic warfare. Protectionism has the additional effect of contracting the world economy by diminishing world trade. Benefits initially attained by those adopting protectionist measures are usually short-lived. In any event, if the industrialized states close their doors to goods from the indebted developing nations, their chances for escaping the debt trap are greatly reduced. One of the contradictory aspects of the policies of the industrialized states toward these indebted developing countries is that, on the one hand, they discourage imports from them because they are concerned about their own imbalance of payments and declining industries, and on the other hand, they extend them loans to compensate for their inability to export goods to gain solvency.

Although indebtedness is decidedly the central issue in the international political economy, it is also important to address the imbalance of payments from instability. Trade imbalances are a source of continuing difficulty in the relationships among some of the industrialized states. Ongoing efforts are directed at rectifying these imbalances, which have caused considerable friction even between states that are otherwise strongly allied with each other, such as Japan and the United States.

Exchange rate instability has exacerbated the problems of imbalance in trade and international indebtedness. Since the major currencies fluctuate so dramatically and unpredictably over short periods of time, no country can be certain that the currency it accepts today in exchange for goods or services will hold its value. Indebted countries find the difficulties of repaying foreign loans heightened by exchange rate fluctuations. Even the industrialized states suffer from the continual fluctuation of currencies, which has been detrimental to the international economic order, has inhibited expansion of trade, and has spawned enormous international movements of capital. Most of the industrialized states in 1987 formally agreed to take measures to stabilize currencies, and informally agreed to halt the further decline in the value of the dollar.

As the foregoing analysis suggests, the fate of the developed and developing states is clearly linked. When the developed states suffer from poor economic performance, they are less inclined to make funds available for loaning to or investing in the developing countries, and they even resort to protectionist measures to curb imports which threaten their domestic economies. On the other hand, when the indebted developing states suffer from poor economic performance, they are unable to repay their loans, much less develop. In either case, the international trade system may shrink in size, launching both the developed and the developing states on a downward spiral from which recovery may prove far more costly than prevention.

The articles in this section reveal the dimensions of some of the problems participants in the international political economy face. Private investment in lesser developed countries by multinational corporations (MNCs) is, for example, on the wane because of restrictive investment policies in the host countries. Although new international strategies have been created to encourage greater MNC investment, the immediate prognosis is not good (Article 39). For its part, US bilateral aid has, in many instances, improved the life-style of a small ruling elite, and has given local governments more control over their citizenry, but has not advanced economic development (Article 42).

Thus, both aid and investment strategies have fallen short of their intended goals, with the result that there is little impetus to provide more help to the LDCs in either form. Nevertheless, the director of the IMF feels that progress has been made in addressing the debt problem. A turnabout has occurred in current account deficits of the Latin American countries, facilitated by more realistic exchange rates, and the decline of international interest rates by six percentage points since 1982. Of further benefit to the indebted countries has been the strengthened financial basis of commercial banks which loan to other countries. On the other hand, the global economic environment in 1986 was not particularly hospitable to development, largely because of the threat of expanding protectionism (Article 43).

In the international trade sector participants in talks on the General Agreement on Tariffs and Trade (GATT) are making every effort to resolve disputes over unfair trade practices, protectionism, and other issues which diminish the willingness of countries to engage in expanded trade (Article 40). The Soviet Union is angry, however, that it continues to be left out of these multilateral trade negotiations for what it believes are reasons of political bias. The Soviet Union sees this as an effort to thwart it from expanding its trade with the industrialized states of the Western alliance (Article 41).

Looking Ahead: Challenge Questions

What are some critical dilemmas that stand in the way of resolving the present debt crisis for developing countries? What are the respective views of private banks, national governments, indebted countries, and international lending institutions on the best solution to the crisis? What are the stakes if the debt crisis is not resolved? Who will be the major losers? Is cancelling debts owed by certain countries a possible solution? What would be the effect if indebted countries simply refuse to repay their international debts?

Where does developmental aid fit into this picture of indebtedness? What forms of bilateral developmental aid have proven to be most effective in advancing sustained growth in the recipient countries? Is military aid a necessary and beneficial form of aid to developing countries?

Evaluating the MNC Contribution

Timothy W. Stanley
Stephen E. Thomsen

Timothy W. Stanley is a lawyer and a political economist. He is Chairman of the Board of the International Economic Policy Association and President of the International Economic Studies Institute. He is also a member of the State Department Advisory Committee on International Investment, Technology, and Development, and the author or co-author of numerous books, articles, and studies on multinational and international economic and security problems. Dr. Stanley previously served in government in various capacities, including the White House Staff, the Office of the Secretary of Defense, as Defense Advisor and Minister at the US Mission to NATO, and as an arms control negotiator in Vienna.

Stephen E. Thomsen has an M.I.M. from the American Graduate School of International Management. He has been an economist with the International Economic Policy Association since 1983 and has recently published a report entitled International Capital Flows and the United States: Palliative, Panacea or Pandora's Box?

Relations between multinational corporations (MNCs) and less developed countries (LDCs) have evolved since the hostility of the early 1970's, but a fundamental dichotomy remains. On a bilateral basis and in discussions with multinationals, the third world seeks to promote foreign investment in their countries, while multilaterally, they push for restrictive codes of conduct for MNCs. The multilateral debates bring up the complex question of jurisdiction over a multinational (a difficult term to define). While recognizing the sovereign rights of each country to regulate activities within its own borders, to what extent can "codes of conduct" be anything but voluntary guidelines? The essential point is that with increased pragmatism and trust on each side, the MNC can play a vital role in alleviating the genuine distress of the poorer countries, while also benefitting its home country. In other words, it *can* be a positive, rather than a zero-sum game.

The Debate Over Foreign Investment

In principle, at least, the multinational corporation is not that much different from any other kind of business enterprise; it has a product, a process, or a service that it tries to sell at a profit. The key difference for internationally oriented companies is that the markets are primarily abroad. Generally speaking, they would prefer to service them from a US production base if that is feasible. But increasingly, when faced with impediments such as the common tariff barrier of the European Community or the elaborate systems of exchange and other controls of Latin America, or when distance and shipping costs put them at a competitive disadvantage, companies have tended to produce abroad for those markets and, urged by the host country's desire to earn foreign exchange, to export to third countries.

The arguments in favor of foreign direct investment in developing countries by multinational corporations are well known and well documented. They need only be summarized here. In general, MNCs bring capital, technology, expertise and employment to LDCs. By purchasing goods and services locally and by paying above-average wages, MNCs also serve to stimulate growth in those countries in which they invest. To the extent that MNCs export their production, they improve the trade performance of the host country. They are, in effect, a ready-made, efficient industry for a country that would have difficulty creating one on its own.

The problem, critics of MNCs state, is that foreign affiliates of MNCs do not belong to the country in which they are located; they are allegedly "pirates without flag or country," with little regard for the host country beyond its profit-making potential. MNCs must bear some of the burden for this misconception. Certain cases of MNC involvement in influencing domestic politics of developing countries have been well publicized. Critics also contend that MNCs may actually hinder economic development by draining the host country of capital, by orienting the economy towards the production of luxury goods, and by employing only outmoded or "inappropriate" technology. If we are to assume that foreign investment in LDCs is a long-term prospect for an MNC, then a continuous inflow of new capital and technology is a necessity. And most of the US firms with which the writers are familiar do invest with a view to decades of solid cooperation with the host country and with its local partners. Those who seek only a "fast buck" usually wind up losing it instead.

Unions argue that foreign direct investment harms the home country of the parent by "exporting jobs" in order to take advantage of cheaper foreign labor and by exporting these goods back to the home market, especially in the United States. Studies have refuted this claim by showing that companies with foreign investments have actually created more jobs at home than those with no international investment, owing to the fact that at least one-third of US exports are to foreign affiliates. Also, the latest available Commerce Department Benchmark Survey (1982) found that only 9.7 percent of goods produced by manufacturing affiliates are exported back to the United States. When transportation equipment from Canadian affiliates (under the US-Canadian Automotive Agreement) is excluded, the figure is closer to five percent. This relatively small figure can be expected to increase in later data as the overvalued dollar forces companies to "outsource" increasingly to overseas locations, owing to the artificially low cost of foreign currencies.

Changing Attitudes Toward Foreign Investment

The MNC debate is an old one, tending to be more emotional than rational. But while the arguments may stay the same, the antagonists are changing. It is no longer surprising for LDCs to publicize foreign investment opportunities in their countries in US business periodicals. Even India still promotes foreign investment in the wake of the Bhopal disaster. What brought on this change of heart among developing countries? One subtle reason is the increased confidence which LDCs now have in dealing with MNCs on a pragmatic basis, in part because the UN's Center on Transnational Corporations makes available to them top-flight legal and negotiating expertise. But the most obvious answer is the debt crisis that erupted in 1982 and that has now grown to almost one trillion dollars, encompassing almost the entire third world. The LDCs' need for foreign capital following the oil price increases in the 1970's was mitigated in part through the recycling of petrodollars by commercial Western banks. In this way, developing countries were able to prolong the period of "miracle" growth that they were experiencing and to retain the illusion that they could develop by themselves, without foreign investment. The rude awakening came in 1982 when Mexico was unable to pay interest on its loans. Developing countries, having opted for debt over equity, now find the debt service a crushing burden, while foreign banks are ever more wary of increasing their LDC exposure through additional loans. Thus, equity capital from abroad has become a much sought-after commodity. But ironically, the same debts which fueled this trend have also discouraged MNCs from investing in the third world. The imposed austerity measures breed uncertainty and instability, and the developing countries' need for foreign exchange leads to restrictions on both the repatriation of investment earnings and the importation of needed capital goods.

Bilateral Investment Promotion

Following the turbulent 1960's and early 1970's, when outright nationalizations and takeovers, often with little or no compensation, were prevalent, the United States has belatedly begun to initiate a series of bilateral investment treaties (BITs). These treaties supplant the outdated "friendship, commerce and navigation" treaties of the pre-World War II era and aid in promoting and securing foreign investment. The United States has lagged behind Europe in negotiating BITs with third world countries, but the gap is narrowing, with half a dozen treaties signed (Haiti, Morocco, Panama, Senegal, Turkey, and Zaire) and several in the works (including Cameroon, Egypt, Indonesia, and Malaysia). The US Senate is expected to ratify several of them this year. The objective of the BITs is to provide for intergovernmental consultation on problems, arbitration of investment disputes, national treatment (non-discrimination against the foreign firm in the local market), reasonable assurances about repatriation of capital and profits, and adequate compensation in the event of nationalization or expropriation. But negotiations have been arduous. With China, for example, there are still issues to be resolved even after six rounds of talks.

Multilateral Investment Promotion

The World Bank has recently established the Multilateral Investment Guarantee Agency (MIGA) that will insure MNCs against various non-commercial risks. Although US MNCs can generally protect themselves against many commercial and political risks through the US Overseas Private Investment Corporation (OPIC), as can many European firms through their governments' analogous programs, the coverage is not complete. Moreover, it is argued, host countries are more comfortable with a multilateral program. Reagan Administration efforts to "privatize" OPIC will increase the need for MIGA. Currently, OPIC is cheaper and offers better coverage than private insurers. If it is privatized, it will probably lose some of its negotiating power in the settlement of disputes.

MIGA will guarantee against four types of risk: restrictions on the amount an MNC affiliate can transfer back home, expropriation, breach of contract by the host country, and war or civil unrest. MIGA will also publicize investment opportunities and offer technical assistance to developing countries. To avoid giving an unfair advantage to MNCs over the local competition, MIGA will cover funds brought into the country by foreign competitors. For MIGA to begin operations, five developed and fifteen developing countries will have to subscribe $360 million. There is some question whether the almost essential US blessing will be forthcoming in spite of Administration support, owing to the need for Congress to appropriate $44 million of the $222 million US subscription. MIGA is intended as a complement to the International Center for Settlement of Investment Disputes (ICSID). Both serve to promote investment—MIGA through guarantees and the ICSID by providing an international forum for dispute settlement.

Regulation of MNC Investment

Even when MIGA is fully ratified (with 11 signatories to date) and wins acceptance, problems between MNCs and LDCs will remain. While developing countries have become much more accepting, they still restrict the ability of MNCs to function independently in the host country. These restrictions often take the form of performance requirements. Companies must sometimes export a certain amount of production, employ a certain amount of local labor, use a certain amount of domestic inputs or only foreign capital, license their technology to local corporations, or share ownership of the affiliate with the host government or local partners—i.e. the so-called "Mexicanization." Such requirements are by no means limited to the developing world.

Although the primary motive for foreign direct investment is to service the local or regional markets, performance requirements can sometimes act as a deterrent. As such, they are actually counterproductive by limiting the amount of foreign exchange that a host country can earn. This explains why the growth of US investment in Mexico and Brazil from 1979 to 1984 was slower than the growth of US investment in almost all other major developing countries in Latin America and Asia. Mexico and Brazil boast the greatest absolute amounts of US foreign investment (excluding finance affiliates) due to their large markets and their proximity to the United States. But their restrictive investment policies, inspired partly by the debt crisis and partly by their fear of US economic hegemony, have scared away the foreign investment that they now need so badly. According to a 1985 report by the US Trade Representative's Office, "Individual companies claim Brazilian price controls, the arbitrary application of the law, remittance controls and other aspects of the investment policy have deterred investments and cut into profits."

US Direct Investment in the Major Developing Countries of Asia and Latin America

	Growth 1979-1984 percent	Position 1984 millions $
Thailand	380	967
Indonesia	270	4,409
Singapore	160	2,232
Colombia	150	2,103
Chile	140	601
Hong Kong	115	3,799
Taiwan	110	828
Malaysia	106	1,153
Argentina	71	3,157
Peru	44	2,220
Brazil	32	9,551
India	22	415
Ecuador	21	366
Mexico	20	5,380
South Korea	19	823
Venezuela	-5	1,711
Philippines	-6	1,185
Latin America	37	25,089
Asia	118	15,811

Source: Commerce Department

Indicative of Latin America's restrictive policies is Decision 24 of the Andean Investment Code. The Decision, approved in 1970, essentially called for the phasing out of foreign (mostly US) ownership of investments in the Andean Common Market. It also prohibited investment in most of the local service industry. According to the USTR, "The impact of Decision 24, along with selective expropriations, burdensome labor laws and now somewhat liberalized restrictions on repatriating profits have reduced the number of US companies willing to invest in Andean nations." It may be significant that the foreign ministers of the five Andean countries plan to meet this March to liberalize their investment rules.

If Latin America wishes to attract US investment, it should follow the example of the relatively open investment policies of the developing countries of Asia. While US investment in South America and Mexico grew by only 37 percent between 1979 and 1984, US investment in the developing countries of Asia grew by 118 percent.

Another potential deterrent to foreign investment is illustrated by India's suit against Union Carbide over the Bhopal disaster. The Indian Government claims that the parent company is *ipso facto* responsible for its Indian affiliate's actions, simply because Union Carbide is a multinational corporation, without having to prove any other criteria for *respondeat superior* or even any negligence. If accepted, this thesis "would shake the foundation of modern international business" and "undermine the availability of much needed investment capital in the developing nations," as was noted in the *Journal of Commerce* last year.

Jurisdiction and International Law

Clearly a sovereign nation can regulate all activities within its borders. But as shown by the Andean example cited above, overly strict regulations can discourage investment. Host countries, especially in Latin America, resist any references to the standards of international law and contest the right of home countries to intervene on behalf of one of their companies in any conflict or legal proceeding. This idea, known as the "Calvo Doctrine," is an emotional hangover from the days of gunboat diplomacy; and while it may be understandable in an historic context, it generates major problems for today's jurisprudence, both bilaterally and multilaterally.

One needs to recall here the emotional debates of the 1970's, not only about MNCs, but also about North-South relations. The LDCs argued that they were being exploited by various neo-colonial means and that they had a "right" to a more fair share of the world's economic pie and to higher prices for their commodity exports by cartel-like arrangements. Many sought unsuccessfully to emulate OPEC, even though they themselves were badly hurt by OPEC's price gouging.

Moreover, the LDCs argued, they were not bound by the traditional concepts of international law, since many of them had not been independent when its main principles were formulated. This view, however, is contradicted by the membership of the LDCs in the United Nations, whose Charter (Article 4) requires all members to accept the obligations of the Charter and, by extension, the legal principles on which it is based.

The poor countries banded together to form the Group of 77, now some 120 countries, as a bloc to confront the rich countries of the North. Their huge majority in the General Assembly enabled them to pass a number of one-sided resolutions: asserting a permanent sovereignty over natural resources; making a "Charter of Economic Rights and Duties of States" (CERDS) in which the advanced countries had most of the duties and the LDCs most of the rights; and establishing a "New International Economic Order" (NIEO) which included demands for multilateral regulation of MNCs, concessional transfers of technology and liabilities for restrictive business practices.

During all of this, a UN standing Commission on Transnational Corporations was formed with a primary mission of establishing a "UN Code of Conduct for Transnational Corporations," whose negotiations still continue, after more than a decade.

There have been five major code exercises, the most successful of which was conducted among the 24 members of the OECD in 1976. That exercise issued a "Declaration on International Investment and Multinational Enterprises" (OECD Doc. C(76)99) to which "Guidelines for Multinational Enterprises" were annexed. Although the guidelines are strictly voluntary in nature, governments have urged their corporations to follow them and many companies have indicated their intention to adhere to the principles. The relative success of the OECD negotiations can be attributed to the analogous interests of the developed countries within the OECD. Similarly, the International Labor Organization was able to agree on a "Tripartite (government, business and labor) Declaration of Principles Concerning Multinational Enterprises and Social Policy."

But in fora where both North-South and East-West actors are involved, the only success has been an UNCTAD "Set of Multilaterally Agreed Equitable Principles and Rules for the Control of Restrictive Business Practices." The title alone suggests the problems encountered with even a relatively simple set of principles, based mainly on US antitrust concepts, augmented by the European Community's concept of "abuse

Brazilian factory

of a dominant market position."

A proposed UNCTAD Code of Conduct on the Transfer of Technology remains deadlocked, as does the UN Code of Conduct itself. Fundamental issues include the nature of the code (voluntary or mandatory), applicability (imposing obligations on host governments as well as MNCs), universality (whether Communist states are included), dispute settlement and international legal procedures (the Calvo ghost again), compensation for expropriation, national treatment (including government owned enterprises), and a number of follow-up or "implementation" issues. In effect, all of these issues remain essentially unresolved today, although gaps have been narrowed in some.

The essential dilemma is the nature of the "code." It can hardly be "mandatory" unless put in the form of a treaty or international convention and ratified as such, or if parallel legislation is passed by all countries concerned, all of which seem highly unlikely, although some "model" statutes have been drafted under UN auspices. For its part, the Soviet Bloc insists that only capitalist countries have transnational corporations, although there are in fact a number of communist joint ventures with firms outside of COMECON which might so qualify. There has been little enthusiasm in any quarter for the suggestion of George Ball and others for "stateless" or supranationally incorporated enterprises. These supranational corporations would be subject to the jurisdiction of an international body.

The "77," often supported by the Communist Bloc, continue to insist on a mandatory, multilateral code, partly as a matter of tactics in bargaining. What, if anything, will emerge is anybody's guess. What is really going on in the "Alice-in-Wonderland" world of the United Nations about codes for MNCs amounts to international politics over economic issues masquerading in false legal garb.

One of the few places where the United States has proposed formal constraints via a treaty has been over illicit payments, in the light of the Lockheed and other bribery scandals involving US firms. But, ironically, this received almost no political support from any quarter in the body most critical of MNCs—the UN General Assembly. The draft treaty continues to languish in ECOSOC. (The United States has, however, enacted its own Foreign Corrupt Practices act, penalizing US companies for actions that are common in many parts of the world.)

If voluntary guidelines along the lines of the OECD's cannot be agreed upon in the UN's North-South, East-West context, it seems to us, the multilateral code of conduct exercises should be abandoned in favor of bilateral investment treaties, made as parallel as possible to avoid giving advantages to one or another country. The most favored nation concept common to trade agreements represents the down-to-earth negotiated contracts between transnational business partners that should be encouraged. In this way, the interests of both host and home countries can be served with minimum risk and maximum gain to both sides.

The problem, then, is to use the available capital and technology to promote economic development and alleviate the misery in which most of the third world's people live, rather than, in the medieval theological analogy, to debate endlessly how many MNCs can be made to dance on the head of a regulatory code.

Rewriting GATT's rules for a game that has changed

The trade talks that begin in Uruguay on September 15, 1986 could last a decade. They will determine whether international trade is "managed" by national governments into the next century, or whether the old and still sound principle of comparative advantage is rediscovered.

The eighth round of talks on the General Agreement on Tariffs and Trade (GATT) is the most complicated trade round yet. The politicians from GATT's 92 member nations, who meet at the seaside resort of Punta del Este in Uruguay next week, know that the world is drifting away from the assumption of free-trading virtue upon which the GATT is based. Are they there to tinker with a set of rules whose time has gone? Or can they use this round to widen and strengthen GATT's articles and so re-establish the faith?

The main problem for GATT is that it has been undermined in recent years by a shift in the basic technique of protectionism. The emphasis has moved on from tariffs, from which GATT draws its name, to subsidies and to market-sharing agreements. Market-sharing goes against one of GATT's main tenets by ushering in selective protectionism. It permits the victims of protectionism to be singled out in flat contradiction of the GATT principle of non-discriminatory behaviour: ie, that a tariff against one country must be a tariff against all.

Market-sharing deals (including so-called voluntary export restraint agreements—VERs) were not dealt with properly during the six years of the preceding round of GATT talks—the Tokyo round. So nations which made concessions to freer trade in the Tokyo round could offset them by negotiating a VER, or its equivalent, to keep their protesting industries happy. The semiconductor agreement negotiated with Japan to protect American chip makers is a recent example. Such arrangements invariably mean higher prices for the unfortunate consumer. Market-sharing agreements today affect around 43% of America's imports, and over half of France's.

The task at Punta del Este is only to set the agenda for the next round of talks. The real struggle begins when negotia-

tions get going in Geneva. The Uruguay declaration on the aims of the next round will probably be close to a draft—the so-called "*café-au-lait*" proposals—presented by Switzerland and Colombia and supported by 41 countries.

This draft seeks to extend GATT's authority to include agriculture and trade in services, an ambition that could by itself cause the talks to founder. But it does not contain what many economists would like to see—a thorough reassessment of the way GATT works so as to strengthen its influence on the world trading system and to permit it to control the growth of market-sharing arrangements, rather than let them spawn in haphazard fashion. To do this, GATT will need a strong set of inter-linked codes with powers to enforce them—through national courts if need be.

In a managed trade system, trade patterns are determined by political clout rather than by comparative advantage, because the terms of market-sharing agreements are more easily influenced by such powerful countries as America and Japan than they are by small but competitive trading nations. Newcomers find it hard to break into new markets. As such a system proliferates, it curbs world economic growth.

This is a grim prospect. Yet there is a chasm between what should happen at Punta del Este, and the Geneva talks beyond, and what will probably happen. It is not yet even clear that the main trading nations want to avoid managed trade. The Uruguay agenda will include the following issues that will test the world's collective will to resist its emergence. Ideally, each requires a bold new approach, but the answer to each of them in Geneva will probably be a fudge.

The **safeguards** question is the most crucial. Safeguards are the measures permitted by GATT for the protection of

domestic markets against "unfair" trade. They are supposed to help a country avoid undue economic hardship, and to allow it to shield itself against subsidised and dumped imports. They also permit protection on an emergency basis, under Article 19. This says (roughly) that if imports suddenly flood into a country in such volumes that a domestic industry is damaged, that industry may be protected. The idea is to create a breathing space for adjustment of industry in the threatened country.

At the very least this GATT-approved route to protectionism needs to be more closely controlled. If it cannot be policed, there is an argument for scrapping it altogether. Article 19 is almost always abused, because "temporary" protection rarely, in practice, encourages adjustment. Look at the Multifibre Arrangement (MFA). It contradicts GATT principles, but was set up by GATT members. It protects the textile industries of industrial countries against cheap third-world imports. It is discriminatory and as time goes by it has become more restrictive, not less.

But instead of tightening up on safeguards, the eighth round will be under pressure to make them more flexible. The EEC wants the central GATT principle of non-discrimination (ie, countries cannot be singled out as targets for protective measures) abandoned on safeguards. Selective safeguards, its negotiators say, should be sanctioned by GATT. That would mean GATT smiling on the nasty market-sharing deals which are now so much in favour.

Too few teeth

Mr Martin Wolf of the Trade Policy Research Centre in London gives three reasons why such official blessing of market-sharing deals would damage the world trading system. Such selective pro-

 From *The Economist*, September 13, 1986, pp. 63-69. © 1986 The Economist, distributed by Special Features.

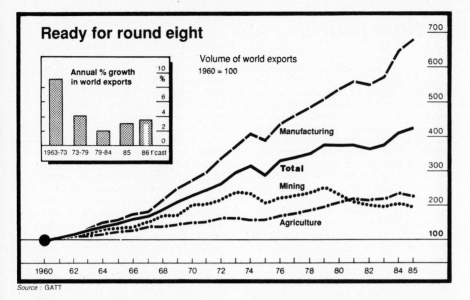

Ready for round eight

Annual % growth in world exports

Volume of world exports
1960 = 100

Manufacturing

Total

Mining

Agriculture

Source : GATT

tectionism increases the politicisation of trade. It allows a protectionist country to side-step a big deterrent to breaking ranks on multilateral trade—the prospect that the United States or the EEC will retaliate. If discrimination were accepted as legitimate behaviour, it would be impossible for GATT to enforce common rules to restrict the spread of protectionism.

The United States is keen to see the strengthening of **dispute settlement** at GATT. The disputes panel, which handles the enforcement of the agreement, has no teeth. Any member state may ask for a panel report on an alleged breach of rules by another member, but putting the panel's recommendations into effect depends on the willingness of the countries involved to implement them. It is not a court of justice.

The panel has worked well in 50 cases out of 52, but the remaining two cases have made it hard for the American administration to argue that the GATT is efficiently enforcing a trading system which is fair to the United States—the usual argument advanced by American administrations against congressional and industrial protectionists. The EEC twice side-stepped recommendations made by the disputes panel on agricultural trade with America (on citrus and soyabeans). Congressmen were cross, saying that GATT was useless if it could be ignored at will by as large a trading block as the European common market.

Some countries think that the disputes panel performs well when allowance is made for the hazy rules it is asked to interpret. Much trade in agriculture is beyond GATT's reach. GATT rules are opaque on such questions as the legal status of the Lomé Convention, which regulates trade between the European common market and many African and Caribbean countries, and the status of the

variable levies which are used to finance the EEC's common agricultural policy (CAP). Make the rules clear, say the defenders of the disputes panel, and the panel will be more effective.

They are probably only half right. Good rules help, but a panel without power of enforcement will always be weak in those areas where trade conflict is greatest—and agriculture is undoubtedly one of them.

Most of the world wants GATT rules on **agriculture** tightened, because subsidies have become so costly and damaging. Farm surpluses are huge and growing. America's grain mountain, for instance, could exceed 200m tonnes within a year. Australia, Canada and Argentina are among the main sufferers. Their farm exports are depressed by sales of surplus crops at giveaway prices in their big markets. Australia wants GATT members to commit themselves in Uruguay to dismantle export subsidies in agriculture within a set time, but finds its negotiating muscle weakened by its own protectionism on trade in manufactured goods.

The EEC can be relied upon to resist the Australian initiative. It says that support for agriculture comes in all sorts of guises, and to make export subsidies the main issue would discriminate against the European Community which happens to favour that approach. Agriculture, according to the EEC, is a special subject which should be tackled separately from other talks on subsidies.

Most countries disagree. First, because the separation of agriculture would provide Europe with a good excuse for sending the CAP theologians from Brussels to Geneva to negotiate. They would have no interest in seeing agriculture as part of a larger negotiation. Second, because GATT talks are all about trading concessions. Surrender of agricultural subsidy is not possible unless plenty of

bargaining chips are on the table. So it does not make sense to keep the scope of talks too narrow. France wants to trade off agriculture against agriculture. Australia and New Zealand simply could not match any EEC concessions on that basis.

Farming lobbies in Europe and America could wreck the Geneva agriculture talks. The sincerity of the EEC in wanting liberalisation is doubted by all, while the Reagan administration is under intense pressure from America's suffering farmers. The best that can be expected from Geneva is some curbs on the more outrageous forms of farm subsidy and other forms of agricultural protectionism.

Anything more would require exorcising the notion that farming should not be subject to market forces. That would require the EEC to recant its beliefs and America to ditch its farm lobby.

The challenge at Geneva will be to come up with some arrangement which does not contradict GATT principles but which the EEC can live with. One possible approach is a transitional arrangement that progressively reduces subsidies for farm products but allows them to be replaced with income subsidies paid to farmers. Such a "temporary" arrangement would run the obvious risk of becoming a permanent part of the trade landscape, like the Multifibre Arrangement. But it would have the advantage of making farm support more visible to the European public because it would take the form of government spending, rather than artificially raised food prices.

Tourism for textiles

Bringing trade in **services** under the GATT umbrella is almost as controversial an idea as the inclusion of agriculture, so the issue will probably appear on the Uruguay agenda in the haziest of forms. Total opposition from a group of developing countries led by Brazil and India would mean that the agenda might have to be established by majority vote in Uruguay—a heretical development for GATT notables, who like to see consensus on all GATT decisions.

The question of services has already split the developing world into two groups. Much of the industrial world is behind America in feeling, with varying degrees of strength, that services (trade in banking, insurance, travel, etc) should be brought into the agreement. In America almost three-quarters of jobs outside farming and the armed forces are in services. The EEC, America and Japan still dominate the service industries worldwide, but their share of world exports of services has fallen to 74% in 1984 from 81% ten years earlier. America reckons that services will be its main provider of economic growth and the

Who wants what this time round

America is the *demandeur* of new trade talks for the world. President Reagan, despite approving new deals to export subsidised grain and sugar, still sees America's interest lying in freer trade, and wants a stronger GATT to open up world markets for American goods and services. His trade negotiators find it useful to present Congress (with some truth) as a fearsomely protectionist force in order to win concessions for freer trade from other countries.

Congressmen delight in drawing attention to protection abroad—Europe's farm subsidies or its market-sharing deals. Such actions, they say, justify retaliation. The EEC flouts rulings by GATT panels; most new forms of protectionism escape GATT rules altogether.

In part to counter protectionists in Congress, the Reagan administration is seeking a stronger GATT with power to set the rules for newer types of trade (services), and to counter newer forms of protectionism (market-sharing agreements). If this initiative succeeds it may prove possible to convince protectionist waverers in Congress that GATT can be relied upon to make world trade fairer and freer. In the short term, the big danger for GATT is that the Reagan administration will give up its crusade and give way to domestic protectionist pressures, before the talks in Geneva really get going.

The main EEC motive for supporting the GATT talks is to please America. It is afraid of having to deal with a protectionist United States should this trade round fail. Europeans (wrongly) tend to see little immediate benefit to themselves in becoming embroiled in a new round. High unemployment and five years of slow growth mean that Europe is keen to cling to managed trade agreements, which restrict competitive imports. GATT will try to outlaw voluntary restraint agreements (VERS) while Europe will want them legitimised.

Europe will not easily give ground in farming. Australia and others want GATT members to agree to the abolition of export subsidies on farm products within a specified time. The EEC will fight this.

Japan supports America's call for a trade round; more precisely, its foreign ministry does. It makes sense for Japan to favour freer trade on a GATT multilateral basis because it is too often at the wrong end of bilateral pacts that restrict sales of this or that (most recently semiconductors) into certain markets. Yet its Ministry for International Trade and Industry has favoured VERS, and that might cause some confusion in Geneva. Like the European Community, Japan sees GATT as a fairly good institutional way of handling America, and fears American protectionism.

The **developing countries** are split.

This is something new. Up until a few years ago, they tried to pursue a common line within GATT, which worried other members who felt a north-south divide politicised the organisation, and held up business. Members want to avoid political divides within GATT because they do not want to see it hamstrung like some United Nations specialised agencies.

Some developing countries, led by India and Brazil, take the traditional third-world line. This means leaving novelties, such as services, off the agenda, and demanding discussions on the improvement of world commodity markets, including the bringing into operation of UNCTAD's plan for a common fund to finance the stabilisation of commodity prices. They also optimistically demand reform of the international financial and monetary system.

A second group of developing countries, 20 strong and including the ASEAN group, have joined forces to support the United States. For the most part, they are not particularly keen to have services discussed, but they are prepared to go along with a fuzzy outcome in that sector if it means a little more free trade for a little longer. Both groups of developing countries reassert the principle that they should not have to make concessions which are inconsistent with their development, financial and trade needs. GATT's director-general, Mr Arthur Dunkel, will have his work cut out trying to get all these discordant voices to sing free-trade's praises.

main provider of jobs for workers idled by the decline of older industries.

The India-Brazil group says that so long as the industrial world is unwilling to budge on protecting its farming and textile industries, developing countries have no interest in opening up markets to American services. If comparative advantage cannot operate in the sectors where we possess it, they say, why should we let it function where we do not?

If the hardliners stand fast on services, the prospects for the next round will look shaky. America has hinted that if it sees GATT becoming paralysed by north-south confrontation, it could abandon this round and look for ways of encouraging trade liberalisation with "like-minded" countries.

There are several fringe issues which America would like to see on the agenda, which would provide fertile ground for rows with the third world. Most prominent are **intellectual property rights**, which involves the protection of copyright and patents, and **industrial counter-**feiting. America would like GATT to crack down on both. Countries such as Thailand and South Korea, where copying foreign designs is big business, do not want to see their style cramped.

But it would be wrong to see the next GATT round only as a minefield of national interests and issues such as these. The round poses one big question—are governments still prepared to commit themselves to freeish, multilateral trade, and to an international agreement which enforces it?

GATT: The Eighth Round

V. ZOLOTUKHIN

A new round of multilateral trade negotiations has started in Geneva within the framework of the General Agreement on Tariffs and Trade (GATT). The decision to initiate them was reached at a special session of GATT member countries in Punta del Este, Uruguay, from September 15 to 20 this year.* The new round, the eighth in GATT's history, was opened by the declaration adopted at the session. The session formed a Trade Negotiations Committee which got down to work at its first meeting in Geneva at the end of October.

THE AGENDA FOR FOUR YEARS

The purpose of the Uruguay-round soon became clear. It was to further liberalize and expand world trade by improving market access and lowering or abolishing tariff and non-tariff restrictions, increase the role of the GATT system in world trade and its ability to respond to changes in the international economic situation, and help debtor nations in the Third World meet their financial obligations.

In the context of these general questions, participants are expected to consider more specific problems, such as the liberalization of trade in agriculture, in tropical and natural resource based products, and in textiles and clothing. It is also expected that they will draw up an agreement on trade safeguards, improve the rules and procedures for GATT member countries, and examine trade related aspects of intellectual property rights, including the right to trademarks and trade related investment measures affecting GATT member countries.

For the first time in GATT's history, the agenda for multilateral talks includes issues related to world trade in services (transport, tourism, insurance, banking operations, construction in other countries, computer data transfer). Also for the first time, multilateral trade negotiations are being linked to international monetary problems, particularly the foreign debt of developing nations. The GATT countries have agreed that while the talks continue they will not introduce new import restrictions and will gradually remove barriers that run counter to the General Agreement. Thus, the Uruguay-round covers the widest ever range of international trade problems, and its decisions will regulate world trade until the end of the century.

The new round is intended to last four years. But in view of the complexity of the problems and the sharp disagreements between the negotiating parties, it may last much longer. This is especially indicated by the divergence in views on the importance and priority of issues on the agenda that arose between industrialized capitalist and developing nations in the course of the preparations for talks. For instance, the question of trade in services was included in the agenda under U.S. pressure, though it was opposed by developing countries, particularly India and Brazil. Under a compromise reached in Punta del Este, parallel talks—on trade in goods and trade in services—will be held. Not formally linked, they will, organizationally, be directed by the Trade Negotiations Committee. For their part, the developing nations have secured a pledge that a moratorium on new import restrictions will be introduced and existing trade barriers rolled back. They also attach great importance to the linking of world trade with their foreign debt.

POLITICAL BIAS

Prompted by the belief that many of the trade policy questions discussed at multilateral negotiations have a bearing on its foreign economic interests, the Soviet Union declared in August 1986 that it would like to take part in these negotiations. Informal consultations on another matter—the granting of observer status in GATT itself—have been in progress between the Soviet Union and the GATT secretariat and its member countries since 1982.

In doing so, the Soviet Union has followed the example of many other countries which, before joining the General Agreement as full members, had participated as observers. The practice, incidentally, is provided for by the rules and traditions of GATT. By making an approach to GATT, the Soviet Union did not intend to remain an observer, regarding this status as merely an initial step.

The countries attending the Punta del Este session had been informed of the Soviet Union's desire to join the General Agreement in the future as a full member on agreed terms. The Soviet Union also explained its aims at the negotiations: to help improve the trade policy climate for international trade and elaborate decisions necessary for this purpose; expand trade between the Soviet Union and GATT member countries and strengthen confidence and cooperation between them; acquire the experience of participation in GATT in connection with the changes now being effected in the management mechanism of Soviet foreign trade in the overall context of restructuring the economic mechanism.

But GATT did not respond favourably to the Soviet request. The participation of the Soviet Union in the Uruguay-round, Western newspapers pointed out, was opposed by some Western countries, particularly the United States. The Soviet Union cannot thus take part in this round because the Punta del Este session limited the number of participants, without regard for the interests of the U.S.S.R. and other non-member countries. This decision is a step backwards from the Tokyo-round, which was open to all interested states. It is also clear that the United States and some other GATT members blocked the Soviet Union's participation for political motives.

Moscow believes, however, that the refusal to admit it to the Uruguay-round is not the final word on the part of this multilateral organization. In the present adverse international situation, the Soviet Union's rapprochement

with GATT does not call for mutual efforts and the clarification of positions.

A SHORTSIGHTED APPROACH

Those opposed to establishing ties between GATT and Moscow claim that the Soviet economic system is alien to the principles, rules and practice of the organization and that the Soviet Union would thus be unable to fulfill the commitments stipulated by the General Agreement. These arguments are clearly dictated by politically biased considerations.

Firstly, GATT does not regulate the economic systems of its member countries. They are freely chosen by their peoples on the basis of national sovereignty. Countries with different socio-political systems, socialist and developing nations included, already participate in GATT. It is also evident that socio-economic structures are not completely identical, even in industrialized capitalist countries.

Secondly, as far as the fulfillment of commitments under the General Agreement is concerned, Western countries take an individual attitude to each state wishing to accede to GATT. This means that the commitments of an applicant state become a subject of special negotiations. By announcing its intention to join GATT in the future

GATT—Background Note

The General Agreement on Tariffs and Trade (GATT), established in 1948, defines the rights and obligations of its member states in international trade. Intergovernmental bodies and a secretariat, based in Geneva, have been set up within the framework of GATT to supervise the implementation of the rules of the organization. GATT is thus simultaneously a permanently operating international organization and a forum for multilateral and bilateral negotiations and consultations between member states on all matters of their foreign trade policy.

As of November 1986, ninety-two countries were full-fledged members of the organization. Among them there are socialist countries: Hungary, Cuba, Poland, Romania, Czechoslovakia and Yugoslavia. As many as 152 countries participate in GATT in various forms. The Soviet Union does not take part in the organization's activities.

The General Agreement is essentially a code of principles and rules governing international trade. Its main principles include most-favoured-nation treatment in trade, nondiscrimination, reciprocity of concessions in trade, balance of rights and obligations, national treatment of foreign goods, transparency in the foreign trade policy of the member states, recognition of customs tariffs as the chief form of protection of the domestic market, and settlement of disputes through bilateral and multilateral negotiations and consultations.

The GATT rules cover such fields of international

trade as customs tariffs of the member states and quantitative import restrictions (quotas, contingents and import licensing), the shipment of goods across borders (including various methods of customs evaluation of goods to determine the tariff or import tax), regulation of foreign trade standards, measures against dumping and government subsidizing of export, safeguard measures used by member countries (that is, import restrictions allowed by GATT's rules), and the use of a preferential regime, that is, preferential terms in trade with developing nations.

Over 85 percent of world trade exchange is now governed by the GATT rules. The General Agreement operates on the principle, recognized by its member countries, that foreign trade should be prompted by economic levers and considerations, not administrative methods or decisions.

Seven rounds of multilateral trade negotiations have been held within the framework of GATT. The first six rounds dealt mainly with the reduction of customs tariffs. As a result, the level of customs tariffs in the member countries has been cut by roughly two thirds. As well as an agreement on a further reduction of customs tariffs, the countries attending the seventh, Tokyo-round of negotiations held from 1973 to 1979, concluded multilateral agreements on standards, import licensing and export subsidies, trade arrangements in a number of agricultural products and civil aircraft.

as a full-fledged member, the Soviet Union is naturally prepared to observe all the rules, procedures and traditions of the institution.

Also untenable is the argument that the Soviet Union's participation in GATT will lead to the organization being politicized. The U.S.S.R. is a major trading nation. Foreign economic ties play a significant part in its economy. Their role in the acceleration of social and economic development will further increase after the foreign economic mechanism has been revamped and cardinal economic reforms have been carried out. In the course of this reconstruction, producer amalgamations and enterprises will be given greater independence in their business ties with foreign partners. They are to be made completely self-financing. The aim of the current reforms in the Soviet Union is to ensure management of the economy by economic levers, not administrative measures. All this will qualitatively influence the Soviet Union's participation in the international division of labour and involve it more deeply in the multilateral trading system on the basis of GATT's principles and rules.

Those opposed to the Soviet Union's participation in the General Agreement have in fact themselves politicized the issue by pursuing an obviously unrealistic objective—the isolation of the U.S.S.R. from international negotiations on the future of world trade. Such a shortsighted approach is not conducive to the promotion of multilateral and free world trade and the renunciation of politically motivated discrimination in it. The negative attitude of some Western countries to the Soviet Union's participation in GATT is equally shortsighted in the light of prospects for expansion in East-West economic cooperation, which could become a dynamic factor in international trade exchange.

The Continuing Failure of
U.S. FOREIGN AID

"Our foreign aid has made life more pleasant and entertaining for government bureaucrats in poor countries. However, it has done little to promote the production of wealth, to breed political responsibility, or to encourage people to help themselves."

James Bovard

Mr. Bovard is a free-lance writer who has written on foreign aid for The Wall Street Journal, Chicago Tribune, *and other publications. This article is based on a report prepared for the Policy Analysis series of the Cato Institute, a Washington, D.C., public policy research foundation.*

FOR 40 years, U.S. foreign aid has been judged by its intentions, not its results. Foreign aid programs have been perpetuated and expanded not because they have succeeded, but because giving foreign aid still seems like a good idea. Yet, foreign aid has rarely done anything that countries could not have done for themselves, and it has often encouraged the recipient governments' worst tendencies—helping to underwrite programs and policies that have starved thousands of people and derailed struggling economies.

In agriculture, in economic planning, in food assistance, U.S. foreign aid has routinely failed to benefit the foreign poor. In Africa, Asia, and Latin America, the U.S. Agency for International Development (AID) has dotted the countryside with "white elephants": idle cement plants, near-empty convention centers,

Above: *Jewelry and other possessions left behind in the presidential palace by former Philippine First Lady Imelda Marcos when she and former Pres. Marcos hurriedly departed on Feb. 25, 1986.* **Below:** *Some of the 2,500 shoes of the former First Lady stored in racks inside the presidential palace. There is considerable evidence that staggering amounts of U.S. foreign aid funds poured into the Philippines were spent on such personal extravagances by Marcos and his wife.*

Reuters/Bettman Newsphotos

abandoned roads, and—perhaps the biggest white elephant of them all—a growing phalanx of corrupt, meddling, and overpaid bureaucrats.

Since 1946, the U.S. has given over $146,000,000,000 in humanitarian assistance to foreign countries. In 1985, the U.S. provided over $10,000,000,000 in non-military aid abroad, ranging from free food to balance-of-payments support to project-assistance and population-planning programs. AID employs over 4,500 employees to administer these programs, many of which have expanded rapidly under the Reagan Administration

Americans have a long tradition of generously aiding the victims of foreign earthquakes, famines, and wars. Before World War II, private citizens provided almost all of America's foreign assistance. After World War II, the Truman Administration decided that a larger, more centralized effort was necessary to revitalize the wartorn economies of Europe. Economic planning was the rage in Washington in the late 1940's, and Marshall Plan administrators exported their new-found panacea. The Marshall Plan poured over $13,000,-000,000 into Europe and coincided with an economic revival across the continent. However, analyses indicate that Europe would have recovered regardless of U.S. aid, and that the clearest effect of the Marshall Plan was to increase the recipient governments' control of their economies.

The apparent success of the Marshall Plan led Truman in 1949 to propose his Point Four Program to provide a smaller version of the Marshall Plan for poor countries in Africa, Asia, and Central and South America. Truman declared that Point Four would be "a bold new program for making the benefits of our scientific advances and industrial progress available for the improvement and growth of undeveloped areas."

In the 1950's, the Eisenhower Administration downplayed humanitarian aid, concentrating on security assistance to strategic allies. In 1954, Sen. Hubert H. Humphrey pushed the Food for Peace program through Congress, but that was the largest innovation in economic assistance during the decade. When John F. Kennedy took the helm in 1961, the stage was set for a huge expansion of foreign aid. In a special message to Congress, Kennedy called for "a dramatic turning point in the troubled history of foreign aid" and proclaimed that the 1960's would be the "decade of development"—"the period when many less-developed nations make the transition into self-sustaining growth." He placed heavy stress on the willingness of recipient governments "to undertake necessary internal reform and self-help." In 1961, AID was created, and the U.S. foreign aid bureaucracy came into its own.

Despite Kennedy's stress on requiring reforms from recipient governments, foreign aid routinely went to countries pursuing policies destined to turn them into permanent economic cripples. Partly as a result of a widespread perception that such aid was usually wasted, it consistently ranked as one of the least popular government programs with the American public.

From the mid-1960's to the early 1970's, South Vietnam received the bulk of U.S. economic aid. In 1973, Congress, concerned about the ineffectiveness of U.S. aid, heavily revised aid-program goals to focus more on social services and less on economic development.

When Ronald Reagan took office in 1981, many observers expected a thorough reform of U.S. foreign aid. Reagan declared in major speech before the annual meeting of the World Bank and Intertional Monetary Fund, "Unless a nation puts its own financial and economic house in order, no amount of aid will produce progress." Since then, despite his tough rhetoric on requiring reform from recipient governments, little has changed. American foreign aid still suffers the same problems it did when Kennedy took office in 1961. Despite countless reforms, foreign aid is still a failure.

Instead of breaking the "endless cycle of poverty," foreign aid has become the opiate of the Third World. AID and other donors have encouraged Third World governments to rely on handouts instead of on themselves for development. No matter how irresponsible, corrupt, or oppressive a Third World government may be, there is always some Western government or international agency anxious to supply it with a few more million dollars. By subsidizing political irresponsibility and pernicious policies, foreign aid ill serves the world's poor.

American foreign aid has often harmed the Third World poor. In Indonesia, the government confiscated subsistence farmers' meager plots for AID-financed irrigation canals. In Mali, farmers were forced to sell their crops at giveaway prices to a joint project of AID and the Mali government. In Egypt, Haiti, and elsewhere, farmers have seen the prices for their own crops nose-dive when U.S. free food has been given to their countries.

AID can not be blamed for all the mistakes made in the projects it bankrolls. However, by providing a seemingly endless credit line to governments regardless of their policies, AID effectively discourages governments from learning from and correcting their mistakes. Giving some Third World governments perpetual assistance is about as humanitarian as giving an alcoholic the key to a brewery. Good intentions are no excuse for helping to underwrite an individual's—or a country's

—self-destruction.

Foreign aid programs appear to be incorrigible. For 35 years, American foreign aid policymakers seem to have learned nothing and forgotten nothing. U.S. foreign aid projects routinely repeat the same mistakes today that were committed decades ago. One telltale ironic report title from the General Accounting Office says it all: "Experience—A Potential Tool for Improving U.S. Assistance Abroad." This study focuses on the failure of U.S. humanitarian aid to achieve its goals. It begins with a close examination of one of the most popular foreign aid programs, Food for Peace. Then comes a review of AID's record in resurrecting the economies of Central America, followed by an analysis of AID's role in African agricultural development. AID's achievements in Egypt and Indonesia are then reviewed, followed by an analysis of AID's role in spurring the development of private business and capitalism in poor countries. The study concludes with an analysis of why U.S. foreign aid has failed in the past and why it will most likely fail in the future. Military aid and security assistance is a different issue and is not examined in the study.

Free food bankrupts foreign farmers

Food for Peace is probably our most harmful foreign aid program. The U.S. is dumping over $2,000,000,000 worth of surplus agricultural commodities a year on Third World countries. Although sometimes alleviating hunger in the short run, the program often disrupts local agricultural markets and makes it harder for poor countries to feed themselves in the long run.

Food for Peace was created in 1954 to help the Eisenhower Administration get rid of embarrassingly large farm surpluses. The program aimed to benefit American farmers and the U.S. merchant marine and at the same time help hungry foreigners. In reality, it removes the evidence of the failure of our agricultural policies, often with little concern for the food recipients.

In the 1950's and 1960's, massive U.S. wheat dumping in India disrupted that country's agricultural market and helped bankrupt thousands of Indian farmers. George Dunlop, chief of staff of the Senate Agriculture Committee, speculated that food aid may have been responsible for millions of Indians starving. According to a 1975 General Accounting Office (GAO) report, massive food aid to Indonesia, Pakistan, and India in the 1960's "restricted agricultural growth . . . by allowing the governments to (1) postpone essential agricultural reforms, (2) fail to give agricultural investment sufficient priority, and (3) maintain a pricing system which gave farmers an inadequate incentive to increase production.''

U.S. food aid is still having devastating effects. A report by the AID inspector general found that food aid ''supported Government of Egypt policies . . . which have had a direct negative impact on domestic wheat production in Egypt.'' AID administrator Peter McPherson has admitted his concern that U.S. food donations are still having an adverse effect on Egyptian agriculture. In Haiti, U.S. free food is widely sold illegally in the country's markets next to the Haitian farmers' own crops. Governments often accept U.S. free food at the same time that they are repressing their own farmers, refusing to pay them what their crops are worth.

Roughly a quarter of Food for Peace giveaways go to the Food for Work program. FFW recipients receive food in return for working on labor-intensive development projects. These projects are intended to increase agricultural productivity, but are often only make-work schemes.

FFW workers often labor to improve the private property of government officials or large landowners. An AID analysis of FFW in Bangladesh, which has the largest FFW program in the world, concluded that FFW ''results in increased inequity'' and ''strengthens the semi-feudal system which now controls most aspects of the village life.'' The workers were paid less than the program promised to pay, and the government used U.S. wheat for other purposes, paying the workers with inferior, infested wheat. A 1975 UN Food and Agriculture Organization report concluded that FFW projects in Haiti ''have extremely deleterious effects on the peasant communities and cause great erosion of the reservoir of mutual service relationships of the traditional peasantry.'' In the Dominican Republic, shoddy AID FFW program management ''led to giveaway programs, a road project that proved to be a footpath leading nowhere, agricultural projects for which FFW incentives were not needed,'' and the usual horde of ineligible recipients. In many places, rural residents neglect their own farms to collect generous amounts of food for doing little or no work on FFW projects. FFW has contributed to a shortage of agricultural labor at harvest time.

Much of the food donated by Food for Peace is targeted for school food or health programs for mothers and children. AID claims that these programs prevent displacement of local production and reduce malnutrition. However, an AID audit of targeted food assistance in India, which has the largest such program, concluded, ''The maternal/child health program has not improved nutrition and the school feeding program has had no impact on increasing school enrollment or reducing the drop-out rate.'' Even though targeted food assistance has been ineffective, CARE (the private voluntary organization that administers it for AID) and AID's India mission ''have resisted efforts to arrange an orderly transfer of program responsibilities to the Government of India.''

AID has done little to discipline the private voluntary organizations that distribute the free food and often blatantly disregard official U.S. policy. A report by the AID inspector general found that free food in Tanzania and elsewhere in Africa had created permanent doles, whereby people who could feed themselves did not bother growing enough food to do so. A priest in Tanzania reported that ''residents of this area could grow all the food they wanted, but had chosen to not produce all they needed'' because of the availability of U.S. free food.

The Catholic Relief Services official policy manual for Food for Peace programs states, ''Any child under the age of five years is eligible to be registered in the program. All children should be encouraged to stay in the program until the age of five.'' AID auditors found that over half the children receiving free food were not nutritionally substandard. AID operations have been passing out free food in some villages for over a decade, and several feeding centers have reported that they would have to give out free food for at least another decade.

AID's mission in Tanzania and the private voluntary organizations have repeatedly refused to make any distinction between needy and self-sufficient families. The result is a program that discourages people from feeding themselves and that has a crippling effect on the development it seeks to encourage. Food for Peace is a handout program designed more to make the donor feel good than to benefit the recipient. Although this problem has been obvious almost since Food for Peace began, the program still suffers from the same fundamental defects that afflicted it in 1954.

Food for Peace is also an administrative nightmare. Recipient governments continually neglect to file reports on how food aid has been used, but AID keeps shipping them millions of dollars worth of free food every year. The Congo, instead of using FFP donations to feed its people, sold free food to buy a small arms factory from Italy. In March, 1984, *The New York Times* reported that AID officials believed Ethiopia was selling its donated food to buy more Soviet weaponry. Mauritius insisted on receiving only the highest quality rice and then used it in hotels catering to foreign tourists. Cape Verde begged for more emergency relief aid at the same time that it was busy exporting wheat donated by other countries. Nothing was done about these incidents, however, and the free-food gravy train kept on running.

Despite all these problems, Food for Peace still has the loyal support of the U.S. merchant marine. The program requires that at least half of all donated commodities be shipped in U.S.-owned carrier vessels. An AID study found that it cost four to five times more to ship raw materials by U.S. carriers than by foreign carriers. In some cases, shipping charges cost almost as much as the food donated. However, even this income has not made the U.S. merchant marine prosperous. A recent Senate Agriculture Committee report concluded, ''Rather than encouraging the development of improved U.S. vessels, the program encourages the continued use of semi-obsolete and even unsafe vessels which are of little use for commercial or defense purposes.''

The salvation of Latin America

AID is playing a key role in the Reagan Administration's efforts to revive Latin America. U.S. aid has poured into El Salvador, Honduras, and other countries in a desperate attempt to buy prosperity for strategic U.S. allies. This great flow of assistance provides a good test of the benevolence of foreign aid.

El Salvador is AID's showcase in the Western Hemisphere, and the biggest game in El Salvador is land reform. In early 1980, the government seized the property of hundreds of the largest farmers, began setting up cooperatives, and promised to eventually turn the land over to small farmers. From the beginning, AID has been fully supportive of Salvadoran land reform, pouring more than $250,000,000 into the cause. In a 1983 *Washington Post* article on land reform, AID administrator Peter McPherson claimed that ''real progress is being made,'' that 500,000 *campesinos* (small farmers) already benefit, that previously poor peasants ''now own their land,'' and that ''agricultural production in the reform sector compares well with pre-reform production.''

McPherson's claims are based on wishful thinking. Since the Salvadoran government expropriated large private farms in 1980, production of coffee, the largest export, has plummeted 30%. Sugar and cotton production have also declined. The government has provided no real compensation to the expropriated landowners—they were given only worthless government land bonds, which can not be redeemed now and whose value is rapidly depreciating as a result of inflation. The small tenant farmers who now plow much of the land are required by the government to wait 30 years before selling any of it, which essentially ties them to the land as though they were medieval serfs. Hence, they lack any real title to their land, contrary to McPherson's claim. The government forces farmers to sell their crops to the state for prices far below the crops' true worth, and often it does not pay farmers for as long as two years after they turn in their harvest.

The government of El Salvador has done an abysmal job of administering economic overhaul. The 1983 harvest was disrupted because the government's central bank failed to make sufficient credit available to farmers during planting season. After expropriating large farms, the government set up hundreds of cooperatives to manage those farms. However, neither the government nor AID knew exactly how many cooperatives existed; 317 was the best available estimate. As of September, 1983, three and a half years after the property had been expropriated and the cooperatives created, the Salvadoran government still had not surveyed the expropriated properties, established the amount and class of lands involved, determined the number of properties expropriated, or established the amounts owed to the previous owners.

The new cooperatives are very poorly managed. The typical cooperative uses twice as many workers as the previous farmland owners did to work the same land. As a result, many cooperative members work only two or three days a week. Much of the land in El Salvador is mountainous and unfit for farming, but the new cooperatives are futilely trying to squeeze harvests out of the worst-quality land—land on which the previous private owners never considered wasting seed and fertilizer. The AID inspector general estimated that three-quarters of the new cooperatives are located on predominantly poor farmland.

AID personnel have apparently made only a minimal effort to investigate how the cooperatives are actually working. The inspector general found that AID officials had visited only one of 41 cooperatives randomly selected for audit. Even though land reform is AID's principal project in El Salvador, AID's post for director of agrarian reform was vacant for 18 months.

Throughout Central America, foreign aid has vastly expanded the size and power of central governments. As Manuel F. Ayau, president of the Universidad Francisco Marroquin in Guatemala City, observed in 1983, foreign aid "has been spent putting governments in the business of power generation and distribution, telecommunications, railroads, shipping or other ventures that invariably end up charging monopoly prices and losing mon-

ey to boot. These ventures not only produce no wealth for their countries, but they also tax economically productive enterprises to cover their losses."

In Honduras, AID is propping up the major cause of the people's misery—the government. A 1985 GAO report noted, "The government's centralized procurement process averages over 100 steps requiring about six months to complete." The economy is dominated by heavily subsidized, inefficient state-owned enterprises. Much U.S. aid is labeled "balance-of-payments support" and is intended to cover the country's trade deficit, which is caused by Honduras' overvalued exchange rate. As Ayau noted, overvalued currency means "the foreign exchange spenders—the exporters—subsidize the foreign exchange spenders—the importers—thus promptly exhausting foreign exchange reserves. Typically, more debt is then acquired to postpone the eventual day of reckoning."

Honduras' overvalued exchange rate is encouraging capital flight because Hondurans recognize that the official exchange rate amounts to a *de facto* expropriation of their foreign-exchange earnings. The Honduran government refuses to adjust the rate because "exchange rate policy actions might imply government mismanagement of the economy," according to GAO. Instead of encouraging the government to reform its exchange rate and stop hindering its own export trade, AID is paying to set up a price-checking unit in the government's central bank to better regulate Hondurans involved in import or export transactions. With AID's support, the Honduran government is repressing the symptoms while continuing to cause the disease.

Africa—foreign aid wasteland

In the 1960's, AID and other donors began a concerted effort to help the newly independent nations of Africa develop their economies. Since 1960, per capita food production in Africa has fallen 20%, roads and bridges have been collapsing across the continent, and Africans' faith in the future has shriveled. As a 1983 *Foreign Policy* article concluded, "Average per capita income in the continent at the end of the 1980's may be lower than it was at the beginning of the 1960's." Despite huge influxes of development aid, export volumes for most African countries actually fell during the 1970's. AID, the World Bank, and other donors helped set up many of the state-owned enterprises and state farms that disrupted African agriculture and contributed to the starvation of thousands of people.

AID's record in Africa is dismal. AID agricultural projects routinely provide little or no benefit to African farmers. An AID inspector general report on AID agricultural programs in the Sahel (a belt of eight poor countries just south of the Sahara) concluded that "no one with a modicum of business sense" could have avoided seeing many of the problems associated with AID projects. According to the report, "Food production projects in the Sahel have accomplished little, if any, desired results." A 1981 AID report concluded, "The Sahelian states cannot effectively use this magnitude of assistance." Yet, AID continues to pour money into the region.

The Operation Mils Mopti project in Mali is typical of AID African agricultural assistance. In 1976, AID launched a project to boost food production and marketing in the Mils Mopti area of Mali. AID plowed over $10,000,000 into this project, which included the usual development array of applied research, more tools and fertilizer for farmers, better roads, and better grain marketing.

Almost everything went wrong, but AID kept financing the program long after its failure was evident. AID paid for the building of 18 warehouses, but five were not built, three were not finished, three collapsed, two had their roofs blown off, and three more quickly crumbled owing to "serious structural deficiencies." Fifty-two open wells with contaminated water were to be sanitized, but only nine were actually improved. One hundred mills for grinding grain were to be constructed; the project managers built and tested one mill, then gave up. The road-improvement project repaired less than one-quarter of the roads scheduled for upgrading.

Operation Mils Mopti sought to increase grain marketing, but the government marketing board paid farmers only the official price for their crops, which was far below free-market prices. To fulfill the marketing goals, the government forced farmers to sell their crops, thereby effectively expropriating their harvest. Instead of increasing sales, Mils Mopti resulted in a fall in total procurement by the government marketing board of over 80% by the time the project ended in 1979.

Although the government refused to pay farmers a fair price for their crops, it did spend $4,900 on a mural to promote the project. AID auditors found the same kind of mural for sale in a nearby gift shop for less than $700. At last report, the $4,900 mural was inspiring the farmers while hanging in the project headquarters' lavatory!

Livestock-production projects in Senegal were equally unsuccessful. In the mid-1970's, AID committed itself to improving the livelihood of Senegal's livestock producers. AID aimed to increase the number of cattle in the Bakel region from 11,200 to 25,000. However, after almost $4,000,000 in U.S. aid had been spent, only 882 more cattle were on the range. A $7,000,000 project in the Sodespt region also sought to boost livestock production and marketing, but managed to sell only 263 cattle. The project was also designed to sell 4,950 goats and sheep, but it failed to sell any.

Both livestock projects sought to stem the deterioration of Senegal's rangeland, which threatens to subvert the entire Senegalese livestock business. They were launched to respond to the devastating droughts that had struck Senegal in the early 1970's, but they assumed that normal climatic conditions would prevail. The projects made no provision for livestock forage in case of renewed drought. In addition, the project was so poorly planned that, although it tried to encourage increased production, it did nothing to alter the grazing use of the public commons area. In 1982, Senegal was again hit by drought, and the country's livestock business suffered greatly.

One report by the AID inspector general observed that AID's Senegal mission felt "considerable pressure existed [from Washington] to program and spend project funds, with a lesser concern for effective use of the monies," and "overstated project objectives were required to gain AID/Washington approval." In asking for a renewal of the project, AID's Senegal mission "disregarded key evaluation findings," insisting that the "project was sound in goal and purpose." As usual in politics, spending money was more important than getting results. The same pressures that led to failure in Senegal are at work in almost all AID projects.

In many African countries, it has been clear that the success or failure of AID agricultural projects could be a life-or-death issue for the citizens. Yet, as is obvious from the AID inspector general's summary on the eight countries of the Sahel and from other reports, AID has bungled its relief efforts. African governments—with state marketing monopolies and policies that force farmers to sell their crops to the government at a loss—bear most at the responsibility. (In some African countries, farmers are routinely shot for trying to sell their crops on the black market.) Nevertheless, AID has continued to bankroll these governments, regardless of their pernicious policies.

The more foreign aid African governments have received, the worse they have tended to perform. As GAO noted, "The large number of donors and their administrative requirements place a considerable burden on recipient governments and strain their already weak administrative capacity." A recent AID analysis noted: "Many African institutions officially responsible for planning and implementing development are saturated with development assistance, paralyzed by administrative inefficiency, staggering beneath a burden of complex and differing donor requirements, and are themselves in danger of becoming obstacles to development."

Some African countries receive their entire investment budget from foreign aid. As GAO noted, "Governments, because of the importance of donor financing, are often more preoccupied with fund raising than structuring effective development plans." As long as the foreign aid keeps pouring in, life will continue to be prosperous for the government employees who administer development programs.

Despite all these failures, African civil servants continue to prosper. No matter how mismanaged the economy, the government can almost always find funds to provide raises for its employees. As one International Monetary Fund official assessed the effect of foreign aid on Zambia, "It is fair to say that what we have done is to allow Zambia to maintain a standard of living for its civil servants [whose payroll amounts to 20% of the country's gross domestic product] which is totally out of synch with the rest of the economy." Yet, no matter how far government extends its clumsy grasp over the economy, foreign aid donors keep pouring in the funds. In Zimbabwe, government spending has increased from 35% to 60% of the gross domestic product since 1980. Nevertheless, Reagan Administration officials continue to boast that U.S. aid is encouraging positive economic reforms. In Zimbabwe, *The Wall Street Journal* recently noted, the media has been nationalized and the government now bans some foreign publications from entering the country.

The champion of Third World business?

Since the 1950's, American foreign aid rhetoric has stressed the need to develop business and private enterprise in the Third World. After 30 years of preaching the virtues of the private sector, however, the U.S. still directs most foreign aid to foreign governments, not private businesses. Furthermore, the aid that does go to businesses has done little to encourage free markets; foreign aid has yet to buy a single country a free market.

AID has obligated over $179,000,000 since 1976 to support the private sector in Egypt. However, a cursory examination of project descriptions shows that AID has some novel ideas about what that means. Part of its private-sector aid package provides money to the Egyptian government "to take equity positions in private-sector industrial projects." Thus, AID is helping the private sector by giving money to the government to buy it out. Over one-third of the $32,000,000 given to the Development Industrial Bank for private-sector support was reserved for aid to state-owned enterprises. AID also gave Egypt $33,000,000 to set up a "Private Investment Encouragement Fund." After five years, the program's only achievement was the hiring of a part-time executive director, a chauffeur, and two part-time employees. Not a single loan to private business had been made. Despite this dismal record, AID has not terminated the project.

Almost all AID private-sector funds are channeled directly or indirectly through the recipient country's government. The 1979 Chrysler bailout is the domestic equivalent of AID's Third World private-sector development. Some private-sector aid may eventually end up in private coffers, but only after political strings have been attached, and the money usually goes only to businesses with political clout. The result is not free markets, but "crony capitalism"—money distributed to the friends and relatives of politicians.

Even at its best, AID private-sector assistance simply buys an industrial policy for the recipient government. AID helps decide which industries are to be developed, where factories will be built, and what prices will be charged for the final products. U.S. assistance thus promotes the kind of government direction of economic development that has been criticized in the U.S. by prominent economists of all political persuasions and that the Reagan Administration claims to abhor. As development expert Melvyn Krauss notes, "There is only one way to privatize the economy, and that is to reduce the role the government plays. Foreign economic aid, because it represents government-to-government transfers, socializes recipient economies." Even when it is ultimately ladled out to private businesses, foreign aid weakens the comparative position of the private sector by increasing the government's revenue and power.

Besides, AID is inherently incapable of efficiently aiding Third World businesses, possessing neither the capability nor the incentive to be a competent venture-capitalist banker. AID employees rarely have any training in banking, and they are unqualified to judge which firms might be creditworthy. Each AID country mission suffers from the usual government-bureau incentive to lend as much money as possible, for otherwise its budget for the following year will be reduced, and the staff's chances for promotion will diminish. AID employees are often promoted according to how many loans they make, not according to how many loans are paid back five years down the road. Thus, AID employees have no incentive to adequately investigate loan applicants.

AID's cheap loans and grants to businesses allow U.S. and Third World bureaucrats to pick winners and losers in village markets. This may be gratifying to the bureaucrats, but it breeds inefficiency in the Third World. When subsidized loans determine which businesses succeed or fail, businessmen spend less time on business and more time on politics.

Foreign aid consists largely of one government "helping" another government by beefing up its budget, increasing its power over the private sector, and multiplying its leverage over its citizens. As economist P. T. Bauer observed, there is an "inherent bias of government-to-government aid towards state control and politicization."

The marvel of foreign aid is that many of the same people who oppose government intervention in the U.S. somehow think we are doing foreigners a favor by paying for it abroad. Many of the people who recognize that Amtrak has been an expensive mistake have no objection to subsidizing state railroads in Africa. The same people who would fight any Department of Agriculture effort to impose ceilings on prices received by American farmers are silent about U.S. financing of African bureaucracies that burden African farmers with exploitative price controls. Some of the same Congressmen who realize that Federal irrigation policies squander billions of dollars worth of water are still enthusiastic about constructing government irrigation projects in Indonesia.

Foreign aid is based on the premise that foreign governments are devoted to their citizens' welfare—an assumption that is even less true of foreign politicians than of the members of Congress. AID projects in Guatemala have failed partly because some Guatamalan government officials oppose improving the plight of the rural poor. A million people may have starved in the Sudan in 1985 because the government-owned railroad refused to transport American-donated food. In Africa, where tribal rivalries often still prevail, AID money is used to prop up the reigning factions in the same way that local American political machines use Federal grants as slush funds. Foreign aid greatly increases the patronage power of recipient governments. As Bauer notes, "The great increase in the prizes of political power has been a major factor in the frequency and intensity of political conflict in contemporary Africa and in the rest of the less developed world."

AID officials often justify the agency's handouts by claiming that they persuade recipient governments to abandon pernicious economic policies. The idea seems to be that the U.S. must bribe foreign governments not to commit economic suicide, but few recipient governments have modified their economic policies in response to AID assistance. Poverty-stricken Burkina Faso imposed a 66% tariff on importation of animal-drawn plows and a 58% tariff on engines used for irrigation pumps. According to *The Wall Street Journal*, in Zambia, the 1985 crop harvest was endangered because the "Zambian state corporation that collects agricultural produce can't afford to buy the bags it needs." As the World Bank recently admitted, preaching about the virtues of free market has so far had little effect on African socialism.

Making U.S. aid conditional on policy reform also can not work simply because AID is probably more anxious to give than Third World governments are to receive. Consider the case of Mozambique. In the last 10 years, Mozambique's Marxist government has thoroughly destroyed that nation's economy. *The New York Times* recently noted that Maputo, the capital of Mozambique, "Lacks virtually everything." Mozambican farm policies pay farmers only a tiny fraction of what their crops are worth, and they are largely responsible for a famine that killed 100,000 citizens in 1984. On the verge of being overthrown by pro-Western guerrillas, the Mozambican government decided to make some modest economic reforms and see what the U.S. would pay. AID rushed in with a $33,000,000 bailout package, even though the country is still full of Cuban troops and Soviet advisers and is still socialist. *The New York Times* commented, "The American change of heart is apparently a result of Mozambique's readiness to accept American aid in its time of despair." For AID, willingness to accept a handout is sufficient proof of a government's good intentions.

There is little that foreign aid can do that private credit can not do equally well or better. As Bauer notes, "The maximum contribution of aid [to development] is the cost of borrowing that is avoided." However, the cost of avoiding interest payments on loans is the transformation of imported capital into a pork barrel for recipient politicians. The costs of politicizing aid are greater than the costs of interest payments on private credit. Going on international welfare is frequently as pernicious to Third World governments as going on Aid to Families with Dependent Children is for struggling American families.

Curbing investment

At the same time that Third World leaders claim they are entitled to international welfare to overcome their countries' poverty, they often close their borders to foreign investors, thus greatly diminishing the amount of capital entering their countries. In 1960, foreign investment accounted for roughly 30% of the net flow of capital to developing countries. Now, despite a huge increase in foreign investment between industrial countries, it accounts for barely 10% of the net capital flow to the Third World. Foreign investment in the Third World in real dollars was lower in 1983 than in 1970.

Many less-developed countries have effectively decided that they would rather stay poor than allow foreigners to share the profits of national development. Governments have expropriated foreign companies, prohibited them from remitting their profits, and cheated them with "official" foreign exchange rates that are simply a disguised form of expropriation. The Mexican government recently rejected a proposed $300,000,000 joint truck-building venture with the Chrysler Corporation because the deal might have endangered the government's control over the Mexican automobile industry.

A *Wall Street Journal* article recently noted, "In most developing countries, would-be foreign investors face a web of restrictions and conditions that would sour almost anyone." In Venezuela, for instance, "Stringent labor laws make it costly to fire inefficient workers. Corruption, red tape and delays abound; and the government frequently changes the rules of the game."

Yet, foreign investment under beneficial conditions would, in contrast to foreign aid, avoid saddling the recipient countries with hordes of inefficient government corporations or getting them mired in debt from government borrowing abroad. Foreign investment played a significant role in the early economic development of the U.S., Australia, and other industrial countries. By bankrolling supermodern factories in Tennessee, Ohio, and elsewhere, foreign investment is helping reindustrialize the present-day U.S.

Foreign aid is extremely fungible—every increase in outside donations frees up an equivalent amount of a recipient government's own revenue to be spent for other purposes. Many less-developed countries routinely squander their own money. Mobutu Sese Seko, president of Zaire, has amassed a multi-billion-dollar personal fortune and has built 11 presidential palaces. Ghana, Brazil, Kenya, and the Ivory Coast have spent billions building new capital cities. Mercedes-Benz automobiles are so popular among African government officials that a new word has come into use in Swahili to describe them: *wabenzi*—"men of the Mercedes-Benz."

6. THE INTERNATIONAL POLITICAL ECONOMY

Of course, not all types of foreign aid are automatically harmful. Private voluntary aid that bypasses a recipient country's political structures can help people in the Third World. The Peace Corps had good intentions, but it is now largely providing bureaucrats and technicians for foreign governments, thereby reinforcing political control over development. Rushing in medical supplies after a major earthquake or tidal wave can help the victims as long as it does not permanently increase the government's power or the people's dependence on politicians.

Our foreign aid has made life more pleasant and entertaining for government bureaucrats in poor countries. However, it has done little to promote the production of wealth, to breed political responsibility or to encourage people to help themselves. American foreign aid usually only strengthens oppressive regimes, allows governments to avoid correcting their mistakes, and bails out bankrupt state-owned enterprises around the world.

Regardless of our future good intentions, American foreign aid programs will still be controlled by politicians anxious to buy goodwill and administered by bureaucrats anxious to meet their quotas of loans, and they will still be received by foreign governments careless of the use of free gifts. As long as the same political, bureaucratic, and economic incentives govern international welfare, the same mistakes will be repeated.

Managing Director's Address . . .

All Participants Must Work Together To Ensure Resolution of Debt Problem

Following are remarks by J. de Larosière, Managing Director of the Fund, before the Latin American Federation of Banks (FELA-BAN) in Quito on November 21, 1986. His address was entitled "Growth and Debt in Latin America."

I am delighted to participate in these meetings. We in the Fund have long had high regard for the role that FELABAN is playing in promoting cooperation among the private banks of Latin America. This morning I want to focus on an issue that is of immediate interest and concern to all of us, namely, how can the indebted countries achieve sustainable growth while continuing to make progress toward the restoration of normal debtor-creditor relationships?

Ever since the outbreak of the debt crisis in 1982, this region has been at center stage. Roughly 40 percent of the total external debt of all capital importing developing countries is accounted for by Latin American countries. No other geographic grouping of developing countries has a share as large. But it is not just that. With ratios of total debt and of debt service to exports that are almost twice as high as for all developing countries, Latin America's debt burden is an unusually heavy one. Finally, with the exception of Africa, there is no other region in the developing world where the case for combining improved creditworthiness with durable growth is more compelling. Even after the better than 3 percent a year average growth performance of 1984–86, the level of real per capita gross domestic product (GDP) in Latin America is still below that of 1980.

I shall divide my remarks into three parts. First, I shall survey the progress that has been made in handling the debt problem and identify the difficulties that remain. Second, I shall outline the policies and actions needed to make the reinforced debt strategy succeed. Finally, I shall discuss the role that the International Monetary Fund is playing in this overall strategy.

Where Do We Stand?

1. The debt problem did not arise overnight. It cannot be solved overnight either. Still, this should not obscure the considerable progress that has been made to date.

(i) To begin with, the last four years have witnessed a sharp turnaround in external positions. In 1982 indebted Latin American countries had a combined current account deficit equal to 34 percent of their exports; by 1985–86 that ratio had been reduced to less than 8 percent. Whereas non-debt-creating capi-

tal flows financed only one sixth of the combined deficit in 1982, they covered nearly half of it in 1985–86.

This dramatic improvement in the external accounts could not have taken place without key policy adjustments in the indebted countries themselves. Overvalued real exchange rates that had produced a bias against exports and had unduly encouraged imports were brought down to more competitive levels. In fact, the region's real effective exchange rate depreciated by about a third between 1982 and mid-1986. This was an important contributory factor to the 40 percent increase in the value of non-oil exports over the same period. Public sector deficits that had been allowed to more than double over the 1979–82 period were trimmed. In practically all of the region's largest economies, government deficits are now substantially lower than they were at the outbreak of the debt crisis. Low—and often negative—real interest rates that had weakened incentives for saving and the efficient allocation of investment were in many cases raised to more realistic levels. And last but not least, several high-inflation countries—Argentina, Bolivia, and Brazil come immediately to mind—have recently launched bold and comprehensive corrective actions. The region's (weighted-average) inflation rate—while still too high—is expected to decline from its 1985 peak of over 145 percent to less than 90 percent this year. In short, some of the domestic policy weaknesses that figured so prominently in the run-up to the debt crisis are being tackled.

(ii) A second notable area of progress concerns the behavior of international interest rates, which have declined by more than 6 percentage points from their 1982 level. This carries particular significance for Latin America because roughly two thirds of its external debt is subject to variable interest rates. Each 1 percentage point decline in international interest rates saves the indebted countries of this region approximately 2¼ billion dollars in net interest payments on an annual basis. It is significant that the ratio of Latin America's interest payments to its export earnings has been on a steadily declining trend since 1982—and this despite a 20 percent increase in the size of its external debt.

(iii) A third positive element has been the strengthening of financial positions on the part of both commercial banks and debtor countries. Commercial banks have added to their loan-loss reserves and expanded their capital base. U.S. banks, for example, now have a ratio of claims in Latin America to their capital of about 80 percent; in 1982 it was on the order of 130 percent. At

"All Participants Must Work Together To Ensure Resolution of Debt Problem," *IMF Survey*, December 1, 1986, pp. 374–377. Published by the International Monetary Fund, Washington, DC.

203

the same time, indebted countries in Latin America have seen their international reserves grow by over a third since 1982. These strengthened positions mean that there is now a firmer basis for banks to resume reasonable lending to developing countries and that some debtor countries can now count on an expansion of their imports.

(iv) The final area of progress concerns the effective collaboration that has developed among debtor countries, creditor countries, commercial banks, and multilateral financial institutions. It is this collaboration that has permitted an orderly approach to the debt problem.

2. These achievements should not be underestimated. But we should also acknowledge that there have been setbacks and that some serious problems remain.

". . . the period ahead is likely to be one in which growth will be equally necessary to sustain adjustment and policy reform."

(i) The quantum improvement in the external position of indebted countries did not come without costs. Commercial financing flows to developing countries contracted sharply after the onset of the crisis—at a time of declines in export earnings and increases in real interest rates. Total net private lending to Latin America stood at $55 billion in 1981. By 1983, it had fallen to less than $1 billion. Given the sheer size of the initial disequilibrium and the heavy dependence on private sources for current account financing, these countries had little choice but to make deep cuts in imports and investment. Between 1981 and 1983, import volumes in Latin America plunged by more than 40 percent, while the share of gross investment in GDP fell by more than 5 percentage points. Growth was interrupted; unemployment rose; and real incomes fell. The almost 10 percent expansion of real output during the past three years has put Latin America back on the road to recovery. But social tensions are still there. This is a region where the population and labor force are growing rapidly. Five million new jobs are needed each year just to keep unemployment from rising. As necessary as adjustment was—and still is—to sustain growth, the period ahead is likely to be one in which growth will be equally necessary to sustain adjustment and policy reform.

(ii) A second general area of concern relates to this year's global economic environment, which has been less hospitable to developing countries than many had hoped.

A dominant factor for Latin America has been the pronounced decline in world oil prices. This of course had very different consequences for the region's fuel exporting and non-fuel exporting countries. Whereas the former group saw its terms of trade, export earnings, and current account position all deteriorate significantly this year, the latter group is expected to record a moderate improvement in these variables—and this notwithstanding the further decline in the prices of non-oil primary commodities. The difference in growth performance is equally marked. While fuel exporters endured an estimated decline of almost 2¾ percent in real GDP this year, non-fuel exporters are likely to register a gain of about 5 percent—their highest growth rate since the beginning of the decade. In the aggregate figures, it is the adverse experience of the fuel exporters that predominates. Taken as a whole, Latin America suffered estimated deteriorations of 12 percent in its terms of trade and of 10 percent in its export earnings; a widening of its current account deficit from about 4 percent of exports last year to more than 11 percent this year; a further rise in its debt-to-exports ratio; and, finally, a

slowdown in its growth rate from 3¾ percent last year to an estimated 2¾ percent this year.

"A dominant factor for Latin America has been the pronounced decline in world oil prices."

A disturbing feature of the current global environment is the continuing threat posed by protectionism. If anything, the problem seems to have become more entrenched in the industrial world over the past few years. Subsidies applied to agricultural products, restrictions on textile imports, and voluntary export restraints have been especially damaging to Latin American countries. The effects of protectionism are particularly pernicious in present circumstances when debtors are struggling to earn their way out of debt. If they find their path blocked by restrictions against the very products in which they hold a comparative advantage, what incentive will they have to adopt more "outward-looking" policy reforms?

The large external payments imbalances among the three largest industrial countries are also worrisome. The current account deficit of the United States is expected to be in excess of $120 billion this year, while the surpluses of the Federal Republic of Germany and Japan are together apt to reach more than $110 billion. These payments imbalances are a source of instability and friction—not just to the countries involved but to the entire world economy. They complicate the tasks of achieving exchange rate stability, of beating back the forces of protectionism, and of sustaining economic expansion. Fortunately, help now seems to be on the way. The realignment of major-currency exchange rates that has occurred over the past 18 months should facilitate the efforts to reduce these imbalances. Likewise, prospects for more convergent financial policies are brighter. Of particular importance is the plan put forward for a major fiscal correction in the United States. But we should recognize that exchange rate changes take time to have their full impact on trade volumes and that much remains to be done to translate financial plans into action.

(iii) Yet a third concern is the contraction of commercial financing flows that I alluded to earlier. In 1983 commercial banks increased their net lending to Latin American developing countries by 6 percent. But net new lending has been on a disappointing downward trend since then. In 1984 it expanded by 2 percent. Last year it was virtually flat. There can be no return to the unsustainable rates of bank lending that prevailed in the 1973–81 period. But when growth-oriented adjustment programs are being implemented with courage and tenacity, it is essential that debtors be assured of continued understanding and support on the part of their creditors.

(iv) Finally, a frank and comprehensive assessment would also indicate that some policy slippages have occurred in indebted countries during the past year and that there is still a long way to go to establish the underlying conditions necessary for sustained growth.

"A disturbing feature of the current global environment is the continuing threat posed by protectionism."

The overall public sector position weakened this year in 7 of the 12 largest economies in Latin America. The problem was most pronounced in the fuel exporting countries, where the large drop in world oil prices induced a significant loss of budgetary revenues. In some other cases, the permanence of cuts in budget deficits was undermined by excessive reliance on once-and-for-all revenue measures and by weak control of expenditure.

Taking a longer-term perspective, the existence of both large stocks of public debt and still-high rates of inflation in much of the region acts as an impediment to durable growth and limits the room for maneuver of policymakers. Any internal or external shock that widens the fiscal gap adds to the already heavy burden of interest payments and gives rise to difficult financing problems. Selling yet more debt typically involves even higher interest rates and a crowding out of private expenditure. High inflation generates pervasive uncertainties, weakens the financial sector, and ultimately limits the scope for further revenue from an inflation tax. Attempts to place higher taxes on domestic assets can, meanwhile, encourage capital flight. In the end, there is no real alternative to determined fiscal adjustment and comprehensive programs to fight inflation.

Needed Policies and Actions

The picture of the debt situation that I have just painted serves to bring out the challenges we now face. In my view, the response to those challenges must recognize two fundamental realities. One is that further progress on the debt problem depends critically on each of the major parties pulling his weight. Co-responsibility must therefore remain the cornerstone of the strategy. Second, a satisfactory solution to the problem—not only in Latin America but in the developing world as a whole—is feasible only in the context of durable growth in the indebted countries.

1. Debtor countries can maximize the odds for success by putting in place appropriate macroeconomic and structural policies and by persevering in their implementation. Each country's economic program must be designed for its specific needs and circumstances. Allow me to offer a few guideposts for policy that I think are particularly relevant to the current situation.

(i) Debtor countries need to make the most of their export opportunities. Export earnings are crucial for generating the foreign exchange necessary to service external debt and for stimulating domestic production. Yet exports will only flourish if exporting is sufficiently profitable relative to other economic activities, if exporters have access to the imported inputs they need, and if producers of tradable goods are subject to the proper competitive discipline. This means that real exchange rates have to be continuously maintained at competitive levels and that—where necessary—foreign trade regimes should be liberalized to eliminate excessive protection for domestic producers. In this connection, I would like to draw attention to the positive steps taken by Ecuador to reform its exchange system and to liberalize imports.

(ii) Improved growth also implies more and higher-quality investment. It is noteworthy that those indebted countries that were best able to protect investment during the external adjustment process also registered the strongest growth performances. Given the recent sluggishness of capital inflows and the need to service existing debt, domestic savings have assumed even greater importance as a source of new investment. It is therefore essential to maintain real interest rates at levels that encourage private saving, to ensure that government deficits do not absorb an unduly high share of private saving, and to orient the tax system toward the reward of saving rather than consumption. A receptive attitude toward foreign direct investment would help to unlock more foreign savings. Such investment is not only non-debt-creating and a means of upgrading the level of technology but it also offers greater protection than do borrowed funds against sudden changes in the international cost of capital. Yet

increasing savings—domestic and foreign—is only half the battle. It is equally necessary to see that those savings are put to

> "... there is no real alternative to determined fiscal adjustment and comprehensive programs to fight inflation."

efficient use. Again, realistic real interest rates can help—in this case as a signal for differentiating between productive and less productive investment projects. The relatively high capital-output ratios in countries with recent debt-servicing problems—a characteristic that goes back long before the debt crisis—are suggestive of the considerable scope for improvement in this area.

(iii) Structural, supply-oriented policies are also essential, especially where they spur the development of the private sector. In this regard—an area, I might add, in which Ecuador has been taking actions—the rationalization of public enterprises, tax policies that reward work and investment, the provision of adequate credit to private firms, and efforts to keep real wages in line with labor productivity all have constructive roles to play.

(iv) There is another element in the growth-oriented adjustment strategy. Indeed, it is a prerequisite for all the other elements. I refer to the maintenance of overall financial stability and the confidence it provides to traders, savers, investors, and lenders—be they domestic or foreign. Nowhere is such stability more central than in seeking a repatriation of flight capital. It has been estimated that capital flight almost doubled the financing requirements of Latin American countries over the 1979–82 period. By all accounts, capital flight has declined appreciably since then. For some countries in this region, we are now seeing the beginnings of a repatriation of the large stock of private financial assets held abroad. But further progress in this area cannot be dictated. It will come only with the further strengthening of confidence. Prudent monetary and fiscal policies, accompanied where needed by institutional measures to combat inertial inflation, therefore are indispensable.

2. Adjustment policies in debtor countries—central as they are to the debt strategy—cannot do the job alone. More than 70 percent of Latin America's total exports go to the industrial countries. Moreover, it is the latter's policies that have the largest impact on international interest rates and on the values of the key invoice currencies. A situation in which the real interest rate on debt exceeds the growth rate of debtor countries' exports is not conducive to a declining debt burden or to growth. The industrial countries can provide crucial support by rolling back protectionism and by following sound fiscal and monetary policies that are compatible with healthy, non-inflationary growth in world demand, lower international interest rates, and an appropriate pattern of exchange rates. In addition, they can facilitate financial flows to indebted countries through adequate official export credits and increased official development assistance. The massive transfer of resources from the Third World to the industrial countries caused by recent declines in developing countries' terms of trade—a figure on the order of $80 billion this

> "As much as ever, the Fund is being called on to react quickly and imaginatively to difficult circumstances."

year alone—also means that creditor countries are in an improved financial position to support the growth efforts of the indebted countries.

3. As I suggested earlier, banks' new loan commitments to major debtors during the past year appear to be well short of the amounts implied in the U.S. debt initiative. The large commercial bank financing package in support of Mexico's adjustment efforts provides an important test for the strategy of collaboration. It is encouraging that some debtor countries who had earlier needed the bridge provided by concerted lending to help them through the difficult early stages of adjustment have now graduated to more normal market access. In this respect, the resumption of spontaneous bank lending to Ecuador and to Uruguay—the first such cases in Latin America—is most heartening. We are likewise witnessing a greater readiness to introduce innovative financial mechanisms into the picture. One promising avenue—already under way in a number of debtor countries, including Brazil, Chile, Mexico, and the Philippines—is the conversion of existing bank debt into equity. This growing trend is, in my view, most welcome. We in the Fund are following developments in this field with great interest. The IFC's [International Finance Corporation's] recent initiative should give further impetus to such conversions. Another interesting technique is cofinancing with the World Bank, as illustrated in the arrangements for Côte d'Ivoire and Uruguay. The revolving credit facility for the pre-financing of Ecuador's oil exports also breaks new ground. Given what is at stake, I can only expect that creditors and debtors will increasingly recognize their common interest in arranging farsighted and equitable solutions to financing problems.

4. The final pillar of the reinforced debt strategy is enhanced collaboration between the Fund and the World Bank. The particular strengths of the two Bretton Woods institutions are complements—not substitutes—in formulating growth-oriented programs. Over the years the Bank has accumulated broad practical experience in assessing and monitoring investment programs, the efficiency of public enterprises, pricing policies, sectoral measures, and other supply-oriented policies. The same is true of the Fund with respect to exchange rate, fiscal, monetary, and foreign borrowing policies. But it is precisely by combining the two within a common diagnosis of problems that growth and adjustment—liberalization and stabilization—can best reinforce each other.

The Role of the Fund

I come now to the central role that the Fund has been playing— and is continuing to play—in the debt strategy.

"[Latin America] is a region of great economic promise."

1. From the beginning, the Fund has been assisting the indebted countries in drawing up comprehensive economic and financial programs geared to the particular problems of each case, and in mobilizing the financing needed to carry those programs out. In Latin America alone, the Fund has provided more than $14½ billion in balance of payments financing since mid-1982. Because the Fund's lending is conditional on countries' undertaking adjustment efforts, there has been a "catalytic" effect on other lenders, particularly the commercial banks. About $29 billion in concerted bank lending has been disbursed in the form of new money to Latin American indebted countries since the beginning of 1983; rescheduling of medium- and long-term bank debt for the region has exceeded $184 billion over the same period.

Of the 15 heavily indebted countries mentioned in the debt initiative, more than two thirds have in place, or are now initiat-

ing, policies supported by the Fund, with close World Bank involvement. Twenty other countries are having discussions with the Fund with a view toward arranging Fund support for their adjustment efforts. As much as ever, the Fund is being called on to react quickly and imaginatively to difficult circumstances. Mexico is a classic case in point. Within a short period, it had experienced a fall of more than 60 percent in the price of the one commodity that made up two thirds of its export earnings. After studying all the options, it came forward with a comprehensive program aimed at growth, adjustment, and economic reform. The Fund has decided, with the World Bank and the Paris Club, to assist this courageous effort of the Mexican authorities.

Of course, the Fund can only continue to play its role in the debt strategy if it has the requisite financial means to do so. It is in this light that we appreciate the initiative announced by the Government of Japan at the recent Annual Meetings of the Fund and the World Bank to lend SDR 3 billion to the Fund. I also welcome the agreement reached in the Interim Committee to leave unchanged for 1987 the enlarged access limits. This means that in the period ahead the Fund will continue to be able to provide significant financial support for the strong adjustment efforts of its members.

2. Earlier on, I stressed the enormous contribution that an improved global economic environment would bring to the debt strategy. It is not enough to ask that the large existing external imbalances among the largest industrial countries be reduced. Instead, the objective must be to reduce those imbalances in a way that permits the expansion of output to continue at an adequate pace and that facilitates the further lowering of international interest rates. But experience shows that this cannot be left to "go-it-alone" economic policy management. Instead, each of the countries has to adopt sound policies and frame them in light

". . . domestic savings have assumed even greater importance as a source of new investment."

of international considerations. This is the way to get countries' fiscal and monetary positions to behave in a compatible way, to reduce the excessive variability and misalignment of key-currency exchange rates that have so plagued the world economy over the past six years, and to improve the efficiency and symmetry of Fund surveillance. Put in other words, we need enhanced economic policy coordination.

The Fund is to play an important role in the coordination process. Our analyses of the world economic outlook have been adapted to highlight the interactions of economic policies and the potential sources of economic incompatibilities and tensions among countries. We are also working on the formulation of a set of economic indicators that could be used in a judgmental way to help guide government policies toward consistent and mutually beneficial directions.

3. Fighting protectionism must be everybody's business. The path to expanding economic activity and a diminishing debt burden lies in an opening up—not in a contraction—of world markets. This is why the Fund has consistently lent its efforts toward the promotion of an open trading system. The Declaration agreed at the recent GATT [General Agreement on Tariffs and Trade] ministerial meeting in Punta del Este that launched the Uruguay Round of multilateral trade negotiations is an important step forward. Its coverage is comprehensive, and its standstill and rollback provisions give it real teeth. In the period ahead it is crucial that the commitments in the Punta del Este Declaration be translated into action.

* * * * *

The broad framework of the reinforced debt strategy is sound. The challenge we now face is to achieve better implementation of that strategy. By combining more effective policies in debtor countries with a strengthened global economic environment and with adequate financing, it is possible to transform the 1980s into a period of renewal and growth for Latin America. This is a region of great economic promise. Its ample natural resources, high educational level, solid industrial base and economic infrastructure, and the abilities of its people give it the potential to be a pole of growth in the world economy. It is in the interests of all parties to see that this potential is fully realized. Social progress, financial stability, and, ultimately, the consolidation of democracy are all closely linked to the success of the development strategy.

Latin America's external debt: the limits of regional cooperation

Esperanza Durán

The problem of Latin America's external debt, which came to the forefront of international attention in 1982 and 1983, continues to be serious. Financial and economic collapse at the domestic and international level has been averted by swift action by the creditor banks and some tough austerity policies in the debtor countries—in many cases under the supervision of the International Monetary Fund (IMF). But only temporarily. The 'crisis-management' approach adopted to ease the immediate difficulties has worked, but long-term solutions for what remains a potentially explosive situation have not yet been devised.[1]

Within Latin America, a growing awareness has developed that, despite the diversity of their approaches to economic policy-making, the countries in the region are up against the same problems in negotiations over their foreign debt. This realisation, plus the deterioration of the external conditions in the world economy (rising interest rates, declining terms of trade, growing protectionism in the industrial countries), has prompted Latin American leaders to make pronouncements and engage in a measure of collective action aimed at easing the conditions imposed on them and increasing their bargaining power. Many have argued that the debt problem is no longer a purely financial question and that it has been transformed into a largely political problem. The leaders of the main Latin American countries have made this clear at a series of meetings held to discuss a common strategy on the debt which resulted in the formation of the 11-strong Cartagena group. The group's aim is to establish a political dialogue among the main actors in the debt drama: banks, governments of creditor and debtor countries, and multilateral institutions. So far, the group has had no success. But there have also been more radical statements from the region. Alan García, on his inauguration as President of Peru in July 1985, declared his intention to make debt repayments not exceed 10 per cent of his country's export earnings. Shortly afterwards, Cuba's Prime Minister, Fidel Castro, in the presence of a host of Latin American personalities in Havana, called for the collective default of the Latin American countries' foreign debt. But these spectacular public statements have not, so far, been followed by radical actions by the Latin American countries. Neither the much-feared formation of a debtors' club nor the collective repudiation of financial obligations by the Latin American countries has occurred, although a few individual—and inevitable—'discreet moratoria' by countries like Bolivia and Ecuador have taken place.

This article describes the efforts by the Latin American countries to present a common front vis-à-vis their creditors, and their successes and failures in achieving more favourable terms in their debt renegotiations; points out the limits to collective action and analyses external obstacles to closer cooperation by Latin American countries on the debt issue; and finally, it examines the prospects for more assertive action by the Latin American debtors in the future.

The debt saga: phase one

When the gravity of the debt problems faced by the Latin American countries was fully realised by the creditor banks and

From the May, 1986, issue of *The World Today*, pp. 84-88. THE WORLD TODAY, published monthly by The Royal Institute of International Affairs, 10 St. James's Square, London SW1Y 4LE, U.K. Student discounts for subscriptions.

the governments of the industrialised nations, following the summer of 1982, prompt measures were taken to take control of the situation. The governments, as lenders of last resort, tried to convince the banks to keep their credit lines open to the Latin American debtors in order to keep the financial system running smoothly until some longer-term solutions could be found. The common opinion at this early stage was that the problem faced by the debtor countries was one of liquidity, not of insolvency. Therefore, it was believed that short-term assistance combined with a swift return to sound economic management would lead to the creation of the necessary resources to enable debtor countries to meet their debt-servicing obligations.

Adjustment programmes under the guidance of the IMF were demanded by the banks as a precondition for keeping their credit lines to heavily indebted countries open. Thus, they increased an exposure which on purely commercial individual-bank considerations would have been improbable. IMF stabilisation stressed the need for fiscal and monetary caution and tried to put an end to expansionary economic policies in Latin America, which were regarded by many as one of the roots of the debt crisis. The emphasis was on sharp reduction in public expenditure and anti-inflationary measures, the raising of fiscal revenues and the curtailment of capital flight. On the current-account front, measures prescribed included trade (and domestic-markets) liberalisation and the devaluation of the national currency to boost exports and reduce imports. The chief aim was the achievement of a trade surplus which would enable debtor countries to replenish their foreign reserves and meet their debt repayments.

This type of adjustment programme was supposed to restore internal equilibrium to the Latin American countries and put them back on a sound economic basis. The disbursement of stand-by credits by the IMF and the new finance to be provided by commercial banks was to be linked to the performance targets of the countries under treatment. The expectation was that the implementation of this programme would lead to the eventual restoration of the debtors' creditworthiness which would, in turn, lead to the resumption of voluntary lending.

However, the theory did not match the practice; the IMF-sponsored measures produced a number of negative consequences. The stabilisation policies pursued by the Latin American countries in order to obtain access to further lending created heavy social and political burdens. There was a steady decline in nutritional standards; drastic cuts in public expenditure led to a further reduction of already poor educational, housing and medical services; unemployment increased dramatically. There were food riots and demonstrations in Brazil, violent protests in the Dominican Republic and huge strikes in Bolivia and Peru. Austerity in the eyes of the Latin Americans did not seem a reasonable solution to their problems. Worst of all, these sacrifices did not even look like containing the seeds of a solution in the longer run. The future, just like the present, continued to look dim.

With increasing frequency, over the last year or two, the Latin American leaders kept saying that the region could no longer sacrifice growth in order to repay its $360bn worth of external debt. Latin American officials started voicing their belief that it was not only internal factors that had created the debt crisis. External circumstances and policies in the industrial countries were also to be apportioned part of the blame. Therefore, they argued, it was logical to expect that the burden of responsibility should be more evenly shared. Latin American leaders repeatedly stressed that, despite very high costs in social and political terms, the Latin American countries had made major adjustments in their economies to meet their financial obligations, and called for a parallel reaction by the banks and creditor countries. These declarations seemed to suggest that the way was being paved for a collective Latin American approach to the problem. But it soon became clear that this type of action faced heavy obstacles.

Regional cooperation: the Latin American option

What worried commercial bankers and their governments after the Latin American governments started consultations among themselves about debt renegotiation was the possibility of a polarisation in the debtor-creditor relationship and the eventual formation of a debtor club. The danger there lay in the possibility that such a club adopt a radical posture towards common financial obligations, including the imposition of ceilings to debt-servicing linked to each country's export performance; unilateral interest rate-capping; declaration of grace periods when no capital or interest payments would be made; or even, however improbable, a concerted default. These were the developments banks and creditor governments feared and wanted to avoid. At the very least, the formation of a debtors' club would make the present (and preferred) case-by-case approach unworkable. It would also provide the Latin American debtors with a powerful new addition to their bargaining power.

Six months after the 1982 Mexican financial collapse which triggered the crisis, the then president of Ecuador, Osvaldo Hurtado, appealed to two Latin American economic institutions, namely ECLA (United Nations Economic Commission for Latin America) and SELA (Latin American Economic System), to develop a strategy for dealing with the acute economic and financial difficulties the region was undergoing. These institutions drafted a document outlining the 'bases for Latin American response to the international economic crisis', and sponsored several meetings of representatives of Latin American governments to discuss possible common action.[2]

A major Latin American economic conference took place in Quito, Ecuador, in January 1984, which was attended by the Presidents of Colombia, Costa Rica, Ecuador, Dominican Republic, the Prime Minister of Jamaica and high level officials from 26 Latin American and Caribbean countries. The conference issued a document called the Quito Declaration and a Plan of Action outlining the steps that the countries in the region should take to ease their economic and financial problems. The Plan of Action stated that the responsibility for the current problems posed by a massive foreign debt was shared between debtor and industrial countries, banks and multilateral financial institutions. It went on to propose a comprehensive programme which covered not only debt-related solutions but considerations on trade, regional food security, cooperation on energy issues and services. Specifically with regard to the debt, the Plan called for a reduction of debt-service repayments, interest rates, commissions and other charges which substantially increased the cost of renegotiation. It proposed the lengthening of repayment and grace periods, the maintenance of an adequate flow of fresh finance for the region, more commercial credits and the elimination of the protectionist barriers imposed by the industrial countries.[3]

At this early stage of regional cooperation on the debt, none of the proposals contained in the Plan of Action translated into effective practice. Nor did they have a direct impact on the bilateral negotiations which were taking place around this time between debtors and creditors to restructure the existing debts. But the Quito meeting had created an atmosphere of regional solidarity and provided a common platform for future negotiations.

The first test of this newly found regional identity came during the annual meeting of the Inter-American Development Bank (IDB) in Punta del Este, Uruguay, in the spring of 1984. The governments of Brazil, Colombia, Mexico and Venezuela took the unprecedented step of putting together a $300m loan for Argentina to help it meet overdue interest payments. This Latin American bail-out was a good sample of the options available to Latin American borrowers if they decided to act collectively. However, the next collective action was triggered yet again by an external factor and not by a regional development.

There had been warnings coming not only from Latin America, but from top policy-makers in the United States, such as the then chairman of the Council of Economic Advisers, Martin Feldstein, and the Chairman of the Federal Reserve Board, Paul Volcker, that rapidly rising interest rates, coupled with the Latin American countries' reluctance to accept economic stagnation as the price for new funds, would make the 'crisis-management' approach followed until then unworkable in the medium and long term. Indeed, interest rates had been showing marked increases in a relatively short time. From February to May 1984, the United States prime lending rate increased by one and a half per cent adding up millions to the interest bill of the debtor countries. In May 1984, the prospect of a clash between Latin American debtors and their creditors over interest rates and trade protectionism increased sharply. The Presidents of Argentina, Brazil, Colombia and Mexico issued a joint statement warning western governments that external factors outside the control of their governments, namely high and rising interest rates and the proliferation of protectionism, not only were serious threats to the economic growth of the region, but that they were also jeopardising the progress of democratic trends in Latin America. 'Our countries cannot accept these risks indefinitely. We do not accept being pressed into forced bankruptcy and a prolonged economic paralysis . . .' read the statement.[4] The statement was unprecedented not only because of the severity of its tone, but because it was jointly subscribed by three big Latin American debtors.

Reactions to this and other appeals by the Latin American countries to the western governments to adopt a more flexible attitude towards their foreign debt difficulties and to the suggestion that a debt summit should take place came at the tenth annual economic summit of the seven major industrialised countries in London in June 1984. In their communiqué the call for a debtor-creditor summit was ignored, but the third-world debt problems were specifically addressed. The statement regarding the debt problem reiterated the agreed strategy of the industrial countries for dealing with it: to be flexible in its application and to continue the case-by-case approach. It mentioned that the part industrial nations should play was to help debtor countries to implement the necessary economic and financial policy changes with due attention to political and social problems. The industrial nations agreed that the IMF should continue to play a central role in this process in closer cooperation with the World Bank, whose function in fostering medium- and long-term development should be strengthened. Finally, the communiqué stressed the need to extend multi-year reschedulings of commercial debts, as well as those of governments and government agencies, to the countries which made successful efforts to implement the necessary economic reforms.

The 'Cartagena consensus'

The statement on the debt, issued after the 1984 London summit did little to assuage Latin American countries' worries. Shortly afterwards, the majority of the countries in Latin America sent delegations to Cartagena, Colombia, to try to reach a common position on the pressing problems affecting their debt repayments, particularly the rise of interest rates (which increased by another percentage point in June). Of the countries represented at Cartagena, the one most prepared to adopt a radical attitude towards creditors and IMF-imposed austerity programmes was Argentina, with the possible backing of Bolivia, Ecuador and the Dominican Republic.

It was the economic and political situation in these countries that was behind their possible challenge to the whole IMF-centred international financial system and approach to the problem. President Raul Alfonsín, as the first democratically elected Argentine leader after the long period of military dictatorship, was in no position to accept the IMF austerity package as the condition to obtain new finance. He had already issued a refusal to pay interest accrued on Argentina's debt. It was, in fact, the Latin American loan, as mentioned above, that prevented Argentina's debt from becoming non-performing. Bolivia, for its part, had already declared a moratorium on its foreign debt; payments had already been suspended in 1983. Ecuador had also stopped payments on its foreign debt a month before the meeting, while the Dominican Republic had suspended negotiations with the IMF in the wake of riots which followed the introduction of food price increases. Other possible backers of the radical approach were Peru and Chile, both small and perhaps more vulnerable debtors. Chile, for instance, urged the region as a whole to pay no more than 25 per cent of its export earnings on debt-servicing. Bolivia backed this initiative, which became generally accepted by the Cartagena group as a principle, but was never put into operation. Other participants at the meeting were less inclined to take a confrontational attitude, which had a lot to do with their own economic situation and the state of their bilateral negotiations with the banks.

But the real obstacles to achieving a collective clout, were the relatively better conditions then enjoyed by several countries. Mexico was expecting to be the first country to obtain the much-sought multi-year rescheduling of its official debt in exchange for its willingness to abide by the austerity measures directed by the IMF. Brazil was expecting similar treatment, given that it had been making efforts since early 1983 to implement major changes in wage, fiscal and monetary policies and was achieving impressive trade surpluses.

Thus, there was not much common ground among the 11 Latin American countries gathered in Cartagena to take concrete collective actions. There was a strong interest, particularly among the large debtors (with the exception of Argentina), in the maintenance of the autonomy of individual countries in their negotiations with the banks, and in the adoption of only a general declaration of principles. In the end, this position won the day. The moderate line was adopted. All agreed against the creation of a debtors' cartel, and against a general moratorium. The final document, known as the Cartagena Consensus, reiterated the Quito declaration on the need to bring down interest rates and reduce trade protectionism, but also demanded a rate cap on loans to debtor countries, the lowering of the 'spreads' (the difference between borrowing and lending rates), the stretching of the maturities of loans and compensatory payments to countries hit by variable interest rates.

A significant concrete result achieved in the process was the institutionalisation of the 11-nation Cartagena group[5] as a permanent regional forum for consultation on debt matters, in particular addressed to securing an efficient exchange of relevant information. The next meeting of the group took place in September 1984 in Mar del Plata, Argentina. There were no new initiatives over the debt as such, but the invitation to the industrialised countries to engage in a direct political dialogue with the debtors was renewed. The Argentinian delegation, in contrast to its attitude at Cartagena, this time adopted a cautious approach, avoiding statements which could harm its own negotiations. The Latin American representatives present at this meeting agreed that the Interim and Development Committees within the IMF and World Bank respectively were inadequate forums to move forward on the debt issue. These committees were essentially of a technical character, whereas the debt problem was firmly placed within the political sphere. Any radical change in strategy would need to involve bodies with a wider competence. The reaction to this proposal was varied. The United States and Britain rejected the idea of a special conference on the debt stressing that it should be kept within the established forums, such as the UN, and the IMF and World Bank committees. However, other governments, including France and Canada, informally supported the idea. Among the proposals the Mar del Plata meeting agreed upon was that for the creation of a compensation fund within the IMF for use by less developed countries whose debt repayments had risen substantially owing to high interest rates. There were also suggestions for increasing the lending capability of the World Bank. Changes were proposed on the guidelines of the IMF for negotiating austerity packages in order to accommodate longer-term solutions as well as considerations of social costs involved. The Latin American representatives also objected to the practice of prior agreement with the IMF before renegotiation of loans that commercial banks have traditionally insisted on.

Between the period of the Mar del Plata meeting and the following gathering of the Cartagena group in Santo Domingo in February 1985, the debt situation of several countries moved in the right direction. Mexico achieved in September 1984 a much publicised restructuring of $48·7bn of its public debt on very favourable terms, and Brazil and Venezuela, and perhaps also Argentina, were in a good position to follow in Mexico's steps. In Santo Domingo, Latin American delegates decided to stop pressing for the idea of a summit with western governments in order to await the results of the IMF's Interim Committee and World Bank's Development Committee due to take place in Washington in April 1985. Some interpreted this moderate position as the result of the fact that Mexico, Argentina and Venezuela had had major successes in their official debt negotiations. But these developments triggered the launching from Santo Domingo of a call for this treatment to be extended to the rest of the debtor countries.

The maverick approaches

The summer of 1985 brought some unpleasant surprises for bankers and creditor governments alike. These were: Peru's decision to limit foreign debt payments to 10 per cent of its export revenues; and Fidel Castro's large and notorious Latin American gathering in Havana, where he made an appeal to the Latin American governments to repudiate their foreign debt. Although no serious immediate consequences ensued from García's and Castro's much publicised statements, they added a new element of urgency to the regional debt negotiations.

Alan García's challenge to Peru's creditors, made in his presidential inaugural address, took everybody by surprise. It was the first case of a major country taking unilateral action to implement one of the proposals suggested by the Latin American countries in their regional meetings—the proposal to put a ceiling on debt payments in relation to the countries' export earnings. Moreover, the ceiling announced by García was far more drastic than the 25 per cent limit proposed by Chile at the Cartagena meeting. Other Latin American debtors reacted quickly to Garcia's statement. High-level delegations were present in Lima for the inauguration, six of them headed by the Presidents of their respective countries. The members of the Cartagena group rejected the Peruvian President's initiative to cap debt repayments. Although the idea of linking debt payments to exports had been endorsed by the Cartagena group as a principle, no country had dared carry it out, let alone announce it, so defiantly. The other tough part of his statement, that Peru would not accept the conditionality of the IMF, did not cause so much consternation. Other countries (for instance Venezuela) had kept their distance from the IMF, while Brazil and Argentina had maintained only intermittent relations with the Fund.

García's statement did not unleash a wave of attacks on the prevailing strategy for managing the debt, but it did serve to reinforce the view that Latin American countries should engage in harder bargaining with the banks and should not accept great sacrifices for their populations and stagnant economies as a matter of course.

Another maverick initiative came from Cuba's leader, Fidel Castro. In Havana at the end of July 1985, Castro hosted a conference for 1,500 delegates, including ex-presidents, ex-prime ministers, political and religious leaders and prominent businessmen, but few of the region's policy-makers. Castro's contention was that the debt was unpayable and that, therefore, Latin America should repudiate all its financial obligations. His appeal fell on deaf ears. The general reaction in Latin America was that it was all very well for Castro to urge a global repudiation of the debt when the bulk of Cuba's debt was to the Soviet Union which was not insisting on regular Cuban repayments. As far as Cuba's $2bn debt to western governments was concerned, it was noted that Cuba had worked hard to achieve a rescheduling agreement with its creditors within the framework of the Paris Club and generally showed that it was most interested in maintaining its creditworthiness.

The Baker initiative: too little, too late?

The repeated collective appeals of the Latin American countries for easing the burden of their external debt, and their call for a debt summit with the creditor governments, appeared to go unheeded. Real interest rates remained relatively high. But the debate on the basic nature of the problem began to spill over to the North. There were second thoughts about the strategy advocated until then for handling the debt problems. It is difficult to assess to what extent this change was due to the impact of Cartagena, and its repeated calls for the reactivation of the Latin American economies. However, it was surely no coincidence that the United States appeared to be ready to adopt a new approach to the Latin American debt problem.

The new approach was outlined by the American Secretary of the Treasury, James Baker, at the meetings of the IMF and World Bank in Seoul in October 1985. His proposal was to make available about $29bn net new lending over a three-year period to ease the financial problems of the 15 middle-income most indebted countries. Of this sum, private creditor banks were expected to contribute $20bn, which would be matched by an equal amount in loans from the World Bank and the multilateral development banks (in the case of Latin America, the Inter-American Development Bank), raising lending levels by 50 per cent. This inflow of much needed fresh funds would take place under the continuing supervision of the IMF, although the policies of the debtor countries would be geared at fostering economic growth.

The Latin American response to the Baker initiative was prepared at another meeting of the Cartagena group in December 1985, this time in Montevideo, Uruguay. The group proposed a set of economic 'emergency measures' to alleviate the economic stagnation in many countries by fostering the revival of economic activity. The main demands of the group, contained in the so-called 'Montevideo Declaration', included a call for larger fresh funds than those envisaged in the Baker initiative. Among their demands, the Cartagena group similarly reiterated the need for reducing American interest rates to 'historic levels' by the end of 1986. They also called for a reduction in commercial banks' profit margins, as well as an increase in trade finance and new credits from banks beyond the levels proposed by Baker and the maintenance of their exposure to the region. With regard to the Baker plan, the group described it as 'positive and useful' but 'insufficient'. An ad hoc group composed of Brazil, Mexico, Argentina, Colombia and Venezuela was formed to monitor the progress of the Latin American developments and to propose alternative measures in case of non-fulfilment of the stated objectives.

Similarly, the banks' reaction to the Baker initiative was not enthusiastic. In general, the banks seemed to be reluctant to increase their exposure to deeply indebted third-world countries, and stressed the need for a balance between the contributions of the commercial banks and those from governments and multilateral institutions. A number of banks were not satisfied with the contribution the governments of the industrial countries had made to easing the difficulties created by the Latin American (and third-world) debt. In the banks' view, the governments had not done enough to enlarge the export credits available via export credit guarantee schemes, nor had they matched the banks' offers of multi-year reschedulings of officially guaranteed debts. The banks attached certain conditions to their eventual support of the Baker initiative. Credit would continue to be provided on a case-by-case basis, and this only after the debtor countries had adopted sound economic programmes. A particularly critical and tricky request was that the debtor countries, in the banks' view, should make efforts to halt capital flight as well as to improve the investment climate for prospective foreign investors.

There were some points of coincidence between the two 'opposing ends' of the Baker initiative, i.e. the banks and the Latin American debtors. For example, on the necessity for governments of industrial countries to ease the difficult situation by providing more export credit and easing trade flows, and the need for a higher profile to be given to the management of the debt problems. But there were many more points of divergence. This was particularly true of the banks' reluctance to increase their exposure without sufficient guarantees which, in the Latin American view, amounted to the continuation of the much debated and not too successful approach of recent years.

The impact of declining oil prices

The continuous decline in oil prices, particularly felt at the beginning of 1986, has had a devastating effect on the two major oil producers in Latin America, Mexico and Venezuela. The fact that these two countries are also among the region's big debtors raised international concern over their continued ability to keep servicing their foreign debts.

In an effort to keep its oil market, Mexico was forced to respond to the general level of spot prices and cut its own by an average of $4 per barrel in early February. This price-cut meant that oil revenues (accounting for more than 70 per cent of Mexico's total export revenues) would decrease by $2·2bn on a yearly average. Only a fortnight later, Mexico was again forced to reduce a further $4·68 a barrel, with another possible drop of $3bn in revenue amidst a downward trend expected to continue. Mexico's drastic moves led to speculation that in view of these extremely adverse circumstances Mexico would decide either to declare a moratorium or to ask its creditors to accept a cut in interest payments.

Before reaching a decision, Mexico attempted to involve the Latin American collective forum in dealing with the bitter new phase of the debt problem. A meeting in Cancun, Mexico, between the Presidents of Mexico and Venezuela, Miguel de la Madrid and Jaime Lusinchi respectively, prepared the ground for an emergency meeting of the Cartagena group. A preliminary meeting of the Cartagena group took place in Washington, the first time such a gathering took place outside Latin America, after a call from Mexico and Venezuela. It was agreed then that the members of the monitoring committee should meet again in early March in Punta del Este, Uruguay.

Mexico, Argentina and Brazil seemed to agree on the need to reduce interest rates on past loans, whilst applying market rates to any future borrowing. This was one of the main topics to be discussed at Punta del Este, and Mexico was seen to be on the verge of declaring its intention to cap its interest payments. However, there was no agreement among the monitoring committee as to whether it should spell out a specific rate cap or only to issue vague proposals without specific figures, as had been done in the past.

Nevertheless, when the finance ministers of the steering committee met, after discussions by the foreign ministers on the peace process in Central America, there was a certain lack of rapport among them. Mexico gave the impression of having devoted more time and attention to negotiating bilaterally with its foreign creditors and American Administration officials than to the preparation of a document for discussion at the meeting with its Latin American partners, or to keeping them informed of what strategy it wished to adopt. Perhaps as a result of this, the Punta del Este meeting ended with a short communiqué supporting Mexico in its negotiations with the banks and creditor countries on the emergency financial package.

Declining oil prices, while creating severe problems for oil-exporting countries, help other debtors who have been paying exorbitant oil import bills since 1973. Lower oil prices may have a very positive effect on the world economy, with particular benefits for less developed countries, and even the oil exporters. With low oil prices, world markets will be (and are already being) stimulated. Smaller oil import bills of industrial countries will aid economic recovery, with likely increases in internal demand. This will be a stimulus to international trade, with increased demand for products of less developed countries.

A second possible side-effect of the fall of oil prices may well be an increased readiness in industrial countries to liberalise trade or to grant 'preferential' status to debtor countries; indirectly, competitivity may change in their favour. Though Latin American oil exporters may find it very hard to adjust to the drop of oil prices, other Latin American debtors, particularly Brazil, may find this a very welcome development.

Conclusions

The debt crisis, which has engulfed the Latin American countries in severe economic and financial problems since 1982, has led to a marked increase in regional contacts and to the formation of a Latin American forum, the Cartagena group, for the discussion of their financial problems and the adoption of common postures. Latin American countries realised that the formation of a 'debtor's cartel', implying a confrontational attitude vis-à-vis their creditors, was not in their interest. The actions and pronouncements of the Cartagena group have up to now remained within the bounds of moderation.

The Cartagena group's success in having its demands to the international community met has been mixed. On the one hand, the Cartagena group's proposal for a debtor-creditor summit has been rejected; interest rates still remain high; international trade has not so far received the boost necessary to ease the inflow of foreign exchange from exports to the debtor countries; and the increase of fresh loans to the region has not materialised. The amounts offered under the Baker initiative were considered insufficient, and six months after its announcement no country has yet benefited from it. But on the other hand, the Cartagena group's impact has not been negligible. Its repeated appeals for policies that would foster economic recovery and growth in Latin America have been accepted by banks and creditor countries, at least in principle. And, very important, the Cartagena group has helped to keep up the momentum in the search for long-term solutions to the debt problem.

Collective action, however, has met many obstacles. Solidarity and cooperation seem to operate only when no specific commitments are made. Because it is in each debtor's interest to maintain the maximum level of autonomy when negotiating with creditors, cooperation with regional partners takes second place. A commitment to collective action could well limit the scope of the debtor's bargaining ground. Regional cooperation ends when bilateral negotiations begin.

[1] For general background, see Roland Dallas, 'Democracy and debt in Latin America', *The World Today*, April 1984; Andrew Hurrell, 'Brazil, the United States and the debt, *ibid.*, March 1985; and Esperanza Durán, 'Mexico: economic realism and political efficiency', *ibid.*, May 1985.

[2] On the origins of Latin American collective action on the debt issue, see Riordan Roett, 'Latin America's response to the debt crisis', *Third World Quarterly*, April 1985, pp. 228–34.

[3] CEPAL, Notas sobre la economia y el desarrollo en America Latina no. 389/390, January 1984, 'Declaracion de Quito y Plan de Accion'.

[4] Andrew Whitely, 'Latin Americans step up demands on debt and trade', *Financial Times*, 21 May, p. 1.

[5] The 11 countries represented at Cartagena were: Argentina, Bolivia, Brazil, Chile, Colombia, the Dominican Republic, Ecuador, Mexico, Peru, Uruguay and Venezuela.

The Arms Race, Arms Control, and Deterrence

The Soviet proposals in 1986 and 1987 for complete disarmament by the year 2000 set a new tone in arms control and disarmament discussions. These proposals, the most conciliatory and progressive ones offered thus far, go beyond American proposals for eliminating all medium-range missiles, to addressing the elimination of all ICBMs, defensive systems, and chemical weapons, and even to negotiating about conventional force reductions in Europe. In addition, the Soviets have, for the first time ever, agreed to on-site inspection to assure the United States of its compliance with treaties on nuclear weapons. They have dropped their earlier demand that British and French missiles be included in any agreement to remove Soviet and American intermediate range missiles from Europe, and substituted a request that the British and French simply freeze their nuclear missiles. Gorbachev's offer to sign a separate pact on elimination of medium range missiles in Europe even dropped the earlier precondition that arms negotiations be predicated upon the end to American research in the Strategic Defense Initiative (SDI) program, commonly known as "Star Wars." Further, in spite of the American refusal to accept the Soviets' proposal to freeze weapons testing and deployment while negotiations were taking place, the Soviets unilaterally continued their own test ban until February 1987.

These series of proposals and decisions by the Soviets have put the Reagan administration on the defensive. Even America's allies have been critical of the US for violating the SALT II Treaty limits on bombers and missiles as a symbol of the Reagan administration's decision that it would no longer informally adhere to the Treaty's provisions. In addition, they have been even more critical of US efforts to reinterpret the 1972 ABM (Anti-Ballistic Missiles) Treaty in order to justify the deployment of the SDI space-based defense missile system.

The United States does have other issues to resolve before agreeing to Soviet proposals on disarmament. Most notable is the need to address Korea's and Japan's concern that they do not include a similar complete elimination of medium-range weapons east of the Soviet Union's Ural Mountains. Earlier, Reagan tried to address the Japanese concern by proposing fifty percent reduction of Soviet medium-range missiles in Asia, with the deployment of the remaining missiles confined to Soviet Central Asia. From there, they could not reach Japan or Korea, but could reach China. Since China is not a participant in the disarmament negotiations and maintains a substantial nuclear arsenal of its own, disarmament proposals are more likely to address Soviet concerns about maintaining an effective deterrent to the potential Chinese threat.

On the other hand, although the Europeans responded very positively to Gorbachev's March, 1987 proposal for the complete elimination of Euromissiles, they remain concerned that medium-range missiles east of the Urals could still hit parts of Europe, and that NATO conventional forces are substantially weaker than Warsaw Pact conventional forces. The problem with strengthening NATO's conventional forces to compensate for elimination of medium-range nuclear forces, and perhaps even battlefield short-range missiles, is the vastly greater expense of conventional forces. The increased costs of maintaining a significantly larger standing army and paying for the costs of larger payloads which conventional weapons must carry to deliver the same destructive impact as nuclear weapons seem prohibitive in a period of American commitment to decreasing the national deficit and balancing the budget. It is most unlikely that the military budget will escape the budget ax, much less that it will be increased to provide for larger conventional forces.

Of course, the costs to humankind of an actual outbreak of nuclear war in Europe would be far greater than the costs of the increased conventional forces that would permit NATO countries to feel comfortable in eliminating intermediate-range nuclear forces. But there is no guarantee that an increase in NATO conventional forces would not be met by a proportionate increase in Warsaw Pact forces. In any event, it is virtually impossible to quantify the actual power of either side were war to occur, due to the importance of such factors as the strength of the political and military leadership, the economic and industrial power of each side, the location of the conflict, and the morale, skill, and training of the soldiers.

The Reagan administration has thus far responded only to the first part of the Soviets' comprehensive disarmament proposals. Clearly the elimination of Euromissiles is easier than the elimination of ICBMs for the US; for Euromissiles add little, if anything, to the overall strategic capability of the US, or to its own protection. There are also advantages to the elimination of Euromissiles from the European perspective: eliminating Euromissiles decreases the likelihood of Europe becoming the major battleground for World War III, or of an accidental nuclear war occurring.

The long-term costs and effectiveness of the SDI are of concern to both Americans and Europeans. Thus far in the history of the development of armaments throughout the world, every advance in the development of arms by one side has been matched or surpassed with advances by the other side. It would be most unlikely that the Soviets would not respond to the SDI either with their own defensive shield or with a build-up in offensive weaponry that could overwhelm the American-built shield. Regardless of the economic strains on the Soviet economy, the leadership will not stand idly by while the United States makes a major breakthrough in technology.

Finally, the legality of the SDI in the context of the ABM Treaty and the Outer Space Treaty (1967) is questionable. Any defense so complete that the potential victim of nuclear strike would not be able to retaliate and inflict unacceptable damages on the attacker would mean the end of deterrence. Deterrence, premised upon "mutual assured destruction," is the very heart of the ABM Treaty. For this reason, the SDI is, in fact, not defensive but offensive. By permitting the United States to attack without fear of retaliation, the Soviet Union is put in an untenable position. The logic of strategic thinking suggests, moreover, that if a country believes it has lost its "second strike" capability, it will be tempted to initiate a preemptive strike to gain an advantage. Further, the SDI would violate the Nonproliferation Treaty by transferring X-ray laser capabilities to American allies who participate in the SDI effort. Even if treaty violations were not the issue, the effectiveness of the SDI would be. Many scientists insist that the SDI cannot provide even a near-perfect defense system, and is highly vulnerable to countermeasures such as decoys.

For those states which either cannot afford nuclear weapons or have no access to weapons-grade plutonium, there is another deadly alternative: chemical weapons. Chemical weapons are far easier and cheaper to manufacture than nuclear weapons, making proliferation among the lesser developed countries far more likely. Even if the world manages to eliminate most nuclear weapons, it may be faced with the virtually uncontrollable spread of chemical weapons. Were this to happen, the elitist "nuclear club," with hindsight, might come to be viewed as the preferable alternative.

The articles which follow discuss these and other issues related to arms control, disarmament, and deterrence. The major problem which the United States and, of course, the Soviet Union face is that although deterrence thus far appears to be the result of the existence on both sides of nuclear weapons adequate to prevent a "first strike" capability, this balance could easily become destabilized by advances on one side. The Reagan administration believes it has done much to reverse what were dangerous destabilizing trends in the military balance by strengthening both conventional and nuclear deterrent forces (Article 45). Critics of the Reagan administration's buildup believe it has made a big mistake in forcing NATO to rely on nuclear first use, and that this doctrine should be dropped

in favor of strengthening the capacity of conventional forces to successfully fight a conventional war (Article 51). The Soviets, on the other hand, believe that the US strengthening of its nuclear forces has been destabilizing and has forced the Soviet Union into a continued nuclear arms race (Article 54). The Soviet Union has offered to negotiate a separate treaty on eliminating American and Soviet medium-range missiles from Europe (Article 48). The Chinese dismiss these Soviet proposals, as well as American proposals, for disarmament as mere propaganda (Article 52).

If alternatives to the continuation of the nuclear arms race are to be viable, they must be rooted in cooperation between the US and the USSR to build a mutual shared security. If either side feels its security is jeopardized, disarmament simply is not possible (Article 46). Some analysts would argue, however, that a nuclear-free world is not necessarily desirable, since it increases the risk both of a conventional war in Europe and of the possibility that any one state which cheated and acquired just one nuclear weapon would be able to blackmail all other states (Article 47).

Certainly in the present environment of distrust, the US does not feel comfortable with disarmament. Although non-compliance cannot be verified, it has continued nuclear tests because it believes the Soviets have violated testing bans (Article 49). But some analysts believe that President Reagan's allegations of Soviet cheating are false, and in any event, that the US has also violated the very same arms control agreements (Article 50). For their part, the Soviets insist that their new initiatives have disposed of verification as an issue, and that the real obstacle to a treaty on the total prohibition of nuclear weapons tests is the US (Article 53).

Looking Ahead: Challenge Questions

What motivation does the Soviet Union have in negotiating complete disarmament? Does the US stand to gain anything from disarmament? What factors cause the US to hesitate to negotiate complete disarmament? How will the US and the USSR deal with one of the final stumbling blocks to complete disarmament: namely, that several other countries have, or could easily get, nuclear weapons and that they are not part of the disarmament agreement? What steps could the US and the USSR take to ensure that they are not the future targets of nuclear blackmail by another state? What are the prospects for a successful conclusion to the present arms negotiations between the Soviets and the Americans? Should the Chinese become a part of these negotiations at some point?

Nuclear Weapons, Arms Control, and the Future of Deterrence

Secretary Shultz

Following is an address by Secretary Shultz before the International House of Chicago and the Chicago Sun-Times *Forum at the University of Chicago, Chicago, Illinois, November 17, 1986.*

I'm delighted to be back here at the pinnacle, and I come here to the University of Chicago to talk about nuclear weapons, arms control, and our national security. These issues have been given special timeliness by the President's recent meeting with Soviet General Secretary Gorbachev in Reykjavik. In years to come, we may look back at their discussions as a turning point in our strategy for deterring war and preserving peace. It has opened up new possibilities for the way in which we view nuclear weapons and their role in ensuring our security.

Questions for the Future

We now face a series of questions of fundamental importance for the future: how can we maintain peace through deterrence in the midst of a destabilizing growth of offensive nuclear weapons? How can we negotiate a more stable strategic balance at substantially lower levels of offensive forces? How can we use new defensive technologies to contribute to that stability? How can the West best seek to reduce its reliance on offensive nuclear weapons without running new risks of instability arising from conventional imbalances?

These are exceptionally difficult and complex issues. They go to the heart of our ability as a democratic nation to survive in a world threatened by totalitarianism and aggression. These questions should engage the best minds in American society, and, of course, they have to be treated at reasonable lengths so the best minds have to have a halfway decent attention span. So that's why I have come to speak to this particular audience at the University of Chicago. So this isn't going to be an easy speech, or a short one. I'll ask that you listen carefully, and I hope that you'll reflect at greater length on the text of my remarks.

Forty-four years ago, and about 200 yards from where I am now standing, mankind generated its first self-sustained and controlled nuclear chain reaction. Enrico Fermi's crude atomic pile was the prototype for all that followed—both reactors to generate energy for peaceful uses and weapons of ever-increasing destructiveness. Seldom are we able to mark the beginning of a new era in human affairs so precisely.

I'm not here tonight to announce the end of that era. But I will suggest that we may be on the verge of important changes in our approach to the role of nuclear weapons in our defense. New technologies are compelling us to think in new ways about how to ensure our security and protect our freedoms. Reykjavik served as a catalyst in this process. The President has led us to think

seriously about both the possible benefits—and the costs—of a safer strategic environment involving progressively less reliance on nuclear weapons. Much will now depend on whether we are far-sighted enough to proceed toward such a goal in a realistic way that enhances our security and that of our allies.

It may be that we have arrived at a true turning point. The nuclear age cannot be undone or abolished; it is a permanent reality. But we can glimpse now, for the first time, a world freed from the incessant and pervasive fear of nuclear devastation. The threat of nuclear conflict can never be wholly banished, but it can be vastly diminished—by careful but drastic reductions in the offensive nuclear arsenals each side possesses. It is just such reductions—not limitations in expansion but reductions—that is the vision President Reagan is working to make a reality.

Such reductions would add far greater stability to the U.S.-Soviet nuclear relationship. Their achievement should make other diplomatic solutions obtainable and perhaps lessen the distrust and suspicion that have stimulated the felt need for such weapons. Many problems will accompany drastic reductions: problems of deployment, conventional balances, verification, multiple warheads, and chemical weapons. The task ahead is great but worth the greatest of efforts.

This will not be a task for Americans

Reprinted from *Current Policy*, No. 893, November 17, 1986, pp. 1-5, United Stated Department of State, Bureau of Public Affairs, Washington, DC.

alone. We must engage the collective effort of all of the Western democracies. And as we do, we must also be prepared to explore cooperative approaches with the Soviet Union, when such cooperation is feasible and in our interests.

The Evolution of Our Thinking About Nuclear Weapons

Let me start by reviewing how our thinking has evolved about the role of nuclear weapons in our national security.

In the years immediately after Fermi's first chain reaction, our approach was relatively simple. The atomic bomb was created in the midst of a truly desperate struggle to preserve civilization against fascist aggression in Europe and Asia. There was a compelling rationale for its development and use.

But since 1945—and particularly since America lost its monopoly of such weapons a few years later—we have had to adapt our thinking to less clearcut circumstances. We have been faced with the challenges and the ambiguities of a protracted global competition with the Soviet Union. Nuclear weapons have shaped, and at times restrained, that competition; but they have not enabled either side to achieve a decisive advantage.

Because of their awesome destructiveness, nuclear weapons have kept in check a direct U.S.-Soviet clash. With the advent in the late 1950s of intercontinental-range ballistic missiles—a delivery system for large numbers of nuclear weapons at great speed and with increasing accuracy—both the United States and the Soviet Union came to possess the ability to mount a devastating attack on each other within minutes.

The disastrous implications of such massive attacks led us to realize, in the words of President Kennedy, that "total war makes no sense." And as President Reagan has reiterated many times: "a nuclear war cannot be won and must never be fought"—words that the President and General Secretary Gorbachev agreed on in their joint statement at Geneva a year ago.

Thus, it came to be accepted in the West that a major role of nuclear weapons was to deter their use by others—as well as to deter major conventional attacks—by the threat of their use in response to aggression. Over the years, we sought through a variety of means and rationales—beginning with "massive retaliation" in the 1950s up through "flexible response" and "selective nuclear options" in the 1970s—to maintain a credible strategy for that retaliatory threat.

At the same time, we also accepted a certain inevitability about our own nation's vulnerability to nuclear-armed ballistic missiles. When nuclear weapons were delivered by manned bombers, we maintained air defenses. But as the ballistic missile emerged as the basic nuclear delivery system, we virtually abandoned the effort to build defenses. After a spirited debate over antiballistic missile systems in the late 1960s, we concluded that—on the basis of technologies now 20 years old—such defenses would not be effective. So our security from nuclear attack came to rest on the threat of retaliation and a state of mutual vulnerability.

In the West, many assumed that the Soviets would logically see things this way as well. It was thought that once both sides believed that a state of mutual vulnerability had been achieved, there would be shared restraint on the further growth of our respective nuclear arsenals.

The Anti-Ballistic Missile (ABM) Treaty of 1972 reflected that assumption. It was seen by some as elevating mutual vulnerability from technical fact to the status of international law. That treaty established strict limitations on the deployment of defenses against ballistic missiles. Its companion Interim Agreement on strategic offensive arms was far more modest. SALT I [strategic arms limitation talks] was conceived of as an intermediate step toward more substantial future limits on offensive nuclear forces. It established only a cap on the further growth in the numbers of ballistic missile launchers then operational and under construction. The most important measures of the two sides' nuclear arsenals—numbers of actual warheads and missile throw-weight—were not restricted.

But controlling the number of launchers without limiting warheads actually encouraged deployment of multiple warheads—called multiple independently-targetable reentry vehicles (MIRVs)—on a single launcher. This eventually led to an erosion of strategic stability as the Soviets—by proliferating MIRVs—became able to threaten all of our intercontinental ballistic missiles with only a fraction of their own. Such an imbalance makes a decision to strike first seem all the more profitable.

During this postwar period, we and our allies hoped that American nuclear weapons would serve as a comparatively cheap offset to Soviet conventional military strength. The Soviet Union, through its geographic position and its massive mobilized conventional forces, has powerful advantages it can bring to bear against Western Europe, the Mideast, and East Asia—assets useful for political intimidation as well as for potential military aggression. The West's success or failure in countering these Soviet advantages has been, and will continue to be, one of the keys to stability in our postwar world.

Our effort to deter a major Soviet conventional attack through the existence of opposing nuclear forces has been successful over the past four decades. It gave the industrialized democracies devastated by the Second World War the necessary "breathing space" to recover and thrive. But there has also been recurring debate over the credibility of this strategy, as well as controversy about the hardware required for its implementation.

Over time, we and our allies came to agree that deterrence required a flexible strategy combining both conventional and nuclear forces. This combined strategy has been successful in avoiding war in Europe. But our reliance for so long on nuclear weapons has led some to forget that these arms are not an inexpensive substitute—mostly paid for by the United States—for fully facing up to the challenges of conventional defense and deterrence.

Sources of Strategic Instability

The United States and our allies will have to continue to rely upon nuclear weapons for deterrence far, far into the future. That fact, in turn, requires that we maintain credible and effective nuclear deterrent forces.

But a defense strategy that rests on the threat of escalation to a strategic nuclear conflict is, at best, an unwelcome solution to ensuring our national security. Nuclear weapons, when applied to the problem of preventing either a nuclear or conventional attack, present us with a major dilemma. They may appear a bargain—but a dangerous one. They make the outbreak of a Soviet-American war most unlikely; but they also ensure that should deterrence fail, the resulting conflict would be vastly more destructive, not just for our two countries but for mankind as a whole.

Moreover, we cannot assume that the stability of the present nuclear balance will continue indefinitely. It can deteriorate, and it has. We have come to realize that our adversary does not share all of our assumptions about strategic stability. Soviet military doctrine stresses warfighting and survival in a nuclear environment, the importance of numerical superiority, the contribution of active defense, and the advantages of preemption.

Over the past 15 years, the growth of Soviet strategic forces has continued unabated—and far beyond any reasonable assessment of what might be required for rough equivalency with U.S. forces. As a result, the Soviet Union has acquired a capability to put at risk the fixed land-based missiles of the U.S. strategic triad—as well as portions of our bomber and in-port submarine force and command and control systems—with only a fraction of their force, leaving many warheads to deter any retaliation.

To date, arms control agreements along traditional lines—such as SALT I and II—have failed to halt these destabilizing trends. They have not brought about significant reductions in offensive forces, particularly those systems that are the most threatening to stability. By the most important measure of destructive capability, ballistic missile warheads—those are the things that hit you—Soviet strategic forces have grown by a factor of four since the SALT I Interim Agreement was signed. This problem has been exacerbated by a Soviet practice of stretching their implementation of such agreements to the edge of violation—and, sometimes, beyond. The evidence of Soviet actions contrary to SALT II, the ABM Treaty, and various other arms control agreements is clear and unmistakable.

At the same time, technology has not stood still. Research and technological innovation of the past decade now raise questions about whether the primacy of strategic offense over defense will continue indefinitely. For their part, the Soviets have never neglected strategic defenses. They developed and deployed them even when offensive systems seemed to have over-whelming advantages over any defense. As permitted by the ABM Treaty of 1972, the Soviets constructed around Moscow the world's only operational system of ballistic missile defense. Soviet military planners apparently find that the modest benefits of this system justify its considerable cost, even though it would provide only a marginal level of protection against our overall strategic force. It could clearly be a base for the future expansion of their defenses.

For well over a decade—long before the President announced 3 years ago the American Strategic Defense Initiative (SDI)—the Soviet Union has been actively investigating much more advanced defense technologies, including directed energy systems. If the United States were to abandon this field of advanced defensive research to the Soviet Union, the results 10 years hence could be disastrous for the West.

The President's Approach: Seeking Greater Stability

President Reagan believes we can do better. He believes we can reverse the ever-increasing numbers and potency of nuclear weapons that are eroding stability. He believes we can and must find ways to keep the peace without basing our security so heavily on the threat of nuclear escalation. To those ends, he has set in motion a series of policies which have already brought major results.

First, this Administration has taken much-needed steps to reverse dangerous trends in the military balance by strengthening our conventional and nuclear deterrent forces. We have gone forward with their necessary modernization.

Second, we have sought ambitious arms control measures—not agreements for their own sake but steps which could seriously contribute to the goal of stabilizing reductions in offensive forces. In 1981, the President proposed the global elimination of all Soviet and American longer range INF [intermediate-range nuclear forces] nuclear missiles. Not a freeze or token reductions, as many urged at the time, but the complete elimination of this class of weapons.

The following year, at Eureka College, the President proposed major reductions in strategic offensive forces, calling for cuts by one-third to a level of 5,000 ballistic missile warheads on each side. Again, this was a major departure from previous negotiating approaches—both in the importance of the weapons to be reduced and in the magnitude of their reduction. Critics claimed he was unrealistic, that he was not really interested in arms control. But the President's call for dramatic reductions in nuclear warheads on the most destabilizing delivery systems has been at the core of our negotiating efforts. The Soviets have finally begun to respond to the President's approach and are now making similar proposals.

Finally, the President also set out to explore whether it would be possible to develop an effective defense against ballistic missiles, the central element of current strategic offensive arsenals. To find that answer, he initiated in 1983 the SDI program—a broad-based research effort to explore the defensive implications of new technologies. It is a program that is consistent with our obligations under the ABM Treaty. He set as a basic goal the protection of the United States and our allies against the ballistic missile threat.

Since then, we have been seeking both to negotiate deep reductions in the numbers of those missiles, as well as to develop the knowledge necessary to construct a strategic defense against them. It is the President's particular innovation to seek to use these parallel efforts

in a reinforcing way—to reduce the threat while exploring the potential for defense.

Reykjavik: A Potential Watershed in Nuclear Arms Control

All of these efforts will take time to develop, but we are already seeing their first fruits. Some became apparent at Reykjavik. Previously, the prospect of 30%, let alone 50%, reductions in Soviet and American offensive nuclear arsenals was considered an overly ambitious goal.

At Reykjavik, the President and General Secretary Gorbachev reached the basis for an agreement on a first step of 50% reductions in Soviet and American strategic nuclear offensive forces over a 5-year period. We agreed upon some numbers and counting rules—that is, how different types of weapons would count against the reduced ceilings.

For INF nuclear missiles, we reached the basis for agreement on even more drastic reductions, down from a current Soviet total of over 1,400 warheads to only 100 on longer range INF missiles worldwide on each side. This would represent a reduction of more than 90% of the Soviet SS-20 nuclear warheads now targeted on our allies and friends in Europe and Asia. There would also have to be a ceiling on shorter range INF missiles, the right for us to match the Soviets in this category, and follow-on negotiations aimed at the reduction in numbers of these weapons.

Right there is the basis for an arms control agreement that doesn't just limit the future growth of Soviet and American nuclear arsenals but which actually makes deep and early cuts in existing force levels. These cuts would reduce the numbers of heavy, accurate, multiple-warhead missiles that are the most threatening and the most destabilizing. These ideas discussed at Reykjavik flowed directly from the President's longstanding proposals. They are a direct result of his vision of major offensive reductions as a necessary step to greater stability.

At Reykjavik, the President and the General Secretary went on to discuss possible further steps toward enhanced stability. The President proposed to eliminate all ballistic missiles over the subsequent 5 years. Mr. Gorbachev proposed to eliminate all strategic offensive forces. They talked about these and other ideas, including the eventual elimination of all nuclear weapons. The very scope of their discussion was significant. The President and the General Secretary set a new arms control agenda at Reykjavik, one that will shape our discussions with the Soviets about matters of nuclear security for years to come.

Of course, make no mistake about it. Tough, and probably drawn-out, negotiations will still be required if we are to nail down any formal agreement on offensive force reductions. For example, the Soviets are now linking agreement on anything with agreement on everything. But the fact that we now have such reductions clearly on the table has only been made possible by:

- Our steps to restore America's military strength;
- Our firm and patient negotiating efforts over the past 5 years;
- The sustained support of our allies; and, not the least,
- By our active investigation into strategic defenses.

The prospect of effective defenses and our determined force modernization program have given the Soviet Union an important incentive to agree to cut back and eventually to eliminate ballistic missiles. Within the SDI program, we judge defenses to be desirable only if they are survivable and cost effective at the margin. Defenses that meet these criteria—those which cannot be easily destroyed or overwhelmed—are precisely the sort which would lead Soviet military planners to consider reducing, rather than continuing to expand, their offensive missile force.

But only a dynamic and ongoing research program can play this role. And for their part, the Soviets are making every effort to cripple our program. Thus, there were major differences over strategic defenses at Reykjavik. The President responded to Soviet concerns by proposing that, for 10 years, both sides would not exercise their existing right of withdrawal from the ABM Treaty and would confine their strategic defense programs to research, development, and testing activities permitted by the ABM Treaty. This commitment would be in the context of reductions of strategic offensive forces by 50% in the first 5 years and elimination of the remaining ballistic missiles in the second 5 years, and with the understanding that at the end of this 10-year period, either side would have the right to deploy advanced defenses, unless otherwise agreed.

But at Reykjavik, the Soviet Union wanted to change existing ABM Treaty provisions to restrict research in a way that would cripple the American SDI program. This we cannot accept.

Even as we eliminate all ballistic missiles, we will need insurance policies to hedge against cheating or other contingencies. We don't know now what form this will take. An agreed-upon retention of a small nuclear ballistic

missile force could be part of that insurance. What we do know is that the President's program for defenses against ballistic missiles can be a key part of our insurance. A vigorous research program will give the United States and our allies the options we will need to approach a world with far fewer nuclear weapons—a world with a safer and more stable strategic balance, one no longer dependent upon the threat of mutual annihilation.

Next Steps With the Soviets

In the short term, our task is to follow up on the progress arising out of the Reykjavik discussions. For our part, we are energetically seeking to do so. Our negotiators in Geneva have instructions to pick up where the two leaders' exchanges left off. We have formally tabled our proposals, based on the progress at Reykjavik, and we are ready to discuss them.

To give additional impetus to that process, I met with Soviet Foreign Minister Shevardnadze in Vienna at the beginning of this month to continue our exchanges—not just on arms control but on the full agenda of U.S.-Soviet issues, including those regional and human rights problems which are so critical to building trust and confidence between our two nations.

Our negotiating efforts—and the President's own discussions with the General Secretary—have been based on years of analysis of these issues and on our frequent exchanges with the Soviets. The Reykjavik meeting, for instance, was preceded by extensive preliminary discussions with the Soviets at the expert level in Geneva, Moscow, and Washington. We have had our senior negotiators and best advisers at all of these sessions—as well as at our most recent encounter in Vienna.

So we have been well prepared to move. But whether we can achieve concrete results now depends on the Soviets. General Secretary Gorbachev has spoken positively of the need to capitalize on the "new situation," he called it, created by Reykjavik. But at Vienna 2 weeks ago, the Soviets seemed primarily interested in trying to characterize SDI in the public mind as the sole obstacle to agreement. Mr. Shevardnadze was quick to accuse us of backsliding from the Reykjavik results and to label our Vienna meeting "a failure" because of our unwillingness to accede to their demands to cripple SDI. We will doubtless hear more such accusations over the coming weeks.

So all of this will take time to work out. But that's to be expected in negotiating with the Soviets. We are

serious about our objectives, and we are determined to hold firmly to them. We have a clear sense of how our two nations might be able to move toward greater strategic stability. We are ready to move quickly to that end, but we are also prepared to be patient.

The Challenges of a Less Nuclear World

The longer term implications of the Reykjavik discussions may prove even more challenging for us. Thus far in the nuclear age, we have become accustomed to thinking of nuclear weapons in terms of "more bang for the buck" and of the high price for any possible substitute for these arms. But to my mind, that sort of bookkeeping approach risks obscuring our larger interests. We should begin by determining what is of value to us and then what costs we are prepared to pay to attain those ends.

The value of steps leading to a less nuclear world is clear—potentially enhanced stability and less chance of a nuclear catastrophe. Together with our allies, we could enjoy a safer, more secure strategic environment.

But we would not seek to reduce nuclear weapons only to increase the risks of conventional war or, more likely, of political intimidation through the threat of conventional attack. Therefore, a central task will be to establish a stable conventional balance as a necessary corollary for any less nuclear world.

How would a less nuclear world, one in which ballistic missiles have been eliminated, work? What would it mean? It would not be the end of nuclear deterrence for the West. With a large inventory of aircraft and cruise missiles, the United States and NATO would retain a powerful nuclear capability. In a sense, we would return to the situation of the 1950s, when strategic bombers served as our primary nuclear deterrent force. But there would be an important difference in the 1990s and beyond. Our aircraft would now be supplemented by a host of new and sophisticated technologies as well as cruise missiles launched from the air and sea. It would be a much more diverse and capable force than in previous decades.

In such circumstances, both the United States and the Soviet Union would lose the capability provided by ballistic missiles to deliver large numbers of nuclear weapons on each others' homelands in less than 30-minutes time. But Western strategy is, in fact, defensive in nature, built upon the pledge that we will only use our weapons, nuclear and conventional, in self-defense. Therefore, the loss of this quick-kill capability—so suited to preemptive attack—will ease fears of a disarming first strike.

For our friends and allies in Europe and Asia, the elimination of Soviet ballistic missiles—including not just the Soviet Union's strategic ballistic missiles and its many SS–20s but also the shorter range missiles for which we currently have no deployed equivalent—would remove a significant nuclear threat.

But it would also have non-nuclear military benefits as well. Today, the Soviet Union has ballistic missiles with conventional and chemical warheads targeted on NATO airfields, ports, and bases. The elimination of ballistic missiles would thus be a significant plus for NATO in several respects.

The nuclear forces remaining— aircraft and cruise missiles—would be far less useful for first-strike attacks but would be more appropriate for retaliation. They would be more flexible in use than ballistic missiles. The slower flying aircraft can be recalled after launch. They can be retargeted in flight. They can be re-used for several missions. We currently have a major advantage in the relative sophistication of our aircraft and cruise missiles; the Soviets have greater numbers of these systems and are striving hard to catch up in quality. They have given far more attention to defense, where we have a lot of catching up to do. But our remaining nuclear forces would be capable of fulfilling the requirements of the Western alliance's deterrent strategy.

The West's Advantages in a Less Nuclear World

The prospect of a less nuclear world has caused concern in both Europe and America. Some fear that it would place the West at a grave disadvantage. I don't think so.

In any competition ultimately depending upon economic and political dynamism and innovation, the United States, Japan, and Western Europe have tremendous inherent advantages. Our three-to-one superiority in gross national product over the Warsaw Pact, our far greater population, and the Western lead in modern technologies—these are only partial measures of our advantages. The West's true strength lies in the fact that we are not an ideological or military bloc like the Warsaw Pact; we are an alliance of free nations, able to draw upon the best of the diverse and creative energies of our peoples.

But dramatic reductions in nuclear weapons and the establishment of stronger conventional defenses will require a united alliance effort. In light of the President's discussions in Reykjavik, we must join with our allies in a more systematic consideration of how to deal with a less nuclear world. To my mind, that sort of process of joint inquiry is healthy for the alliance, particularly since we remain firmly agreed on the basics—the alliance's fundamental principle of shared risks and shared burdens on behalf of the common defense.

All of these steps—deep reductions of nuclear weapons, a strong research program in strategic defense, improvements in conventional defenses, and negotiations with the Soviet Union and Warsaw Pact—will have to be closely synchronized. This will require a carefully coordinated political strategy on the part of the alliance to deal with these interrelated aspects of the larger problem of stability and Western security. We will begin a preliminary discussion of just such an approach during my next meeting with my NATO counterparts in Brussels at the December session of the North Atlantic Council.

Conclusion

This is a full and complex agenda for all of us to consider. Is it ambitious? Yes. Unrealistic? No. I think that, on the basis of the progress made at Reykjavik, substantial reductions in Soviet and American nuclear forces are possible, and they can be achieved in a phased and stabilizing way.

But we need to think hard about how to proceed. We are taking on a difficult task as we seek to create the conditions in which we can assure the freedom and security of our country and our allies without the constant threat of nuclear catastrophe.

And, of course, our work to achieve greater strategic stability at progressively lower levels of nuclear arms is only part of our larger effort to build a more realistic and constructive relationship with the Soviet Union. We cannot pursue arms control in isolation from other sources of tension. We will continue to seek a resolution of the more fundamental sources of political distrust between our nations, especially those in the areas of human rights and regional conflicts.

Progress—whether in science or foreign affairs—often has to do with the reinterpretation of fundamental ideas. That's no easy task. It requires challenging conventional wisdom. And often we find that gaining new benefits requires paying new costs.

Just as what happened 44 years ago in the squash court under old Stagg Field opened up both new horizons and new dangers, so we now see new possibilities for protecting our security, as well as new risks if we don't manage them well. So it is up to us—working together with both allies and adversaries—to ensure that we use these new opportunities to achieve a more stable and secure peace.

Are There Alternatives to Nuclear Threat Systems?

Searching for areas of agreement, rather than disagreement, is the key to superpower coexistence

JOHN MARKS

John Marks is a former foreign service officer and Senate aide. He coauthored the bestselling CIA *and the* Cult of Intelligence *and is the author of* Search for the Manchurian Candidate. *He currently serves as executive director of Search for Common Ground in Washington, D.C.*

This article is adapted from a speech Marks delivered at the Forty-fifth Annual Conference of the American Humanist Association in April 1986.

I used to make my living writing books critical of the Central Intelligence Agency. I was very effective at throwing monkey wrenches into the old system. Indeed, I was a world-class monkey-wrench thrower. With no apologies for that kind of adversarial approach, what I was doing was a lot like punching a pillow or rearranging deck chairs on the *Titanic*.

About seven or eight years ago, I discovered another possibility: that there was an alternative kind of politics—a politics of building rather than of tearing down. I tell you this as somebody whose formative years came opposing the Vietnam War and as somebody who had a long record of extending a raised middle finger toward the "powers-that-be." What happened to me is that I discovered another alternative: the idea that politics can be transformed, that it did not have to be simply a rearrangement of the old system but that it might be possible to get beyond that system.

Please look at the simple diagram in FIGURE I. It is adapted from one first drawn by Jonas Salk, the inventor of the polio vaccine, and it represents the idea of *discontinuous change*. It's really very simple; it demonstrates how life goes on in a straight-line basis. A, B, C, D: you get up in the morning; you put on your clothes; you have breakfast. It's predictable. It's a straight line. It's linear. You come up to a certain point, though, and, instead of the line continuing, it emerges in a different plane. It goes A, B, C, D and emerges at M, N, O, P. It's the same sort of jump as from believing the world is flat to believing it's round.

In science, Thomas Kuhn has written about this idea, which he called a *paradigm shift*. For example, Newtonian physics takes place on one side of the shift, and Einstein broke through to the other side with the theory of relativity. His discovery was not a linear extension of what happened before. It was a discontinuous change. It's very important to realize that, when this kind of shift occurs, it doesn't necessarily rule out the old part. Newtonian physics still exists. It wasn't invalidated by Albert Einstein; it was transcended.

There's another aspect, too, which is also very important. The first awareness of this kind of shift seems to occur on the intuitive, viscerel level. Intuitively, we sense there must be some other way. Our vision lets us make a leap of faith. Yet, intellectual processes still play a part in this kind of shift. For Einstein to have made the shift to relativity, he had to be thoroughly rooted in the old notion of Newtonian physics. "Knownothingism" didn't get him over the hump. He had to know what he was doing in the *old* paradigm in order to discover the *new* paradigm. *At the same time, no amount of rearranging within that old framework would have gotten him into the new one.*

And it's this same model that I am working to apply in the nuclear, international security arena. Millions of people around the world know that there has to be a better way. I don't think that the nuclear question is totally an intellectual problem. I do not accept the idea that there is an incremental piece of knowledge which is going to get us over the top. It seems to me that we are talking about some much more fundamental issues here. These are on the emotional, psychological level. Anybody who tells you that the nuclear arms race is only about missiles and bombs is out of his or her mind. I think there are other, much more deep-seated factors behind the arms race, some of which we know about and some of which we don't. The question we have to answer is how to we get from A, B, C, D, to M, N, O, P—from insecurity to security? My organization, Search for Common Ground, is dedicated to finding specific ways to make that leap, to get from here to there.

This article first appeared in *The Humanist* issue of September/October 1986, pp. 22-25, 32, and is reprinted by permission.

7. THE ARMS RACE, ARMS CONTROL, AND DETERRENCE

I used to write books for a living, and I'm rather fond of metaphor. A large part of my present job is to search for metaphor. Giving people a way to frame a new reality seems to be the key to having the new reality take hold. The following long, involved metaphor describes the nuclear arms race. You may have heard the first part already. The nuclear arms race is like two little boys standing knee deep in a room full of gasoline. One little boy holds ten matches, and one holds seven matches. Somehow, the one with fewer matches wants to get more matches, and the one with more matches feels more secure because he's holding more matches. To the peace movement, the overwhelming threat is that *one match will set off the whole room*. The mix of matches—of weapons—is not that important in a room full of gasoline. The threat is holocaust.

Now, I would just point out to you that there's another point of view in this country. The people who control the federal government in Washington—President Reagan and people on the conservative side—have another perspective. They look at that same room and see pretty much the same mix of matches. But, to conservatives, the predominant threat is that the other side—the Soviets—will get so many matches, or a qualitatively superior mix of matches, that our side will lose its power. We'll be blackmailed, pushed around, Finlandized; the Soviets will make us do things that we don't want to do—we'll lose control. The world view that many, if not a majority of people in this country, hold is that the overwhelming threat of the nuclear arms race is that the Soviets will blackmail us or make us commit acts against our will.

There is a so-called debate in this country over the nuclear threat. Yet, the two sides are usually talking about different things. One side, the conservative side, sees the nuclear threat as blackmail. The other side, the liberal side, regards the nuclear threat in terms of holocaust. In other words, it's an apples-and-oranges kind of discussion. My own view is that this is not an "either-or" proposition. I think each side shares some of the other's fears.

The way that many people try to deal with that particular threat is by trying to shift the mix of matches. And, that mix is certainly important. There are certain combinations of matches which are self-incendiary or which scare the other side into irrational acts. Those *are* real dangers,

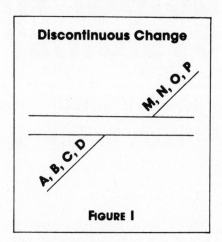

and I fervently hope that they are dealt with.

But I would say that there is another option. And that's the option upon which I and quite a few others are acting. We are not looking for ways to rearrange the mix of matches —of weapons. We're looking for ways to drain the gasoline from the room. We want to shift the climate or the context or the paradigm or the framework within which those matches are being held and whatever is in the heads of those little boys that causes them to be in the room in the first place. In other words, we seek to change the dangerous thinking that leads them to play this game. This, I submit, would be a discontinuous change—a jump from *A, B, C, D* to *M, N, O, P.*

I realize that such a shift might sound completely unrealistic, so I will provide an example of a similar but not exact model. I am referring to the extraordinary change that has occurred in Sino-American relations since 1972. Most adults remember when China was perceived as the enemy, the "Yellow Peril." We fought China directly in Korea and indirectly in Vietnam. Within the framework of Sino-American relations, there was a lot of killing.

But, in 1972, Richard Nixon did

something which was absolutely extraordinary: he unleashed forces which brought about an absolutely fundamental shift in Sino-American relations. It was astounding. It was a paradigm shift—a shift in the way the American people thought about China, and vice versa. President Nixon's reason for acting probably had more to do with ganging up on a common enemy—the Soviet Union—than anything else. Yet, the fact is that almost overnight China was transformed from being the Yellow Peril to becoming a kind of acupuncturing, ping-pong-playing country which Americans suddenly wanted to visit.

What's interesting to me is that the Chinese didn't change at all, *at least at first*. They continued to be radical communists. They kept on oppressing human rights. They even kept invading Vietnam. Only a few years before, when U.S. leaders had perceived that China's proxies threatened South Vietnam, they sent in American troops. In 1979, China actually invaded Vietnam, and our leaders thought it was wonderful because they were teaching an old enemy a lesson. This would seem to indicate that the framework or the *context* within which relations take place is just as important, probably more important, than the actions within it. And if ways can be found to shift that framework, then a different kind of politics is possible. I would call it *transformational politics* as opposed to *traditional politics*.

It's interesting to note that the Chinese started to change not before but after the shift. Recently, they have been moving closer to our system. Look at what happened to the Chinese nuclear weapons: before the shift, while the Chinese had only a comparative handful of such weapons, we were rather threatened by them. Originally, we were going to build the ABM to stop them. We didn't like the idea that our enemy had a nuclear capability. The Chinese still have those nuclear weapons, true. They are primitive, true; they could probably "only" kill thirty or forty million Americans, and then we would obliterate them because we have so many more.

But today, virtually no Americans are worried about nuclear war with the Chinese. Anyone suggesting going to Geneva to negotiate a SALT agreement with the Chinese would be laughed at. It is not a serious proposition. But the fact is it would have been a very serious proposition fifteen years ago. Yet, the Chinese nuclear weapons are still there; they have not been dismantled. And our nuclear weapons are still there; they certainly have not been dismantled. What has changed is how the United States and China look at each other. In the process, each side's nuclear weapons cease to threaten the other. Consider that many people, including me, have shared a knee-jerk notion that the world needs to move to nuclear disarmament, and then consider that the United States and China have retained nuclear weapons and neither feels threatened.

While I am not advocating retaining nuclear weapons indefinitely, I *am* suggesting that there could be some other possibilities beyond conventional wisdom. There may be alternative ways of looking at the nuclear dilemma, of reframing the issue—of shifting the framework within which nations interact. What I do for a living is look for these alternative ways of interacting.

My organization, Search for Common Ground, is trying to identify, in essence, the ping-pong diplomacy of the 1980s. What events might produce that same kind of shift in U.S.-Soviet relations as happened between the United States and China? It is not as easy as sending a ping-pong team to the Soviet Union. The Chinese and the Soviets are not the same. They represent very different problems. There are different historical impediments. There are different cultural impediments. The Soviets are a genuine superpower, with over twenty thousand nuclear weapons. The Chinese never presented that level of threat. These and other differences are profound.

My assumption is only that a fundamental shift *is* possible, not that it is inevitable. Yet such a shift becomes *more* likely as more and more people realize that it is possible. In other

words, as more and more people see the possibility of discontinuous change, the chances of jumping from *D* to *M* increase.

I want to emphasize that I am not Pollyannish. I am not naive about the nature of the Soviet system. I find absolutely reprehensible Soviet policies toward Afghanistan and Poland. As a realist, however, I believe that the following metaphor helps put the relationship between the United States and the Soviet Union into perspective.

If you are walking down the street and somebody sticks a gun to your head, that person is called a mugger. Now, this metaphor makes you uncomfortable. Unfortunately, the given of this metaphor is that the mugger has stuck a gun to your head; the given of the arms race is that the Soviets have stuck a big gun to our head, and we have stuck a big gun to their head. No amount of blustering or threatening or saying that we're going to build a bigger gun is going to make the Soviets drop their gun, nor are we going to drop ours.

Now think about that for a second. If somebody is holding a gun to your head, do you want them to have the shakes with their finger on the trigger, or do you want them to be secure, composed, and calm? Isn't it ironic that *your* vested interest is in *their* security? In other words, the notion that your assailant has a steady finger on the trigger is extremely important when somebody is holding a gun to your head.

That, unfortunately, is not the way that we and the Soviets conduct ourselves in international relations. What we do is almost the exact opposite. I used to work for a Harvard law professor named Roger Fisher, and the way he put it is as follows: Americans and Soviets both have to understand that we are in this boat together and that there is no way that their end is going to sink while ours stays afloat.

Americans and Soviets have to get used to the idea that neither of us controls the forces on this planet. The button that determines whether our country lives or dies is not located in the United States of America. It isn't *our* button. It's *their* button. Whether

or not we survive is determined by people in Moscow. Now, we could do things to make them push their button, and they could do things to make us push our button. But our button is in Moscow, beyond our reach.

Unfortunately, people in power in both countries still act as if they were in control. The fact is they cannot control the situation. Americans and Soviets alike have got to accept the idea that security depends upon the other side and ultimately cannot be won at the other's expense. There needs to be a movement away from a narrowly defined view of national security, a view that our nation makes us secure, toward a much broader notion of common or mutual security—a notion that security is interdependent. Such a shift in thinking, in the long run, is the only way we are going to be secure on this planet.

The notion of mutuality, or commonality of security, is absolutely imperative to survival in the nuclear age. Unfortunately, many of us, myself included, from time to time conduct ourselves in what could be called "adversarial ways." Such ways are driven by a mentality that says, "I win; you lose," and they usually lead to prolonged instability. They do not work on a personal level, and they do not work on the international level. We need to move away from those adversarial "win-lose" kinds of processes into a nonadversarial, win-win, you-and-me-world, as opposed to an adversarial, lose-lose, you-or-me-world.

These are the kinds of assumptions upon which my colleagues and I base our work. On the day-to-day level, we at Search for Common Ground translate such assumptions into specific projects that advance nonadversarial ways of creating real security. One of our fundamental operating strategies is to avoid issues—like MX versus anti-MX or Pershing versus SS-20—in which protagonists are already locked into concrete positions. There is little flexibility or chance for discontinuous change in such issues. Rather, we try to discover and advance creative new ideas for breaking the deadlock and, particularly, to develop specific projects of collaboration between the United States and the Soviet Union—projects that result in the two countries discovering common ground.

For example, in 1985 we started an initiative to get the United States and the Soviet Union to cooperate on a program to immunize the world's children against childhood diseases and thus save five million lives a year. We passed the idea on to Senator Richard Lugar, the conservative, Republican chairman of the Senate Foreign Relations Committee, and Senator Claiborne Pell, the liberal, Democratic ranking member. The two senators introduced it as a resolution which eventually passed the U.S. Senate and was discussed at the Geneva summit. This year, we launched an even more ambitious effort to have the United States and the Soviet Union commit themselves to space cooperation that will lead to a joint manned mission to Mars.

We believe that initiatives of this sort provide a means for reframing national security issues. Another such initiative was the musical play, *Peace Child*, which we launched in 1982 by coproducing it at Washington's Kennedy Center. *Peace Child* is the story of an American boy and Soviet girl who work together, against the resistance of their elders, to establish a peaceful world. The play has had hundreds of performances around the United States, in the Soviet Union, and by nationally televised "space-bridge" between the two countries. Our involvement in *Peace Child* was based upon the idea that the vision of children might move the world when adults have failed.

Since 1982, Search for Common Ground has sponsored an ongoing series of workshops and conferences in Washington and Ottawa to provide an environment conducive to rethinking national security. These events, usually two days long, bring together hawks and doves who interact within a format designed to have them discover new insights and arrive at common ground. At one of these workshops, a marine colonel had a brilliant idea. He said, "What we really need is a military that makes us secure while not making other countries insecure."

Think about that for a minute. The conservatives get what they want in that particular construct: security. (Actually, liberals want it, too, but they don't always know it.) The liberals also get what *they* want, which is a sense that the world isn't insecure and won't blow up. It would represent an extraordinary shift if American and Soviet national security planning was based upon that premise.

If the United States and the Soviet Union started having conversations based upon this premise, both nations would employ very different, non-threatening kinds of defense policies. We're looking for ways to get a premise like this into the intellectual process. How do you reframe the arguments? How do you raise the questions about mutual security so that something happens because of it?

These are a few examples of the kind of work I do at Search for Common Ground. On the personal level, I find it extremely gratifying and good for my mental health. On a larger level, I strongly believe that thinking and action of this sort could, if greatly expanded and intensified, have a profound impact.

Beyond theory to reality: Can the world disarm?

Peter Grier

Staff writer of The Christian Science Monitor

Washington

A world without nuclear weapons sounds like a state of grace, compared with the current condition. Is there any way to reach that world? Would it actually be safer than today's?

Clearly the knowledge of how to construct nuclear warheads will be forever in men's minds. To many people, the arms arsenals themselves seem similarly immortal.

As a symbol of the technological persistence of nuclear weapons, consider what happens to United States warheads when they become obsolete or reach the end of their useful lives. They are not thrown away so much as reincarnated.

When these weapons are retired, as they are every day at the Pantex weapons plant near Amarillo, Texas, parts such as casings and electronics can be simply shredded and buried. But the radioactive core is too expensive and dangerous to dispose of, and instead is recycled into the next generation of weapons.

Thus the plutonium 239 in Titan 2 missiles now being dismantled may become the fissionable soul of tomorrow's MX missile. Thirty years from now it may be transformed into an X-ray laser, and so on, in a progression stretching as far as military planners can imagine.

Will there ever be an end to this line of arms? Do people want it to end? Almost everyone who lays claim to being an expert on the superpower balance will preface opinions with a perfunctory reference to the desirability of a nuclear-free world.

The fact is that most of them don't really mean it, except as the longest of long-term goals. Since the early 1960s, the conventional wisdom of the present and former US officials who are called "the

strategic community" has been that talking about complete disarmament is not quite respectable.

The only people clamoring to turn all nuclear weapons into dust are the most liberal of the peace-group activists – and President Reagan and his loyal followers. (Of course, these opposite political poles differ wildly in how this nirvana is to be reached, and what it will look like when people get there.)

Since the Strategic Defense Initiative was launched in 1983, the President has stubbornly insisted that its goal is to make nuclear weapons impotent and obsolete, nothing less. At the Iceland demi-summit he apparently discussed, albeit reluctantly, the possibility of scrapping all nuclear weapons in the foreseeable future.

The Iceland discussions in particular have galvanized debate in the West about nuclear disarmament. The vast and respectable middle ground of former defense secretaries, think-tank scholars, and European ministers has responded with dozens of opinion and editorial pieces saying it would be a bad thing to rid the world of nuclear arms.

Their arguments, to nonexperts, may seem puzzling. If nuclear war is the worst event imaginable, how can getting rid of the weapons decrease security?

To understand why nuclear strategists think as they do, and why such abolitionists as antinuclear writer Jonathan Schell hold to their own visions of the future, it is helpful to look not just at where they end up, but at where they begin.

Political positions on the abolition of nuclear weapons depend crucially on answers to such questions as why there has not been a general war in Europe in the

last 40 years. Are nuclear weapons a cause of bad relations between the superpowers, or a symptom? If a nuclear war did begin, how bad would things get before it ended?

The following points will give a rough idea of where the poles of debate are on these issues. "Strategists" refers to the bulk of arms analysts, who feel nuclear weapons are necessary for the foreseeable future.

"Abolitionists" refers to peace groups that favor making the complete banning of the bomb an explicit government goal, now. Within each group there are many shades of belief, so the positions presented here are of necessity simplistic.

● Strategists feel that if both the US and the Soviet Union scrapped their nuclear arms, the chances of a conventional World War III on European soil would greatly increase. They say they would rather run the tiny risk of nuclear catastrophe, an admittedly horrific prospect, than a larger risk of a World War II rerun, which they feel would be terrible enough.

Abolitionists feel that this point of view overestimates the Soviet Union's desire to invade Western Europe. They say disarmament would not increase the chances of general war very much.

● On the other hand, abolitionists argue, people must assume that the use of nuclear weapons in anger means the end of the world.

There is a chance, they say, that wide-scale explosion of warheads would lead to the environmental catastrophe known as nuclear winter, and that because the stakes are so high, people cannot gamble that such an event might not occur.

Strategists believe that while nuclear war would be a catastrophe beyond history, in a famous phrase, this does not mean people must operate on the principle that it would be the end of all life. They feel that any nuclear exchange might well be a limited one, and that it is not self-evident that such a war will eventually happen just because the weapons exist.

● Finally, strategists say that if all nuclear weapons disappeared tomorrow, the US and the Soviet Union would still be bitter rivals, and the result would be a world of great tension and suspicion, for in a world of no nuclear weapons, the nation that cheated and acquired just one would be king.

Abolitionists retort that if both sides disarmed, relations between the superpowers would greatly improve, since the fierce arsenals themselves cause much of the friction between the two countries.

Many present and former government officials, even those who are sharply critical of President Reagan's defense policies, consider theorizing about a nuclear-free world to be as big a waste of time as promoting the language Esperanto.

Their reason is not so much the problems that would occur in a nuclear-free world, which they feel are considerable, as the sheer political impracticality of all programs for achieving the goal.

"I just don't see how you get there," says McGeorge Bundy, national-security adviser to Presidents Kennedy and Johnson.

Most of the peace movement devotes its energies not to promoting disarmament per se, but to achieving intermediate steps, like the nuclear freeze and a comprehensive test ban.

Those who do promote disarmament contend that it's time to get past the interminable fights on such points as how to base the MX missile, and push for a public debate on the larger question of what sort of world people are aiming for.

Freeman Dyson, a Princeton physics professor who writes widely on nuclear issues, concludes: "The sooner we all start thinking realistically about the challenges and difficulties of the non-nuclear world, the sooner we may have a chance to bring it into existence."

Gorbachev Offer: 2 Other Arms Hints

BILL KELLER

Special to The New York Times

MOSCOW, March 1 — Mikhail S. Gorbachev's offer to sign an agreement eliminating Soviet and American medium-range missiles in Europe offers tantalizing hints of movement on two other arms-control fronts, according to Western diplomats here.

Mr. Gorbachev's offer, made Saturday, gives two superpowers the prospect of a solid foreign-policy achievement — a medium-range arms pact — when both Mr. Gorbachev and President Reagan, for separate reasons, desperately need one.

Mr. Gorbachev announced his willingness to separate medium-range missiles from other arms issues, including the American "Star Wars" anti-missile program. But he said the Soviet Union hoped for a subsequent arms agreement aimed at "the prevention of deployment of weapons in outer space." In the past, the Soviet leader has always insisted that not only deployment but also development and testing of such weapons, as represented by "Star Wars," must be halted.

Diplomats said it would not be clear until Soviet negotiators presented the details of their proposal in Geneva whether this signaled a new flexibility on the space weapons question.

The second intriguing extra in Mr. Gorbachev's statement, diplomats said, was a gesture of willingness to move quickly on limiting short-range missiles in Europe. The United States and West European leaders have worried that eliminating medium-range nuclear weapons from the Continent would leave the Soviet Union with a large advantage in so-called theater nuclear weapons, shorter-range missiles designed for use on a battlefield.

Promises Good-Faith Gesture

Mr. Gorbachev declared on Saturday

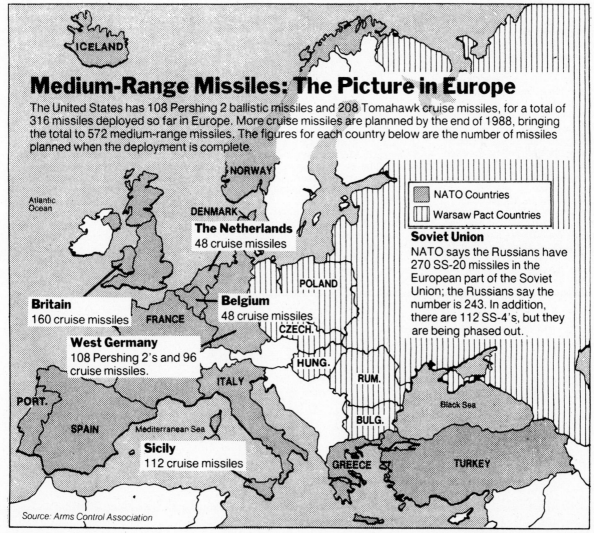

Medium-Range Missiles: The Picture in Europe

The United States has 108 Pershing 2 ballistic missiles and 208 Tomahawk cruise missiles, for a total of 316 missiles deployed so far in Europe. More cruise missiles are plannned by the end of 1988, bringing the total to 572 medium-range missiles. The figures for each country below are the number of missiles planned when the deployment is complete.

ICELAND

NORWAY

Atlantic Ocean

DENMARK

The Netherlands
48 cruise missiles

NATO Countries

Warsaw Pact Countries

POLAND

Soviet Union
NATO says the Russians have 270 SS-20 missiles in the European part of the Soviet Union; the Russians say the number is 243. In addition, there are 112 SS-4's, but they are being phased out.

Britain
160 cruise missiles

FRANCE

Belgium
48 cruise missiles

CZECH.

West Germany
108 Pershing 2's and 96 cruise missiles.

HUNG.

ITALY

RUM.

PORT.

Black Sea

SPAIN

Mediterranean Sea

BULG.

Sicily
112 cruise missiles

GREECE

TURKEY

Source: Arms Control Association

The New York Times/March 2, 1987

that as soon as an agreement on medium-range missiles had been signed, the Soviet Union would withdraw theater missiles from East Germany and Czechoslovakia as a gesture of good faith.

"As far as other theater missiles are concerned," he added, "we are prepared to begin talks immediately with a view to reducing and fully eliminating them."

In his unexpected announcement, made in a statement through the official press agency Tass and read on the evening television news Saturday, Mr. Gorbachev offered to sign "without delay" the tentative agreement he and Mr. Reagan reached at their meeting in Iceland in October. The agreement, as Mr. Gorbachev described it, called for withdrawing medium-range missiles from Europe within five years and reducing each side's total medium-range arsenal to 100 warheads, with the Soviet missiles kept in Asia and the American missiles on United States territory, possibly in Alaska.

Western diplomats said some details — including verification problems and the issue of short-range nuclear missiles — needed to be clarified before any agreement on medium-range arms was reached.

Mr. Gorbachev's proposal seemed to have been shrewdly timed to catch the Reagan Administration at a point when the President will find it hard to resist. The Administration has been staggered by the Iran arms affair, and Mr. Reagan badly needs to show that he can still take charge of foreign policy.

Frustration in Foreign Policy

For Mr. Gorbachev, too, an arms agreement would end a long period of frustration in foreign policy, marked by his failure to halt "Star Wars," to induce the United States to stop testing nuclear weapons or to end his country's entanglement in Afghanistan.

More important, Western diplomats here said today, by breaking the logjam in arms control, he may revive prospects of further arms agreements, including his ultimate arms control ambition, an agreement limiting the "Star Wars'" program.

Thus, diplomats said, Mr. Gorba-

chev's announcement represented a serious concession, but an very nimble one.

The immediate American reaction

There may be Soviet flexibility on 'Star Wars.'

---

was positive, although officials cautioned that important details, such as verification of the removal of the missiles, must be worked out.

The major concession lies in Mr. Gorbachev's willingness to sign a separate pact eliminating medium-range missiles in Europe. He had insisted since October that such an agreement must be part of a package that would include deep reductions in intercontinental missiles and strict limits on Mr. Reagan's Strategic Defense Initiative, as the "Star Wars" program is formally known.

'No Hope of Concession on S.D.I.'

"Gorbachev clearly decided to face the fact that there was no hope of an early Reagan concession on S.D.I.," one diplomat said. "On the contrary, the Reagan Administration has shown every sign of digging in and pushing ahead with space weapons.

"Gorbachev has conceded that if he wants to do any deal with Reagan, rather than waiting three or four years until a new administration has settled in, now is the time to do so."

Even if an agreement on medium-range missiles does not lead to further accord, Mr. Gorbachev may also have calculated that new movement on arms control would reduce the chances of Congressional financing of space weaponry.

"It must have been part of his calculation that the Administration will look less credible in demanding more money for S.D.I. when Congress can see progress being made in arms control," a diplomat said. "Even if Reagan still refuses to bargain on S.D.I., Gorbachev may succeed in outflanking him."

Domestic Problems Cited

Mr. Gorbachev needs an arms control agreement for his own domestic purposes as well.

In his two years as the Soviet leader, he has put enormous stock on his image as a peacemaker. Two weeks ago, in speaking to an international peace forum here, he called for a period of stability in international affairs so his country could devote its attention and resources to repairing its ailing economy.

But he has failed time after time to come up with any concrete arms control pact he could show his people, his military or his fellow party leaders to persuade them that international tensions had diminished.

Despite a series of dramatic gestures, he has failed to slow "Star Wars." Efforts to divide the West European allies have been rebuffed. Last week the Soviet Union resumed nuclear weapons testing after an 18-month unilateral halt, having failed to persuade the Americans to join in a complete test ban.

Few Gains Elsewhere

Nor can he point to any major foreign policy gains elsewhere. Although his approach to foreign policy has been activist and sometimes inventive, 120,000 Soviet troops remain mired in Afghanistan, Soviet overtures to China have yet to pay off, and his effort to make the Soviet Union a player in the Middle East has gone nowhere.

Western diplomats said they believed that the timing of Mr. Gorbachev's announcement was closely related to the resumption of nuclear testing, in two respects.

First, by allowing the military to test again, he may have bought himself some good will in military circles that makes another arms concession more palatable. Military leaders had complained with unusual openness that the moratorium had impeded Soviet military modernization.

Second, a diplomat said, by making his offer on the heels of a nuclear blast, he may counteract whatever public relations damage the resumption of testing may have caused.

Interim Restraint: U.S. and Soviet Force Projections

Following is the President's letter to the Speaker of the House of Representatives, the President of the Senate, and the Chairmen of the House and Senate Committees on Armed Services of August 5, 1986, transmitting an unclassified report to the Congress.

Transmittal Letter

Dear Mr. Speaker: (Dear Mr. President:) (Dear Mr. Chairman:)

Enclosed is an unclassified version of a classified report which I provided on June 19 in response to related Congressional requests, including a request for projections and comparisons of U.S. and Soviet strategic force dismantlements, inventories, etc., in terms of adherence to existing arms control agreements.

As I noted in my letter of June 19 transmitting the classified report, it is clear that SALT II and I codified a very major arms buildup including a quadrupling of Soviet strategic weapons (warheads and bombs) since SALT I was signed in 1972 and near doubling of Soviet ballistic missile warheads from about 5,000 to more than 9,000 since SALT II was signed in 1979.

The report further found that the SALT I and II agreements, even if fully complied with, would not prevent a very substantial further expansion of Soviet capabilities. We believe that, absent SALT II, the Soviets would not necessarily expand their forces significantly beyond the increases already projected *with* SALT II since the Soviet forces are very large and would appear, in our judgment, more than enough to meet reasonable military requirements.

In my letter of June 19, I noted that in view of the adverse implications of Soviet noncompliance for our security and for the arms control process, I had determined on May 27 that, in the future, the United States must base decisions regarding its strategic force structure on the nature and magnitude of the threat posed by Soviet strategic forces, and not on standards contained in the SALT structure which has been undermined by

Soviet noncompliance, and especially in a flawed SALT II treaty which was never ratified, would have expired if it had been ratified, and has been violated by the Soviet Union.

I have also noted that the full implementation of the Strategic Modernization Program is critical both to meeting our future national security needs and to appropriately responding to Soviet noncompliance. However, we will exercise utmost restraint. As we modernize, we will continue to retire older forces as national security requirements permit. We do not anticipate any appreciable growth in the size of U.S. strategic forces. Assuming no significant change in the threat, we will not deploy more strategic nuclear delivery vehicles or more strategic ballistic missile warheads than does the Soviet Union.

I want again to emphasize that no policy of interim restraint is a substitute for an agreement on deep and equitable reductions in offensive nuclear arms, provided that we can be confident of Soviet compliance with it. Achieving such reductions continues to receive my highest priority. This is the most direct path to achieving greater stability and a safer world.

Sincerely,

RONALD REAGAN

Unclassified Report

REPORT TO THE CONGRESS ON U.S. INTERIM RESTRAINT POLICY AND REPRESENTATIVE SOVIET AND U.S. DISMANTLEMENT AND STRATEGIC FORCE PROJECTIONS WITH AND WITHOUT SALT I AND II

I. Introduction: U.S. Interim Restraint Policy and U.S. Responses to Soviet Noncompliance

This report is an unclassified version of a report forwarded to the Congress on June 19, 1986, in response to the requirements of the fiscal year 1986 Department of Defense Authorization Act (Title X, Section 1001 (b)) for a

report on certain data and assessments related to U.S. and Soviet strategic offensive forces and on possible Soviet political, military, and negotiating responses to changes in the U.S. policy of interim restraint. As requested by this legislation, the report covers a 5-year period. It is provided in conjunction with material including the President's statement of May 27 and a White House fact sheet of the same date on "U.S. Interim Restraint Policy: Responding to Soviet Arms Control Violations."

The U.S. policy of interim restraint as first announced by the President in 1982 has been that, in spite of the flaws inherent in the SALT [strategic arms limitation talks] agreements and in an effort to foster an atmosphere of mutual restraint conducive to serious negotiations on arms reductions, the United States would *not undercut* the expired SALT I Interim Offensive Agreement of 1972 or the unratified SALT II Treaty of 1979 *so long as* the Soviet Union exercised *equal* restraint.

In three detailed Administration reports to the Congress on Soviet noncompliance, and through diplomatic channels including the U.S.-Soviet Standing Consultative Commission, the President has consistently made clear that this U.S. policy required Soviet reciprocity and that it must not adversely affect our national security interests in the face of the continuing Soviet military buildup and uncorrected Soviet noncompliance.

In accordance with U.S. interim restraint policy and our efforts to build a framework of truly mutual restraint, the United States has not taken any actions that would undercut existing agreements. We have continued scrupulously to live within all arms control agreements, including the SALT I and II strategic arms agreements. Unfortunately, while the United States has been

Reprinted from *Special Report*, No. 151, August 5, 1986, pp. 1-4. US Department of State, Washington, DC.

229

attempting to hold to the structure of SALT through our policy of interim restraint, the Soviet Union has undercut the very foundation of that structure through its continued violations.

In June of 1985, the President went the extra mile. He decided to dismantle a U.S. Poseidon submarine, in order to give the Soviet Union adequate time to correct its noncompliance, reverse its unwarranted military buildup, and seriously pursue equitable and verifiable arms reduction agreements in the Geneva negotiations. Regrettably, the Soviet Union has so far failed to move constructively in these three areas.

In spite of our expressed concerns and our diplomatic efforts for corrective Soviet actions, the Soviet Union has not corrected its noncompliance. Concerning SALT II, the President's most recent report, of December 23, 1985, to the Congress cited as Soviet violations: (1) the development of the SS–25 missile, a prohibited second new type of intercontinental ballistic missile (ICBM); (2) extensive encryption of telemetry on ICBM missile flight tests, which impedes verification; (3) concealment of the association between the SS–25 missile and its launcher during testing; and (4) exceeding the SALT II numerical cap of 2,504 strategic nuclear delivery vehicles (SNDVs). In addition, the President's report cited three areas of ambiguous Soviet behavior as involving possible violations or other problems with regard to SALT II: (1) SS–16 ICBM activity, (2) the Backfire bomber's intercontinental operating capability, and (3) the Backfire bomber's production rate. Concerning SALT I, the President's report cited a violation in the Soviet use of former SS–7 ICBM facilities in support of the deployment and operation of the SS–25 mobile ICBMs. These SALT II and SALT I violations and other ambiguous situations involving these treaties remain matters of serious concern, as does Soviet violation of the Anti-Ballistic Missile (ABM) Treaty of 1972 and of other major arms control agreements.

The Administration has now concluded a comprehensive review, and extensive consultations with our allies and friends abroad and with Members of the Congress on the continuing Soviet pattern of noncompliance, the Soviet strategic arms buildup, and the lack of progress by the Soviets at the Geneva negotiations. The President announced on May 27 that in the future the United States would base decisions regarding its strategic force structure on the nature and magnitude of the threat posed by Soviet strategic forces, not on standards contained in the flawed SALT structure, which has been seriously undermined by Soviet noncompliance.

In his May 27 announcement on U.S. interim restraint policy and on the U.S. response to continued Soviet non-compliance, the President pointed out the inappropriateness of continuing with the SALT II agreement. SALT II codified continuing major arms buildups. It was considered by a broad range of critics, including the Senate Armed Services Committee, to be unequal and unverifiable in important provisions. It was never ratified by the U.S. Senate and was clearly headed for defeat before the President's predecessor asked the Senate not to act on it. *With* SALT II the Soviets have nearly doubled their strategic ballistic missile warheads from about 5,000 to 9,000, and *with* SALT II they could legally undertake a further significant increase. Even if SALT II had been ratified, it would have expired on December 31, 1985.

Finally, continued Soviet violations have seriously undercut the agreement for several years in spite of repeated U.S. requests for corrective Soviet action. (Concerning SALT I, this agreement expired in 1977, and since it was signed in 1972, the Soviet Union has quadrupled the number of its strategic nuclear warheads. As for the United States, even if we did not retire older systems, the United States would, under current plans, remain in technical observance of the SALT I numerical limits until mid-1989.)

The President made clear in his May 27 announcement that the United States would continue to exercise utmost restraint in the future, seeking to meet U.S. strategic needs, given the Soviet buildup, by means that minimize incentives for continuing Soviet offensive force growth. The President stated that, as we modernize, we will continue to retire older forces as our national security requirements permit and that we do not anticipate any appreciable numerical growth in U.S. strategic forces. He also indicated that, assuming no significant change in the threat we face as we implement the strategic modernization program, the United States will not deploy more strategic nuclear delivery vehicles or more strategic ballistic missile warheads than does the Soviet Union.

The President also noted that, as a result of his decision to dismantle two older Poseidon submarines, the United States will remain technically in observance of the terms of the SALT II Treaty for some months. He continues to hope that the Soviet Union will use this additional time to take the constructive steps necessary to alter the current situation. Should they do so, the President has stated that this would be taken into account.

Needless to say, the most essential near-term response to Soviet non-compliance remains the implementation of our full strategic modernization program, to underwrite deterrence today, and the continued pursuit of the Strategic Defense Initiative (SDI) research program, to see if it is possible to provide a safer and more stable basis for our future security and that of our allies. The strategic modernization program, including the deployment of the second 50 Peacekeeper missiles, is the foundation for all future U.S. offensive force options. It provides a solid basis that can and will be adjusted over time to respond most efficiently to continued Soviet noncompliance. The SDI program represents our best hope for a future in which our security can rest on the increasing contribution of defensive systems that threaten no one.

In his May 27 statement, the President emphasized that no policy of interim restraint is a substitute for an agreement on deep and equitable reductions in offensive nuclear arms, provided that we can be confident of Soviet compliance with it. Achieving such reductions has received, and will continue to receive, his highest priority. We hope the Soviet Union will act to give substance to the agreement reached by the President and General Secretary Gorbachev at the summit meeting last November to achieve early progress in the Geneva negotiations. It was agreed to focus, in particular, on areas where there is common ground, including the principle of 50% reductions, appropriately applied, in the strategic nuclear arms of both countries, as well as an interim agreement on intermediate-range nuclear forces. If the Soviet Union carries out this agreement, we can move now to achieve greater stability and a safer world.

The classified report transmitted to the Congress on June 19 provided a comparison of representative U.S. and Soviet strategic weapons dismantlement that would be required over the next 5 years if both countries were actually to observe all of the quantitative limits of the SALT I and SALT II agreements. It then presented representative projections of the strategic offensive forces of the two sides, assuming that the SALT I and SALT II limits no longer apply. Finally, it provided an assessment of possible Soviet political and negotiating responses, insofar as these are understood and anticipated at present. For security reasons, the present, unclassified version provides the information concerning U.S. and Soviet forces in substantially abbreviated form.

At the outset, it must be noted that there are important uncertainties in the assessments presented herein. With respect to the data on Soviet forces, the projections represent broad trends—based on both evidence and assumptions —and are not intended to be precise forecasts. On the basis of U.S. experience, it is unlikely that Soviet strategic forces 5 years from now will be identical (or necessarily even extremely close) to these force projections. Nevertheless, we believe that Soviet strategic forces in the next 3–5 years can be reasonably characterized, based on evidence of ongoing programs that would be difficult to alter radically in this timeframe.

By contrast, the size and complexion of future U.S. strategic forces are relatively easier for the Soviets to determine. We must contend with potential *increases* in Soviet strategic programs and capabilities. However, the principal source of uncertainty for Soviet planners about the scope and size of future U.S. strategic programs is, in all likelihood, the extent to which future U.S. programs may be *reduced* by congressional or executive branch action.

The data presented here assume *full* implementation of the Administration's strategic modernization program. It is absolutely essential that we maintain full support for these programs. To fail to do so would be the worst response to Soviet noncompliance. It would immediately and seriously undercut our negotiators in Geneva by removing the leverage that they must have to negotiate equitable reductions in both U.S. and Soviet forces. It would send precisely the wrong signal to the leadership of the Soviet Union about the seriousness of our resolve concerning their non-compliance. And, it would significantly increase the risk to our security for years to come. Therefore, our highest priority must remain the full implementation of these programs.

II. Projected Soviet and U.S. Dismantlements

This section of the report provides representative projections on dismantling that would result if SALT limitations were extended. They should be considered to be approximations and would be subject to alteration by policy decisions or programmatic adjustments by either side. It should be pointed out that, as documented in the President's December 23, 1985, report to the Congress on "Soviet Noncompliance With Arms Control Agreements," the Soviet Union's SALT-accountable strategic nuclear delivery vehicle level is above the SALT II cap of 2,504, in violation of the Soviets' political commitment not to undercut the treaty.

Representative Soviet Dismantlements. The Soviet Union has several programs underway to introduce new strategic delivery systems that would necessitate dismantling of older systems if the Soviets were to restrict their overall force to SALT levels. Under a representative projection of such programs, consistent with SALT limits over the next 5 years the Soviets would deploy significant numbers of new delivery vehicles, including SS–25 and SS–X–24 ICBMs, Typhoon- and Delta-type SSBNs, and Backfire bombers and ALCM [air-launched cruise missile] carriers.

If SALT I and II limits were to be complied with, these actions would necessitate dismantling some older systems in the Soviet inventory, as well as some more modern systems. The older systems include SS–11 and SS–13 ICBMs, SS–N–6 SLBMs [submarine-launched ballistic missiles] on Y-class SSBNs, and Bison and Bear aircraft. Because the Soviets already are very close to the SALT II sublimit of 820 MIRVed [multiple independently targetable reentry vehicle] ICBM launchers, deployment of the MIRVed SS–X–24 would require dismantling of existing MIRVed ICBMs—most likely SS–17s and possibly some SS–19s—to stay within the ceiling. Similarly, with the continued deployment of SS–N–20 and SS–N–23 SLBMs, their total of MIRVed missile launchers would exceed the ceiling of 1,200 in a year or two; then they would need to dismantle more MIRVed ICBMs or some SS–N–18 launchers on relatively new D–III-class SSBNs to continue observing the cumulative sublimit of 1,200 MIRVed ICBM and SLBM launchers. They have, for some time, been at the limit of 62 modern SSBNs established by SALT I; thus deployment of new SSBNs would require continued dismantling of older submarines.

The dismantlements that would derive from these actions probably would total over the next 5 years slightly more than 600 strategic nuclear delivery vehicles, with some 1,000–1,200 associated ballistic missile warheads. (The SNDV figure also includes heavy bombers judged to have a capacity for some 300 nuclear weapons.) Some dismantling of older systems would occur eventually in any case, with or without SALT limits. These projected dismantling actions do not take into account the Soviet potential for *additional* cheating, while nominally observing SALT numerical limits. This might be intended to avoid compensatory dismantlement of other ICBMs, including MIRVed ICBMs.

Representative U.S. Dismantlements. With respect to U.S. programs and dismantlements, full implementation of the strategic modernization program would require continued dismantlements under SALT of U.S. older strategic program systems, most of which are nearing the end of their useful life based on both military and economic considerations.

III. Projected Soviet and U.S. Strategic Forces

Projected Soviet Forces. In projecting Soviet strategic offensive force deployments, assuming SALT limits no longer apply, the caveats discussed above regarding assumptions and uncertainties underlying such projections are relevant.

To place these figures in historical perspective, since 1972 when SALT I was signed, there has been a fourfold increase in the number of Soviet strategic nuclear weapons (missile warheads and bombs) and nearly a doubling of Soviet ballistic missile throw-weight. Indeed, since the signing of SALT II in 1979, the number of Soviet strategic ballistic missile warheads has nearly doubled from about 5,000 to more than 9,000. This great expansion of Soviet strategic forces has been possible for the most part with SALT. (The agreements limited launchers and only indirectly affected deployed weapons.) As noted, however, the Soviet Union has also violated the arms control limitations imposed by these agreements.

The Soviet Union now has about 10,000 strategic nuclear weapons (missile warheads and bombs). The SALT I and II Treaties, even if fully complied with, would not prevent a very substantial further expansion of Soviet capabilities. Even assuming future Soviet compliance with SALT II—other than the continuation of current Soviet violations—deployed Soviet weapons are projected to increase to over 12,000 in the next 5 years. Moreover, by further violating the agreements, the Soviets could plausibly add in the same time period a relatively modest increase of even more weapons to their forces.

It is difficult to predict precisely what the Soviets might do absent SALT constraints. They would not necessarily expand their forces significantly beyond the increases discussed above, which are very large and would appear, in our judgment, more than enough to meet reasonable military requirements. Thus there might well be little appreciable difference, in terms of total weapons, between the forces that the Soviets might deploy with and without SALT constraints. It is reasonable to expect that in the absence of SALT, the Soviets would not dismantle all their older systems as rapidly as under SALT. Some classes of weapons (e.g., SSBNs) might not be dismantled at all during the next 5 years without SALT constraints. Given the great extent of the Soviet strategic modernization program, however, many of these older systems would have relatively little impact on the overall threat to U.S. security.

The Soviets have the potential to expand their forces somewhat further, should they decide to do so for either military or political reasons. If a deliberate effort were made by the Soviet Union to expand its strategic forces beyond SALT II levels, they might increase their forces somewhat further, to about 15,000 weapons by 1991.

However, the costs associated with such an expansion of capability, on top of an already very aggressive and expensive modernization program, would be a disincentive against any such Soviet effort.

With or without SALT, the Soviets are, in any case, likely to modernize their intercontinental nuclear attack forces further by replacing most of their currently deployed land- and sea-based ballistic missiles and heavy bombers by the mid-1990s. This impressive Soviet modernization program, which will result in significantly improved survivability, flexibility, and hard-target capability, has been in train for a long time.

Projected U.S. Forces. The United States could achieve roughly 14,000

weapons by fiscal year 1991 in a no-SALT environment by introducing the full strategic modernization program without undertaking the dismantlements that would otherwise be required by SALT.

IV. Soviet Political and Negotiating Reponses

It is difficult to predict specific moves the Soviets might decide to take politically or in the negotiations to try to increase criticism of, and build pressure against, the President's May 27 decision. They have already leveled a propaganda campaign against the decision. Ironically, in light of ongoing Soviet violations of SALT II, including violation of the strategic nuclear delivery vehicles numerical limit, they have warned that they will go beyond the SALT limits if the United States does. While they have stated that they would take the "necessary practical" steps, e.g., increasing missiles and warheads, it is not at all clear that they would further expand their forces beyond the increases already planned, as discussed above. However, they are likely to portray *any* expansion, including that already planned, as a response to U.S. actions.

The Soviets may decide to make political or negotiating moves as a matter of tactics that seek to discredit the U.S. decision. However, the May 27 decision is not likely permanently to alter their basic, overall objectives for negotiations or for a summit. These objectives include increasing opposition to the U.S. modernization program, particularly the Strategic Defense Initiative, and weakening the Western alliance.

We hope that the Soviet Union will join us in a framework of *truly* mutual restraint. For its part, the United States will continue to exercise utmost restraint in the future, seeking to meet U.S. strategic needs, given the Soviet continuing buildup, by means that minimize incentives for continuing Soviet offensive force growth. As we modernize, we will continue to retire older forces as our national security requirements permit. Assuming no significant change in the threat we face as we implement the strategic modernization program, the United States will not deploy more strategic nuclear delivery vehicles or more strategic ballistic missile warheads than does the Soviet Union.

No policy of interim restraint is a substitute for an agreement on deep and equitable reductions in offensive nuclear arms, provided that we can be confident of Soviet compliance with it. We hope the Soviet Union will act to give substance to the agreement reached by the President and General Secretary Gorbachev at the summit meeting last November to achieve early progress in the Geneva negotiations.

Our objectives in Geneva remain the same as stated at the summit: to seek common ground in negotiating deep, equitable, and verifiable reductions in strategic and intermediate-range offensive nuclear arsenals and to discuss with the Soviet Union how we could enhance deterrence and stability by moving toward a world in which we would no longer rely exclusively on the threat of nuclear retaliation to preserve the peace. We hope the Soviets will negotiate seriously with us toward these important goals.

Do the Soviets Cheat?

Rich West

What is the basis for the President's charges that the Soviets have repeatedly violated agreements with the West? How valid are they? Those concerned about arms control need to understand the charges the Administration has made, because they are central to the future of our cause. What follows is a summary of allegations lodged by the U.S. against the U.S.S.R. since the signing of the SALT I treaty in l971.

Allegation: By upgrading their SS-11 ICBMs to SS-19 ICBMs, the Soviets violated SALT I's prohibition on converting light ICBM launchers to heavy ICBM launchers.

Comment: This charge is problematic because the SALT I agreement did not specify what constitutes a "heavy ICBM." After the treaty was signed, the U.S. issued a statement defining heavy ICBMs. The Soviets never accepted that unilateral statement. Nevertheless, the U.S. contends that the Soviets understood U.S. terms and that, by deploying the SS-19 missile, they were "defeating the stated U.S. object and purpose of limiting the throwweight of Soviet ICBMs." The U.S. charge has some substance but little force, since the U.S. negotiators failed to clarify the matter at the bargaining table.

Allegation: The Soviets failed to meet a 1974 deadline for dismantling 41 excess ABM launchers, thereby violating SALT I launcher limits.

Comment: When the U.S. filed the charge the Soviets apologized for the delay and proposed a six-month extension on the deadline. The U.S. accepted the amended terms. In the intervening 10 years, the Soviets have adhered strictly to launcher limits.

Allegation: In 1976 the Soviet Union failed to meet a deadline for dismantling ICBM launch silos before deploying new ballistic missile-firing submarines (SSBNs), thereby violating the SALT I Interim Agreement.

Comment: Before the U.S. filed the charge, the Soviets acknowledged the problem, apologized for the discrepancy, and accepted a U.S.-proposed compromise that stipulated delaying further SSBN deployment until the requisite silos were dismantled. The terms of the compromise were fulfilled.

Allegation: In the mid-1970s the Soviets deployed the ABM-X-3 system with mobile radar components, a violation of the ABM treaty's ban on mobile radar systems.

Comment: The Soviets denied the charge. The State Department has since issued a report on compliance that states that while the radar could be installed more rapidly than previous systems, the process still requires several months, and consequently the system cannot be considered mobile.

Allegation: The Soviets violated the l972 multilateral Biological and Toxin Weapons Convention and the 1925 Geneva Protocol by maintaining an offensive biological warfare program and by their involvement in the production, transfer, and use of toxins in Laos, Kampuchea, and Afghanistan.

Comment: This charge, leveled repeatedly by the U.S., is corroborated, at least circumstantially, by independent sources. The Soviets deny producing or using biological and toxin weapons.

Allegation: The Soviets have built a large phased-array radar (LPAR) in Krasnoyarsk, Central Siberia, in violation of the ABM treaty.

Comment: The Soviets deny that the radar was built for ABM purposes. Rather, they maintain, it was built for space surveillance, one of LPAR's capabilities. Since the U.S. lodged its objections, the CIA and the British government have determined that the radar is not for ABM purposes, but for early warning of incoming SLBMs. The radar's siting and orientation make this use a violation of the ABM treaty. The Reagan Administration, however, has never filed formal charges.

The Soviets have countercharged that the four U.S. PAVE PAW phased-array radars might "provide a base" for missile defense, prohibited by the ABM treaty. The U.S. contends the PAVE PAW radars are part of an early-warning system explicitly allowed by the ABM treaty.

Allegation: Soviet installation of a new ABM test range in Kamchatka in 1975 was a direct violation of the the ABM treaty.

Comment: The Soviets argued that the range had existed when the ABM treaty was signed and therefore did not violate treaty limitations. The U.S. has accepted the Soviet defense.

Allegation: From 1973 to 1975, the Soviets conducted SA-5 radar tests "in an ABM mode" in violation of the ABM treaty.

From *SANE World Newsletter*, Vol. 25, No. 3, May/June 1986, pp. 4-5. Reprinted with permission from SANE World, a publication of SANE, Committee for a SANE Nuclear Policy.

Comment: The U.S. made this allegation despite ambiguities in its monitoring data. The Soviets explained that the radar was being used to prevent aircraft from straying into the test area, a permissible radar function under the ABM treaty. Immediately after the issue was raised, the Soviets discontinued the practice anyway.

Allegation: In 1973 the Soviets began building additional ICBM silos, a violation of SALT I's freeze on offensive missile launchers.

Comment: The Soviets claimed the silos under construction were for command and control, in other words to house technicians and computers, not ICBMs. Soviet documentation and further intelligence reports led the U.S. to accept the Soviet explanation.

Allegation: In 1974 the Soviets were covering SSBN and SLBM construction facilities to inhibit surveillance.

Comment: After the U.S. raised the issue, the Soviets removed the covers. In 1973 the Soviets made a similar charge against the U.S., alleging that the shelters being erected over several Minuteman silos in Montana hindered surveillance. The U.S. said the shelters were for wintertime construction. The Soviets apparently accepted the U.S. explanation.

Allegation: The Soviets are engaging in increased encryption of telemetry data in violation of SALT II.

Comment: The SALT II provision on encryption was deliberately vague because the issue is highly contentious. Both sides have the right to encode any information they want so long as the other side can still verify treaty compliance. Air Force Chief of Staff Charles Gabriel has said, "It is misleading to use the level of encryption as a guide for determining how well we can verify what they are doing. More critical is the 'nature' of the encryption, that is, what missile functions are being encrypted and what functions are being transmitted in the clear." The U.S. does have other means of verification that do the job just as well. The Soviets deny that their encryption impedes verification, and American officials refuse to clarify what data we are having trouble reading, claiming that would uncover confidential intelligence secrets.

Allegation: By developing the SS-25 ICBM, the Soviets are violating the SALT II restriction that limits each party to one new type of ICBM. (They had already declared the SS-24 as their new type.)

Comment: The Soviets contend the SS-25 is not a new missile, simply a modification of the SS-13 (SALT II permits such refinements). The issue remains unresolved. The Soviets have in turn charged the U.S. with the identical violation because of our development of the MX and the Midgetman missiles.

Allegation: The Soviets have deployed the SS-16 mobile ICBM at the Plesetsk Test Range, violating the SALT II ban on deploying this type of ICBM.

Comment: The Soviets contend the SS-16 is not operational. U.S. intelligence confirms that no SS-16 tests have been performed since 1976 (and that the last test was a failure). General Gabriel testified in 1983, "We do not believe mobile SS-16s are deployed."

Allegation: The Soviets have conducted underground nuclear tests in excess of the 150-kiloton limit set by the Threshhold Test Ban treaty.

Comment: The Soviets deny the charge. In April 1986 the CIA announced that it was revising its procedure for estimating test yields, because its method had overestimated the yields. The revision significantly undercuts the U.S. charge.

Allegation: The Soviets failed to take the necessary precautions to prevent radioactive matter, vented from their underground tests, from spreading beyond Soviet territory, a violation of the Limited Test Ban treaty.

Comment: The U.S. doesn't contend that the careless venting was deliberate. Moreover, the U.S. is also guilty of this act. While such accidents reflect inadequate precautions, they carry no military significance. Neither government has ever regarded the act as a serious treaty violation.

BACK FROM THE BRINK

McGeorge Bundy, Morton H. Halperin, William W. Kaufmann,
George F. Kennan, Robert S. McNamara, Madalene O'Donnell, Leon V. Sigal,
Gerard C. Smith, Richard H. Ullman, and Paul C. Warnke

Here is an arms-control plan, based on a new nuclear strategy, that requires no negotiations, no treaties, and no verification—a plan that the United States and its allies, taking arms control into their own hands, can implement unilaterally, thereby immediately reducing the risk of a nuclear confrontation.

OR THE PAST FORTY YEARS THE UNITED States and its allies have wielded the threat of initiating the use of nuclear weapons as a substitute for the deployment of conventional forces sufficient to deter and, if necessary, to defeat potential enemies. This policy has proved costly to U.S. security: it has increased the risk of nuclear war, damaged relations with our allies, and undermined the fighting ability of our conventional forces. Moreover, despite four decades of effort, no one has been able to develop plans for using nuclear weapons that would either increase the prospect of military victory or produce any outcome short of the destruction of the United States and its allies. It is time for U.S. policy on "first use" of nuclear weapons to be re-examined.

We propose an alternative that we believe merits serious public debate. Briefly, it is this: *The United States should base its military plans, training programs, defense budgets, weapons deployments, and arms negotiations on the assumption that it will not initiate the use of nuclear weapons.* We believe that adoption of this principle would reduce the risk of nuclear war, improve the prospects for arms control, strengthen public support for policies pursued by NATO, and ultimately lead to improvements in conventional capability that would enhance the security of the United States and its allies.

In 1982 four of us wrote an article calling for debate on a similar but not identical proposition (McGeorge Bundy, George F. Kennan, Robert S. McNamara, and Gerard C. Smith, "Nuclear Weapons and the Atlantic Alliance," *Foreign Affairs*, Spring 1982). The proposals we put forward were not new, but we hoped they would spark a public debate on the proper role of nuclear weapons in our security policy. Our aim, we stated, was not to end a discussion but

to begin one. We have come together in a larger group in the hope of advancing that discussion.

Much has occurred since 1982. Pershing II and cruise missiles are being deployed in Europe, over strenuous public objections. The deployment has been billed as a victory for the cohesion of the alliance. President Ronald Reagan, meanwhile, has proposed the Strategic Defense Initiative (SDI), calling on the scientific community to render ballistic missiles impotent and move toward eliminating all nuclear weapons. The SDI has potentially serious implications for extended nuclear deterrence.

The most noteworthy development since 1982, with respect to the issues raised here, has been a new emphasis on the importance of conventional forces as an alternative to nuclear first use. In our view, a broad consensus has emerged in support of significantly reducing reliance on nuclear weapons. President Reagan himself has said, "For too long, we and our allies have permitted nuclear weapons to be a crutch, a way of not having to face up to real defense needs. We must free ourselves from that crutch. Our goal should be to deter, and if necessary to repel, any aggression without a resort to nuclear arms."

Prominent religious groups have called for alternatives to the first use of nuclear weapons—alternatives that would not increase the threat of war. Two congressional authorities on defense, Senator Sam Nunn and Representative Les Aspin, have urged the West to reduce its reliance on nuclear weapons. Experienced military officials, including the Supreme Allied Commander in Europe, General Bernard W. Rogers, have concurred. The United States has taken a modest but significant step toward a diminished reliance on nuclear weapons by reducing their number in Europe. Even after the planned reductions are completed, however, there will be some 4,500 U.S. warheads based in Great Britain and on the Continent.

The yearning of the American public for a change is reflected in its positive response to the SDI, which promises a "shield" against nuclear attack, as well as to proposals that would eliminate nuclear weapons altogether. While both of these approaches are based on unrealistic political and technological assumptions, we believe, the reaction to them does demonstrate the receptiveness of the public to new ideas. It also highlights the importance of developing an alternative to the current policy before the desire for change produces an irresistible pressure either to retreat from U.S. commitments abroad or to maintain them dangerously.

In the short run the United States can and should move toward a diminished reliance on nuclear weapons by reducing and relocating vulnerable nuclear forces currently deployed near the NATO–Warsaw Pact border. We believe that eventually the United States, in concert with its NATO allies, should formalize its commitment not to initiate the use of nuclear weapons and should alter its deployments, war plans, and attitudes accordingly.

Current U.S. Policy: The Threat of "First Use"

ANY AMERICANS ARE NOT WELL INformed about the nature of U.S. policy on the use of nuclear weapons. According to one survey conducted in 1984, for example, 81 percent of Americans polled believe that current policy is to use nuclear weapons "if, and only if, the Soviets attack the United States first with nuclear weapons." This is a fundamental misunderstanding.

In fact the possibility of first use permeates all aspects of American defense policy. In the European theater and elsewhere, the United States contemplates and plans for a first use of nuclear weapons in response to conventional attack. U.S. military and civilian officials draw up war plans and buy and deploy weapons on the assumption that the President will initiate the use of nuclear weapons "if necessary." U.S. foreign commitments, as well as calculations about the forces needed to meet those commitments, are based on the assumption that the United States would in some circumstances be the first to use nuclear weapons. Successive Administrations have rejected arms-control proposals that might limit the nation's capabilities with respect to first use.

Current American policy relies heavily on the threat of first use despite the conspicuous lack of a plausible set of circumstances in which nuclear exchanges would not gravely risk catastrophic damage to the United States and its allies. Most experts agree that even the most limited use of nuclear weapons could lead quickly to vast destruction in the United States and Europe. Decision-makers would be under great pressure during a crisis. There would be a strong incentive to fire off nuclear weapons before

they could be destroyed on their launchers. Command, control, and communications would deteriorate once a nuclear war had begun, leaving decision-makers with incomplete information on rapidly changing battlefield conditions. These factors make it likely that authority to use nuclear weapons would have to be delegated to field commanders soon after the onset of a nuclear conflict, or perhaps even before it began. Such a policy offers little room for error and leaves little time for rational response.

The only effective and durably credible role of nuclear weapons is to deter others from using them. Yet the threat of nuclear first use has remained a part of U.S. policy ever since the United States acquired nuclear weapons, persisting through its loss of a nuclear monopoly in the late 1940s and its loss of nuclear superiority over the Soviet Union some two decades later. A continuing commitment to such a policy might ultimately present the United States with the choice of initiating the use of nuclear weapons or seeing a bluff called. Either way, the consequences could be disastrous.

A clear U.S. decision that nuclear weapons will not be used first in any conflict, or will not be used early in a nuclear conflict, would contribute to U.S. and allied security in a number of reciprocally reinforcing ways. When integrated into all aspects of military planning, such policies would reduce the risk that nuclear weapons would be used in the heat of crisis, would reduce political tensions that give rise to such crises, and would improve the operational effectiveness of existing conventional forces.

How a First-Use Doctrine Harms Allied Security

HE RELIANCE BY NATO ON NUCLEAR first use directly and adversely affects its capacity to fight a conventional war. Owing to statutory limits that the United States imposes on the number (326,414) of its soldiers in Europe, some American conventional forces are being sent back to the United States in order to make room for those given nuclear missions. As General Rogers testified in May of 1985, "What is happening is as I eat the spaces for the ground-launched cruise missiles, nuclear weapons, I am bringing in nuclear weapons . . . and sending conventional forces home."

Plans for first use of nuclear weapons further limit the artillery and aircraft available for conventional operations. Tactical (short-range) nuclear forces in Europe rely primarily on launchers, such as howitzers and tactical aircraft, that are "dual-capable"—capable, that is, of launching either conventional or nuclear weapons. In the event of a conventional conflict, and even if full conventional strength were required, a number of these launchers would be held in reserve for nuclear missions. In fact, the incentive to withhold "dual-capable" artillery and aircraft would increase as the fighting intensified—the very point at which they would be most urgently needed.

The destructiveness of nuclear weapons also places a number of restrictions on NATO units to which such weapons are assigned. In peacetime, nuclear-certified units must be trained in extensive safety-and-control procedures. Nuclear munitions, for example, require command, control, and communications arrangements separate from those for conventional munitions. They require extensive security precautions against accidents and terrorism. All of these requirements place heavy demands on limited resources. In forward units the elaborate management procedures that necessarily accompany nuclear systems not only consume scarce manpower but also increase the risk that nuclear weapons would be used, if at all, in the heat of the moment, rather than as the result of careful deliberation.

Much of NATO's nuclear arsenal, despite security precautions, remains vulnerable to purely conventional attack by Warsaw Pact tactical air units. To conserve personnel and resources, all U.S. tactical nuclear munitions are concentrated in a relatively small number of storage facilities. Because of their concentration and visibility, these sites would be attractive targets and are highly vulnerable to attack. The Western alliance is thus posed with a dilemma. If NATO, during a political crisis in Europe, felt that a conflict was imminent, it might move to scatter its vulnerable nuclear assets in order to protect them. Soviet leaders, however, might very well interpret such an action as preparation for a NATO nuclear attack. NATO's alternative would be to allow those weapons to remain concentrated and vulnerable to a pre-emptive Warsaw Pact strike—nuclear or conventional. In either case Soviet leaders would be under pressure to destroy the weapons quickly—and NATO field commanders would be under pressure to use them quickly.

Perhaps the greatest cost to and most important prejudice against conventional capabilities is one that Robert S. McNamara has identified: "The reliance on NATO's nuclear threats for deterrence makes it more difficult to muster the political and financial support necessary to sustain an adequate conventional military force. Both publics and governments point to the nuclear force as the 'real deterrent,' thus explaining their reluctance to allocate even modest sums for greater conventional capabilities." In a world of finite resources and political constraints, the investment in nuclear forces serves not as a military backup to conventional forces but as a political replacement for them. The problem is compounded by the integration, in front-line combat units, of nuclear and conventional weapons, undermining the effectiveness of a conventional defense. This imposition of a nuclear capability on conventional forces means that the threat of first use of nuclear arms, intended to create a possibility that deters, may in the end drive decision-makers in a crisis to authorize the firing of nuclear weapons.

NATO has become, in effect, a captive of its war plans, its training programs, and its authorization and management procedures. Despite the current doctrine of flexible response in Europe, NATO military planners have warned that in reality the response during a crisis would hardly be flexible. The deployment of battlefield nuclear weapons in forward areas could, in fact, negate the doctrine, because it could require that a decision to "use or lose" nuclear weapons be made very early—even before a purely conventional defense had been attempted. General Rogers has stated that whatever his actual authority, he would be forced to "escalate fairly quickly to the first use of nuclear weapons" if war broke out. For this reason he has supported a no-early-use policy in Europe coupled with an improved conventional capability.

One of the fundamental assumptions underlying a first-use policy is that the explosive power of nuclear weapons can substitute for NATO manpower. First-use proponents suggest, for example, that nuclear weapons will be available as a last resort to avoid a defeat by conventional arms if NATO forces are outnumbered and in danger of being overrun. But since avoiding conventional defeat is the goal, substituting nuclear weapons for fighting men is not the answer. Nuclear weapons cannot make up for manpower deficiencies. They cannot hold ground. Many studies have suggested that a NATO escalation to nuclear war would favor the side with greater manpower, because of the tremendous number of casualties that would occur on both sides.

It is NATO's contention that first use could be used as a *political* signal of the alliance's strength and resolve in the midst of a conventional battle, a means of restoring deterrence and convincing the adversary that further aggression is useless. But the vulnerability of NATO's nuclear weapons to pre-emptive attack, and the fact that they could not reverse the tide of a losing battle, belie these arguments. NATO's leaders must realize that nuclear weapons used against a conventional threat offer no net military gain.

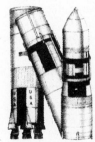

ATO'S STRATEGY OF RELYING ON THE FIRST use of nuclear weapons has, in our view, not only diminished its ability to respond with conventional forces but also increased the likelihood that at the height of a crisis NATO would resort to nuclear weapons. In the opinion of many first-use proponents, this dependence on nuclear weapons is precisely what is required to deter a conventional attack by Warsaw Pact forces and thus to avert war in Europe, either nuclear or conventional. The best way to avoid a nuclear war, first-use proponents argue, is to avoid the conventional war from which it might evolve.

In order to reduce the risk of conventional war, the argument continues, NATO must increase the risk of nuclear war; it must integrate nuclear and conventional forces, deploy vulnerable nuclear systems in forward areas, and create a situation that is likely to get out of hand soon after the beginning of any conflict. We recognize that these circumstances may prompt a measure of hesitation among Soviet decision-makers. But NATO cannot afford to continue to base its forces and its strategy on this prospect alone.

First, even if the specter of "nuclear accidents waiting to happen" instills a greater measure of caution in Soviet leaders, it cannot guarantee that the East and the West will never stumble into war. It *must* guarantee this, however, because a single failure of NATO's first-use policy could all too easily escalate to global nuclear war. There are many examples throughout history of wars beginning not through a rational calculation of potential benefit and cost but through a miscalculation at the height of a political crisis. If, as a result of ambiguous NATO activities or an intelligence failure, the Soviet Union became convinced that the West was about to commit an act of conventional aggression, then it might well take some military action regardless of a possible nuclear response. In addition, NATO's first-use posture would increase the danger that any unauthorized use of nuclear weapons, or their use by a third party against the Warsaw Pact or NATO countries, could be misinterpreted and spiral out of control.

There is a second reason why NATO should not rely on nuclear first use. What is most important in keeping the peace in Europe is the political self-confidence of the West. The decisive consideration in the Soviet calculus is whether pressure against NATO will be met by a united alliance with the ability and resolve to respond firmly. Certainly, doubts about the loyalty of East European forces enter into NATO calculations. While first-use proponents warn that a fundamental shift away from current policy would threaten the unity of the alliance, it is in fact current policy that presents the greater long-term threat to that unity. NATO's first-use policy, rather than providing a foundation for a united and self-confident defense, has become a growing source of distrust and dissension.

The divisive impact of the first-use policy is apparent in the major conflicts that have dogged the alliance since its formation. NATO has never been able to agree, for example, on the shape that "follow-on" use of nuclear weapons should take if "demonstration" use is not successful in persuading the adversary to halt and withdraw. After the deployment of U.S. tactical and intermediate-range nuclear weapons in the 1950s and 1960s, NATO was likewise unable to reach agreement on military plans for their use. Plans to deploy the neutron bomb in the late 1970s met with strong resistance in Europe. More recently, bitter and divisive debates have taken place between the United States and its European allies, and between European governments and much of the European public, over the deployment of Pershing II and ground-launched cruise missiles in Europe, scheduled for completion in 1988.

Both the United States and the Soviet Union have now put forward proposals to eliminate medium-range nuclear weapons in Europe. The European reaction to improved prospects for an agreement, despite earlier calls for progress in arms control, has been cautious at best. Reportedly, one German official has commented, "The whole idea of bringing the missiles over here was to reinforce the nuclear link between Europe and the United States. After all the agony and protests over deployment, we will probably go through a new debate now over how credible is the American nuclear umbrella." This is just the most recent example of the ways in which NATO's first-use policy forces an unfortunate choice between maintaining the cohesion of the alliance and reducing the risk of war through arms control.

Needless to say, peacetime tensions within the alliance do not bode well for NATO's performance during an East-West military confrontation. As a 1983 report by the North Atlantic Assembly stated: "Few experts believe that the NATO political consultation process could possibly function effectively in time of crisis. In this sense the close proximity of battlefield nuclear weapons to the potential combat zone increases the urgency of the decision-making process and places an unnecessary and undesirable pressure on the Alliance political leadership."

Uncertainty about NATO's ability to respond effectively in a crisis undermines conventional deterrence. According to most experts, there is little risk that NATO would fail to receive early warning of Warsaw Pact preparations for an attack. There is a significant risk, however, that the alliance, out of fear of alarming the Soviet Union and provoking an attack, would fail to authorize prudent actions in response. The commingling of nuclear and conventional forces would reinforce this tendency toward inaction among Western leaders. Proposals to give field commanders, in advance, the authority to respond incrementally by increasing readiness are politically unacceptable and unwise. However, delays in NATO mobilization and reinforcement would significantly shift the conventional balance in favor of the Warsaw Pact and would present the worst possible conventional scenario.

Such a situation, in the context of a serious political crisis in which the Soviets felt strong incentives to take military action, would undermine conventional deterrence and could increase the risk of a "smash-and-grab" maneuver. The best deterrent to such an action is to have a conventional defense in place and ready, not an "immobilized" nuclear NATO. As Field Marshal Lord Carver, the former Chief of the British Defence Staff, has warned: "It is folly for the Organization to base its defense on a policy which, in time of real tension, would divide it. It must find a policy on which it could remain united—and that can only be one which does not rely on being the first to use nuclear weapons." To discourage limited Soviet military actions NATO can continue to rely on a nuclear deterrent of low credibility or it can emphasize a conventional response of high credibility. The second alternative provides a more reliable deterrent and promises a lower risk of nuclear war.

Toward an Alternative NATO Nuclear Policy

AISING DIFFICULT QUESTIONS ABOUT the long-run effectiveness of NATO's nuclear deterrent is essential. Such questions will continue to bedevil the alliance as long as its strategy is based on false assumptions about the nature of nuclear weapons and implausible scenarios for their limited use. The most promising means of strengthening the alliance's cohesion and confidence lies in reducing, and then removing, its reliance on first use.

One essential component of a new consensus is that NATO allies be reassured as to the firmness of the U.S. security commitment. Yet one lesson of the Euromissile controversy is that in the minds of many Europeans, greater reliance on nuclear weapons no longer provides this reassurance—quite the opposite. The proliferation of nuclear-weapons systems has aroused strong and growing concern about the risks of nuclear war. As long as the United States relies on nuclear weapons to "reassure" its allies, it will be caught in conflicting European currents: on the one hand, concern that the United States would not employ nuclear weapons soon enough, and, on the other hand, concern that the United States would use them too readily. As the British defense analyst J. Michael Legge has written, "It was never entirely clear whether the Europeans wanted a finger on the nuclear trigger or on the safety catch." Europeans want to feel confident that the United States would not actually start a nuclear war in Europe but would like the Soviet Union to believe the opposite. It is a difficult task to show such resolve to the Soviet Union and hide it from the people of Western Europe.

The only way to reconcile these conflicting demands is to seek alternative means of demonstrating the commitment that this country has consistently felt. Relying on conventional forces to meet conventional threats means a redefinition, not an abandonment, of shared commitment and shared risk. It would still be necessary for the United States to be ready to reply with American nuclear weapons to any nuclear attack on its European allies.

The most tangible and non-provocative evidence of U.S. commitment is the presence of U.S. forces in Europe. As Michael Howard, the military historian, has argued, "The United States is 'coupled' to Europe, not by one delivery system rather than another, but by a vast web of military installations and personnel, to say nothing of the innumerable economic, social, and financial links that tie us together into a single coherent system." These links ensure that any war in Europe—nuclear or conventional—would immediately be an American war. If our allies require additional reassurance, then a formal permanent commitment of U.S. forces to the defense of Europe may offer the best evidence that a desire to reduce reliance on nuclear weapons does not indicate a reduction of the U.S.

commitment to the security of its European allies. It is precisely because this commitment is felt so strongly that we are concerned about the form it takes.

It is time that the responsibility for avoiding war returned to where it belongs—with political leaders. Avoiding war is a matter of managing conflicting interests and ensuring that alternatives to military force exist. There is no technological "fix" to substitute for the complex process of managing political relations. The best way to avoid war in Europe is to ensure that Soviet political interests would not be served by it.

What would Europe be like without its nuclear "crutch"? Would Western Europe be made "safe for conventional aggression," as Alexander Haig has warned? Whether considering a "smash-and-grab" maneuver or a full-scale attack, Warsaw Pact forces would be likely to confront a united NATO that had formidable conventional strength. The greater economic resources of the West suggest that Warsaw Pact forces would face a long conventional war even if they decisively won the first campaign. British and French nuclear forces would remain under independent control and capable of initiating the use of their nuclear weapons in a crisis—but they would not be compelled to do so, given their survivability and their distance from the East-West border.

NATO leaders would have to consider what diminished reliance on nuclear weapons would mean for Soviet behavior in a crisis. A NATO shift in policy, after being reflected in NATO force planning, might encourage Soviet leaders to adhere to their own declaration of no first use and might reduce their incentive to launch pre-emptive attacks on NATO nuclear assets at a time of crisis. At the very minimum, such a shift would improve East-West relations and increase the opportunity for progress in arms control.

But would Soviet leaders have such confidence in the NATO no-first-use policy that they would be encouraged to launch a conventional attack? We believe that the answer is no. First, there are grave political considerations—such as fear of convulsion in Eastern Europe and respect for the internal political strength of the NATO nations—that make a Soviet decision to attack Western Europe exceedingly unlikely under any present or foreseeable conditions. But quite aside from this fundamental reality, which is in fact better understood today in Western Europe than in Washington, we believe that no change in Western doctrine could or should give the Soviets reliable assurance that NATO's nuclear weapons would not be used if the fighting got out of control.

The Soviets have repeatedly stated their determination not to be the first to use nuclear weapons, but no NATO planner would take such public statements at face value. NATO continues to anticipate the possibility that the Warsaw Pact will initiate the use of nuclear weapons, and the Warsaw Pact would do the same if there were a no-first-use declaration by the West. With or without such a declaration, any Soviet leader would be hesitant to mass Warsaw

Pact divisions for an offensive and thereby create valuable targets for NATO nuclear weapons. So long as nuclear weapons remain available to the alliance, the possibility of their use exists and cannot be discounted by the East or the West. A new NATO policy could not remove this risk altogether, but it could reduce it.

Concrete Steps
That the West Can Take

HE FUNDAMENTAL PROBLEM OF THE current first-use policy is that it misconstrues the nature of nuclear weapons. It assumes that nuclear weapons can fulfill conventional war-fighting roles. But even their most limited use carries an unacceptable risk of escalation to general war. How have nuclear planners responded to this problem? They have redoubled their efforts to make a first-use policy credible. They have sought to buttress first-use threats by integrating nuclear and conventional forces, by deploying vulnerable nuclear weapons that would have to be used early or not at all in a conventional conflict, by developing systems—for example, the neutron bomb—that attempt to blur the line between conventional and nuclear weaponry, and by expressing a determination to defend U.S. allies with nuclear weapons. None of these efforts changes the basic nature of nuclear weapons. All of them, however, increase the risk of nuclear war and strain relations within the alliance.

The immediate step to take, therefore, is to re-examine the proper role of nuclear weapons and redirect efforts away from buttressing first-use policies and toward making a safe, stabilizing transition to a nuclear posture designed to deter nuclear use. Such a transition would have to be carefully planned but would certainly be less dangerous than attempting a transition from "threat deterrence" to "defense dominance," as epitomized by the President's Strategic Defense Initiative. There is evidence that a shift away from an over-reliance on nuclear weaponry is already under way. In Europe attention is focusing on efforts to improve the effectiveness of conventional forces and to "raise the nuclear threshold." A growing awareness of the limitations of nuclear deterrence is also apparent within the Reagan Administration. In 1984 General John W. Vessey, Jr., then the Chairman of the Joint Chiefs of Staff, observed, "If we are sincere about avoiding an early nuclear decision or surrender, we should emphasize more reinforcement capability rather than less. Even if one views NATO's current conventional posture as little more than an extended trip wire—and I do not—a major retrenchment in U.S. ground reinforcements for NATO would leave little recourse other than the nuclear alternative. That is a cure that is worse than the disease."

While there is consensus on the need to reduce reliance on nuclear weapons, there appears to be little consensus on how best to proceed. The approach suggested here is that when formulating its military plans and setting nuclear and conventional force requirements the United States should assume that it will never be in its interests or in the interests of its allies to initiate the use of nuclear weapons. More specifically, the United States and its allies might move toward a more durably credible defense posture in Europe, and elsewhere, by taking the following steps.

As an initial measure the Western alliance could adopt a policy of no early use. A no-early-use policy, when reflected in NATO force planning, would improve the effectiveness of existing conventional forces by increasing their flexibility and lightening the burden of nuclear-weapons safety and control procedures. Because such a policy would require NATO to pull back its vulnerable, forward-based nuclear systems, it would both expedite the withdrawal of nuclear weapons agreed to by NATO in October of 1983 and facilitate further reduction in the number of nuclear weapons deployed among NATO forces in Europe. Those weapons that raise the most serious problems relating to release authority and early use—some short-range nuclear artillery, atomic demolition munitions, and nuclear air-defense systems—could all be rapidly withdrawn and their storage facilities secured against conventional and other forms of non-nuclear attack. The repositioning of battlefield and theater nuclear weapons well away from the NATO–Warsaw Pact border would ultimately allow the West to propose negotiations on a verifiable agreement establishing a carefully defined zone on both sides of the border in Europe, beginning in the central region, within which no nuclear munitions would be deployed.

As another interim measure NATO could halt any weapons-modernization programs, such as those to produce and deploy new generations of nuclear artillery shells, that are predicated on a strategy of early use of its nuclear arsenal. This would, among other things, avoid the damage to relations within the alliance which would certainly come from attempts to deploy such weapons in Europe. Elimination of dual-capable launchers is also desirable. Such launchers, particularly tactical aircraft, should be uncoupled from a nuclear role, and nuclear weapons should be sharply differentiated from conventional systems. Nuclear forces could be placed under a separate command and provided with separate alert procedures, as William W. Kaufmann has suggested.

A logical next step would be a policy of no early second use. This would enhance stability by requiring that the United States and its allies identify the location, source, and extent of any nuclear explosion before responding.

When it is ready, the alliance should declare its intention not to be the first to use nuclear weapons—that is, tactical or theater nuclear weapons—in Europe. The United States should make a similar declaration, or at the very least a declaration of no early use, with respect to American nuclear weapons deployed in other theaters. Although the fact is not widely understood, American policy in Asia, the Middle East, and elsewhere contemplates the first use of nuclear weapons. The United States threatened or considered the use of nuclear weapons outside Europe on a number of occasions in the 1950s, when it was official U.S. policy to initiate the use of nuclear weapons in any large-scale conflict. More recently, in 1975, the Ford Administration made public the fact that the United States had stored nuclear weapons in Korea and had explicitly threatened to initiate the use of nuclear weapons, if necessary, to defend South Korea. Presidents Jimmy Carter and Ronald Reagan have both implied that the United States would use nuclear weapons, if necessary, to counter Soviet aggression in the Persian Gulf. Under a no-first-use policy the United States could scale down the number of nuclear weapons stockpiled outside the United States and Europe, or eliminate them altogether. Either measure would give the United States added leverage in pursuing nuclear arms control and nuclear nonproliferation.

We would argue, finally, that the United States should adopt a policy of no *strategic* first use—a commitment not to initiate the use of American strategic weapons based on the U.S. mainland or at sea. Declared American policy, with regard particularly to Soviet aggression in Europe, retains the option of launching a strategic strike against Soviet forces before the United States itself has been attacked and even before the Soviets have used nuclear weapons locally. The approach suggested here would move policy away from the initiation of any such attacks, whether on the battlefield or upon the Soviet homeland.

Adoption of a no-strategic-first-use policy would have profound consequences. It would mean, first, that there would be no rationale for deploying highly vulnerable systems—for example, the MX missile—that could not survive a first strike. Second, it would significantly alter targeting criteria and the forces needed to destroy those targets. Under an assumption of no strategic first use the United States would not require the capability to destroy large numbers of Soviet "hard" targets. Only a small number of hard targets could be usefully hit in a U.S. second strike. Because Soviet missiles in silos would be sitting ducks for such an attack, the Soviet Union, on warning of a U.S. retaliatory strike, would in all likelihood fire those missiles rather than allow them to be destroyed on the ground. Only a disarming first strike could possibly catch Soviet missiles in their silos. Thus, if the United States rules out the first use of nuclear weapons, there would be little purpose in targeting the majority of these silos.

Changes in targeting would reduce the requirements for systems designed to destroy hard targets. It would also make certain additional systems, such as the Trident D-5, unnecessary, since their main function is to supplement this capability. Finally, a no-strategic-first-use policy would permit an alteration of the criteria by which strategic-arms-control proposals are evaluated. It would reduce U.S. reluctance to trade away destabilizing systems for equivalent Soviet weapons. Current opposition to a total

test ban, for example, is based on the need to retain and develop reliable weapons for a pre-emptive strike, as well as on the need to develop and refine tactical nuclear weapons.

Needless to say, a policy of no first use presupposes the abandonment of the Strategic Defense Initiative. Although we share the President's hope for a diminished reliance on nuclear arms, we do not believe that his proposals will safely take us in that direction. The danger of the SDI is that it attempts to provide a technological, or "hardware," solution to a fundamentally political problem; in the nuclear age there can be no security in the East or the West unless it is mutual security. The Strategic Defense Initiative threatens to erode allied unity, and confidence in American guarantees, by raising the prospect of a "decoupling" of Western Europe from the United States. At the same time, the SDI will consume billions of dollars that might be used to upgrade conventional capabilities. Moreover, if the Soviet reaction to the Strategic Defense Initiative is to build more nuclear weapons to overcome U.S. defenses, as the Department of Defense suggests that it may be, then the SDI will have been a step not toward a world without nuclear weapons but toward a world with more of them. These considerations aside, it is highly unlikely that the United States will be able to develop strategic defenses of any reliable effectiveness.

 T HAS LONG BEEN THE POLICY OF the United States to retain the option of initiating use of nuclear weapons to defend its security and that of its allies. Yet even today military planners are hard pressed to describe precisely how the first use of nuclear weapons would contribute to that security. That military planners have persisted in seeking sensible uses for nuclear weapons is, to some extent, understandable. Policy-makers have sought to harness the tremendous destructive power of nuclear weapons to strengthen U.S. security. With the first-use policy, they have failed.

While nuclear weapons do not cost more money than conventional weapons, they are in many other ways more costly. A reliance on nuclear weapons to deter conventional aggression has diverted money and manpower from other areas, hampered the effectiveness of conventional forces, contributed to East-West antagonism, and weakened the unity of the alliance. First use has remained U.S. policy largely because its costs are intangible and indirect. That is so only as long as no war or crisis is in prospect. But once either is, the results could well be catastrophic for the United States and its allies. The alternative approach recommended here would increase U.S. and allied security by reducing the risk of nuclear war, increasing the U.S. capability to fight conventionally, and improving the prospects for arms control.

US and Soviet Responsibility

for Disarmament

Si Chu

Two draft resolutions on nuclear and conventional disarmament submitted by China have recently been adopted by the 41st session of the United Nations General Assembly by an overwhelming majority of 150 to 0 with 2 abstentions in one case and by consensus in the other. This is the first time that China has solely sponsored and put to the vote important draft resolutions on disarmament at the UN. This is another manifestation of China's independent foreign policy and of its contribution to the maintenance of world peace.

The resolution on nuclear disarmament urged the United States and the Soviet Union, which "possess the most important nuclear arsenals," to "discharge their special responsibility for nuclear disarmament" by "taking the lead" in halting the nuclear arms race and reaching an agreement on the drastic reduction of their nuclear arsenals at an early date. The resolution on conventional disarmament stressed that the United States and the Soviet Union "have a special responsibility in pursuing the process of conventional armaments reductions," and that they and their respective military blocs should negotiate in earnest with a view to reaching early "agreement on the limitation and gradual and balanced reduction of armed forces and conventional weapons under effective international control." The key to disarmament lies in whether the two superpowers will fulfill the special responsibility they have by taking the lead in disarmament. The widespread support given to the two resolutions shows that China's views and proposals are reasonable and practical, and reflect the common desire of people from all parts of the world.

At present, the continuous escalation of the nuclear arms race poses a grave threat to world peace. Over the years, the two superpowers have fiercely vied with each other in the field of nuclear weapons, and are now extending their arms race to outer space. The various kinds of nuclear weapons in their hands now account for over 95 percent of the world's total. Obviously, it will therefore only be possible to relax international tension and reduce the danger of nuclear war if the USA and the USSR take the lead in disarming. Any viewpoint that neglects, or evades or denies the special responsibility of the superpowers will thus prove unacceptable to the world community.

Under great pressure from the people of all countries, including their own, both the United States and the Soviet Union have advanced various proposals on nuclear arms control and disarmament. Both have declared that a nuclear war cannot be won and must never be fought; and both admit their special responsibility for nuclear disarmament. Both have also declared their willingness, in principle, to take the lead by reducing their nuclear weapons by 50 percent. However, all this has so far added up to no more than mere propaganda and a succession of "peace offensives." Six rounds of arms control negotiations between the two in Geneva have resulted in no agreement. And summit talks in Geneva and Iceland between President Ronald Reagan and General Secretary Gorbachev proved disappointing. As a result, the international community is becoming increasingly concerned about the escalation of the nuclear arms race and is demanding that both the United States and the Soviet Union adopt constructive and flexible positions and engage in serious negotiations to reach an agreement on the significant reduction of nuclear weapons which both helps relax international tension and does not infringe upon the interests of other countries.

While laying the emphasis on nuclear disarmament, China's resolution on conventional disarmament also points out the serious threat to world peace and international security presented by conventional arms, and the need for conventional disarmament. In the age of nuclear weapons, there can be no absolute demarcation between a conventional and a nuclear war. If a war breaks out in an area with a high concentration of nuclear arms, it is likely to escalate into a nuclear war. And with the advance of science and technology, conventional weapons have become increasingly deadly and destructive. Conventional wars since World War II have claimed tens of millions of lives and inflicted incalculable damage to property. It is a fact that all foreign interference in and aggression against sovereign states has been carried out with conventional forces. Conventional and nuclear disarmament are hence closely related and mutually complementary. China's resolution pointed out that the United States and the Soviet Union, "with the largest military arsenals," "bear a special

Reprinted by courtesy of *Beijing Review*, Vol. 29, No. 52, December 29, 1986, pp. 16-17.

responsibility in conventional armaments reduction." The possession of the largest and most advanced conventional arsenals by the two superpowers, coupled with the tension and confrontation between them, directly threatens world peace, and it is therefore necessary to urge the United States and the Soviet Union to be the first to reduce conventional arsenals.

Ardently desiring peace and firmly opposing war, the Chinese people urgently need a peaceful and stable international environment in which to pursue their programme of socialist modernization. China has always stood for the complete prohibition and total destruction of nuclear arms and has declared it will never be the first to use nuclear weapons, and will never use them against nuclear-free zones and non-nuclear-weapon states under any circumstances.

A Soviet official on verification

Roland M. Timerbaev

Roland M. Timerbaev, Soviet deputy ambassador to the United Nations, was formerly deputy director of the Department of International Organizations in the Soviet Foreign Ministry. He has been involved in negotiations on the SALT I and Non-Proliferation Treaties and toward a comprehensive test ban and is the author of a number of books on disarmament and foreign policy.

THE OCTOBER 1986 issue of the *Bulletin* carried a critical review of my book on verification of arms limitation and disarmament, which I wrote in 1981 and published in 1983. That review contained some misconceptions and misinterpretations of the Soviet view of verification. Without going into a discussion of these misperceptions, I would like to give the readers of this magazine a first-hand description of the Soviet Union's approach to verification. This, in my view, is especially important today, for the Soviet government has recently adopted a new approach to this crucial issue.

The importance of verification is now greater than ever before. It derives from the pressing need to achieve a breakthrough in the international situation; to overcome the negative, confrontational trends, which have been growing in recent years, and to clear the way for winding down the arms race on earth and for preventing it in outer space; for an overall reduction of the danger of war; and for building trust as an integral component of relations between states. To achieve this new political thinking is necessary—that is to say, the recognition of the fact that in the present situation people can no longer act the way they did before. This fully applies to the problem of verification as well.

That was reaffirmed by the Reykjavik meeting last October during which the problem of verification was also discussed. Having expressed its willingness to go ahead with deep cuts in nuclear weapons, the Soviet side favored the strictest possible verification in any form. In a postnuclear situation, verification must be even more stringent and of the kind that would provide full assurance of reliable compliance with agreements during every stage of arms reductions.

As a result, this issue too was settled in principle. The deficit of new political thinking in the U.S. position, however, foiled the success of the Reykjavik meeting. As a consequence, the historic chance to negotiate a whole package of reliably verifiable agreements was missed.

ONE OF THE PRINCIPAL lessons of Reykjavik is that new political thinking for nuclear age realities is an important condition for finding a way out of the critical situation in which humanity has found itself at the end of the twentieth century. In materializing such new thinking, the Soviet Union attaches particular importance to the problem of verification. We have stated, on more occasions than one, that the Soviet Union is open to verification and that we are interested in it no less than others.

The attempts that are being made to use verification issues to avoid agreements on arms limitations and disarmament are immoral and sanctimonious, as well as basically destructive. Broadly speaking, the problem of verification is no longer on the agenda as some kind of obstacle to agreements. What is needed now is to deal constructively with that problem.

The fruitfulness of new approaches and the need for their implementation have been convincingly demonstrated by the results of the Stockholm Conference on Confidence- and Security-Building Measures and Disarmament in Europe. These results have proved that even in a complex situation understandings can be reached on the problems of security, provided that there is the political will and desire to do so. The practical significance of the Stockholm accords lies in the fact that a set of political and military-technical measures has been agreed upon to reduce the risk of war in Europe and to strengthen security and confidence among the participants in the agreements that have been reached. In fact, what is involved here is the first major agreement in the politico-military field since the signing of the SALT II Treaty. A foundation has been laid for new agreements, including those on substantial reductions in armed forces and armaments in Europe, as proposed by the Warsaw Treaty member countries at their meeting in Budapest last year.

In Stockholm, the Soviet Union materialized in practice its new approach to verification issues, thereby confirming that today the problem of verification, as such, does not exist, provided that there is indeed an earnest intention to seek mutually advantageous solutions which would lead to the lessening and elimination of the danger of war.

The new political philosophy underlies also the Soviet initiative for a sizeable reduction of conventional armaments and armed forces in Europe. The Soviet Union and its Warsaw Treaty allies advocate reliable verification at all stages of that process. That may involve both national technical means and international forms of verification, including—where necessary—on-site inspections. The Soviet Union also offered a similar approach for verifying the implementation of the program for complete elimination of nuclear weapons everywhere in the world by the end of this century. The verification of armaments to be destroyed or limited would be carried out through both national technical means and international procedures, up to and including on-site inspections.

We have also proposed that in the process of carrying out the nuclear disarmament measures provided for in this program special procedures be worked out for destroying nuclear warheads, as well as for dismantling, converting, or destroying delivery vehicles. In all the stages of eliminating nuclear weapons, the amounts of the weapons to be destroyed as well as the sites where they will be destroyed, are to be agreed upon. Of course, there should be reliable verification, including international procedures, of the destruction or conversion of such weaponry.

WITH THE UNILATERAL Soviet moratorium on nuclear explosions in effect for a year and a half now, no one—including even those who assert otherwise—could fail to see that the main impediment to concluding a treaty on the total prohibition of nuclear weapons tests is not at all the issue of verification.

The U.S. equipment located near the Soviet test site and the foreign reporters who have been there registered the complete absence of Soviet nuclear explosions. This is yet another clear confirmation of the fact that the problem of verification and openness, which has been used by opponents of disarmament in the past, now lends itself to effective solution.

The Soviet Union is prepared at any time and in any place to sign a treaty on the prohibition of nuclear weapons tests. We favor strict verification in that area and are ready to use the valuable recommendations on that question made by the nonaligned summit conference in Harare, Zimbabwe, last September. We are ready to support the proposals advanced by six countries on five continents in regard to the monitoring of compliance with the obligation not to conduct nuclear explosions, and we are ready to accept the recommendations worked out under the auspices of the United Nations.

The Soviet Union has put forward concrete proposals on seismic verification and has come out in favor of conducting more profound research in the field of the international exchange of seismic data with a view to enhancing the effectiveness of such exchange. We have proposed that a system for the expeditious transfer of wave form data be worked out and that an international experiment in that area be conducted.

In our view, an effective solution can also be found to the problem of how to verify the prevention of the spreading of the arms race to outer space. If an agreement to prohibit the introduction of arms into outer space is reached, the Soviet Union will be prepared, on a reciprocal basis, to open its laboratories for verification of such an agreement. One is bound to say that as far as verification is concerned, the Star Wars program, if implemented, will create virtually insurmountable difficulties. A number of questions inevitably arise, for example: By what criteria should one be guided in differentiating between offensive and defensive space arms? How can assurances be provided that a space platform, with missiles, X-ray lasers, or other technical devices, will not be used for a first strike? How will the problems of inspection be solved? Thus, the SDI program would negate the very idea of verification, including verification of compliance with the existing agreements.

THE CONSTRUCTIVE potential of the Soviet position on the verification issue is also manifested in the negotiations to ban chemical weapons. The Soviet Union favors the speediest possible and complete elimination of chemical weapons and of the industrial base for manufacturing them. Such elimination should be carried out under strict control, including international on-site inspections. My country favors continuous or systematic international inspections of the destruction of chemical weapons stockpiles and of the production of highly toxic and lethal chemicals for allowed purposes. Last year, at the Geneva Conference on Disarmament and in the United Nations, the Soviet Union introduced additional far-reaching proposals designed to insure effective verification of the destruction or dismantling of chemical weapons production facilities and also proposed that a provision be made for carrying out systematic on-site inspections of those facilities. In this context, the cessation of the functioning of each chemical weapons production facility would be insured by means of strict verification, including systematic or continuous international inspections. Thus, we operate on the assumption that systematic or continuous international on-site inspections will become the major form of international verification of compliance with the key provisions of a future convention on the prohibition and elimination of chemical weapons.

The main purpose of verification is to promote implementation of arms limitation measures, to strengthen confidence in each other—which is inherent in the fact of their entering into such an agreement— and to provide objective information on the real situation as regards compliance.

The practice of arms limitation negotiations, including those between the Soviet Union and the United States, shows that when there is genuine willingness to come to agreement, verification presents no obstacle. The Soviet Union demonstrates such willingness in practice. There are no weapons that our country would not be prepared to limit or ban, on a mutual basis, and subject to most effective verification.

THE QUESTION OF verification is closely related to the problem of compliance with agreements on arms limitation and reduction. The U.S. government proclaims its willingness to comply with agreements designed to promote security and international stability, and has even submitted resolutions to that effect in the United Nations. Those, however, are empty words, since in actual deeds it is precisely the United States that is undermining the regime of the existing agreements—in particular the SALT I, SALT II, and the ABM Treaties—which constitute the foundation of strategic stability.

The United States asserts that compliance can be determined only by verification. Without minimizing the importance of verification of compliance with agreements, it has to be stated, nevertheless, that sometimes compliance or noncompliance is obvious without any verification—for instance, when there is a unilateral renunciation of an agreement, as is the case with the SALT II Treaty or when the ABM Treaty is interpreted in such broad terms that the meaning of the agreements reached is in effect reduced to zero. A U.N. resolution, adopted on the initiative of a number of Western and socialist countries, including the

United States, by the forty-first session of the General Assembly in December 1986, stressed that "any weakening of confidence in such agreements diminishes their contribution to global or regional stability and to further disarmament and arms limitation efforts." But renunciation of existing international legal instruments and circumvention of treaties directly weaken such confidence. It is regrettable that none other than a country that cosponsored that resolution has been acting in this way.

The Soviet Union believes that the question of complying with the agreements on arms limitation and reduction is of fundamental importance, especially when it involves such basic agreements as the SALT I and SALT II Treaties and the 1972 ABM Treaty. We stand for strict compliance with the obligations under the agreements concluded and for preserving everything positive that has been achieved so far in the field of arms limitation under effective international control.

The main purpose of verification is to promote the implementation of arms limitation measures, to strengthen the parties' confidence in each other—confidence that is inherent in the very fact of their entering into an arms limitation agreement—and to provide objective information on the real situation as regards compliance with it. For this reason, the principal requirement that we make as far as verification is concerned is that it should be effective.

The Soviet Union is convinced that verification should be used to insure the viability of disarmament agreements. Therefore, in addition to being effective, another requirement that we make of verification is that it should be adequate. The principle of the adequacy of verification measures— which has been confirmed by the experience of compliance with international agreements in the field of disarmament— is enshrined in a number of universally accepted international instruments, including the final document of the 1978 First U.N. Special Session on Disarmament, which was adopted by consensus.

The Soviet Union is for effective and adequate verification, is in favor of considering and solving all disarmament and verification problems in a business-like and concrete manner, and advocates a dynamic approach to finding mutually acceptable solutions. The Soviet Union is ready for such solutions.

IRRESPONSIBLE ACT

At 11 hours 59 minutes on November 28, 1986, the 131st B-52 bomber took off from the Kelly air base, San Antonio, where it had been converted, and headed for the Carswell air base, Texas, to be armed with nuclear cruise missiles there. The U.S. thus exceeded the quotas set by SALT-2. The move came as part of Washington's persistent efforts to undermine the present system of strategic stability.

It will be recalled that in 1979 the U.S.S.R. and the U.S. committed themselves, in Vienna, to an agreement not to seek military superiority as it would bring only dangerous instability, generating higher levels of armaments with no benefit to the security of either party. The leaders of the two states gave this solemn pledge when signing SALT-2 in the Austrian capital. For the first time ever in the arms limitation process, the treaty set a quota of arms totals for both sides. The ceiling for intercontinental ballistic missile launchers, submarine-carried ballistic missile launchers, and heavy bombers armed with cruise missiles and air-to-ground ballistic missiles with ranges of over 600 km was set at 2,400 units.

Since the signing of SALT-2, the opponents of disarmament in Washington have been determined to destroy the letter and spirit of the treaty which they find abhorrent. First, the Senate refused to ratify it. Subsequently, efforts were made to bury the treaty by which both sides had agreed to abide.

Here is an example. In June 1985 the National Security Council met in a session to decide the fate of SALT-2 which interfered with the commissioning of the latest weapons. Defense Secretary Caspar Weinberger, a civilian, objected to it on the grounds that it was "senseless." Even the Joint Chiefs of Staff winced at the epithet. The generals were more discreet and suggested to the President that the U.S. should observe the treaty, but feel free to violate some of its provisions.

A year later the issue of SALT-2 observance cropped up again, in connection with the routine testing of another Ohio-type submarine. At that time the White House did not venture beyond the limits set by SALT-2, but threatened to do so when arming another B-52 with cruise missiles. "The President has travelled the last mile, we are no longer bound by that flawed agreement," Weinberger said. The last mile was travelled late in November. The breaching of the treaty caused a considerable stir. The traditional allusions to SALT-2 violations by the Soviet Union did not work this time— many Congressmen were indignant at the White House's arbitrary decision. The Senate and the House of Representatives supplemented a war budget bill with a call to the government to continue to observe SALT-2 which, in their opinion, served the interests of U.S. security. Many U.S. allies in NATO also insisted on its observance, as had been the case on many previous occasions.

What is making Washington bust the treaty now that Reykjavik has held out the prospect of getting the nuclear disarmament issue out of its blind alley and that Soviet initiatives have won widespread recognition? One thing is clear: Washington is determined to undermine the opportunities of reaching an agreement. By showing open defiance to the Soviet Union, it incites us to complicity in the arms race and seeks to wrest concessions from the U.S.S.R. at negotiations. Finally, the move is a reaction to "Irangate." Responsibility for it is borne not so much by the President, of course, but by those whose interests he represents. It is the forces behind him that are gambling on international stability, unmindful of the dangerous consequences their actions could have both for the American people and the world.

The U.S. Administration's decision is commented upon, at our request, by Lieutenant General Victor PAVLOV:

"The decision to breach SALT-2 is a new manifestation of U.S. power politics. I would call it a reckless move dictated, to my mind, by the interests of the military-industrial complex who are seriously worried by the glimmer of a hope of reaching an agreement emanating from Reykjavik. Washington has plainly demonstrated its intention to reduce to nought the progress made in the field of arms limitation and reduction in the 1970s, and at the Reykjavik summit.

"A legitimate question arises: how can one reach a new agreement by trampling previous ones underfoot? It is time the U.S. leadership realized that SALT-2 is of equal benefit to the U.S. and the U.S.S.R. Attempts to justify this adventurist move by allusions to imaginary violations of the treaty by the U.S.S.R. are untenable. I think Washington should harbour no illusions as to any possibility of gaining military superiority over the Soviet Union in that way. We shall certainly never allow the military-strategic balance to be upset. By undermining the SALT treaty the White House bears full responsibility for all the adverse consequences this move may have."

International Organization and International Law

The health of the international order in most functional areas depends upon international law and universalistic world organizations like the United Nations and its agencies. Unfortunately, these organizations' ability to manage the world order has been challenged in the last few years. The United States and Great Britain have withdrawn from UNESCO; the United States refused to submit to the jurisdiction of the World Court on Nicaragua, a practice common to many states when they believe the Court will decide against them; and the various committees and agencies of the United Nations are hamstrung by poor management and political bias.

Even if little more than talk and diplomacy occurs at the United Nations, however, this does not mean it is ineffective. As an international forum to which all states have access, it provides an outlet for anger, frustration, and conflict that is quite helpful in creating an appreciation of some of the sources of hostility and directing international efforts toward eliminating them. Although wars continue to erupt, this need not be considered as evidence of the total failure of international organizations. Their role goes far beyond conflict avoidance to promoting a more effectively functioning international system.

Efforts to improve the world and to maintain peace are not solely the work of large formal international organizations. "International regimes" have contributed at least as much as international organizations. International regimes, comprised of the agreements, rules, and organizations which certain states make for advancing their own interests in specific issue areas, are the institutionalized practices and policies which states adhere to in order to protect their common interests. Thus, while the United Nations seems helpless to address such highly politicized issues as arms control and disarmament, the major nuclear powers have constructed an international nonproliferation regime which deserves most of the credit for limiting the proliferation of nuclear weapons to a mere handful of countries in the more than forty years since atomic weapons came into existence. A fledgling international sea regime addresses the issues of access to resources, transit, and the emplacement of things in the oceans. The international economic regime is one of the most diverse and complicated, with institutions such as the IMF and World Bank playing major roles in the complex issues of debt restructuring, development, and trade protectionism. Multinational corporations and individual governments also participate through tech-

nology transfer, investment, and aid programs. In addition, the international energy regime may prove to be of considerable value in monitoring energy supplies and averting international energy crises.

International regimes thereby contribute significantly to "functional cooperation," a first step toward world integration: states relinquish a certain degree of their sovereign national control over policy in functionally specific areas, such as health, education, technology, finance, trade, and agriculture, in order to reap the greater benefits of international cooperation. In an age of growing interdependence of states, brought about by rapid communication and transportation, and by the fact that so much of a country's life must transcend its own territorial boundaries, states' policies must have the support of other states if they are to be of value. States are, as a result, more ready to consider international cooperation at the expense of narrowly defined sovereign rights. States gain far more by adhering to the rules of the General Agreement of Tariffs and Trade (GATT) and the Nonproliferation Treaty than they do through trade protection and the selling of nuclear weapons technology. Although greater international integration and interdependence cannot guarantee the elimination of war or the pursuit of national interests, there is evidence of the many achievements of internationally coordinated efforts in creating mutually shared interests. As more and more states benefit from multilateralization and internationalism, attempts to advance individual national interests through war become less attractive.

The improvement of human rights is an area in which unilateral national actions have proven more effective than internationally coordinated efforts. Effective international legislation is impeded by fundamental differences in values and ideologies among states. The concept of human rights varies dramatically depending upon a state's ideology or religion. Socialist states believe the interests of the collective take precedence over the rights of individuals. They believe, further, that the definition of human rights is class-based, and, therefore, that a state ruled by the capitalist class cannot define human rights for a state ruled by the working class.

Of course, right-wing dictatorships also resist the interference of other states in their internal affairs on behalf of alleged violations of human rights. For these governments, individuals or groups who oppose the government and threaten its overthrow have abdicated their rights. If

states concerned about human rights issues have a bilateral relationship with these governments, they have sometimes made progress in addressing human rights abuses in these countries. Usually the instrument of persuasion is the withdrawal of support, such as economic, financial, or military aid. Such instruments have proven far more effective when the intervening country does not really need the cooperation of the violator of human rights for a strategic location, military base, or strategic resource. Reasons such as these have inhibited the United States from taking effective action against the South African government to end its policy of apartheid, or to improve the human rights situation in the Philippines before Marcos was ousted.

The articles in this unit address a number of the issues which international organizations and international regimes face today. The international sea regime, in its concern for a more equitable distribution of the resources of and access to the sea to all countries (Article 57), has incurred resistance from the maritime states that want to protect their special rights and are concerned about the erosion of the concept of freedom of the seas (Article 56). A new international regime may be developing to address terrorism. This regime requires international cooperation, at the expense of some amount of sovereign control. One proposal for addressing terrorism is an international criminal court and criminal code for dealing with terrorists (Articles 58 and 59). But if a criminal court is no more able than the World Court has been to assert its jurisdiction over the parties involved (Article 55), its contribution to controlling international terrorism would be seriously in doubt. Although the international legal order still faces formidable problems, the willingness to consider addressing common problems through international cooperation is rapidly growing.

Looking Ahead: Challenge Questions

What kinds of issues have been addressed most effectively by international organizations and international regimes? Why are some issues better addressed by international regimes than by international organizations? Why are human rights abuses so much more difficult to address at the international level? What kinds of international instruments might be created to deal more effectively with human rights abuses? To what degree does internationalism come at the expense of national sovereignty?

World Court Supports Nicaragua After U.S. Rejected Judges' Role

PAUL LEWIS

Special to The New York Times

THE HAGUE, June 27 — The International Court of Justice ruled today that the Reagan Administration had broken international law and violated Nicaraguan sovereignty by aiding the anti-Government rebels.

The Court, the judicial arm of the United Nations, ordered Washington to halt the "arming and training" of the insurgents and to pay Nicaragua for damages caused by military attacks, some of which it said had been carried out by the United States itself.

The judgment, which was widely expected, came after 26 months of litigation on Nicaragua's complaint.

U.S. Rejects the Verdict

In Washington, a State Department spokesman said the United States rejected the Court's verdict, and said the body was "not equipped" to judge complex international military issues. The American spokesman added that "we consider our policy in Central America to be entirely consistent with international law."

In January 1985 the Administration said it would defy the Court and ignore further proceedings in the case because of its view that the World Court, as it is commonly called, has no jurisdiction to decide cases involving ongoing armed conflicts. The Court rejected this position last November.

Throughout the case, the argument that the United States was giving military aid to the contras was never in serious dispute. However, before Washington formally withdrew from the case, it argued that Nicaragua was actively seeking to subvert its neighbors, and that this activity justified actions on behalf of El Salvador, Costa Rica and Honduras.

The Court's findings were announced the day after the House of Representatives endorsed President Reagan's plan to provide $100 million in new aid to the rebels, with $70 million earmarked for military assistance.

The Court that decided the Nicaraguan case consists of 15 judges: one, the chief judge, from India; two from France, and one each from Poland, Argentina, Nigeria, Italy, Brazil, Senegal, Algeria, China, Norway, Japan, the United States and Britain. The American, British and Japanese judges dissented on the most important issues in the case.

The Court deferred a ruling on Nicaragua's petition for $370 million in damages from the United States, saying it wished to give the two countries a chance to negotiate a settlement themselves. However, the Court said it would step in if no accord materialized.

In New York, Nora Astorga, Nicaragua's chief envoy to the United Nations, said that her Government had asked for a Security Council meeting to discuss how to make the United States comply with the ruling.

A legal counsel for the Managua Government said today in Washington that as a result of the ruling, Nicaragua intends to sue the United States for more than $1 billion in damages in United States courts.

"On the monetary damages, we intend to seek its enforcement in the courts of the United States," said Abram Chayes, an American law professor and counsel for Nicaragua.

The Court has no enforcement powers. It depends on voluntary compliance with its rulings by states coming before it.

The Court ruled against the United States on 15 counts.

The Court found the United States violated customary international law and Nicaragua's sovereignty by "training, arming, equipping, financing and supplying the contra forces." It also found the United States guilty of direct attacks on Nicaraguan oil installations, ports and shipping in 1983 and 1984.

It held that the United States broke international law by authorizing overflights of Nicaraguan territory and by mining Nicaraguan ports and harbors in 1984. The Court also ruled that the United States trade embargo against Nicaragua, decreed in May 1985, violates a 1956 treaty of friendship between the two countries.

The Court also condemned the United States for allowing distribution of a Central Intelligence Agency manual on guerrilla warfare techniques to the contras, saying it encourages "acts contrary to the general principles of humanitarian law."

A majority of judges rejected the American claim that it was acting in the "collective self-defense" of El Salvador, Costa Rica and Honduras because Nicaragua was supporting rebel movements in these countries.

The Court said Nicaraguan aid to rebels in El Salvador was mainly in 1980 and 1981, before the United States stepped up its assistance to the contras, and did not constitute an "armed attack" on these countries under international law. As a result, the United States' response was judged disproportionate and unnecessary.

The Court said the United States was responsible in a general way for damage caused by the contras but not for specific acts by the rebels since it does not control them.

It also said the United States has no right to seek the overthrow of the Nicaraguan Government because of its political ideology. But to the surprise of some lawyers, it then added that this doctrine does not apply to "the process of decolonization," suggesting that wars of national liberation may be justified in international law.

The Nicaraguan Foreign Minister, the Rev. Miguel d'Escoto Brockmann, said he hoped the United States Congress would now agree to stop new aid going to the contras. "We want the U.S. to comply with the ruling so that there will be no more killing of our people," he told a news conference.

If the United States fails to respect the judgment, Father D'Escoto said, its "reputation as a member of the international community will be tarnished, perhaps irreparably."

The Foreign Minister said he would discuss the verdict with the United Nations Secretary General, Javier Pérez de Cuéllar, in New York next week before returning to Nicaragua for talks with the other leaders of the Government on their next move in the dispute.

Although the World Court lacks the means to enforce its judgments, diplomats here say that Nicaragua can still use today's judgment in its favor to cause the United States some diplomatic embarrassment. This could first occur in a demand to the Security Council for United Nation-authorized sanctions against the United States if it fails to comply. The United States would then be forced to exercise its Security Council veto to block the Nicaraguan resolution.

The United States walked out of the Court proceedings last year, saying they were biased in favor of Nicaragua.

In announcing that it did not recognize the Court's jurisdiction in January 1985, the Reagan Administration noted that the Soviet Union and most other nations had never assented to the World Court's jurisdiction, as the United States did in 1946.

But the World Court proceeded with the Nicaragua case, in accordance with its rules, as it did when Iran refused to recognize its jurisdiction in the United States' suit over the seizure in 1979 of American diplomats in Teheran as hostages. The Court ruled for the United States in that case.

The Nicaraguan case is widely seen by legal scholars as the most politically sensitive the World Court has ever adjudicated as well as representing its first involvement in an international conflict that is still under way.

The Court's verdict on most key issues was strongly challenged on

Excerpts From Rulings by the World Court

THE HAGUE, June 27 (AP) — Following are excerpts from the rulings today by the International Court of Justice on Nicaragua's complaint against the United States:

The Court, by 12 votes to 3, rejects the justification of collective self-defense maintained by the United States of America in connection with the military and paramilitary activities in and against Nicaragua, the subject of this case.

By 12 votes to 3, decides that the United States of America, by training, arming, equipping, financing and supplying the contra forces or otherwise encouraging, supporting and aiding military and paramilitary activities in and against Nicaragua, has acted, against the Republic of Nicaragua, in breach of its obligation under customary international law not to intervene in the affairs of another state.

By 12 votes to 3, decides that the United States of America, by certain attacks on Nicaraguan territory in 1983-84 has acted, against the Republic of Nicaragua, in breach of its obligation under customary international law not to use force against another state.

By 12 votes to 3, decides that, by laying mines in the internal or territorial waters of the Republic of Nicaragua during the first months of 1984, the United States of America has acted, against the Republic of Nicaragua, in breach of its obligations under customary international law not to use force against another state, not to intervene in its affairs, not to violate its sovereignty and not to interrupt peaceful maritime commerce.

Production of Manual

By 14 votes to 1, decides that the United States of America, by producing in 1983 a manual entitled "Operaciones sicologicas en guerra de guerrillas," and disseminating it to contra forces, has encouraged the commission by them of acts contrary to general principles of humanitarian law; but does not find a basis for con-cluding that any such acts which may have been committed are imputable to the United States of America as acts of the United States of America.

By 12 votes to 3, decides that the United States of America is under a duty immediately to cease and to refrain from all such acts as may constitute breaches of the foregoing legal obligations.

By 12 votes to 3, decides that the United States of America is under an obligation to make reparation to the Republic of Nicaragua for all injury caused to Nicaragua by the breaches of obligations under customary international law enumerated above.

By 14 votes to 1, decides that the form and amount of such reparation, failing agreement between the parties, will be settled by the Court, and reserves for this purpose the subsequent proceedings in the case.

Unanimously, recalls to both parties their obligation to seek a solution to their disputes in accordance with international law.

varying grounds by Judge Stephen M. Schwebel of the United States, Sir Robert Jennings, the British judge, and Judge Shigeru Oda of Japan.

The dissenting judges first challenged the Court's competence to hear the case. The issue was whether the Court could hear the case since the United States specifically refused it authority in 1946 over cases brought under international treaties. Nicaragua claims the United States violated its international obligations under the United Nations and Organization of American States charters.

A majority of judges said this restriction applies but argued that the principles of noninterference in other countries' affairs and respect for national sovereignty, which are enshrined in the United Nations Charter, have now become part of the wider body of customary international law.

The Court, the majority ruled, is therefore competent to judge.

Judge Oda argued that the dispute was not "legal" but "political" and is "more suitable for resolution by other organs and procedures." Lawyers said this suggested that that Judge Oda be-

lieved that the dispute should be judged by the Security Council.

Judge Schwebel's dissent emphasized that the Court had underestimated the gravity of the Nicaraguan Government's involvement in El Salvador.

"I find the Court's statement of the facts to be inadequate," he wrote, "in that it sufficiently sets out the facts which have led it to reach conclusions of law adverse to the U.S. while it insufficiently sets out the facts which should have led it to reach conclusions of law adverse to Nicaragua."

Who Will Protect Freedom of the Seas?

John D. Negroponte

Following is an address by John D. Negroponte, Assistant Secretary of State for Oceans and International Environmental and Scientific Affairs, before the Law of the Sea Institute, Miami, Florida, July 21, 1986.

Today, I would like to consider the question: "Who will protect the freedom of the seas?" I intend to put aside the fine points and phrases of the law of the sea and, instead, speak as a layman to this question.

The world's oceans are vital to mankind in diverse ways. We are just beginning to understand their environmental significance. We have always used their fishery resources. We have begun to learn how to exploit some of their other resources. And through the centuries the world's oceans have been essential as waterways, and now airways, necessary to preserve the peace and to move world trade and commerce.

The freedom of use of the world's marine waters is what we mean by the freedom of the seas. It is perhaps our oldest customary international law doctrine.

The freedom of the seas was not given to mankind. It was won—won through scholarly and legal debate and in naval engagements. Over the years, the freedom of the seas has undergone some changes and refinements. Its exercise has become geographically compressed; its composition has been broken into fragments, and some of those have been lost. So, today, when we speak of the freedom of the seas, we

mean, primarily, the freedom of movement on the world's seas and oceans by navies and maritime commerce: the freedom to navigate and to fly from one continent to another over broad expanses; the freedom to navigate and to fly from one sea to another through even the narrowest of straits.

Without the freedom of the seas, the world would be a different place. Maritime commerce as we know it would not exist. The global balance of power would be unalterably shifted.

Threats to Freedom of the Seas

The freedom of the seas has come under attack, traditionally, because of two considerations: coastal security and resource requirements of coastal communities. Security considerations have played a role in promoting new coastal state jurisdictions. Both the legal regimes of the territorial sea and the continental shelf were justified on security grounds. And coastal state resource considerations have justified virtually all forms of maritime jurisdiction.

Thus, in spite of its traditions and benefits, the freedom of the seas is confronted by something called the coastal state. The coastal state regards the sea as a resource—its resource. Some coastal states go beyond that, seeing in the sea a means of providing a security buffer for their territory. The upshot is that the coastal state seeks to bring within its grasp as much of the offshore area and resources as it can justify.

The coastal state is assisted in its

efforts by some of our finer professions: scientists, engineers, lawyers, and politicians. Marine science's search for knowledge is resulting in many new discoveries of the ocean's potential. Engineers find in the ocean the opportunity to invent and to apply new technologies to capitalize on that potential. Lawyers find ample opportunities to create "new" law, quietly whispering how to justify exploiting that potential without, as they say, "adversely affecting" the freedom of the seas. And, then comes the politician, weighing the issue, and, as he or she does so, we must ask: "Does he hear an advocate for the freedom of the seas?"

The technique which coastal states have used for many years to assert control over area and resources, while ostensibly not "adversely affecting" the freedom of the seas, is to draw a distinction between the interest of the coastal state and that of the international community. The normal pattern is that the coastal state acknowledges that the international community has a certain right to navigate off its coast, if the resource- or security-related jurisdictional claim by the coastal state is accepted by the international community.

In concept the distinction between resources use and navigation is a reasonable approach which provides a basis for balancing the interests of all states. And the balance which exists between coastal state security concerns and the rights of the international community also has justification. In fact,

Reprinted from *Current Policy*, No. 855, July 1986, pp. 1-3. United States Department of State, Bureau of Public Affairs, Washington, DC.

however, over the years the international community has had a hard time protecting its navigation rights. The fine points of the law, the subtle distinctions which are often the key to concluding negotiations, often are lost sight of in practice. The result is ironic. Instead of coastal state jurisdiction being an exception—a limited encroachment on the freedom of the seas—we find the opposite to be true, at least in terms of political emotions: the freedom of the seas becomes an exception or encroachment upon the rules of coastal state jurisdiction.

This trend, which has been going on for some time, further endangers the freedom of the seas. It does so by creating a new way of thinking about the oceans in the minds of scientists, engineers, lawyers, politicians, and others. We begin to think in proprietary terms about the sea off our coast, and, in doing so, the freedom of the seas takes second place to coastal state jurisdiction.

Examples of this process are evident in the law of the sea. Once the freedom of the sea applied to all marine waters. Then the concept of the narrow territorial sea developed—in which there is the right, or some would call it an exception, of innocent passage. Later the concept of straight baselines found its way into state practice and a right (or exception) of innocent passage was recognized where it had previously existed. Later came the resource claims—first the continental shelf, then the narrow and later the broader fishing zones, all ostensibly not "adversely affecting" the freedom of the seas. More recently, we have seen the development of broader 12-mile territorial sea claims together with a straits navigation regime called transit passage that is not supposed to "adversely affect" the freedom of the seas. The list goes on to include the archipelagic states principles, together with the regime of archipelagic sealanes passage. And, finally, there is the exclusive economic zone, and if you find the appropriate cross-referenced passage in the 1982 convention, you will find that the exercise of jurisdiction in that zone, also, is not supposed to "adversely affect" the freedom of the seas.

The freedom of the seas seems to be lost in a welter of coastal state jurisdictions. I remember a cartoon from the *New Yorker* magazine about the time the Third UN Law of the Sea Conference was beginning. It showed a group of diplomats around a conference table. Standing in the doorway at the back of the room was Neptune. One diplomat was speaking, and the caption said something like: "Before we begin our conference on dividing up the sea, there

is a gentleman here who wishes to be heard."

Well, would you say that from Neptune's perspective the third conference was a success or failure? A lot of ocean and resources got divided up by the coastal states at that conference. The conference's attempt to deal with the resources beyond coastal state jurisdiction failed to achieve the agreement of all states. And the promotion and protection of the freedom of the seas, under the convention the conference developed, may only be found by proper legal interpretation of subtle points and phrases.

Why is this so? Why could not the maintenance and preservation of the freedom of the seas be expressed in categorical terms throughout the convention text? Why were so many points disguised?

Perhaps the reason is that there is no one group of states for which the freedom of the seas is that group's exclusive interest in the law of the sea. There are no exclusively maritime states. All the maritime states are coastal states, as well. They must balance their interests. One aspect of their national interest must be balanced against the other. Yet, it is this group of states that is the principal user of the sea—for coastal resource exploitation and for international navigation. From the practice of this group of states, the customary law of the sea emerges. Thus, the freedom of the seas—the freedom that presumably Neptune would have us preserve—has no advocate that does not have other interests and responsibilities.

Avoiding Further Setbacks

The Third Law of the Sea Conference was called, in part, because of the interest of the United States and the Soviet Union in stopping further erosion in the meaning of the freedom of the seas. The conference didn't halt it—look at what happened during the conference—but it may be said to have stabilized matters for a period. But for how long? If the freedom of the seas is not to suffer further setbacks in the wake of the third conference, the maritime states must do two things and do them well.

The first of these is not to be afraid to assert the freedom of the seas in their activities around the globe. The rights and freedoms of the sea will be lost over time if they are not used. There may, from time to time, be political costs in exercising such rights; but these costs cannot be avoided if the right is to be preserved. Deference to coastal states in the exercise of rights will only make it more difficult to exer-

cise the right in the future, since the political cost of using the right will increase in the absence of usage.

In this regard, it is particularly important that the maritime states utilize the rights set forth and identified in the 1982 convention. Many of the rights making up the freedom of the seas are somewhat obscured by the coastal states' orientation of the convention text. If the maritime states do not remind others from time to time of the existence or meaning of the significant commas, phrases, and words found in the text, the freedoms they represent will be lost to sight.

The second thing that must be done by the maritime states is that they must keep their own houses in order. If they let their coastal state personality get the better of them, the freedom of the seas will founder. The danger I see is that there is a tendency for each state to see the waters and circumstances off its coast as in some way unique. In this way the coastal state justifies assertions of new or broader forms of jurisdiction to satisfy its coastal appetite.

This tendency, which has been dubbed "creeping uniqueness," is the latest threat to the freedom of the seas. A maritime state will not do good service to the freedom of the seas if it gives in to calls to consider its coastal waters as unique, justifying a new and creative legal approach. And it is worse still if that creative legal approach goes beyond or severely strains the principles laid out in the 1982 convention, thus destabilizing the balance between the freedom of the seas and the interests of the coastal state that are reflected therein.

The U.S. Role

How does the United States stack up in all of this? The United States does, after all, have a split personality when it comes to the law of the sea.

On the first point, the United States has been at the forefront in exercising the freedom of the seas in spite of occasional political costs. In particular, the Navy's routine assertion-of-rights program has received quite a lot of notoriety in recent weeks, given the events in the Gulf of Sidra. It is important to note that the program was developed in the late 1970s, during the Carter Administration. Thus, it has a bipartisan character. Also, it is important to point out that the program was developed in anticipation of the successful conclusion of the Third Law of the Sea Conference. It was believed that, even with a widely ratified Law of the Sea Treaty to which the United States was party, it still would be necessary to exercise the rights set forth in the convention in order not to lose them.

It goes without saying that it is even more important that we exercise our rights today. The 1983 presidential ocean policy statement commits the United States to this course. The exercise of rights—the freedom to navigate on the world's oceans—is not meant to be a provocative act. Rather, in the framework of customary international law, it is a legitimate, peaceful assertion of a legal position and nothing more. If the United States and other maritime states do not assert international rights in the face of claims by others that do not conform with the present status of the law, they will be said to acquiesce in those claims to their disadvantage. What is particularly difficult in this situation is to understand that the more aggressive and unreasonable and provocative and threatening a claim may be, the more important it is to exercise one's rights in the face of the claim. The world community can't allow itself to be coerced—coerced into lethargy in the protection of the freedom of the seas.

On the second point, as well, the United States gets good marks—but perhaps not straight As. In general, the United States has taken a conservative approach to its coastal state claims. In making its claims, it has made clear that there is no intention to "adversely affect" the navigation rights of other states in the waters off the coast of the United States. Both the 1945 Proclamation on the Continental Shelf and the 1983 Proclamation of the Exclusive Economic Zone make clear in specific language in the proclamations themselves that the resource claim is not intended to affect the international rights and freedoms of other states.

The United States has maintained its narrow territorial sea at 3-miles breadth. It has chosen not to draw straight baselines. It conservatively exercises its right under Article 7 of the 1958 Convention on the Territorial Seas and Contiguous Zone to claim juridical bays less than 24-miles wide at the mouth. It has only very few small spots of historic waters, which are of no consequence to the international community and which could have been incorporated in a straight baseline system had it chosen to do so. Contrary to what some foreign press reports have said, the United States has not drawn baselines between the islands of the Aleutians or of Hawaii. Foreign vessels of all states—commercial or military—navigate off the U.S. coast routinely, consistent with their rights under international law.

The United States has taken a conservative approach to its maritime claims for several reasons, one of which is the desire to lead by example. By its action it hopes to encourage similar conservative approaches by others.

But the United States has been known to put its coastal state hat on from time to time. For the most part, though, it has resisted the creation of rules to meet its unique concerns. As the United States moves into the implementation of its exclusive economic zone, it must bear this in mind. We must recognize that one cannot slice the pie too thin. We must stand for principles—recognizable principles that are not riddled with self-serving exceptions.

The present challenge before the freedom of the seas is that its traditional defenders have begun to think of the oceans as a resource rather than as the world's highway. Science and technology have opened to us the ocean's resources. We must not expect that mankind will be denied the opportunity to exploit them. As mankind does so, satisfying its needs and using its capabilities, the freedom of the seas will continue to come up against coastal state demands. If the freedom of the seas is to survive—not to be subject to further inroads—we must be energetic in its promotion and protection. As we face the challenges that science and technology bring us, we must meet them bearing in mind the question: "Who is protecting freedom of the seas?"

Highlights of the Convention on the Law of the Sea

Adopted on 30 April 1982 by the United Nations Conference on the Law of the Sea (by 130 votes to 4, with 17 abstentions) after more than eight years of preparatory work, the *Convention on the Law of the Sea* lays down rules for all parts and virtually all uses of the oceans. While a large part of the Convention deals with the international areas of the sea, there are important provisions recognizing the jurisdiction of States in a number of areas. The Convention will come into force when it has been ratified by sixty States, but a number of States have already altered their own national legislations to bring them into line with its provisions. Below, some of the key features of the Convention.

• Coastal States would exercise sovereignty over their territorial sea of up to twelve miles in breadth, but foreign vessels would be allowed "innocent passage" through these waters for purposes of peaceful navigation.

• Ships and aircraft of all countries would be allowed "transit passage" through straits used for international navigation, as long as they proceeded without delay and without threatening the bordering States. States alongside the straits would be able to regulate navigation and other aspects of passage.

• Archipelagic States, made up of a group or groups of closely related islands and interconnecting waters, would have sovereignty over a sea area enclosed by straight lines drawn between the outermost points of the islands. They would have sovereignty over these archipelagic waters, while ships of all other States would enjoy the right of passage through sea lanes designated by the archipelagic State.

• Coastal States would have sovereign rights in a 200-mile exclusive economic zone with respect to natural resources and certain economic activities, and would also have certain types of jurisdiction over scientific research and environmental preservation. All other States would have freedom of navigation and overflight in the zone, as well as freedom to lay submarine cables and pipelines. Land-locked States and "States with special geographical charac-

teristics" would have the right to participate in exploiting part of the zone's fisheries when the coastal State could not harvest them all itself. Delimitation of overlapping economic zones would be "effected by agreement on the basis of international law...in order to achieve an equitable solution". Highly migratory species of fish and marine mammals would be afforded special protection.

• Coastal States would have sovereign rights over the continental shelf (the national area of the sea bed) for the purpose of exploring and exploiting it without affecting the legal status of the water or the air space above. The shelf would extend at least to 200 miles from shore, and out to 350 miles or even beyond under specified circumstances. Coastal States would share with the international community part of the revenue they derive from exploiting oil and other resources from any part of their shelf beyond 200 miles. Delimitation of overlapping shelves would be on the same basis as for the exclusive economic zone. A Commission on the Limits of the Continental Shelf would make recommendations to States on the shelf's outer boundaries.

• All States would enjoy the traditional freedoms of navigation, overflight, scientific research and fishing on the high seas. They would be obliged to adopt, or co-operate with other States in adopting, measures to manage and conserve living resources.

• The territorial sea, exclusive economic

zone and continental shelf of islands would be determined in accordance with rules applicable to land territory, but rocks which could not sustain human habitation or economic life would have no economic zone or continental shelf.

• States bordering enclosed or semi-enclosed seas would be expected to co-operate on management of living resources and on environmental and research policies and activities. Land-locked States would have the right of access to and from the sea, and would enjoy freedom of transit through the territory of transit States by all means of transport.

• States would be bound to use "the best practical means at their disposal" to prevent and control marine pollution from any source. The text defines which categories of States (coastal States, port States and flag States) would be responsible for preventing pollution and punishing polluters, particularly when pollution originated on board vessels, and what kinds of enforcement action were allowable. States would be liable for damage caused by violation of their international obligations to combat marine pollution. They would be bound to co-operate globally and regionally in formulating rules and standards of environmental protection, and would commit themselves to promote technical assistance to developing countries in this area.

• All marine scientific research in the exclusive economic zone and on the con-

Reproduced courtesy of *Unesco Courier*, February 1986, pp. 30-31.

Diagram taken from the *U.N. Chronicle*

Limit of territorial sea
over which a coastal State
has sovereign powers

International
Sea-Bed Area

Limit of Exclusive
Economic Zone

The International Sea-Bed Area

The longest part of the Convention concerns the future regime for exploring and exploiting the bottom of the deep ocean in areas beyond the continental shelf of any State.

Of main economic interest in this area at present are polymetallic nodules lying on or just below the sea-bed at great depths, composed of manganese, copper, cobalt and nickel, although the Convention extends to all resources of the area, including any which may be discovered or which may become economically exploitable in the future.

The Convention would establish a "parallel" system for exploring and exploiting the deep sea-bed. Under this system, all activities in the area would be under the control of the International Sea-Bed Authority, which would be authorized to conduct its own mining operations through an organ called Enterprise. At the same time, the Authority would contract with private and State ventures to give them mining rights in the area so that they could operate in parallel with the Authority. The resources of the area would be managed as a "common heritage of mankind".

Of all the minerals known to exist in and under the seas the most valuable at the moment is oil. About one fifth of total production comes from the continental shelf within 200 miles of the coast of about 75 countries and under relatively shallow water. Many such areas have not yet been tapped and vast reserves are suspected under much deeper water.

Nodules rich in nickel, manganese, copper and cobalt are the most valuable resource now known in the International Sea-Bed Area.

tinental shelf would be subject to the consent of the coastal State, but those States would be obliged to grant consent to foreign States when the research was to be conducted for peaceful purposes and fulfilled other criteria laid down in the Convention. A coastal State could deny permission for such research or insist on its cessation, but only under circumstances defined in the Convention; in the event of a dispute, the researching State could require the coastal State to submit to international conciliation on the ground that it was not acting in a

manner compatible with the Convention.

● States would be bound to promote the development and transfer of marine technology "on fair and reasonable terms and conditions". This would be done with proper regard for all legitimate interests, including the rights and duties of holders, suppliers and recipients of technology.

● States would be obliged to settle by peaceful means their disputes over the interpretation or application of the Conven-

tion. When they could not agree on the means of settlement, they would have to submit most types of disputes to a compulsory procedure entailing decisions binding on all parties. They would have four options: an International Tribunal for the Law of the Sea, to be established under the Convention, the existing International Court of Justice, arbitration and special arbitration procedures. Certain types of dispute would have to be submitted to conciliation, a procedure whose outcome is not binding on the parties.

Wanted: An International Criminal Court

Paul Wilkinson

Paul Wilkinson, head of the Department of Politics and International Relations at the University of Aberdeen and author of "Terrorism and the Liberal State" (Macmillan), excerpted from the bi-monthly "New Democrat" of London.

NewDemocrat

Democracies are vulnerable to terrorist attacks because of their open societies and the ease of movement across and within their frontiers. Western Europe is especially at risk from international terrorism spilling over from the Middle East. Europe presents a variety of symbolically important and accessible targets for fanatics. Moreover, through our tolerance and laxity we have allowed the so-called embassies of countries such as Libya, Syria and Iran to abuse their diplomatic status and operate as command posts for murder and mayhem.

There is no case in modern history in which a European democracy has been destroyed by a terrorist group. However, terrorism can be damaging to democratic governments. For example, in Northern Ireland and Spain terrorism not only attacks innocent life and rights; it also aims to undermine democratic values, institutions, processes and rule of law. Unchecked terrorism can easily escalate to civil war.

The threat to Western freedom from the spread of terrorism in Third World areas is especially serious because terrorism in unstable regions is likely to undermine fragile democratic governments, which could alter the regional balance of power. That could also threaten Western economic interests, such as access to oil and raw materials and lines of maritime communication at strategic points.

In a world of sovereign states, effective international cooperation is inherently difficult, particularly in the sensitive areas of internal security and law and order. Countries have traditionally taken the view that the national government has sovereign control.

Western politicians and judiciaries are as chauvinistic in this regard as other states.

A major difficulty is the lack of a single forum for Western democratic cooperation. The European Economic Community does not include all the major Western countries, and it is primarily concerned with economic matters. NATO, though it has a larger membership, remains an intergovernmental organization whose members jealously guard their national sovereignty. It has been left to the Council of Europe to mount the European Convention for the Suppression of Terrorism, but the Council lacks political weight and its convention remains unratified by key countries such as France and is unenforceable.

Some Western democracies have little or no experience of terrorism and cannot see the importance of the problem. Enthusiasm for action often dissipates once a specific outrage has died away. Some Western governments are unwilling to endanger commercial outlets or sources of oil by taking tough action against pro-terrorist countries such as Libya. Others, afraid of attracting revenge attacks, hope to buy security with appeasement.

There is a need for improved international cooperation within the democratic community. Terrorism is inherently international in character. Unfortunately, we still lag badly in applying on an international level the hardline policy that has worked so well in countries such as Italy. There is a need to upgrade the coordination of policy, sharing of intelligence, pooling of counterterrorist expertise and technology, and cooperation in police investigation and extradition of suspects.

Improving extradition is a popular slogan in all Western pronouncements on international cooperation against terrorism. When the U.S. Senate still refuses to pass a measure that would extradite fugitive Irish Republican Army murderers from the U.S. to Britain, and when France is still giving shelter to terrorists on the run from other European countries, we have good reason to

be cynical about these promises.

The Western alliance should urgently consider setting up an international criminal court and code that could deal with the investigation, trial and sentencing of international terrorists. This would avoid the delays and uncertainties of relying on extradition procedures among a confusing variety of diverse national legal systems.

On the matter of sanctions, governments should combine to shut down the diplomatic network resources of terrorist states by severing diplomatic relations with them until they mend their ways. Concerted economic sanctions would have a tremendous effect in forcing the dictators of terrorist states to reconsider the utility of continuing terrorism. These measures have not yet been tried by the West. It is high time that they were. They are fully compatible with international law.

We must also make progress in negotiations and diplomacy to resolve some of the underlying conflicts in the international system that inevitably fuel violence. For example, a settlement of the long and bitter conflict between Israel and the Arab states on the Palestinian issue is a long way off. Even if we were to achieve it by some miracle of diplomacy, Middle East terrorism would still not be eradicated. But at least it would be substantially reduced. Instead of despairing young Palestinians in the camps flocking to terrorist groups like the Abu Nidal movement, their energies could be channelled into creating and developing their own homeland.

International terrorism is more than an attack on the rights of the innocent and the rule of law. It constitutes a real threat to peace and civilized international relations. The response of liberal states, at an international as well as national level, should be firm and courageous.

Cosmetic gestures and pious statements of good will are no longer enough. How many more innocents have to die at the hands of terrorist murderers before we learn to act effectively together? (May 1)

COUNTERING THE THREAT OF TERRORISM

Rushworth M. Kidder

European Community nations aren't selling any more surplus butter to Libya.

Business executives abroad are turning in their highly visible limousines for modest sedans. Engineers in Massachusetts are developing a "sniffer" that can detect even the tiniest scent of explosives. United States Army bases in Germany are being guarded against intruders by loud-honking geese.

In these and other ways, Western nations are learning to counter the threat of international terrorism.

But terrorist attacks are on the rise worldwide. And few terrorists have been brought to justice. A report from the Jaffee Center for Strategic Studies at Tel Aviv University in Israel notes that terrorists were captured or killed in action in only about 1 of every 10 incidents in 1984.

Authorities on terrorism generally reject the notion that terrorism can be wiped out entirely. For the immediate future, they see it as a problem to be managed, not solved. But they insist that much more can be done to control it.

From scores of interviews with terrorist experts in recent months, the following broad conclusions emerge about countering terrorism:

Diplomatic measures

"The single most important step," says Italian authority Franco Ferracuti, "is international cooperation." But such cooperation is difficult, he cautions, because nations have different traditions, laws, and economies. Intelligence services hesitate to share information, fearing leaks abroad. Courts are concerned that extradition could help bring a foreign government's political enemies home for punishment. Politicians fear that sanctions against nations backing terrorism could disadvantage their own economies.

There are differences, too, in the definition of terrorism. European nations, with a history of domestic terrorism, tend to see it as a criminal problem. But Israel, which is at war with its Arab neighbors, sees it as a form of warfare demanding a military response—a view increasingly prevalent in America.

An international consensus is growing, however, about ways to deal with the problem. For example: the six-point statement issued earlier this month by the heads of the seven industrial nations at the Tokyo summit. Galvanized by the US bombing of Libya April 15 and the European Community decision of April 21 to impose sanctions against Libya, summit leaders agreed to ban arms sales to terrorist-sponsoring nations, deny entry to suspected terrorists, improve extradition procedures, impose tougher immigration and visa requirements, and improve cooperation among security organizations.

They also agreed to impose size limits on diplomatic staffs from offending nations. Since the US bombing of Libya, Libyans have been expelled from Britain, West Germany, France, Italy, Spain, Denmark, Belgium, the Netherlands, and Luxemburg.

Experts, in fact, pinpoint embassies and consulates as an essential link in the terrorism support system. "The European Community generally has been far too weak in using its rights under the Vienna Convention," says Paul Wilkinson of the University of Aberdeen.

◼ COUNTING THE COSTS OF TERRORISM

Mapping trends in terrorism around the world is a task complicated by substantial differences in the definitions of terrorism used by the nations sampled. The graphs below do, however, highlight some important aspects of the effort to reduce terrorism. In Northern Ireland, the level of violence has steadily diminished under consistent application of the rule of law. In Italy, antiterrorist efforts were ineffective until the public was aroused. Terrorism in West Germany continues at high levels, fueled by a hard core of disaffected youth and the cooperation of fellow Euro-terrorists. Israel has had periods of relative success in controlling terrorism, often after extensive military action, but has not found any permanent solutions. Incidents against the United States tend to rise and fall with US visibility as a party to issues of concern to terrorist groups.

◼ UNITED STATES:*

*International terrorist incidents against US citizens and property

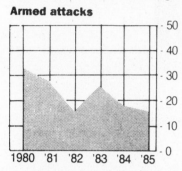

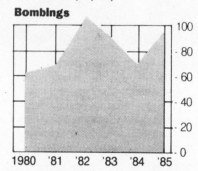

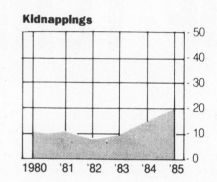

Source: US Department of State, Washington

◼ ISRAEL:

Major domestic incidents of terrorism in which Israeli citizens were casualties, 1969-85

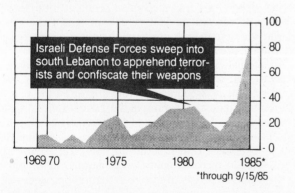

Israeli Defense Forces sweep into south Lebanon to apprehend terrorists and confiscate their weapons

*through 9/15/85

Source: Israeli Defense Forces, Tel Aviv

◼ WEST GERMANY:

Cooperation among "Euroterrorists" from Germany, France, and Belgium, has sustained high levels of terrorism.

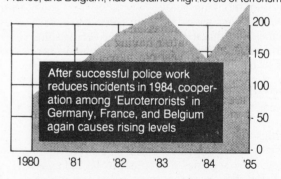

After successful police work reduces incidents in 1984, cooperation among 'Euroterrorists' in Germany, France, and Belgium again causes rising levels

Source: Federal Office for Protection of the Constitution, Cologne

That convention, dating from 1815, establishes rules concerning diplomatic immunity and the diplomatic pouch. Under those protections, Libya, Iran, Syria, and other terrorist-sponsoring nations have harbored terrorists, stored and transported weapons, provided false documents, and operated networks of agents ready to commit terrorist acts within a host country. There are increasing calls for rethinking these provisions.

Intelligence gathering

"The only effective way of beating terrorist activities," says Federal Bureau of Investigation (FBI) assistant director Oliver (Buck) Revell, "is to have intelligence on their operations, their organizations, their membership, their motives, their philosophies, their ideology."

The word intelligence, however, is an umbrella for

■ NORTHERN IRELAND:

Terrorist incidents, 1969-85

Deaths

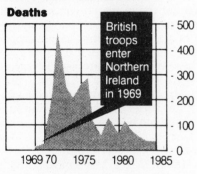

British troops enter Northern Ireland in 1969

Explosions

Imprisoned IRA member Bobby Sands dies during hunger strike

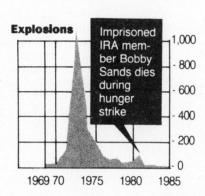

Shootings

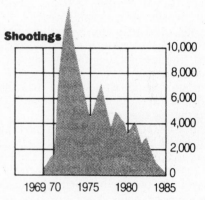

Source: Royal Ulster Constabulary, Belfast

■ ITALY:

Incidents of terrorism, 1969-85

Attacks

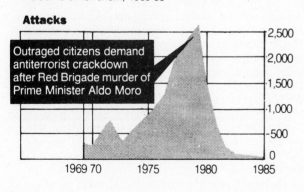

Outraged citizens demand antiterrorist crackdown after Red Brigade murder of Prime Minister Aldo Moro

Attacks causing bodily injury

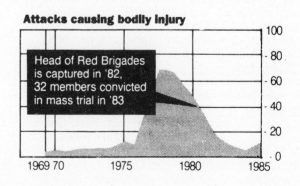

Head of Red Brigades is captured in '82, 32 members convicted in mass trial in '83

everything from a whispered comment to a super-computer.

It covers an informer's tip in September 1984 that the Valhalla, a 77-foot trawler, would shortly leave Boston carrying seven tons of arms destined for Irish Republican Army (IRA) terrorists. It also covers the US spy satellites and British Royal Air Force Nimrod aircraft that tracked the ship and the transfer of arms to an Irish boat, the Marita Ann, before the Irish Navy made the interception.

Most observers agree that effective counterter-rorism requires human intelligence gathering — and that overemphasis on electronic means has hampered efforts to build an effective network of human agents. Because of emphasis on the use of computers, says Reinhard Rupprecht of West Germany's Ministry of the Interior, "we are in danger of neglecting the police on the beat."

But since terrorist organizations tend to be small and highly secretive, some of the best leads come from the simplest measures. "You pay a lot of little ladies to keep their ears and eyes open [and] to send you information," says former Central Intelligence Agency chief Stansfield Turner. "The false alarm rate will be tremendous," he adds. "Hopefully, we're skilled in sifting data."

Some of that sifting is now being done through Interpol, whose central computer facility in Paris is proving useful in tracking the movements of terrorists and weapons.

Security measures

From his office in Rome, Judge Rosario Priore can look out his window at the Tiber River — through thick, bulletproof glass. One of several magistrates responsible for cracking down on the Red Brigades and other Italian terrorist groups, Judge Priore, a bachelor, lives under constant threat.

"You get used to doing everything with a bodyguard" he says, "[because] in every hideout of the Red Brigades, [the magistrates] found maps of their own houses and streets."

Terrorism experts, while noting that physical protection by itself is not sufficient, agree that it is an essential part of the formula.

At its most expensive, protection can involve reconstructing entire buildings: The US State Department is, for example, asking Congress for $4.4 billion to build 79 new embassies and renovate 175 others.

Airports are beefing up security measures. Once situated in open fields, they are now increasingly surrounded by high fences, sometimes illuminated (as in Belfast) by bright lights every few yards. Baggage checks, too, are becoming more thorough, with some security forces using dogs trained to sniff out explosives. New kinds of X-ray and low-level neutron radiation scanners are being pioneered for hand-luggage searches. Israeli officials routinely pass checked baggage through a low-pressure chamber, to trip pressure-sensitive bomb detonators on the ground rather than at 30,000 feet.

But with factories, airline offices, communications facilities, and power and water distribution points added to the list of possible targets, the problem of providing physical security becomes vast. Rand Corporation analyst Brian M. Jenkins, a highly regarded observer of trends in terrorism, estimates that $21 billion is spent annually in the United States for security services and hardware — a number he sees rising to as high as $60 billion by the end of the century.

Some experts offer a suggestion for the future: Require new facilities to take security issues into account just as they do environmental issues. "We ought to have a security impact statement on what kind of security the site offers," writes Neil Livingstone in a recent issue of Terrorism: An International Journal. "We do that for defense contractors, but we do not do it for basic infrastructure targets."

Legal and social measures

At bottom, many observers agree that terrorism is a highly mental phenomenon. "If we're going to prevent terrorism movements from re-creating themselves in the jails, in the universities, in the society at large," says Professor Wilkinson, "we have to win the battle of ideas."

To do that, he says, Western societies need to undertake "a strengthening of democracy in all its various ramifications."

One often-cited example is the Green party in West Germany, which has a number of former terrorist sympathizers in its ranks. Party affiliation allows them to pursue their sometimes radical political philosophies through nonviolent, democratic means.

Such channels, Wilkinson says, give some people an alternative to violence, because they provide "legitimate and potentially effective [means for] altering and reforming the conditions of their own lives."

He and other scholars see several phases to countering terrorism. The first involves cutting off the recruiting process. Jerrold M. Post, a Washington-based psychiatrist, observes that "one should have a broad-ranging program designed to make the terrorist career less attractive for the alienated youth. A great deal in a constructive way could be done to demythologize [terrorism]. I'm really not talking about propaganda [but about] available information."

A second phase involves what Professsor Ferracuti calls "a way to redirect terrorists." Amnesty programs, used effectively in Italy, have enabled hardline terrorists to reenter society rather than continue in the only life they may have known.

Public awareness

The central bus station in Tel Aviv is awash with humanity: old women with shopping bags, young men in short jackets, Israeli soldiers with automatic weapons, Palestinian laborers, rabbis. They have one habit in common, however: When they board a bus, they glance under the seat and in the overhead rack — checking for suspicious packages.

Officials of the Israeli Defense Forces say that more than 80 percent of bombs in public places are dismantled, "because of the awareness of the public that there is such a thing as a suspicious object."

Such awareness is growing across Europe as well. Signs on London subways urge riders to watch for abandoned packages. Pierre Verbrugghe, director general of the National Police in France, tells of a passenger who, finding such a package on the Paris Métro recently, hurled it out the window. He did the right thing: It contained four pounds of explosives and two pounds of nails.

Such awareness extends to individuals as well as packages. Italian officials note that, after the murder of Prime Minister Aldo Moro in 1978 by the Red Brigades, terrorism in Italy began its steep decline — in part because the public, repulsed by that act, no longer kept quiet about suspicious activities.

Military and police actions

Rescuing hostages held by terrorists requires small, fast-acting commando units, such as West Germany's GSG-9, Britain's Special Air Services (SAS), and the US Delta Force.

Preempting terrorist incidents can require actions

ranging from the arrest of would-be terrorists to the invasion of terrorist-sponsoring nations. Such measures rely heavily on sound intelligence, and demand sophisticated military and police operations carried out by experienced personnel.

Such measures work with varying degrees of success. The freeing of the hostages from a Lufthansa airliner hijacked to Mogadishu, Somalia, in 1977 was a stunning success for the GSG-9. But the 1980 effort to rescue US hostages held in Tehran, Iran, was a disaster, as was the attempt by Egyptian troops to recapture an EgyptAir airliner hijacked to Malta last fall.

The best sort of police action, authorities agree, is the successful preemptive measure. Ambassador Robert B. Oakley, head of the State Department's counterterrorism activities, notes that more than 120 terrorist attacks against US citizens at home and abroad were foiled in 1985.

Military and police measures, however, can also be used for retaliation — a use drawing criticism from some terrorism specialists. One difficulty, says Dr. Post, is that terrorist groups often consist of "troubled individuals who have a hard time working together cooperatively." Retaliation, far from deterring future action, may solidify a previously unstable group.

Controlling arms and explosives

Terrorism requires weaponry. Sometimes, as in continental Europe and Northern Ireland, the devices are homemade. Royal Ulster Constabulary officials note that bombings by IRA terrorists could be drastically reduced by one step: finding a new sort of fertilizer. Because of its high nitrogen content, the powdered fertilizer commonly used in Ireland is explosive. Packed into milk cans, it forms the powerful bombs placed by terrorists under culverts and in cars. Scientists in Britain and Ireland are said to be searching for new, nonexplosive fertilizers.

But sometimes the weapons are highly sophisticated. According to Edward C. Ezell, a weapons specialist with the Smithsonian Institution, materiel captured from the various Palestine Liberation Organization factions during a sweep into Lebanon by the Israeli Defense Forces in 1982 included 150 antiaircraft weapons; 1,193 antitank weapons; 7,507 rockets; and 51,637 mortar bombs.

So far, US, European, and Israeli security officials say they have seen little evidence of terrorist involvement in chemical or biological warfare. And while they are alert to the threat of nuclear terrorism, they see it as improbable. Nuclear devices are hard to build and almost impossible to test secretly, and their use could call forth immediate retaliation against nations suspected of sponsoring terrorism. Nor do such weapons serve the terrorists' purposes very well. "Terrorists want a lot of people *watching*," says Mr. Jenkins, "not a lot of people *dead*."

Media self-regulation

When Muhammad Sadiq al-Tajir was discovered safe and well at a south London address Jan. 17, it was the first the world had heard about his kidnapping.

But it was not the first the press had heard of it.

Mr. Tajir, the brother of the United Arab Emirates' ambassador to London, was ransomed for $3 million after having been kidnapped Jan. 7. But under a 10-year-old agreement between Scotland Yard and the British press, no word of his kidnapping was published until it was resolved, although editors were kept informed along the way.

Keeping kidnappings out of the news, both editors and police officials say, seems to help keep the crime from spreading. Britain's rate of kidnapping for ransom, eight cases in 11 years, is very small compared with rates for West Germany, Italy, or Spain.

Such regulations can backfire, of course. When British television stations carried a picture of a Greek child returned unharmed after a kidnapping, one woman phoned the British Broadcasting Corporation to say that the picture should have been broadcast earlier: She had seen the child playing outdoors at a neighboring house, where there were usually no children.

Most observers feel strongly that state censorship is an anathema. Many, however, feel that the media must engage in self-regulation. Television journalists and news executives interviewed for this series spoke of common problems in covering terrorism. So far, however, no international forum has been devised to bring journalists together to discuss them.

Maintaining public composure

Finally, experts point out that terrorism needs to be kept in perspective. "Don't panic," says the FBI's Mr. Revell; "don't let the notoriety reach a state of hysteria. [Terrorism] is an important phenomenon. But it is not threatening the American way of life or the Western democracies, and it won't as long as we don't let it. But if we let it, it causes us to develop a siege mentality and almost unilaterally curtails our own freedom."

Wilkinson, after years of teaching university students who have been roughly the same age as many terrorists, puts the emphasis on prevention rather than cure. "We have to win the battle in the classrooms and in the seminars, just as we have to in the political hustings — not by crude propaganda and counter-ideology, but by opening people's minds to other ideas and showing them how to criticize and how to grow intellectually."

"The open society," he concludes, "is the best antidote to terrorism."

NEW BOOKS ON TERRORISM

• Cline, Ray S., and Yonah Alexander. **Terrorism as State-Sponsored Covert Warfare.** Fairfax, Va.: Hero Books. 1986. *Two well-known terrorist experts at Georgetown University's Center for Strategic and International Studies detail the reasons for looking at terrorism as a form of war.*
• Hubbard, David G. **Winning Back the Sky: A Tactical Analysis of Terrorism.** Dallas: Saybrook Publishers. 1986. *A short*

study of skyjacking in layman's terms, written by a psychiatrist who has interviewed scores of terrorists.

• Livingstone, Neil C., and Terrell E. Arnold, ed. **Fighting Back: Winning the War Against Terrorism.** Lexington, Mass.: Lexington Books. 1986. *Sixteen well-documented essays by various authors on ways that the United States can respond to state-sponsored terrorism; includes studies of legal, moral, diplomatic, military, and media-related issues.*

• Netanyahu, Benjamin, ed. **Terrorism: How the West Can Win.** New York: Farrar, Straus & Giroux. 1986. *Assembled by Israel's ambassador to the United Nations, these 38 mini-essays are by such well-known public figures as George P. Shultz, Daniel Schorr, Eugene Rostow, and William H. Webster.*

• Ra'anan, Uri, Robert L. Pfaltzgraff Jr., Richard H. Schultz, Ernst Helperin, and Igor Lukes, ed. **Hydra of Carnage: The International Linkages of Terrorism and Other Low-Intensity Operations.** Lexington, Mass.: Lexington Books. 1986. *Five Tufts University professors have drawn together 18 essays by various authors, followed by 300 pages of captured documents and testimony by defectors showing the extent of state (especially Soviet) sponsorship.*

• Wright, Robin. **Sacred Rage: The Crusade of Modern Islam.** New York: Simon & Schuster. 1985. *A former correspondent for the Monitor, CBS News, and the Washington Post, Wright draws on her Middle East experience to paint a probing and highly readable study of the terrorism inspired by Islamic fundamentalism.*

Abbreviations

ABM: Antiballistic missile
ACDA: Arms Control and Disarmament Agency (USA)
ACP: African, Caribbean, and Pacific Countries
AID: Agency for International Development (USA)
ALCM: Air-Launched Cruise Missile
ANC: African National Congress (South Africa)
ANZUS: Australia, New Zealand, and the United States
ASAT: Anti-satellite
ASEAN: Association of Southeast Asian Nations
ASW: anti-submarine warfare (DOD)
AWACS: Airborne Warning and Control Systems
bbl: barrel
BMD: Ballistic Missile Defense
C³ (C-cubed): command, control, communications
C³I: command, control, communications, and intelligence
CBW: chemical and biological weapons
CCD: Conference of the Committee on Disarmament (UNO)
CCP: Chinese Communist Party
CD: Committee on Disarmament (UNO)
CIA: Central Intelligence Agency (USA)
CIEC: Conference on International Economic Cooperation
CMEA: Council on Mutual Economic Assistance
COCOM: Coordinating Committee for Multilateral Export Control
COW: Committee of the Whole (UNO)
CPE: Centrally Planned Economies (communist industrial)
CPSU: Communist Party of the Soviet Union
CSCE: Conference on Security and Cooperation in Europe
CTB: Comprehensive Nuclear Test Ban Treaty
CW: Chemical warfare
DC: developing country
DIA: Defense Intelligence Agency (DOD)
DOD: Department of Defense
DTA: Democratic Turnhalle Alliance (Namibia)
EC: European Community
ECDC: Economic Cooperation among Developing Countries
ECOSOC: Economic and Social Council (UNO)
ECU: European Currency Unit
EEC: European Economic Community
EFTA: European Free Trade Association
EMS: European Monetary System
END: European Nuclear Disarmament
FAO: Food and Agriculture Organization (UNO)
FBS/FOBS: Forward based systems (strategic)
FDR: Revolutionary Democratic Front (El Salvador)
FMLN: Farabundo Marti National Liberation Front (El Salvador)
FRG: Federal Republic of Germany (West Germany)
G-77: Group of 77
GATT: General Agreement on Tariffs and Trade
GCC: Gulf Co-operation Council
GDP: Gross Domestic Product
GDR: German Democratic Republic (East Germany)
GLCM: Ground-launched cruise missile
GNP: Gross National Product
GWP: Gross World Product
IAEA: International Atomic Energy Agency
ICA: International Communication Agency (USA)
ICBM: Intercontinental Ballistic Missile
ICJ: International Court of Justice
ICNT: Informal Composite Negotiating Text (UNCLOS)
IDA: International Development Association (World Bank)
IEA: International Energy Agency (OECD)
IFC: International Finance Corporation (World Bank)
IGO: Inter-governmental Organization
IISS: International Institute for Strategic Studies (London)
ILO: International Labor Organization
IMF: International Monetary Fund
IRBM: Intermediate Range Ballistic Missile
JCS: Joint Chiefs of Staff (DOD)
KT: Kiloton
LDC: Less Developed Country

LLDC: Least Developed Countries
LOS: Law of the Sea
LRTNF: Long-range theatre nuclear forces
MAD: Mutual Assured Destruction
MARV: Maneuverable Re-entry Vehicle
MBD: Million of barrels per day (oil)
MBFR: Mutual and Balanced Force Reductions
MDB: Multilateral development banks
MFN: Most Favored Nation
MIRV: Multiple Independently Targetable Re-entry Vehicle
MNC: Multinational Corporation
MRBM: Medium-range ballistic missile
MSA: Most Seriously Affected Countries
MTN: Multilateral Trade Negotiations
MX: Missile Experimental
NATO: North Atlantic Treaty Organization
N-bomb: Neutron bomb
NGO: Non-governmental (international) organization
NIC: Newly Industrializing (industrialized) country
NIE: National Intelligence Estimate
NIEO: New International Economic Order
NIO: New (international) Information Order
NPT: Non-Proliferation Treaty
NSC: National Security Council
NSM: National Security Memorandum (NSC)
NTB: Non-tariff barrier
OAPEC: Organization of Arab Petroleum Exporting Countries
ODA: Official development assistance
OECD: Organization for Economic Cooperation and Development
OPEC: Organization of Petroleum Exporting Countries
OSD: Office of the Secretary of Defense
PD: Presidential Directive
PGM: Precision-guided munitions
PLO: Palestine Liberation Organization
PQLI: Physical Quality Life Index
PRC: People's Republic of China
PZPR: Polish United Workers (Communist) Party
RDF: Rapid Deployment Forces
RV: Re-entry vehicle
SAC: Strategic Air Command (DOD)
SALT: Strategic Arms Limitation Talks
SDR: Special Drawing Rights
SIPRI: Stockholm International Peace Research Institute
SLBM: Submarine-Launched Ballistic Missile
SLCM: Submarine-launched cruise missile
SRBM: Short-range Ballistic Missile
SSBN: Submersible Ballistic Nuclear (Nuclear Ballistic Submarine)
START: Strategic Arms Reduction Talks (Reagan)
SWAPO: South-West African People's Organization
TCDC: Technical Cooperation Among Developing Countries
TNE: Transnational Enterprises
TNF: Theatre Nuclear Forces
UN: United Nations
UNCLOS: UN Conference on the Law of the Sea
UNCTAD: UN Conference on Trade and Development
UNDP: UN Development Programme
UNEF: UN Emergency Force
UNEP: UN Environment Programme
UNESCO: UN Educational, Scientific, and Cultural Organization
UNGA: UN General Assembly
UNHCR: UN High Commissioner on Refugees
UNICEF: UN Children's Fund
UNIDO: UN Industrial Development Programme
UNITAR: UN Institute for Training and Research
UNO: United Nations Organization (the whole UN system)
UNRWA: UN Relief and Works Agency for Palestine Refugees
UNSC: UN Security Council
UNU: UN University
WHO: World Health Organization
ZPG: Zero population growth

Glossary

This Glossary*contains primarily technical, economic, financial, and military terminology not usually defined in most World Politics textbooks.

—A—

Absolute poverty: The condition of people whose incomes are insufficient to keep them at a subsistent level. If affects some 800 million people who are without adequate food intake (calories and proteins), water safe from disease-carrying organisms and toxins, minimum clothing and shelter, any kind of education, health care or employment. They are concentrated in certain areas such as the Sahel and the Horn of Africa, and Bangla Desh, but they also exist in almost all LDCs, including *middle-income countries*.

African, Caribbean, and Pacific Countries (ACP): Fifty-eight countries associated with the European Community through the *Lome Convention*.

Airborne Warning and Control System (AWACS): Flying radar stations that instantaneously identify all devices in the air within a radius of 240 miles and detect movement of land vehicles.

Air-Launched Cruise Missile (ALCM): A cruise missile carried by and launched from an aircraft.

Antiballistic missile (ABM): A missile that seeks out and destroys an incoming enemy missile in flight before the latter reaches its target. It is not effective against MIRVs.

Apartheid: A system of laws in the Republic of South Africa that seeks to preserve for the white minority population the absolute political, economic, and social control over non-whites who are variously classified as Coloureds (of mixed blood), Asians and Bantus (native Africans). Bantus are forced to settle in reservations known euphemistically as homelands or Bantustans. They must always carry passes to be appropriately stamped for work outside their area of domicile.

Appropriate technology: Also known as intermediate technology. It aims at using existing resources by making their usage more efficient or productive but adaptable to the local population.

Arms control: Any measure limiting or reducing forces, regulating armaments, and/or restricting the deployment of troops or weapons.

Arms race: The competitive or cumulative improvement of weapons stocks (qualitatively or quantitatively), or the build-up of armed forces based on the conviction of two or more actors that only by trying to stay ahead in military power can they avoid falling behind.

Association of Southeast Asian Nations (ASEAN): A regional regrouping made up of Indonesia, the Philippines, Singapore, and Thailand.

Atomic bomb: A weapon based on the rapid splitting of fissionable materials thereby inducing an explosion with three deadly results: blast, heat, and radiation.

Autonomy talks: Intermittent negotiations between Egypt and Israel, as provided in the *Camp David Agreements,* with the USA as intermediary and with as an objective the development of self-rule among Palestinians of the West Bank and the Gaza Strip. These autonomy talks are considered a sham by the Arab world, as Israel rules out a national homeland, not to say a state, for Palestinians.

—B—

Backfire: US code name for a Soviet supersonic bomber that has a range of 5,500 miles and can carry nuclear weapons. US experts disagree as to whether or not Backfire should be classified as a strategic weapon.

Italicized terms are defined elsewhere in the glossary.

Balance of Payments: A summary of the international transactions of a country over a given period of time, including commodity, service, capital flows, and gold movements.

Balance of trade: The relationship between imports and exports.

Ballistic missile: A payload propelled by a rocket, which assumes a free-fall trajectory when thrust is terminated. Ballistic missiles could be of short range (SRBM), intermediate range (IRBM), medium range (MRBM), and intercontinental (ICBM).

Barrel: A standard measure for petroleum, equivalent to 42 gallons or 158.86 liters.

Basic human needs: Adequate food intake (in terms of calories, proteins, and vitamins), drinking water free of disease-carrying organisms and toxins, minimum clothing and shelter, literacy, sanitation, health care, employment, and dignity.

Bilateral: Between two nations.

Binary (chemical) munitions/weapons: Nerve gas canisters composed of two separate chambers containing chemicals that become lethal when mixed. The mixing is done when the canister is fired. Binary gas is preferred for its relative safety in storage and transportation.

Biosphere: The environment of life and living processes at or near the earth's surface, extending from the ocean floors to about 75 kilometers into the atmosphere. It is being endangered by consequences of human activities such as air and water pollution, acid rain, radioactive fallout, desertification, toxic and nuclear wastes, and the depletion of non-renewable resources.

Brandt Commission: An independent commission on international economic issues created in September 1977 and headed by former West German Chancellor Willy Brandt.

"Broken arrows": Pentagon code word for accidents involving US nuclear weapons.

Buffer Stocks: Reserves of commodities that are either increased or decreased whenever necessary to maintain relative stability of supply and prices.

—C—

Camp David Agreements/Accords: Agreements signed on September 17, 1978 at Camp David—a mountain retreat for the US President in Maryland—by President Anwar al-Sadat of Egypt and Prime Minister Menachem Begin of Israel, and witnessed by President Jimmy Carter of the United States of America. They are "A Framework for Peace in the Middle East" and "A Framework for the Conclusion of a Peace Treaty between Egypt and Israel."

Cancun Summit: World leaders' meeting on October 22-23, 1981, in the Mexican resort of Cancun to discuss global economic issues—a major event that could make or break the North-South dialogue. The agenda item: whether to launch a new round of *Global Negotiations.*

Centrally Planned Economies (CPEs): As distinguished from free-market economies, countries generally included in this category are industrialized Communist countries: the USSR, East European countries, and the PRC.

Circular error probable (CEP): The radius of a target circle within which half of the enemy weapons are projected to fall.

Cold war: A condition of hostility between the USA and the USSR in their struggle to dominate the world scene since the end of World War II.

Commodity: The unprocessed products of mining and agriculture.

Common Fund: A fund to finance 18 commodity buffer stocks as proposed in the 1976 Nairobi *UNCTAD* IV integrated program for *commodities.*

Common Heritage of Mankind: 1970 UN declaration states the "seabed and ocean floor, and the subsoil thereof, beyond the limits of national jurisdiction. . ., as well as the resources of the area, are the common heritage of mankind."

Common Market: A customs union that eliminates trade barriers within a group and establishes a common external tariff on imports from nonmember countries.

Compensatory Financing Facility: An IMF program established in 1963 to finance temporary export shortfalls, as in coffee, sugar, or other cyclically prone export items.

Concessional loans: Loans given to LLDCs by MBDs which can be repaid in soft (non-convertible) currencies and with nominal or no interest over a long period of time.

Conditionality: A series of measures that must be taken by a country before it could qualify for loans from the International Monetary Fund, such as: (1) devaluing its currency, in an attempt to boost exports and restrain imports; (2) controlling the rate of expansion of the money supply in order to dampen inflation; (3) reducing government spending, especially human services expenditures; (4) imposing wage controls, while eliminating price controls; (5) raising interest rates in order to encourage savings; (6) increasing taxes; (7) reducing or dismantling barriers to foreign private investment and to free trade in general.

Conference on International Economic Cooperation (CIEC): A conference of 8 industrial nations, 7 oil-producing nations, and 12 developing countries held in several sessions between December 1975 and June 1977. It is composed of four separate commissions (energy, raw materials, development, and financing). It is the forum of the *North-South dialogue* between rich and poor countries.

Conference on Security and Cooperation in Europe (CSCE): See *Helsinki Agreement.*

Confidence-building measures (CBMs): Understandings (called for in the Final Act of Helsinki) to give advance notice of NATO or Warsaw Pact military maneuvers and major troop deployments.

Consensus: In conference diplomacy, a way of reaching agreements by negotiations and without a formal vote.

Contact Group: See *Western Five Contact Group*

Coordinating Committee for Multilateral Export Controls (COCOM): Composed of representatives of 14 NATO countries and Japan, it sets restrictions on the transfer of Western technology to communist nations with direct or "end use" military applications.

Council on Mutual Economic Assistance (CMEA OR COMECON): Founded in Moscow in 1949 as a counterpart of the Marshall Plan (European Recovery Program), today it is comprised of the USSR, the countries of Eastern Europe, Mongolia, Cuba, and Vietnam.

Counterforce: The use of strategic nuclear weapons for strike on selected military capabilities of an enemy force.

Countervalue: The use of strategic nuclear weapons for strike on an enemy's population centers.

Cruise missile: A small, highly-maneuverable, low-flying, pilotless aircraft equipped with accurate guidance systems that periodically readjusts its trajectory. It can carry conventional or nuclear warheads, can be short-range or long range, and can be launched from the air (ALLUM), the ground (GLCM), or the sea (SLCM).

—D—

Declaration of Talloires: A statement issued in 1981 by Western journalists who opposed the UNESCO-sponsored *New World Information and Communication Order,* at a meeting in Talloires, France.

Delivery systems or Vehicles or Launchers: Land-Based Missiles (ICBMs), Submarine-Launched Missiles (SLBMs), and long-range bombers capable of delivering nuclear weapons.

Democratic Turnhalle Alliance (DTA): A party in the Namibian dispute, set up by South Africa as a political alternative to SWAPO. The DTA is considered as a puppet creation of South Africa by the United Nations. Its leader is Dirk Mudge.

Denationalization: A policy of the government of South Africa to declare certain reserved areas as "homelands" or "Bantustans" which it then recognizes as separate "national states." The black population is forcibly transferred into one of these "independent homelands" and declared to be its citizens, whether they like it or not. Once that is done, Blacks are no longer considered as citizens or nationals of South Africa, and thus become, in effect, foreigners in their native land.

Detente: A French term meaning the relaxation of tensions or a decrease in the level of hostility between opponents on the world scene.

Deterrence: The prevention from action by fear of the consequences.

Developed Countries: (DCs): Countries with relatively high per capita GNP, education, levels of industrial development and production, health and welfare, and agricultural productivity; 24 OECD members and 6 centrally planned economy countries of Eastern Europe, including the USSR.

Developing Countries (LCDs): Also *Less Developed Countries;* these countries are mainly raw materials producers for export with high growth rates and inadequate infrastructures in transportation, educational systems, and the like. There is, however, a wide variation in living standards, GNP's, and per capita incomes among LCDs.

Development: The process through which a society becomes increasingly able to meet basic human needs and assure the physical quality of life of its people.

Disappearance: Government kidnapping of individuals without leaving a trace. A violation of human rights occurring in alarming proportions under various dictatorial regimes, whereby individuals would be taken away by government agents, unbeknownst to their family, friends, or co-workers. Where they are detained, what they are charged with, whether they are still alive or are dead is not known. Usually attempts to inquire about their fate are futile or result in the disappearance of those making inquiries.

Disinformation: The spreading of false propaganda and forged documents to confuse counter-intelligence or to create political confusion, unrest, and scandal.

Dumping: A special case of price discrimination, selling to foreign buyers at a lower price than that charged to buyers in the home market.

Duty: Special tax applied to imported goods, based on tariff rates and schedules.

—E—

East (as in the East-West Struggle): (a) A shorthand, nongeographic term that includes non-market, centrally planned (communist) countries; (b) In a more restricted sense, the Warsaw Pact (military)/ CEMA (economic) bloc of the USSR and Eastern European countries under its sway.

East-West conflict: The military, economic, political, and ideological worldwide struggle between the communist countries and the industrial democracies. Also known as the Cold War.

Economic Cooperation among Developing Countries (ECDC): Also referred to as intra-South, or South-South cooperation, it is a way for LCDs to help each other with *appropriate technology.*

Escalation: The stepping up of the level of conflict, either qualitatively or quantitatively.

Essential equivalence: Comparing military capabilities of two would-be belligerents, not in terms of identical mix of forces, but in terms of how well two dissimilarly organized forces could achieve a strategic stalemate.

Eurodollars: US dollar holdings of European banks; a liability for the US Treasury.

Euromissiles: Shorthand for *long-range theatre nuclear forces* stationed in Europe or aimed at targets in Europe.

European Community (EC): Composed of the nine European Economic Community (EEC) members; it has a Council of Ministers, an elected European Parliament, a European Court of Justice, a European Investment Bank, and a European Monetary System.

European Currency Unit (ECU): The common unit of valuation among the eight members of the European Monetary System (EMS).

European Economic Community (EEC): Also known as the European Common Market. Founded in 1957 by France, West Germany, Italy, Belgium, the Netherlands, and Luxembourg for the purpose of economic integration. It was joined in 1973 by the United Kingdom, Ireland, Denmark and in 1981 by Greece. Spain and Portugal have also applied for membership. Its main features include a common external tariff, a customs union on industrial goods, and a Common Agricultural Policy. Full economic and monetary union remains an objective.

European Free Trade Association (EFTA): Austria, Finland, Iceland, Liechtenstein, Norway, Portugal, Sweden, and Switzerland. Each member keeps its own external tariff schedule, but free trade prevails among the members.

European Monetary System (EMS): Established in 1979 as a preliminary stage toward an economic and monetary union in the European Community. Fluctuations in the exchange-rate value of the currencies of the participating countries are kept within a 2¼ percent limit of divergence from the strongest currency among them.

Exclusive Economic Zone: As proposed in *ICNT,* a belt of sea extending 200 nautical miles from coastal state. In this area coastal state would have rights and jurisdiction with respect to the resources of seabed, subsoil, and superjacent waters.

Exports: Products shipped to foreign countries.

Export subsidies: Special incentives, including direct payments to exporters, to encourage increased foreign sales.

General Agreement on Tariffs and Trade (GATT): Created in 1947, this organization is the major global forum for negotiations of tariff reductions and other measures to expand world trade. Its 83 members account for four-fifths of the world's trade.

Generalized System of Preferences (GSP): A system approved by GATT in 1971, which authorizes DCs to give preferential tariff treatment to LCDs.

Glemp, Archbishop Jozef: The Primate (top leader) of the Roman Catholic Church in Poland.

Global: Pertaining to the world as a whole; worldwide.

Global commons: The Antarctic, the ocean floor under international waters and celestial bodies within reach of planet Earth. All of these areas and bodies are considered the common heritage of mankind.

Global Negotiations: A new round of international economic negotiations started in 1980 over raw materials, energy, trade, development, money, and finance.

Golan Heights: Syrian territory adjacent to Israel that occupied it since the 1967 war and that annexed it on December 14, 1981.

Gross National Product (GNP): The total value of all goods and services produced by a country in a year.

Gross world product: The sum of all gross national products.

Group of 77 (G-77): Initially a group of LDCs which issued a "Joint Declaration of 77 Developing Countries" at *UNCTAD I* in 1976 in Geneva. Now, made up of 122 countries, it remains the caucus of LCDs. Synonymous with the "South" in the North-South dialogue.

Hegemonism: Any attempt by a larger power to interfere, threaten, intervene against, and dominate a smaller power or a region of the world.

Hegemony: Domination by a major power over smaller, subordinate ones within its sphere of influence.

Helsinki Agreement: A declaration adopted on August 1, 1975 by 35 nations, including the USA and the USSR, participating in the *Conference on Security and Cooperation in Europe* that started in Helsinki, Finland, on July 3, 1973. Its main document is the Final Act in which signatories pledged to respect each other's sovereign equality and individuality, to promote detente, fundamental human rights, economic and social progress and well-being for all peoples. They also pledged not to use force or the threat of force and subversion in relations among themselves and with other nations. Three follow-up conferences took place in Belgrade in 1978 and in Madrid in 1980 and 1982. They have provided a forum for diplomatic confrontation between the USA and the USSR.

Horn of Africa: The northeast corner of Africa which includes Ethiopia, Djibouti, and Somalia. It is separated from the Arabian peninsula by the Gulf of Aden and the Red Sea. It is plagued with tribal conflicts between Ethiopia and Eritrea, and between Ethiopia and Somalia over the Ogaden desert. These conflicts have generated a large number of refugees who have been facing mass starvation.

Human rights: Rights inherent to human beings, including but not limited to the right to dignity; the integrity of the person; the inviolability of the person's body and mind; civil and political rights (freedom of religion, speech, press, assembly, association, the right to privacy, habeas corpus, due process of law, the right to vote or not to vote, the right to run for election, and the right to be protected from reprisals for acts of peaceful dissent); social, economic, and cultural rights. The most glaring violations of human rights are *torture, disappearance,* and the general phenomenon of *state terrorism.* The basic documents of human rights are: the Universal Declaration of Human Rights (1948), the Genocide Convention

Farabundo Marti National Liberation Front (Frente de Liberacion Nacional Farabundo Marti; (FMLN): The unified guerilla command of El Salvador, comprising five groups; Popular Forces of Liberation.

Finlandization: A condition of nominal neutrality, but one of actual subservience to the Soviet Union in foreign and security policies, as is the case with Finland.

First strike: The first offensive move of a general nuclear war. It implies an intention to knock out the opponent's ability to retaliate.

Fissionable or nuclear materials: Isotopes of certain elements, such as plutonium, thorium, and uranium, that emit neutrons in such large numbers that a sufficient concentration will be self-sustaining until it explodes.

Foreign policy: The process and the substance of preserving one's national interests in the tangled maze of global relations that are constantly changing.

Forward based system (FBS or FoBS): A military installation, maintained on foreign soil or in international waters, and conveniently located near a theatre of war.

Fourth World: An expression arising from the world economic crisis that began in 1973-74 with the quadrupling in price of petroleum. It takes the least developed countries (LLCDs) and the most seriously affected countries (MSAs).

Front-line states: As regards to Namibia, the expression refers to Black African states immediately adjacent to it, namely Angola, Zambia, Zimbabwe, Mozambique, and Tanzania. Nigeria and Kenya, being leading states of Black Africa, also consider themselves part of this anti-South Africa group, even though they are located over 1,500 miles away from Namibia.

(1951), Convention on Political Rights of Women (1952), the International Covenant on Civil and Political Rights (1966), the International Covenant on Economic, Social, and Cultural Rights (1966), the International Convention on the Elimination of All Forms of Racial Discrimination (1969), the European Convention for the Protection of Human Rights and Fundamental Freedoms (1954), the [Inter-]American Convention on Human Rights (1969), and the Declaration on Protection from Torture (1975). An international covenant against the use of torture is near completion in 1981.

Hu Yaobang: Chairman, Chinese Communist Party, succeeding Hua Guofeng.

Imports: Products brought into a country from abroad.

Informal Composite Negotiating Text (ICNT): Prepared in July 1977; officially only a procedural device serving as basis for negotiations, but functions as draft law of the sea treaty.

Innocent Passage: In a nation's territorial sea, passage by a foreign ship is innocent so long as it is not prejudicial to the peace, good order, or security of the coastal state. Submarines must surface and show flag.

Intercontinental Ballistic Missile (ICBM): A land-based, rocket-propelled vehicle capable of delivering a warhead to targets at 6,000 or more nautical miles.

Interdependence: An increasingly obvious characteristic of current world politics and economics whereby no country, however powerful, is totally immune from the consequences of actions and events happening in other countries, no matter how small and weak.

Intermediate Range Ballistic Missile (IRBM): A missile with a range from 1,500 to 4,000 nautical miles.

International: Between or among sovereign states.

International Development Association (IDA): An affiliate of the World Bank that provides interest free, long-term (50 years) loans to developing countries in support of projects that cannot obtain funding through other existing sources. Its lending may be curtailed if the USA, as announced, reduces its contribution from $3.2 to $2 billion for the 1983 fiscal year.

International Energy Agency (IEA): An arm of *OECD* that attempts to coordinate member countries' oil imports and reallocate stocks among members in case of disruptions in the world's oil supply.

International Finance Corporation (IFC): Created in 1956 to finance overseas investments by private companies without necessarily requiring government guarantees. The IFC borrows from the *World Bank*, provides loans and invests directly in private industry in the development of capital projects.

International Monetary Fund (IMF): Conceived of at the Bretton Woods Agreement of 1944 and in operation since 1947, its major purpose is to encourage international cooperation in the monetary field and the removal of foreign exchange restrictions, to stabilize exchange rates and aid in balance-of-payment problems.

Interstate: International, intergovernmental.

Intra-South: See *Economic Cooperation among Developing Countries.*

Jaruzelski, General Wojciech: Succeeded Jozef Pinkowski as Poland's Prime Minister, then succeeded Stanislaw Kania, as First Secretary of the Polish United Workers (Communist) Party. A pragmatic and moderate leader, he was caught in the middle by hardliners within the party's Central Committee on one side, and by the hard-liners in the Solidarity independent trade union on the other. Due to the ultimatum adopted by the Executive Committee of Solidarity on December 12, 1981, Jaruzelski imposed martial law on Poland on December 13.

Kampuchea: The new name for Cambodia since April 1975.

KGB: The Soviet security police and intelligence apparatus, engaged in espionage, counterespionage, anti-subversion, and control of political dissidents.

Khmer Rouge: Literally "Red Cambodians," the communist organization ruling *Kampuchea* between April 1975 and January 1979 under Pol Pot and Ieng Saray.

Kiloton: A thousand tons of explosive force. A measure of the yield of a nuclear weapon equivalent to 1,000 tons of TNT (trinitrotoluene). The bomb detonated at Hiroshima in World War II had an approximate yield of 14 kilotons.

Launcher: See *Delivery Systems*

Least Developed Countries (LLDC): Countries that in 1979 had a per capita income of $370 or less and where the basic human needs cannot be met for the bulk of the population.

Less Developed Countries (LDC): (Previously called underdeveloped countries, and later, developing countries.) Countries where the basic human needs are not fully met, yet are well on their way to development.

Linkage: Putting together two separate issues in diplomatic negotiations.

Lome Convention: An agreement concluded between the European Community and 58 African, Caribbean and Pacific countries (ACP), allowing the latter preferential trade relations and greater economic and technical assistance.

Long-Range Theatre Nuclear Forces (LRTNF): Recently developed nuclear weapon systems with a range greater than 1,000 kilometers (or 600 miles) such as the US Pershing II missile or the Soviet SS-20.

Low-income countries: According to the World Bank there are 36 such countries with per capita income ranging from 80 to 370 US dollars per year. They account for 2.26 billion people, of which 1.62 billions are in China and India.

Maneuverable Re-entry Vehicle (MARV): A ballistic missile re-entry vehicle equipped with its own navigation and control systems capable of adjusting its trajectory during re-entry into the atmosphere.

Medium-range Ballistic Missile (MRBM): A missile with a range from 500 to 1,500 nautical miles.

Megaton: The yield of a nuclear weapon equivalent to 1 million tons of TNT (approximately equivalent to 79 Hiroshima bombs).

Microstates: Very small countries, usually with a population of less than one million.

Middle-income countries MICs): According to the World Bank, there are 60 such countries, with annual per capita income (PCI) ranging from 380 to 4,380 US dollars. Twenty-five of these countries have an annual PCI of less than $1,000; 23 of these countries have a PCI ranging from $1,000 to $2,000; and 12 countries have a PCI ranging from $2,000 to $4,380. This is a most unsatisfactory classification, as the highest PCI of MICs is $4,380 while its lowest PCI is only $380, which is only $10 more than the highest PCI in the low-income country group.

Ministates: Small countries, usually with a population of less than five million.

Missile experimental (MX): A mobile, land-based missile that is shuttled among different launching sites making it more difficult to locate and destroy.

Most Favored Nation (MFN): In international trade agreements, a country granting most-favored-nation status to another country undertakes to make available to that country the most favorable treatment in regard to tariffs and other trade regulations that it makes available to any other country.

Most Seriously Affected Countries (MSA): Low-income countries that import their energy needs and that were hurt the most by the OPEC price increases in 1973.

Multilateral: Involving many nations.

Multilateral Development Banks (MDBs): These are the World Bank Group that include the *International Development Association* (IDA) and the *International Finance Corporation* (IFC), the Inter-American Development Bank (IDB or IADB), the Asian Development Bank (ADB), and the African Development Bank (AFDB).

Multinational: Doing business in many nations.

Multinational corporation: *See* Transnational enterprise.

Multiple Independently Targetable Re-entry Vehicle (MIRV): Two or more warheads carried by a single missile and capable of being guided to separate targets upon re-entry.

Mutual and Balanced Force Reductions (MBFR): The 19-nation Conference on Mutual Reduction of Forces and Armaments and Associated Measures in Central Europe that has been held intermittently since 1973.

Mutual Assured Destruction (MAD): The basic ingredient of the doctrine of strategic deterrence that no country can escape destruction in a nuclear exchange even if it engages in a pre-emptive strike.

—N—

Namibia: African name for South-West Africa.

National Intelligence Estimate (NIE): The final assessment of global problems and capabilities by the intelligence community for use by the National Security Council and the President in making foreign and military decisions.

Nautical mile: 1.852 kilometers.

Neocolonialism: A perjorative term describing the economic exploitation of Third World countries by the industrialized countries, in particular through the activities of multinational corporations.

Neutron bomb: Enhanced radiation bomb giving out lower blast and heat but concentrated radiation, thus killing people and living things while reducing damage to physical structures.

New International Economic Order (NIEO): The statement of development policies and objectives adopted at the Sixth Special Session of the UN General Assembly in 1974. NIEO calls for equal participation of LDCs in the international economic policy-making process, better known as the *North-South dialogue.*

New World Information and Communication Order: A highly controversial proposal made in 1980 by the UNESCO-sponsored Commission for the Study of Communication Problems (McBride Commission) to promote a "free and balanced flow of information and news" through "effective legal measures designed to circumscribe the action of transnationals by requiring them to comply with specific criteria and conditions defined by national development policies." The "transnationals" referred to here are the West's Big Four news agencies, namely the Associated Press and the United Press International (USA), Reuters (UK), and Agence France-Press, plus major Western broadcasting companies. This attempt to legitimize state censorship of foreign media by Third World countries provoked a response by Western journalists known as the *Declaration of Talloires.*

Nonaligned Movement (NAM): A grouping of nations that have deliberately chosen not to be politically and militarily associated with either the West or the Communist bloc. Started with Bandung in 1955, six nonaligned summit meetings have been held—Belgrade (1961), Cairo (1964), Lusaka (1970), Algiers (1973), Colombo (1976), and Havana (1979). Interim leadership of the nonaligned countries rests with the country that last hosted a summit meeting. There were 94 members in the NAM in 1981.

Non-alignment: The concept or policy of remaining neutral in the cold war; not taking sides with either the USA (West) or the USSR (East).

Non-nuclear (weapons) state: One not possessing nuclear weapon.

Non-proliferation of Nuclear Weapons Treaty (NPT): Under this Treaty, the non-nuclear-weapon states pledge not to manufacture or acquire nuclear explosive devices and agree to international verification. Nuclear-weapon states, party to the NPT, pledge not to transfer nuclear explosive devices to any recipient and not to assist any non-nuclear-weapon state in the manufacture of nuclear explosive devices.

Non-tariff barriers (NTBs): Subtle, informal impediments to free trade designed for the purpose of making importation of foreign goods into a country very difficult on such grounds as health and safety regulations. Japan as of 1981 had 99 categories of NTBs.

Normalization of relations: The reestablishment of full diplomatic relations, including de jure recognition and the exchange of ambassadors between two countries that either did not have diplomatic relations or had broken them.

North (as in North-South dialogue): (a) A shorthand, non-geographic term for the industrialized countries of high income, both East (the USSR and Eastern Europe) and West (the USA, Canada, Western Europe, Japan, Australia and New Zealand.) (b) Often means only the industrialized, high-income countries of the West.

North Atlantic Treaty Organization (NATO): Also known as the Atlantic Alliance, NATO was formed in 1949 to provide collective defense against the perceived Soviet threat to Western Europe. Its members are Belgium, Denmark, France, the Federal Republic of Germany (West Germany), Greece, Iceland, Italy, Luxembourg, the Netherlands, Norway, Portugal, Turkey, the United Kingdom, Canada, and the United States. France has an independent striking force not integrated into NATO. Greece intends to withdraw militarily from NATO.

North-South dialogue: A wrangling between the industrial Western countries (North) and the LDCs (South) for trade preferences, and economic and technical assistance taking place in Conferences on International Cooperation (CIEC). The Soviet Union and its allies generally remain aloof from the North-South dialogue, arguing that LDC problems are the result of past colonialism and capitalism and, therefore, are the sole responsibility of the West. It was started in 1974 with the *Third World's* call for a new international economic order.

Nuclear free zone: A stretch of territory from which all nuclear weapons are banned.

Nuclear Non-Proliferation Treaty (NPT): A treaty that, among other things, binds those non-nuclear countries adhering to it to forego the acquisition or production of nuclear weapons and forbids the transfer of such weapons to a non-nuclear state.

Nuclear proliferation: The process by which one country after another comes into possession of some form of nuclear weaponry, and with it develops the potential of launching a nuclear attack on other actors.

Nuclear reprocessing: The separation of radioactive waste (spent fuel) from a nuclear-powered plant into its fissile constituent materials. One such material is Plutonium, which can then be used in the production of atomic bombs.

Nuclear terrorism: The use (or threatened use) of nuclear weapons or radioactive materials as a means of coercion.

—O—

Oestpolitik: Literally, Eastward politics, it is the West German foreign policy of *detente* aiming at cooperative relations with the Soviet Union and East European communist countries, with the intermediate goal of normalization of relations with East Germany and the ultimate goal of reunification of the two Germanies.

Official Development Assistance (ODA): Government contributions to projects and programs aimed at developing the productivity of poorer countries. This is to be distinguished from private, voluntary assistance, humanitarian assistance for disasters, and most importantly from military assistance.

Ogaden: A piece of Ethiopian desert populated by ethnic Somalis. It has been a bone of contention between Ethiopia and Somalia, a war that contributed significantly to the refugee and starvation problems in the Horn of Africa.

Organization for Economic Cooperation and Development (OECD): Composed of 23 Western countries plus Japan. All have democratic political systems and, except for a few, have high-income industrial economics. Also referred to as the "North" as in the North-South dialogue.

Organization of Arab Petroleum Exporting Countries (OAPEC): A component of OPEC, with Saudi Arabia, Kuwait, the United Arab Emirates, Qatar, Iraq, Algeria and Libya as members.

Organization of Petroleum Exporting Countries (OPEC): A producers' cartel setting price floors and production ceiling of crude petroleum. It includes members of OPEC plus Venezuela, Iran, Ecuador, Gabon, Nigeria and Indonesia.

Osirak: Site of the Iraqi nuclear power plant near Baghdad that was destroyed by Israeli bombings on June 7, 1981. The site was constructed with the assistance of France, which has pledged to rebuild it.

Overkill: The capability of the USA and the USSR to kill not only each other's population several times over, but the world's population as well.

—P—

Palestine: "Palestine" does not exist today as an entity. It refers to the historical and geographical entity administered by the British under the League of Nations mandate from 1918 to 1947. It also refers to a future entity in the aspirations of Palestinians who, as was the case of the Jews before the founding of the State of Israel, are stateless nationalists.

Palestine Liberation Organization (PLO): A coalition of Palestinian groups united by the dedication to the goal of a Palestinian state through the destruction of Israel as a state.

Payload: Warheads attached to delivery vehicles.

People's Republic of China (PRC): Communist or mainland China.

Perez de Cuellar, Javier: The fifth Secretary General of the United Nations. His 5-year term began on January 1, 1982.

Pershing II: US MRBMs to be deployed in Western Europe to counteract Soviet SS-20s.

Petrodollars: US dollar holdings of capital-surplus OPEC countries; a liability for the US Treasury.

Physical Quality of Life Index (PQLI): Developed by the Overseas Development Council, the PQLI is presented as a more significant measurement of the well-being of inhabitants of a geographic entity than the solely monetary measurement of per capita income. It consists of the following measurements: life expectancy, infant mortality, and literacy figures that are each rated on an index of 1-100, within which each country is ranked according to its performance. A composite index is obtained by averaging these three measures, giving the PQLI.

Polisario: The liberation front of Western Sahara (formerly Spanish Sahara) that is fighting against Morocco claims over that territory. The USA supports King Hassan of Morocco in this war in return for staging rights of Rapid Deployment Forces in the Middle East/North African area.

Polish United Workers Party (PZPR): Poland's communist party's name since 1948.

Post-industrial: Characteristic of a society where a large portion of the work force is directed to non-agricultural and non-manufacturing tasks such as servicing and processing.

Precision-Guided Munitions (PGM): Popularly known as "smart bombs." Electronically programmed and controlled weapons that can accurately hit a moving or stationary target.

Pre-emptive strike, attack: To attack an enemy before one is attacked. A nuclear attack launched in the expectation that an attack by an adversary is imminent, and designed to forestall that attack or to lessen its impact.

Proliferation: Quick spread, as in the case of nuclear weapons.

Protocol: A preliminary memorandum often signed by diplomatic negotiators as a basis for a final convention or treaty.

—Q—

Quota: Quantitative limits, usually imposed on imports or immigrants.

—R—

Rapprochement: The coming together of two countries that had been hostile to each other.

Recycling: As used in recent international finance, it means the flow of money from capital-surplus OPEC countries (Saudi Arabia, Kuwait, Libya, and Iraq) into private or *multilateral development banks* (MBDs) for relending to poorer countries. Recycling resulted from the capital surplus accumulated by certain OPEC countries due to the quadrupling of oil prices in 1973-74 and subsequent price hikes.

Re-entry Vehicle (RV): That portion of a ballistic missile designed to carry a nuclear warhead and to re-enter the Earth's atmosphere in the terminal portion of the missile trajectory.

Regionalism: A concept of cooperation among geographically adjacent states to foster region-wide political (OAS, OAU), military (NATO, Warsaw Pact) and economic (EEC, EFTA) interests.

Rejectionist Front: In the context of the Arab-Israeli conflict, the front consists of Arab countries that reject any solution to the Palestinian question short of the establishment of a Palestinian state in place of the state of Israel. It is made up of the PLO, Syria, Libya, Algeria, and to a lesser degree all other Arab states except for Egypt and the Sudan. They also rejected the Camp David Agreements.

Reprocessing of nuclear waste: A process of recovery of fissionable materials among which is weapon-grade plutonium.

Resolution: Formal decisions of UN bodies; they may simply register an opinion or may recommend action to be taken by a UN body or agency.

Resolution 242: Passed by the UN Security Council on November 22, 1967 calling for the withdrawal of Israeli troops from territories they captured from Egypt (Sinai), Jordan (West Bank and East Jerusalem), and Syria (Golan Heights) in the 1967 war, and for the right of all nations in the Middle East to live in peace in secure and recognized borders.

Resolution 435: Passed by the UN Security Council in 1978, it called for a cease-fire between belligerents in the Namibian conflict (namely SWAPO, Angola and other front-line states on the one side, and South Africa on the other) and an internationally supervised transition process to independence and free elections.

—S—

SALT I: The discussions between the US and the USSR on the limitation of strategic armaments that have been under way since 1970. They have resulted in (1) a treaty limiting the deployment of anti-ballistic missile (ABM) systems; (2) an agreement setting ceilings on intercontinental ballistic missiles (ICBMs) and submarine-launched ballistic missiles (SLBMs) for a five-year period; and (3) the Vladivostok Accord, setting ceilings on all strategic nuclear delivery systems (including heavy bombers) and on MIRVs (multiple independently-targetable reentry vehicles).

SALT II: The SALT II agreement consists of three parts: (1) A treaty, to last through 1985, which, inter alia: sets initial equal aggregates of 2,400 on the total of strategic nuclear delivery vehicles; mandates further reductions in the overall ceiling down to 2,250 before expiration of the treaty; sets equal subceilings on several key categories of systems; restricts the number of warheads that are allowed on each missile; and limits each side to one new type of ICBM. (2) A protocol to last through 1981, which covers issues not ready for longer term resolution. (3) A joint statement of principles and guidelines for subsequent SALT negotiations. SALT II never went into effect, as it was not ratified by the US Senate.

Second strike: A nuclear attack in response to an adversary's first strike. A second-strike capability is the ability to absorb the full force of a first strike and still inflict unacceptable damage in retaliation.

Shatt al Arab: The body of water located between Iran and Iraq, and claimed by both. The dispute over Shatt al Arab was one of the causes of the Iran-Iraq war.

Short Range Ballistic Missiles (SRBM): A missile with a range up to 500 nautical miles.

Solidarity: Independent self-governing trade union movement started in Poland on August 22, 1980 and terminated on December 13, 1981 after radical members of its Presidium passed a resolution on December 12 calling for a national referendum to see whether the communist government of Poland should continue to govern. Individual members of the Presidium also called for the establishment of a provisional government.

South (as in North-South dialogue): A shorthand, non-geographic term that includes economically less developed countries, often represented by the Group of 77.

South-South: see *Economic Cooperation among Developing Countries*

South-West African People's Organization (SWAPO): The guerilla organization fighting against South Africa's illegal occupation and exploitation of Namibia. SWAPO is recognized by the United Nations as the authentic representative of Namibia.

Sovereignty: The ability to carry out laws and policies within national borders without interference from outside.

Special Drawing Rights (SDRs): Also known as paper gold. A new form of international liquid reserves to be used in the settlement of international payments among member governments of the International Monetary Fund.

SS-17, 18, 19: Soviet ICBMs.

SS-20: New mobile Soviet medium-range nuclear missiles aimed at Western Europe.

Stabex Program (stabilization of export receipts): An EEC program that provides financial assistance to selected developing countries that experience temporary export earnings shortfalls.

State: Regarding international relations, it means a country having territory, population, government, and sovereignty, e.g. the US is a state, while California is not a state in this sense.

State terrorism: The use of state power, including the police, the armed forces, and the secret police to throw fear among the population against any act of dissent or protest against a political regime. Such state power includes extraordinary measures such as martial law (military rule), revolutionary or military tribunals ("kangaroo courts"), summary executions, mass killings either by face-to-face firings or indiscriminate use of artillery, and bombings against wide areas that contain civilian settlements. It also includes the use of physical, biochemical, medical, and psychological torture on political prisoners or prisoners of conscience. State terrorism is a phenomenon of modern technology, practiced by totalitarian and authoritarian regimes, by communist and non-communist regimes alike.

"Stealth": A code name for a proposed "invisible" aircraft, supposedly not detectable by hostile forces, and that would be the main US strategic fighter-bomber of the 1990s.

Strategic Arms Limitation Talks: See *SALT I* and *SALT II*

Strategic balance or parity: A concept used in nuclear planning and debate to determine the equivalence of forces between two armed blocs, e.g. the US vs. the USSR, NATO vs. the Warsaw Pact. Opposite of strategic imbalance that could be either superiority or inferiority.

Strategic consensus: An elusive objective of forging an anti-Soviet alliance pursued by the Reagan administration in the Middle East. It would link together such entities as Israel, Egypt, and Saudi Arabia, except that Israel and Saudi Arabia consider themselves enemies. Jordan, which was also courted by the Reagan administration, would have no part of it.

Strategic minerals: Minerals needed in the fabrication of advanced military and industrial equipment. Examples are uranium, platinum, titanium, vanadium, tungsten, nickel, chromium, etc.

Strategic nuclear weapons: Long-range weapons carried on either intercontinental ballistic missiles (ICBMs) or Submarine-Launched Ballistic Missiles (SLBMs) or long-range bombers.

Strategic stockpile: Reserves of certain commodities established to assure that in time of national emergency such commodities are readily available.

Submarine-Launched Ballistic Missile (SLBM): A ballistic missile carried in and launched from a submarine.

Superpowers: Countries so powerful militarily (USA, USSR), demographically (PRC), or economically (Japan) as to be in a class by themselves.

Supranational: Above nation-states.

—T—

Tactical nuclear weapons: Kiloton-range weapons for theatre use. The bomb dropped on Hiroshima would be in this category today.

Tariff: A tax levied on imports.

Technetronic: Shorthand for technological-electronic.

Technical Cooperation Among Developing Countries (TCDC): A clearinghouse and a coordinating body through which less developed countries (LDCs) may help each other solve similar problems by low-capital, appropriate technology applications.

Territorial Sea: The territorial sea, air space above, seabed, and subsoil are part of sovereign territory of coastal state except that ships (not aircraft) enjoy right of *innocent passage*. As proposed in ICNT, a coastal state's sovereignty would extend 12 nautical miles beyond its land territory.

Terrorism: The systematic use of terror as a means of coercion.

Theatre: In nuclear strategy, it refers to a localized combat area such as Europe, as opposed to global warfare involving a US-USSR nuclear exchange.

Theatre Nuclear Forces (TNF): Nuclear weapons systems for operations in a region such as Europe, including artillery, cruise missiles, SRBMs, IRBMs, and MRBMs.

"Thinkables": Nuclear strategists who believe that one should plan in terms of nuclear war actually occurring, and for its aftermath.

Third World: Often used interchangeably with the terms *less developed countries, developing countries,* or the *South,* its two main institutions are the *nonaligned movement* (which acts primarily as the political caucus of the Third World) and the *Group of 77* (which functions as the economic voice of the Third World).

Tokyo Round: The sixth and latest in the series of GATT trade negotiations, begun in 1973 and ended in 1979. About 100 nations, including nonmembers of the GATT, participated.

Torture: The deliberate inflicting of pain, whether physical or psychological, to degrade, intimidate, and induce submission of its victims to the will of the torturer. It is a heinous practice used frequently in most dictatorial regimes in the world, irrespective of their ideological leanings.

Transnational: An adjective indicating that a non-governmental movement, organization, or ideology transcends national borders and is operative in dissimilar political, economic, and social systems.

Transnational Enterprise (TNE) or **Corporation (TNC):** Synonymous to *Multinational Corporation* (MNC). An enterprise doing business in more than one country.

Triad (nuclear): The three-pronged US strategic weapons arsenal, composed of land-based *ICBMs,* underwater *SLBMs,* and long-range manned bombers.

Trilateral: Between three countries or groups of countries, e.g. USA, Western Europe and Japan; USA, USSR, and China.

—U—

Unilateral: One-sided, as opposed to bilateral or multilateral.

United Nations Conference on Trade and Development (UNCTAD): Was convened in 1964 in response to growing concern among LDCs over their effort to bridge the standard-of-living gap between them and DCs. Meetings were held in 1968, 1972, 1976, and 1979 and have focused on North-South economic issues.

"Unthinkables": Nuclear strategists who believe that a nuclear war, once begun, is likely to create a disaster of such magnitude that it is not meaningful to plan in terms of its actual occurrence.

—V—

Venice initiative: The Declaration by the European Community foreign ministers, on June 12, 1980, backing Palestinian "self-determination" and participation in Middle East negotiations; calling for an end to Israeli occupation of the Gaza Strip and the West Bank and to Israeli settlements there; and condemning Israel's proposed change in the status of Jersualem.

Verification: The process of determining that the other side is complying with an agreement.

Vulnerability: As used in strategic planning, it refers to the condition under which US silo-based ICBMs can be targeted for pinpoint hits by Soviet missiles.

—W—

Walesa, Lech (pronounced vah-wen-sah): Leader of the independent trade union movement known as Solidarity, which came into existence in August 1980 and was dissolved in December 13, 1981 by the martial law decree imposed.

Warhead: That part of a missile, projectile, or torpedo that contains the explosive intended to inflict damage.

Warsaw Pact or Warsaw Treaty Organization: Established in 1955 by the Soviet Union in response to the inclusion in NATO of the Federal Republic of Germany (West Germany). The members are the Soviet Union, Bulgaria, Czechoslovakia, the German Democratic Republic (East Germany), Hungary, Poland, and Romania.

West (as in the East-West conflict): A short-hand, nongeographic term that means (a) in economic matters, the *OECD* countries; (b) militarily, *NATO,* France, and *ANZUS.* Basically the market-economy, industrialized, and high-income countries that are committed to a political system of representative democracy. The three main anchors of the West today are North America, Western Europe, and Japan, also known as the Trilateral countries. Australia and New Zealand are also parts of the West.

Western economic summits: Annual meetings of the leaders of seven Western industrialized nations (the USA, the UK, France, West Germany, Japan, Italy, and Canada) with the president of the Commission of the EEC in attendance. These meetings were first held at Rambouillet, France, in 1975. The latest was the Ottawa Summit in 1981.

Western Five Contact Group (re Namibia): Five Western countries acting as intermediaries between South Africa, SWAPO and Front-line States to work out procedures for the independence and future government of Namibia. They are Canada, the Federal Republic of Germany, France, the United Kingdom, and the United States. The European nations are more pro-SWAPO while the USA is more pro-South Africa.

"Window of vulnerability": An expression often used, but not consistently defined, by Ronald Reagan and his associates since the Presidential campaign of 1980. Military specialists use the word to refer to a period of time in the future (in the late 1980s) when US silo-based ICBMs can be accurately hit by Soviet missiles while the mobile MX system (now scrapped) will not yet be operational, and when the aging B-52 bombers are no longer serviceable while the *Stealth* aircraft will not yet be operational. Mr. Reagan approved a plan to close this "window" by MIRVing the silo-based ICBMs, by hardening their concrete covers, and by building B-1 bombers.

World Bank (International Bank for Reconstruction and Development-IBRD): Makes loans, either directly to governments or with governments as the guarantors; and through its affiliates, the International Finance Corporation and the International Development Association.

World Politics: The sum of all those actions and interactions of some 160 nation states and scores of non-national and trans-national actors in terms of political, diplomatic, military, and economic policies.

—X—Y—Z—

Yield: The explosive force, in terms of TNT equivalence, of a warhead.

Zero option: President Reagan's proposal made on November 19, 1981, that the US would cancel its plan to deploy MRBMs (Pershing II and GLCMs) in Western Europe if the USSR agreed to remove those it has already emplaced in Eastern Europe and Western USSR.

Zhao Ziyang: Head of government, People's Republic of China.

Zimbabwe: Formerly Rhodesia.

Index

accommodation, Chinese-Soviet, 118-123
ABM, see anti-ballistic missile
Afghanistan, 44, 69, 111, 177, 180
Africa: economy of, 132; race politics in, 137-142; influence of Soviet Union in, 44, 45, 133-136; U.S. aid to, 199, 200
African National Congress (ANC), 137-141
Agency for International Development (AID), and U.S. foreign aid, 162, 196-202
agriculture, and GATT, 191
alcoholism, in Soviet Union, 64
allies, see Atlantic Alliance; Western alliance
Angola, 133, 134, 179
anti-ballistic missile (ABM): 217-219, 233, 234,; treaty, 246
apartheid: 137-142; and U.S. foreign policy, 28-33
Arab-Israeli War: 167; and Soviet Mid-East policy, 43-44; Soviet vs. U.S. views on, 71, 73
Arab states, and Palestinian conflict, 175-183
Argentina: 156; U.S. foreign policy on, 27
arms control: 216-246; Europe's view of U.S.-Soviet negotiations on, 81-83; and new Soviet diplomacy, 37; and U.S. relations with China, 110; verification, 244-246; see also, nuclear disarmament; SALT I; SALT II
arms sales, to China, by United States, 111, 112
ASEAN, 94, 109
Asia: U.S. foreign policy concerning, 10; see also, South Asia; Southeast Asia
Association of Southeast Asian Nations, see ASEAN
Altantic Alliance: and German-American relations, 88-90; and Greece, 91-92
autocratic regimes, U.S. foreign policy and support of, 17-20
authoritarian regimes, vs. totalitarian regimes and human rights, 24-25

Basic Law, and Hong Kong, 150
Beijing, 108, 109, 111, 115, 117, 118, 119, 120, 143, 144, 149
benign detachment, as foreign policy ideology, 20-21
bilateral investment treaties (BITs), 187
black market, in Soviet Union, 65
blacks, and race politics in South Africa, 28-33, 137-142
Botswana, 137, 140
bourgeois liberalization, and China, 129

Calvo Doctrine, 188
Camp David Accords, 172, 180
Carter administration: foreign policy of, 10-11; human rights policy of, 24
Castro, Fidel, 18, 45
Central America: and Contadora Treaty, 156-160; Soviet influence in, 45; U.S. foreign policy on, 16-18; and U.S. foreign policy toward Nicaragua, 27
Central Committee, role of, in Soviet Union, 61-62
Chernobyl, nuclear accident at, 39-41
Chile: human rights violations in, 26-27; U.S. foreign policy toward, 18-19
China: burgeois liberalization in, 129; disarmament resolutions by, 242-243; and Hong Kong, 143-150; and nuclear war, 222, 223; reforms in, 129;

relations of, with Soviet Union, 111, 112, 114-123; relations of, with United States, 20-21, 108-113
Commission on Verification and Control, 156, 158, 159
communism, effects of, on Soviet economy, 60-65
Communist party, changes needed in Soviet Union's, 66-67
containment, policy of, 10
Contadora treaty, 156-160
contras, Central American opposition to U.S. aid to, 27
Convention on Law of the Seas, 256, 257
Costa Rica, 156, 160
Cuba: as Soviet ally, 45; and U.S. foreign policy, 18

death-squad, 161, 162
debt crisis: in Latin America, 203-213; in Mexico, 153-155
defense spending, and Japan, 104-105
Democratic Kampuchea (CGDK), and invasion of Kampuchea by Vietnam, 151-152
Democratic party, isolationist ideology of, 10-12
Deng Xiaoping, 109, 110, 111, 119, 143
détente, Reagan administration's dismissal of, 80
disarmament: nuclear, 216-246; see also, arms control
discontinuous change, and debate over nuclear threat, 221, 222
disinvestment, consequences of, in South Africa, 30-31
Dobrynin, Anatoly, on foreign policy, 37

East-West relations: and Soviet view of world war, 51-59; see also, U.S.-Soviet relations
economic assistance: U.S. vs. Soviet, to Third World, 42-47; see also, foreign aid
economic reform, Soviet, under Gorbachev, 60-65
economic sanctions: role of, in foreign policy, 19-20; against South Africa, 30-32
Egypt: and Islamic revivalism, 167, 168; and Palestine conflict, 178; Soviet view of U.S. relations with, 72
Egypt-Israeli peace treaty, 172, 178
El Salvador: 156, 158, 160; economy of, 163; role of United States in, 161-164
England, see Great Britain
Ethiopia, 133, 134, 179
Eurocentric foreign policy, 14-15
Euro-communism, 96
Europe: communism in, 96; and nuclear weapons, 227-228, 235-241; and Palestine conflict, 180, 181; and terrorism, 98-101; U.S. foreign policy and alliances with, 14-15
European Economic Community (EEC), 83
evangelical Protestantism, and El Salvador, 162
exports, Soviet oil, 48, 49

first strike, and U.S. policy on use of nuclear weapons, 236, 237
foreign aid: 162, failure of U.S., 196-202; see also, economic assistance
foreign investment: by multinational

corporations in less developed countries, 186-190; of U.S. in China, 109, 110
foreign policy: and ideology, 8-15; open door, of China, 108-123; Soviet, in Third World, 42-47; importance of Western alliance to U.S., 14-15
France, and terrorism, 99
freedom of the seas, 253-255
freedom: role of, in foreign policy, 13-14; and human rights policy, 22-24

General Agreement on Tariffs and Trade (GATT), 154, 190-195
German-American relations, and future of the Alliance, 88-90
Gorbachev, Mikhail: 63, 116, 117, 227, 228, 242; changes in Soviet diplomacy under, 36-38; Soviet economic reform under, 60-67
Great Britain: and Hong Kong, 143-148; NATO and out-of-area security, 93-95
Greece: 96; and Atlantic Alliance, 91-92; and terrorism, 99

Haiti, U.S. foreign policy toward, 27
Harmel Report, 88
health effects, of Chernobyl nuclear accident, 41
Helsinki Final Act, human rights provisions of, 28
Honduras, 156, 160
Hong Kong, 143-150
human rights: apartheid and violations of, 28-33; definition of, by Cyrus Vance, 22-23; and U.S. foreign policy, 22-29
Hungarian Socialist Workers' Party, interview with General Secretary of, 125-128
Hungary, 125-128
Hussein, King, 173, 178

ICBMs, see intercontinental ballistic missiles (ICBMs)
IMF, see International Monetary Fund (IMF)
imports, Soviet need of, 48
India, Soviet relationship with, 44
Institutional Revolutionary Party (PRI), 154, 155
insurgency, against Third World Marxism, 42-47
intercontinental ballistic missiles (ICBM's), 230, 234, 247
Interim Restraint Policy, U.S., 229-232
International Atomic Energy Agency (IAEA), conference on Chernobyl nuclear accident, 39-41
International Corp. of Inspectors, 156, 159
International Court of Justice, and U.S. involvement in Nicaragua, 250-252
internationalization, and Japan-U.S. relations, 101-103
international law, International Court, concerning U.S. involvement in Nicaragua and, 250-252
International Monetary Fund (IMF), and Latin American debt, 203, 206-211
international terrorism, 258, 259-264
international trade, see trade
interventionism, 8-15
Iran, and Islamic revivalism, 168, 169
Iran-Iraq War, 176, 179; and Soviet-Middle East policy, 43